INDIAN RITUAL AND BELIEF

The Keys of Power

SPINNING OUT THE THREAD

The women of Kashmir are famed for their beauty, but your first impression is that they have been overrated. However, after you have seen them at their various tasks and recreations, noted their erect carriage, the undulating grace of their movements, and their flashing eyes, you realize that they have a charm distinctively their own.

INDIAN RITUAL AND BELIEF

The Keys of Power

J. ABBOT, B.A. (Oxon)

INDIAN CIVIL SERVICE

WITH NUMEROUS DIAGRAMS

MANOHAR

2000

This work was originally published in 1932 under the title
The Keys of Power: A Study of Indian Ritual and Belief

First published in India, 1984
Reprinted, 2000

ISBN 81-7304-339-6

Published by
Ajay Kumar Jain for
Manohar Publishers & Distributors
4753/23 Ansari Road, Daryaganj
New Delhi 110002

Printed at
Mehra Offset Press
1979, Ganj Mirkhan
Chandni Mahal, Daryaganj
New Delhi 110002

PREFACE

THE conservatism of the East gives a peculiar interest to a study of Indian customs, for the sanction of the great religions of India has not concealed phases of primitive thought; beneath the animism of Hinduism and the monotheism of Islam lies a culture of dim centuries which still dictates a commanding ritual. This conservatism, however, is not without its limitations. There is in India a mass of custom protected by the conservatism of a priestly class and the force of communal sentiment, that changes little from year to year; on the other hand there are customs without such protection which are fast disappearing before the disruptive force of modernism. The ritual of agriculture in particular is changing fast. In Lower Sind and in Gujarat the change has been great, and in the Deccan I have myself witnessed in the last decade customs derided and discarded by the present generation and left to an older generation to preserve. This disappearance of such custom is the more impressive because it is precisely the older culture which has been preserved in many rites of agriculture, and its loss entails the greater prominence of rites which find their basis in a philosophy of animism.

It is not the object of my book to offer directly any analysis of animism or of the religion of the Prophet, still less to follow any of the many side-tracks taken by Hindu philosophy, but primarily to record as many customs as possible before it is too late, and to attempt to show how far the concept of a supernatural cosmic power dominates popular practice. The reader will find few references to customs collected by other writers, and this because I cannot but think that the circular questionnaire which has so often been the means of gathering information has led to many errors. It is impossible in my opinion to accept as a rule the statement of a member of one caste about the customs of another caste, and even more impossible to expect to find second-hand the rayat's explanation of his practices.

In a very deep sense this book is the result of co-operation, for to a multitude of Indian friends I owe any confidence with which I have endeavoured to explain underlying belief, and I have voiced no explanation, however controversial it may seem, which does not faithfully represent local belief.

The glossary is intended to serve as an index of reference to the English reader unacquainted with Indian words, and attempts only the minimum definition of words constantly recurring. The transliteration of vernacular words follows the scheme of Transliteration given in the *Journal of the Bombay Branch of the Royal Asiatic Society* (New Series, Vol. iv, Nos. 1 and 2). In some cases, however, it would have been pedantic to correct a spelling of long usage.

As typical of Muhammadan belief I have taken the customs of Sind and not those of the Muhammadan in the Presidency proper where Muhammadan custom has been influenced by Hindu example. In Sind the Muhammadan says 'He who imitates a sect is one of them', and on the whole an investigator of Sindi customs can safely presume that Muhammadan practice is not a mirror of Hindu belief.

MENTON, FRANCE — J. ABBOTT

January, 1932

CONTENTS

APPENDICES

GLOSSARY

Abhiṣek . .	The ceremonial bathing of an image.
Akṣat . .	Unbroken rice grain.
Amāvāsyā .	The new-moon day.
Ankurāropaṇ .	The ceremonial sowing of seed; 'Gardens of Adonis'.
Ārtī . .	A lamp the waving of which is a frequent feature of ritual.
Āsan . .	A seat used to insulate śakti from the ground.
Aśmārohaṇ .	The standing on a stone during a marriage ceremony.
Āvāhana .	The invocation of śakti.
Āvarana . .	A proxy.
Bahuḻ . .	Dark, applied to the dark half of a month.
Baḻī . .	An offering to appease.
Bāśing . .	The coronet of the bridegroom.
Chillā . .	Retirement for forty days of a Muhammadan saint.
Dakṣiṇā . .	A gift of cash.
Darśan . .	The beholding of embodiments of śakti.
Dikbāndha .	The fortification of the quarters against evil.
Dṛṣṭi . .	The evil eye.
Fāt'ha . .	An invocation with the hands stretched out and the palms turned upwards.
Ghātvār . .	A day of danger.
Ghōrō . .	'Heavy' with kudrat.
Haḻad . .	Turmeric.
Hōma . .	A sacrificial fire.
Jap . .	The silent muttering of prayer.
Kalaśa . .	A water-pot.
Kankaṇ . .	A wristlet worn by the bridal pair.
Kari . .	'Evil time.'
Khaṇ . .	A bodice cloth. Folded in a triangle as an offering.
Kharif . .	The earlier of the two cultivating seasons.
Kula devatā .	The family god of the Hindu.
Kumārikā .	An unmarried virgin.
Kuṇḍ . .	A pit used for a sacrificial fire.
Madhupark .	A mixture of curds and milk, ghee, water, honey and sugar.
Manḍap . .	Booth.
Mangalsnān .	An auspicious bathing of purification.
Mangaḻsūtra .	The necklace of the married woman.
Muḍadoṣ .	The anæmia a child contracts from contact with a woman in her menses.
Muhūrtta .	An auspicious moment arrived at by detailed calculation.
Naivedya .	Anything fit for offering. Offerings to gods, spirits, friends and guests are naivedya.
Nāndi . .	The Brahmin devak.

Niṣkramaṇa . The going of a Hindu woman after her delivery to a temple.
Nivāḷī . . The waving and the casting away of articles to avert evil.
Oṭī bharaṇī . Filling the lap or the fold of the sari of a girl or woman with fruit and grain. In Sind the custom is called God bharna; Rajputs call it Kholo bharani.
Pādā . . Footprint.
Paṇatī . . A light of one wick lighted on a death.
Pancpālvi . Five leaves.
Parvakāl . A moment of juncture; a moment of power.
Pāṭ . . A low stool or board, square in shape, used to insulate śakti from the ground.
Pāyguṇ . . A man's inherent potentiality.
Pīḍā . . Evil; applied to the evil influence of the planets.
Pinḍa . . Balls of cooked rice offered to the pitṛs.
Pitṛ . . Manes.
Pūrṇimā . The day of full moon.
Prāṇpratiṣṭā . Installation of an image.
Prasād . . The transferred śakti of a god. It includes leaves used in worship; naivedya offered to an image; sandal paste used in worship; water in which the image has been bathed; incense burnt before the god and lights waved before the image.
Prayascitta . A purification with water.
Pūjā . . Worship.
Puṇya . . Usually translated as merit.
Puṇyavant . A man who has acquired puṇya.
Rabī . . The second and later season of cultivation.
Rās . . The pile of gathered grain on the threshing floor.
Samāvartan . (Soḍamunja) The due return of the Brahmacārī to his father's house for marriage at the close of his studentship of twelve years which should follow his munji. This ceremony is performed three days or more prior to his marriage. The boy's parents install Nāndi; then a hom is performed to atone for any breach of rule since the boy's thread ceremony. The boy is shaved and bathed; then with fire from the first hom the samāvartan hom is celebrated. The boy then pretends to go on a pilgrimage to Benares and sets out with an umbrella, walking-stick and a bundle of rice flour and pulse. He is dissuaded from going by a maternal uncle or friend or relative and told that he will be given a bride.
Samprokṣaṇ . A purificatory rite in which a gift is purified by the sprinkling over it of water.
Sankalpa . The declaration of the object of a rite by the celebrant; water is poured on the ground and mantras are uttered in confirmation of the declaration.
Sanskāra . A ceremony that makes a man complete; adds something that is missing and qualifies him to take up a new state. There are twelve principal sanskār, but sixteen are recognized.
Śānti . . Rite of propitiation.
Saubhāgya . The happiness of married life.
Śrāddha . . Obsequial rites.

Sud . . Suddha; applied to the bright half of the month.

Suher . . The impurity attached to birth.

Surgi . . The thread tied round pots at four corners of a square within which the bridal pair take their mangalsnān. The bathing itself is called the surgi bathing.

Sutak . . The impurity attached to death.

Suvāsinī . The married woman.

Svayambhū . Self-existing. A term applied to certain symbols the śakti of which is greater than that of symbols into which man invokes power.

Tīrth . . Water with acquired śakti.

Tulsī . . Ocimum sanctum. Every Hindu household keeps a tulsī plant.

Tulsīvṛandāvan The square enclosure of the tulsī.

Ugra . . Fierce. Applied to certain forms of gifts which transfer evil and sin.

Utsavmūrtti . A duplicate image of a god which in substitute for the main image is taken in procession.

Utāra . . The removal of evil; that is its transference.

Vanvāha . The Muhammadan bridal pair 'sit in Vanvāha' for the period in which they must not be exposed to the sun.

Varāt . . The bridegroom's procession.

Vaṭu . . The boy at his thread ceremony.

Visarjana . The formal dismissal of invoked śakti.

Viṭāḻ . . The impurity of a woman in menses.

Yajamān . The person who has undertaken the performance of a rite.

Yantra . . From a root 'to restrain'. Something that curbs; an amulet against evil.

A brief note will assist the English reader to approach a correct pronunciation of Indian words.

'ṣ' or 'ś' will be pronounced like the English 'sh'.

Long 'ā' will be pronounced as the 'a' in 'father', and the short 'a' like the 'u' in 'but'.

Long 'ī' has the sound of the double 'e' in 'meet'; 'o' has the sound of 'o' in 'hole'. The vowel 'e' has the sound of the 'a' in 'mate'.

THE KEYS OF POWER

CHAPTER I

LIFE AND POWER

BY strange chance the most primitive thought in the Bombay Presidency is found close to its great metropolis, for the settlements of the *Kātkarī* come down to within thirty miles of Bombay, and are scattered over the two adjoining districts of Thana and Kolaba.

The *Kātkarī*, himself entirely without gods, has borrowed the gods of Hinduism; quite without a calendar of his own he has taken the holy days of his Hindu neighbours, but his borrowed creed sits lightly upon him and it is still possible to trace many of his primitive concepts in his daily ritual. Dismissed usually as an animist he really represents a much earlier stage of thought when such objects of Nature as attract man's attention are endowed with life and its potencies. The *Kātkarī* believes in *jīva* or 'life', giving it a very limited connotation which does not approach the wider meaning given to it by Hinduism.

Jīva the *Kātkarī* finds in things that come to an end, that die. He sees the ocean ebb and flow; he sees the monsoon clouds break on the rugged peaks around him; he sees the rivers flow to sea; he sees the sun and moon rise and set and the stars' regular courses he has in some cases detected. Yet in none of these does he recognize *jīva*. The ocean's movement is constant; the clouds pass slowly away; the rivers never cease to work their way to the sea; and the heavenly bodies always reappear. There is movement in these natural objects but there is no death and without death there is no *jīva*. A lucid explanation of his conception of *jīva* is provided by his attitude towards rivers; the river that without interruption unceasingly flows to the sea has for him no interest, but if a river comes suddenly out of a rock, or if in the hot weather its bed becomes dry, he finds a beginning and he finds an end and accordingly attributes *jīva* to the river. On the other hand, he can attribute *jīva* to an inanimate thing; life is not synonymous with motion. His theory of *jīva* is not drawn from observed movement. He has the Tongan and West African notion that inanimate objects may be 'alive' and that they die when they are broken or destroyed. His funeral ceremonies illustrate his belief that his weapons of the chase have *jīva*.

The *Kātkarī's* funeral rites are unique in the Presidency if not in India. The body of the deceased is carried a short distance out of his house by women who hand it over to men bearers, when a stone called *Jīvkhaḍā*, 'stone of life', is kicked up from the ground. This stone or pebble enshrines the *jīva* of the dead; under different names it appears in the funeral ritual of many castes, but only in the Konkan is it known as the 'stone of life'. Another feature in the obsequies of a *Kātkarī* is the erection of a miniature 'house of the dead' on a large stone placed over the ashes collected from the pyre. There are several patterns of this house. The more elusive *Dhōr Kātkarī* makes a house of four poles with no door but with an open side; the *Sōn Kātkarī* makes his house circular with a central pole and six smaller side-posts covered with a thatch of paḷas (Butea frondosa), or as an alternative pattern puts two posts in the centre and three posts at the side, the central posts being connected by a cross-beam. Into this house of the dead the *Dhōr* puts boiled rice, milk and liquor; and the *Sōn* four hollow pieces of bamboo containing spirit, water and milk. If any of the articles which were burnt with the dead have not been completely burnt their remnants are also placed in the house of the dead.

It is these things burnt with the dead that give another illustration of the *Kātkarī's* concept of *jīva*. He burns with the dead the smoking utensils of the deceased, a sickle to provide him with a weapon of defence in the next world, and the bow and arrows the deceased has used, and these last he breaks into pieces before he puts them on the pyre. The weapons are broken [1] to take their *jīva* out of them so that a jīvaless set of weapons may follow a jīvaless dead to the other world; unless the weapons are broken the *Kātkarī* thinks they cannot follow the dead.

The *Jīvkhaḍā* and the broken weapons burnt with the dead thus provide two illustrations of the *Kātkarī's* concept of *jīva*. Beyond

[1] Cp. *Religion and Folklore of Northern India*, W. Crooke, 1926, p. 233: 'There seems to be little or no evidence to show that as in other parts of the world, articles dedicated in this way are intentionally broken "to take the life out of them" and thus adapt them for the use of the spirit.' The author was apparently unaware of the general prevalence of this practice among the *Kātkarīs* of the Karjat taluka Kolaba district.

these he recognizes *jīva* in animals and in all trees and similar growth and believes that on death all such *jīva* passes back again to the earth from which it springs forth again in some new form.

From this concept of *jīva* with its limited embrace we pass to the Hindu concept of *śakti* and the Muhammadan concept of *kudrat*. It would be hard to find a concept more comprehensive than the Hindu idea of *śakti*. Various concepts of a diffused supernatural cosmic power prevail in different ethnic areas of the world, and as a general term applicable beyond the local limits of its origin, the word *mana* has been applied by scholars to these concepts and has not lacked precise definition. In the treatment of the ritual and belief however of India animism has played so prominent a part that the moulding of religious phenomena has been narrowed and the dominance of Indian practice, magical and religious, by a concept earlier than animism has received insufficient attention.

Śakti is a creative dynamic force or power in everything visible and invisible; in things animate and inanimate. It pervades everything assuming a separate entity in individual things in which it becomes a transmissible personality. It pervades thoughts and ideas; embodied in thoughts it may be the power of benediction; it is developed by the common will of many; gratitude transmits it as does a curse. It is a power which acts both for good and for evil. Its good effects are *barkat*, its bad effects are *aniṣṭ* or, as women pronounce it, *ariṣṭ*. It is a dangerous element and cannot be lightly treated, but from one point of view the whole of man's endeavours in magic and in religious ritual are concentrated on getting control of this power, using it for his own benefit and accumulating a fund of it as a potential source of all forms of blessing.

A definition of *kudrat* must follow the same lines. A concept of power older than Islam is intimately connected with the religion of the Prophet, just as it cannot be divorced from the animism of Hinduism. All *kudrat* must come from God and *Kādir* or *Kadīr*, meaning 'possessed of *kudrat*,' are terms applied to God only and not to man. When *kudrat* produces good its effects are *barkat*, the same term as the Hindu uses; when it produces evil that evil is the anger of God, it is also *harkat*. *Halāl men barkat, harām men harkat.* 'In the hallowed there is blessing, in the unhallowed there is impediment.'

There are many terms applied by the Hindu and the Muhammadan to entities to which they attribute 'power'. Royalty approaches divinity very nearly in Indian thought. *Na Viṣṇu pṛthvīpata,* 'without the power of Viṣṇu a man is not a king', or to quote from the speech of a modern politician, 'there is the spirit of God in our King-Emperor!' According to Manu, a king incarnates the *śakti* of the guardian deities of the cardinal points; according to a Muhammadan, every ruler has the *kudrat* of forty saints.

The word 'king' is used by both Hindu and Muhammadan to emphasize the possession of abnormal power. In Sind seed is called *shāh* and *bādshāh,* 'king'; in the Deccan it is called *rājā,* 'king'. The river Indus in Sind is the royal river, *darya shāh*; a saiyid, a fakir and a saint are called 'king' and the child is *bādshāh*; the bridegroom is *var rājā,* 'the royal bridegroom', or *navshāh,* 'the new king'. The sacred soma plant of the Hindu is called *Somarāj* and the same term *rājā* is applied to a walking-stick.

Another honorific denoting the possession of power is the word *Pīr,* 'saint'. Milk to a Muhammadan is *khir pir*; the Indus is the *darya pir* or saintly river; a tree to which rags are usually tied because of its innate power is called *Thigri pir* or *Chindhi pir,* 'the rag saint'; particular trees such as kando, the kabbar and the sirih are called *pir,* and even spirits are called by the same name. A parallel to the use of the word *pir* by the Muhammadan is the use of the word *svāmī* by the Hindu; in some districts the 'devak' which enshrines the *śakti* of the family god is called *kul svāmī.*

Various words meaning 'heavy' are used by the Muhammadan to imply 'heavy with power'; *ghoro; vazandār; bhāro,*[1] the opposite to which is *halko* or 'light'. Before cutting a tree which he regards as *ghoro* a Sindi ties to it a talisman to make it *halko.* The step of a guest is 'heavy with power'; so is a marriage; hours such as those of an eclipse, of sunset, noon, midnight are *ghoro,* as is also the day of the new moon. Trees such as the pipal (Ficus religiosa), the lasuri (Cordia Myxa), the ber (Zizyphus vulgaris) and in general all trees that excite wonder by their great age or their isolation are *ghoro.* The same word is applied to a shrine, to a saint, a pregnant woman, to a child, a bridegroom, a graveyard and a house. It is applied to a pilgrim, to an old person, to a woman for forty days after her delivery; to a learned man, a saiyid, pir or fakir and to a maiden; to milk, bread, salt, water, fire, a lamp, and to a dead body before it is buried.

[1] In the *Indian Antiquary,* June, 1895, p. 156, Sir James Campbell interprets *bhāri* as applied to a marriage as meaning heavy-laden with spirits. My chapter on the bridal pair will demonstrate how far this interpretation is incorrect.

The Hindu speaks of an image or a place or tree to which he attributes *śakti* as *jāgṛt* or 'awake', and the word *jāgṛtsthān* he uses in connexion with the temple of a god, the shrine of a saint, trees, rivers, wells and tanks, big hillocks and the site of buried treasure. The word *parva* meaning 'knot' or 'juncture' applied to time indicates the presence of 'power'; *baliṣṭh*, 'strong', is used in the case of time, gods and stars, whilst *śaktisthān*, 'the abode of power', is confined to temples of powerful goddesses.

Above all words, however, used by the Hindu to express 'power' the commonest is the word *dev* or 'god'. Sometimes a person with special power is called by the name of some individual god, not exactly meaning that the human being is the incarnation of that god, but that even as that god is in the realms above so is he on earth. In this way the *Agnihotrī* is called *Agnināráyaṇ*, saints and sannyāsīs are called *Nārāyaṇ* and the *munjā* or boy at his thread ceremony is called *Viṣṇu*, whilst the bride and bridegroom are compared to *Lakṣmī* and *Nārāyaṇ*. More frequently no individual name is given to express power, but a person or thing with innate power is called *dev*. This word is used both as a suffix and as a prefix. The guest is *Atithidev*; the *Marāṭhā* child is *Dev*; the bridegroom is *Navardev*, 'the god bridegroom', *Devaru*, 'god' or *Bhūsur*, a divine incarnation, a term applied equally to the pilgrim. The tulsī plant (Ocimum sanctum) is called *Tulsīdev*, and in general anything out of the common and difficult to explain is called *dev*. The most numerous examples of this use of the word are found in the wilder tracts of the Presidency where strange natural features and objects are called *dev*. Trees with power to which rags are tied are called *cindhyā dev*, 'rag god'. A big mountain is *devagiri* and as a prefix the word *dev* comes to mean little more than 'the best of', whilst used as a suffix to personal names it is a mere honorific, and it is not always easy to distinguish between the ordinary and the exceptional meaning implied in the prefix or suffix. Parents are called *pitṛdev*, *mātṛdev*, and probably in these words the ordinary and the exceptional meet.

POWER AND HEAT

Indian literature abounds in accounts of superhuman power acquired by the penance of ascetics to which the term *tapas* or 'heat'[1] is applied. A Hindu deity with great power is called

[1] In Melanesia men and objects with 'mana' are said to be hot, *saka*, and in the Ewe language magic power is called *dzo* or 'heat'. In *The Island Builders of the Pacific*, W. G. Ivens, 1930, p. 137, similar Lau terms are given; *ako*, hot, and *si ere*, 'fire', as meaning 'magically powerful'.

prakhar, 'very hot', *jājval*, 'burning' or *jvalit*, 'having fire'. A Muhammadan uses the word *tab* or heat to mean *kudrat*. Sindi Muhammadans believe that a man in communion with God becomes 'hot'; a man who performs miracles is *joshavāro* or *sahib-josh,* and *jōsh* means boiling; *jazbo* means excitement produced by heat, and *jazbevāro* is one word for one who performs miracles; *garmash* means heat, and a man with special *kudrat* is called *garmashjo manhun*; the curse of a saint is spoken of as his fire, and when cursed by a saint one is consumed by his fire.

Etymology apart, there are many Hindu and Muhammadan practices directed admittedly towards making hot and dangerous power cool, *thado*, *thaṇḍa*, *śānt.*

Power radiated or transmitted from gods is hot and dangerous. The linga of Śiva is supposed always to be in a condition of heat and requires to be cooled with showers of Ganges water and the cooling leaves of the *bel* applied throughout the day. Before a thread or a marriage ceremony some Hindu families in the Karnāṭak propitiate *Ambabai.* Various food preparations are served in a shallow dish and *suvāsinīs* or married women sit around; on these articles of food in the dish a small silver or golden image of *Ambabai* is placed before which lights are waved. These lights rest on small cakes of *huraṇ*, a preparation of cooked gram, dal and jaggery. In the final stages of the rite the *suvāsinīs* insert their hands in the food and rub it all into a mixture which is called *boḍaṇ* and which the goddess is supposed to eat when the food is given to a cow. The detail of this ritual, however, of importance for the moment is the extinguishing of the lights with milk and ghee to cool the hot *śakti* which they have acquired from proximity to the goddess. After a marriage *Lingāyats*, *Raddis* and all castes which have *Virbhadra* as their family god, and devotees of Śiva called *Puravanta* perform a ceremony called *Guggul*, walking over live embers to demonstrate the power of Śiva. One detail of this rite is the carrying of pots bearing earth and lumps of burning camphor. When these pots are removed from the heads of those that bear them, milk and ghee are used to extinguish the light and are also sprinkled on the heads of the bearers to cool their hot *śakti* which they have derived from the god. In a similar way the torches with which devotees of *Mailardev* play; the fire-torch with which a *Gondhali* plays in the temple of Mahālakṣmī at Kolhapur; the *nandādīp* or lamps used at Navrātri must all be extinguished with milk and ghee. The light again which is kept burning throughout the night of the worship of *Gaurī* is extinguished with milk and ghee and dismissed with the words *śānt raha*, 'remain cool'. Some families worship *Gaurī* through the medium of a pebble brought from a river; milk and ghee are poured on the feet of those who bring the pebbles in order to cool the unknown *śakti* of the goddess. The thread worshipped in *Anantapūjā* is also dismissed with milk and ghee. On the eighth of Āśvin on Durgaṣṭamī newly married girls worship Durgā, through the medium of a pebble brought from near a tulsī plant; the worshipper wears a thread of silk sixteen fold with a knot (tātu); this thread after completion of the rite is preserved till the fourteenth sud Āśvin and then after renewed worship is sprinkled with milk and ghee and buried in the basin of the tulsī plant.

Muhammadans associate the *kudrat* of a saint with heat. When pilgrims visit the dargāh of a saint they sprinkle water round the tomb, *thado karan*, to make it cool. In the month of Rajab Persian Muhammadans in the name of Ḥaḍrat 'Ali put various foods into seven, twenty or forty pots; when the food has been consumed the pots are thrown into water 'to make them cool' because they are hot with the *kudrat* of the saint. The fires which at some shrines in Sind are maintained perpetually are supposed to represent the *kudrat* of the saints.

Death is associated with hot power. The *Kātkarī* pours milk upon a grave to make the dead cool or at peace, *śānt*; the Muhammadan pours milk upon a grave to make it cool. During *Muḥarram* at the place where the tazias which represent biers are fashioned, water is poured on the ground to make it cool; in the Karnāṭak after *Muḥarram* water is poured on the Ālāwā pit which represents a grave. Hindus pour milk and ghee on the ashes of the pyre before they collect them; the spot where a person actually breathes his last is sprinkled with water to make it cool; a rainy day after the celebration of *Holī* is welcomed as cooling the hot *śakti* of that day. On the third day after the funeral of a Hindu milk and ghee are poured on the shoulders of those who carried the bier to cool their hot *śakti*. Before using the water of a well in which some one has been drowned the hot *śakti* of the impurity of death must be cooled by pouring milk and ghee into the well. *Vaddars* sprinkle mourners on their return from a funeral at the house of the deceased with milk by means of hariali grass (Cynodon dactylon). When a Hindu receives intimation of the death of a near relative he is required to take a cold bath and in some castes to eat curds in order to cool his hot *śakti*.

Illness and disease also are associated with hot power. The Muhammadan sprinkles water over the sick to cool their hot *kudrat*; water in which the hands of children after taking food have been washed; water from seven wells. The hands of the sick are also dipped in water and this water is thrown on their faces and at the foot of a tree; in the case of smallpox coming to a household all the members of the house soak their clothes every evening with water and throw the water at the root of a tree to cool the hot *kudrat* causing the disease. The Hindu on an outbreak of smallpox pours water on the '*pādukā*' representing the feet of the goddess responsible so as to cool her hot power.

The menses of a woman is supposed to be caused by hot power. Immediately after her bath on the fourth day she is given curds to cool her hot *śakti*. The impurity of birth again is a form of hot power. On the seventh day after the burial of the severed navel-cord of a child milk and ghee are sprinkled over the site where it was buried to cool its hot power. The grate (*śegaḍī. Mar. aggiṣṭi. Kan.*) used by a woman during her confinement is put aside after her delivery and sprinkled with milk and ghee to make it cool, and that this is not an act of cleansing only is clear from the fact that before this is done the grate is washed. A bath again is given to the child and this a hot one with the hope that the *pāṭ* and the *pōṭ* of the child may remain cool, *pāṭ pōṭ thanḍa aso*; that the dangerous *śakti* in the back of the child which causes the death of successive births, and that in the stomach, *pōṭ*, which affects the child alone, may be cooled.

The wristlets and garlands of the bridal pair are by Muhammadans thrown into water to make them cool, after contact with the hot *kudrat* of the bride and bridegroom; the Hindu after removing the *kankaṇ* of the bridal pair dips them in milk to cool their hot *śakti*. The Hindu throws milk and ghee on the floor of a cattle-shed before he tethers therein his cattle; in the storehouse where he intends to stack his cakes of dry cow-dung; in the spot where he intends to stack his fodder; on constructing a house he places milk and ghee beneath the first layer of the wall and on the frame-work of the roof before he applies the thatch. In all these cases the object is to cool hot *śakti*. On the sixteenth day after a marriage milk is thrown on the marriage *manḍap* or booth to cool its hot *śakti*; milk is sprinkled on a shrine; milk and ghee are poured on the pole of the threshing-floor before it is removed; milk is thrown on the feet of an animal newly purchased and sprinkled round a house when entered for the first time.

The power inherent in grain suffuses with hot *śakti* the sowers who sow the seed; the pole of the threshing-floor and the cattle that tread the grain are likewise made hot, and as described in another chapter this hot *śakti* has to be cooled.

The ritual again followed at some *jatrās* or fairs illustrates the conception of *śakti* as hot. On the night before the fair begins a firepit is dug, *Agnikuṇḍa*, and fire is kindled therein. The next morning at an early hour the *utsavmūrtti* or the processional and duplicate image of the god worshipped at the fair is carried in a palanquin round the fire three times. The recognized worshipper of the god, the pujārī, crosses the fire the same number of times without harm as he is protected by the *śakti* of the god; he is then lifted above the heads of the worshippers. Then to protect the village from harm, to cool the image and make its potentiality beneficent the image is taken to a well or river and bathed. After this the worshippers bathe in a river and water is sprinkled over those who are unable to bathe.

The offering of *naivedya* or food to a deity has as its object the cooling of the *śakti* of the deity. In greater detail the object is a complex one; it is given out of devotion; it is offered as a *baḻī* to remove evil; it is given to pacify the ugra or fierce *śakti* of the deity. There are some gods that require a specific quantity of food every day and evil follows if less than this amount is given. In these cases the *naivedya* offering cools the hot *śakti* of hunger, the *Jaṭharāgni*. The various kinds of *baḻī* again offered to spirits and to gods make them *śānt*, 'cool' or appeased. When milk is offered to standing crops this again may be a *naivedya* to cool the *śakti* of Lakṣmī with whom crops are identified, or it may be because the crops are considered to be pregnant, but here again it is possible to surmise that a pregnant woman has hot *śakti* which requires cooling.

Power therefore in many forms is associated with heat, the power of divinity, of a saint, of a bridegroom; the innate power of *pāyguṇ* discussed later, the power inherent in grain; but heat is also associated with certain forms of impurity which normally are destructive of power. The concept of heat, in fine, produces a link between the unclean and the holy which will be emphasized in other chapters of this book.

POWER AND MERIT

Man, according to Hindu belief, cannot accomplish anything without a fund of *puṇya* or merit; if he has children, health or wealth, his fortune is attributed to *puṇya*. A *puṇyavant* or person with acquired merit can accomplish anything; his words are prophetic and come true; his blessing confers longevity, his power confers *barkat*. He may even accomplish evil and when he tyrannizes over an innocent person, several popular phrases say that the power of the *puṇyavant* can accomplish anything. *Puṇyad balā ade enu māḍiḍaru naḍitade* (Kan.) and *Puṇyāci jor āhe tyāmuḻe keltari cālte* (Mar.). The mere sight of a *puṇyavant* uplifts and he can bring salvation to the meanest person.

The abnormal *śakti* attributed to a child raising it to the rank of a god is inseparable from its supposed innocence. Faithfulness to her husband brings a wife special *śakti*. The worship of a pious man adds to the *śakti* in an image, and the invocation of power into an image, *pratimā*, by the pious draws into the image greater *śakti* than the ordinary man can draw. This correlation of piety to *śakti* is frequently emphasized in the ancient literature of Hinduism. In the *Manasara Silpa-Śāstra* the master-builder was to be of unblemished character; in the *Nāṭyaśāstra* poets, singers and dancers were to be of stainless character. In the *Institutes of Viṣṇu* a long list of persons is given who were to be excluded from a *Śrāddha* ceremony for the dead and the practice of to-day repeats the same emphasis. At a *Śrāddha* ceremony to-day the Brahmins chosen to represent God or the manes are to be of good character.

In agricultural operations the choice of a good man to begin a work is common; it is quite common indeed for several land-holders to use the same ploughman to initiate their ploughing because of his reputation for piety. Seed sown by a good man always fertilizes, and grain measured by a pious man shows the greatest increase. Piety again is essential to the control of *śakti*; saints who depart from the path of virtue lose *śakti* and mantriks who practise a magic art of healing find their charms without effect if they lead bad lives. There are well-known families in several districts with such power of healing obtained from some saint in the past, some members of which are powerless because of their irregular manner of living.

In one set of practices the efficacy of a rite depends upon the number of the celebrants, and this not merely because common wishes and common will create or invoke *śakti*, but because in a large number of persons there is fair hope that there will be at least one pious person. To the hair of a pious woman is attributed the power of averting evil-eye or of ameliorating its effects. As it is not given to man to divine who is really pious and who is not, the hair-combings of many women are collected and tied to the necks of cattle as a protection against evil-eye; amongst so many women, it is hoped, one will transfer the power that her piety engenders. This same idea enters into the practice of wrapping an infant in clothes collected from many households to guard it against the evil-eye ; though other ideas may enter into this custom there is also the supposition that one household will be a pious one and through the clothes it has parted with will transfer *barkat*. In the same way when an expectant mother finds difficulty in delivery a long line of persons is formed from a well and down this line is passed in silence a pot of water which is eventually given the mother to drink ; somewhere or other the pot must have passed through the hands of a pious person whose piety will confer *śakti* on the woman in her travail.

When piety is credited to a person his *śakti* is deliberately sought. Water in which the back portion of the *dhotar* of a pious man is washed is given to a woman in her travail to drink, with the object both of averting from her evil-eye and of giving her *śakti*. Certain castes and communities have a reputation for honesty or other virtue and are employed by others in the initial stages of an important work. *Kurubas*, because of their traditional honesty, are used to make a nominal ploughing on New Year's Day ; residents of a village in which *Kurubas* reside will not begin sowing until a *Kuruba* has sown some little seed. Shopkeepers consider themselves fortunate if their first transaction in any day is made with a *Kuruba* or a *Raddi*. Village officers of Government, when they collect the land revenue demands, collect first from a *Kuruba* so that the collection work may proceed without hitch, and on one occasion when I staged a drama in aid of local hospitals my subordinate staff sold the first tickets of admission to *Kurubas* and attributed the success of the drama to their prescience. *Kudurakkligars*, a subcaste of Lingāyats, are another community whose supposed piety brings *barkat* to any work begun through their assistance.

All these fundamental ideas can be paralleled in Muhammadan practice and belief. In making *barani nimāz* or prayer to bring rain a man with the *kudrat* of piety is chosen to lead the prayer ; relatives of the dead choose the most pious man they can find to conduct the funeral prayer which is to solace the departed, and if in the agony of his dying the *sūratu yā sīn* is recited by a pious man it relieves the dying man. The turban of a saint on his assuming the *gādī*, that is taking up his charge, is tied by the most pious man procurable. Charms vary in their efficacy according to the piety of the person using them and in counteracting the effects of evil-eye a pious man is chosen.

A stricter parallel even than these to the Hindu customs I have described is afforded by the following Muhammadan practices. On the third, seventh or fortieth day after a funeral Mullahs and

Maulvis are feasted in honour of the dead, but the dead loses *barkat* if those so feasted are not of good character. In Sind every good work should be begun by a good man, whether this be the digging of a new well, measuring grain, tying the turban of the bridegroom, stitching the clothes to be worn by the bridal pair, obtaining control of spirits, *Ḥāḍrāt Jinn*, or making a transference of evil *Ghorā*. In Sind, besides wrapping a baby in clothes collected from many houses, the infant is placed in a cradle bought with money collected from many houses. If there be an epidemic a whole congregation will blow in the direction from which it is expected the epidemic will approach; every member too of a congregation will blow after prayers on a pot of water which is then given to the sick. At a Muhammadan funeral the mourners throw earth on to the body of the dead and the grave in the hope that the *kudrat* of one pious person will secure the dead absolution. On the last Friday of *Ramaḍān* people come to mosques with pieces of paper and get forty members of the congregation to write out the first chapter of the Koran and then use these papers as an amulet to protect a new-born child from evil. The same hope of obtaining power from the piety of some chance-invited guest, along with the other idea that common will begets power, underlies the hospitality which embraces a large number of guests.

As these two ideas go so closely together I will give a few more examples of practices in which power and its concomitant *barkat* is sought through the agency of a large number of persons. At a Hindu marriage or thread ceremony *akṣat* or unbroken rice is thrown on the bridal pair and on the *vaṭu* by all the guests; before the *vaṭu* or boy whose thread ceremony is being performed is invested with the sacred thread it is passed through the hands of many priests and *Brahmacārīs*; before the bridegroom ties the *mangaḷsūtra* or auspicious necklace to the neck of the bride it is passed by many *suvāsinīs* or married women from hand to hand; the *akṣat* of blessing, *mantrākṣat*, thrown on the principal figure in a ceremony, the *yajamān*, by priests, is first passed through the hands of priest after priest; in rites intended to bring rain hundreds of people go to a nulla or stream to hold a feast, *parva*, and again *barkat* is hoped for in their numbers. The greater the number of mourners who attend a Muhammadan funeral, the greater the hope that the dead will win *barkat*; the multitude of guests at a wedding convey *kudrat* to the bridal pair; in times of famine big processions are formed by Muhammadans bearing holy books to bring rain, and at a Muhammadan wedding the bridal pair measure grain, and at this time all their relatives and as many old persons as possible touch their hands.

The possession of 'merit', therefore, is clearly associated with the simultaneous possession of 'power'. One can speak of a 'power of *puṇya*'. There is, however, another aspect to the intimate relation between *puṇya* and *śakti*. The winning of *puṇya* is dependent on *śakti*; it cannot be won under circumstances which destroy *śakti* and it is lost by the same factors which destroy *śakti*.

Though *puṇya* can be won at other times, there are portions of *parvakāl* which are called *puṇyakāl*; the greater the *śakti* of a moment, the greater the possibility of winning *puṇya*. Rāmanavami, for instance, is a day of *śakti*, a *parvakāl* and the time therein when the birth of Rāma is celebrated is a *puṇyakāl*. There is, of course, the inherent danger in a *parvakāl* which makes it, unless it coincides with a *muhūrtta*, a bad time for winning *puṇya*, but a *muhūrtta* derives its auspiciousness from *śakti*, and there are certain days more or less devoid of *śakti* such as the *Kṣayatitha* and the *Kṣayamās* when it is difficult to win *puṇya* because of the absence of *śakti*.

Puṇya again can be won as is *śakti* by contact. By applying to his person earth or water from the *Tulsīvṛndāvan* a man may obtain *puṇya*; on his death if his body be burned with dry tulsi sticks he acquires *puṇya*. The touch and sight of a cow confer *puṇya*; by sprinkling over his person the urine of a cow or water found in the footprint of a cow a man wins merit. The sight and touch of certain trees bring *puṇya*. *Puṇya* is obtained by bathing in a river particularly at a *parvakāl* when the *śakti* of water is greatest; by stepping in the precincts of a sacred shrine; by touching a temple or things which are in contact themselves with divinity; *darśan* or the sight of entities with power confers *puṇya*, the *darśan* of images, even the sight from afar of a temple spire or the sight of holy men. Contact with power through wearing things possessed of power brings *puṇya* to the wearer; beads of ark (Calotropis gigantea), beads of tulsī (Ocimum sanctum) worn as rosaries confer *puṇya*; the Agnihotrī to win *puṇya* wears ornaments of gold, *karṇakuṇḍal*, with two rudrākṣa (Eleocarpus ganitrus) beads, whilst the wearing of a *Śāligrām* stone or linga also confers *puṇya*. Touching sacred books; touching the feet of priests, of saints, of the bridal pair and even touching the dead confers *puṇya*.

Prasād and *tīrth* are both examples of transferred *śakti*. Leaves and flowers used in worship; the offerings of food, *naivedya*, made to a god; the coconut broken before an image; sandalwood paste used in worship; incense, *dhūpa*, burnt and waved before an image; lights waved round a god, *ārtī*. *dīp.*; water in which an image has been bathed, *tīrth*, are all *prasād.* They have all derived *śakti* from contact with divinity and these when touched or taken by a worshipper convey *puṇya.*

The highly developed ritual of Hinduism, confusing on a first study with its meticulous detail, appears more simple in form if its injunctions and multitudinous prohibitions are summarized as nothing but a code of rules by which the *śakti* essential to the winning of *puṇya* can be preserved or enhanced, and on the other hand by which acts that destroy *śakti* or beneficent *śakti* and bring evil *śakti* or *pāp*, 'sin', can be avoided. *Dharma. adharma.* is the tie with which the *śakti* of *puṇya* and *pāp*, of merit and sin, is bound round the soul of man. 'The Keys of Power' are the keys of *puṇya.* Breach of the law of Dharma is sin, *pāp*; it is the loss of that *śakti* which brings *puṇya.*

The rules as to ritual cleanliness are as applicable to the winning of *puṇya* as they are to the fruition of a more mundane object. A person polluted by the virus of death or birth, *sutak* or *suher*, cannot add to his store of *puṇya*, though if he die his destination in the next world is determined by the store of *puṇya* he has previously acquired. Chastity is essential before performing rites intended to produce *puṇya*; before a sacrifice or before a *vrata* or vow. A sacred book cannot be read nor its recital by others listened to, nor can silent prayer, *jap*, be performed when unclean. Here again *puṇya* is like *śakti*; it cannot be won when unclean. If mourners are not clean, the dead loses *puṇya.* Sleep which is an unclean state destroys *puṇya* as it destroys *barkat.* The goddess *Mohinī* steals from a person who has earned *puṇya* by the fast of Ekādaśī all his *puṇya* if he sleeps after the midday meal the next day. To prevent such loss of *puṇya* during sleep, if the *yajamān* feels himself overpowered by sleep, before sleeping he applies ghee to his feet in the belief that *Mohinī* will be deceived and on licking the ghee will assume she has stolen his *puṇya.*

Puṇya is lost by every impure contact, by any evil form of *śakti.* If the stone-of-life be placed on the ground the dead loses *puṇya*; the curse of a guest causes loss of *puṇya* to his host; the touch of unclean persons destroys *puṇya*; to be beaten by a shoe or to beat another with a broom is to lose *puṇya.* *Puṇya* is lost by any form of *himsā.* The contact of iron destroys *puṇya*, and if iron be used in a *Śrāddha* ceremony the dead loses *puṇya.*

Puṇya, accordingly, not only gives its possessor *śakti* but can be acquired only by the possession of *śakti.* As *śakti* can be transferred, so *puṇya* can be obtained by contacts which effect a transference of *śakti*. Further than this, when won, *puṇya* can, like *śakti*, be transferred to another.

THE TRANSFER OF PUṆYA

Hinduism accepts the belief that *puṇya* can be earned [1] by one person for another to whom it is transferred. Half the *puṇya* earned by a husband goes to the wife, though she cannot earn any *puṇya* for her husband; children acquire *puṇya* from the acts of their parents. If a woman dies without having observed the *Ṛsipancmī vrata* she is reborn again as a woman, and to avert such a reincarnation her son can observe the *vrata* for her and transfer to her the *puṇya* he earns. In certain recitals of scriptures, *Saptaśiti Pārāyaṇa* and *Gurucarita Pārāyaṇa* and certain *jap*, a proxy is given to a priest to earn *puṇya* for one who cannot earn it direct; a deity can be worshipped by one person for another and certain vows can be observed vicariously.

If one has earned *puṇya* by a vow, one can transfer this *puṇya* to another by pouring water over tulsī-leaves on to the hands of the other, to the accompaniment of mantras; another practice is to make a gift of a betel-nut saying 'whatever *puṇya* I have earned be transferred to you', to place this in the right palm of the recipient and then in confirmation of the gift pour water on to the nut.

Muhammadans have ideas somewhat similar. Shi'ahs send others on pilgrimage to Mecca to earn merit for themselves and

[1] In the *Padmapurana*, in a dialogue with his consort, Śri Kṛṣṇa speaks about the transfer of *pāp* and *puṇya*. A quarter of the *puṇya* earned by a pupil goes to his teacher; if one earns *pāp* or *puṇya* by following the advice of another, one-sixth of it goes to the latter; a king claims one-eighth of earned *puṇya*. A debtor dying in debt transfers his *puṇya* to his creditor; merit acquired by a deed performed with the monetary aid of another wins *puṇya* in some share for the latter; by taking the services of another in some cases *puṇya* is transferred. By speaking ill of another an exchange of *puṇya* and *pāp* is made; the slanderer loses his merit and gains the *pāp* of the other. Sexual congress or dining from one plate results in an equal partition of sin and merit; by contact with the breath of another, by touching him, talking with him or sitting on the same seat with him, a transfer of sin and merit is effected.

In the *Vritarāj* is a story of a Brahmin Devasvāmī who had a daughter Gunavati destined to become a widow by losing her husband in the middle of a Saptapadī rite. The father was advised by a saint that Soma could avert her widowhood, so he brought Soma to his daughter's marriage. In the course of the Saptapadī Gunavati's husband died. Then Soma made a gift of the *puṇya* she had herself earned by observance of the Somvati *vrata* to Gunavati and by this gift Gunavati's husband was restored to life. By her gift, however, Soma lost her *puṇya* and in consequence her own husband died, but she again won *puṇya* and the restoration of her own husband by worshipping the aśvath tree.

defray the expenses of their pilgrimage; on a death, mourners make a recital of the whole of the Koran and then get a Mullah to pray for the deceased and in his prayers to include the gift of the merit acquired by them through their recital of the Koran. This transfer of merit is alluded to directly in the words, 'I make a gift of my merit to the dead'. Just too as the Hindu child derives *puṇya* from its parents, so the Muhammadan child inherits merit from its parents.

Ideas associated with charity show how both *puṇya* and *pāp*, merit and sin, are related to *śakti*, the former beneficent and the latter evil. At the various *sanskār* of a Hindu specific gifts are made to priests. Different months again are connected with different forms of gifts; at the close of *vratas* gifts are also made to priests. In all these cases of making a gift the priest loses *śakti* by his acceptance of the gift, *pratigraha*, and to recoup himself for this loss of power he has to perform a *prayascitta*, the ordinary form of which consists in making a thousand *jap* or silent recitals of the Gāyatrī mantra. When he accepts food from the *yajamān* at a *jātkarma* he has to observe a *cāndrāyaṇa vrata* in which for fifteen days as the moon increases he adds to his food, and for fifteen days as the moon wanes proportionately reduces his food.

A person accepting a gift becomes the bondsman of the donor and loses his own individual *śakti*. Even after accepting hospitality a guest becomes unclean through loss of *śakti* and cannot strictly worship a god until he has performed a purificatory ceremony. The acceptance of a gift may mean even more than this. On the twelfth day of any of the months forming *Caturmās* there are persons who conceal a gold, silver or pearl ornament in a vessel filled with rice and give this to a priest without telling him what has been hidden therein; this gift is called *guptadān*, the 'secret or concealed gift', and by it the donor frees himself from his secret sins. There are also *ugra* or fierce gifts made deliberately with the object of passing on evil or sins to others. Particular things are appropriate objects to offer to each of the planets through the medium of a priest to avert their evil influence, their *pīḍā*. These gifts are *ugra* and reduce the *śakti* of the recipient. During obsequies various gifts are made to a priest in the interest of the dead; these are very baneful for the recipient. He loses *śakti*, and should he accept as a gift the bed of the deceased, he can never be reborn as a man in another birth as he has lost so much *śakti* and he must perform all his *sanskār* over again. At various *parvakāl*, at an eclipse, at the sankramaṇa of the sun and at other hours of *śakti*, gifts are made to free oneself from evil and to transfer one's sins.

The acceptance of a gift, then, means a loss of *śakti*. The *Laws of Manu*, iv, 187–91, speak of the danger of accepting a gift: 'Without a full knowledge of the rules prescribed by the sacred law for the acceptance of presents a wise man should not take anything even though he may pine with hunger. But an ignorant man who accepts gold, land, a horse, a cow, food, a dress, sesamum, grain or clarified butter is reduced to ashes like a piece of wood. Gold and food destroy his longevity, land and a cow his body, a horse his eyesight, a garment his skin, clarified butter his energy, sesamum grains his offspring. A Brahmana who neither performs austerities nor studies the Vedas yet delights in accepting gifts sinks with the donor into hell just as he who attempts to cross over in a boat made of stone is submerged in the water. Hence an ignorant man should be afraid of accepting any presents for by reason of a very small gift even a fool sinks into hell as a cow into a morass'. 'As he who attempts to cross water in a boat of stone sinks to the bottom, even so an ignorant donor and an ignorant donee sink low' (194).

The practice of to-day is still based on the same idea as to the danger inherent in the acceptance of a gift. At holy places of pilgrimage in India charitable persons open *chatras* or lodging-houses where a pilgrim may obtain food or if he wishes to cook his own food, may have the loan of cooking utensils. In their anxiety to obtain the benefits accruing from making a gift, of which I will speak later, the owners of these houses press their charity upon the pilgrims, but many pilgrims resist their blandishments and refuse to accept any charity lest they should lose the *puṇya* they have won or hope to win by their visit to the holy place. It is again a practice to perform certain *sanskār* of others at one's own expense in order to win the advantages that the donor of charity obtains. *Dharma munja* and *dharma vivāha* are thread and marriage ceremonies of the poor performed during the similar ceremonies of some one else and at the expense of the latter. At one *Lingāyat* marriage that I attended two poor children hardly older than infants were married in order to bring *barkat* to the bridal pair of the main marriage. There is, however, a very definite limitation to this form of charity; there can be no charity funeral, for the interests of the dead have to be considered.

The acceptance of a gift thus results in a loss of *śakti* or of *puṇya* to the person who takes it. On the other hand, it confers

2

puṇya on the donor of the gift. The sacred books of Hinduism describe almsgiving as conferring merit, as destroying sin. The fact that it is the donor of a gift who acquires *puṇya* accounts for the value that a Hindu gives to articles that have been stolen; the use of these does not bestow *puṇya* on any donor. In fire festivals the fuel for the fire is usually stolen and as I have explained later stolen articles are even used in worship. Hospitality as a form of charity also brings *puṇya* to the host, and the counter danger to the guest is illustrated by the phrase *parānn varj yet*, 'avoid accepting the food of others'.

The *puṇya* won by charity can be won only through *śakti*. When a man is unclean he cannot by making a gift obtain *puṇya* for himself; a mourner, for instance, can win *puṇya* by charity only for the dead. The occasion too on which charity is given is also very important; alms given at an eclipse are very effective, whilst alms given at sunset bring no *puṇya* to the donor. In other ways too this *puṇya* is correlated to *śakti*. In the gratitude and good wishes of those who receive charity is *śakti* and this produces *puṇya*; contrariwise ill wishes or curses destroy *puṇya*. 'A man who eats before his guest consumes the *puṇya* of his family' (*Apastamba*, II, 3, 7, 3) and a guest turned away with disappointment takes away from a householder his *puṇya* and throws on him his own guilt (*Institutes of Viṣṇu*, lxvii, 33).

If *puṇya* be *śakti*, as many Hindus with whom I have discussed the problem admit, or if it be as others assert merely inseparable from *śakti*, *pāp* or sin is equally so. *Dharma* prescribes certain rules of conduct the breach of which is *pāp*. Bathing in holy waters or uttering the name of a god or shrine when unclean; stepping over *prasād*, *tīrth* and other things possessing beneficent *śakti*, placing objects which possess such *śakti* on the ground and showing disrespect to persons possessing abnormal *śakti*, are all examples of *pāp*. In all these instances *pāp* or sin is nothing but the effects which follow the revolt of outraged *śakti*. The *śakti* which if respected produces good, when disrespected produces ill, and this good and this ill are called *puṇya* and *pāp*.

Pāpa, again like *śakti*, is transferable and this is implied in the common Hindu belief in vicarious suffering. If a wife sins, her husband shares half the punishment of her sin; if her sin be unfaithfulness, forty-two ancestors of her husband's family and that of her father go to hell. Should a man shave on a Monday, the life of his sons is shortened; if he wears his sacred thread on the wrong shoulder, he shortens the lives of his parents. If a married woman has a full bath on the day her husband shaves, his life is shortened, and if he shaves after she has taken a complete bath, her life is shortened. A guest who leaves his nail-parings in a house brings his host to poverty. If anyone writes letters or makes marks on the ground with charcoal, the outraged *śakti* of the ground brings the owner of the house into debt. If fire be taken behind a man's back and he does not correct the affront by looking at the fire at once, the resentment of the *śakti* of the fire brings harm to his brother. If a *yajamān* blows on fire it is the priest helping him who suffers. If the bridal pair go into the sun, the parents come to grief. Sneezing on the threshold means a shorter life for one's maternal uncle; one's next-door neighbour suffers if one hears the sound of grinding at certain times. A dishonest servant who misappropriates money entrusted to him to give in charity ruins his master financially, and a disciple who sells the knowledge he has acquired from his guru involves the guru in sin. A woman who sews on Monday reduces the days her son will live. If a man declines to eat a dish of *khīr* already served to him his mother dies the sooner, and he reduces his mother-in-law to poverty if he does not eat rice and whey at the close of his principal meal.

From the point of view I have adopted *puṇya* and *pāp* are but *śakti*, or at least inseparable from *śakti*. Every moment a man lives is a drain upon his store of *puṇya*. The term *puṇya sancaya* or 'fund of merit' is applied to *puṇya*, but one never speaks of a fund of *pāp*. This last is merely destructive of *puṇya*. If a man does not constantly perform rites to add to his store of *puṇya* he loses *śakti* with which to fight the *śakti* of evil. The maintenance of a fund of *puṇya* brings him happiness in this world; at his death according to his store of *puṇya* is his bliss in heaven from which he descends to be reborn again when his fund of *puṇya* has become exhausted. As however the soul attains *mukti* or absolution only when there is no balancing of *pāp* against *puṇya* and heaven itself is impermanent, *puṇya* becomes detrimental to attaining the final goal of Hindu endeavour.

CHAPTER II

THE POWER OF MAN

EVERYTHING in a cosmos ruled by power has its own inherent qualities. The Sindi says *kathi kathi lachan ahe,* 'every piece of wood has a different quality'; *lakria lakria bhag ahe,* 'every piece of wood has its own fortune.' A change of the peg with which an animal is tethered may alter completely the condition of the animal; the substitution of one door for another may bring a complete change of fortune to a householder. A belief that every portion of a house has its own *kudrat* leads the Sindi to move a woman in her travail from one part of her room to another, in the hope that she may benefit from that part of the house which has the greatest *kudrat.* The debris of a house a Hindu will use for repairing another house, but never for building a new house, and earth must not be carried, attached to the plough, from one field to another. Sindi Muhammadan women when cooking grain will not throw a single grain away, for it is not known in which grain most *barkat* resides. *Dane dane barkat ahe.*

Man's inherent qualities are called *Pāyguṇ* (Marāṭhī); *Kālguṇ* (Kanarese); *Pagalyā* (Marwari); *Paglān* (Gujarātī), and associated with his foot or leg, but how loosely is seen from the fact that the same terms are applied to the qualities of a house or of a broom, or in fine any other thing that comes for the first time into contact with man. These qualities of the leg or foot in the case of man are determined by the conjunction of stars at his birth; they may be betrayed in man, woman or animal by inauspicious and auspicious markings,[1] but often permit of no valuation till some event

[1] Bad *pāyguṇ* is betrayed in a man by a speck, *macce,* on his left side; in a woman by black lips, pillar-shaped legs, drum-like waist, flat feet, broad forehead, irregular teeth or a masculine appearance. A cow which always nods its head, butts the tethering-post or sheds tears betrays its evil *pāyguṇ. Koḍu baḍiyo danā iṭṭare keḍu tappadu* (Kan.), 'Disaster must follow if animals butt with their horns.' A she-buffalo with the appearance of a male, with thick hide or tail, three nipples or a single horn bending forwards brings evil. There are in all seventy-two inauspicious markings of a horse, *gom* or *khoḍ.* Curls of hair,

permits of a *post hoc ergo propter hoc* decision. The stellar control of *pāyguṇ* is evidenced by the propitiation of the planets which is one way of removing the ill effects attributed to it.

There are other terms which signify the inherent qualities of man as distinct from the *hātguṇ* or the resulting effects of his actions. *Pāycāl* is the evil foot of some ill-starred person passed on the road which explains the failure of a purpose or the aggravation of a disease. In the Karnāṭak as an alternative to *kālguṇ*, 'the qualities of the leg', there is the word *kāldhūḻi*, 'the dust of the leg', another expression of somewhat indefinite connotation as it is also applied to evil-eye. The Sindi speaks of a person with evil foot or evil eye as *manhūs*, which means influenced by an inauspicious star, and the person with a lucky foot as *saïd* or *masaūd*; the foot is *sadoro*, 'lucky', or *nindoro*, 'unlucky', the *kadam* or 'step' is *ghoro*, 'heavy with *kudrat*', and when this power is for evil he speaks of *perchanva*, 'the shadow of the foot'.

Pāyguṇ operates without the volition of the person in question. He may warn even those he meets that he radiates evil, but such warning would not avert his evil influence. The effects of *Pāyguṇ* are known but tardily, for to every happening a cause is attributed after the event. With a tendency however to anticipate evil, man looks upon the *pāyguṇ* of his fellow-men with suspicion and takes measures of precaution to forestall its baneful activities, which destroy fortune and may bring a sequel of illness or death. Its effects approximate to those of the evil-eye. It makes flour watery and thin; it spoils the preparation of food; it reduces the milk an animal yields; it affects adversely the increase of the grain on the threshing-floor or the quantity of wool obtained when shearing. It turns honey and sugar-cane juice sour; it aggravates a disease and can cause a boat to sink. In general, only calamities affecting the family are attributed to *pāyguṇ*, but in Sind disasters

suḻī, reveal the nature of its *pāyguṇ*. A horse with a curl on its eyebrows, cheeks, back, thigh, shoulders, stomach, the tip of its nose or of its ears, at the side of its eyes, on its crest brings nothing but disaster to its owner. Disaster comes also to the owner of a horse with a cluster of black hair covered by a white cluster or a white cluster covered by a black one (*Dhankanio*); one with two clusters of hair on the throat (*Galkatu*); one that always sheds tears (*Ansudhor*); one with a small cluster of hair covered by a larger one called 'breaker of water-pots' (*Behanrafod*). Auspicious markings are white marks on the feet and forehead (*Panckalyāṇ*); a mark on the chest (*Devmand*); a small cluster of hair over a larger one (*Behara Chahadau*); a mark on the neck (*Kantabharan*); white specks on the forehead smaller than a rupee (*Satar Peśani*); a uniform colour with two white forelegs (*Jaska*); two white forelegs and a long white mark down the face (*Fatehjang*). The Cāndaṇi with a white star on the forehead brings the master bad fortune as do the wall-eyed horse (*Kairāḍoḻā*); the horse with a black roof to its mouth (*Kṛṣṇatāḻu*); one with the mark of a centipede on one flank (*Kusgom*) and one with a ring of hair on one flank only (*Kuśavratt*).

such as a flight of locusts affecting a whole district are attributed to the *pāyguṇ* of a bride, and to the *pāyguṇ* of the British was attributed the timely rain that after a period of scarcity followed the British conquest of Sind.

Avoiding contact with other men is the safest precaution and this has the advantage, further, of giving protection against evil-eye. The exclusion of strangers is characteristic of both Hindu and Muhammadan practice. When a woman milks a cow she should be alone; when she churns, the presence of others will reduce the quantity of butter obtained or make it thin. The preparation of a meal involves the exclusion of others, and the admittance of strangers to the threshing-floor whilst grain is being threshed or measured is controlled by precise restrictions. Strangers too are excluded when implements are worshipped by the Hindu.

When the presence of others is unavoidable many measures are taken to render innocuous the potentiality of the stranger or visitor. A host may require his guest or visitor to wash his feet before entering his house, or pass first some time in the sacred precincts of a temple or mosque. He may take food and wave it thrice vertically before the new-comer and then throw it away in two opposite directions. He may mix water with turmeric in a plate and wave round the head of the intruder, finally throwing it at his feet. The stranger may be required to step into the house the right foot foremost and as he does so to kick over a measure of grain placed on the threshold and coloured white and red. Iron nails are driven into the threshold or where the stranger within the house first placed his left foot; iron horse-shoes are fastened on the door or threshold to avert the evil potentiality of *pāyguṇ*. And when a visitor is departing, black *rāḻā* (Panicum Italicum) is thrown behind him, or a black sooty pan or pot is dashed to the ground behind him. Earth too is collected from one of his foot-prints and thrown into fire or at the junction of meeting roads. Lastly, when a visitor has gone, one brushes the steps of the house well with water; one strikes the steps with a broom and one turns all the chairs and tables he has used (Sind). Nim leaves (Melia azadirachta) are hung over the door of a room wherein an expectant mother is confined to render innocuous the *pāyguṇ* of visitors, and the same leaves are used to sprinkle water on their feet. The *Kātkarī* washes the feet of all visitors at a marriage with water, using the leaves of five trees.

A bride comes to her new home with the mystery of the unknown. Even the marriage may be interrupted by some cause such as death or illness, which is attributed to the foot of the bride. To avert the evil effects of her *pāygun̥*, before the bridal pair in Sind arrive at the bridegroom's house a fowl is killed and its blood spread on the threshold and over this the pair have to step. This averts, too, any evil that may follow from the *pāygun̥* of the bridegroom. At the threshold of her husband's house the Muhammadan bride is stopped; a silver or gold coin is placed in her palm covered by a small lamp of earth, *diya*, which she carries lighted into the house. When the bride arrives *Talwārs* and *Vaddars* drive nails into the threshold. Another Sindi custom is for seven married women to place a kind of milk pudding in the left hand of the bride when she reaches the bridegroom's house, and for one of the women to kick it out of the bride's hand. When the bride goes to her father-in-law's house for the first time it is a common practice to throw aside a tumblerful of black and yellow water and to drive a nail at once into the threshold. To protect her husband's house against her evil potentiality the bride is required to press with her right foot a two-seers measure of grain placed on the threshold and to push some of the grain into the house with her foot, entering the house her right foot first.

In a similar way the *pāygun̥* of a newly purchased animal causes apprehension. To render it harmless *Talwārs* and *Vaddars* make an offering of food to the tail of their new purchase; *Talwārs* wash the tail of the animal; *Bhils* give the animal grain to eat with the same object. Other precautions taken are the waving of five plantains before the animal and their throwing away to the inauspicious south; the washing of the feet of the animal and touching these with gold and pearls; the waving of bread round the animal and the throwing of it away before the animal is admitted to its stall. Milk is also poured on the feet of an animal to make its *pāygun̥* white or auspicious. In Sind when a new animal is purchased the purchaser takes with him a rope and a bunch of green grass so that the luck of the animal may remain green and auspicious; gold is also dipped in water and this is then sprinkled over the purchase, or the forehead of the animal is touched with a piece of gold. If in spite of these precautions misfortune continues to befall the purchaser of an animal, natural proof that its *pāygun̥* is evil, the animal is sold even at a loss.

To avert the evil *pāygun̥* of a child it is given to others to nourish; nine kinds of grain, representing the nine planets, are given along with a cow, a pumpkin and cloth to priests as an additional measure of precaution. *Kurubas* on payment stall their sheep in fields at night to provide manure; if any sheep or goat wandered in the night it was until quite recently given away as its *pāygun̥* was evil and would destroy the *barkat* of the flock; to-day the errant sheep or goat is sold even at a loss if necessary.

SHADOW AND REFLECTION

A shadow is most intimately related to the object which throws the shadow. The Sindi explains the *kudrat* of the shadow as due to its containing an emanation from the body (*hamzat*). A man's innate power is greatest when his shadow is longest, and this is one reason for the choice of the hours of sunset and dawn for the practices which are directed to gaining power. On the other hand, when man has little or no shadow as at noon,[1] his power is negligible and at this hour a series of restrictions forbids his doing acts which reduce power. As a man approaches death his shadow grows smaller and astrologers claim they can measure a man's longevity by studying his shadow. According to popular Muhammadan belief, the Prophet was the only man who had no shadow.

A shadow transfers to the object overshadowed the power of the object casting the shadow, for it is itself but a part of that latter object. There are accordingly shadows that confer *barkat* and shadows that destroy power. The shadow of a *puṇyavant* or person who has won *puṇya* or merit, and that of a saint confer *barkat*. To a Muhammadan the shadow of a virgin, of a small child, of a Pir, a Saiyid, a Maulvi or a fakir has the same effect. A good shadow may even turn a bad man into a good one, and when people succeed in all they attempt they are said to have

[1] Sir James Frazer (*Taboo and the Perils of the Soul*, 1922, p. 88) suggests that noon was chosen by the Greeks as the hour for sacrificing to the shadowless dead, because of the diminished shadow of man at noon. Hindus believe that when a ghost becomes one of the manes it loses its shadow. The Hindu *Śrāddha* is not, however, performed precisely at noon, though very nearly so. *Pitṛtarpaṇa* or the oblation of water to the manes is made at noon, but the *piṇḍapradān* and other important rites in the *Śrāddha* are performed within the *aparānhakāl*, the fourth kāl of the five kāl into which the day is divided from sunrise to sunset. Each kāl is made up of six *ghaṭikā* of twenty-four minutes each. In the *piṇḍapradān* darbha grass is spread on the ground, the tips of the blades pointing towards the south, the direction in which lies the abode of shades. The *yajamān* first pours water and til on the grass and then places thereon a *piṇḍa* or ball of cooked rice in the name of the deceased whose *Śrāddha* he is celebrating. Then he places two other similar *piṇḍa* in the names of the father and grandfather of the deceased, or if the deceased be a woman the names of her mother and grandmother. *Akṣat* or unbroken rice is then thrown on the *piṇḍa* with an exclamation uttered on making an oblation; more *akṣat* is thrown and this with the word of invocation *āvāhan*. The *śakti* of the manes is thus invoked. When this *śakti* is dismissed the *yajamān* first obtains the permission of the officiating priest to dismiss the *śakti* and then moves the *piṇḍa* with his hand. If a *pinda* should crack of its own accord before its dismissal, the death of the *yajamān* occurs at a short interval.

fallen under the shadow of the great. The shadow of a good man is often allowed to fall on the sick in the hope of effecting their cure.

There are trees whose shadow is distinctly productive of good. In general, all trees with a milky sap are considered by the Hindu to have good shadows and the absence of such sap condemns the tree and its shadow. The Muhammadan, believing the shadow of a nim tree (Melia azadirachta) to confer *barkat*, plants it over the graves of the dead. A Hindu writing a charm, *yantra*, to assist the delivery of a woman, seats himself as he writes in the shadow of a kaṅgal tree (Pongamia glabra) in order to draw from the power of the tree.

Of evil-working shadows the number is legion. There are animals that at certain definite moments, but not always, have a very evil shadow. The shadow of a newly fledged sparrow when it makes its first flight falling on children will make them lose a limb. In the Konkan if a certain bird, *bhil kavḍā*, drink of the water which is carried to and sprinkled on a pyre and having drunk, casts a shadow on animal or man, it breaks the back of its victim. To the *Pancāḻ*, the Muhammadan and others in the Karnāṭak, the shadow of a black drongo disturbed when hatching will cause one horn of a cow to wither away, and falling on a man will twist and paralyse half of his face. A bat's shadow at dusk gives children a disease called *hakkidoṣa* from which they pine away and die. One symptom of this disease is that the child lies with its hands and feet behind its head like a bat. To effect a cure jvārī, rice, wheat, uḍīd and black sesamum are ground into flour from which a cake is prepared and baked; the middle of the cake is then cut away, leaving a rim through which the child is passed three times. The rim is then tied to a tree frequented by bats so that bats may also pass through it and complete the cure. The shadow of a *halakki* bird produces deformity should it fall on a child or pregnant woman, and so children, and women who are *enceinte* avoid walking abroad at sunset when this bird flies about. The shadow of an owl is also considered bad in Sind.

There are trees whose shadow is dangerous. In Sind the shadows of the bar, sirih, lai and lao are bad. A Hindu is forbidden to go in the shadow of a biba tree (Semecarpus Ancardium) and should a Brahmacārī do so he must perform his thread ceremony again. Throughout the Karnāṭak, the bridal pair in all castes is not allowed to pass under a tamarind tree. A woman who is *enceinte* will avoid the shadow of a pipal (Ficus religiosa) and of other big trees, or that of a white *kaṅgal* at noon. To the Sindi the pipal, ber (Zizyphus vulgaris) and lasuri (Cordia Myxa) trees are *ghoro*, 'heavy with *kudrat*', and considered dangerous.

The shadow of a man often effects evil. In Sind if a person misbehaves they say a bad man's shadow must have fallen on him, and if a man is hopelessly bad they ask whose shadow has fallen on him. As the falling of a shadow on to anything makes a contact between two objects, and as all contacts enable power to be transmitted from either end, it is as dangerous to let one's shadow fall on to something evil as to be directly overshadowed by that evil thing. A man should not at a funeral allow his shadow to fall on the ashes of the dead, for this will lead to his being haunted by the ghost of the dead. If the shadow of a menstruous woman fall on a dying man she herself is harmed (Sind). A Muhammadan will not sleep in the shadow of another person. Evil-eye operates in the same two ways, for the sense of sight is both active and passive and the same result follows from seeing a dangerous thing as from being seen.

Children are not allowed to play with shadows, and are not to sit in anyone's shadow. The bridal pair must not sit in any shadow, and as their shadows to the Sindi Muhammadan are *ghoro*, they must not allow their shadows to fall on others. The peculiar power possessed by a woman when *enceinte*, by a woman in her menses or by a girl on first attaining puberty, transfuses also their shadows, which are *ghoro*. The shadow of a menstruous woman falling on a Hindu woman observing a *vrata*, 'vow', vitiates the vow, and persons on whom it falls must bathe before performing any kind of worship. The shadow of a widow must not fall upon a bride; that of a woman who has lost several children must not touch a woman in confinement; the shadow of a barren woman made more deadly by her menses falling on a child, kills that child and transfers the vitality of the child to the woman giving her issue. The shadow of a pregnant woman renders a snake blind and causes harm to children, particularly if they are her own. The shadow of a woman in menses harms a pregnant woman; gives anæmia and dysentery to a child; reduces the power of an image of a *yantra*, or of a sacred book; it must not fall on a marriage *manḍap*, on the bridal pair, on a child at its tonsure ceremony, or on a boy at his thread ceremony. It must also not fall upon a saint, on the bel and tulsī trees nor where any sacred fire, *hom*, is lighted. A woman even as a woman, quite apart from any moment when she has special power, has a mysterious potentiality; she is often avoided and, *ergo*, her shadow also. There are charms that a Muhammadan will not write if there be near the shadow of a woman. When *Kolis* make an offering to *Hiroba* all women must retire, for their shadow would pollute the offering. Similarly, when *Lamānis* offer *naivedya* annually to *Venkatramana*, the shadow of a woman is avoided. A strict regulation of the *Śrāddha* rite requires that the cooking be all done by the *yajamān* himself, for should the shadow of a woman fall on the food the manes will not be satisfied and the dead will lose *puṇya*. The shadow of a woman must also not fall on food offered to *svāmīs* and *gurus*.

A scavenger's shadow falling on one who has small-pox would aggravate the disease. The shadows of a *Telī*, 'oilman', a *Dhobi*, 'washerman' or of a barber whose professions all involve *himsā* are strictly avoided by anyone dealing with charms. The shadow of a sinner reduces the *śakti* of a person under vow of chastity, and like that of a pregnant woman will cause a tree to wither. The shadow of a mother-in-law is avoided. Even spirits are harmed by the shadows of men A Brahui story is that a man wandered near Kelat and losing his way found a woman baking bread. She was in reality a spirit and fainted when his shadow fell upon her, so other spirits gathered and drove away the man by making a human figure and mutilating its hands.

One reason why the innermost shrine of a Hindu temple is without windows is the protection of the *śakti* of the image from inauspicious shadows. The Muhammadan likewise protects his Koran from all shadows. In performing many a magic rite a man must choose the hour before dawn, before the sun rises to give him a shadow. If he attempts to cure intermittent fever by tying a white thread to a bor tree he must do this before dawn, for his shadow would reduce the *śakti* of the tree and therefore the efficacy of the charm. A man who collects pieces of a rui tree (Calotropis gigantea) to assist the delivery of a woman, must not let his shadow fall on the tree, or the charm will be without effect.

Food is very susceptible to impure contacts. The shadow of a dog or of a person impure from the contagion of death or birth makes poisonous the food on which it falls. When, too, several persons dine together, if one person finishes eating before the others, he must not rise till all have finished their meal lest his shadow fall on their food.

Even the shadow of an object possessing beneficent power may have to be avoided. The *darśan* or sight of a sacred object confers *barkat*, yet the shadow of a temple or image should not fall on a dwelling-house or the inmates thereof will be in danger. To prevent certain shadows such as those of a temple, a single stone image, a tree, a well and a tall post falling on a house, the house should be built so as to leave between it and these objects a distance equal to twice the height of the house.

A shadow is so intimately a portion of a man's being that to do something to the shadow is equivalent to doing the same thing to the man himself. Harm done to a man's shadow harms also the man, and benefit can accrue to the man from action taken respecting his shadow.

To harm a man a mantrik prepares images of earth and puts them on the shadow of the man and pricks them with nails or the thorns of jali (Acacia Arabica), bagni (Caryota urens) and ankli (Artocarpus hirsuta). Alternatively he drives nails into the man's shadow or digs a hole where the shadow has passed and puts in it charmed lemons, bones, nails, and rice of different colours. It is bad for some one else to step on one's shadow. Magicians recite charms and follow the shadows of their victims and strike them with their heels; then taking away the earth which has adhered to their heels burn it to harm the owner of the shadow.

The treatment of the sick through the medium of their shadows is a common practice. When a man has an abdominal tumour he is sent to a mantrik in the Belgaum district, who cuts the sick man's shadow with a knife. If a man has a headache his shadow is made to fall on a post or on a wall, and on this the juice of a marking nut is sprinkled. A man with a headache is cured if his shadow merely falls on certain trees. If a man is possessed by a spirit his shadow is beaten or pinned with a nail to a tree. To expel a spirit or cure a headache *Pancāḻs* drive a nail into a man's shadow. To cure a half-headache or spleen a cross is made on the shadow of the sufferer, on the head of the shadow, and on it is smeared butter and the juice of the marking nut. When a child suffers from *muḍadoṣa*, an illness attributed to the touch of a woman in menses, its shadow is allowed to fall on a tree and then the shadow is pierced with one of the child's earrings, following which the tree withers and the child is healed. Sindi Muhammadans place a loaf on the shadow of a sick man and then cut it in four pieces and throw these to the cardinal points. Measuring shadows or branding them is a Sindi method of expelling disease. When a man is victim of evil-eye he is asked in Sind seven times, 'May I cut your nazar ?' (evil-eye), and then when he says yes, his shadow is cut seven times. If a man is victimized by evil-eye, four lemons are placed on his shadow; these have to be cut all at one blow and the pieces thrown in four directions, care being taken than no two halves of any one lemon are thrown in the same direction.

Sometimes to cure illness or evil-eye a fire is lighted on the shadow of the patient, and seven grains of pepper are thrown into the fire. A man suffering from stomach disease is placed in the sun on a Sunday, and his shadow is marked in lines with a piece of iron which is supposed to cut the disease in shreds.

The reflection of a man is as his shadow, a part of himself. In some vernaculars there is only one word to express reflection and shadow. Any evil that besets a man may be projected into his reflection, and then cast away or transferred to others. A sick man looks at himself in oil or ghee and burns the oil or ghee before an image, usually that of Maruti. Similarly, if afflicted by evil-eye or persecuted by ghosts he burns his own reflection. When a man is suffering from the evil influence of Saturn he looks at his reflection in oil, and sends this to a temple to be burnt in one of the temple lamps. As Sunday is to the Hindu an inauspicious day, anyone going a journey on that day or going out with an object, prevents the frustration of his purpose by looking into a mirror before he sets out.

If a child suffers from *mutadoṣ* contracted by contact with the impurity of a woman, it is made to urinate in a pot and gaze therein at its own reflection, which is then thrown on a jali bush (Acacia Arabica). Proof that a transfer of sickness has been made is given by the subsequent withering of the tree. At an eclipse evil is transferred by looking at one's reflection in oil, then lighting wicks in the oil and giving it away. To avert the evil of meeting a barber one should look into the barber's mirror, and then return it to him. The Sindi bridal pair look at their joint reflections in a mirror, which is then broken, assuring them of the dispersing of their evil. In some *śānti* ceremonies the *yajamān* looks at his own reflection in oil or ghee, and then gives this away to others to avert evil (*nivāḻi*). When a child is born under the *Mūlā* constellation it is presage of the death of one of the parents. When a daughter is born after three sons, or a son after three daughters, the parents are again in danger. To avert evil the father makes gifts to priests and amongst the things he donates is a pot of ghee in which he has looked at his own reflection. In Sind if a man is possessed or sick he looks at his own reflection in oil or milk and then throws the oil or milk at the root of a tree, transferring his evil to the tree. The Brahmin father in the Karnāṭak is not allowed to see his first-born son until he has seen his own reflection in a dish of sweet-oil or in a mirror, and rendered harmless his own evil potentiality which might be roused to activity by his love and admiration of the child. A child suffering from anæmia is made to see its reflection in oil and then the oil is thrown on a golgolki bush.

The whole potentiality for good or evil of a person may be projected into his reflection, and through this his good and bad qualities transferred to another. Among *Śimpīs* after a marriage the bride's mother comes to the bride's house with milk, in which the bridegroom looks at his reflection ; this milk is then distributed to all those present, especially the women guests, and confers on the recipients *barkat.* A person seeing the reflection of the face of a saint is believed to acquire some of the merit of the saint. To improve the unchaste character of a woman her face is smeared with ghee, oil and jaggery, and a harlot is asked to see her reflection in a mirror. By this measure the unchastity of the first woman is transferred to the woman of loose morals. A quainter illustration of the possession of qualities by a reflection is the belief that the reflection of a rainbow produces *Gorocan* [1] in a cow, only those cows having this which graze where the rainbow is reflected or drink its reflection in water.

The same idea that something is projected into a reflection underlies other customs. Sick and dying persons are not allowed to look into a mirror as their *śakti* would be transferred to their reflection, and this at a critical time, when they cannot endure a reduction in power. At a death mirrors are covered up and the chief mourner must not look into a mirror. A man who looks into a mirror after sunset shortens his life, and it is a general practice to cover up all mirrors before retiring to sleep. One who sees his own shadow or reflection in a mirror at night becomes a spirit or liable to the attacks of spirits, and in his next life is reborn as a concubine. Fear of spirits also makes it dangerous to look at one's reflection in water.

Though, too, a man may, to avert evil, deliberately look at his own reflection, doing this is always attended with some danger. The *Śāstrā* prescribe three *Arghyas* to be offered daily, but in practice Brahmins offer four, and one explanation given me of the additional one is that it is offered to avert the evil acquired during the day by unavoidably seeing one's own reflection.

PERSONAL MEASUREMENTS

The measuring of a man's shadow is one way of transferring any illness to another. In the actual length of the shadow there is

[1] *Gorocan* is a yellow pigment found in small quantities in the bodies of cows. It is used in the worship of gods and is applied to the forehead in the same way as sandal-paste. It is also administered to young children and mothers after their delivery and is considered a valuable drug.

something that is part of the self of the man himself, and if this be so, still more is the measurement of the man's body or part thereof an intimate portion of the man's individuality. A man's power passes into a thing made according to his measurements.

In Hindu ritual the *yajamān's angulī* or the width across his four fingers is often a unit of measurement. The sacred thread of a Hindu is ninety-six *angulīs* long; the raised seat of earth prepared for a *hom* or sacrificial fire in *yajna* is measured from the *yajamān's angulī*, being one *angulī* high and eighteen *angulīs* square. In the Agnistoma *hom* the seat is thirty-six *angulīs* high and five cubits of the *yajamān* square. Sometimes the sacred *hom* is placed in a pit one cubit square measured from the elbow of the *yajamān* to the tip of his little finger. The *yajamān* is called the *yoni* (Muliere pudendum) of the fire, and if his measurements are not taken, the offerings are taken away by spirits and destruction comes to the worshipper. An *Agnihotrī* lays out his fire-room according to his own measurements; the raised seat or *bahule* used by the bridal pair at a wedding is measured according to the *angulī* of the bride; the measured *angulīs* must be odd in number, not more than twelve and not less than six. In some castes the marriage *maṇḍap* is square, its measurements being an odd multiple of the cubit of the bridegroom or of some male member of his family. At a wedding again a *dikbāndha* of two white threads is tied round the *maṇḍap* to keep away spirits by the bridal pair themselves or by priests on their behalf, and of these two threads one is measured by the bride's measurement and the other by that of the bridegroom. The threads are said to represent the soul, the thread-of-life passed on from parents to child.

Personal measurements figure prominently in practices adopted to cure sickness or transfer evil. To cure evil-eye, in Sind the victim is measured his whole length with a tape; this tape is then cut in pieces and tied to the sufferer. To avert the same evil, red, black and white thread the height of the supposed victim, is tied to a sirih tree (Albizzia Lebbek). At an eclipse three or five arms' lengths of thread by the measurement of a sick man are taken, tied in three knots and thrown into a well to cast away his sickness; the thread is tied to a tree if it be a case of fever and to a sirih tree if it be one of headache. If a man suffers from rheumatism, at a solar eclipse a thread as long as twenty-five, thirty-five or forty-five of his cubits is wound round a pipal, nim, or bar tree to transfer to the tree the man's rheumatism. At a Muhammadan marriage in Sind both the bride and bridegroom are measured by a thread ten or twelve times from head to foot, and the thread is thrown into a well or running water that the calamities of the pair may be drowned. Besides the practices already described to avert evil-eye, there are other methods of averting this evil which involve the use of the measurements of the victim. A thread is taken the exact length of the victim's height and tied round a copper pot which is filled with milk and put on the fire. If there be actually evil-eye present, the thread will not burn, and then the thread, the pot and its contents are all buried. A simpler method is to measure a thread the height of the victim and hang it up, and as it is suspended cut it in pieces, thereby cutting up the evil-eye. A black thread, the height of the patient, is also cut with a knife, and the evil which besets the victim is finally transferred to the earth by striking the ground with the knife.

Corn, new cloth, and even timber is measured in Sind by the hand to obtain *barkat*. On the first night after a marriage the ground on which the married pair sleep is measured by the height of the taller of the two, and a thread in odd multiple of the same measurement is tied round on all four sides to form a *hisār* or barrier against evil. Before marriage the Muhammadan pair are measured from head to foot and from the measured thread pantaloon strings are made to keep the bridal pair together in love. If a child is slow in beginning to walk, big loaves are prepared and cut into pieces measured by the child's foot and then distributed to friends. Before the distribution of the bread the seven loaves are piled one on another and a cord is placed on the top of them; the child's foot is placed on the pile and the maternal uncle at one blow has to cut with a knife the cord and at least one cake. This practice is called *per mānī*. If a man recovers from a severe illness it is supposed he has special 'power', so as he lies down the length of his body is measured with loaves which are finally distributed to friends, transferring to them special *kudrat*. This is a Persian custom called *nūn-posh* but followed by other Muhammadans. At a Muhammadan marriage the bride measures the height of the bridegroom ten, twelve or twenty-one times and by this measurement makes for herself a pyjama belt.

SALIVA

The human saliva contains power the intensity of which varies with the power of the person in question. The saliva of a saint can transfer to another any quality the saint possesses such as oratorical ability. It is said that the great Muhammadan saint, Sharif Saheb Sisavinhal, in the Shigaon Taluka of the Dharwar District, got all his learning from his teacher Guru-Govind by licking the spittle of the latter in his dying moments. Saints cure the sick by spitting into their mouths or on to their wounds. In Baluchistan [1] a holy man able to charm away locusts passes on his power to his successor by spitting in his mouth. No saint who is diffident of his power will spit in the mouths of pilgrims or in any such way waste his power. Sometimes a Muhammadan saint appoints from among his disciples a vicegerent or Khalifa, giving him *barkat* by wetting his own finger with his spit and applying it to the mouth of the disciple, who in turn acquires the power of bestowing *barkat* on others in the same way. A saint can confer *barkat* on food by his spittle and make a stock of food originally small inexhaustible. Saints have rewarded the piety and hospitality of poor devotees by applying their spittle to their scanty supplies. By spitting into his mouth a saint can make a schoolboy quicker in learning his lessons, or an apprentice more apt in learning his trade. In Sind on the birth of a child, a saint, or an old person sucks honey or a date and then puts the honey or date into the child's mouth, or sometimes merely transfers saliva to bring the child *barkat,* which in the case of this being done by an old person connotes longevity.

If a married woman or *suvāsinī* spit on a pomegranate-tree it forthwith blossoms and bears fruit, for through the medium of her spittle her creative power has been transferred to the tree. In the Deccan amongst almost all classes of Hindus a mother spits on her child when she bathes it, or mixes her saliva with oil and with it smears its body, not merely to avert evil, but also to transfer to it her own longevity. Barren women swallow if they can the saliva of young infants, in order themselves to obtain issue.

Through spitting one continues to exercise power. To spit upon another man is supposed to bring him under control. A Kanarese saying is to the effect that a man obeys implicitly a spitting man *ugaḻu hākidare daṭuvadillā.* To make his wife faithful a man applies his saliva to her breasts when she sleeps. To win over her mother-in-law a woman mixes her spittle in oil and rubs the mixture on the head of the mother-in-law when she is combing her hair. A Sindi Muhammadan going a journey spits into the hand of his child so that it will not worry about his absence from home. If a woman lends her comb to another she spits on it before parting with it; a woman also spits on her hair-combings before throwing them away and this is supposed to make her hair grow the better. The Sindi spits on his own penis to keep his wife

[1] *Census of India,* 1911, vol. iv, Baluchistan, I, 67 f.

in subordination. When women kill lice they spit on their own finger-nails to prevent the appearance of other lice.

Spitting is resorted to to avert evil. If A congratulates B on his good health, B at once asks A to spit to avert evil-eye. Sindis spit on drunkards, prostitutes and people with an evil eye as a protection against evil influences emanating from these persons. Spitting affords protection, too, when one is suddenly frightened or smells something unpleasant. When people return from a cemetery in Sind they spit outside their house before entering it. Mantriks when uttering charms spit to avert evil-eye and keep away spirits. To prevent quarrels a Sindi Muhammadan woman, should she borrow the comb of another, must spit upon it. If a Muhammadan has a nightmare he spits three times to the left and tells no one about the dream. A woman spits on a child to avert from it her own evil-eye. If a child falls accidentally, earth from where it fell is waved round it thrice, the child spits on the earth which is then thrown away. Another alternative practice is for some one who is with the child to spit on the ground and throw on it a copper coin. In lieu of spitting in the face of a crying child to avert evil-eye it is sufficient to say *thu nayi*, 'spit dog'. A father in Sind spits at his own child to keep from it the evil of his own glance.

A number of Hindu practices accept the same principle that spitting averts evil. As one passes articles of *nivāḻi* or *utāra* left at cross-roads with the object of transferring disease or evil to others, one spits, as one does also at a place where an ass has wallowed, to avert contagion, or the stomach pain which comes if perchance one has stepped in the same spot. When a man is persecuted by a ghost of a very wicked person a number of persons spit upon him when he shows signs of being possessed, in order to scare the ghost. To render useless the tricks of mantriks who utilize earth where a man has urinated to do him harm, a man will spit where he urinates. While burning things to avert evil-eye both the victim of the evil eye and the person who waves things round him to cast out the evil, spit. If a child is precocious, the mother spits to avert from it evil-eye.

A mantrik uttering charms to cure a victim of evil-eye runs a grave risk of finding he has effected a transfer of the evil effects to himself; a warning of this having happened he receives in the form of a water-brash. To cast away the evil he spits freely. When things are waved round a person affected with evil-eye the victim spits on them before they are thrown away. A man who shows signs of casting evil-eye is made to spit in the hope that he will render his own glance innocuous.

Spitting effects the contact of two powers. It is therefore dangerous to spit on some things because the power of the thing spat upon is communicated to the person spitting. A person spitting on another who suffers from itch himself acquires itch. Spitting on one's own excreta, or in a cattle-shed, exposes one to the danger of acquiring throat disease. The power in objects possessing power reacts against spitting and there are many things on which a Muhammadan will not spit for fear of the resentment of their innate *kudrat*. A Sindi Muhammadan will not spit upon fire, a lamp, cooking-pots, flowers, fruit, water, bread, tea, sweets, milk, animals, on a green tree, on a bed, a carpet or mattress ; on corn, on implements, salt ; on a pen or ink or paper, a hat or a turban, in a well or river, on shoes, on milk, curds, butter, ghee or oil. He will not spit in a mosque, a graveyard or in the enclosure, *dargāh*, of a saint. He will not spit on a grinding-stone or on a winnowing-fan ; on the pestle and mortar or the collyrium pot and needle ; on a box or a water-pot ; on bricks, lime, a stone or even mud. He will not spit on glass, a fireplace, tobacco or the ornaments of a woman. Typical of the reaction of power to spitting is the blistering of the tongue which follows spitting in fire. The reverse action of spitting is illustrated by the loss, in Hindu belief, of *puṇya* a saint experiences if he is spat upon.

By his spittle a man may convey his wishes to another, be they evil or good. At an eclipse charms are made to hurt others by spitting in water. Spitting adds to the efficacy of a curse. Merely to say 'I spit upon you' is a curse conveying an evil wish. Spitting adds likewise to the solemnity of a vow. If A makes a vow to B, the latter may ask A to spit in confirmation of his promise. On the other hand, just because spitting conveys the wishes of the spitter, spitting is resorted to to make an oath less serious. If a man is made to swear against his wish he spits as he swears to reduce the intensity of the oath, to make as it were a mental reservation. If an oath is taken by another person, that person spits to render the oath inoperative so far as it affects himself. Children in particular, by whom oaths are frequently taken, spit when any one swears by them ; a mother, too, to protect her child against the sequel to an oath taken by its head or blood will spit. Spitting, in fine, has the same effect in reducing the potency of an oath as has the giving of charity.

By spitting on rags and then throwing these on to stones one may transfer one's fatigue to the stones ; this is done by pilgrims to Hampi.

If the spittle of saints and other persons possessing special power confers *barkat*, that of ordinary persons is not without a similar efficacy. To cure itch, leaves of the bekkintaraḍu creeper are chewed into a paste and this is applied to the body. Leaves of the bitter pumpkin creeper are boiled with olive oil and spittle and applied to a carbuncle. The mother of a child which has sore eyes applies her spit to its eyes without first washing her mouth, in the morning, at which time spittle has the greatest curative power.

There is power in the spittle of animals. Honey is considered to be the spittle of bees and is widely used in Hindu ritual as a holy thing. The honey that brings *barkat* is that of the female bee; the honey of the male is supposed to destroy *barkat*. Honey is used for the *abhiṣeka* or ceremonial bathing of images, in the preparation of the *Śrāddha* meal; it is used in the offering of *madhupark* to the bridegroom, a king or a saint, it is used whenever the *pancāmṛt* are used and in all these cases conveys *barkat*. Bees again suck honey from flowers which become therefore the leavings of bees, and holy because they have drawn power from their spittle. The milk of a cow used in many rites such as the offering of *madhupark* and of *pancāmṛt* must have been in contact with the spittle of the calf, or is not holy. Before wringing the udder of the cow the calf must be allowed to suck for some time, and the udder must not be washed before the milk is drawn.

Spit dies quickly and in the belief that this characteristic will produce an effect more or less similar, spit is used to hasten the achievement of a desire. To allure a woman to come to him quickly a Sindi Muhammadan spits on a charmed pipal-leaf or on a stone, and believes that ere the spit dries the woman will come to him. Whenever he goes out with a definite object he spits that he may fulfil his object before the spit dries, and on returning with his object gained he spits before entering his house to show his purpose accomplished.

THE BREATH

By the breath of a man his power with all its qualities is transmitted. Breath which confers or conveys good is called *Daiviśvās*, and the breath which transmits evil is *Āsuriśvās*. The Muhammadan likewise distinguishes between *pāk dam* and *nāpāk dam*, that is, pure and impure breath.

The breath of a saint purifies sinners. Water on which a saint has breathed is used to free a victim from spirit possession. The sick are taken to saints to be blown upon. A saint, besides putting some of his saliva into the mouth of a disciple to transfer to him power, also blows upon him. One who can recite the whole of the Koran by heart, a *Hafiz*, has also special *kudrat* and can confer *barkat* by his breath; on the twenty-third, the twenty-seventh or the thirtieth of *Ramaḍān* at night a Hafiz is brought dates, sweetmeats and collyrium to blow upon. The dates and sweetmeats are preserved to obtain *barkat* and the collyrium is applied to the eyes of the recipients, men or women. Congregational worship again produces *kudrat* and on Fridays after the congregational prayers children stand at the gates of mosques with pots of water for the worshippers to breathe upon and transfer to the water a power which will make it a panacea for all forms of illness. On the fortieth day after a child is born it is taken to a mosque where after the day's prayers are finished the *imām*, or leader of the prayers, and any old man present of reputed sanctity, breathe into the child's mouth. Sometimes on this day an old woman of unquestioned sanctity is brought to the house to breathe into the mouth of a child. A Hindu mother, after she has given a bath of oil to her infant and before she puts it to sleep, breathes on its head to transmit to it her own longevity. If a Muhammadan accidentally hurts an animal and wishes that it should feel no pain, he blows across his palm, thus transferring the power of his kindly wish to the animal.

In all these cases the innate power of the person breathing is transmitted by the breath. In a very large number of cases the breath is charged with the power of sacred passages, and it is this power that confers *barkat* on the person breathed upon. The recital of particular *surahs* of the Koran as a preliminary to breathing with the object of conveying the *kudrat* of those *surahs* is a common Muhammadan practice in Sind. Mere recital of *surahs*, however, in itself confers little *barkat* unless the reciter has mastered them and has *amal* over them, and to obtain this mastery the user of the *surahs* must have the permission of his *pir* to repeat the *surahs*, must be regular in prayer, chaste, truthful and clean. When these conditions are fulfilled, and then only, it is possible by breath to transmit at will the power of the *surahs*.

At the *Jilwa* or ceremony of presentation the Muhammadan bride and bridegroom recite the *sūratu'l-ikhlās* three times, a recital which is equivalent to a reading of the whole of the Koran, and then breathe on each other to excite their mutual love. By reciting the *surah Muzzammil* forty-one times over milk and then blowing on the milk and giving this to a woman one may assist her to obtain issue. To cure small-pox the *sūratu yā sīn* is recited over pulse; this is then breathed upon by the reciter, who mixes it with butter and gives the patient to eat. In Sind madmen are considered either saints or possessed by spirits, the latter being called *jinatjo asar*, 'the result of spirits'. To tell which of the two a madman is, one should recite three times behind his back the *Salwat sharif* and then blow in his direction. If the madman be really a saint he will turn round in resentment.

The first chapter of the Koran is a cure for all diseases if recited forty-one times between the sunset and morning prayers and then blown over the sick. *Qul auz birra-binnas* recited until one is breathless and then blown over the part bitten by a scorpion three times, removes the pain of a scorpion-bite. When there is an epidemic a Mullah or Maulvi is brought to read verses of the Koran and then to blow into the mouth of a goat, which is killed and eaten to obtain *barkat.* This practice of Sindi Muhammadans is called *dam*, 'breath'. During epidemics recitations of sacred verses are made and blown over milk which is then distributed to as many people as possible. A *pīr* confers *barkat* on his congregation by reciting *Salwat sharif*, to which the congregation replies '*Salwat sharifjo isharo kijo*', and blowing across his hand to the worshippers. If a Muhammadan hears bad news from an absent friend he recites the Koran and blows in the direction where he thinks his friend is at the moment. Before having an interview with a person of great importance a Muhammadan fortifies himself by blowing recited Koranic passages over his own person. Before retiring to rest at night recitals of the Koran are blown over a room or any object or person which needs protection; the same measure of protection is taken to cure the sick or protect a man setting out on a journey. To obtain a boon from another a suppliant will recite the *sūratu'l-ikhlās* and blow in the direction of the person from whom he hopes to get his request. By blowing recitals of the Koran in the direction of another, without his knowledge one may subdue that other person to one's will. If this be done for a good object the other person can but comply, but if it be done with a bad object and he is cognizant of what has been done, he can free himself by blowing over himself the *āyatu'l-kursī.*

The blowing of recited verses of the Koran is resorted to to discover a thief. One measure is to place the suspected persons in a circle, and in front of them drive into the ground till buried an iron bar. This bar is four sided and on the sides are written the words *Suvad val Koran, Kaf val Koran, Yasin val Koran ul hakim* and *Kaf, Ha, Ya, Ain suvad.* Then two *surahs* of the Koran are recited and the practitioner blows over the suspected persons and asks them to rise; the thief will be unable to get up. Another measure is to make sticks of wheat flour and put them in a pot of water. One after another, pieces of paper with a *surah* and the names of the suspected persons are dropped in the pot. The *Salwat* is recited ten times; the *āyatu'l kursī* and the first part of the *sūratu yā sīn*, once, *Ho Allah* a hundred times, and the names of Gabriel, Michael, Israel and Israfil four times. Then the sticks are blown upon and all will sink save that one which belongs to the actual thief.

In a similar way Hindus think that breathing preceded by the recital of a mantra or Vedic verse transfers *barkat*. To cure children affected with evil-eye, mantras are breathed over their mouths three times, the while a charm with five threads is tied to their head or neck. *Kān phunkṇen* is the breathing by a *guru* into the ears of a child after making recitation from a sacred book. A mantrik attempting a cure breathes on the part affected after each incantation, but he must breathe downwards or his charm will be without effect. In exorcising a spirit or in bewitching a medium the mantrik blows his recitals into the eyes and ears of the medium. Mantras are repeated and at each repetition a Hindu will blow upon water which is then sprinkled on the sick or drunk by them. Besides, moreover, the *śakti* of sacred words, the *śakti* of things possessing *śakti* may be transferred to others by blowing. On Thursdays and Sundays ashes are blown on the face of any one stricken by evil-eye; cotton-seeds and salt are used when blowing upon milch cattle that will not give milk; persons persecuted by ghosts are freed from their attentions by blowing ashes over them. By blowing the *śakti* inherent in certain *barkat*-giving things over persons or into some form of comestible that they can eat, there are few ills that cannot be cured. In the Karnāṭak on the twelfth day after a birth gram is placed under the anus of the child. Before naming the child the mother eats a little of the gram and then blows into both the ears of the child to secure it for ever against deafness.

So much for the transfer of *barkat* by the breath. There remains for illustration the breath that conveys evil. The breath of a widow who lost her husband very soon after their marriage is dangerous; the breath of a barren woman or of one who has lost all her issue brings death to all children it falls upon. In Sind one proof that a bad woman has breathed on a child is that the child grows more and more talkative. To the Hindu ungrateful persons, liars and backbiters, and those who constantly indulge in abuse, transmit nothing but evil by their breath. Orthodox

Hindus take a bath if they happen to come in contact with the breath of the wicked.

Breath therefore transmits both evil and good qualities. It effects, however, a contact between the breather and the thing breathed upon, in consequence of which there may arise a conflict of two powers. Certain persons and things accordingly which possess more power than usual must be protected from the power transmitted by the human breath and the restrictions which forbid the breathing on certain embodiments of power approach in detail those which prohibit their being stepped over.

A Sindi Muhammadan will not breathe on milk, water, curds, butter or ghee, bread or grain, cooked food ; on a fire save to fan it, or on a lamp ; on green verdure or on flowers. He should not breathe on the Koran, on the earth, on any animal, on fruit, salt, oil, fish or meat. He avoids breathing on all implements, on carpets and mattresses and beds ; on his cooking-pots and on new cloth. *Lingāyats* will not breathe on food, on a lamp or on fire ; on an *āsan* or seat which protects *śakti* from contact with the ground. They will not breathe on materials to be used in worship ; on any image or on such persons as a child, guest, saint or on the bridal pair. To prevent the breath falling on images during worship, on the sacred conch, or on flowers (which last cannot be offered to gods if breathed upon), or on offerings, *naivedya*, a cloth is worn over the mouth by the worshipper. When performing *Prāṇpratiṣṭā* by which *śakti* is invoked into an image the Brahmin covers his mouth. In the temple of Venkoba at Tirupati such a covering is worn every day of worship, as it is thought that the deity comes to the temple without invocation. When offering food to a god ; when performing *jap* or silent prayer ; when teaching a sacred mantra to another *mantropadeśa* the Brahmin covers his mouth. The teacher who teaches a pupil the Gāyatrī mantra shrouds his own face as well as that of his pupil. Saints and *svāmīs* when worshipping shroud their faces leaving uncovered only their eyes.

THE NAME

The name of a man is the very essence of his power. There are stories in the sacred books of Hinduism that give the name a power even greater than that of its possessor. Hanuman was building a bridge whereby he might cross to Lanka by throwing into the sea stones on which he had written the name of Rāma so that they would not sink. Rāma himself watched Hanuman with interest doing this and to test the power of a stone, threw one into the sea without writing his name on it, whereupon it sank at once. Then he turned to Hanuman for an explanation of the failure of his stone to float and Hanuman replied that Rāma's name had more power than Rāma himself.

Repetition of the name of a god puts pressure upon the god and forces the grant of a request. *Puṇya* or merit is obtained by the mere uttering of sacred names. There is a story of Rāmdās about a prostitute who taught her parrot to say Rām and so won *puṇya* for herself. Ajamal acquired *puṇya* because he called his son Nārāyaṇ, and when addressing his son constantly used the holy name. Valmiki was a *Koḻī*, a murderer and robber who kept a record of the murders he had committed by placing in seven earthen vessels a pebble for every murder committed. Even he lost his sin when he called Rāma Rām and eventually became a sage.

A saint's *kudrat* can be coerced in a similar way through his name. In Sind the Muhammadan, to obtain the protection of saints, ties knots in his hair the while he utters their names ; when any difficulty arises he ties knots in his clothes and utters, if he be a Sunni, the name of Piran Pir of Jilan, his chief Pir. A Shi'ah likewise ties a coin in a knot in his clothes as a safeguard against all evil invoking the power of Imam Jamin, one of his twelve *imāms* through his name.

A quarrelsome man is called *Narāda* and quarrels ensue if this name be uttered. To mention the names of spirits after sunset is to invoke their presence ; to utter the word barber is to bring at this time the ill luck that is associated with his profession. An orthodox Hindu rinses his mouth with water to remove the defilement of having mentioned by chance the name of a wicked man.

The name a child is given may influence its future for good or for evil. If a child is not named at all it is not taken as a member of the family, and so if previously born children in any family die soon after birth, a later-born child is not named at all at the usual time but given a random name much later, in the hope that having no name at the age when the other children died, it may escape death. Theophoric names bring a child into the closest relation to the deity whose name it bears. Astrological names likewise give the child the protection of the house of its nativity ; it may be given a name from the month of its birth, from the presiding deity of that month or from the zodiacal sign of nativity. Hindus give their children the names of their family or village gods. A Hindu child born at Dasarā is called after Arjun ; one born on Ramanavami is called Rāma ; a child born in Āśvin is called Kṛṣṇa, and one born on Nāgpancmī is called after the snake-god Śeṣa, whilst one born on Śivrātra is called Mahādev. By these names the infant wins the *barkat* of the day in question. Different families of Hindus call their children after particular deities; when their general practice is broken, calamity befalling is attributed to this negligence and the child's name is changed accordingly. A Hindu child is given also the names of deceased ancestors who died at a great age so that the child may acquire their longevity, and the custom, though dying out, is not yet quite dead of avoiding the names of living relatives in fear that either the child or the relative whose name it bears should die. To bestow on a child longevity, when many children have died in a household, the name of *Maruti* or *Martapa*, a god associated with longevity, is given to the child.

The Sindi Muhammadan equally believes that the name given to a child influences its future. In the hope that a child may become a pilgrim it is called *Haji*; that it may become rich it is given the name of a rich man. In fulfilment of a vow a Muhammadan child is given the name of the kando tree, and that the child may live long the name of a deceased grandfather who died at a great age is bestowed. To secure the favourable influence of the planets their names are given to children; the name of *Zahra* from Zuhrah or Venus, Kamar the name of the moon; Shama that of the sun and Najm, meaning planet. Similarly, the names of days, Sumar, Jumah, Achar, are given to bring the child the *barkat* of auspicious days, but the names of days such as Saturday, Tuesday and Wednesday, which are associated with evil, are strictly avoided. There are particular names to which special *barkat* is attributed. Of all names that of *'Abdullah* has the greatest *barkat*, for Allah is the only absolute name of God, all other names expressing only his attributes, like the name Karim sometimes given to a child. Other names in which there is special *kudrat* are Fāṭimah and Khadijah, the names respectively of the Prophet's daughter and first wife. There is *barkat*, too, in all names derived from Muhammad, such as Mhammed, Mahmud, Aḥmad and their diminutives; in Sind the single name Muḥammad is not used, but compound names such as Ghulam Muḥammad, Yar Muḥammad, Dost Muḥammad are common. Like the Hindu the Muhammadan also calls children after the day on which they are born; children born on any *'Id* are called *Idan*; those born on Friday *Jumah*, and those during *Ramaḍān* by that name.

When a Hindu has lost anything he utters the name of *Kārtivi-ryārjuna*, a mythical king who lost and regained his kingdom several times. If cattle are lost, this same name is written on a board placed near the tethering-peg and the cattle return to their stall within three days. If a house be pestered with snakes, a Hindu writes on the walls the name of the sage Astika or the name of Śiva, *Kalbhairav*. The names of great mantriks such as Basappa of Betigeri and of gods such as Dattātreya have the power of driving away spirits.

By uttering the name of a person as one does something, one may transfer to him the intended sequel to the action taken. In the riddance of evil by transfer to a tree the name of the victim or patient is usually taken at the moment when the transfer is supposed to take place. In the Karnāṭak charms are recited over trees and plants on Sundays and Thursdays and then these are uprooted in the name of a person suffering from constant fever or from glands. To ensure success the action is repeated three or five times, numbers which are associated with finality. If a man has fever another man looks first at the patient and then goes into the forest and finds a pikjali (Acacia Farnesiana) which he pulls up as he utters the name of the sick man; then he ties to the patient a piece of the bark of the tree. In the same way when nails are driven into trees to transfer illness the name of the sick person is uttered, or the names of the patient and of his mother are uttered over a thread which is tied to a tree. If one utters not the name of the patient but of some other person, the evil transferred is conveyed to the person whose name is uttered and is not transferred to the tree.

Evil is averted by the uttering of certain words or names. When a man sneezes he says '*Nārāyaṇ*,' '*Kṛṣṇa*' or '*Govind*'; if he sneezes at mealtime others ask him the name of his birthplace and he mentions this; when bad news is received many holy names are uttered; when a man hears a lizard chirp he repeats four or five times the name of Kṛṣṇa.

If the uttering of a name sets in motion a power which leads to definite sequels, it is not difficult to understand why certain names must not be uttered. If a name be uttered with the deliberate intention of setting in motion a train of consequences, the avoidance of a name is equally logical when it is desired to avert those consequences.

The names of inauspicious animals are often avoided and in their place some other word or phrase is employed. A snake is seldom called by its usual name. When *Thakurs* meet a snake they must not speak in any way about it; other tribes and castes allude to it in many ways of varying deviousness. It is called *pan* or *pāṇḍharā*, 'white,' though it really be of another colour; it is called 'ox' or 'ghost' or 'the live thing,' *Jivānu*. In Kanara it is called *hula* or insect or worm; *Marāṭhās* call it the long thing, *lāmbda* or merely *janāvar*, 'animal'. Sindi Moslems call it *rasi* or rope. When a person is bitten by a snake one says 'the insect has touched him'. The ordinary word for an owl is *gugi*, but in the Karnāṭak it is usual to speak of this ill-omened bird as *hakki* or merely 'bird'; the Sindi calls it the 'night-bird', the 'bad animal' or 'that whose name one would not utter'. A donkey is called *lāmbkāne*, 'long-eared', instead of *gadav*. In the Panch Mahals the *Bhils* speak of the panther as a dog.

Diseases are not alluded to by their names. Leprosy is spoken of as 'the great disease'. The word for convulsions, *śaṭabyāni*, and that for the impurity caused by the touch of a woman in menses, *muḍadoṣ*, must not be uttered. In the first instance one speaks merely of the children's disease and in the second of the 'touch'. The word again for consumption, *kṣaya*, must be avoided. Periphrases are used when speaking of death; the direct word for 'he died', *mela*, is never used save in a curse, and in lieu of it one says *varala* or *devadnya jhali*, 'God's command has come', or *gumvala*, 'is lost'.

Another set of periphrases are those which avoid on many an occasion an expression of finality. When a woman's bangles break it is habitual to say they have 'increased', and similarly the *mangalsūtra* or necklace of the married woman is said to have increased when in reality it has broken. When the stock of saffron is running short it is said to have increased, and instead of *sampila*, one says *vadala*. In just the same way, instead of saying that the mark put on the forehead has fallen off, the mark is said to have grown bigger. In the Karnāṭak one says *baḻi hecyitu*, 'the bangle has become greater', in lieu of *baḻi vaḍitu*, 'the bangle has broken', and *kunkuma bekitu*, 'the *kunkuma* has increased', instead of *kunkuma cellitu*. Sindi Moslems have much the same method of avoiding saying that a thing is finished with or has ended. If a Koran falls to the ground they say it has become bigger, *vadi payo*; if it has been torn badly it has become a martyr, *shahid thiyo*. When the threshing of grain has been completed on the threshing-floor the Muhammadan says it has increased; even when a tablecloth is removed from a table it is said to have increased. When food, too, is taken out of a vessel they say the food has increased. In the Karnāṭak almost identical phrases are used among Hindus to avoid saying that a thing has finished. When the heap of grain on the threshing-floor has come to an end the heap is said to have increased, *rāśi belitu.* *Marāṭhās* in the same way speak of winnowing grain as *dāṇā vadhavine,* 'to increase the grain'. The word 'to increase', indeed, appears in all the vernaculars of the Presidency, used to express the very opposite of its real meaning, to conceal in other words or disguise the fact that a thing has diminished or come to an end altogether.

A very large number of phrases with an inverted meaning are connected with the sanctity of fire. The Kanarese word for fire, *benki,* must be avoided altogether on the threshing-floor as suggesting a disaster, and in its place one must speak of *hulgyā* or 'increase', or *dhupa kenda* or *Agni.* Euphemisms are habitual in all the different language areas of the Presidency when speaking of the extinguishing of a lamp. In Gujarāt, instead of saying 'Extinguish the lamp' one says 'Make the lamp king (Rānā)'; in the Deccan the *Marāṭhā* says '*Diva vadva*', 'Make the lamp big' or '*Divā nirop dyā*', 'Say farewell to the lamp'. In the Karnāṭak one says '*Doḍḍadu māḍu*', 'Make the lamp big' or '*Śānta māḍu*', 'Make cool'. In Sind the Muhammadan putting out a lamp is told to make it green, *bati sai karyo,* and when he extinguishes a fire he is said to have made it cool. Other phrases used to express the putting out of a lamp or fire are *bati vadi kar,* 'Make the lamp big'; *bah ujhan,* 'Cool the fire'; *bati gul karyo,* 'Make a rose of the lamp'. Persians say 'Kill the lamp' or 'fire', Arabs say 'Cool the fire'.

On the threshing-floor inauspicious words are carefully avoided. The ordinary word for a broom is avoided in the Karnāṭak and in lieu of *kaśarigi* the word *śāḻu* is used; instead of the phrase *kasahoḍi* for sweeping the floor, *śāluhoḍi* or *kanatattisu* must be used. If rubbish is to be burned the phrase used is 'apply increase', *huligyanna hachchu,* and if the wind required for winnowing fails, *huligyā bisavallā,* 'increase is not blowing', is said.

It is inauspicious to speak of closing a shop. Gujarātis and Marwaris say *dukan mangal karo,* 'Make the shop lucky', whilst *Marāṭhās* say *dukān vadva,* 'Make the shop big'. Throughout the Presidency the departing guest when he means to say he is going away, actually says 'I am coming'. People whose name is *Devbhankar* are unfortunate in that scarcity of livelihood would follow their using their own name in the morning, at which time they have therefore to speak of themselves as *Motya Gharace,* 'of a big house'. In the afternoon it is unlucky to speak of shaving as, save when a relative dies, shaving is prohibited in the afternoon. Euphemisms are used to avoid actually using inauspicious words. Illnesses are spoken of by words of disguise. Small-pox is

Mātā, 'mother', *motā makārāj*, 'great king' or 'uncle' or 'grains'; measles are the 'good sickness'. Somewhat akin to this is the Sindi habit of calling ugly men and women Yusuf and Zuleikha because Joseph and his wife were famous for good looks. A curious sequel follows the practice of avoiding the word *dahana.* The correct word for charity is *dāna*, but peasants generally pronounce it carelessly as *dahana.* This latter word, however, means also a burning, and so on auspicious occasions has to be avoided, with the result that on occasions of importance the peasant is driven to pronounce the word for charity correctly, and at other times mispronounces it. To say that a person eats excrement is a form of curse; in actual practice, though a person speaking ill of another means to imply this, he says the other is eating sugar.

Numbers have power and the mere mention of a number brings definite consequences. Numbers are therefore often not mentioned, particularly on the threshing-floor where the mention of anything inauspicious will reduce the yield of grain. Instead of one *lābh,* or profit is said throughout the Presidency by Hindu and Muhammadan alike; the number five is an auspicious number, but the Muhammadan alludes to it as *ganj* or wealth. The word *barkat* is substituted for one by the Sindi Muhammadan and for two in Khandesh. *Bālāji* is a substitute for *lābh,* to mean one in Khandesh. The Sindi speaks of *vadha nave,* 'big nine', when he means ninety-nine; in the Karnāṭak the ordinary word for seven, *yelu,* is avoided, because it is also an exclamation, 'rubbish', or can mean 'go to the dogs', and *aru huli,* 'six and more', or *mattondu,* 'one more', is used in its stead. Instead of eleven, *hechchu,* meaning increase, is used, and in lieu of seventeen, *hadi naru huli,* 'sixteen and more'. In ordinary conversation many a substitute is used for numbers. One is spoken of as 'earth', two as 'solstice', three as 'eyes', four as the Vedas or Yugas, five as 'arrow', six as 'enemies,' seven as 'days' or *rishis,* eight as 'directions', nine as 'planets', ten as incarnations, fourteen as 'jewels', fifteen as 'fortnight' and eighteen as 'Purāṇas'.

Sometimes a temple is so sacred that its name may not be uttered. That of *Dharamsthal* is alluded to as the place beyond the river, *Pelataḍi.*

Names are also avoided to prevent a failure of purpose. Not infrequently when creepers and plants are used as magic cures the person who makes from them a charm must not utter their names, but describes them merely by their characteristics. In the sphere of religious ritual the names of gods must not be revealed when a Brahmin performs *jap,* for the silent prayer loses its efficacy at once if this be done. When a *svāmī* prays during a car procession as he is seated in the sacred car, he must keep secret the names of the gods he prays to.

Proper names are often concealed. A wife is forbidden to utter her husband's name; that of her parents-in-law, her husband's elder brothers, uncles and aunts; her mother-in-law's sisters and their husbands. Husbands avoid the names of their wives. The wife of one named *Kallappa* will not use the word *kallu*, 'a stone', nor the wife of one *Dhondi* the word *dhoṇḍā*, 'a stone'. A son avoids repeating the name of his father and a disciple that of his *guru* or preceptor. Every Hindu has names which he keeps concealed either permanently or until he has passed a certain crisis in his life. *Kātkarīs* do not permit a mother to use her husband's name till after the birth of a child. If either the husband or wife uses the name of the other, in this tribe, before others, there is a cry of *paij ali*, 'A penalty has been incurred', and the offender has to distribute the kernel of a coconut to all present. The mother-in-law among *Kātkarīs* is called by a nickname *phui*; the father does not call his eldest son by his name; elderly persons are not called by their names, and among the *Dhōr Kātkarīs* the names of the dead are often avoided. A *Kātkarī* must address his younger sister as *sālī*, cannot use the name of his younger brother's wife, and calls his father *bābā* or 'master.'.

The *Janmanām* or *Nāvarāsnām*, 'the birth-name', of a Hindu is a secret one based on the stars under which he was born. *Navarasnām* is possibly a corruption of *Navraśinām*, the name of the constellation in which the sun was at the time of the man's birth. There are twenty-seven stars each with four quadrants called *pād*. All these one hundred and eight sections have initial letters, to be found in any Hindu almanac, and the birth-name is decided by the initial letter of the particular section. For example, the first *nakṣatra*, namely *Aśvini*, has four *pād* with the letters *cu*, *ce*, *co*, and *lā*; corresponding to these initial sounds the secret names of persons born under these respective quadrants would be *Cuḍamaṇi*, *Cediś*, *Coleś*, *Lakṣman*, each beginning with the letter or sound of the quadrant. This name is kept secret permanently, though it is muttered by Brahmins during their daily *sandhyā* prayers. By the possession of this name the whole horoscope of the person bearing the name would be known, but another reason given for the care with which it is guarded is that it forms part of the *sandhyā* worship to which taboo restrictions apply. At his thread ceremony the father communicates this name to his son in a whisper, the father and son at the time both being enveloped in a single cloth. At the later marriage of the boy the name is used to tally the horoscopes of the boy and of his bride.

A second secret name is the *Abhivādanīyanām*, a name the son utters whenever he bows to his parents. This name is given to the son by his father and is known to none save the father and mother till the thread ceremony of the boy is over.

In addition to these two names, a Hindu may have other names called *laukik* or 'public' as contrasted with those he guards from public knowledge. There is the *Vyavahārikanām*, his proper name that he uses in addresses and writing; this may be taken from a temple, elephant, horse, tree, well, market, a poetical work, a poet, an animal, a palace and many other things. Another name is the *Kuldevatānām* given to the child by the father and based on the name of the family god. Then every Hindu has one or other of the twelve names Kṛṣṇa, Anant, Achyut, Vaikunṭh, Janārdan, Vasudev, Hari and others corresponding to the twelve months during one of which he was born. This is the *Māsnām* or month name. Finally, there are the *Guptanām* and the *Sānketiknām*; the former a compound name such as Chandragupta, Samudragupta, Devaśarma and the latter a conventional name known only to a few intimate relatives.

The change of a name may change the fortune of a child, and on the principle of allopathy opprobrious names are given to a child to preserve it from evil, and in particular from death. When a child is born to parents very late in their married life, or after previous issues have died, such names are given that it may survive. Similarly, to avert evil, second wives are given opprobrious names such as *Huchchi*, 'mad woman', *Mudiki*, 'old woman'. The Sindi Muhammadan protects a son by calling him *Ghudbi*, 'dunghill' and a daughter *Ghudasab*, or by giving them the name of a slave. Throughout Sind and the rest of the Presidency there is a striking similarity in the names of contempt given to children as a safeguard against expected evil. They are called *Gunḍappa*, *Dundappa*, *Dagadya*, *Dagdia*, *Dhondia* or 'stone'; *Tirkappa*, *Fakkira*, *Bhikari*, 'beggar'; *Tippanna*, *Tippa*, 'inhabitant of the dunghill'; *Giriyapa*, *Guddapa*, *Dongaria*, 'mountain or hill'; *Śedappa*, *Arlappa*, *Dhulappa*, *Mannapa*, 'dirt', 'mud', 'dust'; *Hadakia*, 'a bone'; *Heggappa*, *Dodo*, 'rope'; *Kanthapa*, *Kanthewa*, 'thorn'; *Kenchappa*, 'simpleton' and *Huchappa*, 'madman'; *Adivappa*, *Kadapa*, 'jungle'; *Sudugadappa*, 'cemetery'; *Bhutia*, 'ghost'; *Cindappa*, 'rags'; *Norjappa* or *Norjawa*, 'fly'; *Heggappa*, *Undria*, 'rat'; *Munjri*, 'cat'; *Kutria*, 'dog'; *Tukdia*, 'a piece of bread'; *Menasava*, 'pepper'; *Musya*, 'black monkey'; *Mugappa,* 'nostril' and *Mukarapa,* 'nose-ring', as also *Nathia*; *Kariyapa, Kalia,* 'black'; *Budapa,* 'ash', and *Huligapa,* 'fire'; *Ambia,* 'mango'. The names of despised castes are also given and the names of lowly occupations; *Mahāria; Dhedia; Bhilia; Cambharia; Dhangar; Bhangi*—the names of castes; *Jekkapu,* 'a carrier'; *Totappu,* 'a gardener'; *Gopal* or *Dhorkia,* 'a cowherd'. Other names are *Naktia,* 'deep-nosed'; *Ranjania,* 'an earthen water-pot'; *Rumālia,* 'turban'; *Bandepa,* 'rock'; *Kattepa,* 'the raised platform in front of a house'; *Kotepa,* 'fort'; *Gadigepa,* 'platform'; *Supli* ,'winnowing-fan'; *Amavasyappa,* 'as black as a night of no moon'; *Singapa,* 'lion'.

There is a stock answer given by parents to those who inquire why their child bears such an opprobrious name; this answer is, 'Let it live as an insect in the dunghill'. The change of name is accompanied by other measures of protection. Boys are dressed as girls and girls as boys for three years; the child is placed in a winnowing-fan before it is called *Supli*; it is handed to a beggar and from him received back before it is called *Fakir*; it is clad in clothes given by others and then called *Bhikārī*; it is weighed against grain and the grain is given to a sweeper before it receives the name of *Bhangi*; it is passed through a hole in the door to a *guru* before it is called *Bhikṣappa,* 'given as a gift'. A boy's nose may also be bored, his hair cut like that of a girl, and he may be given earrings.

Customs and taboos are often decided by a play on the meaning of a word or name. In the Atharva Veda charms are decided by puns. The similarity between the names of Marāṭhā families and their 'devaks', there is evidence to suggest, is possibly to a larger extent than has been surmised, due to punning. The enlargement of the meaning of a particular symbol such as *dhār* is certainly due to punning on a verbal meaning. *Dhār* means edge and as a 'devak' the edge of a blade; some Powars with a sword to represent their *dhār* avoid using clothes with a coloured border, 'dhār'. To certain trees a dangerous power is attributed, and those who plant them are supposed to die and this merely because their names suggest other words that mean destruction.

SMELL

The smell of a man contains his properties; it contains power. Man in this respect is in no wise different from other things. When flowers have been offered to a god, from contact with the sanctity of the deity they acquire a transmitted power. This power is radiated by their smell, and the smell of flowers that have been so offered to an image, *nirmālya,* confers *barkat.* Sindi Moslems believe the smell of a rose brings *barkat* because it was created from the sweat of the Prophet. The idea of contagion associated with a smell makes it advisable not to smell flowers that have been brought from a cemetery.

A transmission of power is made by the smell just as it is by the breath, by the shadow or other parts of a man's being through which a contact is effected. Parents smell the heads of their infants just as they breathe upon them to transfer to them their own longevity. On the other hand, to smell the person of another shortens one's own life, and if a stranger smells the unshaved head of a child the child falls ill.

The same idea of a transmitted power appears in the prohibition, common to Hindu and Muhammadan, of smelling flowers which are to be offered to power. A Hindu cannot smell flowers which he intends to offer to a god ; a Muhammadan cannot smell flowers before offering them to a tomb or mosque, and in contrast to the Hindu will not smell them even after the offering. The power of the worshipper must not be brought in contact with the power of the god or mosque. Another example of transmitted power is the supposed effect of smells upon a woman who is *enceinte.* If a pregnant woman smells the urine of a horse she will have the prolonged period of pregnancy of a mare and in consequence will die.

THE NAVEL-CORD

The primitive thought which still underlies Indian practices and customs, visualizing the power of man as personality, assumes that a transmission of this power can be effected by portions of his organism, and also that anything which has once formed part of the man retains its connexion even after actual severance.

In Hindu sacred works the navel is connected with the breath of life, and India has many illustrations of the world-wide custom of disposing with care of the navel-string and placenta, under the belief that if any harm happens to these parts of the child, the child itself suffers loss of vitality.

The severed umbilical cord and the placenta contain power. When disposed of they must not be allowed to come in contact with the ground, for they would by such contact lose *śakti* and the child would suffer in a corresponding degree. When *Deśastha Brahmins* dispose of these parts they bury them in an earthen pot, the midwife doing this secretly. *Kātkarīs* bury them in a corner of the house or putting them in a pot with oil throw them into a perennial river ; in the Karnāṭak they are placed in a new earthen pot along with turmeric, betelnut and *akṣat* and buried in the back yard covered with a lid. *Marāṭhās* bury them in a pot close to the mother's cot. When several children of the child's mother have died before the last birth, the parts of the last child are enclosed in a dry gourd shell and buried. *Mahārs* bury the severed navel-cord in the dung-heap. On the analogy of the throwing of other things on to dung-heaps to acquire from the dung-heap which is always increasing in size the power of increase, the navel-cord is thus thrown to add to the *śakti* of the child. The placenta of a cow or the cord of her calf are similarly thrown or buried in an anthill because an anthill is always growing in size.

Different castes attribute different evils as a sequel to any carelessness in allowing the contents of the pot to touch the ground. *Marāṭhās* say that should the severed cord touch the ground the child will suffer from prolonged nausea, but whatever it may be, some harm or other will befall the child if the power inherent in the buried parts is lost by their contact with the ground. If the cord is enclosed in a vessel to secure it from contact with the ground, the actual burying protects the child from the malign magic of mantriks who, by repeating charms over the navel-cord, can effect the ruin of the infant. The protection of the cord from animals also secures the life of the next-born issue.

How closely the preservation of the power within the severed parts is bound up with the conservation of the power of the child itself, is further evidenced by the practice of planting a tree over the buried parts. In Kanara a plantain or an ālu plant (Marsaṇigi) is planted over the buried pot; in the Karnāṭak *Deśastha Brahmins* plant a banyan, a śami or a bel tree. These trees are planted with the object of increasing through the medium of the buried parts the *śakti* of the child, and it is significant that the planted trees are not tended at all after the short period of six or seven days during which the buried parts retain *śakti*. This practice of planting a tree over the buried parts is purely a Hindu custom, for the Muhammadan must see that there is no tree near the spot of burial, as the proximity of a tree would make the mother of the child suffer. The enclosing of the cord and placenta in a dry gourd is somewhat akin in meaning to this practice of planting a tree, for the object of using a gourd, a fruit associated with prolificness, is to prevent the death of the infant and of succeeding births.

Similar care is taken with the last piece of the umbilical cord which remains for some time after the severance of the cord. This piece also may be buried, but more commonly is wrapped in cloth and tied to the cradle of the infant, or to the legs of the mother's bed. After five or six days, if the infant be a first-born, the piece of cord is enclosed in a casket, *tāyat*, of gold or silver, and tied to the neck of the child to wear throughout its life. Its sovereign power protects the child from illness and from thunderbolts, to the adverse influence of which first-born children are peculiarly subject. Not infrequently, however, the child never gets this protection, for a barren woman to obtain issue will attempt to secure this cord of a first-born son, either to eat it or to wear it herself in a *tāyat*.

One further custom affords protection to the child. On the seventh day after the burial of the severed cord, milk and ghee are sprinkled over the site of burial as a *śānti*. This brief ceremony is called *kuil kuni*, 'navel-cord hole' and its purpose is to cool the hot *śakti* within the buried parts before they are abandoned.

The power of the navel-cord conveys power to the instrument with which it is cut. This instrument in the Karnāṭak is insulated from the ground and placed on a plank, receiving worship with *akṣat* and turmeric for twelve days. It is this instrument which is placed so generally under the pillow of the mother or that of the child, or is carried for some days by the mother as a protection against spirits. Another aspect of the power of the severed cord is its dangerous potentiality. If it be cut with a blunt knife and during the cutting any fluid therefrom spurts into the eye of the child, the child henceforth will have an evil eye. There is an element of impurity in the cord, for save for the presence of the cord the child is pure at birth. The nurse or relative who buries the cord is impure from its contact and must bathe immediately; before, too, she can re-enter the house she must wash her feet, and water must be sprinkled over her. Though not a universal practice, it is quite common to find the person who buries the cord forbidden to look backwards after doing this. A site, too, for burying the cord is chosen where it will be difficult for any one to step over it, for not only will the child be harmed if any one step over the buried parts, but the person stepping over them will be harmed by the resentment of the *śakti* therein. To lessen the possibility of any such disaster, thorns are scattered over the place of burial, and with this and the additional object of keeping away spirits, *Kātkarīs* stick an arrow in the ground.

THE HAIR

There is more than the ordinary sympathetic connexion between a man and his hair. Hair grows of its own volition; its cutting is a destructive act of *himsā*, it destroys power. A man's *śakti* is peculiarly bound up with his hair. To reduce the power of a witch her hair is cut short, and one repeatedly comes across stories in India of some ghost, such as that of *Heḍalī*, whose visitations were stopped by her victim cutting her hair and putting the clippings in a cleft of a tree or pillar of wood. In the Karnāṭak is a saying that when the hair of birth is cut away the child grows weaker and weaker, *huttu kụdlu tegdu bitta hudga vanagi kota hoda*. When therefore at the age of three the hair of boys is cut, the hair between the temples and ears and on the forehead is left, this is called *tāḷū*, as a retreat into which the power of the child's hair may retire, and similarly, when at the *munja* or thread ceremony the whole head of the child is shaved, a tuft, *śenḍī*, in the centre at the back of the head is left to retain the boy's *śakti*, and this tuft is kept until death by all save sannyāsīs.

On the other hand, when evil *śakti* causes the illness of a child its health can be restored by shaving off its hair.

The cutting of hair, particularly in the early years of a child's life, is a ceremony surrounded with many restrictions. In Sind when the Muhammadan child, girl or boy, has its hair cut for the first time, this is done at the gate of a mosque, at the *dargāh* of a saint or sometimes in the shade of a kandi tree (Prosopis spicigera). The clippings of hair are buried at the gate of a mosque with sweets and coins in multiples of five, and henna; when the hair of a Hindu boy is cut at the age of three, the severed hair is buried so that it will not be stepped over, that the wind may not bear it to a dirty spot, and to prevent the child getting anæmia. Burying the hair does not, however, mean the contact of the hair with the ground, for as the hair is cut the Muhammadan gathers it in a cloth, and the Hindu collects it in a plantain-leaf. In lieu of burying the clippings they are sometimes thrown into running water, a practice common in parts of the Konkan; in the Karnāṭak I found the custom of tying the first cut hair of a child to the roof of the house. The clippings of the hair of a sannyāsī are placed in a cloth or a leaf and then buried at the root of a tree. *In primis*, protecting the hair from contact with the ground protects the child; there is danger, however, even to others in fallen hair, for if any one sleeps near hair that has fallen to the ground he has bad dreams. After the tonsure of a child, alms must be given at a definite interval of eight or forty days or three months; the alms must be equal in weight to the cut hair. The object of the almsgiving is to avert calamity, for all charity averts calamity according to Muhammadan belief. Offerings to saints at their tombs are called *niyāj* or *harakī* (Kan.); these include the first-cut hair of a child, which in fulfilment of a vow is placed near a saint's tomb, or tied to a tree growing near.

If hair is found in any food, the food is abandoned. Sometimes a mere change of dishes follows, but the more orthodox Hindus will fast the whole day, and not leave the house for any purpose or make a journey. In a *Śrāddha* ceremony should any hair be found in the food which is to be offered to the priests the whole ceremony must be performed again. It is never easy to say what are the precise borrowings made from Hinduism by tribes that are slowly assuming the ritual of Hinduism. The *Kātkarī* has no calendar of his own and so borrows the feast days of the Hindu as dates easily memorized for the celebration of his own rites. *Sarvapitṛī Amāvāsyā*, which he celebrates once or thrice a year on Hindu holidays, he claims is entirely his own. In this communion with the dead he insists that no hair should fall into the food which through the medium of crows is offered to the departed. The woman who prepares the food is not allowed to comb her hair for some time before she begins preparing the offering; with the same object no faggot that protrudes out of the fire can be burnt to the end as this might cause ashes to fall into the food. The *Kātkarī* offers the same explanation for the one prohibition as for the other; namely, the preservation of the food from contamination. Another illustration of the contamination of food by hair is that if food in which hair has fallen is eaten by cattle they fall ill.

The fact that a man's power suffuses his hair and that this retains a sympathetic connexion with the man even after its physical severance, explains two species of practice; the practice that secures control of another through the possession of part of his hair, and the practice that secures control of that other by putting him in intimate contact with one's own hair. *Anvari*, a poet of the time of the emperor Akbar, was given two hairs by a friendly jinn; whenever these were heated the jinn appeared to carry out any behest, and on one occasion, story relates, assisted a servant of the emperor to find a drinking-glass encrusted with diamonds which had been lost. If two persons have a quarrel or dispute, that one of the two will be the winner who obtains a piece of the hair of the other. The idea, too, that control of a person may be obtained through possession of his hair accounts for the care with which hair clippings are disposed of, so that they will not fall into the hands of others; the same care, in fine, with which the severed navel-cord is protected. Love charms afford many an illustration of the converse practice. A typical illustration is the Sindi practice of attempting to make a woman eat the ashes of one's own hair to secure her love, or an enemy to do the same to reduce him to subjection. On the first Monday of any month, a day called 'green Monday', a man who has either of these objects must declare his object early in the morning; then in the evening of the same day he goes to the fields, plucks a small plant, returns home and cuts his hair and nails and burns the clippings with the plant. It remains afterwards merely to watch for an opportunity when he can administer the ashes of the burnt clippings to his enemy or the woman whose love he covets. Eyelashes are used in much the same way to effect harm or capture love.

Apart, however, from the supposed retention by the severed hair of a sympathetic connexion with the original possessor of the hair, hair has naturally a power which partakes of the characteristics of the person from whom it has been cut. The hair of a woman who for many years has enjoyed a married life of happiness, a *suvāsinī* who has had many children is eagerly sought by younger women who wish to share the same bliss to braid in their hair. To secure issue, again, barren women will eat with butter the hair of young boys, just as they will eat a fragment of the navel-cord of the first-born son of another if they can secure it. Merely retaining the lock of a child which has healthy brothers and sisters brings a woman issue. A woman's hair is credited with the power of averting evil-eye; it is placed in gardens to protect creepers, it is tied to milch cattle or burnt before them, and it is tied to a house, when it is entered for the first time, to render innocuous the potentiality of the unknown for evil. As a barren woman from unsatisfied longings is supposed to inflict evil-eye, on the principle of inoculation, that is affording protection by assimilation to the object which causes injury, the hair of a woman without issue is particularly powerful to avert evil-eye. When children suffer from convulsions, to reduce the evil *śakti* which has attacked the children, they are made to inhale the smoke from the burnt hair of a woman. In Sind if a barren woman burns her hair and mixes it with honey, she can increase her husband's love for her by giving the mixture to him to eat. The ashes of burnt human hair cure burns; human hair is burnt before a woman in confinement to assist her easy delivery; hair-combings are burnt before a possessed person to exorcize the spirit.

The transfer of evil may be effected by disposing of hair to others, or by bringing it in contact with some object with inherent power to which it can be conveyed. In Sind, tying the hair or the cut nails of a sick person in a cloth to a tree, in order to transfer the illness to the tree, is a practice of both Hindu and Muhammadan. When the Muhammadan bridegroom in Sind goes in procession on a horse, a lock of his hair is buried under a tree to transfer all his evils to the tree. When a Hindu is approaching death a new black blanket is taken and on it are placed a pumpkin, a piece of iron and the hair and nail-clippings of the sick man. These things are then made into a bundle, adorned with red flowers and worshipped, uncoloured and unbroken rice and black-sesamum are thrown on them before they are given to a priest who waves the bundle three times round the sick person and throws it away. By this means it is hoped that the sick man will get rid of the contagion of death which passes to the priest who, should the steps taken prove effective, must not see the invalid for three months later. In the practice of *utāra*, the riddance of evil, the commonest form of which is the waving of articles around or over the person whose cure or release is attempted, and then throwing the waved articles with their supposed burden of ill at cross-roads in the hope that passers-by will stumble on them and take to themselves the transmitted evil, the use of the hair or the nails of the stricken person is extremely common.

Whatever, though, the manifold uses to which the severed hair of a man may be put, its potentiality for evil is always there. The place where hair cuttings or combings are blown should be purified with cowdung. If the hair be cut by a Muhammadan on 'green Monday' and burned with salt and the leaves of the nim-tree (Melia azadirachta) and its ashes put in water and thrown at the root of a fruit-tree, the tree will never bear fruit. If a man tie clippings of his hair around a lemon and throw where others will see it, he works them evil. A guest must not cut his nails or hair in the house of his host, for he thereby endangers his host. When her husband is sowing, reaping, measuring grain, ploughing; when he has gone on a journey of business or pilgrimage, when too he is ill, a wife must not comb or braid her hair. Pulling out the hair adds to the dangerous power of a curse. This, however, brings us to the broad question of *himsā*, which will be treated in another chapter.

The clippings of nails and the combings of hair if left about bring evil spirits into a house; they are also among the things given when the intention of a donor is to make an *ugra*, gift.

THE NAILS

The nails of a man are as much a part of his self as is his hair. To a Muhammadan the nails are *manhūs*, bearers of bad fortune; they are the surviving relic of the dress that Adam wore in Paradise. They must never be cut in a holy place such as a mosque, and even when cut in a house the clippings must be carried out of the house. The ashes of his burnt nails are used by a Muhammadan to secure the love of a woman or subject an enemy, just as those of his hair-clippings are used; by his nail-clippings he may transfer his evil to others or to a tree. In short, nail-clippings may be substituted for hair-clippings in all or nearly all of the practices described in the previous paragraphs on the use of hair-clippings. To cure jaundice the hair- or nail-clippings of the sufferer are bottled up in a hole in a marking-nut tree or a babul tree (Acacia arabica) with the object of transferring the illness to the tree; a Sunday is chosen for doing this. When a Muhammadan takes an oath, an enemy to make the consequences of the oath more serious for the swearer, burns the hair-combings and nail-cuttings of the taker of the oath.

THE TEETH

A loosened or extracted tooth likewise retains its connexion with its possessor. In the Karnāṭak an old tooth is thrown to the sun [1] in order that the owner may have a new white one. *Chapparbands* and others throw the first tooth of a child to fall out on the roof of the house of a pregnant woman, that through the contact of that tooth with the power of the woman, a new tooth may grow quickly. In Gujarāt the cast tooth is thrown on an ant-hill or dung-heap. An ant-hill and a dung-heap grow in size and, *ergo*, it is hoped that a new tooth will grow. Clippings of the nails and hair are also thrown on a rubbish-heap, not as refuse, but that the original hair and nails may grow as the rubbish-heap grows. In Sind the Muhammadan, like some castes in the Karnāṭak, throws the cast tooth on to the roof of the house of a pregnant woman, if the child loses its tooth before the age of twelve, and as he does so says, 'Am I going to get a new tooth first, or this woman a child?' If a tooth is lost after the age of twelve it is thrown in a graveyard. The burial of lost teeth is also common among Hindus and Muhammadans alike, whilst Muhammadans sometimes

[1] Cp. *The Golden Bough. The Magic Art*, vol. i, p. 181 (1926), for the custom of the Arab and of the peasants of Lebanon of throwing a tooth towards the sun. *Ritual and Belief in Morocco*, E. Westermarck, vol. i, p. 120, for a similar practice in Morocco, Algieria, and British East Africa.

preserve them and bury them with the owner when he dies. Brahmins, when children lose their teeth, or the teeth of an elderly person are extracted, cover the teeth with cowdung and throw them on a roof. Like the severed navel-cord extracted or fallen teeth are sometimes thrown into running water.

EXCRETIONS

On the same principle of transmission of power various other parts of a man are used in the control of power. To make his wife faithful to him a man applies his semen to her left foot when she is asleep. In Sind if a woman can make some one eat anything dipped in her seminal discharge that person falls under her control, and the same result follows if a man uses his semen in this way. Prostitutes use betelnut soaked in their menstrual blood, giving this as a *viḍā* to their lovers to secure their undying devotion. A man similarly mixes ground betelnut with his semen and gives to a woman to eat, that she may have love for none but himself. Childless women mix their menstrual fluid with food and give to the child of another woman, to cause the death of the child and the transfer of its vitality to issue of their own. A barren woman will also fling the *sāḍī* which she wore during her menses on the face of a lady with many children to effect a transfer of creative power. In Sind the cloth soiled by a girl's first menses is cut in pieces and mixed with food, and this, if given to another woman to eat, gives her irregular periods or creates love.

Defeated wrestlers make water over the shorts used by a successful wrestler with the object of rendering him powerless and transferring his skill to themselves. The urine and even the excreta of sick children are thrown on the roofs of houses to cure the children, and transfer their illness to the occupants of the houses. Low-class Muhammadan women in Sind make their husbands drink their urine to retain their love. To make a bride fertile in Khandesh a child is allowed to urinate on the bride's clothes. The urine of some holy men when applied to the body of a sinner has the power of washing away the sinner's sins. To obtain the urine of another or earth on which he has micturated is to obtain a means whereby one can effect his harm. To protect butter from a *ceṭakiṇ* or witch, Hindus remove the pelt of a squirrel, cut off the mouth and remove the flesh, making a pouch which they stuff with earth from where the victim has urinated. The pouch is then sewn up, beaten and placed near the rod to which the ropes of the churn are attached. It is supposed that this causes the body of the witch to swell, restricting her activity. Almost similar is the test that is made of a woman suspected of witchcraft. Earth on which she has urinated is stuffed into the pelt of a squirrel, whilst with the right hand the operator holding a shoe upwards beats the lintel of a door. Whichever side of the lintel he beats, should the woman be a witch, will be reflected in the swelling of the witch's body on the same side. Mantriks on *Amāvāsyā* take earth on which a man has urinated and at a cremation ground make a human image therefrom, and worship with a thousand Kangal flowers, after which by the consequent subjection of one of the spirits of the ground they can work the man any harm they wish. By burning the urine of a man or sewing up earth on which he has urinated in a squirrel's pelt, charmers can prevent a man urinating and cause his death.

On the principle of inoculation, if one boy has bitten another boy the former is made to urinate on the bitten part to cure the wound. Other practices are explained in the same way. The tail of the snake that has bitten a man is bitten; the excreta of rats or of cats are applied to wounds caused by a rat or cat. To cure a bruise caused by the pinch of a shoe the ashes of a burnt piece of leather are applied to the sore; the fat of a tiger is applied to a wound caused by a tiger; a piece of the bone of a dog is ground in water and the paste formed applied to a wound caused by a dog; honey is applied to cure the sting of bees; a scorpion is fried in hot oil and when powdered is applied to a scorpion-bite. To cure cholera the *Kātkarī* applies externally scrapings of the skins of tigers and panthers, as he thinks these animals immune from cholera.

A mother's milk is used for many purposes. Made into an ointment it restores to consciousness a person who has fainted; it is poured on the head of a child to give it health; grain ground in it is used to cure a headache, and in a variety of medicines it cures eye diseases and other complaints.

BONES

The bones of a woman who dies pregnant have the special *śakti* associated with the state of pregnancy. It is common to find conjurers pretending to make, on demand, one rupee into many by using the skeleton of a hand which is said to be the hand of a woman who died pregnant which they have compelled to leave the grave. If a woman dies in childbirth the tusks of wild pig are fixed at the four corners of her grave to defeat magicians. On a Sunday coinciding with an *Amāvāsyā* mantriks go to a burial ground naked, repeat mantras near the grave of such a woman and make offerings they would offer to a spirit. The buried woman rises from her grave naked, eats the rice which is offered her and then stretches forth her forearm for the mantrik to sever, after which she returns to her grave on her dismissal by mantras. In Sind *Amils* try to obtain control of the spirit of a *Telī* woman who dies in childbirth on a Saturday.

Powdered human bones are applied to the sores of leprosy.

Man may differ from man, as one atom from another, in the degree to which he possesses power; he may direct his constant endeavour towards the acquiring of greater and still greater power, but there are moments when, without any volition on his part, he enjoys the possession of abnormal power, and shares in the characteristics of royalty or divinity. As a child he begins his life in an atmosphere of divinity; heaven lies around his infancy. If he live long his closing days again invest him with special sanctity. And finally there are occasions during life when for the moment he ceases to be an ordinary man; as bridegroom, guest or pilgrim, at his thread ceremony or his circumcision he is above the ordinary rules that govern the relation of men, and is himself a potentiality of mysterious power, a blessing and yet also a possible danger to others.

THE CHILD

An Indian child is given many names. Many of these emphasize its innocence. Sindi Moslems call it *maasum* or innocent and the Kanarese *hasi-kūsa* has the same meaning. In the Deccan the child is *gṛhratna*, 'the jewel of the house'. To the Muhammadan it is an angel or like an angel, God-sent *Firishta*; it is *Rajul Baraka*; it is *Bādshāh* or king. The Marāṭhā calls the child *Dev* or *Devāsārakhā*, 'like unto a god'. Amongst *Bhils* one finds the word *Devji* applied to a child, but as this is not general it is probably a borrowed term.

In the Deccan a common saying is that everything that exists exists for the welfare of a child, *je ahe te sarve balakancarhita karita ahe.* To a child a Muhammadan attributes a knowledge of the secret of immortality which unfortunately it cannot convey to man before with growing age it itself loses it. To a Hindu its babbling is its conversation with God; its tears a sign of its pain at finding itself enmeshed in the illusion, *māyā*, of life. In the pure and absolute light of the womb the child exclaims *Soham*, 'I am He, the deity and I are one'; on birth into this world with its nescience, illusion and dark acquired notions of personality and individuality, the child exclaims *Koham*, 'Who am I?'.

By reason of its innate power a child is above ordinary pollutions of contact. It can eat with impunity in the presence of a corpse; it requires no bath after being touched by a woman not ritually pure; it can be suckled by an outcaste nurse. According to Muhammadan belief, every child is born in the fold of Islam and it is its parents who decide whether it should remain a Muhammadan or take another creed. A Hindu child is therefore not unclean, *mushrik*, and a Muhammadan child can be suckled by a Hindu woman. A child, too, can take asses' milk without defilement, though this is forbidden to a Muhammadan adult. A child, however, is not immune from the evil effects of contact with a woman in menses, though it requires no bath thereafter, for *muḍadoṣ* is a disease of children contracted by contact with such a woman. An unmarried girl, before she attains puberty, and a boy, before his thread ceremony, are not impure even if a birth or a death occur in their family. A child may even confer this freedom from pollution on others, for the ordinary Muhammadan rule that no marriage can be celebrated in a home within a year of a death in that family, is broken if within that period a child is born to the same household.

A child is itself pure. It need not bathe before touching images of gods. It can touch things that have been put aside to avoid pollution. Its shoes do not pollute and can be taken even into the inner kitchen. The urine of children is given in Sind to horses to drink and contact with it does not necessitate an ablution before prayer. When the Muhammadan child dies no prayers are said that its sins may be washed away; it is not compelled to pray and before prayer needs no ablution.

The innate power of a child gives it, further, an immunity from harm and enables it to do with impunity things an adult would fear to do. It can eat first-fruits [1] before they are offered to the *kul devatā*, 'family gods' or other gods, and by this offering robbed of their danger; it can sit without harm on the threshold and it can eat the fruit which has been placed in the lap of the Hindu bride. Muhammadans say a child can touch fire and a snake without being burnt or bitten.

[1] *Gamvakkals* offer these first to their gods and to the *Sarvapitṛs*. Children accompany the owner to the fields with music; then five handfuls of grain are cut and placed on a decorated *pāṭ*, 'board' or in an earthen pan (*ghadig*) or on tender plantain leaves which must have their points intact (*halakai*) and then carried by children. Sometimes the first-fruits are given to children. The danger of eating first-fruits is illustrated by the custom in some communities in Kanara of giving them, when not given to children, to untouchables, to women of the *Mukri*, *Hulsar* and *Kotiger* communities, or to *Jogis*.

A child's *kudrat* or *śakti* confers *barkat*. The Muhammadan gives the Koran to a number of children to read aloud for the benefit of the sick, as their prayers are heard by God. On the third morning after a death *ziārat* is performed; the Koran is recited by children, and such children as are too young to do this peel off the husk of gram seeds or dates and when the recital is over these are distributed to all present to confer *barkat*. When a child is smitten with small-pox other children are fed on milk and rice, after which their hands are washed with water which is then sprinkled over the sick child with the repetition of the word *chuto*, 'released', signifying the expulsion of the disease. When a Persian wheel is erected in Sind; when the construction of a new well is begun; when a house is built or entered upon for the first time; when an epidemic rages; when sowing or reaping is commenced; when the river Indus is low and a poor inundation is expected; when a man sets out on a journey; when a man is sick, and at all important ceremonies of life such as a marriage, circumcision or a birth, children are fed to acquire *barkat*. There are some Sindis, indeed, who confine all their charity to gifts to children. The first sheaf of a new crop is often given to a child so that the crop may be a good one. Young children are brought to the funeral of a Muhammadan to give *barkat* to the dead, and fruit and food given to them transmits *barkat* to the dead. At a marriage coins are thrown among children, and charity to children on Fridays is common.

The use of children in Hindu ritual is very common. On the sixth night after a birth children are fed to give long life to the new-born child; when one loses many children in succession young children are feasted in the hope of averting the contagion of death; on the death of a child after the third day but within a month, children of the same age as the dead child are fed to bring *barkat* to the dead and the surviving children. Every Monday after a birth for a month children are fed to give *barkat* to the infant. On the twelfth day after a birth and before the naming of a child it is the custom in the Karnāṭak to put the child to sleep in a cradle. Grain of gram cooked without destroying the grains is placed under the anus of the child. After the naming is over the mother eats some of the grain and then blows, as I have said before, into the ear of the child as a specific against deafness. The remaining grain is distributed among the guests present to confer *barkat*. The preparation of gram is called *helguguri* (*helu* is excreta; *guguri* is preparation); it is often stolen by childless women who desire issue.

Barren women, to obtain issue, feast young children with curds and rice, or offer to give its name to a new-born infant. When a man is dying a child is brought near him in the hope that it will gaze at him fixedly. Its fixed gaze is called *Deva dṛṣṭi*, ' the look of God,' and averts the evil of death ; the sick man, however, dies if the child is indifferent. When small-pox comes to a household, seven children of tender years and one unmarried girl are feasted. *Kātkarīs* have a variant of this custom and on the ninth day after the appearance of the disease call seven girls and a boy ; the boy is given a bamboo stick and each girl a winnowing-fan, coconuts and rice. The children feast and then garlands which have been hung over the patient previously are thrown into a river. At the naming of a child on the twelfth day *Marāṭhās* give boiled rice and sugar to a number of children. At their obsequies of the dead, *Kātkarīs* bathe five young boys over the ' stone-of-life ' in which is enshrined for the time being the *jīva* of the dead, and when the obsequies are performed of a *Kātkarī* who died away from home, five children are employed to call out the name of the dead. *Naikdas* on the ninth day after a funeral feast five children.

Acts performed by *kumārikās* or young unmarried girls or the feasting of such girls have a special significance. During the *Navrātri* festival unmarried girls between the ages of two and ten are worshipped *kumārīpūjā* ; their feet are washed, *akṣat* and saffron are thrown on them, and they are feasted. The number of girls feasted must increase from day to day during the nine days. When preparing charms the feasting of a *kumārikā* is often one of the necessary preliminaries. *Kātkarīs* employ a girl who has not attained puberty when they try to stop rain, and in general in rites intended to produce or to stop rain young children play a prominent part. *Kumārikās* are used to wave *ārtī* round the images of goddesses, round the bridal pair or round elders at Divāḻī. Among *Naidus* and *Pancāḻs* at *Divāḻī* at dawn elders throw rupees into the plates of *kumārikās* to obtain *barkat* from them. At the same festival *Pancāḻs* worship their instruments, keeping a lamp for ten days and nights near the instruments ; on the last of the ten days girls complete the worship of the deity and implements by *mangalārtī*. On the seventh sud. Māgh young girls not above five years of age go from house to house and give plantains and brinjal to *suvāsinīs*. For an *abhiṣek* of images to bring rain, two boys unmarried and below twelve years of age are used to bring the water from a river in a jar which they carry first round the village on their heads. At *Nāgpancmī* girls worship the thresholds of their relatives. When the marriage of the tulsī plant is performed a *kumārikā* is given a present and is bathed in oil.

A child independently cannot perform any religious rite, but if the *yajamān* be a *suvāsinī* with child, or a parent with a child, the rite cannot be performed without the child's presence. When the husband offers oblations to a *hom* the wife has to touch him and also hold her child in her lap; every time parents bow to a god or to an elder they must have their child, if any, with them.

In getting control of spirits *Hāḍrāt Jinn* Muhammadans employ children who have not attained puberty. A very small child fills with water the pot that is often placed on the *Hoḷī* fire. Both Muhammadan and Hindu use children in the taking of omens or the drawing of lots. To find out whether a woman will have issue or not, women take a washed plate of bell-metal, smear it with soot and oil and place it vertically on a board with the back resting against a wall. The plate is worshipped with *akṣat* and *kunkuma* and a lamp fed with ghee is placed near it. Then a child is told to look into the plate without blinking. If there is to be a birth the child, it is believed, will see in the oily surface the figure of a baby, a fruit-bearing tree, or a bunch of fruit or flowers. This divination, called *Harputaḷi*, must be done at night. At a birth the infant is placed by Hindus in a winnowing-fan containing grain with the object *inter alia* that the child's power may bring an increment of grain to the household.

Scares that children are being kidnapped for sacrifice [1]; that they are being buried in the foundations of some construction, arise in India from time to time. In the Karnāṭak there is a festival that is a memory of the sacrifice of a child to bring rain to fill a tank. In almanacs it is usually called *Śirāḷ Pūjā*; traditionally it is known as *Śirāḷ Śetti Pūjā* and *Makkaḷ Habbā*, 'the festival of children'. A small pond is made of earth and in it are placed a cradle and an image of a child. Another image representing a

[1] In the *Ratnagiri* of March, 1929, p. 29, a Kanarese periodical, there is an article about the trial of one Nāgabhusan and one Kṛṣṇamūrti in the Kumtur district for the murder of a boy of eight. Mahālakṣmī, the wife of Tatya, was a snake-worshipper and used to worship daily an anthill in the garden of Kṛṣṇamūrti. One day she saw a snake in the house of the latter, and thought it had appeared to test her devotion; saying that she would take the snake to the anthill and mentioning to her friend the site where she wished to be buried if she died in doing this and expressing a hope that her tomb should be worshipped, she wrapped the snake in cloth and carried it away. Whilst she was carrying the snake to the anthill it bit her and she died. After some days another woman declared with great fervour publicly that barren women would obtain issue and wealth would increase if a human life were sacrificed at the tomb of Mahālakṣmī. Kṛṣṇamūrti was without issue, so for her sake Tatya and Tatya's son, Nagabhusan, took a boy named Mangaya and murdered him at the tomb.

mother who sacrificed her child at the request of her father, called *Cangal̲*, is seated in an adorned *maṇḍap* for twenty days and on the last Monday of the month of *Śrāvaṇ* is taken in procession. This ceremony is begun on the sixth day of the bright half of the month of Śrāvaṇ; among Brahmins the *pūjā* is done by married girls. Its object is to bring rain. Śiriyāl was a king who dug a new tank into which no water would come, so his daughter sacrificed one of her many children and abundant rain followed. Non-Brahmins call the festival *Cangal̲habbā* and seat the image of Cangal on the sixth day till the last Monday of the month when it is taken in procession and thrown into a well; during the interval of time they indulge in masques.

The transference of evil is no ordinary operation, but predicates the presence of power. The use of children for the transference of evil by Hindu and Muhammadan is yet another illustration of the power of the child. In Sind copper coins are touched by the sick and then given to children, transferring to them the sickness. Hindus take the scales of a small-pox victim, this in the Karnāṭak, mix with rice and curds and surreptitiously give the mixture to a child of another family. Another example of *utāra* is the luring of the child of another to the presence of a sick person, the waving of the child round the sick person and the sending of the child away with its supposed burden of ill.

Every child has power beyond that of ordinary man, but certain children have even more power than others. In Sind children born on Thursday night or Friday morning are called *Juman*, *Jumani*, or *Juman rati sayad*, and these have special *kudrat*. A Hindu child born feet foremost, *pāyāl̲ū*, can see spirits and hidden treasure if ointment be rubbed on its eyes; by the touch of its foot it can cure rheumatism, but it is always in danger from water and lightning and brings evil to the midwife, so that care is called for to prevent infanticide. *Koravas* tie round its neck the guts of a fowl and throw these away on a dung-heap in an effort to render its power innocuous.

There remains always, however, the reverse aspect of power. The child's power is no exception to the general rule that there is an element of danger in power otherwise beneficent, that the same power which confers *barkat* may also confer evil, and that the correlation of good and evil is so close that a real separation of the two cannot be made. In the rivetting looks of a child there is evil-eye, though inconsistently with this belief the Hindu welcomes the fixed gaze of a child on a dying man as *devadṛṣṭi*. A man who steps over a child falls ill within a month. The

Hindu will not blow or breathe on a child save when such breathing is calculated to transfer *barkat* to the child; a Hindu mother cannot touch a child the while it eats for six months after birth nor kiss it after a meal. If accidentally one touches a child with one's foot one must touch the child with one's hands and bow to it.

With the attainment of puberty the boy and girl are merged in the mass of ordinary human beings; the sanctity which once was theirs is lost. The thread ceremony of the boy must be completed before he attains puberty, and after this he must work out his own salvation by obeying the laws of power, studying the keys of power; he has been born again, he is *dvija*, 'twice-born'. *Munjī*, as the thread ceremony is called, is performed when the boy is from six to ten years of age.

An oath of a serious form is taken by a child. *Maasumjo kasm*, as it is called in Sind. When the oath is taken the child may be touched. The Hindu takes an oath by stepping over a child; by holding the child; by placing his right hand on the child's head. As he takes his oath he says, 'If I do this I will be drinking the blood of my child', 'A child is near me', 'I hold a child with my hand', 'If I do this I will eat my child'. The child is sometimes taken to a temple and laid before the image of the god. The Muhammadan employs a child to enforce the grant of a request. A young girl is left with the person from whom a boon is expected until the boon is granted. A son is placed in his father's arms with the words, 'Here is his *mair*'. The power that a virgin girl possesses when used in the practice of *mair* is equal to that of seven Korans.

Omens are drawn from the involuntary action of a child. If of its own volition it sweeps the house a guest is expected, as also if it washes its own face. If a child sits in a winnowing-fan and sneezes, its maternal grandparents must fill that winnowing-fan with cakes and give them to other children to eat to avert impending evil.

OLD AGE

One of the most pleasing features of Indian family life which some lament as passing away, is respect for old age. It is not the prerogative of any caste or tribe but a feature of family life among the most primitive and backward as in more advanced communities. Sindi proverbs say of an old man that his beard has not been whitened in the sun, nor whitened with curds. 'If an elderly person says something and a young man does not heed it, then even his settled things are unsettled by God.' 'An old camel is worth two young ones.' 'What the old man can see through bricks young men cannot see through mirrors.' A very common saying of Hindus is 'We are happy in the *puṇya* of our parents.'

Muhammadans call an old man *Rajul Baraka* or *Buzrug*. If a Hindu priest is old he is given the suffix *dev*, 'god', as an honorific.

As man begins his days with more than the ordinary measure of power, so he receives again in his old age a power that surpasses the ordinary. In Sind an old man's blessing and also that of an old woman, is taken before any new undertaking. At a marriage the bridegroom's turban is tied on his head by an old man, and it is an old man who cuts out the cloth from which the gala clothes of the marriage are made. At a circumcision an old man ties the turban or clothing of the boy. When a new animal is purchased the owner finds an old man to be the first to tie up the animal or ride it. Old people are brought to the funeral of a Muhammadan to confer *barkat* on the dead, and contrariwise as many people as can gather at the funeral of an old man or woman to receive *barkat* therefrom. When a parent has lost several children in succession the next infant born is placed in the clothes of an old man or woman. When grain is measured an old man is preferred as measurer. When an old man or woman dies his worn-out clothes are sought by others to obtain *barkat*. A Koran once possessed by an old man is one of the most valuable presents one can give away. The mere possession, apart from their use, of implements and instruments once the property of the old, confers *barkat*, and a bride's dowry often includes the weaving implements of some old person deceased. 'Receiving *barkat*' is the object of all these practices which seek to draw advantage from the power, the *kudrat* of an old person.

The same governing idea rules the practices of the Hindu. The blessing of an old man is taken before the first ploughing; before a new employment is taken up; before going out with a particular object; when a gift is made; when work is begun; when the foundations of a house are laid. At the birth of a child the oldest person present, man or woman, dips something of gold into honey and gives to the child to suck. After their marriage and their worship of the *kul devatā*, the bridal pair take the blessing of the oldest person present among the priests or visitors. When lamps are lighted in the evening the elders of the house are bowed to by those who kindle the lamps. *Lingāyats*, if several children die soon after birth, take a piece of string from the bier of a very old person and tie to the waist of the next-born if it be a boy, or to its arm if it be a girl, to avoid the contagion of death. *Lingāyat Kumbhārs* cut up the clothes of old people on their death and use them to clothe their own children.

Because of their innate power old people are used to plant fruit-trees such as the mango and the coconut. In the Karnāṭak when an old person dies there is a rush to secure some of his ragged clothes, the mere possession of which confers *barkat* on the possessor. Clothes that have been worn by aged and saintly persons are actually worshipped with *ārtī*, *naivedya*, *akṣat* and flowers, as things possessed of special *śakti*. At a birth such clothes ought to be the first clothes worn by the infant when it is placed in a winnowing-fan.

The value of a gift is enhanced if it be made at the hands of an old person; the farewell to a departing guest or family member is given by the aged members of the household. If a guest is leaving his host's house, an old man presents him with a betelnut; if a member of a house is leaving and does not expect to return quickly, an old lady, preferably one with a husband living, puts curds in his right hand as he leaves. One incidental restriction on the departing person that he must not wash his hands after receiving the curds, emphasizes the transfer of *barkat*, for washing is an act of destruction, and prohibited whenever indulgence in it would entail the loss of *barkat*. At the beginning of *Navrātri akṣat* is given to the aged, who touch it and return it to bestow *barkat* on the donors.

In ritual that is more definitely religious old people are chosen for important initiatory functions. When mantras are uttered, though younger priests may recite the greater part of the mantras, the first part which includes the invocation of divine power must be recited by an old priest. In *Śrāddha* ceremonies old Brahmins are chosen to officiate when possible to add to the *barkat* of the dead. The worship of an image is a means whereby its *śakti* may be enhanced, but the increment of power attained by the worship of an old man is considerably greater than the increase which follows the worship of the young. Even among the backward primitive *Bhils* some tribes will not allow any one to worship the family god save the old men of the tribe.

The *śakti* or *kudrat* of the old is illustrated by several other classes of practices. There is a popular belief that they are seldom attacked by evil spirits; in any case there are evils enough which their power automatically averts. Throughout the Presidency, including Sind, there are trees the planting of which by the young is limited by many restrictions, and avoided when possible, as an act fraught with the danger of death. None but the old in the Karnāṭak will dare to plant the alli tree (Memecylon edule), the banyan (Ficus bengalensis), the atti (Ficus glomerata), the niral (Eugenia jambolana), the bāli (Musa sapientum), or the nuggi (Moringa pterygosperma). The betelnut is never planted by the young. In Sind only the old would plant the lai (Tamarix Indica), the sirih (Albizzia Lebbek), and a small variety of nim (Melia azadirachta). *Bhils* also will allow none but old men or men without issue to plant a plantain tree.

A similar line of reasoning leads to the employment of the aged in the practice of *utāra* (*nivāḻi*, *sadqā*, *ghorā* (Sin.)) by which evils are lifted from the afflicted and transferred to others. Typical of this practice is the waving by an old man or woman, round the head of a patient suffering from an abscess, of a yellow-stained rag containing three kinds of grain, uḍīd, bājrī and karad, and its final throwing at the meeting of three roads. There are dangers in this practice which it is safe for the aged only to risk. Old men, too, are employed to wave a *baḻī* round the sick. A *baḻī* consists of an open basket with leaves at the bottom, in which one or more balls of boiled rice are placed with turmeric, red flowers, and lighted wicks. The *baḻī* should not touch the ground, and the man who carries it to a river should not look back, and as he goes water is sprinkled behind him until he reaches a road.

The Muhammadan consults the old and asks for their prayers when he wishes to interpret dreams that worry him; the Hindu, when one who claims to be a *svāmī* proposes to visit him, takes advice from an old person whether the claims of his visitor are genuine or spurious. In the absence of a learned man or one who knows the Koran by heart, any old man can be the *Imām* who leads a congregation of Moslems in prayer. In Sind, at the birth of a child, a saint or aged person sucks honey or a date and then transfers it to the mouth of the child, or may even transfer only his saliva. When ill a Hindu receives his medicine from the hands of the old; it is old men who tie *yantras* and charms to the person of the sick, and on the sixth day after a birth it is an old lady with a husband who ties round the neck of the child its neck ornament. In war the Muhammadan is supposed to do no harm to the old even if they be amongst those he counts as *mushrik*.

Because of their power, old persons are used in the Muhammadan practice of *mair*, to impose a conditional curse upon those who refuse a request. Oaths are taken by the aged, and in Sind particularly by grey-beards, and even as the power of the old gives force to an oath, so the curse of the aged is amongst the worst of curses.

The reaction of power to any form of affront is evidenced by some of the restrictions governing the relations of others with the aged. To step over the bedding of an old man or woman is to shorten one's life. The temper of an old man must never be met with temper. It is forbidden to have sexual congress in a room adjoining that of an elder. One must not smoke in the presence of the old, a rule still practised strictly among the *Kātkarīs*, though with little significance among more advanced classes.

THE GUEST

The hospitality of India is proverbial. It is probably one of the factors which disseminate news with a rapidity that outruns the ordinary means of communication, and so frequently baffles explanation. When wandering in the wilds of Baluchistan I have found the stranger received with a whole series of questions asked in a regular order, the last of which was a demand for the latest news. Every man again has innate power which operates involuntarily, his *pāyguṇ*, and anything new that befalls after the departure or coming of a guest is attributed to the power of his *pāyguṇ*. Every guest, therefore, may effect a change in the fortunes of his host, but the possibility of change is the greater if the guest be an uninvited one. If a holy man be invited expressly to the bed of a dying man he may be unable to save him from death, but if without knowing that any one in the house is ill a holy man suddenly inflicts himself on the household as a guest, the dying man will be saved and even one who has died may be restored to life. To the unexpected, uninvited guest the Hindu gives the name of *Atithidev*, 'the god guest'. To the Sindi Muhammadan the guest is *ghoro*, 'heavy with *kudrat*', as is also his *kadam* or step.

A halo of mysterious possibility encircles the stranger guest in many countries. The folk-lore of Europe down to modern times identifies the unknown visitor as Jesus Christ or as his mother. In the north of England in the border counties there still lingers the habit of placing at the Christmas feast a vacant chair in the hope that Christ may come in the form of an unknown guest. According to Homer, the gods in the likeness of strangers from far countries wander through the cities, and in the Epistle to the Hebrews advice is given to entertain strangers, for thereby some have entertained angels unaware. The Sindi says, 'Feed a pigeon, a partridge and a dove in hope that one day a phœnix may turn up', the phœnix being a bird whose shadow turns a pauper into a king. In the Deccan the householder every day mutters *Atithideo bhav*, 'May a god guest come '. If a sādhu should come uninvited the day is as auspicious as the festival of Dasarā or Divāḻī. *Sādhu sant yeti ghara toc Divāḻī Dasrā.* Stories of the coming of gods in disguise as beggars are very common. The *Kātkarīs* have the story of Hedrabai. Mahādev and Pārvatī disguised themselves as beggars and first went to the house of a Brahmin and asked for prepared food. The Brahmin said they should wait outside and then could eat what he left himself. They waited a little and then Pārvatī said they could not eat leavings, so they went to a poor woman, Hedrabai, who gave them the best gruel without even retaining any for her children. To test her Mahadev asked for more and more until they had finished all the poor woman possessed. The next day the Brahmin invited the beggars to dinner, but they went late, found he had dined without awaiting them and refused again to eat his leavings, and went once more to Hedrabai. When they left Hedrabai the second time they asked for some rice which they returned to her, telling her to put it in a pot, which to her surprise she found filled at once. The Brahmin became a pauper and the poor Hedrabai enriched.

The duty of hospitality is enjoined by the sacred books of Islam and Hinduism. Traditions of the Prophet make the same emphasis and popular adage repeats the same message. 'He whose tablecloth is open will never be bankrupt,' is a Sindi saying, *Janhinjo dastarkhan khulial hundo so kadahin na khutindo.*

The host should make no inquiries about his guest and should receive even an enemy. 'On even an enemy arrived at the house becoming hospitality should be bestowed' (Hitopadesa). In Sind tablecloths are inscribed with these verses

Adime zamin sufrai am ost
Bare khani yaghma chi dushman chi dost.

'The whole world is the common table of God; the friend and the foe are alike.'

Sindis have, too, a story of Abraham turning away a guest of whom he did not approve, for Abraham never took his meals in the morning without a guest, and hearing a voice from heaven rebuking him for not tolerating one who had been the guest of God for seventy-five years, Abraham fell at the feet of the guest and apologized.

A guest is a God-sent blessing; his arrival to a Muhammadan is *rahmat.* Printed on tablecloths in Sind are these words in Persian

"Thank God that your guest takes his own food at your table."

There is a story of the Prophet being visited suddenly by an unexpectedly large number of guests, and of his friend Abu Bakr complaining that there was not enough food in the house. Whereupon the Prophet asked him to arrange the guests in groups of three and set before them what food there was. The food so distributed was ample, proving that the food of the guests came from God.

A guest confers immediate blessing and *barkat* on his host. As a Hindu guest leaves his host's house he says *annadātā sukhi bhav*, 'He who gave me food remain at peace'. The Muhammadan guest as he departs should say, 'May God give you recompense in both worlds'. The guest confers *barkat*. In the Karnāṭak when a revered guest comes, water is poured on his feet, and this is then sprinkled over the heads of the inmates of the house, and even over the house itself, for such guests are *bhūsur*, 'gods on earth'. *Lingāyats* offer a guest dates, plantains and coconuts for him to touch and return. Though by no means a general custom among Hindus, there are non-Brahmins who eat the food left by a guest, considering it *prasād* which transfers to the eater the *śakti* of the guest. Even among Brahmins women and children will eat food left by *svāmīs* who come as guests. 'The remnants of food left by a Muhammadan are always full of cure', and this is still more so in the case of a Muhammadan guest, who is expected to leave uneaten some of the food served him by his host, so that his host may acquire *barkat* by eating it himself.

This idea that a guest confers *barkat* comes out clearly in one or two quaint agricultural customs of wide prevalence. The ordinary sugar-cane press makes a not unmusical sound when turned, which is heard from quite a long distance. At its sound it is the habit of neighbouring agriculturists to flock to the field in which sugar-cane is being pressed and partake of the pressed-out juice. *Śakti* is increased by a common will, and the gratitude and thanks of the self-invited guests are sought as a means of increasing the yield of sugar. A Government Department which essays to popularize a new form of sugar-cane press more economical and effective in its working than the usual pattern, but unfortunately more silent, meets at once an opposition based on the belief that its silent working deprives the agriculturist indirectly of *barkat*, as no far-reaching sound summons the guests. In much the same way a guest is welcomed at the threshing of grain. There is no moment in the gathering in of a crop when man's care may not materially add more to its outturn than the moment when it is brought to the threshing-floor to be threshed. On the threshing-floor the moderate yield in the field may, with proper precautions, be increased by even fifty per cent., and the estimate or *annevāri* made by Government officers in the field, may prove, in the eyes of the peasant, eventually no true measure of the crop's return. If one takes backward communities, such as *Bhils* and *Mavchis* in Khandesh, one finds them prohibiting any guest who arrives unexpectedly whilst the grain is being gathered to the threshing-floor, from departing before the grain is stored in the granary, and entertaining him right regally. In the Karnāṭak the stranger who passes by a threshing-floor, when grain is being threshed or measured is not allowed to depart, or if depart he must, is required to leave behind him a thread from his clothes, or to throw a leaf on to the floor, which is supposed to represent him in his absence, and continue to shower *barkat* on the grain. On no account must a guest or stranger visiting a threshing-floor wash his feet before the threshing is complete, for the washing would wash away the *barkat* he has brought.

The departure of a guest when some member of the host's family has just died, is not allowed by the *Kātkarī* until the funeral is over, for fear that such departure would do harm to the dead. On the other hand, the Muhammadan would welcome the departure of a guest on an inauspicious day, such as Tuesday, in the belief that the guest will take away with him the evil of the day. Persian Muhammadans will not allow a guest to depart on Friday lest he take away the *barkat* of the day, and will not allow him to come to them on a Tuesday lest he bring with him evil.

The reception of a guest is a religious act.[1] In Sind the feast to a guest is called *ziyāfat*, which is interpreted as meaning an inclination towards or an approach to God. To the Hindu the reception of a guest is a sacrifice.[2] He is received as 'lord of the householder'. He is worshipped by the Hindu with *madhupark*[3] and flowers, and given food such as he chooses, *icchābhojana*, and none may eat before him save a bride, an unmarried damsel, the sick or the expectant mother. Muhammadans say, 'If a guest is come and finds the master of the house, the master tells him "You are the master of the house and I am your guest"'. The fruit of welcoming a guest is *barkat* and this is so comprehensive a word

[1] 'The reception of guests is an everlasting sacrifice offered by the householder to Pragapati' (*Apastamba*, ii, 3, 7, 1).

According to *Manu*, the hospitable reception of guests is *Manusya Yajna*, one of the five great sacrifices (*Manu*, iii, 68–74).

[2] 'A guest rules over the world of Indra' (*Manu*, iv, 182).

'A guest is the lord of a householder' (*Institutes of Viṣṇu*, lxvii, 31).

[3] A drink of honey, water, curds, ghee and sugar used in the reception of kings, saints, pilgrims, bridegrooms and Brahmacāris.

that it connotes every form of blessing or weal. In the sacred books [1] of the Hindu the results of hospitality are immunity from misfortune, the averting of evil, wealth, fame and long life in this world and heavenly bliss in the world to come. In Sind the sayings of Shaikh Atar are well known. 'The guest brings his own food but takes away the sins of his host.' 'Any one who receives a guest well befits himself for the *dargāh* of the Almighty.' 'God will regard that man as an enemy who turns away a guest.' 'Brother, keep your guest with respect that you may have respect from God.'

To the power of a guest from which so many blessings flow there is the usual reverse side. His power makes his curse the worse. A curse destroys *puṇya,* the merit or accumulated power of the person cursed, and the fear of the guest's curse accounts largely for the courtesy shown him, just as fear of the curse of the bridegroom explains the royal treatment he receives. The curse of a guest, if unhappily he curses, is a thing the host is powerless to avert. If a host avoids a quarrel with his guest he secures for himself absolution of his sins, but if he turns away a guest disappointed he loses all his merit or *puṇya,* gained in the past, and acquires the guilt of the guest. According to the *Aphorisms of Apastamba*, an offended guest might burn the house of his host with the flames of his anger; he comes to the house indeed resembling a burning fire. In Sind the Muhammadan says, 'If a beggar asks for food and you do not give it, at least do not anger him', *na de na ranjai.* There are many Hindu stories to illustrate the danger of angering a guest. There was once a devotee of Śiva called Śirala to whom the god appeared to test him, and as a beggar demanded a meal from the flesh of his son. Śiral and his wife Canguna in fear of the beggar's anger killed their son and served up his flesh, from which they even partook at the beggar's request. The beggar then refused to eat of the dish as being one

[1] 'The hospitable reception of guests procures wealth, fame, long life and heavenly bliss' (*Manu*, iii, 106).

'The hospitable reception of a guest is a ceremony averting evil' (*Vasistha*, xi, 13).

'The reward for honouring such a guest is immunity from misfortunes, and heavenly bliss' (*Apastamba*, ii, 3, 6, 6).

'He who entertains guests for one night obtains earthly happiness, a second night gains the middle air, a third heavenly bliss, a fourth the world of incomparable bliss, many nights procures endless worlds' (*Apastamba*, ii, 3, 7, 16).

'By honouring a guest he obtains heaven. He obtains better abode after death than even by daily recitation of the Veda, by the Agnihotra, by austerity or sacrificing' (*Institutes of Viṣṇu*, lxvii, lxviii).

'He who prepares food for himself alone eats nothing but sin' (*Manu*, iii, 118; *Institutes of Viṣṇu*, lxvii, 43).

prepared by a pair without issue; they thereupon invoked Śiva, who appeared along with the murdered child and gave them absolute bliss. Another story is that of Anasuya. Once upon a time the sage Nārada, to annoy the wives of Brahma, Viṣṇu, and Śiva, who were always boasting that they were models of fidelity, praised the virtue of Anasuya the wife of one Atri. The three wives thereupon persuaded their husbands to attempt to deprive Anasuya of her chastity. With this object the gods went as mendicants to the hermitage of Atri and demanded a dinner, adding a condition that Anasuya should serve them nude. Anasuya took a cupful of water, washed her husband's feet with the water and then sprinkled the divine guests who at once became babies. She was then able to discard her *sāḍī* and lifting up each baby proceeded to suckle them, placed them in a cradle and lulled them to sleep. The gods were powerless to resume their ordinary form. Their wives, distracted by their prolonged absence, went in search of them, and at the meeting-place of three roads that led to the three heavens, met Narada, who said he had seen their consorts going to the hermitage. The goddesses went then to the hermitage where they found the infants, but were unable to identify which infant was which god, and provoked laughter by their efforts to find their respective husbands. Finally, Anasuya was persuaded again to wash her husband's feet in water and sprinkle this over the infants, who regained their original shape, blessed Anasuya and left with their crestfallen wives.

The host's fear of offending the guest enables the latter to coerce the former into granting a request by refusing to drink water offered by the host, until the request is granted.

Various taboos on the conduct of a guest also demonstrate his potentiality for evil. He must not leave the cuttings of his nails in his host's house. He must never count the rafters in the roof, *khallya gharce vase moju naye.* He should neither praise nor criticize the food that is offered him. He should not sit save where he is asked to sit, nor get up without the permission of the host.

Besides these taboos on his conduct, various measures are taken to nullify the evil potentiality of a guest. His possession of great power is no assurance that he does not also possess an evil eye. As a protection against this, therefore, the Muhammadan host reads the *Āyat ta in yakad.* In the Karnāṭak a gardener will require a guest to wash his eyes and mouth before entering his fruit garden. The guest may also have evil *pāyguṇ*, in other words, without any volition on his part may bring with him a train of evil sequel. To avert this the Sindi takes earth from beneath the heel of the guest, or the hoofs of the animal he rides and, mixing with salt, throws it into fire. He also reads an *āyat* beginning Hasbun Allah. In the Dharwar district the guest must wash his feet before he enters a house. Even after a guest has departed one does not cease to protect oneself against his possibly evil potentiality; grains of black *rāḻā* (Panicum Italicum) are thrown behind the departing guest, as they are thrown after a corpse, or a black sooty earthen pot is dashed to the ground and broken behind him. And when he is quite gone the steps of the house are well brushed with water, and in Sind the chairs and tables he may have used are turned.

Another category of protective measures is that of practices adopted to render innocuous the potentiality of the guest by imposing on him a conditional curse. Brahmins and Rajputs offer him salt, as do Sindis. Still more commonly milk is presented to the guest when he arrives. Should he, after accepting this offer of salt or milk, still conceal an evil intent, the power innate in the salt and milk will harm him. In the Karnāṭak he may even be asked to sit awhile in a temple before he is admitted to a house. The sanctity of the temple is supposed to render harmless the potentiality for evil of the guest. Even so the pilgrim on return from his pilgrimage has to spend some time in a mosque or temple before he is admitted to a house. The Sindi Muhammadan bridegroom is taken before the marriage ceremony really begins, to a mosque to reduce the potentiality of his curse, which is the more potent because he goes into *vanvāha.* And a Muhammadan who has visited a graveyard is required to make himself fit for association with his fellow-men by spending some time in a mosque before he enters a house.

With all his potentiality for good and for evil, however, familiarity with a guest soon robs him of the mystery arising from his being an unknown factor. Traditions relate that the Prophet said special hospitality should be for one night and a day only, the *mudat-i-takalluf*; the full period of hospitality should be three days, after which keeping the guest would be but charity. A Brahmana, according to the *Institutes of Viṣṇu* and according to *Manu,* is an *Atithi* [1] when he stays for one night only. Popular sayings vary somewhat in detail, but in general make one day

[1] *Atithidev,* vid. *Institutes of Viṣṇu,* lxvii, 34, and *Manu,* iii, 102. *Atithi* is one who does not stay for a whole *tithi* or lunar day. A Brahmana who stays for one night only as a guest is called *atithi* because he does not stay for a long time; because he stays (*sthita*) not long (*anityam*).

the really important day of entertainment, and three days the limit. In the Deccan the *Marāṭhā* says: '*Pahile divasi pahuna, dusare divasi pai, tisare divasi rahil tyala akkal nahi.*' 'On the first day a guest is a guest; on the second he is unimportant, and he who stays until the third day has no sense.' Even the wandering sannyāsī is not expected to stay more than three days in any one village save during the rainy months, *caturmās*. A Muhammadan says a guest is dear but only for three days, *mihman aziz ast magar ta si roz.* In Kanarese-speaking districts one finds the vulgar saying *vandu divasa nenṭā; erdu divasa nenṭā; mura divasa nenṭā; nalkane divasa śanṭā.* 'On the first day a relative; on the second day a relative; on the third day a relative; on the fourth day shameless' (lit. pubic hairs).

THE BRIDAL PAIR

Honorifics of royalty[1] or divinity given to the bridegroom and less frequently to the bride, proclaim the special power of the bridal pair. In Gujarāt the bridegroom is generally called *Var Rājā*, 'the king bridegroom'; *Bhāts* give the bridal pair the names of ornaments used at a royal coronation. *Bene Israels* and *Muhammadans* call the bridegroom *Navshah* or 'the new king', and his garland is called by the latter *Sultāni Sehra*, 'the royal garland'. *Lamānis* call the bridegroom *Vetadu*, 'king', and the bride, *Navaleri*, 'queen'. The *Kan Divar* and the *Madival* regard the bridal pair as possessing for six days the *śakti* of a goddess.

[1] 'The Hebrew name for the bride is Kallah, which etymologically implies the idea of a crown. The bridegroom is, on the day of his wedding, deemed a spotless man. . . . The Canticles describe the Israelitish bridegroom as wearing a crown on the day of his espousals—an honour which in later times was extended to the bride. Mishnah records that during the war of Vespasian the use of crowns was forbidden to bridegrooms, and that during the war of Titus brides were included in the prohibition, in token of the intense grief of the Jews at the ruin of the nation and of its Temple' (*Journal of the Bombay Branch of the Royal Asiatic Society*, vol. iii, New Series, p. 181.—Professor Ezekiel Moses Ezekiel).

'There are some interesting customs which show both the taboo character of bride and bridegroom, and also an attempt at disguising them by fictitious change of identity. The Malay wedding ceremony, even as carried out by the poorer classes, shows that the contracting parties are treated as royalty, that is to say, as sacred human beings, and if any further proof is required in addition to the evidence which may be drawn from the general character of the ceremony, I may mention first the fact that the bride and bridegroom are actually called *Raja Sari* (i.e. 'the sovereigns of a day') and secondly that it is a polite fiction that no command of theirs, during their one day of sovereignty, may be disobeyed. During the first week of marriage the Syrian pair play at being king and queen; they sit on a throne and the villagers sing songs' (*The Mystic Rose*, E. Crawley, vol. ii, p. 50).

There is nothing in Indian thought to suggest any disguise of the bridal pair; the ascription of royalty or divinity to them is parallel to the general ascription of these qualities to things or persons with special power.

Divinity is indeed ascribed to the bridegroom and bride in many parts of the Presidency. In Kanara the father-in-law continues to call the bridegroom *Devaru* or 'god' even after the marriage. In the Karnāṭak the bride and bridegroom are *Bhūsur*, 'incarnations of divinity', and the *anśa* or essence of Lakṣmī Nārāyaṇ. In the Deccan the *Marāṭhā* calls the bridegroom *Navardev*, 'the god bridegroom'. There are, it is true, many primitive castes such as *Ghantichors, Bestars, Dang Dasaris, Ghatti Vaddars, Māng Garuḍis, Haraṇśikārīs*, which do not give any special title to either of the bridal pair, but somewhere or other in their marriage customs is reflected the idea that a bridegroom or a bride is not an ordinary personage.

The exceptional power which the bridegroom possesses for a limited time confers *barkat* by contact and radiation. In Sind on the third day after a marriage Muhammadans send the bridal pair dates, sweetmeats and coconuts which the bridal pair merely touch and then return, having by their touch infused them with some portion of their own *barkat*-giving power. This gift is called *mura*. In the same way the family of the pair on the third day feed the pair with butter, honey and dates and then consume the remnants of their repast. During the marriage itself the Muhammadan bride and bridegroom sip milk from a common dish, and then pass this to the assembled guests for them to sip from it, touched as it has been by the lips of the bridal pair. The lap of the bride is filled with sweets and coconuts, and these are then distributed among the visitors to confer *barkat*; after, too, the bride has been brought to her husband's house sweets are put in her mouth and then eaten by married women. Yet another example of the radiation of power by the bridegroom is his transmission of power to the water in which his feet have been washed. To obtain a son, Muhammadan women who have no issue drink the water in which the feet of the bridegroom have been washed by a sister or other female relative. In Bombay Persian Shi'ahs make the bridegroom wash the feet of his bride with milk, and then sprinkle this all over the house.

A Muhammadan bridegroom, and sometimes the bride, is taken to a spot where a work of construction such as the building of a well or bridge, has begun in order to bless its inception; he is taken to a garden the trees of which are barren and asked to water them and make them fertile; his touch will make a buffalo that has failed in giving milk yield a good supply of milk; his prayers will cure a sick man and when the Sindi bride sits in *vanvāha* she is usually asked to pray for others, as her prayers are always heard.

If the bridegroom but lights the lamps of others, offers or touches food before it is distributed, he confers *barkat*. If he allows another to wave money round him before throwing it away he makes that man eventually opulent.

The underlying principles of Hindu customs are similar to those of the Sindi Muhammadan. *Kanyādān* is the gift by her father of his daughter as a bride; this mere gifting confers *barkat* on the father. Mere attendance at a wedding secures *barkat*; the sight of a bridal procession or that of the bridegroom himself confers *barkat*, for the *darśan* of a bridegroom is as that of a god. The water in which the feet of the bridegroom have been washed is to the Hindu holy; it is *tīrth*, *pādōdaka* or *caraṇ-tīrth*, though only on the one occasion of *varapūjā*, 'worship of the bridegroom', and then only to the parents-in-law. When this water is thrown away it must be thrown where it will not be trodden upon. This water with its acquired power scares away spirits. *Kuravers* and *Vaddars* sprinkle this water and that in which the feet of the bride have been washed, all over the house. Parents of the *Beldar* bride wash the feet of the bridal pair and drink the water so used. In the Karnāṭak many non-Brahmin castes sprinkle this water over the heads of the bride's parents. Among *Lamānis* the mother-in-law drinks a handful of the water which drips from the hair of the bridegroom, when with the bride he takes his ceremonial *surgi* bath.

This auspicious bathing, *mangaḻsnān*,[1] of the bridal pair affords another way in which *barkat* can be obtained through indirect contact with the bridal pair. Relatives of the bride and bridegroom sit near the pair, so as to be sprinkled by the water that is poured over the pair, and at one *Bedar* wedding that I attended this bath was postponed for several hours, because several relatives had not appeared, and would have resented the loss of a special opportunity of acquiring *barkat* which would have been entailed by holding the *mangaḻsnān* in their absence.

To the Muhammadan idea of acquiring *barkat* through food touched or left by the bridal pair, one may find a few Hindu parallels. The *Korava* bridal pair eat from one large dish with five married women, and whatever these leave uneaten is consumed by the relatives. *Kurubas* place rice and coconut in the

[1] The *Kan Divar* and *Madival* have a curious *Mangaḻsnān*; this is a merely nominal bathing of the bridal pair and no relatives attend to share in it. A few drops of water are allowed to drop on the heads of the bridal pair who are dressed in their best clothes, and are wearing their head ornaments. This water is to fall on them through a plantain-leaf. The rest of the water must not come in contact with them and is thrown on the ground.

lap of the bride and then dividing these in two equal portions distribute to the two families of the pair to eat. *Śimpīs* have a practice called *suna mukh.* During the actual marriage the mother of a Śimpī bride is not allowed to see the bridegroom, but after the ceremony is over she comes to the house of the bride with milk and plantains. She then holds the milk for the bridegroom to look at his reflection therein, after which both the milk and the fruit are distributed to confer *barkat,* particularly among any women present. The *Naik-Maklu* bridal pair on the first two days of the marriage are invited out by many householders, and served with food which they merely touch, and leave others to eat, or presented with fruit and sweetmeats to distribute to others. *Kall* or *Adivi Koravas* place five measures of rice, five lemons, five dates, five betelnuts, five pieces of coconut and five pieces of turmeric in the lap of the bride. On the sixth day of the marriage when the bride returns to her house, the dates are given to children, the pieces of coconut mixed with ghee and rice are given to five young married women, and any one may share the lemons.

These Hindu customs, however, showing *barkat* acquired through food touched or left by the bridal pair are few in comparison with the customs which are based on the assumption that there is great danger in eating such food. In these latter practices we reach the second axiom, as we might call it, related to the power of the bridal pair. Power is at all times, and even when beneficent, a dangerous entity ; the greater the power, the greater its inherent elements of danger, and even so is the great power of the bridal pair. It may be beneficent, it may confer *barkat,* but it remains none the less a dangerous force against which precautions must be taken. This emphasis of the dangerous element in the power of the bridal pair appears in varying degree in the customs of the Muhammadan and the Brahmin, but is most marked in the practices of the non-Brahmin.

The power of the bridal pair in the Konkan and the Karnāṭak must not come in contact with that of another bridal pair. Brahmins will perform several marriages at the same time: *Lingāyat Kumbhārs* will celebrate several marriages in the same house, and one Sindi bridegroom may meet another without disaster, but among non-Brahmins in general if two bridal processions meet, the respective bridegrooms must cover their faces. *Gollars, Lamānis* and *Kabbars* think that if one pair see the *bāśing* or crown of another pair it will die. *Bhāts* forbid marriages in opposite houses and should two brides or bridegrooms accidentally meet during a wedding, or when on their way to a temple, a *naivedya* has to be offered at once in a temple to avert the evil consequences. In Kanara there is the same idea that their lives are endangered if two brides or bridegrooms meet, and a general belief that if a man or woman marries a second time, the children by the former marriage die if they see the *bāśing*.

In Sind the shadows of the bridal pair are *ghoro* and no one should sit in their shadows. The curse of the bridal pair is very bad because of their innate power, and in order to prevent the bridegroom cursing any one he is taken before the marriage to a mosque. Whilst the Muhammadan bridegroom sits in *vanvāha* his speech is feared; he is therefore taken to those from whom some boon is desired and used as *mair* to force the granting of the request. As, too, the efficacy of an oath is correlated to power the Muhammadan, as does the Hindu, swears by a bridegroom. A famine of wide extent follows any breach by the Muhammadan bridal pair of the restriction imposing silence at certain stages of the marriage ceremony. In the Deccan the Muhammadan shares with the Hindu the belief that if whilst they wear their wristlets the bride and bridegroom touch a pot of water with their foot, it will break almost immediately, a belief to be contrasted with the custom prevalent in the Deccan of making the bridegroom deliberately touch an empty pot of water, a full measure of grain and a broom to bring *barkat*. At the stage when the clothes of the bridal pair are tied together, *Mahārs* rush away all small children, for if a child of two and a half years of age or less be carried by or pass by at this moment it would die.

The leavings of food left by persons possessing power are often eaten by others to obtain *barkat*. Food left by great saints, *gurus* and *svāmīs*, is eaten by others to get *barkat*; food left by a husband is eaten by his wife; the leavings of a child are eaten by others; childless women eat the leavings of women with issue, but the leavings of a pregnant woman and of the bridal pair are not eaten in general by the Hindu. In many ways his attitude towards such leavings is the same as his attitude towards first-fruits, the eating of which is fraught with danger. *Marāṭhās*, for instance, think that only a child with its special power can eat with impunity the rice and coconut placed in the lap of the bride. *Lamānis* wave these things round the bridal pair and then throw them away, thinking it too dangerous for any one to eat of them. *Pancāḻs* offer the rice and coconut first to their family gods, before which they remain for five weeks ere they are eaten by the families of the bridal pair. *Lingāyats* place the unbroken rice and coconut in the lap of the bride on the first day of the marriage; they are then placed before the *kul devatā*, and after the marriage is over the rice is given to the *jangam* priests and the coconut remains in the god-room. If the coconut is lost or if either the rice or coconut be eaten during the marriage, disease or death will come to the bridal pair. In Kanara the *Kan Divars* and *Madivals* tie a coconut and rice in a new cloth to the waist of the bride; on the third day the coconut is broken before the *hālgamba* and then the offering with jaggery is boiled and eaten by all the relatives, saving the parents of the bride. *Raddis*, *Koravas*, *Calvadis*, *Macchigars* and others like the *Lingāyats*, offer the rice and coconut first to the family gods. *Vaddars* restrict the eating of these things to the household of the bridegroom or to the bridal pair themselves. Even the *Bhil* will not allow any one to eat the balls of cooked rice which, after the marriage is complete, are placed in the hands of the bridal pair.

The consumption of these comestibles is not, however, fraught with danger merely to those who eat them without precautions, for the belief is widespread that disaster befalls the bridal pair also. *Gollars* and *Kabbars* believe that if the bridal pair should eat of these things they will consume their own issue, or in other words, have no issue. *Pancāḻs* think that harm befalls the bridal pair if the offerings are eaten before being offered to the *kul devatā*, and *Lingāyats* prophesy the same harm if any one eat them during the marriage ceremony. The prosperity and even the life of the bridal pair are connected with the coconut. *Lingāyats* preserve this in the god-room and its loss brings disease or death to the bridal pair. Among *Brahmins*, when after the marriage the bride leaves her mother's house to go to that of her husband, she is given a coconut which must have its cover intact, *asolī nāraḻ*. This same nut is used at all subsequent presentations and the bride must take it with her wherever she goes for a year, at the end of which year is a ceremony called *varṣāsan* in which she is given again the coconut, which then may be broken. Some Brahmins throw this coconut into a well and when it sprouts plant it in a garden; non-Brahmins do not use a coconut in this way but present rice, dates, fruit and copra which on no account must the bride eat.

Another illustration of the dangerous element in the power of the bridal pair is the restriction which forbids the *Lingāyat* mother to see the face of her son or daughter when *akṣat* is thrown on them at a wedding. The mother must not see the *haṇi akki* or the grains of rice mixed with curds which are applied to the foreheads of the bridal pair before the guests throw the unbroken rice.

Haḍadā ki haṇi akki noḍabaradu. Should she see these, she or her husband will die within three years. As, however, the mother cannot refrain from joining in the benedictory throwing of *akṣat* on the pair, she does this from such a distance as prevents her seeing their foreheads.

Actual contact, *sampark, sansarg,* transmits to things brought near to persons possessing *śakti* or *kudrat* something of their innate power. This transmission entails the diffusion of that power with all its potentiality for good or for evil, and Indian customs often appear inconsistent because attention is for the moment concentrated on one only of the two aspects in which such diffusion can be regarded. Whilst the Muhammadan respects the leavings of food left by the bridal pair as sharing in their beneficent power, the Hindu generally sees only the possibility of a transference of evil. Even the Hindu, however, visualizes the transference of *barkat.* There is *barkat* transferred by the water in which the feet of the bridal pair are washed; contact can be established by sight and the *darśan* of the bridegroom confers *barkat*; the water that falls from the hair of the bridegroom as he takes his *surgi* bath or splashes from the heads of the bride and bridegroom as they make their *mangaḷsnān,* also confers *barkat.* These illustrate among non-Brahmins the transfer of good and not of evil. When, too, measures are taken to nullify the possible evil *pāygun* of a bride as she enters for the first time the house of her husband (*ghar bharaṇī*), she is required to kick over at the threshold a measure of rice, and this rice is added to the family's stock of grain to bring it increase.

A multitude of customs of another category illustrate the same transference of power by contact. Sindi Muhammadans preserve carefully the pillows and beds used by the bridal pair on their first night of married life, and significantly secure these from touching the ground. The gala dress worn by bride and bridegroom is also preserved and kept away from the ground, and given to younger members of the family when in turn their marriage takes place. Even ornaments worn during the marriage are treated with the same care, and the mirror used by the bride must never be broken, or the death of some one of the family will follow.

There can be no surer test whether an object is believed to possess power than its protection from contact with the ground, and this test is particularly applicable to the wristlets and coronets which the bridal pair have worn during the marriage ceremony. A Muhammadan bride and bridegroom wear a wristlet of red thread, *ghāna, dastiyūn,* which cannot be placed on the ground, and after use is finally thrown in a river or well to prevent its touching the ground or being stepped over. The Hindu bridal pair wear wristlets, *kankaṇ*, made out of the *surgi* thread which has averted evil from the bridal pair whilst they took their *mangaḻsnān*, forming an enclosure around them. At all moments a power of great potentiality, the *śakti* of the Hindu bridal pair is never more powerful than it is when they wear their wristlets or *kankaṇ*, and with this power the *kankaṇ* are naturally suffused. After a Hindu marriage, therefore, the wristlets must be carefully preserved. *Talwārs* and *Vaddars* tie them to a beam in the roof and leave them there until they perish of their own accord. *Vaiṣṇava Brahmins* bury them entire in the god-room; *Lingāyats* place them before the *kul devatā* for five weeks and then throw into running water. *Deśastha Brahmins* present them to the family gods and then throw them in a clean place or in water. *Sarasvat Brahmins* dismiss their *śakti* and then tie them to the roof. In Kanara *Kan Divars* and *Madivals* tie the *kankaṇ* on the third day of the marriage to their *hāḻgamba*, leave them so tied for a fortnight and then throw both the *hāḻgamba* and the *kankaṇ* under a tree that has milky juice. *Konchi Koravas* throw their *kankaṇ* into a running stream. *Marāṭhās* tie the wristlets to a post of the marriage *manḍap* for a week or two, and then take them into the jungle where they throw them in a bush so that they will not be stepped over, or send them to a holy place to be preserved for a year. *Calvadis* have a more elaborate custom. They first remove the piece of turmeric [1] which was tied in the wristlets and with it mark the faces of the bridal pair and of the *suvāsinīs* present among the guests, transferring to these last *barkat*, and then tie the wristlets to the linga of the bridegroom and the *mangaḻsūtra* or marriage necklace of the bride. When either the bride or bridegroom dies, the *kankaṇ* is buried along with the deceased. *Vaddars* have several customs alternative to the one of tying the wristlets to a beam; they tie them to the hanging rack used for the storage of their milkpots, or the day after the marriage the bridal pair

[1] Before tying the *kankaṇ Vaddars* go to water and soak the wristlets invoking *Gangā*; the *śakti* of Agni (fire) is also invoked into the wristlets. The *kankaṇ* represents a vow to abstain from anything impure or destructive of *śakti*. *Kankaṇ* are tied to the wrist of the *yajamān* at Yajnas and at car festivals; they tie up the *śakti* of the person wearing them. Whilst they wear the *kankaṇ* the bridal pair must not bow to any one, not even to an elder when *ārtī* is waved. The *kankaṇ* must not be lost and whilst wearing it the bride or bridegroom must not work, or death or disease will follow. The marriage *kankaṇ* has a knot in it in which is a piece of turmeric. This turmeric has one or more branches and is accordingly called 'the root bearing children', *makkaḻberu*. By the *kankaṇ* the bridal pair are made partners with the fertility of the turmeric.

go to the temple of Hanuman, and there untying the wristlets themselves throw them in running water or a well. *Deśastha Brahmins* sometimes give the *kankaṇ* to a priest, who places them in a pot with coloured *akṣat* and throws them away, or after removing the turmeric which is usually tied in the *kankaṇ*, throw the *kankaṇ* into the tulsī plant which every Hindu household keeps. Another Brahmin custom is to worship the removed *kankaṇs* with *akṣat* and give them to a priest, who returns them for preservation to the bridal pair with a betelnut. *Bhils*, whose *kankaṇ* are made of thread and boiled wheaten flour, hang them after the marriage to the roof.

The *kankaṇ* are made from the *surgi* thread; any portion of the thread remaining after the *kankaṇs* have been prepared receives the same protection as the wristlets. It is not allowed to touch the ground, is tied to a post of the marriage *manḍap* until the *manḍap* is dismantled, and generally is later put with the *kankaṇ* and *bāśing*.

The bridal coronet or *bāśing* is of many types. Brahmins make it of plantain-leaves with hanging flowers; the Sarasvat *bāśing* is of cork and tinsel. Bendi (Kydia calycina) is used for it in Kanara; *Haranśikārīs* stitch together seven leaves of alli (Memecylon edule) in three lines with a ball of cotton-wool in the centre. Coloured paper in many cases is the chief material used. In some backward castes no *bāśing* is used. Where a coronet is used, its disposal is on lines similar to those followed in preserving the *kankaṇ*. Sindi Moslems tie garlands to the foreheads of the bridal pair called *mora* or *sehra*. These, after use, are hung on a peg until dry and then thrown into water or are preserved in a box; both methods of disposal preventing their contact with the ground. *Koravas* and *Naidus* also use a garland of flowers which are renewed every day of the marriage and after use are thrown into water. *Raddis, Macchigars, Colvadis, Vaddars* and also *Koravas* tie the *bāśing* to a vertical pillar until it perishes. *Vaiṣṇava Brahmins* keep the *bāśing* in a box for a year and then throw it into the compound of a temple. *Lingāyats* keep the crown in an upper story of the house or in a basket fastened to a beam for three years or longer, and then throw into water. *Pancāḷs* place their *bāśing* in a basket suspended from the roof, place it whenever removed from the basket near the family gods on an *āsan*, and eventually throw into water. *Lamānis* of Ron tie the *bāśing* to the roof until some member of the *Tambore* family visits them, when they give him the *bāśing* in alms. In Kanara the *Kan Divar* and the *Madival* tie their *bāśing* of bendi on the sixth day of the marriage permanently to a beam ; *Calvadis*, whenever the bridegroom sleeps, remove the *bāśing* and place it in a basket before the family gods. *Kurubas* tie it to a beam in the roof for three or five years, and then throw into water. *Deśastha Brahmins* tie the coronet to the roof and leave it there, or offering it to the *kul devatā* throw into water or on some pure spot. Even amongst *Tamil Christians* this idea survives of the transmission of power from the bridal pair into the coronets or garlands they have worn. The bride's mother ties gold leaves round the foreheads of the bridal pair ; these leaves must finally be thrown in a well or running water. In church the bride and bridegroom also wear garlands of flowers ; in the evening when the pair sit in the marriage *maṇdap* these garlands must be hung on a peg and on the third day of the marriage are thrown into water.

Muhammadan, Brahmin, and non-Brahmin alike, therefore, recognize the transfer by contact of power from the bridal pair to the coronets and wristlets they have worn, and the Christian convert has retained the same idea. A variety of ways adopted in disposing finally of these ornaments emphasizes that these ornaments with their acquired power must not be brought into contact with the ground save where that ground has special sanctity, and that they must not be stepped over. Should any one other than the bridegroom step over these ornaments he loses in sequel his own *śakti*. The commonest method of securing the protection of power is to throw things that possess or once possessed power after use into water, and this is the most usual way of disposing of *bāśing*, *ghana*, *kankaṇ*, and *sehra*. In one other respect also Muhammadan and Hindu customs demonstrate the power in these ornaments. The power of one *bāśing* cannot, suffused as it is with the power of one bridegroom, be brought in conflict with the power of another bridegroom. No *bāśing* can be used in two marriages ; no *sehra* can be used for one bridegroom after it has been worn by another. Sindi Muhammadans apply these same axioms of conduct to the henna with which the feet and hands of the bridal pair are covered. This henna can be touched by the bridegroom's sister and by her alone, and any henna left over must be carefully protected until it is finally thrown into water.

There is yet another significant meaning in the practice of throwing wristlet and *bāśing* into water after use. These ornaments which have been in the closest contact with the person of the bride and bridegroom are hot with power. After their removal, therefore, the Hindu dips them in milk, because as they are, they are a potential factor of evil ; they are a possible source of danger and must be cooled. The Sindi Muhammadan does not use milk in this way but considers that the water in which his *sehra* and *ghana* are thrown cools the hot *kudrat* they possess; he throws them into water not merely to prevent their being stepped over or their touching the ground, but also *tanda karna, thaḍo karan* (Sin.), 'to make them cool'. There could be no more lucid illustration of the dangerous power which has been transmitted from the bride and bridegroom.

To return to the bridal pair. If inanimate things with power acquired from them by contact require protection, still more logically must the source of this power be preserved from harmful contacts. The bridal pair, in the first place, must as far as possible be preserved from contact with the ground. In practice this means that they cannot during the marriage ceremony, or at critical moments thereof, such as that when the *akṣat* is thrown on them, sit on the ground. Hindu marriage rites all show in some way or other variants of this common restriction; the pair must sit or stand on something that insulates them from the ground. They may sit on *pāṭ* or flat boards of wood and always square in shape; on low stools sometimes made of wood specially chosen such as mango; on baskets of bamboo, or they may stand in baskets. Their insulation from the ground is further made the more secure by sprinkling on these *āsan* some form of grain; on the *pāṭ* or the black blanket used rice, jvārī or wheat is scattered, the baskets are filled with grain or the husk of grain. *Marāṭhās* construct in the marriage *manḍap* a series of five steps of earth which are covered with cowdung, red earth and chunam and crowned with a twig of the auspicious mango. In front of this pyramid or *bahul* a square is formed, at each corner of which stands a pile of earthen pots, five in number and of diminishing size from the bottom to the top; these pots are also adorned with mango twigs, and stalks of sugar-cane or jvārī rest against them. In the middle of this square the bridal pair sit when *akṣat* is thrown, on an *āsan* of red rice.

In general, too, the bridal pair must wear shoes. A wedding is the only occasion among Brahmins, exclusive of Vaiṣṇava Brahmins, when the *yajamān* must wear shoes; the boy at his thread ceremony, in spite of his power, need not wear shoes. *Talwārs* require the bridal pair to wear shoes for nine days; *Vaddars* for five days, as also *Calvadis* and *Koravas*. *Lamānis*, a wandering tribe, once the carriers of India, always show many modifications of any general practice; the period their bridal pair must observe in retaining their shoes varies considerably even within the limits of one district (Dharwar). In some places the period is three days, in others it is as long as a month. The wearing of shoes is so strictly enforced that they can be removed only when the wearers go to bed; even then the shoes must be placed in the bedding whilst some *Lamānis* insist on shoes being worn by the bridal pair even when they sleep. Amongst *Lamānis* the bridegroom is met at the gate or boundary of the bride's village, where he leaves his old shoes and puts on new ones; in alternative he goes to the bride's house wearing his old shoes but carrying two new pairs for himself and his bride. At the marriage of *Lamānis*, *Marāṭhās* and *Muhammadans* in the Deccan the brothers of the bride try steadily to steal the shoes of the bridegroom, and exact a penalty for their restoration.

Another measure taken to protect the power of the bride and bridegroom from contacts which would destroy it, is to forbid their going into the sun, or if this be unavoidable to protect them, when in the sun, by a covering such as a black blanket. In the adoption of this measure the non-Brahmin, as he does on many other occasions, meets the Sindi Muhammadan and actually parts from the Brahmin. The Brahmin does not prohibit his bride and bridegroom from going into the sun, nor does he require them, should they do so, to wear a black blanket. When, however, the Brahmin bridegroom goes to the house of the bride he is enveloped in a coloured *śelā*, a woman's garment which covers him entirely save for his face. He is further protected by *abdāgīr* or truncated parasols. The Brahmin is, in fact, strictly speaking, less logical or thorough in working out his theory of the special power of the bridal pair; he does not emphasize with the emphasis of the non-Brahmin the dangerous element in that power, and is not so comprehensive in the measures he takes to protect it. One reads so much, one might almost say *ad nauseam*, of the imitation of Brahmin customs and ideas by the non-Brahmin that no excuse is needed for stressing that an examination of many Hindu customs often shows a parallel to non-Brahmin thought and practice not in any Brahmin rite but in the customs of the Muhammadan. If the assumption be natural that the more primitive will usually show the greater consistency and that inconsistency of practice often follows a borrowing of ideas, then there are many occasions on which one might conjecture the taking of a custom by the Brahmin from the non-Brahmin, and not the reverse.

Be this as it may, the Muhammadan and the non-Brahmin protect the bridal pair from the inimical power of the sun; the Brahmin who recognizes in other practices the destruction of *śakti* that follows its exposure to the sun, does not approach either Muhammadan or non-Brahmin in consistency. In Sind the bride and bridegroom withdraw for some days into confinement, or to use the local phrase they 'sit in *vanvāha*'. This means that the bride for seven or nine days sits in a room apart, from which she can go out only if protected by a covering; the bridegroom should observe the same confinement for one day, but in practice walks about covered. The usual covering of the non-Brahmin bridal pair when they unavoidably have to go out in the sun is a thick black blanket worn over the head, and though one may occasionally find the blanket carelessly thrown over the shoulder in these days of discredited customs, the strictness of the restriction is usually observed. *Gollars, Raddis* and *Kabbars* will not allow their bridal pair to part from their black woollen blanket even in the *manḍap*. A *Jain* bridegroom when he goes out of doors wears a handkerchief on his head in which he puts a lemon. The *Kan Divar* and *Madival* impose their restriction on going into the sun for three days as do some *Lamānis*; *Vaddars*; *Koravas* and *Pancāḻs* for five days; *Talwārs* for nine days and some *Lamānis* for a month. The beginning of the period is often counted from the taking of their *surgi* bath or *mangaḻsnān* by the bridal pair. *Bhils* restrict the period to the time the pair are covered with turmeric. *Muhammadans* extend the restriction to the bridegroom's best man, the *anar*, who is not allowed to go into the sun whilst the bridal pair are in *vanvāha*. *Marāṭhās* prolong the period for ten days subsequent to the marriage. Among *Hālakki Gauḍās* the bridegroom goes in procession to the bride's house and the marriage *manḍap* by night, but as he proceeds an umbrella is held over him. The use of an umbrella by many castes is a minor illustration of the same restriction, and of the ascription of royalty to the bridegroom. Just as common, too, as a single umbrella are ornamental fans or parasols which serve no useful purpose now, but are witness as relics to the same underlying idea of protection of power. To avoid unnecessary exposure to the sun, it is a common practice for the bridegroom to take temporarily a house close to that of the bride. Occasionally, too, one finds families which will not take the bridegroom in procession at all.

THE PILGRIM

A pilgrim returns home after his pilgrimage, in an atmosphere of power. He has visited sacred places and by contact has acquired power therefrom. He has, further, by a strict ordering of his life acquired righteousness; the Hindu has acquired *puṇya* or merit, and the possession of *puṇya* means the possession of power. This power is a means whereby he confers *barkat* on others. Water in which the feet of a Muhammadan pilgrim have been washed is drunk by others; his hands are kissed, for they have touched the sacred walls of the *Ka'bah*. A *Haji* is used to force a request; it is the essence of the practice of *mair* in Sind that the agent of coercion should possess power.

In a similar way the Hindu attempts to obtain *barkat* from the returned pilgrim. His feet are washed and the water is sprinkled over people near; it is taken home and sprinkled over the house and over children. Dust is collected from under his feet and with this his friends anoint their bodies. He is invited to feasts, and food he has touched or left uneaten is consumed by others.

And yet just as it is true of other manifestations of power, the power of a pilgrim is a potential source of danger to others. The Muhammadan calls him *ghoro* or 'heavy'; the Hindu considers him *Bhūsur* or an incarnation of divinity. His power is above normal and in corresponding degree his potentiality for evil is the greater.

A Muhammadan pilgrim is feared for forty days; to avoid his curses he must be humoured in every way, not excited nor allowed to work. Before he enters a house on his return from pilgrimage he must first go to a mosque and must wash his hands and face. He must on no account sleep with his wife for a week. The Hindu guards against the potentiality of the pilgrim in much the same way. He is received with respect at the village boundary and given milk, but he must pass a night or two in a temple before he will be received in a private house, or if he arrives by day at least some hours in a temple outside the village bounds. When, too, he first enters a private dwelling his feet are washed and grain is thrown over him. His evil eye is feared by gardeners, who will not allow him to enter their gardens until he has washed his eyes and mouth. The water in which his feet were washed must not be thrown over the elders of the family of the pilgrim himself.

CIRCUMCISION

A *sanskār* is a Hindu ceremony which qualifies the Hindu to discharge properly the duties of the next status into which he passes through that ceremony; a *sanskār* makes complete or perfect by the addition of something that was wanting. Now just as during some of his *sanskār* the Hindu boy is credited with special inordinate power, so the Muhammadan attributes unusual power to a boy at his circumcision. The Muhammadan boy at his circumcision is *ghoro*, 'heavy with *kudrat*'.

Remnants of the boy's food are eaten by others to obtain *barkat*. After his wound has healed he is taken round newly cultivated fields or to a newly constructed well to promote good crops or a good supply of water. He is asked to pray for others and to bless. His curse is very dangerous and care must be taken not to irritate him.

The similarity between the Muhammadan boy at his circumcision and the Muhammadan or Hindu boy at his marriage is very close. A garland of flowers, *mora*, is given to the Muhammadan boy at his circumcision; this must eventually be thrown into running water. So also when his hands are dyed with henna mixed with water, any henna that falls to the ground must be buried or thrown in running water, and no one save a near relative is allowed to carry it. The *mora* and henna are treated after use with the same care as are the *bāśing* and the *kankaṇ*, the *sehra* and the *ghana*. Even the earthen pot of water with which the wound of circumcision is bathed, must be broken or at least chipped after use, a practice in which I surmise the same assumption as that which appears so often in Hindu ritual, that a broken thing loses its power.

THE THREAD CEREMONY

(*Munjī, Upanayan*)

The Hindu boy at his thread ceremony, the *vaṭu* or *munjā*, has special *śakti*. He is considered to be like Viṣṇu in the avatar of Vāman. The water in which his feet have been washed is *tīrth*. From the virus of a woman not ritually pure or a mother within ten days of the birth of her infant he must be protected, and like the bridegroom he sits on a *pāṭ* during the ceremony. Several boys may perform their thread ceremony or *Munjī* on the same day, but they cannot do this at the same *muhūrtta*.

After his thread ceremony the Hindu boy is in strict rule supposed to undergo a course of training for twelve years in the house of a preceptor. The *Samāvartan* (*Soḍamunja*, Mar.) ceremony, the due return of the boy to his father's house for marriage, marks the close of this period of studentship, after which the boy becomes a householder. From the thread ceremony until his marriage he is a *Brahmacārī* and has special *śakti* which renders him immune from the contagion of death or of birth. His *śakti*, too, is not adversely affected by the taking of *dāna*, 'gifts', and if he be devout his *śakti* makes him immune from the attacks of spirits.

Some families give a feast to a Brahmacārī every Saturday to propitiate Maruti; others to win *barkat* feast him throughout the year or at least during *Caturmās* on dvādaśī days. He is invariably worshipped and feasted in honour of Viṣṇu on Bhādrapad sud. 12. During the thread ceremony of a boy many Brahmacārīs are called and feasted at the *Mātṛbhojan* which is the last meal the boy can take along with his mother. Water in which the feet of these Brahmacārīs have been washed is sprinkled over the heads of the *vaṭu* and of his father.

THE ASCETIC

Marriage is regarded as a duty by all the creeds of India. 'When a servant of God marries', said the Prophet, 'verily he perfects half his religion.' According to the Laws of Manu, marriage is the twelfth *Sanskār* and as a religious duty incumbent upon all. The happiness of a Hindu in the next world depends on his having a continuous line of male descendants whose duty it is to make the periodical offerings for the soul of the dead. If a man dies unmarried he wanders about as a ghost troubling the living; he haunts the bamboo, he dwells in the pipal (Ficus religiosa). Many castes differentiate in their funeral ceremonies between the body of one who dies unmarried and that of a married man. When a man dies unmarried he is buried; when he dies married his body is burned, for this method of disposing of the body alone brings *mokṣa.* Among *Lamānis* at the beginning of a marriage ceremony or a month previous to a marriage a ceremony called *Vadāya* is performed. A priest with a hot needle makes a horizontal mark on the arm of the bridegroom and bores his ears, and this is a sign the boy will for ever afterwards bear as proof that he is married and is not to be buried. To prevent the spirit of an unmarried Brahmacāri in unsatisfied desire troubling the living, Brahmins marry one who dies unmarried to a rui tree or branch, and *Lingāyats* perform the same rite in the case of any youth or maiden who dies unmarried.

Even gods are married. The marriage of a god, as does that of a man, increases the *śakti* of the married. A marriage of a god is conducted in the same way precisely as is that of a human being. There is the same installation of the *devak*, *Nāndi*; the same throwing of *akṣat*, the same *Lājāhom.* The families of the bride and bridegroom are represented by priests. The procession of the sacred car corresponds to the ordinary marriage procession. Unless a god be *svayambhū*, his marriage *jatrā* is necessary periodically to maintain the *śakti* of his image.

There is divided opinion, however, as to whether celibate gods such as Maruti, Gaṇpati and Virbhadra can be married. The possibility of their marrying is denied by some, but on the other hand others admit the marriage of Maruti to Bharati Śakti and of Gaṇpati and Virbhadra to Śiva Śakti. Śiva, Virbhadra and Kumārasvāmī are married to Pārvatī; Maruti to Bharati; Śeṣa to Nāgakanyā; Kanyākumārī and Durgā, Banśankhari and Tuljabhavani to Śiva; Lakṣmī to Viṣṇu and Dyamavva or Durgavva to a buffalo. Brahmins worship images of Lakṣmī and Viṣṇu placed side by side on a small cot of gold, silver, copper, or brass, covered by a silk cushion. This worship is done on vad. 2 of Āṣāḍha, Śrāvaṇ, Bhādrapad and Āśvin, and after the worship is over the images are made to sleep together after the rising of the moon. Ultimately the images are given to a priest with the object that as a wife has been gifted to the god, so the worshipper may always possess a wife and not become a widower. The marriage of trees, the marriage of standing crops again engenders an increase of *śakti*.

This idea that marriage completes and leads to an increase of *śakti* is never quite lost even in the reverence paid to celibacy. Chastity is accompanied by *śakti*. When the delivery of a woman is delayed the loin-cloth of a celibate *guru* is soaked in water by *Lingāyats* and this water is wrung out of the cloth and given to the expectant mother to drink. Another practice known in Marāṭhi as *niri utaraṇe*, 'unfolding the fold of the garment', is to wave thrice over the woman the *dhotar* of any chaste person. The leavings of food left by celibates are eaten as *karuṇa prasād*, *karuṇa* meaning 'grace', and water in which their feet have been bathed is thrown over the heads of others to transfer *barkat*. When *śakti* is invoked into an image by the ceremony of *Prāṇpratiṣṭā* the *śakti* actually suffusing the image is in proportion to the piety of the worshipper. An image, therefore, installed by a celibate Sannyāsī draws more *śakti* than one installed by an ordinary worshipper, because of the special *śakti* of the Sannyāsī. In the Puranas are many gods described as having been installed by great *siddhas* and these called *purāṇaprasiddh* have abnormal *śakti*, and like *svayambhū* gods are above certain forms of pollution. A Sannyāsī again is a suitable person to give *mantropadeś* or instruction in sacred texts, because of his special *śakti*. His *śakti* is so great as to make him immune from the contagion of birth or death.

In spite, however, of his special power a celibate is at times a person to be avoided. A *sanskār* is a ceremony the object of which is to give the celebrant something which he lacks, something which will make him perfect. In such ceremonies the sannyāsī would not be welcomed. He would not be asked to a wedding; he would not attend funeral obsequies; he cannot be present at *Lakṣmīpūjā* or the worship of the goddess Lakṣmī; he would not be selected as a member of a *panc* or committee to settle a dispute. An agriculturist would not allow a sannyāsī on his threshing-floor, although an injunction of continence is common whilst grain is being measured; a man constructing a house would not allow a sannyāsī to lay the foundations, or be present when they are laid. A sannyāsī is also not allowed to pass between two women.

KASHAF-UL-KUBUR

In Sind a small number of people are credited with the power of seeing the dead within their graves, and are sought by relatives of the dead to ascertain whether the dead have obtained peace or are suffering in the grave. I have known members of the Legislative Assembly to whom such power was attributed.

SAINTS AND SINNERS

Svāmī; Muni; Sādhu; Kittadi; Yati; Satpuruṣa; Sant; Mahāpuruṣa; Mahātmā; Siddhapuruṣa; Jogī; Arudha; Arif; Pīr; Olyau; Barkatvāro; Puhtal Śakhs; Amānatvaro; Buzrug; Rajal Allah (Saint).

The miracles that saints can perform are legion, but miracles are much the same all the world over, and I propose therefore merely to indicate the general manner in which a saint's miraculous power is evinced. A saint can move from one place to another in defiance of time; he can be in different places at one and the same time; he can assume any form he pleases; can transport his devotees great distances in a twinkling of the eye and can equally bring distant places into the vision of a suppliant. A saint can make inanimate things animate; can show the sun on a night of no moon; can divert rivers; can fly and disappear into the earth; can sit on the face of the waters without sinking; and can rest in mid-air. The length of a saint's life rests with himself, for he can prolong it as he wills. There is little indeed he cannot do against the ordinary laws of Nature; he can see the past and the future and his vision is prophetic.

One form of miracle commonly attributed to saints is an unnatural curing of some disease. Every district almost has some family credited with a special power of curing some particular illness which it has acquired from some saint in the past. At Dharwar is a family called *Rege*, the members of which can cure a bite of a dog, rat or other animal merely by giving the patient water to drink; at Karkikatti is a mantrik who beats with a whip the informant who comes to tell him that another person has been bitten by a snake, and thereby cures the person bitten, though he be miles away. At Kanjgeri another mantrik, when he learns of some one having been bitten by a snake, beats his own palm on the back of the informant or on the ground, a stone, a tree or wall, and this effects a cure. At Hirehal is a schoolmaster who learnt from a saint the art of curing a snake-bite, and this by making the person who brings news of any person being bitten, drink water.

Tying stones to nim trees is one way of curing snake-bites. Near Miraj is the shrine of a *Pir* who has the same power of healing. When a man is bitten by a snake he picks up a stone, utters the name of the *Pir* and ties the stone to a tree. When the cure has been effected, some one, not necessarily the cured man, carries the stone without allowing it to touch the ground, to the shrine of the *Pir* and there ties the stone to a nim tree, and gives the custodian of the shrine the weight of the stone in sugar.

A saint transfers his power to others in many ways. By a gift of the remnants of his food; by wetting his finger with his spit and applying it to the mouth of another; by laying his hand on the head or heart of another; by blowing on water and giving another to drink. Persons who receive food distributed by a saint are called *prasādika*. By washing the hands of a saint one acquires *barkat*; those who do this in Sind are called *hath dhorya ahin*. A caretaker of a saint's shrine, the *mujāwar*, acquires *barkat* and can transmit it by inheritance. The shadow of a saint falling on another person transfers to the latter *barkat*. Kissing the hand, foot, shoulder and even the garments of a saint confers *barkat*. If a schoolboy drinks the water in which a saint has washed after eating, he will the more easily learn the Koran, for he will have acquired power. The water in which a saint has washed his hands is drunk by others and the vessel he uses for washing is used by others. When a saint visits the house of another he is expected to bring some dried fruit for his host, and if he be offered food, to leave a little for his host to eat and thereby acquire *barkat*.

The feet of a Hindu saint are washed and the water is sprinkled over the heads of his host's family. If a man is seriously ill a saint is sent for; his feet are washed and the water used is sprinkled over the patient and given to him to drink. This same water drives away spirits and for this purpose is sprinkled over a house.

When a saint dies, superfluous or additional clothes are placed on his dead body, and then distributed, conferring *barkat* on all who touch or wear them. His old shoes and his old clothes are preserved and worn by others. His sleeping-cot is preserved; his teeth and hair may be preserved.

There is the same element of danger in the power of a saint as in all power. If one refuses an invitation given by him one loses wealth; if one sits on his bed one must expect to die soon; if one sits in his palanquin one's children will die; to touch him intentionally with one's foot means death, or some disease such as leprosy. If, too, the blessing of a saint brings *barkat* his power makes his curse the more dangerous and only God can remove the ill effects of this *uśśāp*. There is danger, too, in the tomb of a saint. In strict theory Muhammadan women should not visit the tombs of saints as the saint can see their nakedness; in practice they visit tombs, but though a pregnant woman will visit a mosque a pregnant woman will not visit the tomb of a saint for fear harm should befall her child.

The tomb of a Hindu saint is his *vṛndāvan*, *samadhi*, *gadagi*; the sacred precincts of the tomb of a Muhammadan saint are the *dargāh*. Contact with the tomb of a saint effects a transfer of *barkat*. At *Miran Datar*, a shrine in Gujarāt, sick people with illnesses attributed to spirits, and lunatics are tied to trees in the vicinity; they remain tied for days and even months until cured, being fed in the meanwhile by the custodian of the shrine. Until quite recently the *Mihr Shahjo Kubo*, at Shikarpur in Sind, was used in the same way to cure lunacy, and lunatics in Sind are still often called *Mihr Shahi Charyo*. The covering of a saint's tomb, or the knockers on the doors of the *dargāh*, are sprinkled with water, and the water is drunk or applied to wounds. Grain is given to the tame pigeons kept at tombs, and the remnants of the grain are brought home and added to the household store of grain to bring increase. Money is in the same way placed on the tomb and then, with the permission of the caretaker, brought home and added to the stock of cash. Water is taken to a tomb and then brought away and used for watering fruit-trees; earth is taken and placed on a tomb and afterwards distributed. In Sind once a year a big cauldron is placed near a tomb of a saint, a mixture of grain and meat is prepared in it and carried away for distribution. Earth from a saint's tomb is strewn on fields to remove pests. Visitors to a tomb place such earth in their turbans or pockets and carry away for many purposes. Given to the sick it effects a cure; tied round an animal it produces fertility;

it is an amulet against the evil of the eye; eaten or drunk with water it confers *barkat.* It is a sovereign talisman to keep away spirits. In Sind this earth is *udī* or *khāk shafa,* 'the earth of salvation'; the Hindu calls it *mṛttikā* and even *prasād.* The keepers of the shrine keep a stock of earth near the foot of a tomb to supply to visitors.

The milk of animals giving little milk is poured over the tomb of a saint to increase the future yield of milk. Water is poured over a tomb and then becoming *tīrth* to a Hindu, is drunk by or poured over the sick. When visiting a tomb earth is taken from it, is mixed with water and drunk as part of the ritual followed to derive *barkat.*

The Hindu and the Muhammadan encircles his saintly tombs. Going round the tomb of Lal Shabaz at Sehwan a fixed number of times is considered as effective as a pilgrimage to Mecca. The tomb is ordinarily encircled clockwise. Animals that are not fertile are taken round a tomb a certain number of times for several days. In Sind the woman who desires issue makes a miniature cradle and when her hopes are fulfilled hangs the cradle up at the shrine. An extracted tooth is buried or deposited at a saint's tomb to bring strength to the other teeth. If sheep or goats fail in giving milk they are driven round a tomb three or seven times. If a horse be addicted to running away, its halter is left at a shrine and the habits of the horse are changed. Sickly children are left at a shrine for several days to achieve a cure. Cradles of children are also placed on a tomb for several days, and then used in the ordinary way to give *barkat* to the children that sleep in them.

The coverings of a saint's tomb are in Sind called *pur* or *ghilāf*; they are embroidered with words from the Koran. Suppliants tear away pieces of these coverings and preserve them. Knots are tied in these coverings as a means of coercing the saint to grant a request. Kissing the coverings transfers power from the tomb to the suppliant, and with the same object of transferring *barkat* the suppliant puts his hands on the tomb and then on his face.

Trees that grow near a saint's tomb derive power from the presence of the saint. At Kalkaleśvar is a nim tree, the leaves of which, instead of being bitter as nim leaves usually are, are sweet owing to contact with a saint. Knots are tied in the branches of these trees; green glass bangles and red rags are tied to them in order to compel the saint to listen to a prayer. 'My affairs are knotted; unless my affairs are unknotted your affairs will not be unknotted' is said by the visitor to a shrine in Sind who, thus coerces the power of the saint, or imposes on him *mair*. The *abjad* alphabet is written on paper, and then the paper is stuck on a tree and into each letter a nail is driven until the suppliant believes he has secured his object. Stones are placed on the tomb of a saint with the words, 'I will not remove these until my request is granted'. Portions of the Koran are recited at the foot of the tomb instead of in reverence at the head of the tomb, or Koranic verses are read at the tomb from the end to the beginning. Nails are driven into the doors of the *dargāh*. Paper is tied round the neck of the sick, and then thrown on a tomb with the words, 'The cure has begun; you must finish it'. Other methods of compelling the saint to hearken to a prayer are to tie a knot in one's hair as one repeats the name of the saint, or when making an offering to the saint to tie a knot in one's clothes, opening this only when the boon is obtained, *ghand badhan*. The ringing of a bell at a shrine; the beating of a drum, *dhamal*, as at the *dargāh* of Lal Shahbaz at Sehwan, and technical recitations by devotees of the saint compel the *kudrat* of the saint to come at the call of the suppliant (*zarb*, *hukāro*, *naro*). When this is done the Sindhi regards the atmosphere of the tomb as *ghoro*. Merely writing a request on a piece of paper and leaving this tied to a tomb is a form of coercion.

A saint never dies, though he leaves the human body. The Muhammadan says that when saints die they do but change their veil, *burka matain tha*. A Hindu always avoids any expression suggesting that a saint has died; he says *deh bittaru*, 'the saint has discarded his body' or *samadhist adaru*, 'has become merged in spiritual calm'. The saint lives in his tomb; his movements and his worship of God can be heard though he be invisible. Once a year or more often on certain anniversaries light is supposed to flash over a saint's tomb revealing his return to the tomb that day as light. To a suppliant the saint appears in dreams; to a Hindu he gives *mantrākṣat* and coconuts and informs him that his wishes will be fulfilled, or on the other hand tells him that his request cannot be granted and he should return home.

A Muhammadan will go to a shrine to obtain answers to his questions in a dream, and to find out whether a work, if commenced, will be successful. This practice is called *istikhāra*.[1] After morn-

[1] Apart from having recourse to a saint's tomb, *istikhāra* is performed on the night preceding Friday. One practice is to read six *re'kāt* and six *surahs* of the Koran and then write out a petition to God, fumigate this with incense and wrapping with a piece of white thread, place in an earthen pot full of water. One end of the thread is tied to the ear of the suppliant, who sleeps with his face towards Mecca, and gets an answer in his dreams. Another practice is to read two *re'kāt*,

ing prayers on a Friday he goes to a saint's tomb, recites the *sūratu yā sīn*, the thirty-sixth chapter of the Koran, and the *sūratu'l-ikhlās*, the hundred and twelfth chapter eleven times each; pays reverence to the soul of the dead saint, reads two *re'kāt*, the first chapter and the hundred and thirteenth chapters of the Koran forty-one times, and the latter chapter again forty-one times, and then covering his face with a sheet awaits an answer from the saint. An alternative practice is to call the *aḍān* first at the foot of the tomb, then at its head, and then at the right and left sides. The *āyatu'l-kursī*, the two hundred and fifty-sixth verse of the second chapter of the Koran, is then recited ten times at the foot of the tomb, ten times at its head, eleven times at the right side and ten times from the left side. Seven steps are then taken from the head of the tomb with the recital of another passage from the Koran, and a prayer for the solution of the suppliant's perplexity at each step. The visitor then covers himself with a sheet and sleeps at the tomb or goes home and sleeps.

Conditional offerings of many kinds are made to saints at their tombs; a promise of the offering is made conditional on receiving a boon. Such conditional offerings are called *niyāj* or *harakī* (Kan.). If a visitor desires issue he promises on obtaining issue to offer a sheep or goat, to hang a cradle on the tomb, to tie to it the hair of the child born when this is cut for the first time. To cure illness the model of a horse associated with strength is promised. Promises of a fixed number of rupees are made which are later placed on the tomb, or nailed to trees near by; promises of flags, or garlands, of a bridegroom's *bāśing*, of bangles are made should the saint bring about a marriage. The nature of the offering has usually some relation to the boon desired. In some cases the appropriate offering is made before the boon is obtained.

In many details the worship of saints approximates to that of gods. The gods of the Hindu pantheon have their special days on which they should be worshipped, and such timely worship adds to the *śakti* of their images. Tuesdays and Fridays are days for the worship of Durgā and other goddesses; Monday for that of Śiva; Thursday for that of Dattātreya, as is also Saturday which last is the best day for worshipping Maruti. In the same way there are days fixed for paying reverence to the shrine of a saint. The shrine of Rajabagsavar of Yamanur should be visited on

recite the *sūratu'l-fatḥ* and certain isolated words a hundred or two hundred times, when the reciter's head will rock, and if it turns to the right success in his contemplated work is assured. A third method is to read two *re'kāt*, recite *Ya-Khabir* a hundred times and then lie down covered with a sheet.

Thursday or on the fifth day of the bright fortnight of Phālgun; the tomb of Rahimansab at Naregal should be visited on an *Amāvāsyā* or on a Thursday.

Fairs, *jatrā*, are also held in honour of deceased saints. At Sirsi, in the dark half of Phālgun, a fair is held in honour of Svāmī Svadimatha; the installation of the standard *dhvajāropaṇa*, is performed on the tenth of the bright half of the month, and after its installation rice balls are thrown in the air which women desiring issue catch and eat.

A saint need not necessarily have only one tomb. There are saints with several tombs and shrines; sometimes one part of the saint's body is buried separately from the rest of the body. In the Sholapur district there is a low range of hills the crossing of which is avoided at certain times, lest the head of a deceased saint should be encountered as it travels to join the headless body of the saint buried elsewhere. The shrine or *dargāh* may not even contain the body of the saint at all. Shrines are erected where saints did penance or even rested awhile. Certain saints, too, have a very wide celebrity spreading far beyond the country in which they are buried; these, too, have local shrines. Trees such as the nim tree are planted and around them a low platform of stone and rubble, *katta*, is erected; these trees and their platforms are considered to share in the power of the saint, and daily readings of the Koran are made at the *katta*. Wherever there is a large Vaiṣṇava community there is a tomb of Raghavendra Svāmī of Mancali who is supposed to have been the second incarnation of Pralhad, son of Hiranyakaśapu. There are hundreds of graves in all, constructed with a little earth taken from the original tomb.

A tomb does not cease to possess power if it be rifled. It derives its power not from the presence of the saint's body; it has been in contact or supposed contact with the saint and from this derives its miracle-working powers.

Beside his tomb, other places associated with a saint radiate power. Near Shikarpur on the bank of a canal is a khabar tree to which the saint, Pir Saleh Shah of Ranipur, gave *kudrat* by resting under it; the tree is called Khabar Pir, and people pluck its leaves to win *barkat*. Places where Muhammadan saints have offered prayers, or performed *chillā* or retired from the world, are marked with poles to which white cloth is attached; these places are called *chillo*, there are many in the vicinity of Sehwan and people resort to them to get *barkat* in some desired form. At Rohri there is a stone which is supposed to bear the marks made by the feet of Ḥaḍrat 'Ali called *Kadam Mubārak,* and this is kissed by pilgrims. Caves are often associated with some moment in the life of a saint; near Clifton on the shore is a cave where Pir Abdullah Shah prayed and near it a spring of water with miraculous powers. The title *Sharif* applied to a place, in Sind it is not applied to a person, indicates its association with some saintly person. Rohri is called Sharif, for a hair of the Prophet is there preserved.

Besides saints there are other classes of persons who possess special power. *Tāleb* is a student who acquires power by reciting the Koran, which is equivalent to conversing with God; even a schoolboy studying the Koran acquires *barkat*. A *Shahid* is a man murdered for no fault of his own; he, too, is a person of power and one of the names of God is *Habib-ul-Shahid*, 'the friend of Shahids'. In Sind there are many tombs of Shahids around Bukkur, Rohri and Makli which are nameless.

A madman may actually be a saint; if not a saint he is possessed by spirits, *jinatjo asar*. In the world at any one time there are supposed to be forty madmen full of *barkat*, forty *Abdāl*, or as they are more commonly called in Sind, *Masta*. There was one saintly madman at Shikarpur called *Vatu* whose body was frequently found in the jungle in fragments, yet the madman invariably turned up again whole and sound. An *Abdāl* has so much *kudrat* that he can alter the destiny of a man as it is written on the tablet of destiny, *Loh-i-mahfuz*; he is supposed to have licked the ink of this roll of fate and thereby altered it. There is a story of a woman going to the Prophet and asking for a son; the Prophet regretted he could do nothing as it was her destined lot to be without a son, so she went to a madman, paid him his fee and got a son. She then returned to the Prophet who was surprised, but the angel Gabriel came down and told him not to be surprised as the madman had given her one of the twin sons of another woman.

A *Saiyid* is a descendant of the Prophet and in respect the suffix *shah* is usually added to his name. Some, but not all, *saiyids* have *barkat*-giving power.

The reading of the *Purāṇa* gives *śakti* to a Purāṇik, and at the close of a reading the feet of the Purānik are washed and the water is sprinkled over the audience of listeners. The *Lingāyat* priest again has special *śakti*. *Dhūḻpādodak* is water in which the *ayya* who visits the house of a *Lingāyat* for alms dips the big toe of his right foot; this water is used for purification after a birth or a death; it is given to a mother on the first day of her confinement and also on the fifth and thirteenth days after her delivery; it is applied to the tongue of a new-born infant, making it fit to wear a linga. Each *Lingāyat* householder must keep some in his house placed on a stand and it is used when the house is infected with insects. Even holier than this water is *gurupādodak* in which the feet of a *guru* who has taken the holy order are washed, whilst holiest of all is that in which the feet of the *Ayya* are washed after he has put his right foot on a linga, *jangampādodak*. The sanctity of these waters is so great that none of them can be placed on the ground. Similarly, on the anniversary of a death, the feet of the Brahmins who are invited to a *Śrāddha* are washed and the water is sprinkled over the heads of the household members.

If sanctity and piety, however, be accompanied by *śakti* and *kudrat*, wickedness and wrong-doing also connote power. Even God fears a bad man, *badmash se khuda bi darta*. In Sind a Persian proverb is well known : 'A rotten *brinjal* suffers from nothing.' *Durjanam prathamam vande*, 'First bow to a bad man', is another familiar adage.

Any change is supposed to result in loss of power. The conversion of a stingy man to generosity results in his illness ; the irreligious man suffers some form of ill when he becomes religious. A department of Government will find interest in the fact that many a criminal tribe associates an outbreak of plague or other calamity with its abandoning of a criminal life, and its taking to agriculture or other respectable means of livelihood. Until they gave up thieving the *Berad* community was immune from plague.

CHAPTER III

THE POWER OF WOMAN

THE mystery of woman, never greater than it is in the case of the Indian woman, finds some solution if she be regarded as a manifestation of creative *śakti*. At various stages in her life she is regarded as almost divine, as the repository of abnormal *śakti*; as a maiden attaining puberty and as a *suvāsinī* with children she fulfils the law and manifests power. As a woman without issue she is credited with baneful power, and though the position of the widow in India permits of no simple explanation, into the treatment of the widow there enters something of the same idea as underlies the treatment of the childless woman; neither the widow nor the woman without issue is complete, and where there is something missing there must be loss of *śakti*.

Even, however, when woman approaches divinity, when she illustrates the working of *śakti* in the functioning of sex, she remains none the less a potentiality for evil. To the Muhammadan, though Paradise lies beneath the heel of a mother, a woman is the friend of the devil; to a Hindu, though she be given the honorific of *dev* or 'god', she is *rākṣasī*, 'associated with spirits'. Old age may give her the *śakti* of longevity, but it also brings the greater power for evil. The power of a woman, however beneficent, is a power that may work evil. Every form of evil *śakti* is attributed to woman; her *pāygun̥* may be evil; her glance may be evil; she is associated with spirits and with the contagion of uncleanliness. *Rākṣasī*, *dr̥ṣṭi*, *pāygun̥*, *suher*, are all terms used in reference to her which stand in violent contrast to *dev*, *pativratā*, and to *ghori* in one of its attributes. Differentiation of sex may have created the mystery of woman, but sexual activity is only a form of the working of *śakti*. Woman with her power for good and for evil is but an illustration of the antagonism latent in the complex attributes of *śakti*.

PUBERTY

A Brahmin girl on attaining puberty is first taken on a visit to the houses of others, where she is feasted in the company of young girls. After the sun has set or night has fallen she is brought home in procession, bedecked and adorned, and seated in a *maṇḍap* specially constructed where she must remain for three days. In some castes the period of her stay in the *maṇḍap* is five days (*Lingāyats, Nekars, Devangs, Jains*). Within the booth she is to sit on a *pāṭ* or low stool, or on a plank, and this restriction that she must not sit on the ground is observed even by those who do not erect a *maṇḍap*, but seat the girl in some verandah or secluded room, away from the kitchen or the shrine of the family gods. A Brahmin custom in the Karnāṭak is for five old women to make her sit on a prepared seat called *nai*, exclaiming '*Nai yera nai yera*' as she mounts the seat, and pronouncing the names of the girl's father, grandfather, and if she be married those of her father-in-law and his father, and their respective *gotras*. An iron rod or piece of iron wrapped in a leaf or the sheath of a plantain is placed by her side, and thrice every morning is waved over her with the words again of *Nai yera nai yera*. On the fourth day the women ask the girl to descend from the seat, saying, '*Nai hali naili*'. *Yera* means 'ascend' and *hali* 'descend', but the precise meaning of this rite seems to have been lost. As on auspicious occasions, *ārtī* or a light is waved round the girl; she is given sweets and is garlanded with flowers.

She is forbidden to go in the sun for several days; in most Hindu castes for a period of nine days; among Muhammadans in Sind for thirteen days. Should she be compelled to leave her room or *maṇḍap* the Hindu girl must cover herself with a blanket, the Muhammadan girl with a sheet. She cannot prepare food for herself, and this is given her by others. She cannot touch fire or light a lamp; she cannot draw water; sow seed or even pass in front of those that sow; she cannot grind grain; she cannot worship or pray. She must remove from her person any *yantra* or talisman she is wearing. Muhammadans observe practically the same restrictions and do not allow her to touch anything of importance. *Māng Garudis* will not allow her to touch any of their implements.

On the third day in the evening women come and fill her lap (*oṭī bharaṇī*) with rice-pulse, wheat-flour and jaggery. On the fourth day as a rule, but in some castes on the sixth day, she is bathed and a feast is given. In the Karnāṭak on the fourth day in the evening her relatives leave the girl at home, and go to a temple where cooked rice and salt are offered as *naivedya*, and then distributed among those present, and in particular to girls whose puberty is delayed. This is called *uppakki*. If the girl be married, sesamum and jaggery are mixed by married women, *yaḻḻacigaḻi*, and then given to all married women present, but unmarried grown-up girls are forbidden to eat of this preparation lest they should attain puberty before their marriage.

If the girl attains puberty whilst wearing an old *sāḍī*, a red *sāḍī* or one of many colours, it is ominous of ill. It is also a portent of evil if she attains puberty on a Sunday, Tuesday or Saturday, or on the first, sixth, eighth or twelfth day of each fortnight of the months of Chaitra, Jyeṣṭhā, Āṣāḍha, Bhādrapad, Kārttik and Pauṣa. To attain puberty under certain stars, Krittikā, Viśakhā, Bharaṇi, Āsleṣā, Jyeṣṭhā and Ārdra, is equally calamitous. If a Brahmin girl attains puberty under an inauspicious star, or at inauspicious times, a *śānti* has to be performed and, as in all *śānti* ceremonies, *kalaśas* have to be installed. In the north-east corner of his room the *yajamān* places three heaps of rice and on these three pots round which a cloth is wound, and to each of which a thread is tied. Then to the accompaniment of mantras he fills the three pots with pure water, and puts in each *akṣat* and sandal-paste. In the middle pot he puts a variety of grain: barley, rice, sesamum, black and green gram, wheat, *rāḻā*; a large number of different leaves of the umbar, vat, bel pipal, and other trees, kuśa and durva grass, red and white lotus, vekhand, nirgudi and aghāḍā. He adds milk, curds and ghee, and six kinds of earth; earth taken from a cow-shed, from the confluence of two rivers, from the bottom of a deep well, from under the feet of elephants, from a highway and from an anthill. Finally, he puts in *pancpallav*, the leaves of five sacred trees. Then on each *kalaśa* he puts a plate of earth or bamboo, and on the middle pot installs *Bhuvaneś-vari*, on the southern pot *Indrani*, and on the third pot *Indra* through the symbol of golden images. The *yajamān* and priests, after worshipping these symbols, touch in turn the three pots, and perform a *śānti hom* to which they offer wheat, ghee, and durva grass as the Gāyatrī *mantra* is repeated. The water of the pots is then sprinkled on the *yajamān* and his wife by the priests, and some is drunk as *tīrth*. The ceremony closes with the gift to the priests of a cow, a bull and of cash.

The period of the girl's impurity during which she cannot be touched varies from caste to caste. *Marāṭhās* will not touch her for three days; *Vaddars* and *Jains* for five days; whilst *Kurubas* will not do so for twelve days. Even after this period is over, Brahmins consider her, for some purposes, impure until the consummation of her marriage has been accomplished. Until this is effected the orthodox will not eat food prepared by her, nor offer such food to a god as *naivedya*, nor invite her to feasts on special occasions.

If on attaining puberty a girl be married, the husband shares in her impurity. He cannot leave his village; cannot go on a pilgrimage; cannot make or receive gifts; cannot shave; cannot celebrate any *sanskār* such as a marriage or thread ceremony; cannot initiate or complete a vow; cannot take part in any sacrifice; he is forbidden to worship or even take *darśan* of gods in certain temples such as that of Tirupati Venkateś, to perform certain *Śrāddhas* in honour of the dead—the *Tirthśrāddha* or *Mahālaya Śrāddha*—and cannot touch or worship any image he has not already touched or worshipped. He is also not a fit person to be invited to special feasts before the consummation of the marriage is effected.

No simple emphasis, however, of the impurity of a girl on attaining puberty will co-ordinate all the rites associated with her seclusion. The Muhammadan regards her shadow as *ghoro*, as charged with power, whilst Hindu practices include many which lay stress not on her impurity but on her *śakti*. Her power is treated as beneficent. As on other auspicious occasions, *ārtī* is waved round her; in this she is given the respect that a bride and bridegroom receive. Yet even in waving *ārtī* round her the belief that she is impure intrudes. *Ārtī* is not to be waved round a single person, and so as no one will sit beside her because of her uncleanness she takes as a companion a doll, or in Kanara a coconut. Then again the *śakti* of grain has to be protected from the virus of her contact; she cannot grind corn, she cannot pass before those that are sowing grain. And yet if her husband, who shares in her impurity, measures grain on the threshing-floor, the grain will show an increase in measure beyond all anticipation. When her attainment of puberty is suspected, as a test she is asked to touch a tree which withers if she has really attained puberty, but on the other hand, though normally she cannot touch a tree, she may touch on the first day a fruit-tree, and if this should give fruit she will herself have issue. *Gollars* fix a lakki tree (Vitex negundo) in the floor and require her to sit under it for three days. *Masalars* make her touch a rui or a babul tree on the fifth day, whilst *Holayas* require her to touch with her right hand a babul (Acacia arabica) on the fourth day. From time to time, in fact, one or other idea predominates; at one moment the idea that she possesses a mysterious power, at another moment that she is unclean. An eclipse must be protected from all uncleanness, and a pregnant woman may not look at an eclipse; a girl on attaining puberty may, however, go unprotected out of doors if the sun be eclipsed.

There is thus a significant difference in the precautions taken to isolate a woman at menstruation, and those adopted to seclude a girl on her first menstruation. In the former there is a uniformity unbroken by any exception; there is a consistent effort to neutralize the dangerous influences supposed to emanate from woman at this crisis. The latter, however, are linked with rites in which there is no idea of contagion, in which, in fact, there is the underlying concept of power neither inauspicious nor maleficent. The difference is not a small one, for it permits one to explain the rules that a girl attaining puberty should not touch the ground nor see the sun, not as additional evidence of her deadly contagion, but as proof of her power.

PREGNANCY

A woman when *enceinte* has special 'power'. She is, to use the Muhammadan term, *ghori*. She has, according to the Hindu, the combined *śakti* of herself, her husband and of her child.

Her power may confer *barkat*. When sowing is going on, and again when the crops are two or three months advanced in maturity, or just before the crops are reaped, a feast is given to a pregnant woman in the hope that her power will be conveyed to the crops. On the ninth of the bright half of the month Bhādrapad, a pregnant woman in the Karnāṭak is asked to grind at home flour from the grain of the particular crop which is growing in the field; from this flour a boiled concoction is made with water and sprinkled by a man over the field. It is auspicious for a pregnant woman to sow seed or to eat the first-fruits of the harvest. In order that a new tooth may grow, a lost or extracted tooth is thrown on the roof of the house of a woman who is pregnant.

A pregnant woman was in olden times frequently a sacrificial victim. At *Hampi* is a wall still worshipped by women pilgrims in memory of the time when one Mahāpuruṣa Bhistapaya buried beneath the wall his own daughter who was *enceinte* to prevent it falling down as it had previously done several times At Ron in the Dharwar district is a well called *Ajjava*. About two hundred years ago there was a family called *Jakaraddi* of which an elder member built a well which remained dry. In a dream he was told that he would obtain water if he sacrificed his eldest daughter-in-law who was then *enceinte*. He thereupon induced the people to assist him to carry food to the bottom of the well to offer it to the water deity; they descended the well by a ladder and held a feast at the bottom of the well. On some excuse when they had re-ascended from the well, *Ajjava* was left at the bottom and the ladder was drawn up. Water flowed into the well and she was drowned. For long after this cradle songs and the sound of a rocking cradle could be heard from the interior of the well, and for many years the *Jakaraddi* family offered regularly new saris and bodices to the well. Originally it was a step-well and on one of its sides was an image of *Ajjava* which was worshipped whenever children were sick or in trouble. About a hundred years ago this image fell into the water and was lost, but another image was made and placed at the foot of the steps, and when the well was made into a draw-well, about A.D. 1890, transferred to the side of the well. The original image is said to have had round it smaller images of children; the present one has images of two children. This is an account given by an old man and woman of the village aged about ninety years. Quite recently I came across a case in which a wall belonging to a railway company fell down more than once, and a local fakir solemnly advised the burying of a pregnant woman beneath the foundations to prevent a recurrence of the accident.

The bones of a pregnant woman deceased are used by conjurers and her skull fastened on a pole is used to protect gardens.

Her *śakti* can be transferred to others. To obtain issue, barren women take her to a garden or to the bank of a river and feast her; cut off stealthily the ends of her robes, causing her a miscarriage and bringing themselves issue, or eat the ashes that are made from burning her robes.

The *śakti* of a woman in pregnancy adds force to certain acts usually dangerous and makes them still more dangerous. It is always dangerous to scratch lines on the ground with ashes, charcoal or nails; it is always hazardous to sit on charcoal and ashes, and such acts are forbidden to a woman in her pregnancy. Spinning and weaving have their dangers and are forbidden to such a woman after the sixth and third month of her pregnancy. Acts of *himsā* are particularly dangerous. From the moment her pregnancy is known she should not grind corn, cut or break wood or sweep; after her sixth month she should not wash clothes, roast grain or make bread. Her *śakti* again adds force to her oath or to her curse. During her pregnancy she cannot give away a winnowing-fan; she should not go near a tree or through standing crops; go into a dilapidated house, sit on an ant-hill or on bones and hides or step over water in which a corpse has been bathed, or she harms her child.

Her power has an element of impurity. If she looks at an eclipse, which must be protected from all uncleanness, she causes the period of the eclipse to be prolonged. Food that she cooks after six months of pregnancy is impure and cannot be offered to a god; if she sees a snake the snake becomes blind until she delivers. To meet a pregnant woman brings misfortune.

The husband of a pregnant woman is also under many restrictions of conduct. To protect the embryo he must not kill a snake, go shooting, take a sea bath, go a long journey, or after her seventh month cut his nails or hair. Her impurity attaches to him. He cannot cook *naivedya* to be offered to gods; he cannot participate in religious ceremonies and his worship is confined to that of the *śāligrām*. When she is advanced in six months of pregnancy he cannot perform *piṇḍapradān*, or the offering of *piṇḍa* to the manes, and must perform *Śrāddha* without this rite. A fortnight before her delivery he cannot partake of the feast held at another's *Śrāddha*, and after her sixth month he cannot attend a funeral.

THE WOMAN WITHOUT ISSUE

The married woman without issue has defeated the purpose of Nature. She is without *śakti* and is associated with the evil *śakti* of spirits which cause infertility. In her supposed envy of other women fortunate in having issue she is credited with the power of inflicting evil-eye.

Being without *śakti* she is naturally destructive of *barkat*. She is a force consistently operating to render fruitless man's endeavours to obtain *barkat* through the working of *śakti*. She can do things with the object of acquiring *barkat* for herself, but she can do nothing intended to bring *barkat* to others. Her breath brings death to the children of other women; even a woman in her menses will not approach her; from all auspicious ceremonies she is rigorously excluded.

The Muhammadan is as severe as the Hindu in isolating her. She cannot prepare food for her mother and father, for *naivedya* to be offered to gods, or food to be offered to the priests officiating at a *Śrāddha*. The Muhammadan, similarly, will not allow her to prepare food for a saint. Food is a sensitive medium for the transfer of qualities, and the qualities of a barren woman destroy *śakti*. A Muhammadan will not allow her to visit a woman in confinement; to attend a marriage or a ceremony of circumcision; to be present at a birth or at the first hair-cutting of a child. She cannot approach a girl who has just attained puberty until the fourth day; she cannot visit a field whilst seed is being sown, or enter a cattle-shed. To meet a barren woman early in the morning destroys the *barkat* of the day.

The husband, as usual, shares in the restrictions placed upon his wife. He too is destructive of *śakti*. It is a bad omen to meet him when one is setting out on an important task. He cannot tie the wristlets of a bridal pair, he cannot hold the screen or *antarpāṭ* between them; he cannot with his wife install the marriage *devak*; he cannot, in fine, do anything for the bridal pair. To a *Śrāddha* he is not invited nor can he officiate thereat as priest; he cannot instal a deity for permanent worship; he cannot perform *Ankurāropaṇ*, cannot be used as *guru* for *upadeś* or imparting sacred instruction, he cannot maintain *Agnihom* or a sacrificial fire, cannot be employed as a proxy for another in any form of worship or rite. He is not allowed to measure grain on the threshing-floor, plant fruit-trees or sow seed; he is disqualified from receiving certain gifts such as those of a cow, bull or of land; he cannot lay the foundations or erect the first pillar of a house. His lack of *śakti* would destroy the *barkat* of the dead for whom the *Śrāddha* is performed; would destroy that of the bridal pair. His installation of a deity would be without effect, for the invocation of *śakti* is proportionate in result to the *śakti* of the celebrant. His measuring of grain would lead to no increase; the seed he sowed would not germinate nor the trees he planted give fruit. Ceremonial celebrations undertaken by him would lead to no *barkat*, for this can be acquired only through *śakti*. A sacred thread made by him would not be worn by another person. If he be a priest he cannot throw the *mantrākṣat* or *akṣat* of blessing.

The hair of a barren woman is used to protect cattle from evil-eye; in Sind, when burnt and mixed with honey it increases the love of a married pair who eat of it.

THE MARRIED WOMAN

Muttaidi (Kan.); *Suvāsinī* (Mar.); *sohag* (Guj.); *suhāgin bhāgin* (Sin.).

There is special *śakti* or *kudrat* in a chaste married woman. To the Hindu she is *pativratā*; to a Muhammadan, *sachi bibi* or *pāk dāman*.

Her mere presence brings *barkat* to her husband's family or that of her parents. *Barkat* is obtained by appeasing or by pleasing her, and on the other hand her curse is dangerous. To avert the ghost of a deceased wife a black *sādī* is given to a married woman; at a wedding the bride to obtain issue gives a coconut to a married woman. At *Sīmāntanayan* a coconut is given to a *suvāsinī* to prolong the life of the child; when a woman loses a child she gives coconuts and fruit to the children of *suvāsinīs* to prolong the life of her future issue. Every Tuesday and Friday in Śrāvan a young unmarried girl washes the feet of five or ten *suvāsinīs* to obtain *barkat*. If a woman has no issue she invites a *suvāsinī* who has issue with her husband to a feast, *Dampatya pūjā*, in order to obtain issue. Barren women wash the feet of *suvāsinīs*, and wave lights round them to get issue. In Sind the clothes of a *suvāsinī* with issue are given to a barren woman or to a woman who repeatedly loses her children.

In ritual the married woman plays a great part. In Sind she pours water over the head of a woman in travail or gives her water to drink. When rain fails, Hindus take a married woman to a stream and ask her to scoop up water in a winnowing-fan and throw away. If a *suvāsinī* spits on a fruit-tree it bears fruit. *Suvāsinīs* worship the pile of grain before it is threshed in the Karnāṭak, and help to sow seed. At a Hindu marriage *suvāsinīs* worship the pestle and mortar; wave *ārtī* round the bridal pair; give the pair their *surgi* bath; pour milk over the hands of the bridal pair and tie their clothes together. In Sind married women with husbands and children alive, *sada suhāgin*, tie the wristlets on the bride and bridegroom, bring their heads together, *lavan*, wave salt round them and give them milk.

The fire of a *hom*, the Hindu sacrificial fire, is carried by a *suvāsinī*, and *ārtī* is usually waved by her.

The acceptance of gifts involves a loss of *śakti*, but the *suvāsinī* does not lose *śakti* by accepting gifts made to bring her *saubhāgya* or married happiness.

THE UNMARRIED WOMAN

Nyani (Sin.)

A Muhammadan woman before marriage is full of *kudrat*. If chaste she is called *sati*, 'full of truth'. She has greater power than that conferred by old age. To offend her is a sin; an oath in her name is a very solemn oath. Her prayers are sought to heal the sick; she is feasted to bring rain by her blessing; she is the best recipient of alms. To force another to grant a request, maiden girls are taken to him; this method of coercion is *mair* and the *mair* of a virgin is equal to that of seven Korans. Women who always remain maiden are said to be married to the Koran; they are invited to all ceremonies to confer *barkat*; their blessings are asked for and other girls eat the leavings of their food.

THE PROSTITUTE

A prostitute is never without a husband; ironically she is called *akhanḍ suvāsinī*, she brings unbroken married prosperity, *akhanḍ saubhāgyavatī*. It is auspicious to meet a prostitute. In Khandesh the prayers of a prostitute are supposed to bring rain; in the Karnāṭak a prostitute is taken in procession when a cessation of rain is wanted. The first *mangalsūtra* or auspicious necklace worn by the bride in many families in the Deccan and the Karnāṭak is prepared by a prostitute. When the image of the goddess of cholera is taken in a cart to the village boundary, prostitutes, but no other women, accompany the procession; on the full moon day of Māgh *Vaddars*, *Mocis* and others make offering to the goddess Yellamma and give cash to prostitutes. During the performance of *Gondhal* a prostitute is invited to dinner; before dinner is served she wraps herself in grass and dances; before leaving the house she says that jewels lie scattered behind her for others to gather.

WOMAN AND *BARKAT*

The power of woman is destructive of *barkat*. It is inimical to the power of grain. In Sind no woman is allowed to enter the *dera* which comprises several threshing-floors; in the Konkan she cannot enter a threshing-floor when paddy is being threshed; in the Deccan she cannot approach when the best stalks are being threshed for seed. No woman is allowed near, in Khandesh, when rice and nagli are threshed. It is quite a general practice to exclude women when grain is being measured. In the Karnāṭak grain not measured on the threshing-floor is put into baskets, and these are emptied into bags and carts; no woman is allowed where the men are filling the baskets from the pile of grain on the threshing-floor. In Sind after the seed has left the house a woman can have nothing to do with its sowing. In the Deccan, though a woman can put seed into the sieve, she may not touch the sieve. Amongst *Raddis* the men must sow all round the field, and women may sow only in the centre protected by the seed sown around by the men. *Haranśikārīs* allow their women to sow gram only.

Woman is excluded from many a ceremony and sacrifice. *Delhiwal Bauriahs*, a tribe with criminal propensities, when they obtain booty realize one-fifth and spend the proceeds on a feast from which all women are excluded. Out of the remaining four-fifths a small fraction of one and a quarter per cent. is reserved for their *Ladha Pir*, and for the goddess *Mātā*, and this when realized is spent on a feast at which their women-folk alone are present. *Bhils* have a fair in honour of their mountain god

Dongaria, and of their goddess *Devmogri*. Men only go to the mountains which open for those who are ritually clean, allowing them to pass to a river where they bathe and from which they take sand and pebbles, and returning home through the same opening in the mountains add these to their store of grain so that it will never fall short. No woman is allowed to share in the feasts at this fair. When, too, the *Bhil* visits the shrine of his goddess in the *Sagbāra State*, he keeps away from his wife, and will not take food prepared by her for fifteen days previously. A woman cannot be present when the *ḍavrā* sacrifice is made to secure the co-operation of spirits in assisting the gathered grain to increase; at the close, too, of many an agricultural operation a feast is held in the fields, and from this she is excluded. In the Konkan the *Kātkarī* and others make sacrifices to the deities that guard the fields, but in these no woman can share. Before the transplanting of the rice seedlings, *Kātkarīs* choose a field, usually one in which water lingers only a short time, and erect in it a hut some four and a half feet high on the east, and three feet high on the west with a sloping roof. Seven stones are placed in the hut to represent a field deity and on these coconut pieces and cooked rice are placed. The worshippers must approach the hut from the east, and no woman may enter the hut.

Women are excluded from many rites to bring rain, though they are a marked feature of many others. The *Mavchi Bhil* of Khandesh worships his god of rain, *Panabara*, *Kalya*, *Megh*, *Jugadeo*, outside the village bounds with food, slaughtered hens, goats and liquor, but no woman participates in this worship. In the Karnāṭak women are not allowed to participate in the funeral of *Jokumār*.

In the Satāra district women cannot share in the worship of *pitars* through whom the service of spirits is obtained; no woman can worship *Vetāḻ*, prince of spirits; when *Koḻīs* make an offering to *Hiroba*, even the shadow of a woman would pollute the offering. *Lamāṇīs* offer *naivedya* annually to *Venkratramana*; the food must be prepared by men only, the water used in its preparation must be carried by men, and the very shadow of a woman must be avoided. *Vaddars* will not allow their women-folk to join in the worship of their tools which they perform on *Amāvāsyā*. In the Belgaum district when there is a large holding on the border of a village a live pig is buried under a tree to propitiate a spirit, and at the time no woman or child must be present. A common non-Brahmin custom of the Karnāṭak on an epidemic of cholera is to take a miniature cart to the village boundary. A sheep also is taken, and a new winnowing-fan, in which are placed lemons, coconuts, bangles, a comb, groundnuts, *pānsupārī* and untwisted thread. At the boundary the god *Bandevva* is worshipped; the sheep is left to wander away and the other things are abandoned on the boundary. This rite, called *hada par karne*, 'to drive beyond the boundary', is performed at midnight, and any one who chances to pass in front of the procession as it goes to or returns from the boundary, dies within a year. In this rite, performed in strict silence, no woman can take part. Karnāṭak Brahmins have two ceremonies; the *Caturmās yajna* or *Pitṛyajna* performed once in a lifetime, and the *Agniśtoma* which can be celebrated annually. In the former the *Pitṛdevatā* are invoked, and in the latter *Indra*. In both cases the food eaten after the *hom* must not be prepared by a woman; the shadow of a woman would make it impure, nor can a woman serve the food.

A person performing the *abhiṣek* of an image should avoid food prepared by a woman; mantriks preparing *yantras* avoid equally such food and even the sound of a woman's bangles. In special *Mahāyajnas* for the good of a community the *yajamān* avoids food a woman has prepared. A woman may not prepare food offered to *svāmīs* and *gurus*, or the food used at a *Śrāddha* for the dead. At a *Śrāddha* the sound of a woman's bangles is avoided, whilst if a woman's shadow falls on the food used at a *Śrāddha* the dead will lose *puṇya*.

Criminal tribes almost invariably hide their implements of crime from their women-folk, and to make sure of this keep their implements in the jungle, and even bury them in the ground or in the tangled roots of trees. *Kaḻḻ Koravas*, after returning from a dacoity, will not show their booty to their women, and keep it buried until they succeed in securing its disposal. After returning, too, from a criminal expedition they cook for themselves for a week, and for the same period will not enter their houses or see the face of their women-folk. The *Konchi Korava* will not allow a woman to touch a snare or net, or to cut up any animal he catches in the chase. A *Haranśikārī* will not allow a woman to step over a plough, or be present when the plough is worshipped. *Dhangar* women may prostrate themselves before images, but disaster follows should they attempt to worship them or make them offerings.

In Kanara, jire (Cuminum cyminum) crop must not be touched by a woman, nor can she be present when this crop is sown or reaped. In the Deccan if a woman enter a field of san (Crotolaria juncea) the heat of the crop becomes so great that her menses ceases, and if she be *enceinte* she has an abortion. *Gam Vakkals* make children carry to their gods the first-fruits of the fields on a wooden *pāṭ*, and forbid women to touch them. Many medicinal herbs if touched by a woman lose their curative power. A woman must not bathe in wells used for the irrigation of a betel plantation, nor wash in water used for irrigating sweet potatoes and chillies.

Women are not allowed to read the *Veda*; they cannot cut a plantain from a tree; cannot pluck tulsī or bel leaves; cannot cut a whole pumpkin or break a coconut. They cannot worship any deity with Vedic *mantras*. In the Purana are many gods described as installed by great *Siddhas*; these are called *Purāṇ-prasiddh* and have abnormal *śakti* not reduced by the touch of a woman; besides these there are *svayambhū*, 'self-existing', deities the symbols of which can be touched by women. With these exceptions a woman cannot touch images of deities installed in temples; she can, however, worship and touch images brought temporarily for worship, though she must not touch the *Śāligrām* stone.

Sindi Muhammadans exclude a woman when attempting to obtain prophetic dreams at the shrine of a dead saint or elsewhere; when reading a charm to cure the sick; when attempting to get a spirit under control; when throwing portions of a sacrificed animal at cross-roads; when reciting charms at an eclipse. In practising magic even food prepared by a woman is avoided and there are charms which cannot be written if there be near the shadow of a woman, or her bangles be heard. Women are excluded at sowing; at measuring grain; from joining a congregational prayer at *'Īds* in a mosque, or from a party discussing an important issue. They cannot be present at the erection of a Persian wheel; when a well is dug; when the important beam of a house is fixed; when the foundations of a building are laid; when a tree is cut, or when an animal is slaughtered. A woman is never allowed to descend a well; to be present when oil is pressed or sugar extracted from the cane. She cannot witness the first equipment of a boat or efforts made to bring rain; she cannot touch tools or magical herbs nor the first-fruits which are given to a Mulla or Sayad. Until her husband has first touched them she cannot touch her husband's clothes, and she may not touch a newly purchased animal until her husband has touched it. A woman cannot join in the prayer for the dead; cannot be present at the *nikah* when the bridegroom and the bride's agent meet in the presence of two witnesses and the bridegroom accepts the bride. She cannot enter a garden of plantain or betel or bathe in water used for irrigating plantains, beans, or flowering trees such as the champha and moghra, and she would not be allowed to shear a sheep.

CHAPTER IV

THE POWER OF EVIL-EYE

Nazar, *Taka* (Sin.); *Dṛṣṭi* (Mar.); *Kākadṛṣṭi*, 'Eye of the crow' (Kan.); *Keṭṭa-Kaṇṇu*, 'Bad-eye'; *Dṛṣṭi-Doṣa*, 'Pollution by the eye' (Kan.)

EVIL-EYE is a form of evil *śakti* which is transmitted by the contact effected by sight. Sight transmits qualities; the sense of sight, moreover, is both active and passive, and it is as dangerous to be seen as it is to see.

By sight *barkat* may be conveyed. Besides evil-eye there is *Kṛpādṛṣṭi*, the glance that confers *barkat*. In a dialogue between Arjuna and Śiva in Śebarśankarvilas Arjuna says to the god: 'Lord protect me by giving me *śakti* by only a favourable look from your eyes. I do not want more.' It is good to be looked upon by a person possessing *śakti*. On the other hand, it is equally good to look on persons with *śakti*; the *darśan* of a bridegroom, of a saint, of a *puṇyavant* who has won much *puṇya* confers *barkat*; the *darśan* of a sacred image, as also that of a corpse unattended by weeping, confers blessing.

Evil *śakti* may be conveyed by sight. It is dangerous to look back at the place where one has deposited a *baḷī*, or has placed the articles used in *utāra* to avert or transfer evil. Whilst bringing medicinal herbs or charmed water to be used magically to effect a cure, it is forbidden to look backwards. When a mantrik has made an evil spirit leave a possessed person, the latter begins to run and fall down; one of his friends then pours water on the spot where he falls, but after doing this neither the man nor his friend must cast a glance behind him. When returning from a funeral mourners must not look back; when the bier-bearers leave the house of the deceased bearing the corpse they must not look back.

Congregational worship and prayer is not a feature of Hinduism, for the Hindu fears the *śakti* of his fellow-men; he fears lest their sight should destroy the *barkat* of his own worship. Other illustrations of the transfer of *śakti* by sight are provided by the restrictions which caution a pregnant woman against seeing certain things, and by the prohibitions which forbid unclean persons to gaze at the heavenly bodies.

The evil potentiality of *dṛṣṭi* is associated with the eye, as *pāyguṇ* is with the foot or *kālguṇ* with the leg, but with a precision no greater. Evil-eye may be cast by the planets; it may be inflicted by the coconut, the markings of which suggest eyes the power of which destroys the *barkat* of a journey if seen when the journey is commenced. In Kanara there are again trees called *kaṇṇinamargaḻu* with eyes that must be avoided. The evil *śakti* of *dṛṣṭi*, moreover, may be transmitted through speech; it is then called *dānt kasāḻ* or *battiśī* (Mar.) or *karibāyi* (Kan.) or *kāḻ jībh*. More accurately evil speech adds to the virulence of evil-eye because the effects of both are identical. An evil-mouthed person is supposed to speak evil through his thirty-two teeth, which explains the *Mārāṭhī* term *battiśī*. The ominous words of a person with evil mouth destroy the purpose of one who meets him on a journey. When such a person is met it is customary to exclaim 'Would some earth were put in your mouth', *bayag mannu hakali*, corresponding to *kannag mannu hakali*, 'Would some earth were put into your eyes', said when meeting a person with an evil eye. A person with an evil mouth is said to speak like a lizard. When a gardener refuses entry into his garden to guests or pilgrims, from fear of their possible evil eye, he requires them to wash not only their eyes but their mouth. Death again is called the evil eye of time; a man on the point of death is under *kāldṛṣṭi*.

Evil-eye is cast by animals as well as by human beings. The *daman*, a species of harmless snake, an owl, a crow, a cat and a dog possess the same power. After their *Vaiśvadeva* or offering made to all gods through fire, Brahmins offer a portion of their meal to crows, *kākbaḻī*, to avert their evil eye. But the association of this evil power with the eye becomes a mere figure of speech in varying degree, when it is extended to ghosts, spirits, planets and trees.

Not only is the association of *dṛṣṭi* with the eye a loose one, but it is not possible to segregate the evil *śakti* of the eye from other forms of evil power. In the Dharwar district it is very common to find evil-eye spoken of as *kāldhūḻi*, but this specifically refers to evil *pāyguṇ*, and again is used with reference to the evil *śakti* of spirits. *Renca* in the Deccan is a disease caused by the evil *pāyguṇ* of an intruder, but it is also caused by evil-eye. The washing of the feet is a common precaution both against evil-eye and against evil *pāygun̩*. The Muhammadan speaks of both evil-eye and evil-foot as *manhūs*, 'influenced by an inauspicious star'.

In the same way it is impossible to place the evil *śakti* of the eye in its own separate category, and say that it is separate from the evil potentiality of spirits. Spirits themselves inflict evil-eye. The Muhammadan of Sind speaks of *jinn bhūtji nazar*, 'the evil sight of spirits and jinn', and the Hindu mother when she waves salt round her child says, 'May the evil-eye of strangers, ghosts, spirits and also of parents and relatives be averted'. In the Konkan the victim of evil-eye is spoken of as *ceṭakyā*, *ceṭakīṇ* or as *bhūtavli*, *bhūtavlya*, 'possessed by spirits'. The same precautions, too, are taken to avert evil-eye as to scare away evil spirits; when things are thrown into fire to avert evil-eye the names of spirits and of ghosts are uttered. Horse-shoes, needles, lemons are as effective in averting the one form of evil *śakti* as in averting the other. A cock with a reversed comb averts evil-eye, but it is also an offering which appeases *Jhoting*, the ghost of a man who died of violence. Even contagion and evil-eye call for the same measures of defence. The skull of a cow or buffalo, or the horns of a cow or buffalo protect a garden against evil-eye and also against the virus of a woman in menses; a garland of jewels woven in hair from a horse's tail is a charm against evil-eye, but also against the *suher* of a woman in menses. The evil eye of a woman again is the worse on the fourth day of her menses.

It is easy to multiply examples of things that are used both to avert evil-eye and other forms of evil *śakti*. The soot of a lamp and ashes are used to avert evil-eye and scare away spirits; fear both of spirits and of evil-eye is given as an explanation of the avoidance of the sun on many occasions. A broom is used to avert evil-eye and spirits. Old shoes are hung on new buildings and in cultivated fields to avert the evil of *dṛṣṭi*, and pieces of shoes are hung round the necks of milch cattle. Shoes guard the threshing-floor from evil-eye and the waving of shoes round the victim of evil-eye is a common practice. A shoe also keeps away spirits. The shoes that protect the threshing-floor from evil-eye also protect it from spirits; a shoe placed beneath a pillow keeps spirits from causing bad dreams; water poured in a shoe is given to a man possessed by a spirit; a child whose illness is attributed to spirits is weighed against shoes, or a garland of shoes is thrown round its neck and then thrown away.

Although the word evil-eye suggests something very clearly demarcated, it is really capable of an analysis in general terms only. In some cases it may be the whole maleficent potentiality of a man concentrated in a glance, justifying its terminology, but it includes far more than this and is hardly separable from other forms of evil *śakti*.

In yet another aspect it is a vague power. In all power, even when beneficent, there is an element of evil, and beneficent power seems at times accompanied by the evil potentiality called evil-eye. A child's look confers *barkat*; its gaze is *deva dṛṣṭi*, the gaze of a god, and yet the same rivetting look of a child inflicts evil-eye. A Muhammadan saint to acquire spiritual elevation performs penance for forty days' *Chillā* in retirement. At the close of his penance his enhanced power first manifests itself in the power of his eye which inflicts evil. It is therefore imperative to place in front of him an earthen pot filled with water, before his period of penance ends, so that when his penance is complete his first glance will fall on that pot, and shatter it to pieces. Purāṇik stories relate incidents connected with the penance of Hindu ascetics which show that the Hindu has the same conception of the association of good and evil as has the Muhammadan. One *Durvasmuni*, an ascetic, performed penance for twelve years, at the end of which time his glance had acquired such destructive power that there was a danger of the whole world being destroyed. To avert this possibility Śrī Kṛṣṇa sent his wife Rukmini with a supply of rice to place in front of the saint before he completed his penance. Another story is of a prince who wished to converse with an ascetic performing penance, but was afraid to risk harm from his evil eye. The prince therefore placed in front of the ascetic before the end of his penance, a pile of fuel and himself stood behind the ascetic and woke him from his trance. When the ascetic woke his first glance fell on the fuel, which was consumed to ashes, and then the prince was able with immunity to come forward and speak to the ascetic, whose glance was now innocuous.

Even divine images may inflict evil-eye. In the Bijapur district at Chalchagudd there is an image of the goddess *Bana Śankari*, which is avoided by pregnant women for fear of being harmed by her evil eye. At Kundgol the image of a god Bharmappa is worshipped annually and the *pujārī* rubs ghee on the image; at Karajgi a special preparation of gram pulse and jaggery called *huraṇa* is rubbed on the image of the god. The god, it is believed, consumes the ghee and the *huraṇa*, and the *pujārī* has to be blindfolded during his worship, as a protection against the evil eye of the god.

There are persons who more frequently than others possess the baneful power of *dṛṣṭi*. It is usually associated with a man who possesses only one eye, for mutilation destroys beneficent *śakti*; a man with deep-set eyes or with eyebrows that unite over the bridge of the nose, a man with red lines in his eyes, *kurundyā*, inflicts evil-eye. The *Kātkarī* who seldom meets a person with blue eyes attributes the same evil potentiality to blue eyes. Women, in general, are more dangerous than men, though it is sometimes said that a woman cannot acquire this evil power until after her marriage. A *Telī*, a *Dhobī*, a *Sonār* woman, that is the oil vendor, the washerwoman and the goldsmith's wife, is dreaded by many; the epithet *bala* or calamity is applied by the Muhammadan to the *Telī* and to the *Dhobī* woman. Here we have again a fusion of ideas; the profession of these castes is one of *himsā*, to use the Hindu term, and *himsā* destroys *barkat*.

Misers proverbially inflict evil-eye. When I was a district officer in Khandesh there were in the district several notorious misers whose glance brought evil to others. One who met them had to go without food the whole day, and there was a saying that if a man could not find time to take a meal, he must have seen one of these misers. At Nasik there was another miser of equal notoriety. To the Muhammadan misers possess *nahosat* and this is destructive of *barkat*. Gluttons, again, are another class which possess the evil power of *dṛṣṭi*. Envy and unfulfilled desire engender evil-eye in the barren woman, and sometimes in the pregnant woman, and in childless old couples. The hungry man again inflicts evil-eye. In Sind there is a saying that evil-eye comes from the richest and from the very poor. *Taka lagandi ahe sukeji ya saiji*.

Though, however, certain individuals possess this evil potentiality and never lose it, radiating evil against their own volition, or independent of volition, any person may at times possess the same power. Love and admiration, for instance, are strong factors engendering *dṛṣṭi*. In the ordinary Hindu marriage ceremony up to a certain point in the ritual, the bride and bridegroom are shielded from each other by a curtain or *antarpaṭ*, lest in their love they should injure each other. When a *Lingāyat* father is allowed for the first time to see his first-born son, he is required to put on the child an ornament of gold to protect it against the evil-eye fostered by parental pride. In Sind when a *rayat* measures his grain on the threshing-floor he must measure with bent head, and on no account gaze at the pile of grain before him, lest in satisfaction at its size he destroys its *barkat*. The Sindi and the Gujarāti have a special name for the evil-eye occasioned by love or admiration and call it *mithi nazar*, 'sweet sight'. A man may even inflict evil-eye on himself. There is in Sind *pahanji nazar*, 'one's own evil-eye', and this one may obtain by too frequently gazing at oneself in a mirror.

Traditionally the Prophet said: 'Evil-eye carries a man to the grave and a camel to the kettle-pot.' To evil-eye a multitude of evils are attributed. *Pacva* is the return of a disease caused by going out too early and exposing oneself to evil-eye; *Renca* is a nausea caused by an evil-eyed person intruding during a meal. An evil glance makes cattle give blood instead of milk; shatters beams and blocks of stones; makes fruit-trees wither; poisons food; breaks a plough, causes illness and even death. The glance of the evil-eyed met on a journey foils the purpose of the journey.

The power of the evil eye is powerless to harm in the absence of fear. Among the *Kātkarīs* contempt for evil-eye is so common that one may find many *Kātkarīs* who do not even know the word *Dṛṣṭi*, and have the vaguest idea of what evil-eye means. It is possible, too, because fear on the part of the victim of evil-eye is necessary if the evil *śakti* of the eye is to be transmitted, that laughter is considered to destroy the potentiality of the evil eye.

Though, however, fearlessness and laughter may defeat the activity of evil-eye, and though many forms of beneficent power are protection against the evil eye, power itself, however beneficent, however intense, must be protected from the evil eye. The power of trees, water, metals, numbers, colours, bread and grain may be a protection against evil-eye; even the power of days affords protection and one may frustrate the activity of a man with an evil eye by saying 'Born on Saturday' or 'Born on *Amāvāsyā*'. The greatest power remains, nevertheless, susceptible to the evil influence of the eye. A child, though a god or almost so; a bride and a bridegroom regarded as the essence of deities, the *anśa* of Lakṣmī and Nārāyaṇa; the girl on attaining puberty; the mother on her delivery, must be protected from evil-eye. Trees, again, must be protected, and last of all images and symbols into which divine *śakti* has been invoked. When *naivedya* is offered to a god the worshipper must cover his eyes with his right hand to protect the image from the possibility of an evil glance; the *devak* is protected by an axe, bread and leaves, and the protection afforded to the *hālgamba* is very similar in detail.

When a man is ailing and suspects that he is a victim of evil-eye, it is possible to find out the source of its evil effects. Alum is waved round the sick man and thrown in fire; in the fire it is supposed to assume the shape of the person or animal that inflicted evil-eye. With this knowledge of the source it is then possible to mitigate the effects of evil-eye, but strictly speaking, there is no cure whereby a person who radiates evil-eye can be rendered permanently harmless. Measures taken, when based on a knowledge of the identity of the person with an evil eye, are measures to cure the effects of the evil glance, and not to destroy the cause. A piece of the skirt of the *sāḍī* or *ḍhotar* of the evil-eyed person is stolen, and burnt. Earth from beneath his feet is shown to children and then burnt in his name, with the words 'Fie upon his eye'; parings of his nails or clippings of his hair are secured and burnt and their smoke is inhaled with the words, 'May he die'. Another measure of protection is to wear something with the approval taken of the person with the evil glance. If the person inflicting evil-eye is one with united eyebrows, the Muhammadan takes hairs from his eyebrows or beard and burns them. The nail of a horse-shoe is burnt in fire in the name of the evil-eyed, and in Sind, as a temporary cure, if occasion permits, the heels of the person with an evil eye are branded or his eyes are washed. Some of these measures emphasize the similarity of *dṛṣṭi* and *pāygun*, for the Muhammadan takes earth from beneath the feet of a man with evil foot and throws it into fire, and in the Karnāṭak if a man with unwashed feet intrudes on persons eating, his feet are washed and a red-hot trowel is first shown to the sun and then applied lightly to their soles.

All these measures, however, only mitigate the effects of an evil glance. A person with an evil eye continues to radiate evil, and this particularly in the early morning. His evil power, however, is fortunately something like the power of a snake to poison. It can for the moment spend itself; the first glance of the evil-eyed bears the full strength of his evil *śakti*, and after this for some time any glance that follows is harmless. An evil-eyed person entering a festive gathering can but injure one victim.

To catch the first glance of the evil-eyed in some such way as to divert the harm it causes, is therefore the object of many precautionary measures. If a man credited with an evil eye suddenly enters one's presence one should divert his glance at once by saying, 'See what has stuck to the sole of your foot'. It is advisable also to say, 'Would some oil were put in your eye' or 'Would some earth were put in your eyes'. In a marriage *maṇḍap* knives are left about haphazard to catch the first glance of any dangerous visitor; the bride with her saffron and the bridegroom with his *gandha* or sandal-paste make lines and markings on their faces of unusual design to attract attention. Disfigurement always attracts attention and so the cheeks, forehead and nose of a handsome child are disfigured by its parents with earth taken from beneath their own feet. During *Nāgpancmī Lingāyat* women make a clay model of a temple, adding a story each week until it has five stories; this temple is called *Guḻkavvā* or *Guḻḻavvā*, the temple of the god *Basavana*. By the side cf this temple to divert the evil glance of any beholder a rough image of monstrous design called *Goggavā* is placed. In the *Gokak* taluka of the Belgaum district there is a large single stone, carved into three pillars, and a chain which the glance of some evil eye caused to crack some fifty years ago. To protect this from future harm of the same kind an image of a man with huge head and thighs has been placed in front of the *maṭh*. Images so placed as a protection against evil-eye are called *dṛṣṭimūrtti*, 'evil-eye images'. In front of some temples are found stones bearing the imprint of a man's foot; *pādagatti*, 'foot of the god'; these are to draw to themselves and away from the temple or its image, the glance of visitors. On the Indian stage there is a buffoon or jester whose duty it is to protect by his sallies the actor of a part which, attracting the admiration of the audience, will expose the actor to evil-eye. This jester is supposed to come on the stage, before the principal actor enters, and as the actor leaves the stage, his part performed, to provoke laughter which is a sound defence against evil-eye.

Avoiding exposure is naturally the surest defence against evil-eye. When *naivedya* is offered to an image the door of the inner shrine is kept closed. When processions are held and images are carried in pomp, the principal image is left in the temple, and a duplicate *utsava mūrtti*, 'processional image', is carried in the procession. In the Karnāṭak, when the Muhammadan bridegroom during the marriage ceremony goes to a mosque, he wears a garland of flowers over his face, and his face remains covered till his return home. Food when carried out of doors is covered. Doors are shut when meals are prepared. When milk is carried, the putting into it of a piece of charcoal or a blade of green grass, is considered as effective as a complete covering. A father is not allowed to see his new-born child for many days, varying in different castes from five to twelve. The bridegroom draws his *bāśing* or crown down over his face; when the Brahmin bridegroom goes to the house of his bride he is enveloped in a woman's *śelā*; the boy to be circumcised is covered with a cloak. A curtain (*antarpaṭ*) between the bride and bridegroom shields the one from the evil eye of the other. Before tying the *kankaṇ* of the bridal pair *Raddis* cover their faces with a blanket, which is not removed till the wedding is over. When a mare foals, a Muhammadan keeps the mare and the foal in the stable for seven days; a Hindu will not expose the udders of a cow at calving for seven days, and for ten or fifteen days will not take out of doors the first butter made for fear of evil-eye affecting the cow. A barren woman, because of her supposed evil potentiality, is excluded from a naming ceremony, from the ceremony (*oṭī bharaṇī*) in which the lap of a pregnant woman is filled with fruit, and from other auspicious ceremonies. To avoid evil-eye the object of a journey is concealed and an object that excites admiration is given away. The various restrictions which, described elsewhere, are placed on certain persons, forbidding their exposure to the sun, protect these persons also from the evil eye.

There are various ways of testing whether a person has been stricken with evil-eye. Seven chillies, seven small stones picked up from a road; one to seven marking nuts and the hair-combings of a woman are waved three times round the suspected victim, and thrown into fire. If the chillies make a crackling sound this is proof of the presence of evil. Chillies with salt are also thrown into fire, and the crackling of the salt betrays the existence of evil-eye. If it is suspected that a child has been victimized, five chillies, salt, fruit, earth from cross-roads, and small sticks taken from the eaves of a house, are waved over the child and thrown in the fire, in the names of those who saw the child ailing. If the articles thrown thus into the fire give off a bad smell, the Muhammadan thinks that there is evil-eye. In Sind a stone is taken and round it thread is wrapped; verses of the Koran are recited over it and it is thrown into fire by some one other than the suspected victim. If there be evil-eye present the thread will not burn so long as it is attached to the stone, but burns when separated from the stone, cut in three pieces and burnt apart. A Hindu practice very similar to this Muhammadan custom is to wave a circular pounding stone, to which black cotton threads have been tied, round the sick person's head and throw into fire. If the sick man be really suffering from the effects of evil-eye the threads will not burn.

Three pieces of salt may also be waved round the sick person and thrown into a pot of water. If there be evil-eye the salt will not dissolve. Another test is to fill a saucer with water and add earth taken from cross-roads. A pot is taken and in it are placed the fibres of a broom, chillies and salt; this pot is then waved round the sick man and inverted in the saucer. If there be evil-eye the pot will stick to the saucer for an hour. Leaves of nāgdavana (Centipeda orbicularis) and isbanda (Peganum Harmala) are smeared with ghee or oil and black powder, waved round the affected person and thrown in fire; if eruptions appear on the leaves the person has been victimized by an evil eye.

There is a symbolic burning of the evil eye. If there is suspicion that a person has been injured by an evil glance, alum is burned, and the smoke is inhaled by the patient; burnt powdered alum is also smeared in lines across the patient's temples and applied to his legs. As the alum is burnt the *Marāṭhā* says '*Iḍā pīḍā jaḻo*', 'Burn the evil'. When alum is heated bubbles are formed and one current belief is that the evil *śakti* goes into the bubbles; another belief is that the alum assumes the shape of the person casting evil-eye. Besides alum, olibanum is burnt and inhaled; chillies, old brooms, leaves which have been used as dinner plates are burnt. An image of the patient is made of cotton or flour, waved thrice round him and then burnt; cloth taken from the patient's house is dipped in oil and burnt for three successive days in the morning and evening. Fibres of a broom, chillies and wet earth are waved thrice round the sick man; then the ground is spat upon thrice and the articles waved are thrown into fire. When a child is ailing a lump of cowdung is placed on its stomach in the shape of a dish; then another vessel with a lighted wick is waved over the child and inverted in the first. The effects of *dṛṣṭi* vanish if the dish of cowdung breaks. Another remedy is to take cowdung and water in a dish and invert this in another dish containing cinders, on which chillies, salt, broom fibres, nim leaves and mustard have been thrown after being waved round the patient. When the one vessel is inverted in the other, bubbles are formed, through which the effects of the evil-eye are supposed to escape away. In Sind fire is placed on the shadow of a victim and seven grains of pepper are thrown in the fire. Sometimes harmel is burned with alum and the smoke is inhaled; a pair of new slippers in Sind is protected by this smoke. Gum ammoniac is also burned and inhaled.

Fire itself destroys the evil of *dṛṣṭi*. At a birth or at a thread ceremony a knotted thread is tied to the child or the boy by Brahmins, and the *śakti* of *Agni* is invoked by the throwing of *akṣat*, before the knot is tied in the thread; this invoked *śakti* averts evil-eye. Lamps of many kinds are also a feature in measures taken to avert evil-eye.

There is also a symbolic blinding of the evil eye. Lemons by their shape suggest an eye and are accordingly used to blind the evil eye. In Sind four lemons are placed on the shadow of a victim, and then struck with one blow so as to cut the lemons in halves, which are then thrown in four directions, care being taken that the two halves of one lemon are not thrown in the same direction. Sometimes in lieu of doing this the ailing man is asked

'Shall I cut your evil eye?' and when he replies 'Yes', his shadow is cut seven times. In the marriage ceremonies of many communities lemons are stuck on swords as a protection against the evil eye. The *panjā* of the Muhammadan carried during Muḥarram in the Karnāṭak are protected from the evil of the eye by a lemon stuck on their longest finger. Lemons are taken as representing the eye of the person inflicting *dṛṣṭi*, pierced with needles or thorns, waved thrice over the victim and thrown away; if it be known who is the causative source the lemons are thrown over him, or on to the roof of his house. Iron nails; marking nuts pierced with needles and thorny branches are used to protect fodder, or the grain on the threshing-floor; nails are driven at the base of the central pole on the threshing-floor, and marking nuts pierced with needles are placed beneath the pole. Both in Sind and in the Karnāṭak lemons pierced with needles are kept or buried in a house as a

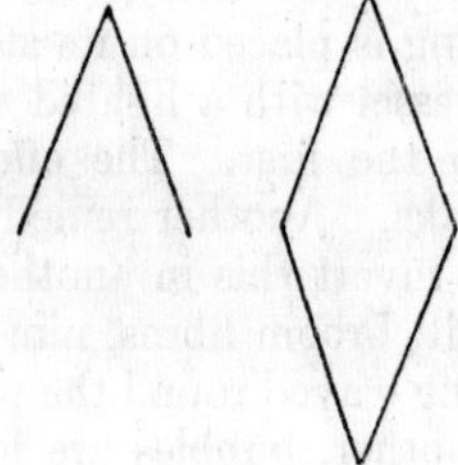

FIG. 1.—*Kevaḍa.*

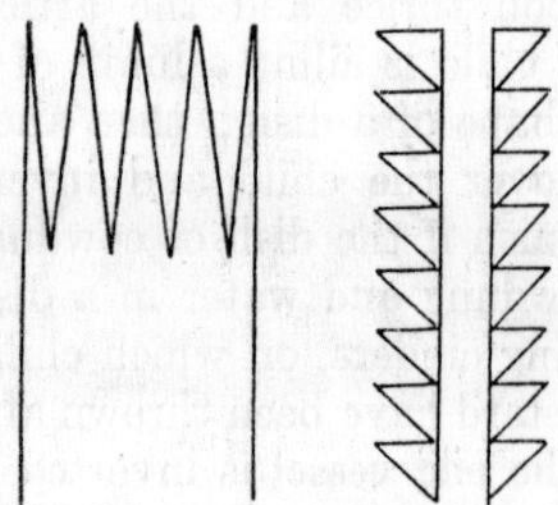

FIG. 2.—Backbone of a fish.

protection. In Sind earth is thrown at a person suspected of possessing an evil eye in order to blind him. In Kanara a pregnant woman finds protection by wearing the sharp quill of a porcupine in her hair whenever she goes out of doors.

The designs of embroidery are full of illustration of measures taken to avert the evil of *dṛṣṭi*. In these the same idea of blinding the evil eye appears. The kevaḍa plant has prickly spikes (Pandanus fascicularis); a single spike is worn as a protection against evil-eye by women in their hair. This same plant is found represented on the saris of women where groups of five spikes are reproduced. A single spike is also represented by a simple triangle, and two triangles joined together produce a parallelogram, the origin of which is betrayed by the retention of the name *kevaḍa*, which is applied to these designs. Besides the spikes of the kevaḍa, the spikey points of the backbone of a fish are also drawn in needlework as charms against the evil of the eye (Figs. 1–2).

The evil *śakti* which is transmitted by an evil eye may like other forms of evil power be transferred. Mantriks when uttering charms over a victim of evil-eye, frequently themselves suffer from water-brash which transfers the effects of *dṛṣṭi* from the original victim to the mantrik. A mantrik, therefore, frees himself from *dṛṣṭi* by spitting. By burying lemons, chillies, pieces of brooms, and baked rice, which have been waved round a victim of evil-eye, the evil *śakti* may be transferred to the earth.

Because a child possesses special *śakti*, drawings of children are made on doors to preserve a house from evil-eye; earth from beneath the foot of a person casting evil-eye is first shown to children before it is burnt. Though, however, a child's inordinate power may be a protection against evil-eye, with an inconsistency not uncommon in Indian ritual, the power of the child requires special protection against the evil power of the eye.

In the belt of a child a few hairs from a bear are tied, and when travelling performers await a train it is no uncommon sight to see other passengers on the station platform covertly pluck out hairs from the bears accompanying the performers. A nail from the left shoe of a man picked up from a road is also attached to the belt of a child. The child is also given an armlet made from the dried intestines of a sheep; one of wool or of five metals is tied with black thread to the child's arm on a Sunday or a Thursday. Blue glass beads are another potent talisman; ornaments made from the hair of an elephant, *hastekansa,* or the claw of a tiger; the last is frequently tattooed on the face and arms. The anklets of the child are no less varied; anklets of gold or iron; of black and white wool; of red, green and yellow silk tied with five knots; rings of copper to which garlic or turmeric is tied. The child's necklace, *dṛṣṭimaṇī*, may be of black glass beads with white spots, a combination of colours that gives power to many a talisman; may include a pendant of iron, gold or ivory, a pentacle of silver, coins of silver, the teeth of a tiger, amber, cornelian and mother-of-pearl. A thread made from the wool of a black sheep is placed crosswise round the child's neck; pieces of broken earthenware found in a cemetery or at a burning ghat on a Sunday or Thursday are perforated and strung on the child's necklace; seeds of ajvān (Carum copticum) are tied in a piece of cloth to the child's neck or a worm, *huli,* dug out of the ground. White, black and red threads or strings of five colours in themselves are potent charms. More than this, the child's body is smeared with the ash of cowdung cakes; betel-leaves burnt in oil with ashes are applied to its fore-head, and periodically at sunset salt, chillies and mustard are waved round the child and thrown in fire. Mantras are written in a reverse direction, and enclosed in a covering of crescent design or half-moon design are tied to the child's hand. These are all precautionary measures; other measures are called for when the child appears to be suffering from the effects of *dṛṣṭi*.

Three images of human shape are made from cotton and shown to the child after spitting on them; they are then attached to a wall and burnt from the bottom upwards. Bread smeared with sweet-oil is shown to the child and then placed on a public road. A marking nut pierced with a needle is held in the left hand, moved upwards and downwards thrice before the child and then burnt in the flame of a lamp. The mother of the child takes her *sāḍī* in her left hand, waves it round the child's face and then shakes it well outside the house, or with the same hand takes the left end of that part of her *sāḍī* which covers the head, waves this thrice below the face of the child and spits on it three times.

A handful of ashes from the hearth and again two handfuls of ashes are shown to the child and thrown at cross-roads; the person doing this must not speak until he has returned and washed his feet. Three twigs of the nim tree (Melia azadirachta), three chillies and earth from below the hinges of a door are shown to the child and burnt. This is done by women who, whilst they do this, must snap their fingers and utter the name of the person with the evil eye, saying 'Fie upon his eye' and at the same time show their left leg to the fire. Red and black water, boiled rice, and two or three pieces of lemon are waved thrice down the child's face; the four fingers of the left hand and the four smaller toes of the left foot are dipped in the water and then the whole concoction is thrown at sunset on to meeting roads. The mother may also take three wicks of black thread steeped in sweet-oil, and lighting each wick in turn visit all the corners of the room; others present ask her what she is doing and she replies, 'Driving away the crying of the child', and throws down each wick in turn. Other measures are to make three holes in an earthen pot, apply oil to the surface of the pot and burn it, apply the soot formed to the forehead, cheek and chin of the child, and then throw the perforated pot at sunset on a road. A lemon may be cut in two and with a piece of bread blackened with the soot from a *tavā* or plate for baking bread, waved thrice round the child and at lamp-time thrown on cross-roads. A shoe of the left foot is waved vertically over the child and then dashed to the ground. Ashes of burnt cotton are applied to the child's cheeks; turmeric and lime mixed in water are poured on rice and this is waved three times over the child. A protection, not necessarily confined to children, is a garland made from the bones of bats which have been killed and buried in a dung-hill.

Charmed ashes of cowdung are placed in one hand and picked up in pinches by the fingers of the other hand. A lemon is cut in three pieces and each piece is daubed with soot and turmeric, the pieces are waved the length of the child's body and then placed where three roads meet, one piece on each road. A custom of *Mahār* women is to bring two flat bones of some animal, and on them place fire, chillies, mustard and earth from cross-roads, and after waving these things over the child throw them where roads meet. In the Karnāṭak a doll is taken; seven kinds of thorns are stuck in it, red dust is thrown on it and after being waved over the child the doll is thrown into a well. A doll may also be made from rags collected from a rubbish-heap; the eye and nose of the doll are marked with black oil; various names are written on paper and tied to the doll, which is then waved over the child, placed in a pit, nailed down and covered with earth. *Kātkarīs* take cooked rice on a leaf with burning wood; as antimony is used for the eyes, they add antimony, wave the whole round the child and throw at cross-roads.

Whilst eating in the presence of others who are not eating, protection against evil-eye is necessary. Two onions are placed before the dishes. Muhammadans are enjoined to serve their servants with the same quality of food as they take themselves to avoid the evil-eye engendered by envy. If food should be spoilt by the glance of an evil eye, the same kind of food is given to the person with the evil eye. When the *Lamānī* bridal pair, on the second day of their marriage, are served with food they are covered with a quilt that no one may see them eat. *Renca* is a nausea or abdominal distention caused by the evil eye of some person who intrudes during the meal of others, and it emphasizes the correlation of evil-eye with other forms of evil power that the same disease is occasioned by the intrusion of some one with unwashed feet or with a watery mouth. When a meal has been finished something is left in the dish; to this the fibres of a broom, grass from the roof of a house, earth from below the hinges of a door, dust from three meeting roads, water, chillies and salt are added and placed in a pot with a lighted wick. This pot is waved thrice round the eater, thrice towards the sun, and thrice round the dish, and is then inverted. This practice is called *rancu*.

Fear of the evil-eye, the evil wishes of the guest, makes it incumbent on the host to give his guest food before he eats anything himself. Even animals are supposed to look on at the meals of men with hungry jealousy and to inflict evil-eye. When one eats, one should throw bits to passing dogs to avert their evil-eye, and the *kākbaḻī* or portion of his meal offered daily by the Brahmin to crows averts their evil-eye.

Animals are protected from evil-eye in many ways. To protect milch cattle worn-out brooms and coconut husks, the horns of a ram, the tusks of a wild boar, small conches, ropes and threads picked up from a cemetery, the horns of a he-goat, the flesh of a tiger, are tied to their neck. *Kātkarīs* tie a piece of old leather to the neck of their animals. Kiru seed is tied to cattle and a rope made from the bark of asina (Briedelia retusa). Animals taken in procession at *Dasarā* are always fumigated before leaving their stalls. Horses are protected by a *bajarbattī* of multicoloured glass beads. Charmed salt is put in the food and fodder of animals and marking nuts pierced with needles are hidden in their fodder. Persons buying cattle in the bazaar tie at once to their legs cowries and black thread; a Muhammadan when buying a horse, cow or mule in the market gives sweets away to spectators to avert all forms of evil, and when his mare foals distributes sweets to every family in the village to avert evil-eye. Bivalve shells are tied to the necks of prized animals; ropes made of jute and cotton with a peacock's feather or a doll of red sandalwood; white, black and red threads; the wool of a black sheep; the hair of a woman, especially that of a woman without issue; dolls made of biti (Dalbergia latifolia) or of sandalwood.

Many things are burnt and with their smoke the animals are fumigated. Madarangi seeds and leaves which have been thrown away after a meal; leaves of the nim tree and of wild onions; the hair of a woman with the wood of tamarind; loban or the resin of Styrax bengoin; mhendi (Lawsonia alba) and biti. On a Saturday or a Sunday wood taken from the roof of three houses is burnt with five or seven chillies after sunset, waved round the animals and thrown on cross-roads. The milk of a cow of one day, the curds of a second day, and the ghee of a third day are offered with a lamp of ghee to the village god, and ashes consecrated in the name of the god are applied to the forehead of the animal, *dipat*. Another precautionary measure is to take a stone which has been found stuck in the branches of a tree, or picked up from a hill which does not adjoin another hill, and bring it home with the left hand and in a state of nakedness; then a bucket of water is placed beneath the udders of a cow and the stone first heated is dropped in the water, causing steam which fumigates the cow.

Buildings are protected from evil-eye by obscene drawings and figures; figures of children are drawn on their doors. Lolasar (Aloe vera) is uprooted and with the roots tied to the entrance of a house. Coins are nailed to thresholds. Lemons and needles are buried in a house. Perforated tiles are kept at the four corners of a house outside. Coconuts tied in a cloth are hung from beams, or marking nuts with baji (Acorus calamus) or pieces of bagni (Caryota urens) or merely old rags.

Fruit-trees and standing crops are protected by garlands of marking nuts and turmeric; the skull of a cow is stuck on a post to protect plantains; *Kātkarīs* hang sandals in their houses and in vegetable gardens; black old cloth or a black and ragged blanket also protect gardens. Isbandari (Plantago ovata) is tied to trees and concealed. *Bedars* tie the hair of women and many castes tie the tusk of a boar, the skull of a monkey, a human skull, old brooms and bones. Creepers are protected by ashes taken from a potter, and the horn of a sheep is burnt amid growing crops.

The bride and bridegroom are protected from evil-eye in many ways besides those I have already alluded to. As a protection against the sun they wear blankets, and that this may be also a protection against evil-eye the blanket must be black. Ashes of burnt betel-leaf are applied to their foreheads. At the beginning and at the end of the marriage ceremony *Haraṇśikārīs* apply water to the eyes of the bridal pair with two betel-leaves. As the marriage procession proceeds, at any cross-roads passed a coconut is dashed against a building or wall; similarly, when the bridal pair go to the house of the bridegroom a coconut is broken in front of them and red and black water with boiled rice on which an oily wick has been placed, is thrown on their path. As a protection to a pregnant woman an egg and red and black water are waved over her and thrown on a road.

The hand and its fingers, and any representation of a hand averts evil, including the evil of *dṛṣṭi*. On an epidemic of cholera *Kātkarīs* make an impression of a hand with soot on a leaf of plantain, and a second impression with red powder; they place on the leaf so marked a ball of rice, wave it from head to foot of any sick person and then, in silence, throw it into a river or into the sea, or abandon it at the boundary of the village that adjoins their own.

An impression of a hand is made on the walls of the mother's room when an infant is born. When a Hindu girl attains puberty a similar impression is made by her on the wall behind her where she sits in her bower. On entering a new house for the first time four rows of such impressions are made ; one row contains five hands, one three, one two, and the fourth row a single hand. *Lingāyats* make an impression of the hand on the pile of grain gathered on the threshing-floor, whilst not infrequently the same mark is made on the floor itself. During *Divāḷī* Hindus make the mark of a hand on the back of their cattle. After a marriage feast women with their soiled hands make the impression of a hand on the walls. On *Baindur Divas*, in the month of Āṣāḍha, when the implements of agriculture are worshipped along with bullocks in the Deccan, the imprint of a hand is made with red powder on the bullocks, lemons are hung round their horns and around their left legs biba nuts and cowries are tied with black thread, as amulets against the evil-eye. In Sind small models of a hand, *panjā*, are worn as charms. The stretching out of the hand in the face of one possessing the evil power of *dṛṣṭi* is called *bujo* or *bhundo.*[1] To the Muhammadan a drawing of a hand has great protective power because this same figure is produced by writing *Ya Allah.*

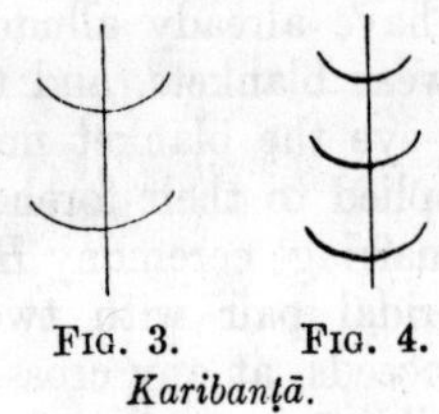

FIG. 3. FIG. 4.
Karibanṭā.

The hand, when used on the threshing-floor, brings *barkat* in the increase of the grain. It is particularly, however, a protection against the evil-eye. The Sindi custom of stretching out the hand in the face of the evil-eyed is also found in the Karnāṭak, where women do this, saying, 'Let fingers be thrust in your eye', '*Ninna kaṇṇaga baṭṭu tivīli*', and in the Deccan where the *Mārāṭha* says, '*Tujhyā ḍolyānt phoḍ pado*', 'May there be a sore in thy eye'.

Crude representations of a hand are drawn to avert evil-eye. In the Malnad parts of the Karnāṭak *karibanṭā* are drawn on the bamboo enclosure in which paddy grain is stored, or with black-coloured grain on the heap of grain on the threshing-floor. On

[1] Cp. *Ritual and Belief in Morocco*, E. Westermarck, 1926, vol. i, p. 471 : 'The gesture with the five outstretched fingers is used against the evil eye in Algeria, Tunis, Syria, and Palestine, among the Sennaarese and the Kababish in the Anglo-Egyptian Sudan, and in modern Greece ; and in the four first-mentioned countries it is accompanied with the phrase "Five in your eye", or "Five on your eye", or "Five on you", or "Five in the face of the enemies". The ancient Romans seem to have used a similar gesture, accompanied with the words, "Ecce tibi dono quinque".'

either side of the door of the room in which a child has been born, on the fifth day after birth Brahmins and non-Brahmins draw the following figures which are called in Kanarese *jīvati gombi*. At the junction of the arms of these figures a little cowdung is applied and a small wick is placed in the dung and lighted. These figures are worshipped, but *suvāsinīs* and women who are *enceinte* must not see these figures, and they are obliterated before visitors come next morning.

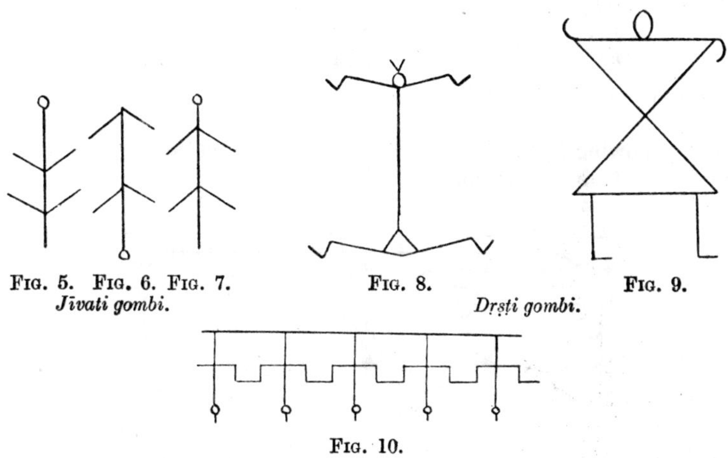

Fig. 5. Fig. 6. Fig. 7. *Jīvati gombi.*

Fig. 8. Fig. 9. *Dṛṣṭi gombi.*

Fig. 10.

Figures with extended arms (Figs. 8–10), dimly suggesting human figures, are found on the pots of potters, and tattoo-marks provide many representations of hands (Figs. 11–17).

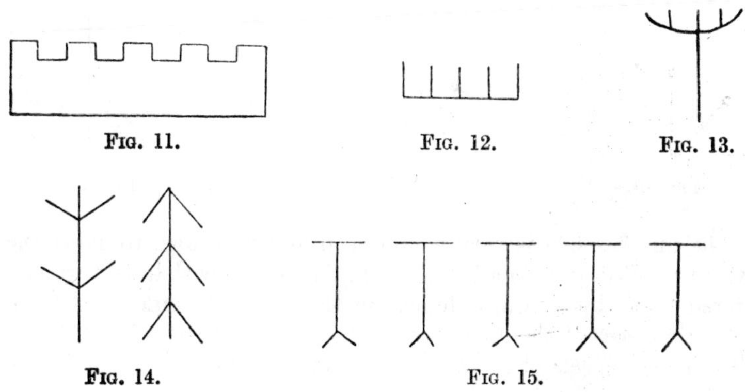

Fig. 11. Fig. 12. Fig. 13.

Fig. 14. Fig. 15.

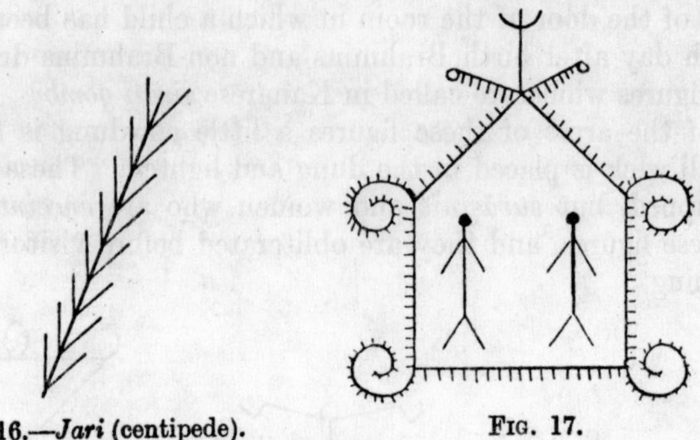

FIG. 16.—*Jari* (centipede). FIG. 17.

The following figure is *ugurina patti*, a representation of finger-nails taken from a piece of embroidery.

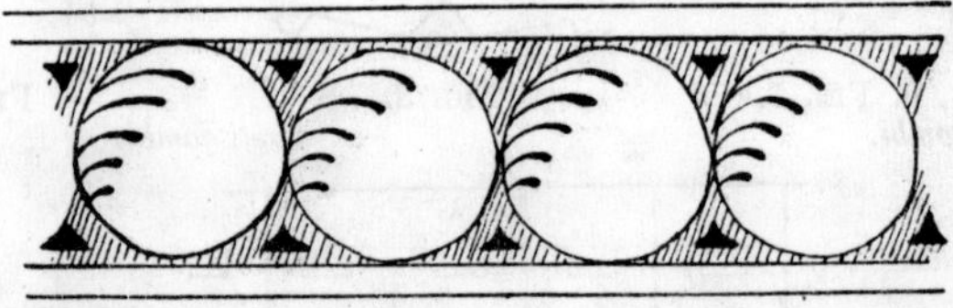

FIG. 18.

On *Karhuṇṇivi*, the full-moon day of Jyeṣṭha sud. 15, to avert evil-eye impressions of hands are made all over the bodies of cattle with wet chalk and red earth, before they go out to graze. Sick cattle are branded with brands called *dṛṣṭibari*, 'evil-eye brands', which contain five fingers (Figs. 19–21).

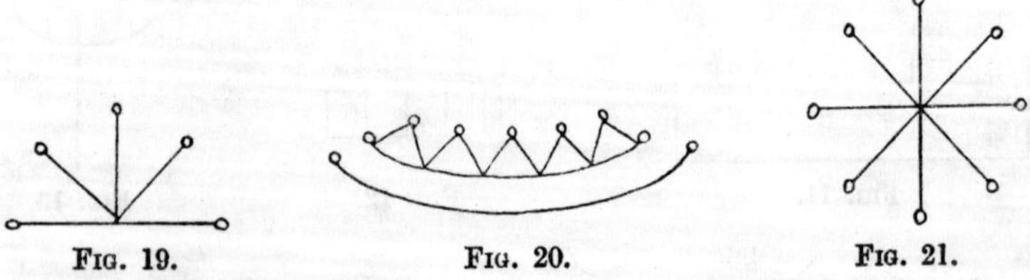

FIG. 19. FIG. 20. FIG. 21.

The number five is very common in designs drawn to avert the evil-eye. Five dots in a line (Fig. 22) are drawn with lime, turmeric or red earth by *Lingāyat* ladies on the threshold and on the top and side pieces of the door-frame. One can find these same marks also on the wheels of carts, on the head of a yoke, on the iron safe of shopkeepers, on iron weights and scales, on the backs of account books, on public motor-cars, on a Marwari's cupboard for storing cloth. When an image is worshipped the same design is drawn on the floor with grains of fried rice, or rice mixed with turmeric

Fig. 22.

powder; when the *Pāṇḍavā* are worshipped or the banni tree is worshipped during the harvest of the *kharif jvārī* the same design is drawn.

The *manganamalaku* (Fig. 23) is another figure allied to the *jīvati gombi* drawn on the newly constructed floor of a house after it has been covered with cowdung, so that the cowdung may not be cracked by the evil-eye of some chance visitor.

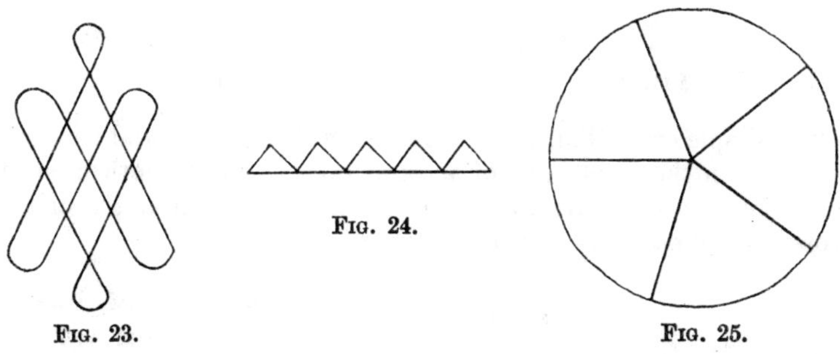

Fig. 23. Fig. 24. Fig. 25.

To protect a threshing-floor *Bhils* and *Koḻis* sprinkle the milk of a goat with five kinds of grains on the floor. To protect a crop of wheat the field is sown diagonally in five rows at the end of the sowing, a sowing that is called investing the field with the sacred thread, *janivārā hākoḍu*. To protect the walls of a new building from cracking caused by an evil glance, five lines are drawn all around the building with water and cowdung; these lines are called *uḍadār* or 'girdle string'. In scaring away spirits one is also averting the possibility of evil-eye, as spirits cause evil-eye, and the number five in design is used as commonly to avert spirits as to avert evil-eye.

Siteyaseragu or the loose end of Śitā's *sāḍī* (Fig. 24) is a favourite tattoo-mark of women intended to scare away spirits..

To scare away spirits on Jyeṣṭha sud. 15 a circle with five radii (Fig. 25) is drawn on the walls of houses near the main entrance.

The next figure is a common design drawn on copper plates

intended to be used as *yantras*, but it is also drawn in front of the woman in confinement to scare away spirits.

A pentacle (Fig. 27) or five-pointed star drawn and finished without lifting the pen from the paper, is a charm against the evil eye. A common ornament which is also a charm is the *kuḍ* (Fig. 28); this to-day contains seven pearls, but the older patterns contain five only arranged in a cross design.

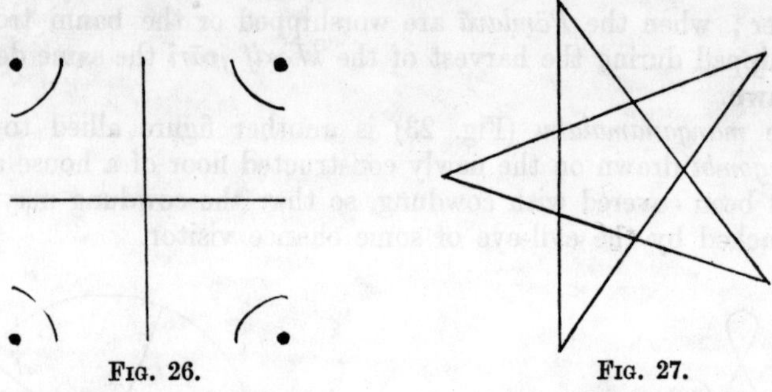

Fig. 26. Fig. 27.

The simple cross (Fig. 29) is drawn on walls, baskets and winnowing fans, on the front page of account books and on cloth used at marriages, to avert evil-eye. On account books variations of the cross are found (Figs. 30–31).

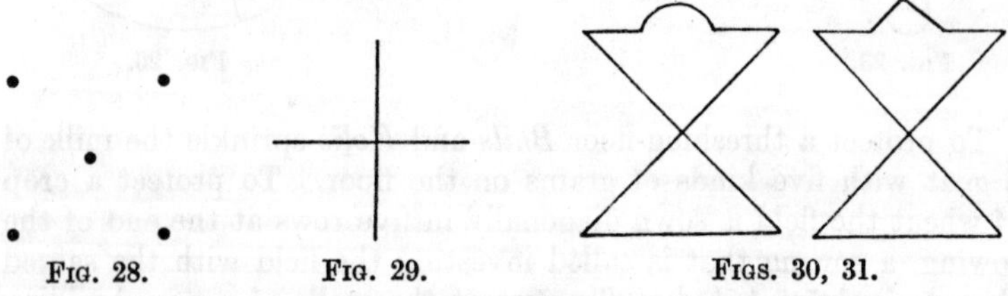

Fig. 28. Fig. 29. Figs. 30, 31.

The *Kātkarī* tattoos his girls after they have attained the age of four or five years, usually between the eyes, with scattered dots on the forehead, hands, cheeks and chin. Tattooing is done on the hands only after the girl has reached puberty. The tattooers come down to the Konkan from the Deccan and strange to say the least advanced section of the *Kātkarīs*, the *Dhōr*, does not tattoo. Though the designs used are not, therefore, the choice of the *Kātkarī*, they do in the Konkan provide some interesting examples of conventional charms in which the number five is very common. The following figures were copied from the faces of *Kātkarī* girls and are charms against the evil-eye.

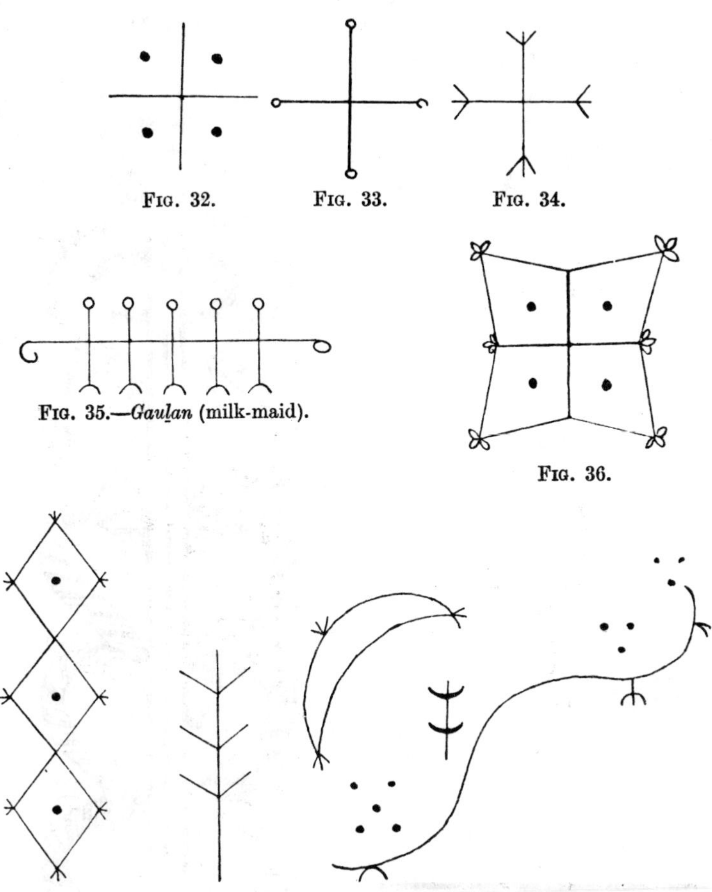

Fig. 32. Fig. 33. Fig. 34.

Fig. 35.—*Gauḻan* (milk-maid).

Fig. 36.

Fig. 37.—Suru tree. Fig. 38. Fig. 39.—Cradle.

In the Karnāṭak appear the following examples of the use of the number five: the first figure (Fig. 40) represents the crown of a bridegroom in a manner suggestive of a five-fingered hand; the second figure (Fig. 41) represents a scorpion, the feelers and sting of which make the number five on each side, and the third figure is called 'the hand of Śiva' (Fig. 42).

Representations of the eye avert the baneful power of the evil-eye. These representations may be realistic or conventional. To protect crops, fruit-trees and flower gardens an earthen pot is fixed amid them on a post; on this pot is drawn with lime a hideous face with prominent eyes. Similar figures are drawn on

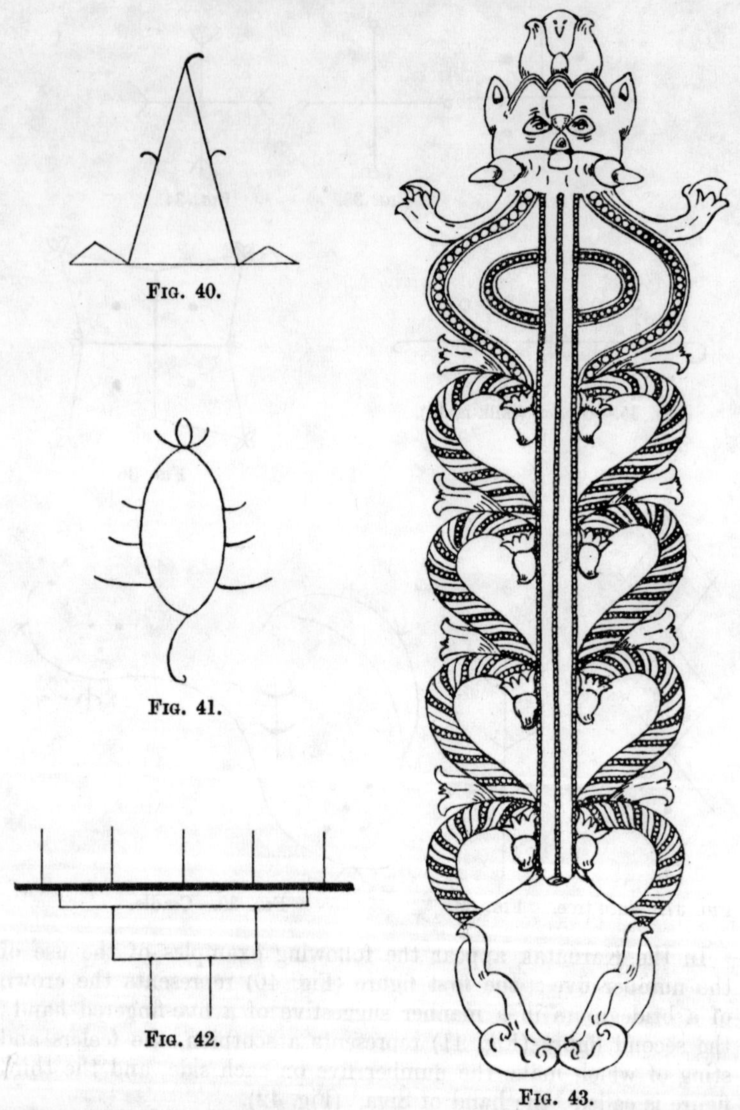

Fig. 40.

Fig. 41.

Fig. 42.

Fig. 43.

stacks of fodder or of cowdung cakes. A sacred car is protected by hideous faces with huge eyes carved amid the carving of the car; faces of dragons with protruding eyes invariably appear in the *prabhāvaḻ* or background against which a sacred image is seated. Similar figures of dragons (Fig. 43) are common on the temples of the Karnāṭak to protect them from the evil-eye of visitors. *Mahārs*, to cure a victim of evil-eye, draw a hideous figure with two eyes on an earthen dish in lime, and putting in it articles usually waved round a victim deposit it at cross-roads.

Many Hindu housewives have a sampler containing designs to be worked on saris and other garments as charms against evil-eye. From one of these samplers the following figures were taken.

Fig. 44.

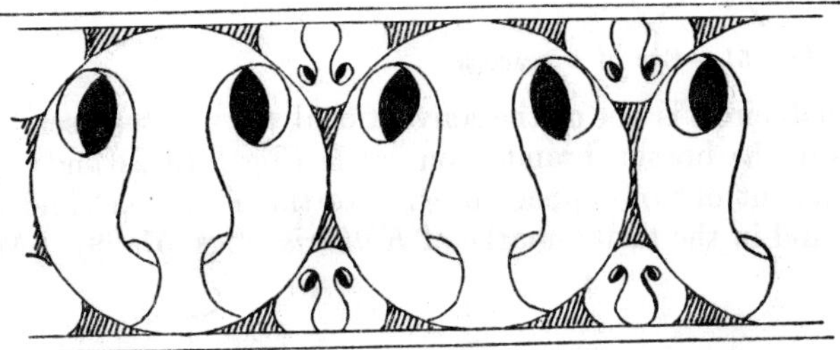

Fig. 45.

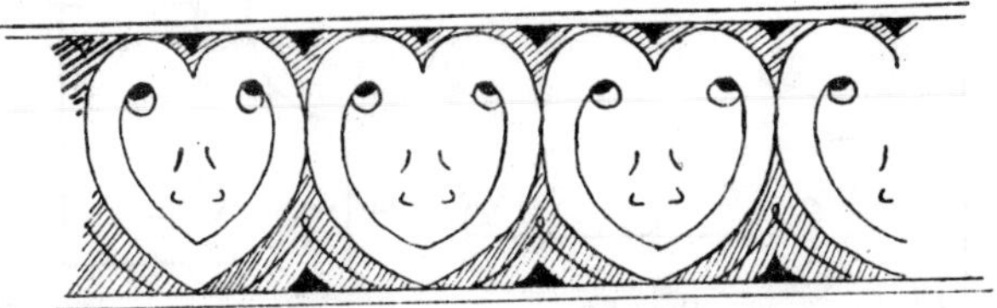

Fig. 46.

Fig. 47.—*Kannina patti*: eye design.

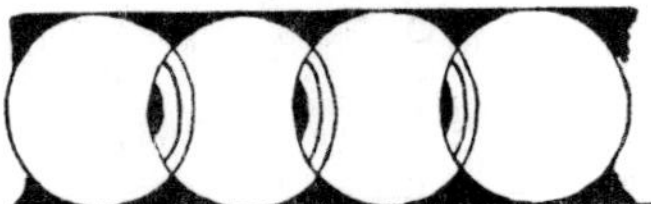

Fig. 48.—*Yettrina Kannina patti*: 'eye of a bull'.

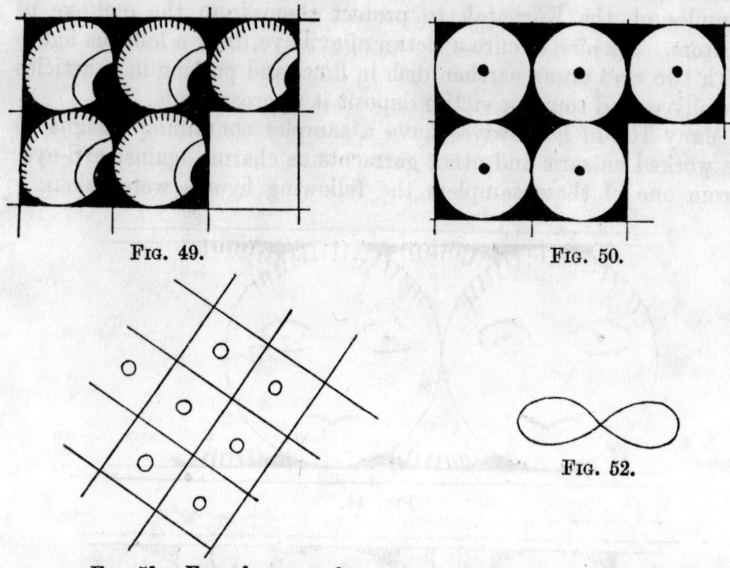

Fig. 49.

Fig. 50.

Fig. 51.—Eye of a peacock.

Fig. 52.

A small circle is one of the conventional ways of representing an eye, as in the brands branded on cattle (Figs. 19–21 and 52); in talismans cut out of copper and tied to the neck of a child (Figs. 53, 56) and in the tattoo-marks of *Kātkarīs* (Figs. 57–69). Among

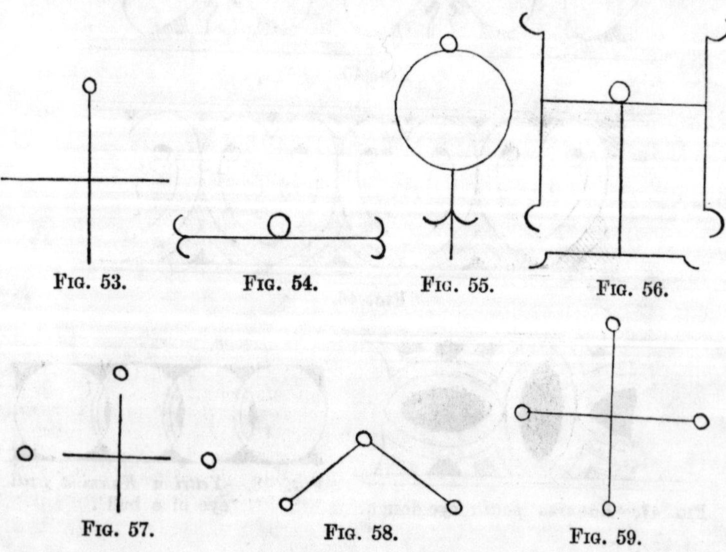

Fig. 53. Fig. 54. Fig. 55. Fig. 56.

Fig. 57. Fig. 58. Fig. 59.

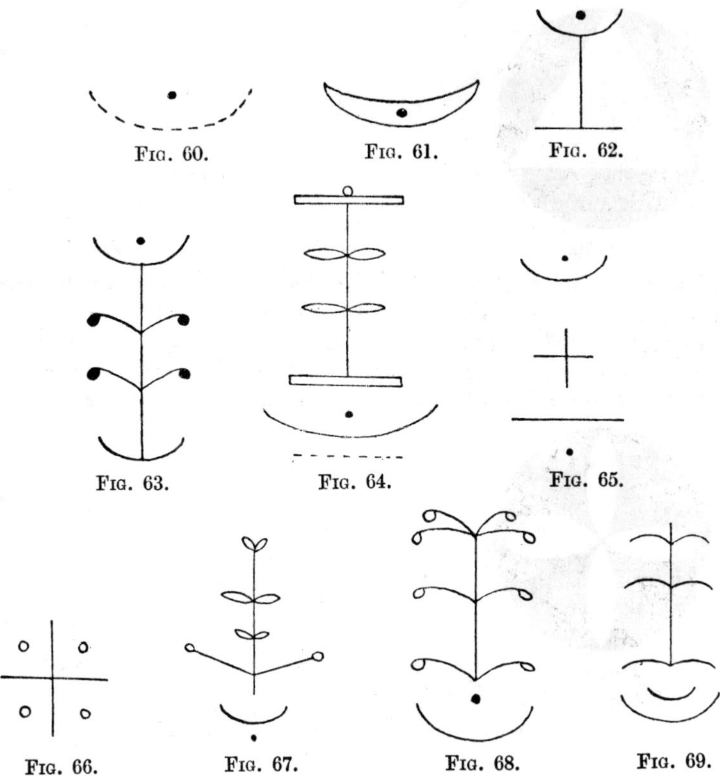

FIG. 60. FIG. 61. FIG. 62.

FIG. 63. FIG. 64. FIG. 65.

FIG. 66. FIG. 67. FIG. 68. FIG. 69.

these figures the *kor* or 'edge of the moon' [1] design obviously represents an eye with its pupil.

Circular holes (Figs. 70–73) are also cut or bored in the doors of temples for visitors to look through to get a glimpse of the god's image, but to do so without harming the image with their evil glance.

If a circle be used to represent an eye, and one representation

[1] Cp. *Ritual and Belief in Morocco*, E. Westermarck, 1926, vol. i, pp. 472–3: 'Sir William Ridgeway has tried to show that the crescent, which has long been and still is a widespread amulet against the evil eye in Mediterranean countries and south-eastern Europe, has evolved from boars' tusks, which have likewise since ancient times been used for the same purpose in those countries; . . . I believe, however, that the crescent may also have an independent origin—quite apart from its traditional connexion with the moon, to which I attach no more importance than does Sir William. It may be an eye-design, a representation of the eyelid; and as I have indicated above, the efficacy attributed to wild-boars' tusks—whether single or two joined together forming a crescent—seems in the main to have a similar origin.'

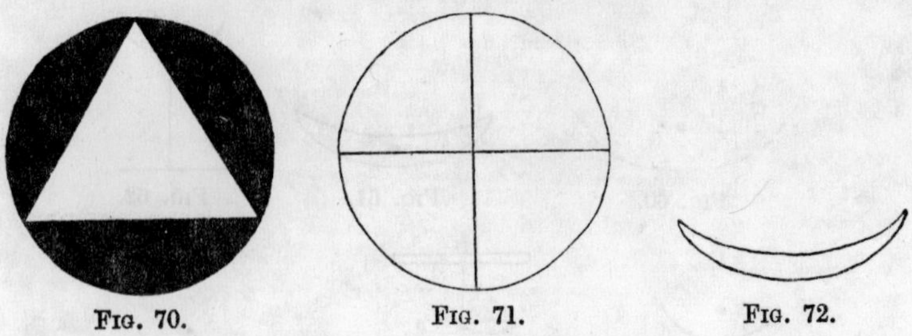

Fig. 70. Fig. 71. Fig. 72.

of an eye is like the crescent of the moon, there are occasions when the circle does in reality represent the sun, and the crescent the moon, regarded as these are, as the eyes of day. In the latter part of the bright half of Māgha until the full-moon day arrives (*Bhārat Huṇṇivi*), *suvāsinīs* in the Karnāṭak draw on the floor of

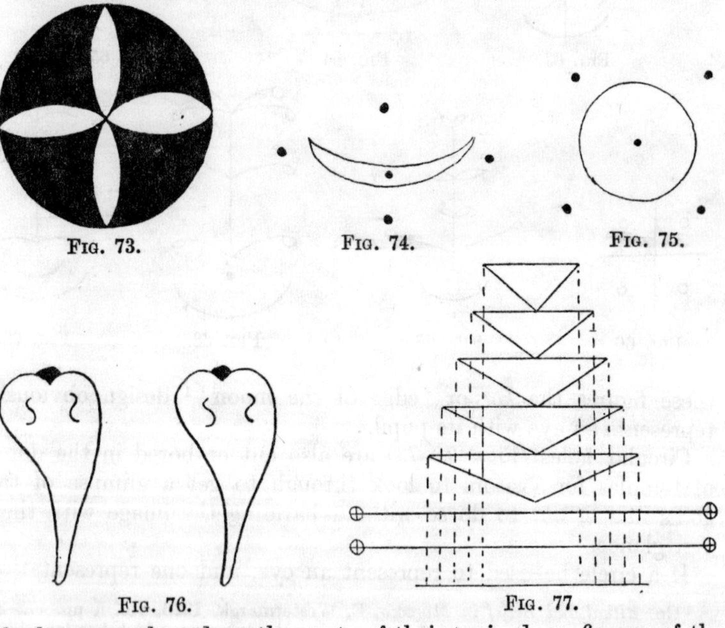

Fig. 73. Fig. 74. Fig. 75.

Fig. 76. Fig. 77.

the house yard, and on the posts of their main door, figures of the sun and moon (Figs. 74–75) with lime. Then on the day following they make other marks below the first representing the footprints of the sun and moon. On the third day two cobras are drawn with expanded hoods (Fig. 76); on the fourth day a figure of a deer and one of a horse as vehicles of the luminaries; whilst on the fifth day two chariots (Fig. 77) are drawn in which the number five is prominent. The object of these designs is to scare away spirits, but the major part of them also averts evil-eye. The crescent of the moon appears in a hair ornament (Fig. 78) worn to keep away evil-eye, and the cobra with two eyes and a hood of five folds also appears in an ornament (Fig. 79).

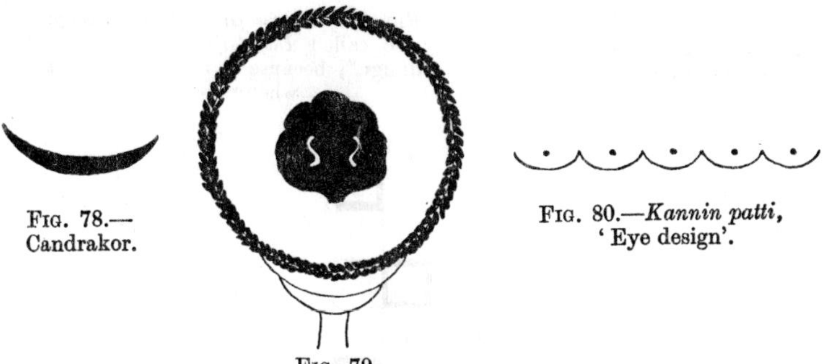

FIG. 78.—Candrakor.

FIG. 79.

FIG. 80.—*Kannin patti*, 'Eye design'.

To avert evil-eye, drawings of the sun and moon are drawn on the pile of grain on the threshing-floor. Women even of the higher Hindu castes tattoo marks representing the sun and moon on their forearm; that of the moon is also tattooed on the forehead and at the outer corner of the eyes so as to enclose the two eyes. These tattoo-marks prevent the wearers becoming evil spirits after death. A dot in the centre of the crescent and dots in the circle of the sun make the former design represent an eye and the latter a face.

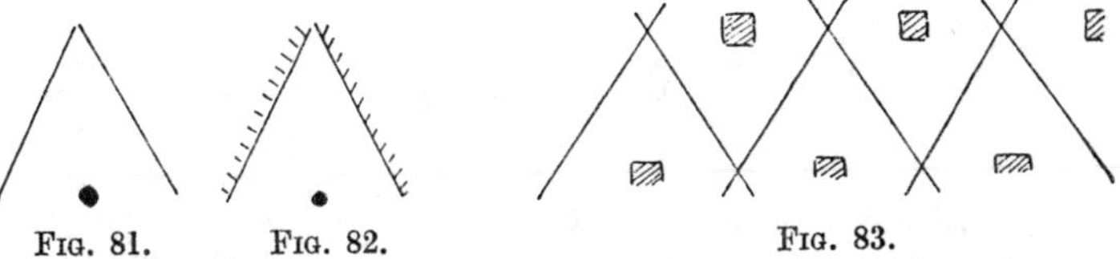

FIG. 81. FIG. 82. FIG. 83.

Navalina Kannu, 'eye of the peacock'.

In embroidery the eye is represented by a lower eyelid and a dot to represent the pupil (Fig. 80).

In the tattoo-marks (Figs. 81, 82) of the *Kātkarī* the eye is frequently represented by a baseless triangle with a pupil in the centre, and this conventional design appears in some patterns of needlework (Fig. 83). Two such triangular representations of the eye joined together produce a diamond with a square in the centre, and this is used to represent the eyes of coconuts or cobras (Figs. 84, 85).

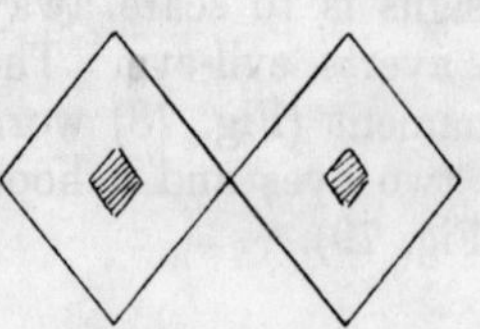

FIG. 84.—*Tengin patti*, 'Coconut design'.

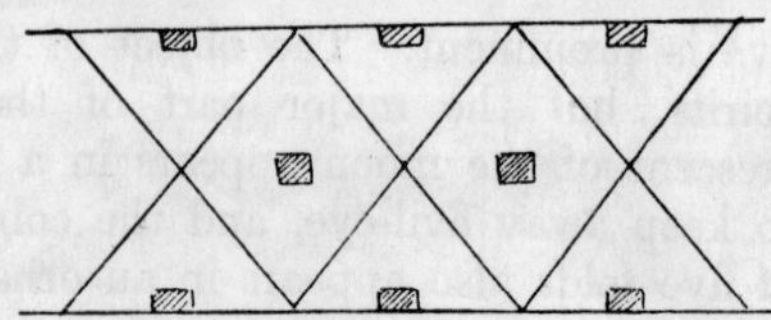

FIG. 85.—*Nagar patti*, 'Cobra design', also called *Dagabaji patti*, 'deceitful design', because it appears the same when reversed.

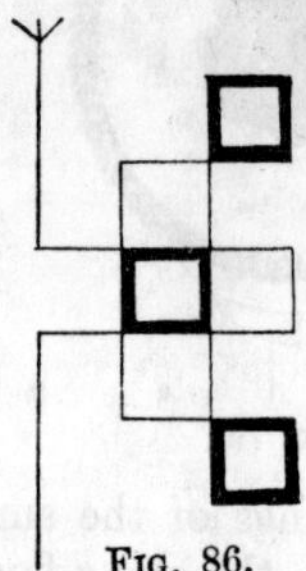

FIG. 86.

A square is used in other ways to represent the eyes of a cobra (Fig. 86). The triangle and the circle are also combined and produce the following design which is named *yettina uchi*, 'the urine of a cow '(Figs. 87, 88).

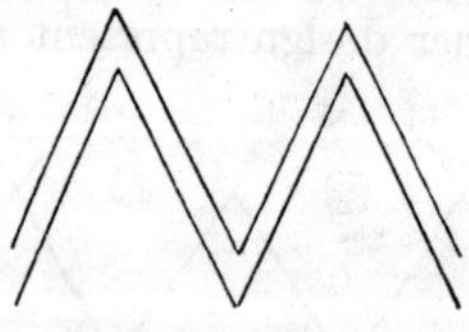

FIG. 87.

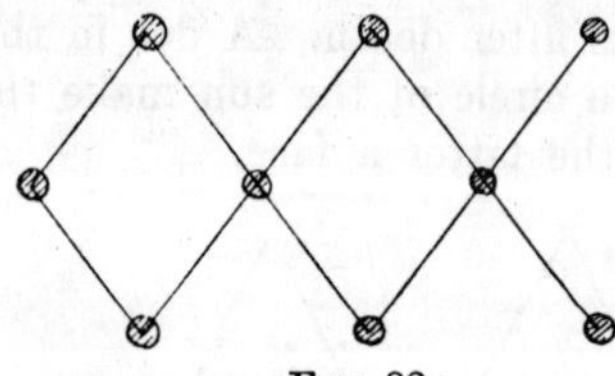

FIG. 88.

The evil power of an evil-eye is frustrated by a representation of a foot, and again the same charm is effective in scaring away spirits. A powerful *yantra* intended to cure spirit possession is rendered the more potent by drawings of feet on the copper plate (Fig. 89).

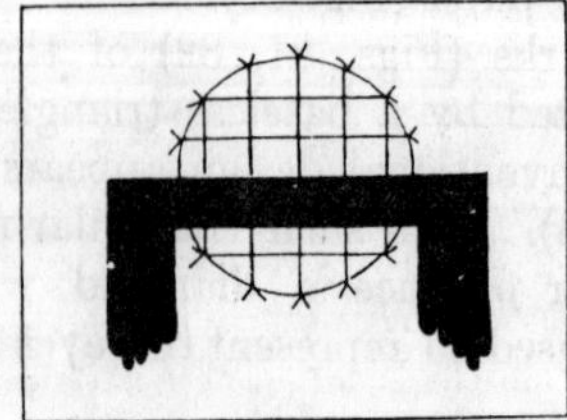

FIG. 89.

Representations of a foot are common in needlework. *Hulikalina* (Fig. 90) is the leg of a tiger; *hakkīkālu,* the foot of a bird, is a very frequent design (Fig. 91).

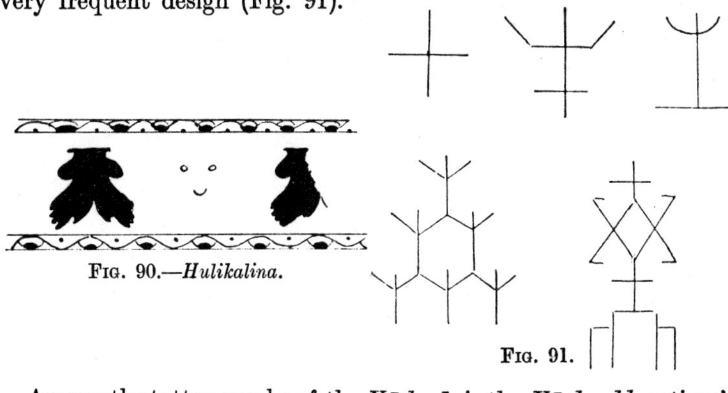

Fig. 90.—*Hulikalina.*

Fig. 91.

Among the tattoo-marks of the *Kātkarīs* is the *Vāghnakh* or tiger's claw (Figs. 92, 93).

Fig. 92.

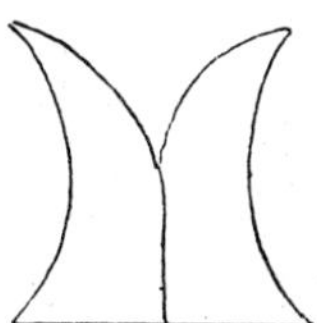

Fig. 93.

The next figure (94) is the footprint of a dog, and is of particular interest because it is often repeated to form a naturalistic representation of a creeper (Fig. 95). Naturalistic objects are often repre-represented in embroidery and tattoing designs. Trees are often represented in embroidery and tattooing by cross-like figures

Fig. 94.

Fig. 95.

(Figs. 96, 97), and the leg of a bird is also the basis of a conventional tree pattern (Figs. 98, 99).

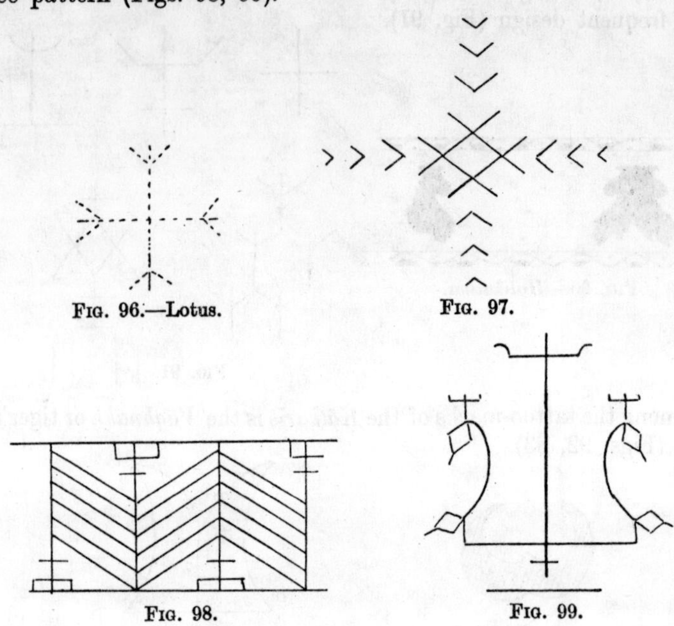

Fig. 96.—Lotus. Fig. 97.

Fig. 98. Fig. 99.

There is one design common to many Oriental carpets called *goḍambi* because of a superficial resemblance to a fruit of the same name. This, however, is really an impression of a foot. In the Karnāṭak it is drawn on the sides of doors by agriculturists; when so drawn it is called *Gaurīpādā*, 'the footprint of Gaurī' (Fig. 100) or *Candappanpādā*, 'the footprint of the moon'. During *Divāḻī* the same figure is drawn in the house yard in numbers by the Hindu and the figures are called *Pāṇḍavar hejje*, 'footprints of the Pāṇḍavās'. Even Muhammadans draw the same figure on their walls with the back of their closed fist which they have dipped in lime. This *goḍambi* design receives many transformations and is the basis of many patterns (Figs. 101–104).

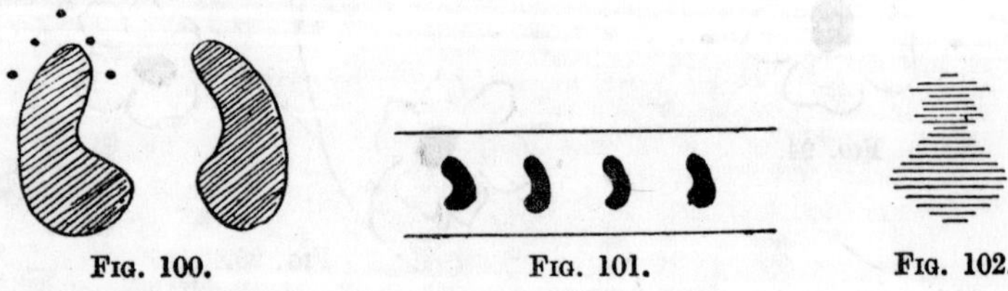

Fig. 100. Fig. 101. Fig. 102.

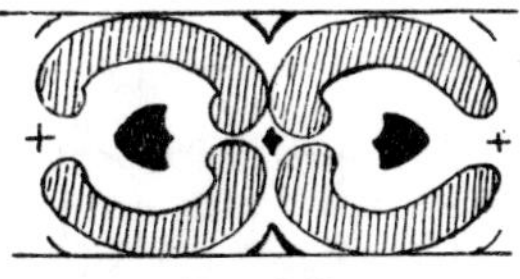

FIG. 103.

FIG. 104.

Representations of seeds and fruit avert evil-eye, and many a design representing a foot, hand or eye also has protective power because it is supposed to resemble also a seed.

The simple cross represents sesamum (Fig. 105).

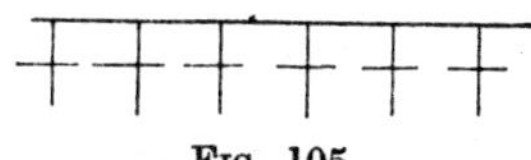

FIG. 105.

A design made up of a bird's feet also represents a grass (Fig. 106).

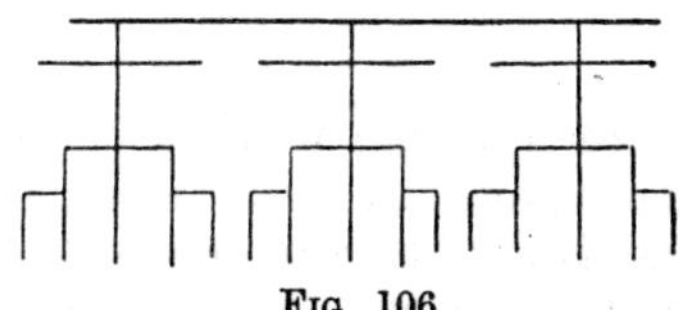

FIG. 106.

Apart altogether from a naturalistic representation in tattoo-marks and in the embroidery of saris, of trees, seeds and fruit, the conventional marks which represent eyes, hands, feet or the number five are used to represent these natural objects (Figs. 107–117).

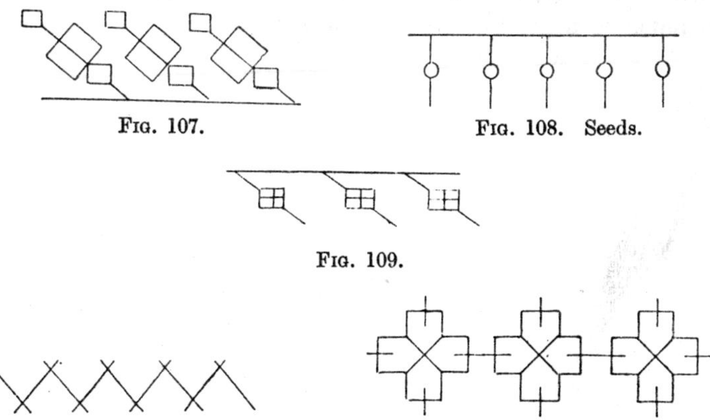

FIG. 107.

FIG. 108. Seeds.

FIG. 109.

FIG. 110.

FIG. 111.—Coconuts.

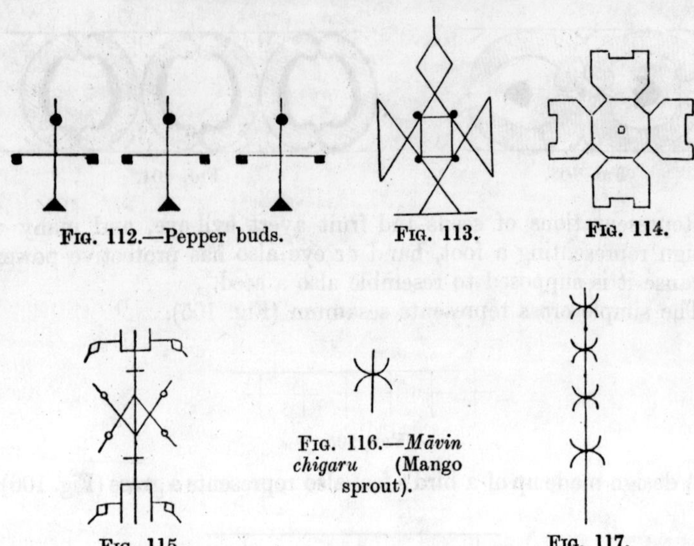

FIG. 112.—Pepper buds. FIG. 113. FIG. 114.

FIG. 115. FIG. 116.—*Māvin chigaru* (Mango sprout). FIG. 117.

In the unusual there is a *śakti* which averts evil-eye. Butter, milk and grain can be protected by a measure inverted; a cock with a comb reversed is not liable to evil-eye; dolls hung upside-down afford protection to a house, and to butter and other comestibles. In a wrestling match to baffle the activities of a witch the shoe of the left foot is worn on the right foot. Herein again we have an illustration of the inconsistencies that arise from finding in a negative the *śakti* of a positive, for if the unusual provides a defence against evil-eye, the evil *śakti* of *dṛṣṭi* is attributed to many forms of the unusual.

CHAPTER V

THE POWER OF THE GROUND

TO the *Kātkarī* the ground is the source and reservoir of all *jīva* or life. When any living thing, a tree, animal or man, dies its life force returns to the ground, and from that again issues in another form. To the Hindu the earth is *bhū mātā*, 'the mother of all things'; it is *dhantari mātā*, 'mother of the crops'; it is *rasa*, 'full of essence'; *sarvasaha*, 'bearing all things'; *vasumati*, *vasundharā*, 'bearing wealth'. It is one of the five primary elements of creation. According to the Koran, man was made from earth and so earth is the mother of man; it is with water, air and fire one of the four elements of creation recognized by the Muhammadan.

Hindus believe that the earth rests on the head of a large cobra, *Śeṣa*, and that an earthquake is caused by the snake nodding its head when it contemplates the sins of the world. Another belief is that *Varāha*, the boar incarnation of Viṣṇu, holds up the earth, and causes an earthquake when he changes his burden from one tusk to another. In popular Muhammadan belief the earth rests on the head of a cow whose head is in the East and tail in the West. The length of the cow from head to tail is as long as the distance a man would travel in thirty thousand years. Another Muhammadan belief is that the earth rests on the horns of a bull which itself stands on a fish; the fish is in water which rests on wind; an empty space supports the wind and the space rests on something known to God alone. An earthquake is caused by the bearer of the earth shifting its burden as it wearies, or is caused by an angel, *Kar-ta-il*, who sits on the Caucasus and holds the veins of the earth; when the angel draws tight the veins there is a famine, when he loosens the veins there is abundance, and when he shakes them there is an earthquake.

To the Muhammadan the earth is a sentient being. To the sky and to the earth as sentient beings God first offered the duty of service, *amānat*, but they declined it, whereupon man accepted it. The earth must not be beaten. Hindus believe that if the earth be beaten, particularly in the evening when it sleeps, crops will be scanty and cattle will not return home from their pasture. The earth should not be beaten for another reason also in that it supports the burden of the world's sins. A wicked man is called *bhūmibhār* (Mar.), 'a burden on earth'. In the Karnāṭak if any one beats the earth some child in his family will get gripes. A Sindi Muhammadan will not beat the earth because some day it will shelter his body, and if beaten will press upon him in the grave and make his grave a hell. No one can escape the punishment of the grave, *Azābu'l-qabr*, and the pressure of the grave mitigates small sins. When a body is placed in the grave it is visited by two black angels with blue eyes, *Munkar* and *Nakir*, who interrogate the dead concerning the Prophet of God. A true Muhammadan will bear witness to the Unity of God and to the mission of the Prophet; a light is then given him in the grave, and the grave itself will expand seventy times seventy yards in length, and seventy times seven in breadth, and the angel will bid the dead sleep until the Resurrection. If, however, the dead be an unbeliever and deny the Prophet, the ground will close upon him, break his sides and cause him great agony until God raises him.

The earth must not be stamped upon. Muhammadans interpret *Surah* xvii, 'The Night Journey', of the Koran as forbidding a Muhammadan to walk pompously on the earth. *Mahārs* think that if one stamp on the ground whilst holding the framework of a door some one in the house will die immediately. Scratching the ground is forbidden in the sacred books of Hinduism.[1] In the Karnāṭak it is thought that poverty comes to any one who scratches the ground. In the Deccan children and pregnant women are not allowed to scratch the ground, or draw lines on it with water, charcoal or flour, and children are not allowed in their excitement to rub their feet to and fro on the ground.

Hindus will not pour hot water on the ground, and Muhammadans observe the same prohibition in the belief that no one should cause death by fire save He who created fire.

A *Konchi Korava* will not dig the ground with an iron tool save when extracting roots from which weavers' brushes are made. In all parts of the Presidency there is a reluctance to use iron pegs to tether cattle, and the aversion to using iron ploughshares is by no means yet a memory.

The earth must be protected from the *śakti* or *kudrat* of fire.

[1] 'Let him not scratch the ground' (*Manu*, iv, 55).
'He must not scratch the ground with a piece of wood or the like' (*Institutes of Viṣṇu*, lxxi, 41).

When a Hindu lights a fire he prepares for it a special hearth, or places leaves on the ground; a Muhammadan similarly puts leaves beneath the fire or sprinkles the ground first with salt. Potters are proverbially unfortunate, and in the Deccan their poverty is attributed to their profession which entails the constant burning of earth. A Muhammadan, save where he has copied the Hindu, will not eat chunam because it is burnt earth. On the other hand, in the Konkan and in the valleys of the Western Ghats that lead down to the coast, there are forms of cultivation, *rāb* [1] and *kumri*, which involve the preparation of the fields by burning leaves and branches.

The earth must be preserved from impure contacts. Sexual congress on the ground is forbidden. When relieving nature [2] the Hindu should place leaves on the ground. The Hindu dead are placed on durva grass; the Muhammadan dead on a mattress or on a plank.

Earth is to the Hindu one of the eight means of purification. In times of scarcity when water has to be taken from any place whatsoever where it can be found, higher castes of Hindus purify the water by pouring it in a hollow on the ground. Falling rain is not considered pure until it has been in contact with the ground. When again vessels have been polluted by an impure touch such as that of a dog, a woman in menses or of an untouchable, they are buried in the ground for three, five or seven days. The Muhammadan also uses earth and sand for purification when water is not available. On the other hand, the conception of the earth's *śakti* as something polluting is not absent from Hindu mythology. One word for the earth is *Medinī*. The Harivansa says that the earth

[1] Rāb cultivation consists in spreading the loppings of trees, dry grass and cowdung on ground selected for seed-beds and firing the whole. The origin of this practice is attributed to a divine curse. The Chitpavan Brahmins insolently claimed immortality and so Śri Paraśram deprived them of this privilege, and after so doing went to meet his brother Lakṣman, who was at the time standing on red laterite soil. Lakṣman accused his brother of deceit and ingratitude, whereupon Paraśram called him up to a large rock, to discuss the matter. Once on the rock Lakṣman lost his petulance and prostrated himself at the feet of his brother. Paraśram asked his brother to descend again to the red soil, which the latter did and again became abusive. A second time he ascended to the rock and became penitent. This time Paraśram sprinkled some red soil on the rock and asked his brother to step on it, which he did and again becoming bad-tempered realized the cause and cursed the red soil, saying 'May it burn'. This curse Paraśram modified by saying 'May it burn and be fruitful', and so the red soil of the Konkan is burnt to make it fruitful.

[2] 'He may ease himself, having covered the ground with sticks, clods, leaves, grass and the like' (*Manu*, iv, 49).

'He must not void . . . on earth which has not been previously covered with grass and the like' (*Institutes of Viṣṇu*, lx, 3).

acquired this name from the *meda* or fat of two demons, Kaitabha and Madhu, who about to kill Brahma were killed by Viṣṇu. In one passage it is said that the bodies of the demons were thrown into the sea, and produced an immense amount of fat, from which the earth was formed by Nārāyaṇa, whilst yet another passage describes their *meda* as covering the earth. This conception of the earth's *śakti* as something unclean is important in considering the belief that contact with the earth is destructive of *śakti*. Nothing is more destructive of *śakti* than uncleanness, and when the *śakti* of the sun or moon is diminished by an eclipse, the same presence of uncleanness is predicated.

Divine *śakti* must not come in contact with the earth. After *prāṇpratiṣṭā* an image becomes a tabernacle of *śakti* which it loses if not insulated from the ground by an *āsan*. The Marāṭhā *devak* and the *hālgamba* of the Karnāṭak, which incorporate the *śakti* of the family god, are also placed on *āsan*, and in the marriage booth are tied to a post. The sacred thread of the Brahmin which in its nine strings embodies the *śakti* of nine gods, and in its knot, the *Brahmagāṇṭh*, that of a triad of gods, must not touch the ground, and is hung by the wearer on the ear whenever it is removed from the neck. The first sheaf intended to be consumed as first-fruits must not touch the ground as it contains the *śakti* of *Prajapati*; even among unadvanced communities in Kanara the first-fruits offered to deities and on certain *Amāvāsyās* to the departed dead, are placed on a wooden *pāṭ*, or on tender leaves of plantain (*Gam Vakkāl, Ghadig, Halakai*). It would be anticipation of another chapter to enumerate more than a few other examples of the insulation of symbols. *Karnāṭakaru Brahmins* tie to a pillar in the marriage *manḍap* the *koḍatī* or wooden hammer which enshrines the *śakti* of *Soma*; *Lingāyat Kumbhārs* place in the marriage *manḍap* an empty pot decorated with a picture of Sarasvati and keep it on a blanket; *Talwārs* at a wedding worship one large and five small pots, four of these being arranged in a square with the others in the centre. The whole figure is called *taigadigi*, 'mother-pot'; the thread which encircles the outside pots of the square is preserved with the *bāśing* and the *kankaṇ* of the bridal pair, and cannot touch the ground. *Kaḻḻ Koravas* place in the marriage *manḍap* a spotted pot of water in which, in the name of Dyamava and Hanuman, a twig of basari has been placed; this pot is insulated from the ground by an *āsan* of jouari grain. To promote the well-being of cattle, *Lingāyats* worship a coconut as an emblem of *Hakkilakṣmī*, guardian of the cattle-shed, and this is replaced by a new one every *Amāvāsyā*. Until the old coconut is broken it cannot be placed on the ground. Whenever, in fine, the *śakti* of a deity suffuses a symbol, that symbol must be insulated from the ground.

Things which have been in contact with divine power cannot be placed on the ground. The *ārtī* or lamp waved round an image is in its plate or *tāmhaṇ* placed on an *āsan* of *akṣat* with red powder; garlands that have been hung round an image; the water in which images have been bathed; the *samīdhas* used in a sacrificial fire or *hom*. Sacred things brought from Benares by the Hindu or from Mecca and Medina by the Muhammadan; the cakes of dust, *Khāk Shafa* or earth of salvation brought by returning *Hajis*; water from the well of *Zemzem* which can touch the ground only when thrown on a grave. A piece of cloth, *ghalaf*, that has touched the *Ka'bah* at Mecca or the tomb of the Prophet must also not touch the ground. A Muhammadan will not place on the ground the Koran or any sacred writing, nor even a book which is consulted before writing a charm.

Contact with the ground destroys the efficacy of religious rites. When the *Agnihotrī* makes fire by friction he and his wife sit on antelope skins or kuśa grass, and all his implements are kept on an *āsan*. The *Lingāyat* places the articles he uses in worship on a cloth known as *gaddagi jāḍi* spread on a mat, *pangticāpi*; the water-pots, the brass or copper ladle used for *arghya*, the plate for burning incense; the brass stand on which lights are placed before a deity; the stone on which sandalwood is rubbed; his rosary and the flowers and leaves used in worship. When the ornamental pitchers to be fixed on the roofs of temples or on sacred cars are worshipped they are placed on jvārī grain. Copper coins when offered to trees in worship are placed on *nāgvel*. *Naivedya* offered to a tree is placed on a board; the *pinḍa* offered to the dead at a *Śrāddha* are placed on darbha grass; lemons, coconuts and flowers offered in worship must not touch the ground. Instruments when worshipped are placed on *pāṭ*; the knife with which the child's navel-cord is severed when worshipped in the Karnāṭak rests for twelve days on a plank. Among *Konchi Koravas* at a marriage, five *suvāsinīs* bring water from a well in a new earthen pot; this has to be kept on an *āsan* of sand. The efficacy of prayer is destroyed by contact with the earth. When a Hindu is performing *jap*, *prāṇāyām* or the daily *sandhyā* he must not sit on the ground; in all *vratas*, *śāntis* and *sanskārs* the *yajamān* must be insulated from the ground. The Muhammadan will not pray on the bare ground save where the sun has shone on it, but uses a prayer carpet or cloak; the Hindu's *āsan* may be a sacred grass, the skin of a deer, or if he be an ascetic, the skin of a panther or tiger.

Meals are taken sitting on *āsan*. *Lingāyats* put their plate on an *āsan*; *svāmīs* put theirs on a leaf. All dishes used at meals by a *Lingāyat* are placed on a wooden or metal stand called *addanagi*, and the person eating sits on a *pangticāpi* or mat with a cloth over it (*gaddagijāḍi, dhābaḻī*). *Gondhalis*, when they worship their gourd, pronged fork and drum, place them on an *āsan* purified with cowdung. The descendant of *Ramdas* worships a *kubdi*, a silver stick with two carved parrots as a head, Ramdas having been called *Rāghūpati* and *Rāghū*, meaning parrot. This stick is used as a rest when *jap* is performed; it is worshipped every day on a *pāṭ* and *akṣat* is thrown on it. It recalls the sword-stick of Ramdas.

Things with innate or acquired power cannot be placed on the ground. A mantra must not touch the ground; sacrificial food; ashes from a temple; a sweet-oil lamp; salt; turmeric. A special altar of leaves protects fire from contact with the ground. The severed navel-cord of the infant is kept from contact with the ground. A Hindu will allow no kind of food to touch the ground, and if food is offered to a dog it must be placed on a prepared mound or given in pieces that the dog will not drop. The wristlets and garlands of the bridal pair, and the crown of the bridegroom are carefully preserved from contact with the ground, nor can the bridegroom's dagger be placed on the ground. Coconuts given to the married pair or to a married woman must not touch the ground; the stone-of-life, the *aśmā* stone; a woman's *mangaḻsūtra* or necklace of married life must not touch the ground. Water used for washing the feet of a *Lingāyat guru* or *ayya* must be protected from the same contact.

Vibhūti (*adhar*) or sacred ashes; holy water from sacred rivers; water over which sacred words have been recited; *yantras* or charms into which power has been invoked; water in which such charms have been soaked; the light of one wick in an earthen plate lighted at a death, *paṇatī*, require the same protection from the ground. If Arabic writing be found on the ground a Muhammadan picks it up and places it in a hole in a wall, or breathing on it the words '*Sala Allaho Salum*', takes it to a *Pir* or a mosque for preservation. If bread be found on a road it is placed in safety away from the ground, and in the Deccan is powdered and thrown to fish to eat. Except in the god-room of a Hindu sacred scriptures cannot be placed on the ground, but require a wooden stand. Coriander and karber (Nerium odorum) are not placed on the ground in the belief that such contact would take away their scented fragrance. A Muhammadan will not place on the ground flowers, perfumes, milk or curds; the dress worn during a marriage by either of the bridal pair or the garlands worn by the boy at his circumcision; a rosary, turmeric or a lamp.

Rain-water enchanted by a *Pir* to cure rabies or snake-bite loses its power if it touches the ground. On the last Friday of *Ramaḍān* Muhammadans pluck leaves of trees, and on these Maulvis write verses of the Koran, and the leaves are then washed in water which is drunk to obtain barkat. Before the leaves are washed they must not touch the ground and so no leaf can be plucked from a branch that itself touches the ground. A stone tied to a tree to cure snake-bite when carried later to the shrine of a *Pir* must not touch the ground, and to prevent such contact is tied round the neck of the person who carries it. Magic practices no less than religious rites depend for their efficacy upon power, and the contact of the earth may render inoperative such practices by destroying power. In the practice of *utāra*, things are waved round a sick person and then deposited at cross-roads. By the waving a contact is assumed to have been made with the sick person, and the article deposited at the meeting of roads has acquired a contagious potentiality. Now it is an invariable custom to insulate these deposited articles from the ground; when the Muhammadan waves curds round a child stricken with evil-eye, he places the curds on a leaf or in a pot (*sānak*) on a public road (*bhānda*). Even more common as an insulator is a winnowing-fan, a tile or a bed of grass. Insulated thus from the ground the deposited articles are a source of danger to any passer-by who accidentally touches them, but they are innocuous if the insulation be destroyed. A passer-by may eat the curds (*bhānda*) which bear the contagion of evil-eye, if he first kick them so as to scatter them on the ground.

In many a magic rite leaves are used which as in the Muhammadan practice during *Ramaḍān* described before, must not have been collected from the ground nor from any branch touching the ground. Coconuts preserved in a niche and worshipped to secure the protection of cattle must be plucked from trees above the ground. The *Koḷī*, when he invokes the *śakti* of *Ind* into five or ten twigs of kalamb (Stephegyne parvifolia), ensures that these twigs have not touched the ground by catching them as they are cut and fall from the tree. In Sind charms that are to be placed in the three elements of fire, water and air (*abi*, *atshi*, *badi*), that is which are thrown in fire, placed in water, or hung to a tree, must on no account touch the ground. Salt brought from a mantrik to be given to a child which has lost its appetite; cotton-seed to be administered to milch cattle that fail in giving milk, and ashes to be sprinkled around fields to free them from insect pests must be brought from the mantrik without their touching the ground. Rags and threads that have been in contact with the sick, must not touch the ground before they are tied to trees or taken to a shrine. From the moment the resolve has been taken to drive a nail into a tree for any magic purpose, the nail must be kept from touching the ground, and the same precaution is applicable to a stone which is tied to a tree to effect a cure.

Many communities, when one of their members dies, make an attempt to find out whether the soul of the dead has acquired peace or not. *Pancāḻs* make an *āsan* of ashes, put on this an earthen lamp and hide it with a basket. This is done as soon as the corpse has been lifted preliminary to bearing it to the pyre; the next day before dawn the basket is lifted and the ashes are examined. Irregular marks on the ashes indicate that the soul of the dead is in trouble; regular markings which can be identified as flowers, horns of bullocks or other well-known things mean that the soul has found a happy reincarnation. *Kaḻḻ Koravas* prepare an *āsan* of sand about the size of an octavo book, and on it place a new earthen pot filled with water. This pot is hidden by a basket till it is examined on the following day; if the pot is still full of water the omen is a good one, if the water has diminished it means that the deceased has drunk of it because he is in trouble. In all such practices an *āsan* is imperative.

The soma herb is a creeper without leaves which grows on the milk-bush; it has no root in the ground and the fact that it does not touch the ground is one of the factors giving it special *śakti.* The juice of the soma is used in great sacrifices only occasionally performed; in these libations of its juice are offered to the sacrificial fire, *hom,* and the juice is drunk by the *yajamān* and assistant priests. Precise ritual determines the manner in which the herb is to be collected. It is brought by a Brahmin in a cart made from tere wood, a species of cedar, and sold to the *yajamān,* who is then forbidden to see the face of this Brahmin until after the completion of the sacrifice. A large number of priests extract the juice with stones and store in vessels of tere wood, which is the same wood from which many of the implements used by the *Agnihotrī* are fashioned. *Konchi Koravas* after killing an animal of the chase will not cut it up on the ground, lest contact with the ground should destroy all future prospects of sport. The animal is placed in the jungle or field on a bed of tarvad-leaves (Cassia auriculata), or if these be not available the animal is taken home and placed on a bed of dāgaḍi creeper (Cocculus villosus).

Persons with special power must not sit on the ground. At no stage of a Hindu marriage can the bride or bridegroom sit on the ground. *Pāṭ* of wood and *āsan* of grain are used as seats, and the Brahmin bride is carried to her *pāṭ* from the shrine of the *kul devatā* by her father. Even when a mock marriage is performed, an *āsan* is imperative. When *kumārikās* or children are fed and worshipped they are not to sit on the ground. At his thread ceremony the *vaṭu* sits on an *āsan*; in the *Garbhādhān* ceremony the bride is placed on an *āsan* and *pāṭ* are used in the ceremony of *Pumsavan* and *Sīmāntanayan*. When a married woman receives a coconut she is required to sit on a stool. Whenever to prolong the lives of their husbands *suvāsinīs* make presents of two winnowing-fans with rice, betelnuts and other things, the recipients must sit on a plank. Before a temple prostitute (*devadasi*, *suli*, *basvi*) takes a paramour she is seated on a blanket over which rice is sprinkled, and an unsheathed sword representing a bridegroom is placed to the right of this *āsan*. Five prostitutes make *ovāḷaṇī* of the girl and her sword; place rice on her thighs and shoulders; tie her *taḷī* or *mangaḷsūtra* round her neck and two small rings to her toes. A leaf which must not be a green one is tied with thread to her right wrist; one to a copper jar, *gundi*, placed in front of her, and one to a stick placed on her left. At the four corners of the blanket on which she sits insulated from the ground, are placed dried coconuts and for each coconut a piece of turmeric and five pice. The rite includes her branding on the arms above the joints, and on her right side above the breast with stamps, *śankh*. The coconuts are then broken in the name of the god to whom she is dedicated and alms are given to the poor.

Mythology would seem to explain this fear of the earth's contact as a fear of pollution. There would also seem to be other explanations of the care with which contact with the ground is avoided. The Hindu to-day offers two explanations. His first explanation is that mere matter, *jaḍ*, such as the earth, should not come in contact with something that derives its *śakti* from mental power. In illustration and support of this interpretation is the undoubted fact that the period of insulating an article from the ground in many a rite, commences from the moment a mental resolve is formed. Stones to be tied to trees to effect cures are picked up from the ground; nails to be driven into trees are taken from any source, but from the moment the actual rite commences neither stone nor nail may touch the ground. The same idea seems to underlie the practice of tying in a cloth to a post money or ornaments which a man promises to give to a god if something particular happens. From the beginning of his vow these pledged things may not touch the ground.

A second explanation offered is that *śakti* is a form of electricity which follows contact and runs into the earth when it can. This, of course, is an explanation which ere this Western writers have suggested (vide *The Golden Bough*, vol. x, pp. 1–18). It is an explanation not only offered by the Hindu himself but one which seems to accord with many an actual practice. I have already described how the things which in *Utāra* are deposited with their burden of evil on highways, are rendered innocuous if they are scattered on the ground and their insulation is destroyed. Their baneful power is drawn away by the earth. An illustration even better than this, however, of the drawing away of power by the ground, is afforded by a practice common in the Karnāṭak. When sowers have finished their task of sowing they are hot with power derived from their contact with the power of the seed; they have to be cooled and with this object have to bathe in cold water, but more than this, they are compelled to sit some time on the ground. Their hot *śakti* is to be drawn away from them by the ground. The shallow brass plate used to receive the water poured on the *linga* held in the hand during worship by *Lingāyats* is placed on the ground. As the water is supposed to cool the heat of the *linga*, the placing of the plate on the ground seems to be another example of drawing away hot *śakti*. Possibly, too, in this category of illustration fall practices in which something charged with injurious power is struck on the ground, that the evil power may go into the ground. In Sind, if a child or other person wields a piece of iron in a menacing manner he is asked to strike the ground with the iron to avert evil. To cure indigestion a broom is waved vertically over a patient, and the ground is then beaten with the broom. If a broom by chance come in contact with any one's person it is beaten on the ground. Shoes and brooms are waved over the sick and then struck on the ground. In Sind, if a man has an evil eye a black thread is measured by the height of the man; this is cut in three pieces with a knife and then the earth is struck with the knife.

In whatever way, however, contact with the ground destroys power, there are practices based on a belief that the ground can impart power which manifests itself it may be in increase. When medicine is taken, some portion is left in the vessel and this is upset on the ground, in order that the ground shall impart increased efficacy to the medicine. In the Karnāṭak a jar of sugar-cane juice, *ras*, is buried in the ground for ten or fifteen days. If the juice be required as medicine it is buried for a year or for two years. The *ras* is deemed to derive increase from contact with the ground. When a cow or buffalo is bought in Sind or in the Deccan, the first milk that it gives is poured on the ground, in order that the future supply of milk may be the greater. Many medicines are kept underground for some time to add to their potency. Though, too, contact with the earth deprives an image of the *śakti* invoked into it by *prāṇpratiṣṭā*, before the installation ceremony it is kept underground for one day by *Lingāyats* that the earth may remove from its dead material its lifelessness, and with the same object kept one day in water, and one day in a heap of grain.

When a child is bathed the water for its bath must not be used without first setting it aside on the ground. At *Divāḻī* when oil is applied to the body the Hindu first sets it on the ground.

Earth is used in the making of images; in many a rite pitchers or dishes are used which must be of earth. Earth is used to augment the power of a curse. The Muhammadan scatters earth when he curses; the Hindu throws earth at a person or on to his roof with a wish that he should die, *mannu turona.* At a funeral in Sind the mourners pick up earth, recite verses of the Koran and then blow on the earth, which is thrown on the grave to give barkat to the dead; such earth is also placed in the *lāhd* or recess in the grave in which the body lies. Earth from beneath the pole of the threshing-floor is, in the Karnāṭak, thrown on the road so that wayfarers may tread it, and confer barkat on the gathered grain.

Many kinds of earth have more than ordinary power. Earth from a saint's tomb is preserved as *prasād*; it is tied to cattle that are barren or fail to give milk. The Muhammadan ties earth from a *Pir's* tomb in a copper casket round the neck of a sick child. Small cakes, about the size of a match-box, of dust from the mosque at Mecca, and the tomb of the Prophet at Medina, mixed with water from the well *Zemzem*, or the holy spring *Ain Zubida* at Medina are used as medicine and carefully preserved. Pilgrims returning from Mecca and Medina keep their travel-stained shirts because they contain the sacred dust of the holy places.

When a child is suffering from *sandubyane* or fits, earth from the junction of three roads is made into a female image. This image is worshipped with turmeric kaṇgal flowers and five kinds of cooked grain, *guggari*, are offered to it; this grain is then waved round the child and thrown on the roof of a house, whilst the image is thrown into a well. When a child suffers from *bālgrah* an image is made from earth taken from three converging streams; the image is female or male not according to the sex of the child but according to its age. The child must not see the image to the neck of which an inscribed plate is attached, and which a man carries in the direction of *Rāhu*, which varies according to the day of the week, and abandons in the open. Earth from the *tulsīvṛndāvan* or the tulsī plant kept in every Hindu house, is applied to the body when bathing. Earth from a tank is used as an altar for all sacrificial fires, and in the ceremony of *Ankurāropaṇ*. Earth from an ant-hill is used to make an image of the snake-god on *Nāgpancmī* day and is used in *Ankurāropaṇ*. In the installation of *kalaśas* earth of seven kinds is used; earth from a highway, from an ant-hill, from a confluence of rivers, from a cow-pen, from a tank, and earth trodden by elephants, and these seven earths are applied to the body when on *Nāraḻi Pūrṇimā* the sacred thread is renewed. Earth from beneath the feet of Brahmins is considered pure, and when Brahmin guests cross the threshold on their leaving their host's house, a cloth is spread on the ground for them to walk over, and any dust that then collects on the cloth is preserved or sprinkled on the heads of the other guests. If a person be bitten by a scorpion, earth from beneath his feet is waved three times over the bitten part and thrown away. If a child fall accidentally, earth is waved round it, is spat upon and then thrown away. Earth from beneath the feet of persons is used by mantriks to work them evil. A Muhammadan mixes earth from a grave-yard with water and gives to a man possessed by spirits. A Muhammadan mother blows earth in alternate directions to avert evil if her child falls. Brahmins blow earth taken from cross-roads across their palm over a sick child.

CHAPTER VI

THE POWER OF WATER

IN the Hindu conception of creation water is one of the five primary elements, the *Pancbhūt, Pancmahābhūta.* In the evolution of the world, water was the fourth element to appear, preceding only *Pṛthvī* or the earth; at its dissolution the world is supposed to assume first the form of water. After the dismissal of *śakti* from things which have been the residence of power, the things are thrown into water, that they may return to the element antecedent to earth from which they evolved. According to the Muhammadan, God has called water *mubārak*; it represents immortality. In the Koran it is the source of life: 'We have made of water every thing living'; the Divine Revelation is compared to water.

Water and milk, the Hindu believes, have a mutual affection. When milk and water are boiled together there is evaporation of water. The milk, not bearing separation, tries to fall into the fire, but is pacified when its friend water is restored to it. In the Kanara district there is the *hāḻkumbha* ceremony (*hāḻu* is milk and *kumbha* is pot). At a marriage two earthen pots, one small and one large, are brought from a potter and kept in the marriage *manḍap*, one on the other. Water is poured into the larger pot and milk into the smaller one, and from these the bride's parents pour alternately milk and water over the hands of the bridegroom. This is symbolic of the union of the bridal pair. One explanation of the *hāḻgamba* rite in the Karnāṭak, the erection of a milk-post, is that originally two posts were erected, the one a barren dry post, *hālh*, and the other a living post, *hasargamba.* On the barren post milk was poured and on the living post water, and eventually the former became known as the milk-post because milk was poured on it.

The power of water must be protected from impure contacts. A *Haranśikārī* will not use water to purify himself after evacuation for fear of disease following the resentment of the goddess of water, *Gangamma.* In the *Institutes of Viṣṇu* (lxiii, 44) it is forbidden to cross a river without need. To-day when a train crosses a bridge over a river passengers throw copper coins into the river. A Sirdar of the Deccan only recently deceased never went out in his car without carrying coconuts and bodice cloths (*khaṇ*), to throw in any river he might have to cross. A Hindu cannot cross a river without removing his shoes; he cannot bathe in it naked; he cannot spit into it, but if he spits first spits on his palm and then washes his palm; when he bathes in a river he turns his head to its source and bows, and before he enters the water sips a little and applies water to his forehead and head. In Sind a Muhammadan will not cross water or dip a vessel into it if unclean. A *Muhāna* or fisherman if ritually unclean will not row or tow a boat; a woman when *enceinte* should not cross a river; for forty days after her delivery a woman may not cross a river, and a woman in her menses cannot wash clothes in a well or river.

The Hindu bride, if she crosses a river, is required to offer it a coconut; a pregnant woman offers it *haḷad* and *kunku* and a coconut. A woman awaiting her delivery cannot wash clothes in a river; after her delivery for forty days or other period, which varies according to caste, she cannot cross a river or wash clothes therein, and before she does so later must take a bath of purification. In her menses the Hindu woman must bathe first in river water obtained from others before she can wash clothes in a river, and when she crosses a river must throw in it betel-leaves and a pice. The *yajamān*, after beginning the obsequies of the dead, cannot cross a river or stream. If food be prepared with water a Brahmin will not touch food touched by a non-Brahmin, nor will a *Lingāyat* eat food prepared by a Brahmin or other non-*Lingāyat* if prepared with water. If a guest who is not a Brahmin comes to a Brahmin's house the host may eat only sweetmeats and fruit left by the guest, for sweetmeats are prepared with milk.

The weighing of water is avoided by both the Hindu and the Muhammadan. In Gujarāt to stop a fall of excessive rain a man with no social ties and no children deliberately weighs water, as a kind of personal sacrifice, for after doing this he can never expect issue.

Water keeps away spirits. When easing himself, if a man is in fear of spirits, he keeps his hand in a pot of water and finally empties the pot, and washes his feet, taking care to wash the entire foot, as spirits attach themselves to any portion left unwashed. If a person sleeps under a pipal tree (Ficus religiosa) he keeps near him a pot of water as a protection against *Munjā*, the spirit of a boy who has gone through his thread ceremony but has died before marriage, which haunts such a tree. The water used in the morning offering of *arghya* is supposed to assist the sun to rise, by becoming arrows which assail the demon of darkness, *Mandeh*, who prevents the rising of the sun, and there are those who think that every *arghya* gives the sun protection against spirits.

A ring of water, a barrier or *dikbāndha*, is used to scare away spirits. At a marriage of *Haraṇśikārīs* four pots are placed in a square formation and untwisted thread is wound round them five times; the water of the pots at each corner is upset so as to form a ring of water, within which the bridal pair take their *surgi* bath. At meal-times after the food has been served a Brahmin sprinkles water round the dishes clockwise, *pradakṣiṇā*,[1] to keep away spirits, *parisincana*. In various other Brahmin rites water is sprinkled in a similar way; it is sprinkled round the offerings of *baḻīharana* and round the sacred fire in *vaiśvadeva*. At a *Śrāddha* water is sprinkled round the offerings made to the *pitṛs* and to the gods, being sprinkled in the reverse way in the case of the offerings made to the dead.

On entering a new house a pitcher of water is placed on a heap of rice and worshipped with saffron and broken coconut, and the water is then sprinkled over the house, *udak śānti*. To keep away *Yakṣa*, a spirit which troubles the bridal pair, the *Lingāyat* invokes *Varuṇa*, the god of water, into his *hasargamba* twig; the Brahmin in many a ceremony invokes *Varuṇa* into a *kalaśa*. *Bhāts* wave a pot of water seven times round the head of the bridegroom, place it in front of his right knee and then throw the water on the ground. Many castes sprinkle in different parts of the house the water in which the feet of the bridegroom or of the bridal pair have been washed. Water in which the feet of a *svāmī* have been washed is sprinkled over a person haunted

[1] A circuit *pradakṣiṇā* is made in the worship of all deities save that to avoid crossing the water-channel of an image of Śiva the circuit of his image is reversed at the channel. The same circuit is made of the pole on the threshing-floor or the central pole of a marriage *manḍap*; A *hom* is encircled in the same way. The bricks of an altar in sequence are laid in this way and whenever five articles are placed in a cross formation the same order is observed. Water sprinkled to the cardinal points is sprinkled *pradakṣiṇā*; dancing on a delayed monsoon follows the same circuit. The Muhammadan makes a *pradakṣiṇā* circuit of his Ālāwā pit at Muḥarram. Things that contain *śakti* are encircled in the same direction and the sacred books of Hinduism (vide *Institutes of Viṣṇu*, lxiii, 26–33 and *Manu* iv, 39) give a long list of objects which must be passed with the object on the right. The opposite circuit, *prasavya*, is followed in the practice of *utāra*; in the waving of things to avert evil; in witchcraft and sorcery this reversed circuit is a method of coercion of evil *śakti*. Stones representing Vetāḻ are placed in this reversed way. A Hindu woman goes round an aśvath tree, *pradakṣiṇā* in worship, but *prasavya* if her object be to obtain issue.

by a spirit. Water is sprinkled by means of two tulsī-leaves (Ocimum sanctum) in the cardinal directions, before any religious rite such as the installation of an image, a marriage or a thread ceremony, or the performance of *jap* or *sandhyā*. To avert spirits water is thrown out of doors as a corpse is carried by; a haunted person, to free himself from the spirit that haunts him, jumps into a river; water is poured in a shoe and given to a haunted person to drink. As water contains fire, it can be used in lieu of fire and be waved round a person as *ārti*, to avert evil. If a man sneeze when standing on the threshold, water is sprinkled on the threshold and the framework of the door to keep away spirits. Washing of the feet is the commonest of practices, for spirits attach themselves to the feet of men and also of cattle, in their efforts to penetrate the abodes of men.

It is not, however, only the evil *śakti* of spirits that water averts. Water, a Muhammadan believes, washes away the sins of a Muhammadan but is powerless to wash away those of a *mushrik*, and as proof of this a horse will drink water in which a Hindu has bathed, but not water in which a Muhammadan has bathed. It is hardly necessary for me to say that a Hindu would not accept this limitation of the beneficent power of water to wash away sin. The *abhiṣek* of a king is supposed to keep away any evil tendencies he would otherwise acquire. The water sprinkled over the *yajamān* by the priests at a *Śrāddha* destroys the evil tendencies of the *yajamān*. Water again is used to deprive *pāyguṇ* of its evil potentiality, and it is used to avert evil-eye. Orthodox Hindus take a bath if they happen to come in contact with the breath of the wicked; they rinse their mouth with water if they happen to mention the name of a wicked person. Water is sprinkled on clothes that return from the washerman before they are used; on articles brought from the market; on flowers before they are used in worship; on the fire which is brought for a *hom*, and on the emptied plate in which it is brought. If a *Śūdra* has touched the rope of a well it is sprinkled with water before other castes will draw water from the well. Utensils given to Śūdras for cooking and other purposes are sprinkled with water before they are received back. Some people on their way to a temple carry a cloth soaked in water, which they wring out or sprinkle as they wend their way.

Water is used in many ways in the strict ritual of bestowing a gift. There is, first of all, the declaration of object, *sankalpa*, by the *yajamān* or *kartā*, accompanied by the throwing of water on the ground in confirmation of his vow to make a gift. Then the gift is purified by water; this ceremony, *samprokṣan*, is a purification with water applied to objects and to images only and not to persons. If, for instance, a Brahmin temple be defiled or an image be defiled by the touch of an impure person, *samprokṣan* is imperative. After the purification of the gift the recipient of the gift is worshipped, and his hands and feet are washed (*arghya, pādya*). Finally, the transfer of the gift is made, water being poured in confirmation on the hand of the recipient over the article itself. A person uttering a mantra sprinkles water on the person for whose good or ill the mantra is recited, to confirm the effect of the recitation. At a marriage the gift of the bride, *kanyādān*, is still made according to this ritual, and *dhāre* [1] or *dhāre ere* is the pouring of water by the bride's father over the right hand of the bride placed in that of the bridegroom. When a child is adopted, *putradān*, the child's natural father pours water into the hand of the adoptive father. Water is invariably sprinkled on gifts made to an image, as without this the *śakti* of the image would be reduced. In strict theory, too, any gift made without this ritual does not confer *puṇya* on the donor. *Konchi Koravas* have a modified form of the *dhāre* ceremony. After the bridal pair have been covered with turmeric powder, *ariśiṇ*, and bathed, the bridegroom entwines his fingers in those of the bride, and their clothes are tied together. They proceed to the bridegroom's house where cold water is poured over their entwined fingers, and the knots in their clothes are undone.

The accepting of a gift has its dangers,[2] and the recipient should purify himself with water. This purification, *prayascitta*, is performed whenever persons have been in contact with impurity. It is absolutely essential when *ugra* gifts with their burden of ill are accepted; when a Brahmin officiates at a *Śrāddha* ceremony,

[1] In Kanarese Dhāra means a string, and Dhāre is applied to an unbroken flow of dripping water. Cp. *Castes and Tribes of Southern India*, E. Thurston, vol. i, p. 166. The author writing of the *dhāre* ceremony among the Bants says: 'This form of gift by pouring water was formerly common, and was not confined to the gift of a bride. It still survives in the marriage ceremony of various castes, and the name of the Bant ceremony shows that it must once have been universal among them'.

[2] Vide *The Origin and Development of the Moral Ideas*, E. Westermarck, 1924, vol. i, p. 593: 'The acceptance of gifts is frequently considered to be connected with some danger. According to rules laid down in the sacred books of India, he who is about to accept gifts, or he who has accepted gifts, must repeatedly recite four Vedic verses called Taratsamandis; or all gifts are to be preceded by pouring out water into the extended palm of the recipient's right hand, evidently because the water is supposed to cleanse the gift from the baneful energy with which it may be saturated.' This seems to me slightly confusing. The purification of the gift is made independently of the final pouring of water into the hand of the recipient.

and in theory every guest accepting hospitality should purify himself in this way.

The purifying power of water is in some degree due to its cooling power. There are many practices of both the Hindu and of the Muhammadan based on the idea that power is heat, and that water cooling this heat renders the power innocuous. To the examples I have given in an earlier chapter (Chap. I) I may add a few more. On the thirteenth day after a death relatives of the dead are sprinkled by Hindus with water, *udalśānt*, to remove the contagion of death. *Tāzias* are wooden structures representing the funeral biers of the martyrs of Kerbela, carried in Sind by Muhammadans during *Muḥarram*; *panjā* are the hands of 'Ali the fourth caliph carried during the same period by Muhammadans in the Karnāṭak. Water is used to cool the hot *kudrat* of both the *tāzias* and the *panjā*. Pilgrims visiting the *dargāh* of a saint sprinkle water round the tomb, *thado karan*, to make it cool; pots in which Persian Muhammadans in the month of Rajab have invoked the power of Ḥaḍrat 'Ali are thrown into water to make them cool.

Water is associated with fertility, one manifestation of the activity of *śakti*. In Sind at the beginning of the flood season of the Indus, the *Abkalāni*, Hindu women sit in the mouths of the canals to catch the incoming river water. Illegitimate children born during the prolonged absence of the mother's husband are called children of the *King River*, though sometimes claimed by the husband as his own because in his absence he sent his *dhotar* to his wife to wear. In the Karnāṭak a woman desiring issue goes to a river, fills a pot with water, worships it and bringing it home, adds it to the water of her daily bath. Another practice is for her to go wearing wet clothes to a deep pool in a river-bed and saying, 'Let there be a lamp [1] in my family, and I will light a lamp in your waters', to make a vow to offer a *parḍī* of seven or five compartments of curds, milk and fruit. In the Sirsi, taluka women, with the object of getting issue, bathe in a river at Svādi and with wet clothes go to the shrine of *Vadirāj Svāmī* which they go round seven times on the day of the saint's car festival, and then standing near the car eat the cooked rice, *dhvajbutti*, which is thrown in all directions as the car is drawn. In many other places bathing with this object is combined with the worship of a locally installed deity; in several cases this is repeated on eleven *Amāvāsyās*. In the Kalghatgi taluka there is a nullah near Ningankop where childless women take a bath, and

[1] Lamp means a child.

worship an image of Śiva which they make from the sand in the stream-bed, offering it a *naivedya* of dates which with their seeds they eat later. In the Sirsi taluka women bathe in the Gudnapur tank near Banavaśi and worship the goddess Kerevva installed on the bank of the tank. Another tank is that of Basavankeri in the Ron taluka where women bathe and worship Basavanna.

A custom of *Mahārs* in Satāra is for a barren woman to go to a river and place five stones in a line on the bank; on each stone she then places a piece of bread, red śendūr and turmeric, and says, 'May the river water come and be my child'. On five successive *Amāvāsyās* a childless woman with her husband will sit in a river, and get another married pair with issue to pour water over themselves so as to fall on the couple without issue. Early in the morning a man without issue will bring water from seven wells and boil it; with this the wife takes a bath, followed by a visit to a temple in strict silence. Before sunrise, too, women bathe in a river and make five balls from the river sand, which they place in a line and worship with coconuts and plantains, promising to give charity if they have issue. In Sind the first water drawn from a new well is supposed to bring issue to a childless woman, as does the water of the Indus taken from near the shrine of *Jind Pir*, 'the living Pir', at Sukkur.

In Sind, water is associated with Khwaja Khizr. Muhammadan women go to the river at Sukkur where is the island shrine of the saint, drink water from the river and pray for children. In the seventh month of a woman's pregnancy, offerings of miniature boats about two feet long, and resembling ancient galleys, are offered to Khwaja Khizr, and this is done also on the fortieth day after a mother's delivery. Among Rajputs on the fortieth day after her delivery a woman carrying her child goes to a well and offers sandal-paste and vermilion and flowers to the spirits of the water. Within a month from the birth of a child, the *Gollar* or *Kabbar* mother goes with five married women to a well, offers coconuts and plantains to the well and bathes the child therein. Among *Raddis*, *Koravas*, *Vaddars* and *Calvadis*, after three months have elapsed, the mother without her child goes with five married women to a well, draws water in a pot which she worships and takes home to drink. Another custom of these communities is to make an image from sand to represent *Gangā*, and leave it in the bed of a river after worship. The period of a woman's retirement after her delivery varies considerably from caste to caste, but it is a general practice at the end of her seclusion for the mother to go to a temple worshipping a well on her way with an offering of milk, flowers and the usual *naivedya*, half of which is thrown into the well, and the other half of which is given to a childless woman to procure her issue.

Water is one of the commonest mediums through which a transfer of power can be effected. Many examples of such transfer I have already given. *Tīrth* is water which has been poured over an image; this, when drunk by worshippers, transfers to them power; it is the *prasād* of the god. Sick people pour water over the tomb of a saint, and sprinkle themselves with this water; water in which the coverings of such tombs have been soaked is also drunk or applied to wounds; water in which the knockers and hasps of the doors of a saintly tomb, *gadagi*, have been washed is used in the same way, for it has acquired power from the saint. The feet of persons with special power are washed and this water is sprinkled over others, over the house and it may be drunk. Such water is *pādōdaka* or *caraṇ tīrtha*. The *caraṇ tīrth* of a sannyāsī is sprinkled over the crowd present; that of the Brahmins invited to a *Śrāddha* over the heads of the household members; that of a *Purāṇik* at the close of a reading of sacred texts over the audience of listeners; that of *Brahmacārīs* invited to a thread ceremony over the heads of the *vaṭu* and his father. The water in which the feet of the bridegroom have been washed is *tīrth* only to his parents-in-law. A boy at his thread ceremony, the *vaṭu*, has also special *śakti* and his *caraṇ tīrth* is sprinkled on the invited guests; that of a pilgrim transfers power to those who come to receive him. Water in which the feet of a husband have been washed is *tīrth* only to his wife, though some castes sprinkle it over the house and over the children. Water sprinkled from *kalaśas* in which *śakti* has been invoked, or which have served as *āsan* for gods, is another form of *tīrth*.

Water poured over a twig of the tulsī (Ocimum sanctum) or umbar (Ficus glomerata) transfers *śakti*. The sword of the great Marāṭhā Śivājī preserved at Satāra has power, and water in which it has been washed is a cure for an obstructed delivery; water in which a gold coin of the emperor Akbar has been washed is given to a woman in her travail. Barren women drink water in which the loin-cloth of a *Brahmacāri* has been washed; water falling from the bodies of a married pair with issue on to a pair without issue transfers power; water from the *surgi* bath of the bridal pair is allowed to splash on to relatives seated near in order to transfer to them power. In the Deccan a woman in travail is given water which has been drawn from a well and passed down a long line of persons, the hope being that in going through the hands of so many it has acquired the *śakti* of one pious person.

On the other hand, water may be inimical to *śakti*. A *yantra* of the Hindu and a *tawiz* or charm of the Muhammadan loses its power if it becomes damp. A bath in fresh water destroys the *śakti* acquired by a bath in the sea; a bath destroys the *śakti* of fire which an *Agnihotrī* has invoked into himself. Many castes will not throw water on a fire to extinguish it, or even on the hearth. There is also in many parts a reluctance to bring water on to the threshing-floor in the belief that it would reduce the quantity of the grain. Strangers can certainly not bring water on the floor, and when measuring, all pots of water save one [1] on the floor must remain empty. In many *Kātkarī* villages water cannot be brought to the threshing-floor; *Mahārs*, however, sprinkle water on and around the pile of grain *rās* to avert spirits. In the Karnāṭak Brahmins will not place a wet cloth on the ground. In another chapter I have explained how washing, although it is necessary in purification, may be an act of destruction to be avoided. *Delhiwal Bhauriahs*, a criminal tribe hailing from the Central Provinces, have a special implement called *gian* made of iron; this is pointed at one end and at the other shaped like a spoon. It bears the mark of the *triśuḻ* and contains the *śakti* of *Devī*. This *gian* remains buried in the ground or in the root of a tree and must never be allowed to get wet.

RAIN

To a Muhammadan rain is *barani rahmat*; the angel Gabriel is in charge of every drop of rain. Rain falling at a funeral means salvation, *bakshishji nishani*; rain-water is sprinkled on the dead or on a bier to give *barkat* to the dead. If within three days of a funeral rain falls it is a sign that the deceased was a person of virtue.

Rain falling as one starts on a journey is auspicious. Rain at a wedding brings *barkat* to the whole community. Arabs and Persians believe that rain falling in *Nisan* is full of *barkat*, cures leprosy and is good to drink when beginning a journey. Charms are soaked in rain-water to cure rabies, and rain-water in which a charm has been dissolved is given a boy to make him learn his lessons.

[1] An empty water-pot connotes failure of purpose. A woman bearing an empty pot must not pass the threshing-floor; a man meeting such a woman must return home and begin his errand again. At a wedding all water-pots must be filled; a full pot of water is kept in a house when first entered upon; at a birth women are asked to bring pots of water and place at the door.

On the other hand, rain should not fall on the Koran nor can a Muhammadan recite the Koran when rain is falling on him. The tombs of saints must be protected from rain, and rain should not be allowed to fall on the bridal pair.

When the Hindu bridegroom at *Soḍamunja* leaves behind him his bachelorhood, he takes a vow in Sanscrit not to run in rain, a vow to which probably little or no attention is paid to-day. The *Konchi Korava* will not hunt deer when the fields are wet with rain. A Muhammadan, however, told me that it is less disrespectful to God to run quickly in rain, than merely to tread on it.

The quality of rain to a Hindu varies according to the *nakṣatra.* In *Hasta* it is poisonous for children; in *Svati* it produces pearls; in *Mṛga* rain-water, if drunk, keeps away disease for four months. In *Viśākha* it begets poisonous creatures, heats the stalks of grain so that animals eating them die. In *Hasta* and *Mṛga* it aggravates a disease; falling in *Citrā* it cures small-pox and chicken-pox. Rain falling at a wedding remains inauspicious in the months of Māgh and Mārgaśīrṣa, but is auspicious even in other months usually inauspicious. Rain is lucky if it fall as one begins a journey; it is of happy omen if it falls after *Holī*, and very much so if it falls when the bridal pair are on their way to the bridegroom's house.

Unless rain has touched the ground it is not to the Hindu pure for the purposes of worship, cooking or bathing. If rain fall on the body of a *svāmī* after he has bathed he must bathe again; if it fall on a man just before he begins any worship he must change his clothes before he can worship; if it fall on the bridal pair the marriage will be without *barkat* and *garjitśānti* is necessary. Rain should not fall on a child, a pregnant woman, a woman after her delivery, a girl attaining puberty or a woman in her menses. It must not fall on things offered to a god; falling on an image it makes it unholy and *samprokṣaṇ* is imperative. Rain-water and hail cannot be offered to a god and saints may not eat hail; it must not fall on a *hom*, and if a sacred fire be extinguished by rain a special *prayascitta* called *punaradan* is performed. Rain decreases the *śakti* of *prasād*, that is of things which have in them the transferred *śakti* of divinity. Rain-water cannot be used for *sandhyā*, *tarpaṇ*, *arghya* or *abhiṣek.*

A stormy day accompanied by thunder and rain becomes a day of *anadhyāya.*[1] On such a day students may not study the

[1] Anadhyāya, 'not studying'. Such days are the first, the eighth, the fourteenth of each month, and Pūrṇima and Amāvāsyā.

Veda. If it thunders and rains on the day of a thread ceremony before the principal *hom* is over, the ceremony is vitiated altogether. The boy is introduced to Vedic study at the time of this *hom* and since the day becomes a day of *anadhyāya*, 'not studying', on account of the thunder and rain, the study of the Veda cannot be begun at the appointed *muhūrtta.* In popular Muhammadan belief a thunderstorm is a time of *barkat,* and the Koran is recited to induce the angels to pray God to send rain. The thunder is caused by the angels calling aloud '*Subhān-Allah*', 'Pure is God'.

THE SEA

The sea is destructive of *śakti.* Though in modern times the rule is not strictly enforced, every Hindu who voyages for three days by sea should go through all his *sanskār* again before he is readmitted to his family. Except on days of *parvakāl,* when the *śakti* of water is enhanced, a sea bath should not be taken. Persons with special *śakti,* such as the boy at his thread ceremony, the *vaṭu,* the bridal pair and a woman in menses, should not touch the sea. Great sacrifices are performed on the banks of rivers, but not on the sea-shore. The Veda should not be studied on the sea-shore. A man with a wife *enceinte* must not take a bath in the sea or he harms the child to come. An *Agnihotrī* who has taken the *śakti* of his sacred fire to himself by *ātmāropaṇ* loses that *śakti* if he swims in a river or in the sea.

At a *parvakāl,* bathing in the sea removes sin. Three sips of sea-water purify the soul. The recital of a *sandhyā* on the bank of a river gives tenfold *puṇya,* on the shore of the sea a hundred-fold *puṇya.* The sea removes the sins of seven lives. The seas are invoked during the *garbhādhān hom* and the mantra then used alludes to them as destroyers of evil.

CHAPTER VII

THE POWER OF FIRE

CERTAIN features of Hindu ritual; its frequent sacrificial fires or *hom* lighted with manifold objects; its fire-festivals of *Divāḻī* and *Hoḻī*, and finally the strict code of rules that guides the conduct of the *Agnihotrī* in his worship of fire, emphasize the Hindu's reverence for fire. The Muhammadan's respect for fire is not so obvious, but he has many practices which entail a following of injunctions similar to those of the sacred books of Hinduism.

Neither Hindu nor Muhammadan will blow on fire or on a lamp to extinguish it. The Muhammadan will blow on fire to fan it into greater flame, but the Hindu will not do even this. A sacrificial fire or *hom* can only be fanned, and should the worshipper blow on it he would harm both himself and the officiating priest. In the case of domestic fires these can be blown upon with a bamboo pipe or across the extended palm, for the use of the pipe and the palm is supposed to rob the human breath of its evil potentiality. A fire which *Marāṭhās* use to boil water for washing a corpse is always fanned with a winnowing-fan, and professional potters, *Kumbhārs*, use the same fan to fan their fire when making pots and bricks. Though *Jains* have no sacrificial *hom*, they will not blow on a fire or lamp. Should a woman *enceinte* blow on a fire, as a result of the resentment of the *kudrat* of the fire she would have an abortion, in the opinion of the Muhammadan.

Extinguishing a fire is no simple matter. In another chapter we have seen the general avoidance by Hindu and Muhammadan of even speaking directly of putting out a fire or a lamp. A fire cannot be extinguished by throwing in it *uṣṭe* water, or water which is left over after a meal; neither can *kharkaṭe* water which contains remnants of food be thrown into fire. The Sindi Muhammadan will not throw into fire dirty water nor even hot or boiling water. Quite general, too, is the prohibition of throwing any kind of water whatsoever on to the hearth. *Haranṣikārīs* will not put out a fire with any kind of water lest in consequence their dead should suffer from lack of food, though on a death throughout the village of the deceased all domestic fires are extinguished by this caste by throwing water on the hearth. A death not uncommonly breaks the uniform application of rule, and among *Kātkarīs* after a funeral the mourners return to the house of the deceased and each of them deliberately throws water into a fire of cowdung fuel. *Ghantichors*, *Bestars*, *Dong-Dasaris* and *Koravas* draw the embers of a fire quite away from a hearth before they extinguish them with water. Extinguishing a lamp is usually done by fanning it, or by drawing the wicks aside.

Fire must be preserved from all impure contacts. As sleep is an impure state neither Hindu nor Muhammadan will sleep near fire; a Brahmin will not have a fire in the sleeping-room, and the common practice of extinguishing a fire before going to sleep is a protection of the fire rather than the protection of the sleepers. One who has just slept must purify himself by a bath before he can approach a fire. If a menstruous woman touches a fire it must be extinguished, all the half-consumed wood must be thrown away, and the hearth must be cleaned with cowdung to make it pure. The Hindu cleans his hearth every day with cowdung; the Muhammadan, who does not think cowdung pure, cleans his whole house with it, saving his place for prayers and his hearth. A pregnant woman must not sit on charcoal or ashes or approach a fire. It is forbidden to spit in fire; the penalty for doing this is a blistered tongue. One cannot relieve nature near fire or approach it after doing this. A fire cannot be stepped over, nor can any one touch it with his feet; the feet cannot even be warmed at a fire, unless so turned that the soles do not face the fire. If a woman throws into fire her hair-combings she loses her hair. The Muhammadan equally strictly avoids throwing in fire cut hair, nail-clippings or any form of ordure.

The power of fire, like other power, must not be destroyed by contact with the ground. A domestic fire usually has its hearth specially prepared, and on this tulsī (Ocimum sanctum) leaves are placed and on these the material of the fire. If a fire has to be lighted hurriedly when travelling, a Hindu will cover the ground with leaves before lighting a fire. A Sindi Muhammadan sprinkles salt on the ground before he lights a fire. In parts of Kanara, leaves of the coconut palm are placed on the ground before lighting the *Hoḻī* fire. Fire must be preserved from the sun. For all *hom* the fire is brought covered with a leaf in a plate of copper or brass. The *Hoḻī* fire, though often to-day lighted in the daytime, should strictly be lighted only after sunset, and its kindling during the day should cause the burning of the whole village within a year.

A lamp is not placed on the ground either by the Hindu or the Muhammadan. A lamp should not be lighted in the sun, and if an *ārtī* is carried out of doors during the day it must be protected. Elsewhere I have described how fire has to be protected from the impure and dangerous contact of iron.

Fire is associated with fertility. To the presence therein of fire is due the fertility of trees. So also there is fire in water and in the sea. The element of fire in the sea is represented by the mythical creation, *Vaḍvāgni*, which is a *devak* in one Marāṭhā family. Because there is fire in water, *agne ra pah*, water can be used in *ārtī*, when a lamp is likely to be blown out. It is so used in the daily worship of gods and when the central figure of a ceremony, such as a bridegroom, makes his first return from a procession or journey, to remove the evil effects of contacts effected by sight. Water can also be used in a *hom*, *av bhrat snān*. In the worship of all gods, but in particular *Maruti* and *Venkoba*, a pit is dug in front of the temple and filled with water coloured with saffron and a kind of camphor. A bathing *abhiṣek* of the god is then made with the water which is finally sprinkled over those present. Then the image is taken to a well, put in a plate and sprinkled with the water of the well, *pāṇī hom*, 'water fire'. Any water which remains in the plate is sprinkled over those attending the ceremony. Women without issue have the image held over them as the water is poured over them. The water, as it contains fire, is supposed to foster fertility. The character again of a gift is determined by the return the donor wishes to obtain. In order to obtain issue a light fed with ghee in a gold or silver stand, *nīlānjan*, is given to a priest.

A number of *homs* are associated with fertility. One *hom* rarely performed nowadays is the *Karyeriṣṭi hom* in the offering to which rice or barley is added. This *hom* should be performed before the sowing of a crop and its object is to produce good crops. Another *hom*, the *putrakameṣṭi*, one celebration of which was performed at Sholapur in 1908, betrays its purpose in its name as that of fostering childbirth; this is seldom performed nowadays because of its great expense, and in its stead are substituted the *Nāgabaḷī* and *Nārāyanbaḷī*. During the marriage ceremony of Hindus, after the *lājāhom* the bride is taken thrice round the fire and she prays *Agni* to bless her with children; during the consummation ceremony again two *homs*, the *Suryopasthān* and *Agnupasthān*, are lighted, and these are supposed to make her *enceinte*. During the marriage ceremony, *Lingāyats* carry lighted torches of ingal (Barringtonia acutangula) to the temple of Virbhadra, son of Śiva; these torches are worshipped by the bridal pair and then thrown on the roof of the temple with the object of bringing the married pair issue and happiness. On the Hindu New Year's Day in Belgaum, pits are dug in the open and fire is brought by *Mahārs* from the patil's house, and thrown into the pits; women then with a prayer to *Agni* to give them children throw into the fire *haḻad*, *kunku* and *akṣat*. Childless *Vaddar* women vow if they get issue to walk through the fire-pit before the temple of their goddess *Huligevvā*, on the day of the goddess's annual car festival. When a Hindu girl reaches puberty, before she is sent to her husband's house she is made to sit with her husband near a *hom*; this is supposed to give her issue, *garbhādhān vidhi*. Fire is so closely connected with the idea of fertility that it can never be carried by an unmarried girl, but is always carried by a *suvāsinī* or married woman, and preferably by one who has borne children.

The Muhammadan also has some practices which are based on a belief that fire fosters fertility. In Sind, if a woman is long without issue she calls many small children and places them all around a fire, feeds them, and asks them to pray that she may have issue. The ashes from the fires maintained at shrines are also brought away, and eaten by women who desire offspring. In the southern parts of the Presidency *Muḥarram* is observed by Muhammadans, in many ways not followed by the Muhammadan in Sind, and perhaps in part copied from Hindu practice. One of the principal features of *Muḥarram* celebrations in the Deccan and in the Karnāṭak is the digging of a large pit called *Ālāwā* which is filled with fire. After the fall of night Muhammadan women, as also Hindu women, come to the pit with a child in their arms, and holding the child crouch under a cloth spread on their heads, whilst a man shovels on to their head the burning ashes of the fire three times and an assistant brushes away the ashes that cling to the covering before they have time to burn through. The children held by the women in their arms may be children of their own born after the taking of a vow, or borrowed from other women for the occasion. In either case the shovelling on to their heads of the fire, and the other practice of walking through the burning wood ashes, distinctly evidence the belief that fertility is a transferrable attribute of fire.

Fire is the semen of the god Śiva. *Tej* is a common word for fire as it is for the human seed. The human seed is produced by the fire latent in the human body. Sacred story relates that *Agni*, weary of his task of transferring the offerings of men, made in fire, to the gods, sheltered in a pipal-tree (Ficus religiosa). The gods found him and churned him out, on which account *Agnihotrīs* produce fire by means of a fire-drill, and women wanting issue go round a pipal-tree both by the right-hand circuit, *pradakṣiṇā*, and by the left-hand circuit, *apradakṣiṇā*. The *śakti* of *Agni* is invoked into the wristlets or *kankaṇ* of the bridal pair, and at one *Lingāyat* marriage I attended I found *Agni* invoked into the *hālgamba*. The production of fire by the *Agnihotrī* is spoken of as the birth of a son, and the fire spark is fondled as if it were a baby, but the simile of sexual creation is not applied merely to the fire created by one under a vow of *Agnihotra*, for the pit or altar constructed for every *hom* should be measured by the measurements of the *yajamān* who is called the *yoni* (Muliere pudendum) of the fire.

The practice of extinguishing a fire in a house when one of its inmates has died, found in many parts of the world, appears in its literal form among some of the more primitive races only of the Presidency. On a death, *Vaddars* take the fire from the domestic hearth and kindling it outside the house prepare on it a pot of *jvārī* gruel. The gruel is taken with the corpse to the burying-ground, and upset on the ground before the body is buried. After preparing the gruel the fire is extinguished, and no fire can be lighted in the house until the mourners return from the funeral, having washed their hands and feet in a tank. *Kātkarīs* on a death, extinguish all fires in the house of the deceased and in the houses of all tribesmen in the village, and allow no fire to be kindled or food taken until the corpse has been buried or burnt. The fire which is taken to the pyre must be freshly prepared as is the custom of many castes. *Haraṇśikārīs* also extinguish all fire in their houses throughout the village on the death of a tribesman. *Brahmins, Lingāyats, Marāṭhās,* and in the southern parts of the Presidency Muhammadans, do not follow this practice. In Sind when a man dies his household cannot light a fire for three days.

At his marriage the Brahmin bridegroom takes an oath in the presence of fire to maintain *Śrota* and *Smārta* fires, the former the fire of *Agnihotra*, and the latter the fire kindled in the *Lājāhom* at his marriage, which should be maintained as long as the husband and wife are alive, and on the death of either should be put on the pyre. This oath is kept by few to-day, so when an elderly Brahmin dies, who has not maintained a perpetual fire since his marriage, a *hom* is prepared from the ordinary household fire and from it fire is taken to the pyre, the object of this being to purify the deceased from his sins. In the Karnāṭak, Brahmins do not forbid mourners seeing fire, but the persons who actually perform the obsequies are not to see fire; in their absence from the house the necessary cooking is done by others, and the house fire is extinguished daily before these particular mourners return and cannot be relighted before they have taken a bath. If a widower, in the absence of grown-up sons, performs the obsequies of his deceased wife himself, he must not see the household fire on his return from the burning ghat. In general, fire is not polluted by the touch of mourners, nor are they forbidden to see it among the more advanced Hindus. Certain fires, on the other hand, destroy the *sutak* or contagion, which usually attaches to mourners. Even though the corpse of an *Agnihotrī* remains in the house, the inmates of the house and other relatives of the deceased are not considered impure. Similarly, *sutak* does not attach, even if they be mourners, to those performing a *yajna* or other sacrifice; they are not considered mourners so long as they are in the *yajnyasata*. The maintenance of a sacred fire is as the performance of any *karma* such as a *Śrāddha* or a marriage; those engaged in such a task are pure until the ceremony is over, when they must bathe and observe mourning. In the case of the death of an *Agnihotrī*, *sutak* does not arise until his body has been kindled on the pyre.

Fire must not be touched by a girl on her attaining puberty. She cannot also light a lamp, Hindu and Muhammadan enforcing the same prohibition. The room in which she is set apart must not be near the kitchen. The Muhammadan protects many embodiments of *kudrat* from contact with a woman in her menses, but he allows her to touch fire; the Hindu, on the other hand, will not allow her even to throw water on fire, protecting fire from the virus of her power, *viṭāḻ*. For a limited number of days a Hindu woman after the birth of her child is forbidden to touch fire; from the *suher* or *suver*, the contagion of birth, fire must be shielded. In some Hindu families the bride for a year after her marriage cannot approach a fire.

It is inauspicious for a Brahmin who has his father alive to touch the ordinary domestic fire, as a Brahmin carries fire for the first time in his life, when he carries it to the pyre on the death of a parent. He should not kindle the ordinary fire for cooking purposes or for heating water. He may, however, kindle and tend the fire of a *hom* or sacrifice, and during many a sacrament is required to worship fire; he may also carry embers from one *hom* to another. The carrying of fire to a *hom* accordingly may be the work of a *suvāsinī*, a married woman or of a man. If fire be taken from a domestic hearth a man cannot touch it and it is brought by a married woman; if the fire be brought from another *hom* a man may carry it in the absence of a *suvāsinī*. If it be brought from the fire of an *Agnihotrī* it is generally taken from its pit by the *Agnihotrī* himself or by his wife, and then carried by a *suvāsinī*, but it may be carried by a man if there be no married woman available.

The power of fire should not be brought in conflict with certain other manifestations of power. From a utilitarian point of view it may be advisable to run no risks by having fire or a lamp on the threshing-floor near inflammable grain, but the rule that fire or a lamp should not be brought on the floor is based on the idea of a conflict of two *śaktis*. In Gujarāt there seems to be no such idea, and lamps are placed on the pile of grain after threshing, as a protection against spirits. In other parts even to speak of fire is forbidden, and fire when alluded to is spoken of as 'increase' or as 'wind'. Salt must not be thrown in fire save deliberately to scare away spirits. Wool must not be thrown in fire. A Muhammadan will not throw in fire flowers, green leaves, curds or milk, nor will he take the Koran near a fire. A written charm cannot be dried near fire. If milk boils over into fire the evil consequences of a loss of milk and the illness of the cow can be avoided by throwing rice-grain into the fire. Fire should not be carried near fruit-trees in blossom, among sheep or into a cattle-shed. The antipathy of fire to rain means that taking fire out of doors uncovered must be avoided when welcome rain-clouds are gathering, but that rain can be brought to an end when desired by throwing out of doors burning embers or torches. When a Hindu is burnt to death his relatives are advised to erect some water-work, by which the spirit of the dead is, as it were, married to the *śakti* of water. Should children throw fire carelessly out of doors they urinate in their beds.

It is bad to turn one's back to fire. If fire be taken behind one's back one must look straight at the fire at once or harm will befall one's brother. If fire be carried from one house to another after sunset the house parting with the fire becomes extinct. Fire carried between two persons promotes quarrels. If fire be taken from under a pot of boiling water a child in the house gets a disease of the scalp, and loses its hair. A lamp that burns ground-nut oil must never be placed on the threshold. A lamp must not be bought on a Saturday or an *Amāvāsyā*; it cannot be lent or given away after sunset. If a lamp goes out while one is eating one must place one's hand on the lamp, remember the sun, rekindle the lamp and eat what was left of one's food in the dish but no more. A lamp with a wick towards the south brings bad fortune, and a disgraceful person is called in Marāṭhī a 'lamp of the south', *dākṣiṇecā divā*. There are Hindus who will never allow others to light their lamps for them.

In Hindu temples *nandādīp* are kept burning night and day; these must not be of iron, nor must they touch the ground; they are suspended or are placed on stands of wood or brass. They must never go out. Their wicks must be single ones or a lamp may have two or four wicks, no one of which must be turned towards the south. Lamps are lighted when *Purāṇa* are recited or when *jap*, 'silent prayer', is performed, and are not extinguished until the recitation or prayer is finished. At some Muhammadan shrines such as that of Kalandar Shahbaz at Sehwan, of Uderolal in Nawabshah district, and of Shah Abdul Latif Bhitai in the Shahdadpur district, perpetual fires are maintained. These fires represent the *kudrat*, the hot power of the saint. Wherever the disciples of these saints settle they maintain a fire; this fire can be brought from anywhere, but it must not be kindled *in situ* with matches. There are shrines, too, such as that of Bachal Shahji Miani near Sukkur, where a lamp is kept and pilgrims give oil for its upkeep for definite periods.

ASHES

Prasād is a term applied to certain things that by contact with divinity or great power have acquired *śakti*. In the glossary of this book I have mentioned some of the things that fall under this definition. Though the ordinary light kept burning perpetually in a temple, and the sweepings of a temple might reasonably be expected to have acquired *śakti*, they are not, however, *prasād*. Now, ashes may be the remains of offerings; they also represent to a Hindu what finally is left after the destruction of the cosmos. They are accordingly *prasād*, 'the favour of God', and to them great power is attributed. They remove accumulated sin; they cure disease; they promote wealth; they bring a man's labours to success; they dispel the evils wrought by spirits; they bring *mokṣa* or release from reincarnation.

Particular ashes have more than ordinary power. The ashes of the *Holī* fire avert the *pīḍā* or the evil influence of the planets; afford protection from epidemics; promote the well-being of children; avert evil from crops and from the threshing-floor. Ashes from a potter's kiln are used in many ways. On Sundays they are sprinkled in silence on brinjal and chilli crops to keep away pests. If a *Vaddar* is bedstricken, his father or an elderly relative first goes to a temple before sunrise, and then brings home ashes from a blacksmith or from a potter or from both, without speaking to any one. Some of the ashes are then applied to the body of the sick man, and the rest are tied in a cloth to a beam above his bed and from them every day till the following Sunday, some are taken and rubbed on the invalid's body. Ashes from a potter's kiln also avert the effects of the evil eye. Potters are reluctant to give their ashes away as they fear a loss of *barkat*, and so potters' ashes are usually stolen. Ashes from a potter are mixed with water and given to a pregnant woman to drink should there be any fear of her premature delivery. Before burying a corpse *Lingāyats* take a potter's ashes and sprinkle round the grave.

Ashes from a pyre are applied to victims of spirit possession; they are administered to the sick to produce sleep; they are mixed with cotton-seed before sowing to ensure a good crop and one free from blight; they are put in a coconut-shell and buried in a cattle-shed to make the cattle healthy; they are rubbed on the bodies of cattle to cure certain diseases or avert the consequences of evil-eye. Contact with ashes from a pyre, it is believed in the Deccan, promotes child-bearing. Some *Śūdras* who have not the right to use *vibhūti* store ashes from a pyre, and apply them during worship to their images but not to their own persons.

Ashes from their furnace are applied by goldsmiths every morning before they begin work, to all their instruments and to their own forehead.

The ashes of particular *hom*, such as *Durvahom*, are particularly efficacious, but the ashes of all *hom* are applied to the body as these ashes possess the power of the Vedic mantras recited when the *hom* were celebrated. Every one who visits a temple of *Maruti* takes ashes from a vessel kept in the temple, and applies them to his forehead or puts a little in his mouth. *Bhairagis* apply them to their whole body. Persons who do this secure a lasting protection against spirits and disease. When setting out on a journey, to ensure success in his undertaking, a Hindu will go to a temple of his favourite deity, and taking ashes therefrom will tie them in a corner of his garments. Ashes from a shrine are given to all who visit the shrine and oaths are taken by these ashes, *angār*.

Some castes use ashes in lieu of cowdung to purify the place where food is taken. To scare away a cobra ashes are strewn all round a house, leaving the circle broken for the cobra to escape;

around a cattle-pen they are strewn to keep away pests. Charmed ashes are used to cure the bite of a scorpion and are blown over a person possessed by spirits; they are given to a child to eat or applied to its body when as a result of evil-eye it cannot eat, or when it cries aimlessly from the persecution of spirits.

For ten days after the birth of a Hindu child a priest repeats mantras over ashes, which are applied to the body of the child to avert evil-eye. When a man is on his death-bed ashes are applied to his feet and hands to create heat. Mantriks use ashes to obtain communion with the dead.

Ashes are applied to images during their worship. *Berads*, *Talwārs* and others use ashes from a pyre for this purpose. Ashes used as *vibhūti* are applied to the forehead and other parts of the body by Brahmins, exclusive of Vaiṣṇavas, and by *Lingāyats*. Brahmin *suvāsinīs* cannot use ashes, but tonsured widows may do so. *Lingāyats* believe that *vibhūti* applied to the forehead effaces the ominous writing of Brahma on the forehead, *Brāhmalikhit*. Smārts use ashes daily, *bhasma*, and when their sacred thread is renewed use ashes for a bath, *bhasma snān*.

The use of ashes to scare away spirits is not confined to the Hindu. In Sind ashes soaked in water are drunk by a Muhammadan when possessed by spirits.

The hearth and its ashes are to the Sindi Muhammadan intimately associated with the concept of *kudrat*. When a hearth is broken he throws it into water. There are three points to a hearth called *mārang*. If one of these be broken it is repaired at once or preserved carefully, for if it should fall into the hands of an enemy, he could destroy the peace of the household by writing on it the names of the family members, and then breaking the *mārang* into pieces. A Muhammadan is reluctant to give ashes or embers from his fire to kindle another, from fear of losing *barkat* thereby. Through ashes strewn on her way he can bring a woman under his control; he can by throwing ashes into the house of another for a period of forty days bring the other all the effects of a curse; contrariwise, if the ashes of his fire be stolen by an enemy he will suffer from the latter's evil magic. A Muhammadan woman when *enceinte* is not allowed to sit on ashes, because of the evil that may be done to her in malice through the ashes.

LAMPS

There are several terms used to describe the waving of things in front of a person to avert evil. *Nicchāvar* is the waving of coconuts, money and other things in front of a person in order to avert evil, especially the evil of the eye; these things so waved are usually given to a *corpus vile*. *Paracchan* is the driving away of spirits; in this rite rice-cakes and other things are waved round the victim with small lighted wicks; chillies, too, are put on burning embers and after being waved are thrown far away. *Nivāḻi* is a waving of cooked rice, salt, pepper, and other things in front of a person or in front of the goddess *Kali* to ward off evil; among the articles waved are sometimes small lighted wicks.

Besides these, there is the waving of a lamp or *ārtī* (*ovāḻaṇī*). This can be performed with water as well as with fire as there is fire in water. The object of waving *ārtī* is *ariṣṭa nivāraṇ*, to ward off evil, and *iṣṭa prāpti*, 'to obtain *barkat*', for *barkat* comes when evil has been averted. Among *Lingāyats* when a man dies, his wife waves *ārtī* round his dead body whilst it still lies in the house, so that the deceased may not become an evil spirit.

Ārtī is usually waved by *suvāsinīs*, that is by married women. *Suvāsinīs* wave it round the bridegroom when he reaches the confines of the bride's village; round the bridal pair at the moment *akṣat* is thrown upon them; at the end of the *lājāhom*, *suvāsinīs* of the bridegroom's relations wave it round the bridal pair, and after the *Mangaḻsnān*, *suvāsinīs* from among the relatives of the bride wave it round the bride and bridegroom. The Brahmin does not wave it round his *devak*, but those castes that have the *hāḻgamba* wave *ārtī* round it in the temple where it is first worshipped, and place it near the *hāḻgamba* in the marriage *manḍap*. At a birth married women wave *ārtī* round the child and the mother; around the child only immediately it is born and round both the child and mother after the child's navel-cord has been cut. At the tonsure ceremony and again at the thread ceremony *ārtī* is waved round the child.

Ārtī is used daily in the worship of the *kul devatā*. It is waved round standing crops and round the pile of grain on the threshing-floor; it is waved round a newly purchased animal. It is waved over a river when it is worshipped. Amongst *Lingāyats* and non-Brahmins a month after the birth of her child a mother goes to a river and waves *ārtī*. Before a *Lingāyat* marriage water is brought from a river for the *mangaḻsnān* of the bridal pair, and at this time *suvāsinīs* worship the river and wave *ārtī*. On Karka Sankramaṇa, Brahmins go to a river and *suvāsinīs* wave *ārtī*.

Ārtī is waved over the site to be executed for a new well. It is waved in front of trees. When an *Agnihotrī* cuts his twigs of aśvath to produce fire he waves *ārtī* round the tree and asks its forgiveness. It is waved round an aśvath tree whenever it is worshipped on an *Amāvāsyā* coinciding with a Monday. During the whole month of Kārttik it is waved round the tulsī daily before sunrise because Viṣṇu then manifests himself in the plant in a greater degree than usual. It is waved on the twelfth sud of the same month when the tulsī is married to Kṛṣṇa. On the twelfth of the bright half of Aṣāḍha it is waved round the tulsī in the evening because Viṣṇu that evening retires to rest. On the full-moon day of Kārttik it is waved round the dhatri (Phyllanthus emblica) because Viṣṇu then manifests himself in that tree. Śiva manifests himself in the bilva tree (Aegle marmelos) on the fourteenth of the dark half of Māgh, so *Lingāyats* wave *ārtī* round the tree at this time, whilst those who have vowed to do so do this every Monday. Smārt Brahmins wave *ārtī* round the atti tree (Ficus glomerata) on the full-moon day of Mārgaśīrṣa because *Dattātreya* manifests himself in the tree on that day. In this waving of *ārtī* both men and women join, an exception to the usual practice which confines the waving of *ārtī* to married women.

On Narakcāturmās during Divāḻī, *ārtī* is waved round the whole family and friends. It is waved round a sannyāsī who comes as a guest; round a child when it is named and on every annual birthday of the child until it attains the age of ten or twelve, and again when it is first given solid food.

An *ārtī* can never be lighted by a widow, though she could light an ordinary lamp. In all auspicious ceremonies, *mangalkārya*, it consists of two small pots, not unlike egg-cups, called *nīlānjan* placed on a dish or *tāmhaṇ*. Each *nīlānjan* has two wicks placed across the top of the pot so as to point towards the four cardinal points. One *nīlānjan* only is used when a lamp is waved over the dead. An *ārtī* is supposed to contain all *śakti*, but if a *nīlānjan* is shaken out of its plate and the light goes out, the *śakti* of the *ārtī* is lost, and death comes to some member of the family using it. When an *ārtī* has been waved before a sacred image it acquires *śakti* from the image, and is considered *prasād*, whereas touching a lamp, *nandādīp*, kept burning constantly in a temple would not give the worshipper the *prasād* of the deity.

Ārtī is waved before a single image. On the thirteenth day of the obsequies it is waved round the chief mourner and round him alone. With these exceptions *ārtī* cannot be waved round anything that is single. When a girl attains puberty and *ārtī* is waved before her, she is required to hold a doll, or in Kanara a coconut to represent a second person. When a bridegroom, a returned traveller or a pilgrim is honoured with *ārtī*, a girl or a boy is required to sit with him or stand by his side.

As the Muhammadan considers it inauspicious to wave a lamp round the head he has no practice parallel to this waving of *ārtī* by the Hindu. A Muhammadan will not even wave a lighted stick lest he suffer from an excess of urine.

Soot formed on a finger when this is put in the flame of an *ārtī* is used to avert evil-eye and spirits. *Lingāyats* apply such soot to the forehead of a child on each of its first eight birthdays; it is applied to the bridal pair, to the boy at his thread ceremony; it is daubed on the central pillar or on a wall of a house entered upon for the first time; it is also rubbed on the bodies of cattle.

Besides the special form of lamp, the *ārtī*, which is so prominent a feature of Hindu ritual, lamps are used on many an occasion to avert evil. In *śānti* ceremonies when a *baḻī* is offered to gods or spirits to avert anticipated evil it contains in its usual form, cooked rice, black gram and a lamp. This lamp is waved round the *yajamān* and his wife and perhaps round his children also, and is then taken to a river without its touching the ground, by a man who must not look back as he goes, and behind whom others sprinkle water. During *Divāḻī* young boys take a lamp in a basket of leaves and wave it before the bullocks saying, '*Iḍā pīḍā jodige yettina piḍā hoḻī dāti hogali*', 'May evil with that of the oxen go beyond the river'. In Kanara among the *Hālakki, Vakkals*, the *Devars, Ambigers, Madivals* and others there is a rite called *Taḻige baṭṭalu*, to which corresponds a rite among *Haviks* called *Bittakki*. The *Taḻige baṭṭalu* is a copper plate containing rice, a pot of water with a mango-twig inside it and a coconut as a cover, and a light fed with oil. This plate has to be carried by the sisters of the bride and bridegroom wherever the bridal pair go, from the beginning to the end of the marriage ceremony, and its object is to avert evil in general, and in particular evil-eye. In the Karnāṭak and in Kanara is another rite called *Airaṇī*. Five squares one within another are drawn with *akṣat* of five colours; at the four corners of the outside square and at the centre of all the squares are placed five *kalaśas*, each with a covering plate on which is a light. The *Airaṇī* is walked round five times by five persons, namely the bridal pair and the parents and the uncle of the bride. At a marriage among *Raddis*, after *akṣat* has been thrown on the bridal pair, a common feast is held (*bhum*). At this twenty to twenty-five plates of cakes (*hoḻiga*) are served, and on many of these lights are lighted. A more general custom on the last day of the marriage, is for the parents of the bride to make a gift to the bridegroom's father of sixteen winnowing-fans, containing cakes of flour on which small lights are lighted.

In the Panch Mahals a lamp is placed on the pile of grain on the threshing-floor as a protection against spirits; in the Konkan with the same object a small lamp of flour is lighted on the grain, *rās*, after sunset. Around the lamp used in the Panch Mahals four other small lamps are arranged according to the cardinal points. A betelnut wrapped in cloth and burning ground-nut oil is used as a lamp, and tied to the post in the marriage *maṇḍap* to which the *Marāṭhā devak* is attached. *Kātkaris* place a lamp near the buried navel-cord of a child. A lamp made of wheaten flour with a wick of cotton burning in ghee is one of the ingredients of a *parḍī* offering before or after the grain on the threshing-floor is measured. A lamp burns night and day in the innermost part of a temple, and the room in which a woman has just given birth to a child is protected for several days by a lamp. In all these cases protection is provided against evil spirits.

In the conception of power, and the correlation of good and evil, as Indian thought pictures it, it is not difficult to find some inconsistency, as manifestations of power are used to avert an evil from which they are not themselves immune. Water is used to avert spirits, yet water is haunted by spirits; trees are susceptible to evil-eye, yet trees and their parts are used to avert the evil of the eye. There is the same contradiction in the use of fire to avert spirits, for fire is haunted by spirits. The Muhammadan believes that *jinn* were created from fire, and that ashes are the food of spirits, and that burning the homes of men is at times the sport of spirits. The Hindu finds the presence of spirits betrayed by sudden fires appearing in the jungle, near water or on the sea-shore; he forbids children playing with fire after sunset lest spirits, *kolli devv*, 'torch spirits', play with it. A Muhammadan again takes great care at a funeral to leave no light or fire near the grave lest a spirit should enter the grave. Sleeping near fire is regarded as dangerous by both the Hindu and the Muhammadan because of the presence of spirits. On the other hand, fire in many ways scares away spirits.

After the *lājāhom* at a marriage a lemon is put at the end of a sword or knife and held in the flame of a lamp placed on the head of the bride's mother. The soot formed on the lemon is applied to the cheeks of the bridal pair to avert spirits and is called *Śindupa*. The waving of *ārtī* prevents a dead person becoming a spirit, and as we have already seen, lamps and ashes are used in many ways to avert spirits. In the Karnāṭak on a birth, a cup of wheat flour if the infant be a girl, and of copra nut if the child be a boy, is placed in front of the mother and baby. The cup has four wicks fed with ghee; the knife with which the navel-cord of the child was severed is held over the wicks, and the soot forming on the blade and on the lemon stuck at the end of it, is applied to the eyes of the mother and child to scare away spirits. *Kaḻḻ* or *Adivi Koravas* bury their dead; one mourner carries a pot of water round the grave and another following makes holes in it with a scythe; then a large stone is placed near the head of the dead and on this the pot is smashed. Fire is also taken in a new earthen pot to the grave and after the burial is thrown near the big stone, with the object of keeping away spirits, and to further this object the more fragrant things are burnt in the fire.

Hālusorog or 'milk-disease' in jvārī and sugar-cane is attributed to the activity of spirits. On a Thursday or Sunday, therefore, at midnight an exorcist or a strong-minded person carries through and round the fields a torch of cotton and hemp, and the disease is supposed in the Karnāṭak to vanish within a week.

When a lamp is lighted for the first time every evening some Hindus repeat a Sanscrit verse, 'Let good come; good health and wealth; let there be no enmity in us. We salute the lighted wick'. This is said with covered head and hands joined in benediction; the young children in the house then bow to the family gods, and then to their elders. In the Karnāṭak Muhammadans also salaam the lamp at lighting-time.

THE AGNIHOTRĪ

In strict theory every Brahmin should take the vow of *Agnihotra*, to maintain a perpetual fire, but the actual number of those who do so is comparatively small, as in the ordinary occupations of life it is impossible to observe the many restrictions that are placed on the conduct of those who take the vow.

Before a man can take this vow he and his wife must be ritually pure, and to ensure this they perform a *Prayascitta* called *Sarvaprayascitta*, and perform also three *hom* ceremonies called respectively *Kūśmanḍ hom*, *Gaṇ hom*, and *Varjā hom*, all of which are an atonement for any omission of observances in the past. This purification ritual lasts a whole day. On the next day the first rites of *Agnihotra* really begin. First of all the man and his wife celebrate *Puṇyāhavācana*. This ceremony is performed by Brahmins at the beginning of every auspicious ceremony (*mangalkārya*) and is an invocation of divine blessing. First of all the god *Gaṇpati* is invoked into a coconut or betelnut. Then a site is embellished with stone powder (*rāngoḻī*) and on it is placed a plantain leaf; on this in turn rice is spread and on this again two water-pots or *kalaśas* containing water, leaves of five trees, *pancpallava,* seven kinds of earth, five kinds of gems and gold. On top of the *kalaśas* are placed two gold, silver or copper dishes containing rice (*pūrṇapātra*). In each dish is put a coconut and these nuts are worshipped by the man and his wife, after invoking the *śakti* of the god *Varuṇa* into each coconut. This is followed by the *yajamān* and his wife offering libations of water to all gods and demi-gods, and invoking their blessing on the ceremony contemplated; finally, one of the priests present pronounces a blessing on the *yajamān,* and after dismissing the *kalaśas* takes water from them and sprinkles over the *yajamān* and his wife.

The next step taken by the *Agniḥotrī,* and this with the aid of his wife, is the installation of *Nāndi, Nāndisthāpan,* that is the worship of *Nandinī, Nalinī, Umā, Maitrā, Paṣuvardhinī* and *Śastragarbha.* He next makes a *hom, Smārt Siddhi hom,* from the fire of the *Lājāhom* which he has tended since his marriage. This fire ought to be maintained by all Brahmins from the day of their marriage; it is not produced by attrition but taken from the family hearth by the *yajamān's* wife. Actually few Brahmins maintain this *Smārtagni* from their marriage, and when later they maintain it have to produce it by attrition. After the celebration of this *hom* the *Agnihotrī* shaves completely and bathes. He then himself cooks rice on the fire of the *hom,* and feeds four priests with the rice and with milk which is called *Brahmodān*; then he heats the *araṇi* pieces of wood over the same fire and puts them aside. Taking half of the fire he puts it in a pit dug in the south-eastern corner of his room and extinguishes the rest of the fire with water (*Śrotriyāgār*). This is followed by a meal with his wife in which spices and salt are avoided, the meal consisting of cooked rice and cow's milk only. The next day he rises about three in the morning; he bathes, as does his wife, and priests are invited and allotted parts to perform.

Assisted by the priests, the man and his wife proceed to produce fire by means of a fire-drill. The upper drill of this instrument, the *uttarāraṇi* and the block in which it works, the *adharaṇi,* must be from a pipal (Ficus religiosa) tree that has grown with a śamī tree (Prosopis spicigera). Such a tree is called *Śamīgarbha,* 'born from the womb of the śamī', the śamī being considered female and the pipal male. The *adharaṇi* is called *yonipātra,* emblematic of the female principle, and in length is one cubit of the *yajamān,* and four to five inches in diameter; the śamī wood is used for the *adharaṇi* and the wood of the pipal for the drill. This idea of sexual union is not confined to the process of making fire by friction. The pestle of an oil-press is made of sagdi (Schleichera trijuga), the lac tree, and the mortar of undi (Calophyllum inophyllum), the Alexandrian laurel, and of these the former is considered male and the latter female. In Sind the component parts of a sugar-cane press are similarly regarded as male and female.

The wood that holds the drill is called *mantha*, and the horizontal beam above it *upamantha*, and both these are made from tere wood, a species of cedar. The upper end of the *mantha*, where it fits into the beam, should be tipped with copper, but in practice it has an iron tip in violation of the strict rule forbidding the use of iron.

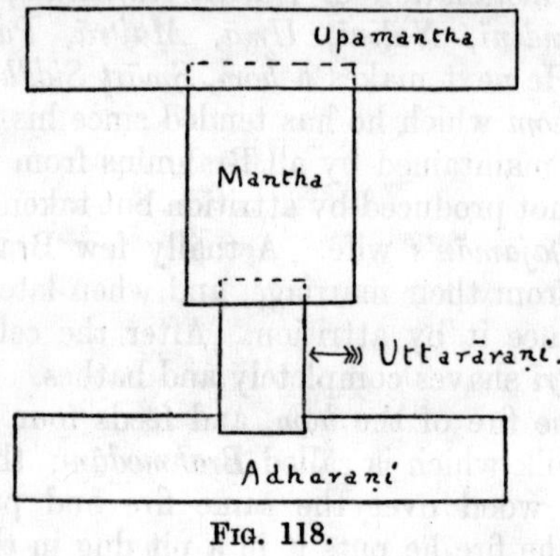

Fig. 118.

It is essential that the attrition should be begun by the man and his wife. A coir string is used to make the drill revolve and this is held by the *Agnihotrī's* wife. Shavings of pipal-wood are kept near to feed the fire. If fire is not soon made, the failure is attributed to the immorality of the *Agnihotrī* and his wife, who must memorize their immoral acts and make a loud recital of them before all who are present. The production of the fire is the birth of a son to the *Agnihotrī* ; the fire spark is at once captured in a copper dish, fondled as a child and fed with pipal-shavings, and dry cowdung cakes. Sandal-wood or the wood of the jack tree may also be used at first, but later any wood may be used except mango and Strychnos nux vomica. When the fire has caught the shavings it is put in a pit, and a *hom* is prepared with nine kinds of grain and ghee, and from this *hom* a second *hom* is prepared in a second pit called *dakṣiṇā* or 'southern'. All the ceremony up to this point must be completed before sunrise, for if longer time be taken, all the rites are vitiated and must be commenced again from the beginning. A third *hom* is made in the *āhavanīya* pit with fire taken from the second pit, and in this offerings of ghee are made just at the moment when the sun is half-above the horizon.

The first fire is the store of *Agni*; the *Gārhapatya*, 'the government of a house', is in the western part of the fire-room; the eastern pit is square, the *Āhavanīya*, 'that which is used for invoking'; that on the south is semicircular, the *Dakṣaṇagni*. The southern pit is for offerings to the *pitṛs*, the square one for

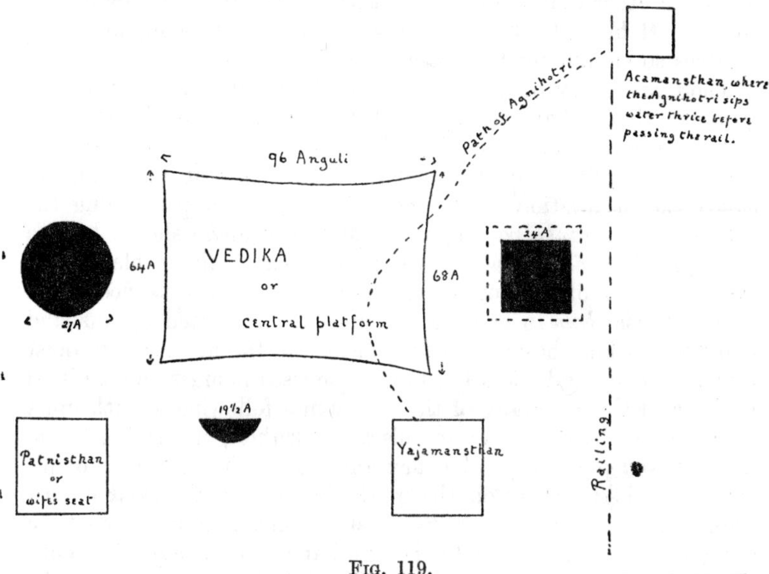

Fig. 119.

The dotted line from the Acamansthan to the Yajamansthan is the path taken by the Agnihotrī, who alone can cross the Vedika.

worship of the gods, and the principal pit for that of their consorts. The first and third fires are called the son and grandson of the second fire.

During the whole of these rites the *Agnihotrī* and his wife are preserved from contact with the ground, for they sit on kuśa grass or the skin of an antelope; they are forbidden to use wooden *pāṭ*, so familiar a means of insulation. The *araṇi* and *adharaṇi* are placed on the same kind of *āsan*; these are kept by the *Agnihotrī* and his wife for life; if they be lost a purificatory *prayascitta* is necessary and the process of creating fire has to be begun again. When either the *Agnihotrī* or his wife dies the pieces are buried with the deceased.

It is imperative that the *Agnihotrī* should have a wife. His wife not only assists in the turning of the fire-drill when the fire is created, but she prepares the rice of the meals, and it is she who finishes the worship of each day, as the last water used therein is put in her hand and she lets it fall to the ground. When the *Agnihotrī* performs special sacrifices on full-moon and new-moon days a girdle of manja grass is tied round the waist of his wife (*mekhalabandh*). The *Agnihotrī* cannot eat any food prepared by a woman other than his wife and, according to some, his daughter-in-law. If his wife die an *Agnihotrī* can marry again, but until he does so cannot tend his sacred fire.

There are many occasions when Hindu ritual demands that the *yajamān* should have living a wife; without a wife he is, as it were, mutilated and therefore loses *śakti*. In all the sixteen *sanskār* excluding the obsequial ones, in *vratas* or vows, and in *śāntis* the declaration of the *yajamān's* object in performing the ceremony, the *sankalpa*, requires that the *yajamān* should have a wife. In *Puṇyāhavācana*, or the invocation of divine blessing at the beginning of all auspicious ceremonies, a wife is necessary. The sacrificial *hom* in many a rite must be celebrated by husband and wife; while the man offers oblations to the fire the wife must touch his hand and when the fire is dismissed it must be dismissed by both of them. Many of the ceremonies following a birth must be performed by the father and his wife together; in the *Jātakarma* the husband puts drops of honey and ghee into the mouth of his new-born child resting on the mother's lap. In the *Niṣkramaṇa* ceremony the woman who has just become a mother must be accompanied to a temple by her husband; in *Annāprāśan* both the husband and wife should give the child its first food. At the tonsure of a child, *Caul*, the father cuts the hair of the child whilst the mother gathers the hair cuttings and mixes them in cowdung before throwing them away. At a thread ceremony or at a marriage a pot of water is taken and in it is placed a smaller pot with a small hole in it. The time the small pot takes to fill and sink is called a *ghaṭikā*, a period of twenty-four minutes, and a number of *ghaṭikā* are counted from sunrise, a finger impression being made with wet *kunku* on the wall to memorize each count. This method of measuring time decides the auspicious moments for celebrating the important rites of these ceremonies. The installation of the two pots, the *Ghaṭikāpātra-sthāpan*, must be done by a man and his wife together. *Kanyādān*, or the gift of the bride to the bridegroom, must be formally made by a relative of the bride with his wife. In the worship again of implements both husband and wife should join, though some tribes will not allow their wives to join in the worship of their implements on *Amāvāsyā*. The *Marāṭhā devak* is brought back from the temple to the marriage *maṇḍap* by the *yajamān* and his wife with their clothes tied together.

In all these ceremonies the essential requirement is that the *yajamān* should actually be a married man with a wife living. Though when present the wife is allotted certain specific duties, the absence of the wife from participation in the rites can be condoned, but the husband must take a proxy, *āvarana*, to represent his absent wife. In Gujarāt, if the wife be absent, the husband takes a doll dressed in a woman's clothes to represent her; in the Deccan he places a supārī-nut in his waist-cloth, or puts somewhere near him an ornament of his wife. If a widower wishes to perform his daughter's marriage and has no married relative available to instal *Nāndi*, he does the installation himself, taking an areca-nut to represent his wife.

The conduct of an *Agnihotrī* after taking his vow is regulated by a whole code of minute restrictions. He is not allowed to go on pilgrimage. He can leave his sacred fire to the care of any member of his family, but must return home every *Pūrṇimā* and *Amāvāsyā*. These are the last days of the two fortnights of the month; they are days for the purification of *Agni* polluted during the intervening days, and on these days the *Agnihotrī* must shave, and without calling any guests offer rice and milk to the fire. The opening days of the succeeding fortnights which follow these days are called *Pratipadā*, and are days on which the *Agnihotrī* is to make special offerings of rice flour and ghee, *Iṣṭi*, 'desire', to the fire in the presence of guests and invited priests. Besides this he must cut his kuśa grass himself on two varying *Amāvāsyā* in the year (*kuśagrahanam*, 'taking kuśa'); the knife with which he does this must be kept by him alone and sharpened by himself. With this knife sanctified when he took his vow he cut the notch in the *adharaṇi*. The *Agnihotrī* uses kuśa grass (Poa cynosuroides) for many purposes. He spreads it round his fire-pits; places his vessels and other things on this grass; the broom with which he sweeps his fire-room or *śrotriyāgār* must be made from this same grass; he uses it as a cover to his various vessels, as an *āsan* for himself and his wife, and with it sprinkles his offerings on the fire. He must cut this grass in a north-eastern direction from his village. The utensils of an *Agnihotrī* include a ladle to serve ghee; a second vessel of the shape of a bird's head with a beak used to hold ghee; a dish out of which *Brahma* represented by a priest takes his share of food, and a small cart in which the *Agnihotrī* and his wife are supposed to go to and return from the abode of the dead, *Indraloka*. These utensils (*sravā, srucā, prasitraharaṇ, śakaṭ*) are all made of tere wood.

His sacred fire an *Agnihotrī* cannot give away, but when offerings to it are complete he can lend fire from it for use in a thread ceremony, or in the *Upakarma* ceremony that follows this after an interval of a year. He cannot accept gifts nor can he eat *parānn* or food offered by others. He is not to wear leather shoes, though he may wear wooden ones; he cannot sleep on a bed but on a mattress of straw, cane or bamboo or on the skins of deer. The selling of things he has made is forbidden him; he must avoid meat and salt and cannot share in a *Śrāddha* meal. Before ever making fire he must maintain chastity for three days, shave and take *pancgavya*, that is the five gifts of a cow, milk, curds, ghee, urine and dung. His own measurements must decide the lay-out of the fire-pits in his fire-room. He may have a knot in his sacred thread, but cannot wear torn garments repaired by stitching or knotting together. These restrictions in general enforce the avoidance of acts which reduce *śakti*.

There is no *sutak* or impurity attaching to the corpse of an *Agnihotrī*, and others can touch it without pollution until it has been placed on the pyre, and this has been kindled with fire taken from his sacred fire. On the death of an inmate of his house the other inmates and their relatives are not impure, even though the corpse be still in the house; the *Agnihotrī*, however, cannot tend his fire, and as it is forbidden to extinguish his sacred fire deliberately, allows it to die out, rekindling it by means of his fire-drill after the period of mourning is over. The three fires of the *Agnihotrī*, his sacred fire as distinct from his household fire, must be protected from certain impure contacts. They must not be touched by a dog, monkey, crow, jackal, by a Śūdra, a sinner, a woman in menses, or even by a woman within ten days of the birth of her child. The touch of these animals and persons would also destroy the *śakti* in the *araṇi* sticks and render them useless.

At the beginning of all *hom* celebrations *akṣat* is kept on a leaf near the fire, and some of this is applied by the *yajamān* to his forehead to get *śakti* by a transfer of the *śakti* of the fire. An *Agnihotrī* can transfer the *śakti* of his fire; when he leaves home for some days he sometimes takes the *śakti* of the fire to himself and believes it accompanies him on his journey. He heats both his palms in the fire as he repeats certain mantras and then rests them on his chest, making a transfer of *śakti*; this is called *Ātmāropaṇ*.[1] Afterwards, when rekindling fire, he takes some *samīdhas* or sacred sticks and brings them in contact with his chest; he recites mantras and kindles the twigs with fire which is supposed to be the fire the *śakti* of which he had transferred to himself. If during the period that he bears the *śakti* of the fire, he swims in a river, a tank or the sea, touches a woman in menses or one within ten days of her delivery, or a Śūdra, he loses his *śakti*. Like every other worshipper he may also preserve the fire of a particular *hom* by transferring its *śakti* to sticks of pipal which he heaps on the fire, and then preserves, extinguishing the *hom* itself. When these sticks are kindled later they are supposed to have the *śakti* of the original *hom*. The transfer of the *śakti* of the *hom* to the sticks is called *Samitsamāropaṇ*, and the process by which this power is again conjured from the wood is called *Pratyavrohaṇa*.

On Āśvin sud Pūrṇimā the *Agnihotrī* pounds fresh ears of the new crops, usually rice, and making preparations from them, offers them to his fire and feeds Brahmins. This is called *Āgrāyaṇī* or *Navānnbhojan*, 'eating the new food'.

FIRE AND POWER

Fire in many cases is unable to harm power. In describing measures taken to test whether a man is stricken with evil-eye, I have given two examples of the inability of fire to destroy other power. The Sindi Muhammadan, to make this test, ties thread round a stone, recites over it Koranic verses and throws into fire. If there be actually present the power of evil-eye the thread will not burn so long as it remains tied to the stone, in contrast to the way articles waved round a person stricken with evil-eye are usually burnt. The Hindu takes a pounding stone some six inches long and ties black cotton threads round it and after waving over the sick man, throws it into fire. In this case also the thread whilst attached to the stone will not burn, if the sick man be really affected by *dṛṣṭi*.

Fiction which pursues the exotic and unusual has made familiar some of the practices of India, in which the celebrant demonstrates his immunity from being harmed by fire. Such demonstration

[1] *Āropaṇama* is applied to the transfer of *śakti* in the throwing of *akṣut* on the bridal pair, *akṣatāropaṇ*; to the installation of the *guḍhī* pole in which the *śakti* of Garuda is invoked, and the poles installed at car festivals, *dhvajāropaṇ*; to the first pillar of a house into which the *śakti* of Vastospati is invoked, *stambhāropaṇ*; the repetition of mantras in the ear of another is *mantrāropaṇ*; the invocation of the *śakti* of Kāma into damanaka grass is called *damankāropaṇ*; throwing the burden of a sin on to another is *doṣāropaṇ*.

that the celebrant possesses a power transferred from a deity, which renders fire innocuous to hurt him, is more common than is usually supposed. In the Karnāṭak is a ceremony called *guggaḷa*, performed by some Lingāyat families, by devotees of Śiva called *puravanta*, and by some Brahmins and others who have *Virbhadra* as their family god. It is usually performed during or after a marriage ceremony. The elders of a family take a large and shallow earthen pot filled with earth, and on the earth kindle large pieces of camphor. This pot is then given to the principal member of the family who carries it on his head to the temple of *Virbhadra*, accompanied in procession by the women-folk of the family bearing small *kalaśas* of water and burning camphor. The celebrant then enters the temple and worships the god and on his exit walks through a pit of burning camphor dug outside the temple. As he walks through the fire he holds in his arms an image of the god. He accomplishes this walk through fire without harm, thanks to his possessing the *śakti* of Śiva. His immunity from harm is supposed to demonstrate that without the power of Śiva, fire itself has no power, as Śiva proved one time when in anger he destroyed a sacrifice on its way to the gods through fire. A vivid emphasis of the celebrant's possession of power is given by the practice of sprinkling over his head, milk and ghee when he removes the pot of burning camphor, and of extinguishing the fire within the pot in the same way, for the milk and ghee are used to cool the hot *śakti* of the celebrant.

At Benhal in the Ron taluka of the Dharwar district a *jatra* or fair is held occasionally at the temple of *Hulgevvā*. A feature of the fair is that a large *Agnikuṇḍa* or fire-pit is prepared and *pāyas*, or rice boiled with water, jaggery and coconut juice is offered as *naivedya* to the goddess. Before this offering is actually made one of the pujāris puts both his hands into the vessel of boiling *khīr*, and takes out some of its contents in his joined palms and puts in a plate. The *khīr* taken out in this way forms the *naivedya*. Having done this the pujārī then throws ghee into the fire-pit, goes round the pit three times, jumps into it and crosses it. His example is followed by others who have taken vows, but these wear clothes which have been made wet. Protected by the *śakti* he has received from the goddess the pujārī escapes harm. The wearing of wet clothes is quite a common feature in Hindu ritual; still wet from a bath these clothes ensure ritual cleanliness, and in the case now described, are not intended to prevent the fire burning the celebrants, save in so far as ritual cleanliness ensures immunity.

At Gadag the pujārī of the goddess *Udacava* walks through

burning embers. On the final day of the Navrātri festival called *Kaulu* one of the pujāris at the temple of Aryadurgā at Ankola, that of Kalyayini at Avursa, of Mahāmai at Sadaśivgad and of Śanterikamakṣi at Kumta, takes out cakes from boiling oil with his bare hands and this without harm.

An annual fair is connected with the Malkarjun temple at Kanakon in the Goa State. Rice is offered as *caru* to the deity and is prepared in this unusual way. Three of the pujāris lie or sleep on the ground with their heads almost touching, but leaving a triangular space between. Their heads are then used as a hearth; fire is kindled between them and on their heads is placed a pot in which the rice is boiled. The pujāris escape all harm unless there be some impurity of man or thing in the vicinity, in which case the heat becomes intolerable, and the cooking has to be stopped.

At Mavinkop in the Dharwar district is a temple of Maruti. On the day following *Guḍhīpādvā*, the New-Year day of the Śālivāhan era, early in the morning the palanquin of the god is taken out preceded by the pujārī bearing a lighted lamp. When the palanquin returns the bearers and some of those who have accompanied it walk some few yards over the levelled and burning embers of a fire.

Muhammadans have the same belief that fire is unable to harm *kudrat*. In Sind stories are common of the burning of houses in which nothing escaped save a Koran, or of that of shrines in which only the tomb escaped. The power of some shrines is an insurance against hell-fire, whilst many Sayads claim that fire cannot harm them, and step over fire or dip their hands into boiling water. In the southern parts of the Presidency the men who bear during *Muḥarram* the panjā, models representing the hands of 'Ali the fourth caliph, are credited with sacred *kudrat* which enables them to walk over fire, or hold red-hot balls of iron between their teeth without harm. Muhammadans believe that if the fat of a frog be applied to a twig of the fig-tree which is a tree of Paradise and full of *kudrat*, and this be buried in the hearth, no fire will burn on the hearth and nothing can be cooked over it.

In contrast to the belief of Muhammadans that fire does not harm great *kudrat*, the Hindu thinks that if one of his temples be burnt, the image therein loses its *śakti* and a fresh invocation of power and a new installation is called for.

HOḺĪ

Hoḻī is the great fire-festival of Western India observed by Hindus at the full moon of the month of *Phālgun*, or as it is sometimes called in the Deccan, *Śimgā*. Like other *Pūrṇimā* or full-moon days *Hoḻī* is a day of *śakti*, a *parvakāl* and, as at other such times, all acts which destroy *śakti* must be avoided during *Hoḻī*. All forms of *himsā* must be avoided. There must be no grinding; no sweeping; no washing; oil must not be pressed; crops must not be reaped nor fruit cut and shaving is forbidden. Like other *parvakāl*, *Hoḻī* is followed by a period of danger which is called *kari*.

Another feature of the celebration of *Hoḻī* is that it cannot be held if it coincides in time with certain auspicious ceremonies, or falls within a certain interval from these. The fair of a deity is a celebration of a divine marriage; a *jatrā* is a *kalyāṇostana*, a ceremony the object of which is *kalyāṇ* or welfare, and no *Hoḻī* fire can be lighted on a day which is the date for such a *jatra*. For a year after a marriage, again, inauspicious acts which might imperil the *barkat* of the marriage are avoided. During this period the bridegroom cannot attend a funeral; the thread ceremony as one of importance less than that of a marriage cannot be performed; even the *Śrāddha* rite which celebrates the anniversary of the death of a kinsman is modified, if it falls within this year, and in lieu of the ordinary food prepared for this ceremony the food of a joyous feast is prepared. The celebration of *Hoḻī* is among the acts tabooed for a period after a marriage, as also after a thread ceremony and even after a death. If either a marriage, a thread ceremony or a death has occurred within the year in any household, that household cannot burn its private *Hoḻī*.

There are two accounts of the meaning of the *Hoḻī* festival, and the practices of to-day, particularly in the Karnāṭak, where the variation of custom is greater than in the Deccan or the Konkan, seem to be based in confusion on these two accounts. According to one story, *Tārakāsura* the son of *Tripurāsura* became too powerful and lorded it like a tyrant over the gods and celestial beings, who realized that his power could be checked only by *Śadanana* the unborn son of the god Śiva. They therefore requested *Kāma*, the god of love and his consort *Rati*, to go to Śiva and rouse in him and his consort *Pārvatī* the fire of love. *Kāma*, with his wife, accordingly went to Śiva and found him performing penance in the company of *Pārvatī*. *Rati* was able to inflame *Pārvatī*, but when *Kāma* stood before Śiva, before he could inflame the god he opened his eyes, and angry at the disturbance of his penance burnt *Kāma* to ashes with a glance of fire from his third eye. Then the followers of Śiva clamoured loudly and shouted abuse, whereupon Śiva restored *Kāma*, but ordered that his punishment of the god of love should be commemorated annually by the burning of *Kāma's* image, and that all who did this should secure escape from the evils that beset them. The second story explains the festival as the scaring away by abuse of a demoness *Ḍhunḍhi*, whose habit it is to bring various diseases to children and the young.

In the Karnāṭak there are two distinct forms of celebration connected with *Kāma*. There is one called *Mojin Kāma*, 'playing Kāma'. This consists in installing two big images of the god of love and his consort in a *manḍap*; before these for five days after their installation there is dancing and the singing of obscene songs, until the night of *Holī Huṇṇivi* when the images are worshipped and deposited, sometimes after a processional march, in the house of the hakdār, or person with the inherited right to their custody, till the next year. The second form of celebration which presents great confusion of ideas, is the *Sudo-Kāma*, the burning of *Kāma*.

Three months before *Holī* a site is chosen for the burning of *Kāma's* image, and is cleansed and sprinkled with water. Then every Sunday till *Holī* a party of men go out for *shikar*; the first expedition with this object being made on the day following the *Sankramaṇa* called *Kari*. On their way to the jungle the men worship an ari tree (Bauhinia racemosa) and place near it their guns, their instruments and even their sticks and scythes, and worship them. When the first animal is shot this victim and the successful hunter are worshipped in the jungle; a procession is formed, women wave *ārtī* round the victim of the chase and the hunters, and the slain animals are all placed on the site where *Kāma's* image is to be burned later. The blood of the slain animals is collected in a tin, and a small spot of blood is daubed on the doors of all the leading men in the village, and a communal feast is made from the flesh of the victims. These formalities are observed only on the first Sunday when the expeditions begin, and are not followed on the succeeding Sundays.

The night before *Holī* people gather and to the accompaniment of music visit every house in the village, and demand old clothes which are taken to the house of a hakdār, whose inherited right it is to burn the image of *Kāma*. The hakdār presents the people with a bamboo which they take to the village carpenter who from the bamboo and from straw fashions an image of a man without a head. The old clothes are then washed and dressed round the headless image, and this is left in the house of the hakdār. Next morning, that is actually on *Holī*, a man is sent with a coconut to a painter who makes a head of earth and paints it and gives to the carpenter to attach to the image. Once again a procession is formed; a coronet or *bāśing* is taken to the site of the pyre, and coconuts and food are offered to the site. Wood, cowdung cakes and old baskets are stolen from all and sundry and at night thrown near the image. On the next day, called *Pratipadā*, and also known as *Kari*, the image is burnt about noon in general, though there is much local variation in the time and the day when this is done.

There is boisterousness enough at *Holī*. Donkeys are ridden till they are exhausted and broken tins are tied to their tails; stamps bearing lewd words are freely used to mark the clothes of onlookers. The stealing, however, of fuel for the pyre is not another example of wantonness. In rites which have as their object the barkat of the community at large, stealing is a common feature. Not only the fuel used at *Holī* but the fire itself is stolen; *Mahār* boys steal the fire with which the first pyre is lighted and from this pyre all the other pyres must be lighted. At the festival of the demon *Kollappa* at *Hampi* the materials of the pyre are stolen. In rites intended to control rain, stealing is again a recurring feature. The *barkat* which accrues from stealing I will deal with later; a thing given bestows *barkat* not on the recipient of the gift but on the donor, and in communal rites it is essential that the benefit of the rites should fall not to any private individual but to the community at large. In communal rites, accordingly, theft is quite a common feature.

After the head of *Kāma's* image falls, coconuts are thrown into the fire and then extracted; the first coconut rescued from the fire is given to the hakdār, who breaks it in pieces and mixing with fried gram distributes among the crowd. A big basket is filled with the ashes of the pyre and freely scattered about the village to protect it from evil. Coloured red water, *vokli*,[1] is sprinkled by the crowd on each other, and in procession the crowd makes its way to a large temple where a coconut is offered to the resident god. The same night there is wild singing in front of the house of the hakdār in which prostitutes join until the break of dawn. The last incidents in the celebration are the distribution of the ashes of the fire to those present, excluding women, and the making of a final expedition into the jungle, after which any animal killed is taken five times round the spot where the image has been burnt.

[1] The throwing of *vokli* always involves among the orthodox a purificatory bath, *mangalsnān*. Celebrants of *Holī* must take such a bath before re-entering their homes; in car festivals *vokli* is thrown on the image of the god, and the image must be bathed in a river or tank before it can be replaced in its temple the bridal pair throw *vokli* on each other, necessitating their *mangalsnān*.

Throughout the festival in the Karnāṭak are practices which associate the burning of the image of *Kāma* with the demoness *Ḍhunḍhi*. In many households at night an image of *Kāma* is drawn on paper and burnt, *Kāmadahan*, to avert the influence of the demoness. That demoness is associated with the diseases of children and it is significant that the fire should be taken from the house of a *canḍāl* in which a woman has within the last ten days given birth to a child, and that the ashes of the pyre are applied to the bodies of children to avert evil, and preserved as a specific against convulsions and other illnesses of children. Children, too, obtain strong teeth by eating the grain of gram fried on the pyre (*Hoḻībuddi*).

The death of *Kāma* is the subject of mock representation. In some few places in the Karnāṭak the obsequies of *Kāma* are still performed on the eleventh day after *Hoḻī*, in a place far removed from human residence, and a grand feast follows the obsequies called *postu*, but this custom along with others is fast dying out. Another custom sometimes found is that of circumambulating the pyre, in which old and young join, carrying persons in their arms and abusing them as if dead. This abuse is supposed to free the abused persons from the *pīḍā*, or evil influence of the planets. At Hubli, in the Dharwar district, four bearers carry a man on a bier of bamboo as if a corpse; the man carried has his forehead plainly marked with red powder. In front of the bier walks a man carrying a pot of fire, and in the wake follow others dressed as women who wail and moan as the mock funeral passes through a crowd of jeering onlookers. The semblance of a funeral is maintained also in small details connected with the communal pyre. Water is sprinkled round the pyre, and the mock mourners produce a dull sound by striking their mouths with the back of their palms. One explanation of the weird sound thus produced, which has been given the onomatopoeic name of ‘ bomb ’, is that it imitates the howling of jackals.

A few other customs are singular and confined to certain of the less advanced tribes. Among the *Vanjāris* of Khandesh the women-folk tie down their men in the cattle-sheds and hold them to ransom; they surround the *Hoḻī* fire and forbid any man to touch it or remove its ashes and pursue and beat any man who is bold enough to attempt to break the prohibition. On *Dhūḻvaḍ*, the day after the full-moon, *Kātkarīs* play a game called *Cenḍū phaḻī*. The *phaḻī* is a conical pyramid of circular stones about six inches in width at the bottom, and tapering to an inch and a half at the summit. The *Cenḍū* or ‘ moon ’ is a ball which is thrown at the cone of stones in a game something like rounders. The captains elect their sides of five players and as each man is added to a side he is asked whether he chooses to be sun or moon, pipal or umbar. Pairs of cognate things are taken, but the first question is whether the sun or the moon is preferred. *Haraṇśikāris* at *Holī* propitiate *Maileva*, the goddess of epidemic. Early in the morning before sunrise the headman of the tribe bathes and fries wheat-cakes in a cauldron of oil. He must take out the cakes with his hands, and offering them as *naivedya* to the goddess, distribute later to all his tribesmen. If the headman does not suffer from burns all will be well with the tribe, but if he be burnt an epidemic will break out.

An erected pole is a common characteristic of the day's celebration in all parts of the Karnāṭak, Deccan and the Konkan. In the Deccan a pole of the castor-oil tree is taken and to it a stalk of sugar-cane is tied. Around this pole is heaped the fuel of the fire. In the northern parts of the Konkan the same pole is used and to it is attached a stalk of sugar-cane and a live hen which last falls into the fire when the cord which ties it to the pole is burned. A betel-tree is used for the pole in parts of Kanara, whilst in the Karnāṭak a thick bamboo or a branch of the Palmyra palm mad (Borassus flabelliformis) forms the pole which is called *Holīgāni*. In the Deccan and in the Konkan the pole is erected in the centre of the pyre; the general practice in the Karnāṭak is to erect it fifty cubits away from the fire. A branch some twenty or thirty cubits long is chosen and it must have other branches and be covered with leaves. Mango-leaves are tied to it for its whole length and a *bāśing* is fastened at the summit; five kinds of grain, saffron and food are offered to it. On *Ugadi* day, the Hindu New Year's Day, the pole is again worshipped and cut down, leaving two cubits of it still standing; the portion cut is thrown away, but the stump is preserved till a new pole is substituted the next year, when the stump may be used for any communal purpose, but on no account for any private purpose. One custom is to tie ropes to the pole when cut from the tree and have a tug-of-war; the power of Mahādev is invoked into the erected pole. When the pole is finally destroyed the village patil takes the upper part, and the lower portion falls to the *meti*, or the first inhabitant of the village; no one from another village would dare to touch it because of its divine *śakti*.

When kindling a private *Holī* the ground in front of the house is swept and covered with cowdung; designs are drawn on it with *rāngolī* powder and *halad* and *kunku* are sprinkled on it. Then a branch of eranḍī is planted in the centre by the head of the household, and around it are piled cakes of cowdung and sandal-paste; flowers and a lamp of ghee are placed near or on the pile of fuel. All male members of the family attend the worship of the twig after which live charcoal is brought from the hearth to light the pyre. To the *Hoḻī naivedya* is then offered, and a coconut is broken before it, pieces of which are later distributed as *prasād*. Around the fire the head of the house, followed by the other male members, goes beating his mouth with his palm. The twig of eranḍī must be cut from the top of the tree and in the Deccan must possess a fork of two branches.

Barkat is attributed to the fire and to its ashes. In the Deccan a pot is placed on the fire and filled with water by a small child; when the water has boiled it is taken away and used for bathing and is supposed to prolong the life of those who bathe in it. Live embers from the fire are also put in a pot, and water heated by pouring over them is used for bathing. Torches are lighted from the fire in the Karnāṭak and used for freeing a house from pests; domestic fires lighted from the fire of *Hoḻī* secure the household permanently from epidemic and other evils. In Kanara, ashes from the pyre are applied to the forehead and afford protection against all evil including the *pīḍā* of planets. The ashes are mixed with the seed of the coming season, are sprinkled in the granary to protect it and also on the threshing-floor. And lastly the divination that is made in all districts as to the future season and its crops, seems but a survival of a belief that the fire itself has an influence on the incidence of rain in the cultivating season. In the Deccan, balls of wet earth are placed beneath the fire, one for each month of the rainy season, and according as one or another ball dries the hardest a forecast is made as to the month which will have the best rainfall. An earthen pot is also placed under the pyre, filled with water and covered tight, and from the evaporation of the water a surmise is made as to the coming rains. The readiness with which the pyre kindled, and the direction in which the head of *Kāma's* image falls when burned are in the Karnāṭak signs by which the season's prospects can be prophesied. If the head of the image falls forward the *kharif* or earlier cultivating season will be a good one; if the head falls backwards the *rabī* or later season will be the best. Until quite recently another method of divination was common in the Karnāṭak. Grain of each of the principal grain crops was mixed with ashes from the pyre of *Kāma*, and tied in a cloth to the top of the *Hoḻīgāni* in front of the *manḍap* in which the images of *Kāma* and his consort were installed, or in front of *Kāma's* pyre. The ashes were supposed to attract moisture which caused one or more of the different grains to germinate, and the agriculturist then chose for sowing those whose germination was the most advanced. Perhaps the peasant has lost faith in the accuracy of this mode of divination, for the custom is among those that have died out.

There is considerable disagreement as to the hour when the pyre should be lighted. I have witnessed the lighting of communal pyres between dawn and noon; in some parts noon seems the favourite hour. The burning by individual households who have the practice of doing this, of an image of *Kāma* drawn on paper seems to be done invariably after dark, and the consensus of written authority is that the *Hoḻī* fire should always be kindled after dark. The Dharamsindhu, the Vrataratna, and the Nirnayasindhu agree on this point, whilst the Jyotirnibandh says that if the pyre be lighted during the daytime, the whole village will be wiped out by fire within the year. If one accept the weight of written authority the celebration of *Hoḻī* affords apparently no support to the 'solar theory' which would explain, on analogies collected from fire festivals in many parts of the world, the kindling of fire as a sun-charm.

It is not difficult, I think, to assume that the more elaborate customs of *Hoḻī* prevalent in the Karnāṭak evidence a confusion of two celebrations. There is a marked absence of any burning of images in the Deccan and in most parts of Kanara; even in the Karnāṭak the burning of an image is not an invariable feature of the festival. In the songs, too, sung at *Hoḻī* in the Karnāṭak there is a recurring refrain, *dhundume basantāj habba*, which unites the destruction of the demoness *Ḍhunḍhi* on the full-moon day of Phālgun, with the worship of the god of love and his consort on the first of the dark half of the same month, at the advent of spring, *vasant*. The images burned indeed are those of *Kāma*, but the fact that they are admittedly burned to secure freedom from the attentions of the demoness, suggests that in reality it is the image of evil *Ḍhunḍhi* and not that of *Kāma* which has its funeral in the celebrations of *Hoḻī*. In the Karnāṭak in the evening of *Hoḻī* all the members of a household sit on a seat covered with a white cloth. The women-folk wave lights before the men and apply sandal-paste to their foreheads. Mango-blossoms are ground in water by means of a pestle of red sandalwood and the water is drunk by the men. This is to bring *barkat* throughout the coming year, and as the words uttered when drinking show, is to inaugurate the coming of spring.

Whether this conjecture be accurate or not, the principal details of the celebration of *Holī* seem to fall into two categories. There are features which seem to permit of no explanation other than that they stress the creative force of generation. It is a married man who has not married a widow who must apply the first fire to the pyre; married couples are prominent among those who dance around the kindled pyre. The fire is supposed to have a direct influence upon the cultivating season, upon its crops and its rains; perhaps, too, it is associated with a plentiful supply of game. Wherever, too, a pole is erected in or near the pyre it must bear the insignia of fertility, forking branches and leaves, whilst Brahmins stick their paper drawing of *Kāma* into a piece of jvārī (Sorghum vulgare). And on the other hand, other features seem just as clearly associated with the belief that with her funeral the evil influence of the demoness *Ḍhunḍhi* is crippled; children play a prominent part in the ritual of *Holī*; the fuel for the fire is taken from a house in which there has been a recent birth and the ashes of the fire are used to protect children from disease.

At Hampi a festival very much like that of *Holī* is celebrated in the month of October, on the full-moon day of *Gaurī huṇṇivi*. The festival is called *Kollappanahabba*; on this day a man hired for the occasion impersonates the demon of illness and evil; he is first made to stand in a central place in the village, is then beaten and badly mauled and driven out of the village by a crowd of hundreds. As the man is being driven away persons meeting him must on no account see his face; villagers of adjoining villages should not see the crowd of pursuers enter their confines, and any one who happens to meet the noisy rabble should turn round and join in the pursuit of the demon. After being driven out of the village far away the expelled man is not allowed to return to his village that same day, but has to pass a night in the jungle.

Just as at *Holī* a large pyre is lighted, the fuel being stolen generally for the purpose. As soon as the impersonator of the demon has been driven away a huge image of the demon *Kollappā* is made out of old clothes collected from house to house, and solemnly burned. Any one who has by chance seen the face of the fugitive must go to the pyre and witness the burning of the image to escape imminent evil.

TRIPURI PŪRṆIMĀ

Tripuri Pūrṇimā, also called *Dev Divālī*, is Kārttik sud. Pūrṇimā, on which day the god Śankara is supposed to have killed a demon called Tripurari. People take a vow on Āśvin sud. Pūrṇimā and end it on this day of Kārttik. The vow is called *Kārttik snān*, and on Tripuri Pūrṇimā they bathe and make a gift of a light to priests to acquire *puṇya*; they must also take their food under the dhatri tree after worshipping the tree and Viṣṇu (*āvaḻi bhojan*). On this day lights are to be lit in temples and at night lights are placed in miniature boats and set adrift on rivers; lights are also placed at the root of trees such as the tulsī (Ocimum sanctum), aśvath (Ficus religiosa), the banyan and the dhatri (Phyllanthus emblica). The lights on the water bring *mukti* to nocturnal birds, to insects, fish and other animals that see the lights; the lights at the root of trees similarly bring *mukti* to the birds.

On this day *himsā* of all kinds is forbidden. Sexual congress, the cutting of trees, reaping, threshing, the plucking of flowers and fruit; shaving or hair-cutting. To obtain the *barkat* of the day, moreover, one should keep awake all night.

DIVĀḺĪ

The lighting of lamps at this festival is supposed to avert premature or unnatural death. *Yamadharma*, the god of death, once inquired of his messengers whether they ever felt pity for the dying, and they related a story of rājā Haima, who died prematurely from the bite of a snake which issued from the nostril of his own father, when the latter sneezed on the fourth day of his wedding. The god, impressed by the sadness of this story, told his messengers to assure those who lighted lamps for five days from Āśvin vad, 13 that they would escape premature and unnatural death. Lighted torches are carried through the streets to the cry '*dīp dīpālyo*', and villagers hand torches to Government officers for them to give to their boys to carry; cowherds make an image of a large hooded cobra out of kanchi-grass, and folding the hood so as to form a niche, place in it a light and carry this from house to house and wave round the cattle. Torches, too, are held high to the sky to provide light to reach heaven to those unfortunate souls that have fallen into hell. On the *Amāvāsyā* of *Divāḻī* in the evening when the cattle return from pasture, agriculturists put across the entrances of their cattle-sheds large bundles of dry sticks and, setting fire to them, make their cattle cross the fires to enter their stalls as a protection from disease for the next twelve months.

The protection of cattle is the object of other rites performed at *Divāḻī*. I have already described the custom of boys waving a lamp in a basket of jvārī-stalks before the cattle in every house to scatter evil 'beyond the river'. In the Malnad tracts of the Karnāṭak both at *Hoḻī* and at *Divāḻī* to protect cattle from wild beasts, lights are waved round a stone placed under certain trees to represent *Hulidev* the tiger-god. Some castes during *Divāḻī* make a large heap of cowdung in their cow-pen and stick in it branches of āghāḍā (Achyanthes aspera). To secure protection of their cattle *Lingāyats* worship a coconut as an emblem of *Hakki-lakṣmī*, guardian of the cattle-shed, and renew the coconut every *Amāvāsyā*, the coconut being placed in a niche which must face west. During *Divāḻī* some families offer this symbol special worship; a small *manḍap* of sugar-cane stalks is erected before the niche and a black blanket and black *sāḍī* are offered to the goddess. Five *suvāsinīs* wave a light known as *tubid ārtī*, and consisting of a *kalaśa* of water with a coconut and betel-leaves as a cover, and five other small pots with betel-leaves, all placed in a shallow dish along with a lamp, *nīlānjan*. Coconuts and rice are offered to the goddess and then distributed. Neither the coconut nor the *ārtī* is allowed to touch the ground.

Early in the morning of *Narakacaturdaśi*, which falls during *Divāḻī*, Brahmins place a light in their privies to celebrate the destruction of the demon *Narakāsur*.

CHAPTER VIII

THE POWER OF METALS

METALS have the power of particular planets; all of them derive potentiality from the sun but secondarily from one or more planets, gold drawing power from Mercury and Jupiter, silver from the moon, copper from Mars, and iron from Śani or Saturn. Another Hindu belief, however, is that metals do not possess *śakti* themselves, but that to each planet some one metal is pleasing, and that the use of the metal secures the co-operation of the particular planet. Gifts of pure metals are therefore made to planets to avert their evil influence; gold is offered to all planets, copper to the sun and to Mars, silver to the moon and to Venus, lead to Rāhu, and iron to Saturn.

Life is a permanent possibility of contacts. Contact with the unknown is contact with a potentiality that cannot be estimated or valued; a power that may lead to a sequel of good but may also induce evil. Everything, inanimate or animate, that enters for the first time into contact with man, brings with it an atmosphere of the mysterious and problematic; its innate power, its *pāyguṇ*, is an object of apprehension, and measures are taken to ensure, as far as possible, that its new contact brings a train of weal and not of woe. In these measures gold is often used to nullify the possibility of an evil working of *pāyguṇ*.

When an animal is purchased a piece of gold is placed on its forehead; in Sind the Muhammadan sprinkles its forehead and feet with water in which gold has been dipped. When a new house is constructed, as soon as the great beam of the roof is placed in position a nail of gold is driven into it. When, too, a Hindu occupies a house for the first time, he takes a piece of turmeric, red-coloured rice and a piece of gold, and knots these in a cloth, which he colours with turmeric and carries with him when first he leaves the house. A bride again comes to her husband's house with all the potentiality of the unknown, enhanced in her case by the fact that she is a woman, and that during her marriage she possesses special power. It is at least an act of caution when she leaves her home for the first time, bearing to her new home all the unknown consequences of her contact, to tie to her arm, that of the bridegroom and even to the arms of their sisters and the guests a coin of silver, copper or gold, an *Imām Jamin* as the Sindi Muhammadan would call it, because the Muhammadan ties knots in it in the name of Imām Jamin, one of the twelve imāms of the Shi'ahs. The Sindi bride is also stopped at the threshold of her husband's house, where a gold coin is placed in her palm covered by a small lamp of earth (*diya*) which she carries lighted into the house.

At a birth gold is used in many ways. There is danger in a *Lingāyat* father seeing his first-born son, a danger to the father as well as to the child, for the child may bring illness to his father and the father may inflict evil-eye on his son. Among Brahmins this double danger is averted by the father, before he sees his son, looking at his own reflection in a mirror or a dish of sweet-oil. The *Lingāyat* father is allowed to see his son only after the child's first hair-cutting ceremony has been performed, and even then he must protect the child by putting on it an ornament of gold. To secure *barkat* for a new-born child an elderly person dips an article of gold into honey, and gives the honey to the child, transferring to it not only the power of the honey, but also the longevity of the giver. In the Karnāṭak when the first food is given to an infant a gold ring is dipped in sweetened milk and with this the child's tongue is moistened before it begins to eat. In Sind on the sixth day after a birth, a day of fateful possibilities, a gold ring or ornament is dipped in milk in the light of the moon or stars, and the milk is sprinkled on the child, and mother, and also drunk by the mother.

To go on a journey is to expose oneself to myriad contacts of unknown character. Whenever a Sindi Muhammadan begins a journey he fastens to his arm an *Imām Jamin* to secure a safe return; this accomplished, he adds more coins to the knot and distributes sweetmeat. The Hindu goes on his journey protected by his knot of turmeric and gold.

To secure fruition of one's object in agricultural tasks, gold is rubbed on the blade of the plough at the first ploughing in the Karnāṭak; when jvārī again is sown the sowers are required to wear rings of gold. In these customs there enters also the assumption that there is a transfer of the colour of the gold to the grain of the future crop.

Gold to a Hindu is a life-giver and form of the gods. In the mouth of the dead it gives absolution from sin. The placing of gold in the mouth of the dead, sometimes along with pearls, is a very widespread practice among Hindus. Castes as far apart in development as the *Brahmin* and the *Tilagar* or *Korava* have this same custom, and in the *Barat* community gold is always fixed in life to one tooth so as to ensure that on death there is gold in the mouth. A Hindu lady, when married, has a *mangaḻsūtra* or necklace containing two pierced beads of gold given to her by her father and her husband's father; on the death before her of her husband she places these beads in his mouth to secure his absolution from sin.

In the Karnāṭak when a child is still-born its ear or nose is pierced with a ring of gold, to prevent the contagion of death passing to the next birth. The dead child is supposed then to pass again into the mother's womb and be reborn. *Satt kūsu hotte yoḻage*, 'the dead child enters the womb'. *Marāṭhās* say '*Ahevācā melā kheḻāvālā gelā*', 'The dead child of a woman with a husband has but gone to play'. *Kātkarīs* mark the thigh, the face or body of a dead child with collyrium and expect to identify the next birth by a corresponding physical mark. Gold is washed in water and this is given to a person with a cold or fever to drink; gold is used to touch the eyes when they palpitate. A sick man in delirium is branded on the forehead with a red-hot piece of gold; when a child is born, water in which gold has been put is given to the mother to drink; gold dipped in water is also given to a woman to assist delivery. The tongue of a sick man is cleansed with gold and the sick wear rings of gold.

Creative power is but one manifestation of *śakti*. Gold may be used to obtain issue. Gifts are determined again by the return desired, and to obtain issue, gold is gifted to priests; thin threads made from gold wire (*yajnopavīt*); images of a cow or calf in gold; a cradle with an image of a child also made of gold, or a ghee-fed light in a stand of gold (*nīlānjan*).

Gold should be worn always on the body so that when a bath is taken the body is washed with water which has flown over gold. At a Hindu marriage I have frequently seen an ornament of gold held in a vase or saucer above the heads of the bridal pair during their *surgi* bath, so that the water of the bath pours over the gold on to the bodies of the pair and their relatives seated near. On every day of one's *nakṣatra* a little gold is shredded and preserved until it becomes a tola in weight, when a finger-ring is made from it and worn as an amulet. At a circumcision Muhammadan women tie to the boy's wrist with five threads, a black glass bead and one of gold to avert the attentions of spirits.

Because of its inherent power, gold is used by the Muhammadan in Sind to effect a transfer of evil. Gold and copper coins used with this object are significantly called *bala-en.* At a marriage women who must not have married twice collect such coins in a plate and give to the minstrels to transfer to them, as to a *corpus vile*, the calamities that threaten the bridal pair. Before the coins are actually given to the minstrels they are first waved round the bridal pair to effect with them a contact. Similarly, at a rite of circumcision the guests wave silver, copper and gold coins round the boy and then present them to the musicians. By the Hindu gold is used for the invocation of the *śakti* of all gods. When a Brahmin dies gold is put in his mouth ; the son of the deceased then throws sesamum on to the gold and invokes the *śakti* of Sarasvati, the goddess of knowledge, into it, so that the deceased will be able intelligently to answer the questions put to him by Yama, the ruler of the world of the dead. When a child is born under the *nakṣatra* of *Mūlā,* which means that he will bring disaster to his parents, the parents perform a *śānti* or rite of appeasing, and taking a piece of gold place it on an *āsan* of sesamum, and throwing on this *akṣat* invoke the śakti of Lakṣmī. On the naming of a child and equally when after a marriage the bride enters the house of her husband, a piece of gold is placed on rice and through the medium of *akṣat* the *śakti* of Lakṣmī, goddess of good fortune, is invoked. At *Vāstuśānti,*[1] performed when a new house is entered upon for the first time, a gold image is prepared of *Vāstupuruṣa,* and into this his *śakti* is invoked with *akṣat.* Gold is also among the *devak* of the *Marāṭhā* into which the *śakti* of the family god is invoked.

Gold is pure. The *Agnihotrī* to win *puṇya* wears ornaments of gold (*karṇakuṇḍal*). Among *Lingāyats* at a *Śrāddha* ceremony the *yajamān* wears a ring with a knot of gold, so that he may be pure, for in all ceremonies connected with the dead purity is an absolute necessity. The purity of gold must be preserved and in no wise

[1] The image should really be buried when the foundations are dug ; in practice it is done when the completed house is entered upon for the first time. An image about an inch long of earth, silver or gold, is put in a box of earth (*peṭikā*), and buried in the south-eastern corner of the central room in a pit one and a half feet deep. The pit is filled with water and it is inauspicious if the water merely sinks into the earth without filling the pit. In the box are placed nine kinds of precious stones, five small pieces of different metals, flowers, darva-grass, moss, curds and cooked rice. The pit is then filled with the original earth. The site is worshipped and the clothes of a man or woman are offered to it. Brahmins call the image *Vāstu-puruṣ* ; non-Brahmins give it the name of a demon, *Kavḍakanṭak.* This would seem to be the relic of an ancient custom of burying a living person beneath the foundations. The image used by non-Brahmins is made of wheat-flour and is of hideous form.

sullied. A Hindu, therefore, should not sleep wearing anything of gold, for sleep is an impure state and destructive of *śakti*; no Hindu, again, will wear an anklet of gold. Muhammadans will not wear gold on any part of the body below the waist; they will not bring gold into contact with the dead, and a strict Muhammadan objects to gold being placed on a mosque or shrine, and considers that his prayers are of no avail if said whilst he is wearing gold.

SILVER

In Sind if a boy is born in sequence to three girls or a girl following three boys, and these earlier-born children have died, disaster to the fourth is expected, so the fourth child called *Trikhar*, 'born after three', is protected against the contagion of death by a silver anklet.

A silver anklet is put on a leg that is diseased in any way to arrest the spread of the disease. Silver is a common charm against the evil-eye, and a silver crescent not unnaturally averts any evil anticipated from the influence of the moon. To obtain issue after taking a vow, rings of silver are worn on the hands and feet (*beḍi*). Silver eyes (*kaṇṇbaṭṭu*) and moustaches (*miśī*) are presented to certain goddesses in fulfilment of a vow, with the object of securing release from some illness, or to get issue. The coming of a bride is considered to be the coming of the goddess Lakṣmī, but this goddess of fortune is proverbially fickle and never rests long in one place, so to tie the goddess down and enforce her prolonged stay in the house silver chains are tied to the feet of the bride (*sarpaḻi*). A bride must always wear ornaments of silver (*kadagā*, *pilyā*; *sutagālugur*). Silver is used for invoking the *śakti* of *Rudra*. When a child is born under the inauspicious constellations of Mūlā, Jyeṣṭhā, Asleśa or Māgha, as a protection against their evil influence the father of the child places a silver image of *Rudra* before a *kalaśa* and throws *akṣat* on it.

COPPER

To both Hindu and Muhammadan copper is a pure metal; to the Hindu it is *pavitr*. It is a substitute for gold, and in the mantra that accompanies the making of gifts to priests, though copper coins may be used they are spoken of as 'flowers of gold'.

The use of copper at a funeral forms a bond of similarity between the rites of many castes and tribes, for though its manner of use may vary considerably, in some way or other, copper is generally used at a funeral to secure the absolution of the dead. It hardly matters what community one takes, some such use of copper will be found. The *Kātkarī* places a copper coin in each hand of the dead, in the shroud behind the neck of the dead, and also on the banks of any rivulet or stream encountered by the mourners. After the funeral is over a copper coin is placed on both banks of the first stream met on the return of the funeral party, and before bathing in a river, to remove the contagion of death, the mourners throw into the river a copper coin. Reminiscent of Roman story is the *Kātkarī's* explanation that he places copper coins near water to furnish the dead with the means to pay the charges of the ferrymen he will meet on the *ohole* or streams that separate the world of the living from that of the dead. The *Kātkarī* also places a copper coin under the *jīvkhaḍā*, 'stone-of-life', which for some time enshrines the life of the dead. *Gollars* and *Kabbars* place five copper pice on a stone at a burial in the name of the dead and ask for his absolution. *Lamānis* tie a copper coin in a knot in the shroud and on their way to the pyre cut off the knot of cloth and throw it away, or alternatively place it at the head of the corpse. *Lingāyat Kumbhārs* write sacred words on pieces of copper numbering fifteen or nine, and place these pieces on the shoulders, knees, chest, head and other parts of the dead. Brahmins at a funeral throw about coins of silver and copper. Among castes which employ Brahmin priests, twelve days after a death the son of the deceased offers to the priests *pṛthvīdān*, giving them the gold, silver or copper plate on which the priests have dined, in order to transfer to him the sins of the dead. *Bhāts* place a copper coin in the mouth of the dead and also in his hand at the burning ghat. Castes, again, that perform a mock marriage to a tree place a copper coin on an *āsan* of nāgvel, and offer it to the tree to free the bridegroom from sin. Should a Hindu unhappily kill a cobra he is absolved from the sin of killing it, if he burns it with a copper coin in its mouth, and if he does this on a Saturday the burnt copper becomes a ring of potent charm to avert spirits.

Sindi Muhammadans have practices illustrating the idea that through the power of copper, sin and other evil may be transferred. At a Muhammadan funeral coins are distributed; these are called *isqāt* or 'unburdening', and many knowing the burden of sin that they bear will refuse to accept them. To avert sickness and evil-eye copper coins are placed at the foot of trees, with the amiable object that others may come along and in their cupidity taking the coins may also effect a transfer to themselves of evil. When children suffer from small-pox they touch copper coins, and these are then given to the poor with the object of transferring to them the illness. With this same object of transferring evil, copper coins are thrown on the graves of saints for others to pick up. Copper coins are placed on graves to make a transfer of sin, and when a man dies, copper utensils are presented to fakirs to secure the absolution of the dead. At a marriage and at a rite of circumcision evil is transferred by copper coins waved round the bridal pair or boy and given to the hired minstrels, and these coins are called, as I said before, *bala-en* or 'calamities'.

At an eclipse a Hindu makes offerings of copper to beggars to make a transfer of evil; this gift of copper, *tāmradān*, acquires the quality of fierceness, *ugraṭa*, from the *śakti* of the hour of the eclipse. To the Sindi Muhammadan copper is called *kari bala* or 'black calamity', a reference to its use in transferring evil which makes the term a close parallel to the Hindu word, *ugra*.

Copper is offered by the Hindu to all gods and is a common ingredient of ritual. At *Śrāddha* ceremonies all pots used must be of copper, as also those used at the annual thread ceremony. When water is offered to Viṣṇu in the daily *sandhyā* the pot and spoon used must be of copper. Copper coins are offered to trees; on the fifteenth of Jyeṣṭha copper coins are placed on leaves of nāgvel in front of a banyan-tree; when the tulsī plant is married copper coins are offered. At sacred bathing-places bathers throw copper coins into the river; passers-by throw copper coins into wells, and travellers into rivers.

Copper to a Muhammadan is the best metal from which to construct a *tawiz* or charm; in the southern parts of the Presidency he constructs from copper the sacred *panjā* or hands which are borne in procession at *Muḥarram.* To a Hindu copper is, similarly, the best metal from which to construct a *yantra,* as this can be taken into shrines where *śakti* is invoked into the *yantra.*

Because of its purity, water is always placed at the bedside in a pot of copper, and the word for water-pot is literally copper. In the Konkan childless women wear a tiny box of copper to keep away the spirit that causes barrenness. A copper bracelet is tied at an eclipse to the arm of an expectant mother to secure her an easy delivery. *Lamānis* bury a copper coin with the severed navel-cord to protect this portion of the child's self. In all the practices of *utāra,* the riddance or transfer of evil, copper coins are waved round the sufferer, and used as the medium for transferring the evil to others. The Sindi equivalent for *utāra* is *ghorā,* and in this copper coins are waved round the sick and then given to the poor.

IRON

Iron to a Hindu is *Hīnloh,* a 'despicable' metal; it is *amangal,* 'unlucky'. To sneeze whilst holding a piece of iron is prophetic of failure of purpose. After a purificatory ablution a Hindu must not touch iron, for it is unclean. In Sind the Muhammadan speaks of the 'deceit of iron'; *loh droh* or *lohani droh.* Even thieves hesitate to steal iron, and those who do so never prosper. To use stolen iron for a ploughshare would mean in Sind the drying up of the later crop. To pick up iron found on the road is to court disaster; the Muhammadan in Sind avoids this as rigorously as the Hindu in the Deccan, whilst in the Karnāṭak any one who finds a piece of iron gives it away at once. A child's play may cause disaster if it should menace any one with a piece of iron, and it is imperative to avert coming evil by striking the iron on the ground. The vernaculars of the Presidency have many a pithy proverb illustrating the baneful power of iron. In Marāṭhī they say that the friendship between a bill-hook and a pumpkin is no friendship; that any calamity is the falling of the axe of heaven, and that the handle of an axe by association with iron brings disaster to its own family, to wit to trees.

Iron is inimical to *barkat,* for it militates against the working of power from which comes all *barkat.* It must therefore be strictly avoided on all occasions when action is taken, in the hope of obtaining an increase of power, with its concomitant barkat. In all rites of religion, in every form of worship or prayer it is absolutely tabooed. An image of a deity after the invocation of *śakti* becomes an abiding place of power; whenever, in fact, power is invoked it is given a temporary and localized residence. As iron drives away *śakti* it follows naturally that no invocation of power can be made into any entity of iron. No image of a god is made of iron save the image of Śani or Saturn with whom iron is associated, and this image cannot be taken into the shrine of the family gods, *kul devatā.* No *yantra* or charm into which divine power is invoked can be made of iron, and this not the less because a *yantra* is taken into a shrine or temple. Among the symbols into which the *Marāṭhā* invokes the *śakti* of his family god, among his *devak* appear several metals, but iron is not one of these. A *svastika* which embodies the *śakti* of the deities that guard the cardinal points cannot be made of iron; the *Lingāyat* makes his *linga* which he carries with him, of silver.

A Hindu temple consists of two parts, the inner part, *garbhārā, garbhagudi, garbhagraha,* and the outer part or *sabhāmanḍap.*

Iron can be taken into the outer part, but never into the inner shrine, the only exception to this being the iron *triśul̲* of Śiva which is kept near his image. In any religious ceremony all iron must by the orthodox be removed from the person of the worshipper, as, for instance, the key of his treasure-box usually worn attached to his sacred thread, and particularly any ring on the hand, as the hand plays such an important part in ritual. No instrument of iron can be taken into the fire-room of an *Agnihotrī*; the hole in his fire-drill cannot be made with iron, and though nowadays there is not so strict an observance of rule, his *araṇi* and *adharaṇi* were formerly fashioned with darbha-grass. In the case of an ordinary *hom* celebration the *samīdha* or sacred twigs with which the fire is fed must be broken by hand, and without the use of any instrument; the fire itself must be brought in a vessel which is not of iron, and as the *Agnihotrī* so also the participant in a *hom* ceremony must wear clothes which have not been sewn, as sewing implies the use of a needle. When a coconut is broken before the family gods, it is either broken with a knife outside the shrine, *Devāci Kholī*, or is broken within the shrine with a piece of sandal-wood, or as by the *Lingāyat Kumbhār* with a washed stone taken into the shrine for this purpose. Iron lamps cannot be used in temples or in the room of a god; during the recitation of *Purāṇa* or when *jap* or *abhiṣek* is performed, the lamps used must be of silver, copper or bronze; these lamps are called *nandādīp* and are placed on stands of wood or brass when not suspended to keep them away from the ground. Iron spoons and pots cannot be used in religious ceremonies, and the sacred conch in every temple rests on a seat, *āsan*, of brass, *Śankhāsan*. Strict orthodoxy, too, requires that all stools used in worship should have nails of brass, and though this rule is now often honoured in the breach, it is still followed by Brahmins in the *Śrāddha* ceremony in which the *pāṭ* used have nails and rings of brass.

Pancāl̲s make a distinction between iron and steel. At noon and sunrise when worshipping *Kāl̲amā* they worship something of steel within their shrine, placing it in insulation from the ground on a *pāṭ* of wood, but when they worship their anvil, as this is of iron they do not take it within their shrine.

Śakti cannot, I have said, be invoked into iron. Every month on the fourth day of the dark half a Hindu takes a *kalaśa* of water with some fruit, usually a coconut, over it, and invokes into the pot the *śakti* of *Gaṇpati*. The water in the pot becomes by contact with the invoked *śakti* itself full of power, and is sprinkled over the head of the *yajamān* and the heads of his family members to bring them *barkat.* The pot used may be of earth and of any metal save iron. On a few occasions when iron or steel is worshipped, it is worshipped without any invocation of power. To avert the evil influence [1] of Saturn an iron image of Saturn is placed in a pot of earth or iron filled with oil; the pot is covered with two black blankets and worshipped with blue flowers, *akṣat,* an offering of cooked rice and sesamum, and finally given to a Brahmin priest of dark complexion on a Saturday. There is no invocation of *śakti* into this image. The image, again, which is usually made from a horse-shoe, is worshipped outside the shrine of the family gods, and is never taken into a temple. Another example of the worship of iron that suggests an exception to the rule that power cannot be invoked into iron is the worship of *Śastragarbha.*

In a marriage ceremony one of the auxiliary ceremonies is the creation of an atmosphere of *śakti* within the marriage booth or *maṇḍap* itself. Amongst Brahmins this is effected by the *Maṇṭap-devatā pratisthāpan,* the installation of a number of *devak.* At the top of the four posts of the *maṇḍap* are installed four *devak, Nandinī, Nalinī, Maitrā* and *Umā,* through the medium of two mango-leaves tied together on which *akṣat* is thrown. In the middle of the canopy a twig of the sacred aśvath tree (Ficus religiosa) to which a pair of mango-leaves is tied, is placed, and represents *Paṣuvardhinī* whose power is invoked by mantras. Last of all, the *devak* is *Bhagvatī Śastragarbha,* a personification of the *śakti* within a weapon; near the middle of the booth a winnowing-fan is placed, surrounded by four jars connected by three threads passing all around, and in their centre is placed a knife or sword. This instrument is worshipped with *akṣat,* saffron and flowers, but it is significant that the word *āvāhayāmi,* 'I invoke', which is used in installing the other *devak,* is not employed in the installation of *Śastragarbha.* Similarly, on the sixth day after a birth an instrument, usually the knife with which the navel-cord of the child was severed, is placed on a board, but the *śakti* of *Śastragarbha* is not invoked therein, a contrast to the simultaneous invocation of the *śakti* of *Gaṇpati* into a betel-nut, and of *Janmadā* or *Ṣaṣṭhī* into a small image of gold. Lastly, on the fourth day of a marriage in the Karnāṭak a sword is worshipped, and the bridal

[1] Every planet for a period dominates all the other planets. This domination is called *daśā*; the sub-rule is *bhukti* or *antardaśā.* Saturn rules some seventeen or nineteen years; his period of mischief is seven and a half years. He has twelve houses. When a man's birth-house comes in the first, second and twelfth of these houses, he is said to suffer from the influence of *sāḍesāti,* 'seven and a half'. Saturn is also dreaded in the fifth and eighth houses.

pair, as part of the *Airaṇī* worship, go round it three times; it represents the weapon with which *Gaurī* released the bride from the clutches of Soma, Gandharva and Agni, but there is no invocation of the *śakti* of *Gaurī*. A woman is supposed never to be without a husband; until she attains four she is the wife of *Candra*, then she becomes in turn the wife of the *Gandharvas* and of *Agni*, after whom she becomes the wife of man.

The avoidance of iron in religious ceremony is further illustrated by the manner of making certain sacrifices.[1] At the fair of *Dyamava* in the Karnāṭak a Mahār called *Potrāj* tears to pieces a small lamb with his teeth, and then mixing the pieces with boiled rice throws them to all the cardinal points to make a *bhūtbaḷī* and keep away spirits. On occasions, again, of a great national calamity such as a famine or drought, sacrifices on a huge scale, *mahāyajna*, are made by a large number of Brahmins. A set of rigid rules controls the choice of the *yajamān*; he must be a man of marked piety and perfect without physical blemish, and possessing both a wife and a son; in other words, he must be possessed of considerable *śakti* and this *śakti* he must not reduce by indulgence in sleep, which is allowed him only at prescribed hours. When the sacrifice is made, two animals, a goat and a pig, are killed, the latter over the body of the former, and it is essential that no iron instrument be used in killing the animals. The animals are done to death by all the Brahmins headed by the *yajamān* pommelling them to death with their fists.

The use of iron in fashioning an image or in chiselling ornamental work would seem inevitable, but scattered all over the Dharwar district in the Karnāṭak are temples constructed, traditionally by *Jakanacārya*, a prince who in penance for accidentally killing a Brahmin, built temples throughout India from Benares to Cape Comorin. These temples are supposed to have been built without the use of any iron [2] instrument, the architect having the art of making stone soft and effecting his ornamental work by moulding. Even to-day one hears of individual sculptors accredited with the same skill. Tradition is that this King of Architects suspected his wife's fidelity and did penance for five years in a forest. The god Śiva bade him erect temples, but he complained he had no such art, whereupon Śiva placed his hand on his head, promised him divine assistance and said he should become famous as the Master Architect. He was also directed by Śiva to employ masons in

[1] *Census of India*, 1901, xvii, 214. When to secure offspring a child was killed a bronze knife was used.

[2] Cp. Exodus xx. 25, and 1 Kings vi. 7.

relays night and day as the divine architects would work for him at night, whilst if he worked only by day people would attribute his energy in building to the co-operation of evil spirits.

In the everyday construction of images the use of iron instruments is common, but the ill effects of using iron are removed after the image is complete by a ceremony called *Angyuttaraṇa Sanskār*, in which the finished image is placed in a copper basin and bathed with milk and water poured over it together. At the time, too, of using an iron chisel, it is worshipped with flowers, a *naivedya* is offered to it, *akṣat* is thrown on it and *ārtī* is waved around it to nullify its inimical power.

Iron, again, should not be brought into contact with things possessed of *śakti*, such as fire, butter, milk, grain and even the earth. The only thing that can be placed in fire without harm is the *tapani* which is heated to melt the ghee used in a *hom*, and this has to be purified by mantras before use. When the *Hoḻī* fire is kindled, the person who kindles it must remove all iron from his person. An *Agnihotrī* takes the fullest precautions to exclude iron from his fire-room, though there is in the modern fire-drill a piece of iron; his pourer and spoon are of the same wood as his drill, and his pot for hot milk is of brass. When fire is blown, an iron pipe or bellows containing iron must be avoided. Against this general rule the blacksmith is, of course, by profession a habitual offender, for he brings iron into contact with the *śakti* of fire; it follows, therefore, that he is always an unlucky wight.

Butter cannot be touched with an iron spoon nor milk be placed in iron pots. In general, no cooking is done by Hindu or Muhammadan in iron vessels. The complexities of modern life make it difficult to avoid bringing iron into contact with the ground, but there lingers an aversion to using iron ploughshares and to iron pegs for tethering cattle. In all parts of the Presidency, exclusive perhaps of Gujarāt, there is some grain crop or other which cannot be reaped with an iron instrument. The Sindi Muhammadan applies this prohibition to his matar crop (Pisum sativum), the Marāṭhā to his major grains. Iron measures, again, are tabooed in many parts; in Kanara the ordinary measure is of wood; in the Karnāṭak baskets are used on the threshing-floor though an iron measure may be used at home; in Khandesh important grains such as nagli (Eleusina Aegyptiaca) are measured in baskets and the older generation avoids iron measures in all cases. In the Deccan there is much local variation in practice. In some tracts the grain is put into bags on the threshing-floor and then measured at home; in other places it is measured at home or outside the floor. In general, a basket is used for measuring, but when the crop is held in partnership more accurate measurement is insisted upon and this leads to the use of metal measures. The use of a basket, apparently, has followed the disappearance of the old wooden measure. In Sind one is forbidden to take iron into the threshing *dera*, and here and elsewhere it is forbidden to store grain in iron vessels, or cut bread with a knife.

Though certainly not now a universal rule, the avoidance of an iron or steel instrument in severing the navel-cord of an infant is quite common. In Sind the cord is usually severed with a stalk of grain or thick grass; in Gujarāt the older generation uses a stalk of jvārī. Many tribes, such as the *Kātkarīs*, merely snap the cord. When scissors are used there is often a pretence maintained that something else actually performs the cutting. *Jains* of the Dharwar district first go through the pretence of cutting the cord with a pair of betel-leaves before they use scissors; Brahmins in the Karnāṭak first touch the navel-cord with the sacred thread of the child's father, and it is this which is supposed to do the actual cutting. On other occasions, too, iron and steel instruments are avoided or their use disguised. At a birth the caul is cut with the bangles of the mother. At a thread ceremony when the boy's head is shaved save for a tuft of hair left at the back of his head, the razor is dipped in milk, and two mango-leaves are tied to the blade, the assumption being made that the hair is really cut by the mango-leaves. In one *Marāṭhā* family I found the custom of cutting, at the time of marriage, the tuft of hair that had been left on the boy's head at the first tonsure, with a razor of gold. When the first hair of a Muhammadan child is cut in Sind, a red or green thread is tied to the razor to protect the child's head from harm.

There are four Hindu ceremonies of hair-cutting. *Jāvaḻ*, generally performed before the child completes a year of age and done in any month that is even in number counted from the birth of the child, is an additional ceremony and not counted among the *sanskār*. The *sanskār* in which a child's hair is cut are three; *Caul* performed at any time after the child has attained three years of age, and before the thread ceremony in its eighth year; the thread ceremony performed in the child's eighth year or failing this before it attains twelve; and the *Samāvartan* which in strict rule should be celebrated after a lapse of twelve years. In all these *sanskār* the same ritual is prescribed and a copper razor is used. Priests bring a copper razor, twenty-one blades of kuśa-grass, butter, curds, a pot of hot water and one of cold water, a shallow dish and materials for a *hom*. The child is made to sit on the right knee of its mother who in her turn sits to the right of her husband, the child and its parents alike facing east. Then the priests with mantras pour hot and cold water separately from the pots into the shallow dish, add to this butter and curds, and mark out the portion of the child's head that is to be shaved, by drawing a line with the butter three times round the head. Then one priest takes three blades of the kuśa-grass, holding the ends pointing towards the west, and holds them near the right ear of the child on the line of butter; a second priest cuts the grass and some of the hair with the copper razor. In this way the priests cut along the butter line, using four bundles of grass on the right of the child's head, and three on the left, exhausting all the twenty-one blades. When the priests have finished this preliminary cutting the barber does the rest, but must use the same water as that used by the priests. He too ought to use the copper razor, but in practice uses his own steel razor.

Iron must be carefully avoided in the gathering of herbs and plants with magical curative power. The thigh-bone of a black sheep killed on a Saturday averts evil-eye, but no such bone has power if the butcher has bored a hole in it before casting it away. In Kanara there are herbs called 'fever-killer' which lose their power if touched by iron; the root of turmeric, haḻad (Curcuma longa), must never be uprooted with iron. Muhammadans will not use iron in pounding antimony. The Hindu pounds his soma-leaves with a stone; leaves of bel and tulsī offered to a god must not have been cut with iron. Charmed lemons are broken with a stone by Brahmins or pierced with a silver needle to extract juice for the sick, but an iron instrument cannot be used for this purpose. To cure diarrhœa or anæmia in a child, attributed to the shadow of a woman not ritually clean, the bark of a tree is removed with a stone at daybreak and in silence; this is then made into paste on a stone with water or the urine of a cow and applied to the child's body. This prescription again loses its efficacy altogether if the bark is touched with iron.

The wearing of unsewn garments is dictated by the same idea that the contact of iron destroys power. This restriction is observed by the Muhammadan pilgrim; by the sādhu; by the Hindu bride and bridegroom; by the *guru*; by the *Vaṭu* at his thread ceremony and the woman at the ceremonies of *Sīmāntan-nayan* and *Phūlśoban*.

In Sind among Muhammadans from the moment the bridal pair sit in *vanvāha* until the marriage is complete, neither of them may eat anything cut with a knife. A Sindi Muhammadan will not beat any animal or threaten it with a piece of iron. *Konchi Koravas* fear the loss of all future sport if they use anything of iron in catching animals for food, and when they kill their captures, beat them to death with sticks. In the Karnāṭak a shopkeeper, to destroy the luck of a rival and prevent his attracting customers, will surreptitiously drive nails into the threshold of the rival's door.

There are Muhammadans who say iron cannot be taken deliberately into a mosque, though iron lamps are hung in mosques; there are in Sind mosques reputed to have no door nails or hinges of iron, and the Sindi Muhammadan will not take anything of iron with him when to win *barkat* he goes to the *dargāh* of a saint. In the Karnāṭak where Muhammadans carry in procession at *Muḥarram panjā* or hands, these cannot be of iron. A Muhammadan will no more bore a hole with iron in a *tawiz* or charm than a Hindu in a *yantra*, nor will he ever enclose a charm in a cover of iron. In Sind if one touches the top of a palm-tree with iron it forthwith withers; in Kanara it is dangerous to eat without soaking in water for hours tufts of bamboo which have been cut with iron.

The similarity between Hindu and Muhammadan ideas about iron is still more marked when we pass to the customs which illustrate how iron is destructive of evil power.

There is, first of all, the evil power inherent in man; his *pāyguṇ* which in spite of himself may work for evil. As a protection against the evil *pāyguṇ* of a guest or visitor a horse-shoe is fastened to the house door; as, too, the stranger enters the house, nails are driven into the threshold or a nail is driven into the spot where first on entering the house he placed his right foot. A more stringent measure, which one can hardly imagine any one submitting to voluntarily, is the Karnāṭak custom of showing a red-hot trowel to the sun and applying it lightly to the soles of the intruder whose *pāyguṇ* is suspect. Or it may be that a man radiates evil by his glance; once again iron horse-shoes, nails, needles and anklets of iron protect others from his evil power.

To protect a man against the evil influence of planets, against their *pīḍā*, a ring is made from a horse-shoe nail picked up on Saturday and inscribed with numbers representing the planets.

8	1	6
3	5	7
4	9	2

In the Deccan an iron nail is taken secretly from a ferry-boat and made into rings on a Saturday, and these serve the same purpose as well as avert spirits. When *Śani* or Saturn is inauspicious, Brahmins make gifts [1] of iron nails and of a *tavā* or iron plate on which bread is cooked. The lamp used in propitiation of *Śani* is invariably of iron, and a man under the *pīḍā* of Saturn wears an iron toe-ring. If a man die under a bad star, an egg and a small piece of iron are thrown into the pyre at his cremation.

Disease is a manifestation of hot and evil power, and iron is a preventive. In Sind if an insect causes inflammation of the eye the bite is touched with iron and the patient mutters, 'Let the iron swell and not the innocent eye'. In cases of intermittent fever women dip seven chains and bolts of doors in water, and drink the water. Red-hot iron is put in water and this is used as a cure for cholera and plague. Iron bangles protect children against illness; cattle are similarly protected by garlands round their necks made up of iron rings, or by iron chains. Epilepsy is cured by water in which iron scrapings have been washed. In the Mallad tracts of the Karnāṭak during an epidemic of cholera, people carry with them axes when they leave their homes; in the case of sore eyes an iron plate is passed over the eyes or the iron filings of a saw mixed with lemon juice are applied. Another practice is to rub a piece of iron with vekhand (Iris pseudacorus) in water on a stone till a paste is formed and then apply the paste to the eyes. Iron toe and finger rings avert rheumatism and piles, and an iron chain attached to a swollen leg arrests the swelling. To cure jaundice iron is heated and dipped in a mixture of curds and turmeric, and this mixture is applied to the soles of the feet and the palms of the hands. The ashes from a blacksmith's shop are valuable in curing disease as they contain iron. They must be collected before dawn by a relative of the sick man, and this on a Sunday. *Vaddars* then tie them in a cloth to a beam above the sick and make daily applications of them to the body of the patient.

Death is visualized in Indian thought as a kind of contagion and against this contagion iron is a powerful antidote. In Sind if several children of one mother die in succession the mother wears an iron anklet or ring made from the nails of a boat that has

[1] These gifts, because of the burden of evil they transfer to the recipient, are *ugra*, or fierce. A gift of iron is not necessarily always *ugra*; its *ugraṭa* or fierceness is determined by the object of the gift and the occasion of its giving. Iron is used to make an *ugra* gift at an eclipse; during obsequies and in *Nārāyaṇbaḷī*, a form of belated obsequies, and when it is intended to remove the *pīḍā* or evil influence of Saturn. An ordinary gift of iron without any object of transferring evil is called *lohadanḍ*; when the gift is *ugra* it is spoken of as *lohakhanḍ*.

sunk, and any child born subsequently is given a nose-ring of iron. After a funeral when the mourners return home, before entering their homes they must walk over a bar of iron. If a Muhammadan dies on the third, the eighth, the thirteenth, the eighteenth, twenty-third, or twenty-eighth of the lunar month, days which are full of *kudrat*, which are *ghoro* or *nahas*, a piece of iron is placed in his mouth to prevent the immediate and successive deaths of his relatives. In Gujarāt a woman who has many abortions, or whose children die young, wears an iron anklet preferably made from a butcher's knife. When a person is dying, to avert death a new black blanket is spread out and on it are placed a pumpkin, the nail-parings and cut hair of the dying man, and a piece of iron. This is all made into a bundle, adorned with flowers, and *akṣat* and black sesamum are thrown on it; the bundle is then given to a priest who waves it thrice over the dying man and throws away. If the dying man recovers, the priest who took to himself the gift must not see the man for three months. In Sind among Muhammadans, if several children have died in succession and yet another dies when born, an iron nail is driven into the ground below the waist of the mother as she lies confined.

It is not, however, always easy to distinguish in customs associated with a death, between those which aim at preventing the spread of the contagion of death, and those which are a protection against the ghost of the deceased. On the death of a *Kātkarī* an arrow is placed at the head of the corpse, and one at its feet, to prevent the return of the ghost. *Kansaras* place a knife near by when the corpse is tied to its bier. In the Karnāṭak Brahmins put a piece of iron on the chest of a woman who dies in childbirth to prevent the return of her ghost, which is amongst the most dreaded in India. In the Konkan when a death occurs in a household a horse-shoe is nailed to a pillar or to the threshold of the house. In Sind if a man dies during *panjak* days, that is between the first and the fifth, or between the twenty-fifth and thirtieth of a month, iron is buried or driven into the ground at the head of the grave; similarly, if a man dies during the three days after the tenth of *Muḥarram*, a piece of iron is buried near the head of the dead. On the death of his wife a *Marāṭhā* carries a knife about with him for five days, keeping it near by whenever he removes it, and in the hair of the deceased he puts five pins; if the woman dies within twelve days of confinement a horse-shoe is attached to the threshold, whilst if she dies in childbirth nails are driven into the ground where she breathes her last, and into the ground around her grave. Nails are also driven into the threshold to keep away the ghost of a deceased wife. In Sind iron is placed near a dead body so long as it remains in the house, and carried by any one who visits the graveyard. On the death of a *Lingāyat*, after the burial the *guru* is made to stand on an iron pick-axe and spade placed on the grave, and his feet are washed with water; this water, it is thought, sinks into the grave, and prevents the deceased becoming an evil spirit. For ten days after a death Brahmins take an iron instrument to the place where the obsequies are performed; this is dipped in water and the water is poured over the last *piṇḍa* offered to the dead, and on the last day the instrument is given to a priest. This affords protection to the soul of the dead on its way to the abode of the dead, *Pitṛlok*, and the gift to the priest increases the barkat of the dead. Non-Brahmins do likewise on the days of their obsequies, which differ from those observed by the Brahmin. It is only, however, at the obsequies immediately following a death that iron is used in this way, for at the later *Śrāddha* ceremonies the *yajamān* cannot wear anything of iron for fear of harming the dead.

There are occasions on which evil power hovers around beneficent power, as moths gather around a light; occasions on which man or woman is by reason of innate power temporarily more liable than at other times, to the attack of spirits. At a birth special precautions are taken to protect both child and mother. In the Deccan nails are driven into the ground at each corner of the mother's bed; in Sind the same protection is afforded by four arrows placed at the corners of the bed. Muhammadans in Sind keep both a sword and a clasp-knife near and a pair of iron tongs, whilst in the child's cradle is placed an iron tripod covered with a cloth. The instrument with which the navel-cord of the infant was severed frequently serves the later purpose of averting spirits when placed under the mother's pillow. In Sind it is kept under her pillow for forty days; *Kumbhārs* keep it under the pillow for eleven days, *Pancāḻs* for five, and *Koravas* for three days. Throughout the ten days following the birth of her child the *Sarasvat Brahmin* mother keeps with her this same instrument, and takes it with her whenever she leaves her room. To protect the mother and her child on the sixth day after a birth, *Vaiśyas* patrol round the house throughout the night with iron instruments in their hands, and beating kettledrums. Iron nails driven into the threshold keep spirits away from a woman's confinement room, and a *Lingāyat* woman from the first moment she becomes *enceinte* wears an iron needle in her hair. The *Vaddar* woman during her confinement keeps a knife in her armpit.

Muhammadans of the Karnāṭak observe the following custom. In front of the mother and child is placed a small lamp with four wicks fed with ghee, the bowl of the lamp being a cup of wheaten flour or a copra shell according as the child is a girl or a boy. The knife with which the child's cord was cut is then taken, a lemon is stuck on its point and it is inserted in the flame of the lamp. The soot with which the lemon is soon covered is used to mark the eyes of the child and mother. With a needle heated in the flame the nurse makes two lines on the head of the child, a sign like a plus on its stomach, and below the chest. Then the mother with the child is taken near the door and asked to look at a star which, when she finds, the nurse chants '*Pīk pāṇī ābād haye*', and sprinkles water over them. As a protection against spirits the mother is covered with a blanket, the knife is held before her as she walks slowly towards the door, and the lemon cut in two pieces is thrown on either side of her path.

When a child is born to *Mahār* parents an iron vessel is placed near its ear and struck with a nail, and water is sprinkled on the child. In the fifth month of pregnancy *Rājputs* put a diadem on a woman's head, and this contains an iron needle.

Precisely because the bridal pair, and in particular the bridegroom, is charged with power; because the whole atmosphere of a marriage is one of power, evil spirits throng around and measures to avert them are a familiar feature of the marriage ceremony in all communities. In Sind iron rings are given to the bride. Before the actual marriage begins the Muhammadan bride and bridegroom 'sit in *vanvāha*', which means that the bride sits for seven or nine days in a room apart and sees no male person. The bridegroom is supposed to remain apart for one day, but in reality walks about with his head covered with a cloth. Whilst the bride and bridegroom are in *vanvāha* they have each a knife; the bridegroom retains his knife until *Sataware*, when after completion of the marriage ceremony he accompanies his bride to her father's house. The best man helps the bridegroom to guard his knife, and when the heads of the bridal pair are brought together during the marriage ceremony the knife is held between the pair and over their heads. In Gujarāt *madanphūl* (Vangueria spinosa), the use of which is supposed to foster love, is tied to the hands of the bridal pair with an iron ring. Among the *Kan Divar* and *Madival* communities the bridegroom must carry a knife in his hand, whenever during the five days of the marriage ceremony he wears his *bāśing*. *Kunbis, Kolhatis, Marāṭhās* and Muhammadans in the Deccan require the bridegroom to carry a dagger with a lemon on its point; the *Kansara* bridegroom carries a dagger when he goes from his own house to that of the bride. *Calvadis* worship a sword before a marriage, and after the marriage the bridegroom takes the sword to a temple, and this sword he must wear the first day he puts on his crown, though not after the first day. In this very common practice of carrying a sword or dagger at a marriage to avert spirits, there would seem to enter the idea of a successful struggle with the mysterious powers, for until quite recently the *Marāṭhā* bridegroom carried a shield as well as his dagger.

Lingāyats, to protect the bride and bridegroom, place beneath their seat a knife, fork, and a piece of iron. Among *Vaiśyas* an iron instrument is tied to the waist of the bridegroom in the *Samāvartan* ceremony performed before his marriage. Among *Lamānis* two earthen saucers filled with parched rice, dates, lemons and iron nails or needles are waved before the bridal pair and thrown away to avert spirits. There are many castes in Gujarāt who offer to or wave round the bridegroom a wooden pestle, a churning stick and also an arrow and a plough. The *Koḻī* bride is brought to the marriage *manḍap* holding an arrow in her hand. At a *Māng* marriage the maternal uncles of the bridal pair stand near them with a knife on the point of which is a lemon.

One feature of a Hindu marriage is the bath, *mangaḻsnān*, which the bridal pair take in the *manḍap*; they do this in a small space enclosed by earthen pots around which thread is wound, forming a barrier against evil. One accepted surmise is that the word *surgi* applied to the thread and to the bath is a corruption of *churikā*, 'knives', which of old protected the pair against spirits. When five married women or the mothers of the bridal pair at a marriage of *Gollars*, *Raddis* and *Kabbars*, go to a well to fetch water for this auspicious bath, a man accompanies them bearing a sickle with a lemon on its point to prevent a spirit entering the water. In Sind among Muhammadans the best man, *anar*, holds a knife over the water-pipe as the mothers of the bridal pair draw water.

Among *Deśastha Brahmins* after the *Lājāhom* and the marriage feast, the party of the bridegroom comes with music to fetch the bride, bringing a jewelled ornament which the bride worships as Lakṣmī, goddess of good fortune. The bride and bridegroom are given new clothes, and a carpet is spread on which the bridegroom's father sits with the bride on his knees. He is called upon to protect the bride and agrees to do so; then water is poured on his head and he puts sugar in the bride's mouth. His example is followed by all the elders of the bridegroom's family, including his mother. The bride is then handed to the bridegroom and both proceed to the family shrine; as they proceed the bride's mother carries a lighted lamp and the maternal uncle holds a sword in the flame of the lamp. After the worship of the *kul devatā* the soot formed on the blade of the sword is applied to the faces of the bridal pair, and then the bridegroom is allowed to take away his bride. This is the *Sade* ceremony.

At his circumcision the Muhammadan boy holds a piece of wood tipped with iron, and a sword is held over him as he sits on an earthen pot. He also wears a ring of iron in a wristlet of thread, and until his wound is healed has a knife which must not touch the ground and which he puts under his pillow when he sleeps.

When a Brahmin girl attains puberty she is protected from spirits by an iron instrument or rod enclosed in a plantain-leaf or sheath, which is kept near her and waved over her every morning and evening for three days. As a protection against spirits during their keeping of penance Hindu saints eat iron filings every day, and have an iron ring fastened to the stick they keep with them. Persons supposed to be possessed by spirits wear iron anklets; mantriks who essay to dispossess spirits wave an iron rod over the victim of possession and beat it on the ground; they also drive nails into the ground in each of the cardinal directions to form a *dikbāndha* [1] or barrier against the intrusion of spirits. A child who is born feet foremost is peculiarly liable to be struck by lightning, so it is protected by an anklet of iron, or a piece of iron tied in its loin-cloth.

In a thunderstorm *Kātkarīs* and others in the Konkan throw iron ploughshares out of doors. Iron is carried on the person as a protection against lightning. So far then from rendering lightning innocuous to man by using iron to determine its path, as is the object of Western science, Indian superstition visualizes lightning as a spirit which iron will scare away. As the Indian practice is supposed to drive away the spirit of lightning, the *Mahār* believes that it protects not only the inmates of the house who are at home, but also those who happen to be away from home. Sindi Muhammadans to avert lightning keep an iron pot in their field or near their house.

Erotic dreams are attributed to spirits, so to avert these brooms

[1] *Dikbāndha* is the fortification of the cardinal regions: east; south-east; south; south-west; west; north-west; north; north-east; *urdhava* (above) and *adhas* (below). In religious ceremonies it is essential first to defend these points against the intrusion of evil. Water is sprinkled in these directions by means of tulsī-leaves; *akṣat* or white mustard seeds are scattered in the same directions. In car festivals the sacred car is protected in this way; in the Mallad tracts of the Karnāṭak houses and other property are protected from thieves by a *dīkbāndha*, and crops are similarly protected.

or iron instruments are kept near the pillow of the sleeper. The agency of spirits is suspected if milch cattle do not give milk, and an iron chain is fastened to one of their horns, and a copper *yantra* filled with filings of a saw round their necks. Fear is caused by spirits, and so when a child shows fear it is given to drink water in which red-hot iron has been dipped, and to wear round its neck an iron knife or ring.

To protect fruit-trees from spirits worn-out shoes with their iron nails are hung on them. First-born children, if boys, are peculiarly liable to the attentions of spirits and accordingly wear a piece of iron in their loin-cloth. Iron horse-shoes fixed on a threshold debar entry to spirits ; non-Brahmins fix the anvil of a blacksmith to their threshold. Horse-shoes are used by mantriks to cure spirit-possession ; iron nails are driven into spots haunted by spirits ; when treasure is buried, care is taken to place it in an iron vessel or to bind the receptacle with an iron chain, that spirits may not interfere with it.

The assumption that iron is inimical to power results in many inconsistencies of practice. These inconsistencies are very marked in the ritual of the threshing-floor, for side by side with practices that enforce the avoidance of iron as detrimental to the innate power of the grain, one finds practices which adopt iron as a protection against the evil power of spirits. In the Deccan if the activity of a witch is feared, and she works with the co-operation of spirits, two to seven nails are driven until invisible into the ground near the central pole of the threshing-floor. Iron is also placed on the ground if any one approaches the floor to avert his evil eye. In Khandesh beneath the central pole of the floor is placed, when the pole is erected, a biba or marking nut pierced with needles, and when the collected grain is placed on the threshing-floor a nail or a piece of iron is placed in the pile, *rās*. Even the more primitive tribes such as those of the *Bhil* and the *Mavchi* put iron in the *rās*, under the belief not only that it scares away spirits, but also that it leads to the increase of the gathered grain. Marking nuts pierced with needles or sickles are often placed surreptitiously in the *rās*. In the Panch Mahals, though no one would enter the threshing-floor carrying a sickle after the grain had been brought in, before the work of gathering the grain begins a sickle is placed on the floor, in the belief that it prevents the scattering of the grain. In Sind again no one may enter the threshing *dera* carrying iron, but a ring of iron is tied to the *nih* or central pole of the threshing-floor, and over the pile of grain a piece of iron is suspended to avert spirits.

In a very large number of customs there is this same inconsistency. If the Sindi bridal pair cannot for several days eat anything that has been cut with a knife, it is because their kudrat must not be impaired by contact with iron, yet the protection of the pair from spirits involves their being brought into a very literal closeness to iron. If iron or steel is avoided in the cutting of the child's navel-cord it is because iron must not be brought near to the *śakti* or *kudrat* of the child, yet the ritual connected with a birth brings iron near the child with the object of protecting it against evil power. The use of iron at the obsequies of the dead to bring the deceased protection and even *barkat* is in contrast with the avoidance of iron at *Śrāddha* ceremonies. It is in contrast, too, to another custom. On a death the son, wife, or other relative of a Hindu deceased lights a lamp at the place where the dead actually expired. The soul of the dead is supposed to take up its abode in this lamp for ten days. On the tenth day the lamp is carefully taken to the burning ghat, and with it is lighted a fire used during the offering of *piṇḍa* to the dead, and the light is then extinguished. This light consists of an earthen plate, *paṇatī*, with a single wick turned towards the south, and can never be of iron. The cord with which a Hindu corpse is tied to a bier cannot be cut by any implement of iron, but only by a stone for fear of harming the *barkat* of the dead, and the coins that are placed under the *jīvkhaḍā* which embodies the power of the deceased are of copper, yet myriad are the examples of the use of iron at a funeral or death to keep away the ghost of the dead, or the contagion of death. In many ceremonies, lastly, the participants must not imperil their *śakti* or *kudrat* by wearing garments which have been sewn, yet iron and steel avert from them evil power.

These apparent inconsistencies arise from the fact that iron is inimical to all forms of power, be it good or evil.

In Hindu thought *himsā* is the destruction of life, and iron is the chief instrument of *himsā*. An act of *himsā* destroys *śakti*, and hence follow rules that forbid grinding, sweeping, washing, shaving and hair-cutting and enforce chastity. The instrument of *himsā*, iron, equally destroys *śakti*. Its presence would prevent *śakti* taking up its abode in a symbol, would render ineffective any act of invocation; its presence would render fruitless any rite, religious or magical, the intended results of which depend for their fruition on *śakti*. On the other hand, iron is equally destructive of evil *śakti*; it averts the evil *śakti* of *pāygun*, of *dṛṣṭi*, of the *pīḍā* of the planets, it averts spirits.

The modern Hindu labours hard at times to make primitive

ideas harmonize with the changed circumstances and necessities of the twentieth century. An ingenious explanation in this way was given me of the use of an iron *ankuśa* to drive an elephant and of an iron bit to drive a horse, and again of an iron *tavā* to roast bread. In each case, I was told, the iron was used to reduce *śakti*; to reduce the *śakti* of the elephant and horse so as to make them manageable and to reduce that of the bread so as to make it edible by man without danger. The explanation at least calls attention to the belief that iron is inimical to *śakti*, and along with it I would give one more.

The practice of driving nails into trees varies considerably in detail in different areas of the Presidency. In Gujarāt the nail is first waved round a sick person and when driven into the tree effects a transfer of evil to the tree, evidenced in many cases by the withering of the tree. This bringing of the nail, however, into contact with a sufferer is not a universal practice; in many cases the nail has never been in any implied contact with the sufferer, it is withdrawn, too, from the tree after a cure has been effected. In these latter cases the driving of the nail into the tree is nothing but a coercion of the power of the tree, *mair* as the Sindi Muhammadan would term it, and paralleled by the practice followed both by the Hindu and the Muhammadan of coercing the power of a saint by driving a nail into the door of his tomb or *dargāh*. A belief I found in the Deccan puts this idea of coercion in a novel form. The tree, it is said, possesses the *śakti* of the sun, iron possesses the *śakti* of Saturn, and the sun and Saturn are inveterate enemies. When, then, a nail is driven into a tree, the *śakti* of the sun, eager to free itself from such an incubus, listens to entreaty and grants a demanded request.

Whether or not the 'innovation'[1] theory which explains the superstitious aversion to iron as a dislike of a new metal is justified, whether or not spirits are essentially creatures of the Stone Age, the apparent inconsistencies of Indian practice seem to find a rational explanation in the doctrine of *himsā*. In a matter-of-fact world with its pressing necessities man has to make a choice, and so sometimes he avoids iron in order to preserve beneficent *śakti* and at other times he employs iron to remcve evil *śakti*; in some cases he is compelled by necessity to commit an act of destruction he would prefer to avoid, the navel-cord has

[1] Vide *Primitive Culture*, E. B. Tylor, 1873, vol. i, p. 140; *Ritual and Belief in Morocco*, E. Westermarck, 1926, vol. i, p. 311; *Religion and Folklore of Northern India*, W. Crooke, 1926, p. 283; *The Golden Bough*, Part ii, 'Taboo and the Perils of the Soul', Sir James Frazer, p. 232; *Encyclopaedia of Religion and Ethics*, A. E. Crawley, vol. viii, p. 590.

to be severed and the hair has to be cut, so making the best of things he adopts a camouflage.

IMPLEMENTS

Upakaraṇ

An implement or instrument is something used by man, the potentiality of which is inseparable from his own power. It is bad to use the implements of another whose fortune is usually bad, and contrariwise it is lucky to use his instruments if he be a man of good fortune. When a man dies his weapons may be destroyed in the belief that it is unlucky for another to use them, or that in the hands of another they will be without power, but they may also be preserved as objects which will transfer to others the power of their first owner. Both these ideas govern practice in India. The *Kātkarī* breaks the weapons of the dead, not only to send them without life to the world of the dead, but also to prevent others using them; the Muhammadan preserves the implements of the old, particularly their weaving instruments, and at a Muhammadan wedding the bridal pair is protected by a dagger of the family handed down from one generation to another.

There is no example, as I have said, of *śakti* being invoked into an instrument of iron, partly because no such invocation into iron can be made, but also in part because there is already *śakti* in an implement and two *śaktis* cannot occupy the same symbol. Instruments are associated often with special deities. Quite apart from the association of the goddess *Lakṣmi* with almost everything a man uses in his daily life to his profit, other deities are connected with implements. The Brahmin calls the *devak* he installs *Bhagvatī Śastragarbha*; criminal tribes such as the *Bauriah* associate their instrument of crime, *gian*, with the goddess *Kāli*, and a familiar example of such deification was that by the Thugs of their pick-axe. *Davris* have a three-pronged fork, a gourd and a dry pumpkin; *Gondhalis* have a torch, a tambourine and a musical instrument called *cavanke*, and in these instruments they believe their respective goddesses *Jotiba* and *Ambabai* reside.

Implements of every kind are worshipped to add to their *śakti* just as images of deities are worshipped with the same object, and this especially at moments full of *śakti*. *Amāvāsyā* is a day taken by many Hindu castes for this worship; holidays such as *Gaṇeśa Caturthī* and *Divāḷī* and *Pūrṇimā* are also days of such worship. *Lingāyat Kumbhārs* worship their implements after an eclipse, During this worship of implements, as during the worship of divine symbols, there can be no act of *himsā*. *Pancāḻs* and *Tiglars*, to give one example, will not during the worship of their implements, allow grinding, the threshing of grain, washing, sweeping or even the cleaning of the house with cowdung, whilst there can be no shaving or cutting of the hair.

In other respects, too, the *śakti* of implements receives the same protection as that of a divine symbol. Instruments must not be stepped over; they must not come in contact with any kind of impurity. From the worship of implements women are on occasions often excluded, as on *Amāvāsyā*, and criminal tribes usually shield their implements not only from the contact of woman but even from being seen by woman. There are, moreover, other restrictions which suggest that further precautions to protect the *śakti* of implements were formerly universal. When the instrument with which the navel-cord of a child was cut is worshipped some days subsequent to the child's birth, it is placed on an *āsan*, on a plank. At a marriage when the services of *Gondhalis* are taken, an *āsan* of red and white flowers or a cross of wheat and pieces of coconut is made on a piece of cloth, and on this their instruments are placed; on the same occasion the *triśuḻ* or three-pronged fork is brought to the marriage *maṇḍap* under a canopy. *Gondhalis* have also an aversion to placing their instruments at any time in the sun, though they only voice a vague fear that the sun will spoil the instruments. Another example of protection given to an implement, after the manner in which *śakti* in general is protected, is the care with which the *gian* of the *Bauriah* is preserved from becoming wet, to ensure which the weapon is kept buried.

The *śakti* of an implement varies according to that of the person using it, in the same way that the *śakti* of an image varies according to the *śakti* of the person who worships it. Man's *śakti* controls, in fine, the amount of *śakti* radiated from an image and no less that radiated from an implement.

CHAPTER IX

THE POWER OF SALT

SALT has *śakti* or *kudrat*. In Kanarese they say, 'There is no better relative than a mother, and no better taste than that of salt.' It is supposed that everything in the universe contains salt. *Uppe uppu*, 'Salt, salt and nothing else', is a Kanarese phrase. In Gujarāt a handsome person is said to have a 'saltish face'; 'on his face is plenty of salt'. An Arabic word, *malih*, is used in Sind to mean both 'saltish' and 'handsome'.

Salt confers *barkat*; when it does not do this, it is said 'In your salt there is no salinity', whilst the Sindi Muhammadan would say, 'Asanje nimakjo doh ahe', 'It is the guilt of our salt', or 'Asanje nimak men harkat ahe'. 'The salt of a disliked person has no salinity', *Nāvaḍtīce mīṭh aḷaṇī* (Mar.). Salt has the essence, *anśa*, of Lakṣmī, the goddess of good fortune; *Lingāyats* will not put grains of salt on their plates as they have the form of a *linga*, and must not be powdered. According to Muhammadan tradition, 'Salt is the Sardar of foods'. Other Muhammadan sayings are: 'Commence your meals with salt and end them with salt'; 'He who begins his food with salt and ends with it, his sins will be forgiven and God will forgive those who take food in his house in this manner'. In the Karnāṭak salt should be served first on all auspicious occasions and last on inauspicious occasions. In Gujarāt salt must be the first thing among the purchases made for a marriage, but in the Deccan with sweet-oil it must be the last of such purchases. Salt is among the *daśadāna* or the ten things which are given away to obtain *mokṣa*, and in the mantra accompanying the gift of salt by a Hindu it is spoken of as 'the best of savoury articles promoting strength'.

Spirits are scared away by salt. The *Lamāni* bridal pair at one moment in the marriage ceremony walk in silence to a heap of cowdung placed towards the south, and bow to it; at that time the priest puts salt on their heads to avert spirits. Among *Lingāyats* salt is put all round a corpse at its burial to protect it from spirits, and salt is carried along with the body in a winnowing-fan to the burial ground. *Lingāyats* also keep four bundles of salt on the four legs of the mother's cot, after the birth of her child, to keep away spirits. To prevent cattle disease, again the work of spirits, salt is tied to the roof of a cattle-shed, and salty water is sprinkled around the shed. As a protection against spirits salt is buried near a newly-dug well or the spring of water which feeds it as soon as it appears. If a Hindu goes to a cremation ground at night he carries with him salt. On a journey when it sleeps at night, a child is protected by salt placed under its pillow, and travellers beginning a journey at night put salt in the tassel of their turbans. A person attacked by small-pox is after his recovery taken to a temple of *Durga* to show his gratitude; at that time he is very weak from illness, and so a bundle of salt is placed on his head as a protection against spirits, and he keeps this till he reaches the temple; he does not require it, however, on his return, as he is then protected by the *prasād* of the goddess. Pilgrims on their return from the temple of the goddess *Yallavā*, take a small bundle of salt and throw it on a stone image near the temple called *Hurakin Yallavā*, to keep away itch. Salt with herbs is put in a bag and hung round the necks of children suffering from *bālgraha*, a disease brought by spirits.

If a child starts suddenly to show fear the mother takes salt, and eating it, blows her breath upon the child to convey to it the *śakti* of the salt. A baby requires special protection, and when carried in a public conveyance is protected by a knot of cloth containing salt tied under its arm. If a Sindi Muhammadan falls under the evil influence of a star he is weighed against salt and the salt is thrown into a river. *Lingāyats* place salt on the spot where the bride puts her right foot on entering her husband's house for the first time after her marriage. When the *Tamil Christian* bride first enters her husband's house, just before she actually enters it the bridegroom's party give her salt to eat, to render her *pāyguṇ* harmless. Similarly, when *Tamil Christians* move from one house to another, salt and a pot of water are placed on the threshold of the new house. Hindus, in general, mix salt with the cowdung with which the floor of a new building is first smeared; salt and mustard are also put in a doll of black cloth and hung, the doll upside-down, in front of a new house. In the Dharwar district if whilst a man is eating, another man intrudes, the former attributes to the *pāyguṇ* of the latter any subsequent pain he feels, and to cure this eats salt with betel-leaves. If the calves of a cow die successively at birth, salt mixed with asafoetida is put in the mouth of the next-born to avert death. Salt is buried at the corners of a haunted house to keep away ghosts (*Kāvakaṭṭodu*), whilst water in which salt has been dissolved is sprinkled in a cattle-shed on the outbreak of foot-and-mouth disease.

Salt averts evil-eye. It is therefore very commonly used at marriages to protect the power of the bridal pair. In Gujarāt the young sister of the bridegroom sits behind him in his carriage, or even on the same saddle, as he goes to the bride's house, and continually waves over his head a bowl containing a rupee and salt. In the Deccan at a Muhammadan marriage the women attendant on the bride tie salt in their own head-dress; five women hold a sheet over the bridal pair and the bride's mother then waves her salt five times over the head of the bride and throws it into water to remove evil-eye (*nazar utarne*). Mantriks mutter charmed words over salt and put this on the tongue of a victim of evil-eye. An everyday precaution against evil-eye is to wave salt with chillies three times at sunset and throw into fire. If a man cannot digest his food, which clearly shows that he is afflicted with evil-eye or victimized by evil *pāygun*, charmed salt is given him to eat. A Sindi Muhammadan attempts to cure one afflicted with evil-eye by mixing earth taken from under his heel with salt and throwing this with chillies into fire, or waves salt, turmeric and an egg over the victim and throws these things at cross-roads or into a graveyard. When a man's sickness is attributed to evil-eye, earth from four roads, pieces of a broom and salt are waved from head to foot of the patient by an old woman, and by her from her palm thrown into fire, and this is repeated again and again until a warning crackling indicates the burning of the evil power.

The power of salt is made use of for many a purpose. If a Sindi goes to his shop, in order to get many customers, before leaving home he takes an egg and a pinch of salt, and waves them round himself, then breaks the egg and throws its interior on to cross-roads, and the shell and the salt into fire. Sindi Muhammadans bury in the bedroom of the bridal pair salt, leaves of the sirih tree and an egg, to increase their love for each other. On the last *Sankramaṇa* called *Mīna Sankramaṇa* or *Lavaṇa*, the Hindu makes a point of giving away salt in the name of the sun to acquire *puṇya*. Hindus and Muhammadans alike add salt to sweet dishes to get *barkat*. On the Hindu New Year's Day as early as three or four o'clock in the morning vendors of salt go from door to door in Gujarāt calling out '*Sabras, sabras*', 'salt', and every one tries to begin the new year with the purchase of salt.

In Sind the Muhammadan bride and bridegroom pour salt into each other's hands in order to have issue in proportion. This is called *phul main*, 'to measure flower'. This measuring of salt is, indeed, done twice; once during the marriage after the heads of the bridal pair have been brought together, and again when the bride enters her husband's house after the marriage. In the Karnāṭak a custom among *Deśastha Brahmins* and others is for the bridal pair to step upon piles of wheat and salt on the fourth day of the marriage; behind each of these piles is drawn an image of an elephant. The elephant is supposed to be the *vāhan* or vehicle of *Indra*, the god of wealth; *akṣat* is thrown on the elephants and mantras invoke therein the *śakti* of the god. The maternal uncle of the bride holds the bridegroom and his wife the bride as they step on the piles. The bridegroom's elephant is called *Bhadramātang* and the bride's elephant *Mattamātang*. The images are worshipped with the words 'Celestial elephant, give benediction to the bridal pair that they may win happiness'. This stepping on the elephants and the piles is called *Gajārohaṇ*, and is done before the bridal pair leave the bride's house for the temple.

Because of its innate power, salt is used in the transference of evil. It is put in an iron pan and given to a priest to transfer the evil accruing from the adverse influence of Saturn in *Sāḍesāti*. It is used in making *ugra* gifts, particularly when an hour such as that of an eclipse favours such gifting. At an eclipse salt is given to the depressed *Māngs* to transfer to them all evil besetting the household of the giver. At an eclipse the Sindi Muhammadan uses salt in a variety of ways. He takes salt to a burning *ghāṭ* where he collects ashes from a funeral pyre equal in weight to the salt, and brings home the salt and ashes, after the eclipse has passed, as a panacea against all illness. He mixes salt with an equal weight of earth from a cemetery and with powdered pulse makes a figure of his enemy, and writing on it the name of his enemy and of his enemy's mother buries the image, encompassing in this way the illness of his enemy. At an eclipse he throws away his old stock of salt, throwing it in a well, and buys a fresh stock to get barkat; he throws salt in a well or at the root of a tree to free himself from illness; he stands neck-deep in water holding a piece of rock-salt till the eclipse is over, then breaks the salt in seven pieces and throwing one piece daily into fire, calls upon his love to come, which she does, of course, before the seventh piece is thrown away. At a funeral Muhammadans give salt to a fakir to remove the sins of the dead, and with the same object

Brahmins give salt to a priest on the first and twelfth days of the obsequies. In Sind the Muhammadan takes to the grave a bag of salt, and after the funeral this is distributed among the poor to get rid of the sins of the dead.

It is typical of everything that possesses power that its power, even though usually beneficent, contains an element of danger. Salt is no exception to this general rule, and many precautions have to be taken to guard against the danger inherent in salt. It is very inauspicious to go out carrying salt or even to meet a person carrying salt; a Hindu when carrying salt cannot salute another. Salt again cannot be received in the hand. When he offers salt to another a Muhammadan puts it in a cloth or on a plate and allows the other to take it up; a Hindu puts it in a cloth or in a pot which he places on the ground. Accepted in the hand the receiver loses his wealth and shortens his life, and enmity and quarrels follow. If unavoidably or accidentally any one places salt in the hands of another, it is imperative to say at once '*valitu*', 'good wishes', to avert impending evil. Salt cannot be given away at night; it should never be put in milk and save to cure the effects of evil-eye may not be thrown in fire.

Neither a Hindu nor a Muhammadan will step over salt. After a meal, if any salt remain on a plate it must be wetted with water before it is thrown away; to throw away salt without this precaution is to run the risk of falling heavily into debt. Salt cannot be thrown on the ground. Throughout the Presidency, exclusive of Sind, the vernaculars all have the same saying that one who throws salt on the ground will have to pick it up at the Judgment[1] with his eye-lashes, a saying that, strange to say, is also found in Syria and in Morocco. Salt cannot be carried at the same time as ghee, nor along with oil. It cannot be sold at sunset, nor can it be purchased on a Saturday or on an *Amāvāsyā*. At a wedding the salt used must on no account be brought from another village, but obtained in the village where the wedding is celebrated. Salt is included in the articles alluded to in the phrase *ras vikrāya*; strictly speaking, it should never be sold and those who sell it are still despised. Though on a night journey as a protection against spirits a Hindu would take the minor risk and protect himself with salt, he would not otherwise begin a journey carrying salt but would make a purchase of salt after starting. Sometimes when one inmate of a household sets out on a journey the rest of the inmates will avoid salt, for salt easily absorbs water and perishes, and its dissolving would entail the failure of the journey's

[1] Cp. *Ritual and Belief in Morocco*, E. Westermarck, 1926, vol. i, p. 115 and note.

object. Practice varies and there are those who will eat salted food on such an occasion and fear no consequences, but would not add salt to their food. When a man cannot begin his journey at an auspicious moment he hangs his provisions for the journey to a peg outside his door as an indication that he has begun his journey, and then sets out later at his convenience, the journey being held to have commenced auspiciously. His provision for the journey includes rice, turmeric, a coconut and pice, but must never include salt.

Hindus think that a person who eats the salt of another begins to think as the other thinks. A Hindu creditor who has just lent money to a debtor goes home at once and touches salt with the same hand as that with which he handed over the money; this ensures the perpetuity of the loan which the debtor is never able to repay in full.

Oaths are taken by salt. An oath by salt is taken by a purchaser when a vendor disputes his payment of the purchase price. It is also common among more primitive communities such as *Koravas*, *Bhils*, *Ghattivaddars*, *Dong Dasaris* and *Bestars*. The power of salt is also useful in imposing a conditional curse. A treacherous man will not eat the salted food of another lest the power of the salt destroy him. One instance of this I came across was that of a gang of thieves who broke into the shop of a jeweller. The leader of the gang, picking up what he imagined was a very fine jewel, tested it between his teeth, but found it to be rock-salt, whereupon he took away his men without touching anything else in the shop. *Brahmins* and *Rajputs* alike offer salt to an unknown guest, who refuses it if his intentions be bad. *Nimak halāl* means 'true to one's salt'; *nimak-khaver* is a loyal man, an eater of salt; *nimak harām* is one who is false to his salt, and these terms still have a meaning in India to-day. Among Sindi Muhammadans a very bad form of cursing is to say '*Luni lagai*', 'May salt affect you'.

One explanation for the avoidance of salt at a *Śrāddha* meal is that the use of salt would mean demanding gratitude from the dead. To discover a thief a Sindi Muhammadan gives cakes of flour and salt to a number of people, including the suspect; the actual thief on eating the salt betrays himself by bleeding at the mouth.

The use of salt is supposed to hasten maturity and foster passion. At the approach of fruit, salt is put at the stem of fruit-trees and then well watered to increase the yield of fruit; it is put at the root of coconut-trees to make them fertile and a mixture of ghee and salt is supposed to increase the human creative power. Ascetics avoid salt. *Agnihotrīs* avoid salt that is not obtained from a mine. It is avoided on the inception of a vow until the vow has been completed; persons who have vowed to perform a fixed number of *jap* avoid it, as also women who take a vow on *Bhādrapad*, sud. 5. From the beginning of the marriage ceremony until the *Gharbharaṇī*, or entry of the bridegroom's house after the marriage, the Hindu bridal pair must abstain from salt.

CHAPTER X

THE POWER OF STONES

ACCORDING to Muhammadan belief, a stone is pure; it prays to God. Stones are placed on a grave to confer *barkat* on the dead, and a grave, as far as possible, is made of stones. Those who cannot afford to construct a grave of stone place pebbles on the grave. Contact with a stone at the time of prayer increases the efficacy of the prayer; the prophet Muhammad used to recite his prayers holding pebbles in his hand, and a learned man's prayers are rendered more effective by his sitting on a stone. To bring rain several men meet and, taking pebbles, recite over them collectively the name of God.

To cure illness verses of the Koran are written on a stone along with the name of the sick person, to each letter of which a numerical value is given, and then the stone is thrown in a well. By taking forty-one stones and reciting over them verses from the Koran one can bring even the fairies to earth to do one's bidding. When evil-eye is suspected a stone is taken; thread is wrapped round it and Koranic verses recited over it by some one other than the afflicted person. Then the stone is thrown into fire; if there be evil-eye the thread will not burn so long as it is round the stone; the thread has to be removed, cut in three pieces and thrown independently into fire. Women bring from Arabia stones called *Kadam Mubārak* on which Haḍrat 'Ali is supposed to have trod; these are dipped in water and the water is drunk to cure illness.

A stone resents any form of uncleanness. It is forbidden to kick a stone. One may not remove any form of impurity with a stone, and when masons saw stones they refrain from sexual congress until their work is finished or the stones will break irregularly and the cuts will not be straight.

Stones are used to coerce power to act according to man's desire. Trees are warned that if a request is not granted within a certain time, stones will be placed on them; if the request is not granted stones are placed on the tree at the stated time to force the tree to accede to the request. Similarly, a Sindi Muhammadan places stones on the tombs of saints as a coercion of their special power. In this practice there enters also the idea that the stone prays to God, and the saint is gratified by the blessing that follows its prayer. A stone is placed on the top of a tree and a promise made to the tree that a flag will be substituted for the stone if the tree listens to a request.

A stone is placed in a cradle to prevent the child crying. If a man goes a journey with a baby, he waves three stones over the baby and then facing the direction of the place he is leaving, throws away the stones. To cure a scorpion-bite a stone is placed on the bite and three times the bitten man says, 'Let not the poison ascend' and then removes the stone. With the object of injuring an enemy a Muhammadan writes the enemy's name and that of his mother on a stone, recites over it *Ism Azam* and then breaks the stone. If a man loves a girl he writes his own name and the names of the girl, her mother and his own mother on a stone, and buries it quietly in her hearth; when the fire is kindled and the stone becomes warm the fire of love is kindled in the girl. If a man wants a girl to come to him he writes these same names on a stone, recites *Ism Azam* and ties the stone to a tree; when the wind blows the tree, the girl is smitten with love and comes to the man. One may also produce heat and cold at will in the body of an enemy; the first by writing the names of the enemy and of his mother on a stone and placing it in the sun; the second by hanging such a stone on a tree or high place in cold surroundings.

Somewhat inconsistent with the recitation of the Koran over stones is the belief that when the Koran is so recited with a good object the stone may break because extremely sensitive to the presence of *kudrat*.

To a Hindu a stone is a thing possessing life and a soul, possessing *śakti*. The cutting of a stone for a building involves the destruction of this life, so, on completion of a house, well or wall or any construction of stone a *śānti* is imperative. Three stones are placed together and on them a pot, *kalaśa*, of water; a *prayascitta hom* is performed and after this the water in the pot is sprinkled all over the house to protect the stone-dressers from the resentment of outraged power.

A stone adds force to an oath or to a curse. The force of an oath is greater when the taker of the oath holds a stone or stands upon a stone. To augment the power of a curse two stones are placed, the one on the other, and then cut. A Muhammadan to make more serious the oath taken by his enemy will grind stones when the oath is taken. In both cases a destructive act is committed. Boundary stones may embody curses upon those that violate the boundaries, the penalty of transgression being inscribed on the stones. In the Deccan, if two persons agree to meet at a certain place, and only one of them keeps his word, he sets up a stone at the meeting-place and this compels the other to regale him and his friends with sweetmeats. *Thakurs* have a form of betrothal by means of a stone; a man wishing to marry a widow throws a stone at her which she picks up and produces before an assembly of elders who enforce the betrothal.

Stones are used by many castes to add strength to the marriage vow. *Raddis* at the time *akṣat* is thrown on the bridal pair make the bridegroom stand in front of the bride, a curtain between them, on a stone used for kneading bread. At a wedding *Simpīs* make the bride and bridegroom alternately stand on a stone and a rope, or place the stone and rope under the respective chairs of the bride and bridegroom. The Brahmin parallel to these practices is the rite of *Aśmārohaṇ*,[1] 'standing on a stone'. A stone, usually the one used for grinding sandal-paste (*sāṇīkallu, sahāṇ*), is placed near the marriage *hom*. The bride's brother brings *lāhyā* in a winnowing-fan, that is fried grain of paddy or jvārī, which is offered to the fire by the bridal pair. At each offering the brother puts a handful into the hands of the bride; on this the bridegroom pours ghee and then both the bride and the bridegroom throw the *lāhyā* into the fire to the accompaniment of mantras repeated by the priest. After the first offering the bridal pair make a round of the fire and then the bride stands on the stone, and the priest utters a mantra on behalf of the bridegroom. Three offerings are made in this way and three times the bride stands on the stone. The mantra is as follows: 'I am unfailing, you who stand on the stone are unfailing. I am heaven and you are the earth; I am Sāmveda and you are Ṛgveda. Let us two be married; may be beget children and live one hundred years dear to each other with our bodily splendour and above all ourselves the pride of the Divine Being.'

[1] There is a curious error in *Primitive Paternity*; E. S. Hartland, vol. i, p. 208: 'A stone called the Ashma or spirit stone, that which is used at the funeral rites of the tribe, and into which the spirit of the dead man is supposed to enter, is kept near the fire and at each circuit, as the bride followed by the bridegroom approaches this stone, she stands on it till the priest finishes reciting a hymn. Here it seems clear that the idea underlying the rite is that the spirit of one of the tribal or family ancestors occupying the stone becomes reincarnated in her.'

Aśmā, though applied to the *Jīvkhaḍā*, merely means stone. The *Jīvkhaḍā*, too, could not be put on the ground and is not preserved. The stone used in *Aśmārohaṇ* has no connexion at all with the dead. This error seems to have been made through quotation.

This stepping on a grindstone is a form of oath by the goddess *Lakṣmī*, for household implements are identified with her. In a similar way the *Marāṭhā* bridegroom goes to the shrine of the *kul devatā* after his marriage bearing on his left shoulder the top part of a sieve used for sowing seed, and the bride carries a *ravī* or butter churn. The *Māng* bridegroom holds a sieve on his shoulder at the entrance to his house when, on the night following his marriage, the bride is brought to him in procession. On the last day of the marriage the bridal pair of the *Arers* go in procession to a temple, the bridegroom bearing a seed drill and the bride the handle of a churn, and bow to the god. On their return home before they enter the house, each of them still holding the same implement pronounces the name of the other. *Vaddars* at a marriage take a *vaniki* or wooden rod used for cleaning rice, apply turmeric and in the evening erect in a hole before the house of the bride. To the top of the rod leaves of atti are tied. This rod the bridal pair circumambulate five times. In all these practices, though other ideas may enter into the rite, the essential feature is the taking of an oath.

On the birth of a child in the Karnāṭak a stone-roller (*varvaṇṭā* (Mar.), *gunḍakallu* (Kan.)) or pestle with which spices are ground, is dressed in a woman's clothes and the head-dress of a child (*kuncī*). This stone is called *Gunḍappa* and is treated as a new-born infant, and a girl in the family pretends to be its mother, *Gunḍappantāyi*, and receives gifts on the twelfth day after the birth. On the twelfth day the stone is placed in the living child's cradle where *akṣat* is thrown on it. A stone is long-lived and it is therefore supposed that by this ceremony the child's life will be prolonged into old age.

In the Bījāpūr district women who have no issue go to the hill of *Sitimani* and thereon build a miniature house or temple. By the side of a hilly track leading from Badami in the same district they place one stone to the right and one to the left and a third stone across the two stones. These stones represent a house and as the women construct it they say, 'I have built a house for you; so you should continue my house', '*Ninage nānu maṇi kaṭṭeni, nannamaṇi nīnu nillisu*'. After a child is born the women return to the site, remove the stones and give a feast.

A stone brought from an isolated hill that does not connect with another rise, or a stone found stuck in the branches of a tree is used to avert evil-eye from milch cattle. It must be brought back with the left hand, the carrier being naked, heated red-hot and placed in water with which the udders of the cattle are steamed.

Priests when they go to villages not their own to conduct funeral rites are said, when they find few deaths with consequent work, to place stones on their books with the object of causing more deaths.

When a man is bitten by a snake a stone is placed on his head to prevent the poison circulating; the stone is stationary and *ergo* the poison will be stationary. Stones are tied to nim-trees to cure a snake-bite, and large stones are piled on jack-trees to make them yield good fruit. When a man is bitten by a scorpion he will be cured if he upsets, without speaking to any one, the first stone he finds. From personal experience I can say that this supposed cure does not work. Near Nāgasamudra is a stone which if inverted by a woman who is awaiting her delivery or by any one on her behalf, gives her an easy delivery. To assist her it is even sufficient to find a stone near the village gate, to worship it as *Huligevvā* and then invert it, again putting it straight after the child is born. In many places are stones called *usargallu*, 'breathing stones', which, if the affected part is rubbed against them, cure sprains. Between Ron and Savadi in the Karnāṭak is a worn stone near a tank; students before going up for an examination, debtors contemplating taking a loan or parents in pursuit of a companion in marriage for their children, attempt to lift the stone; if it be found light they will have success in their object, but will fail if the stone appear heavy. To cure fever a piece of flint is made hot and put in juice obtained from the leaves of gajargoṭi (Bignonia suaveolens), and the juice is drunk by the sick person. To cure a snake-bite five pebbles are waved over the bitten part in the name of *Āḍiguḍi Imāmsāb* of the Bījāpūr district and finally deposited at the saint's resting-place without their being allowed to touch the ground.

There are several ways of transferring fatigue to a stone. In the Konkaṇ on the summit of passes there is often a pile of stones and sticks called *Ṭahāḻdev*, 'the branch-god'. *Kātkarīs* as they ascend the passes carry with them from the bottom of the pass a branch which they throw away on reaching the summit, after which they descend the further side of the pass free from fatigue. In lieu of branches *Thakurs* throw stones on the pile. In Sind also on the ascent of a hill and even on a long journey on the level, a stone or stick is carried and thrown away when the traveller is tired. Pilgrims to Hampi spit on rags and throw these on a stone at the entrance of the village to transfer to it the fatigue of their journey. In the village of *Julkatti* in the State of Hyderabad there are rough-hewn stones called *Kanṭī Basappā* on which wayfarers throw rags with the same object.

Stones are charmed and carried on one's person on a journey to keep away spirits, and those who dabble in the magician's art use four stones to form a *dikbāndha* against spirits.

Primitive tribes such as *Bhils, Mavchis* and *Konkaṇīs* on the remarriage of a man who has lost his first wife require him to carry a large stone engraved with the image of a woman, which stone after the marriage is buried in the cemetery still showing the image above the ground. The object of this rite is to fix the ghost of the deceased wife and prevent its wandering (*vaḍ dakhaṇī*). If a man dies by accident his family members carve a picture of a man on a stone and bury it to half its depth in the ground, with the similar object of rooting the ghost of the dead (*vīr*) to one spot.

A stone can be made the tabernacle of *śakti*. Images of gods are fashioned out of stone,[1] and even into unfashioned stones the *śakti* of gods is invoked. On the sixth or seventh day of *Bhādrapad* five small stones are taken from a well or river to represent *Gaurī*; a hill-god whose shrine it is difficult to reach is represented by five stones. In Marāṭhā villages *Khandoba* is represented by a pile of stones from which each worshipper removes five stones, adding five other stones.

Stones are invested with the *śakti* of gods and placed in cattle-sheds to keep away the spirits that reduce the milk yield of milch cattle. Such stones represent *Pūṣan* or the sun-god under whose protection cattle go to and return from their pasture; the stones are also called *Karevvā*. One of the most familiar examples of investing stones with *śakti* is the invocation of *śakti* into stones which are buried in fields, gardens or houses as a protection against evil. These stones are *Kṣetrapāl*, 'guardians of the fields' or *Dikpālakā*, 'guardians of the directions'. After their burial the stones are placed above ground and are frequently called *Pāṇḍavā*, five in number, representing the five protecting deities of the fields, but also known as *Dharma*, Air, Fire and the *Asvin-Kumārs* or the sun and moon. The ordinary agriculturist invokes *śakti* into his stones not by the uttering of mantras and the throwing of *akṣat*, but by pouring water on the stone, applying lime and red earth, and sandalwood paste, covering them with flowers and

[1] Stone possesses the *śakti* of solemnity and is therefore used for images. The goddess *Durga* is one of the *śaktis* known as *ugra*, 'fierce', and her images are usually of wood which is called *dāru*, 'fierce'. Images used in a house, e.g. images of the *kul devatā*; images used when performing Grahyajni or invoking the *śakti* of the moon, are made of *kānsu* metal. Gaṇpati's image is always of earth; the image of Śeṣa used on Nāgpancmī is of earth, as also that of Śiva in Pārthivapūjā, black soil from the bed of the tulsī being preferred.

leaves, throwing incense into fire and finally by making an offering, *naivedya*, to the stones, an offering which must eventually be buried in the field.

A stone may also have special *śakti* which no neglect on the part of worshippers can impair. It is then *svayambhū* [1] or 'self-existing'. There are many things that possess inherent *śakti* such as trees, water, fire, earth, implements, grain or a cow, but these have not the characteristics of immovability nor have they the conventional marks of divinity. There are again stones such as the *Sūryakānt*, a round vitreous stone which represents the sun; the *Bāṇ*, an elliptical stone representing Śankar; the *Śāligrām*, a round black stone representing Nārāyaṇ, which are worshipped without any previous installation, without any previous invocation of power, but these again are not *svayambhū*. Besides these there are other stones worshipped without any invocation of *śakti*; the red stone representing Gaṇpati, called *Narmada Gaṇpati*, and a white metallic stone, *Suvarṇmukhi*, representing Devī, found in the beds of rivers such as the Narmada and Gandaki. To be *svayambhū* a stone must be immovable and possess the signs of divinity; such stones may be but occasionally worshipped, as many of the stones visited by pilgrims are, but their *śakti* will never diminish. A *svayambhū* deity requires no marriage *jatrā* to keep his *śakti* unimpaired; the *śakti* of the symbol is independent of the piety of the worshipper, and the symbol can be touched by females and by *Śūdras* without reduction of its power.

In funeral rites a stone with various names figures very commonly and this among castes strictly Hindu as well as among those that are barely within the pale of Hinduism. This stone is called in mantras *Śvetśilā*, *śvet* meaning white, for it embodies the *śakti* of the ashes and the bones of the dead. It is also called *Preṭśilā*, 'the stone of the dead'; *Pretrājā*, 'the king spirit', and in the Konkaṇ very generally *Jīvkhaḍā*, 'the stone-of-life'. The general practice is for the file of mourners to kick up a stone on their way to the pyre, and for the bearers of the body then to change places, and among tribes wherein women carry the corpse from the house

[1] There are *svayambhū* lingas at the following places: Saurastra (Somanāth); Sri Saila (Malikārjuna); Avanti (Mahākāl); Mandhatrapur (Onkārēśvar); Paralī (Vaijanāth); Rāmeśvar (Rāmalinga); Dwarka (Nāgeśa); Kāśī (Viśveśvar); Nasik (Trayambakeśvar); Badari (Kedāreśvar); Surādri (Ghusmeśwar). The following lingas are known as *Ātmaling*; that of Mahābaleśvar at Gokarna and the lingas of Chāyāling, and Vāyuling. The following stones are also *svayambhū*: the *pādukā* of Dattātreya at Audumbar and the Virupakṣa at Hampi. There are *svayambhū* gods at Pandharpur (Pānḍurang); at Tirupati (Venkataraman); at Venkatapur (Venkaṭeś) at Udapi in south Kanara (Kṛṣṇa) and at Kolhapur (Mahālakṣmī).

for the women bearers to return home, leaving the men to bear the corpse. With this stone the cords that fasten the corpse to the bier are cut, and the jar which the chief mourner carries round the pyre is broken at each circumambulation. The subsequent ways of dealing with the stone are many, but agree in keeping the stone away from contact with the ground, on the assumption that such contact would destroy the *barkat* of the dead, and his *puṇya*. *Thakurs* who bury their dead on the twelfth day throw the *Jīvkhaḍā* with the *pinḍa* into water, as do *Bhois* and *Lonaris*. *Pancāḷs* when cutting the cords of the bier place one stone under the cords and strike this with another to sever the cords; they then keep both stones apart on grass or in a bush until the third day of the obsequies when they are placed in a pot and hung on a tree till the twelfth day and then thrown with the ashes and bones of the deceased into a river.

In the Deccan, in particular, the stone is called *Aśmā*, but it is not difficult to find communities that have no name for the stone, and use it at a funeral without any formulated idea of the stone enshrining the *śakti* or the life of the dead. Among Brahmins in the Deccan the nearest heir to the deceased breaks with the stone the earthen pot he carries three times round the pyre, and then ties the stone in a cloth and hangs on a tree. On the seventh to the tenth days inclusive the stone is tied round the neck of the *yajamān*; on the tenth day it receives the offerings meant for the dead after which it is thrown, to the accompaniment of mantras, into water. In the Ron taluka of the Dharwar district *Deśastha Brahmins* have the following practice. The lower of the two stones used in cutting the cords of the bier is thrown into water immediately after use; the upper stone is taken home and placed on a matla-leaf. Where the deceased actually expired a pit is dug and in it is placed an earthen saucer of oil with a lighted wick facing south. This light is not allowed to go out for ten days. In another saucer is placed rice mixed with earth near which is put a pot of water. A nail is driven into the wall some three feet from the ground and from it thread is hung with its end in the pot of water. Each day that the obsequies are performed the stone is taken to the *ghāṭ*, and when brought back is placed on the leaf near the pot and saucers. When the *yajamān* dines he sprinkles a little water on the stone and into the pot, and throws a morsel of rice on to the roof of the house. On the eleventh day of the obsequies the stone is thrown into water. The stone loses its *pretatva* when thrown into the water, and to sever their connexion with the dead it is customary for the mourners and relatives of the dead to bathe in the water in which the stone was thrown. During the obsequial rites it is the *Lingaśarīr* that is invoked into the *Pretaśilā*, a subtle invisible body with *śakti*.

Māḻīs tie the stone in a white cloth which they attach to a beam over the spot where the deceased expired and finally throw into a river. *Kātkarīs* have a ceremony distinctly their own; on the fifth day after the death the stone is placed outside the door of the deceased and five boys who have maintained a fast are bathed over the stone. The children call upon the dead by name individually; the dead spirit responds and enters an image made of ashes and water, whereupon the eldest leader of the clan present solemnly pronounces that the dead is dismissed, *mokiḻā*, from the tribe. By means of the inherent power of the stone a *Kātkarī* mantrik can discover the human being, if any, who is responsible for the successive deaths of all the male members of a household.

The grinding-stone, the pestle and the mortar in the words of *Manu* are 'slaughter-houses', they are instruments of *himsā*; their use is circumscribed with rigorous rules intended to preserve *śakti*. On the other hand, they are necessary implements of work; they are associated with the goddess *Lakṣmī* and like all implements must be worshipped to enhance their *śakti*. When the new millet crop is ripe on *Pūrṇimā*, on sud. six of the month or on Pauṣa sud. fifteen, the grinding-stone is decorated and worshipped. Women who must have their husbands alive take and grind new millet and out of the flour make preparations which are offered as *naivedya* to the family god. The day this is done is a great festival and is called *Kuldharma*. When the date of a Hindu marriage has been settled a good *muhūrtta* is found for beginning to prepare the food for the marriage. This found, the grinding-stone is first worshipped; *Gaṇpati* is worshipped and wheat which has been first put in a winnowing-fan is ground, after which the food is prepared. At a Hindu and a Muhammadan marriage alike the grinding-stone is used at particular moments, though grinding is strictly prohibited at other moments during the ceremony. During a Hindu marriage as during a thread ceremony there is a grinding of black gram by *suvāsinīs* on the grindstone and the preparation from its flour of *naivedya* for *Nāndi*. This follows a worship of the stone which is called *Uddinamuhūrtta*. Sindi Muhammadans perform a rite called *Buki*. Seven dates are tied with red thread to the grindstone and seven women who are the only wives of their husbands, turn each the stone and take the dates which are distributed. The same is done separately for both the bride and the bridegroom. Then an old man ties the thread and with it wheat and an iron ring to the wrist of the bridegroom, and the bridegroom's sister does the same for the bride. On the seventh day of the marriage different grains are brought and placed under the grindstone, and the bridal pair are required to touch the handle of the stone so that their love may mingle even as the several kinds of grain are mingled by the grinding, and may always abide as some grain always remains on the stone.

There are several occasions on which the mortar and pestle are worshipped in much the same way by married women. At a thread ceremony the boy begs rice from his mother, a begging which is called *Bhikṣāl̲*, using a copper plate as his begging bowl. The pestle and mortar are then worshipped by *suvāsinīs* before the boy himself pounds the rice therein. The boy then winnows the pounded rice in a winnowing-fan and spreads it on a deer-skin and finally cooks it on the fire of a special *hom*; offers oblations therefrom to the fire and the remainder to priests. In wedding rites the pestle is used as frequently as is the grinding-stone. *Konchi Koravas* on three occasions bathe the bridal pair over a pestle; once on the first day of the marriage when the pair are anointed with turmeric and oil; then again the next day before the *kankaṇ* of the pair are tied, and on the last day before the bridegroom takes home his bride. In some Hindu families during a marriage til and jaggery are pounded in a mortar by married women; after first worshipping the stones the resultant mixture, *yal̲lacigal̲i*, is presented to married women. In Kanara among Brahmins, and usually on the fifth day of the marriage called *nāgavalli*, the pestle and mortar are decorated and worshipped. Rice-flour with water is pounded in the mortar and from the dough five serpents are made and worshipped by the bridal pair. The wristlets of the bridal pair are removed after the formal dismissal, *visarjan*, of their *śakti* and thrown on the serpents, which in their turn are dismissed and with the *kankaṇ* taken away and left in a group of *Nāga* stones (*nāgar bale*), or like so many things which once have possessed invoked power are thrown into water. This is an important marriage rite the object of which is the propitiation of the snake-god so that the married pair may have issue. The appeal to the god is in this wise: 'Oh *Mahābhugin*, protect me from snake-bite and give me long-lived progeny. I have approached you out of devotion. Oh deity most benign, protect me. Knowingly or unknowingly in this life or in any past life, if I myself have or any ancestor of mine has killed a snake, graciously protect me from sin and pardon me the transgression.'

Kātkarīs in the Konkaṇ have a ceremony on the fifth day after a birth to remove the impurity of birth, *suver*. Though several castes worship a grindstone at a birth or during the next few subsequent days, the ceremony called *Pāṭā* is claimed by the *Kātkarī* as entirely his own. On the fifth night after a birth no *Kātkarī* adult can sleep. During the day coconut pieces are sent to all the women in the village to wash their hair and bodies, as the whole village is impure. Five mango-leaves are placed after the arrival of the visitors, on five ways leading to the house and smeared with red, black and yellow powders. Five similar leaves are also placed on the *pāṭā* or stone used for grinding spices, which has previously been placed over the buried navel-cord of the child. In the morning of this fifth day the stone is cleaned; at noon it is covered with rice, red and yellow powder and flowers, and camphor is waved over it; throughout the day it remains concealed by a basket which is removed in the evening, when a burning lamp is placed near it and remains near all the night, which is passed in merry-making.

Stones are frequently used when iron is tabooed. The cords of a bier are cut with a stone; charmed lemons are broken with stones; the soma plant is crushed with a stone and *Lingāyats* break with a stone the coconuts they offer to their gods. To cure the dysentery of a child the bark of a tree is administered, but the bark must be removed with a stone. Precious stones have naturally their individual power. A common test of a precious stone or of the *Sāligrām* is to take rice grain carefully measured and after placing the stone in it remeasure it; if the grain shows an increase in measure the stone is a good one but worthless if there has been no increase. Different stones are offered to different planets to avert their *pīḍā*; the ruby to the sun, the coral to Mars, the emerald to Mercury, the diamond to Jupiter and Venus, and the bluestone to Saturn. Stones taken from a burning *ghāṭ* have a power which is made use of by mantriks.

When cholera breaks out some Hindus fix two small stones, one on either side of their front door and cover them with saffron and flowers. These are to deceive the goddess *Marī* to whose wrath the epidemic is attributed, for when she sees the stones she is supposed to go away imagining she has already visited that house. Mourners on their return from a funeral throw five pebbles towards the site of burial or of cremation to keep away the ghost of the dead. Cairns of stones are very common in the hilly tracts of Sind and on the Baluch frontier, generally on the top of passes or where some death has occurred. In the plains stones are thrown at the shrines of saints and in some cases at temples; at the temple of Kayanath Dev at Halher two or three stones are thrown by every pilgrim who on approaching the temple is not allowed to follow the straight and direct route, though he may take this on his return. The only explanation I have received of this practice is that the throwing of stones is an act of reverence.

CHAPTER XI

THE POWER OF TIME

TIME in Indian thought is no abstract measure but something very real and concrete suffused like other entities with power. There are moments of *śakti* when the movements of the stars and planets produce a *parvakāl*; there are other moments when a combination of elements of time produces a *muhūrtta*, the auspiciousness of which is correlated to the horoscope of the person who chooses those moments for action. On the other hand, there are *dies nefasti*, and in all moments of great power there lurks the element of danger which characterizes all power.

The Hindu day, for the purposes of ritual, is divided into five *kāl*, each of which is made up of six *ghaṭikā* of twenty-four minutes, calculated from the time taken by a measured pot with a hole in it to sink in a larger pot of water. The installation of these pots is a recurring feature of religious ceremony.

Of the five *kāl* of the day two, *sangavkāl* and *aparāṇhakāl*, are comparatively of ordinary potentiality; the other three *kāl*, namely *prantahkāl*, *madhyanhakāl* and *sanyakāl*, are times of great *śakti* and particularly the first forty-eight minutes of each *kāl*. These hours of dawn, noon and sunset are turning-points and are therefore considered *parvakāl*, though not by all. Whether *parvakāl* or not, however, they are hours of *śakti*. The term *parvakāl* is applied without dispute to all *Amāvāsyā* and *Pūrṇimā*, to new and full-moon days, the eighth and fourteenth days of each fortnight; to all the twelve *sankramaṇa* when the sun passes from one zodiac to another; to the eighty-four *sankrānt* when the seven planets similarly change their zodiacs, and to hours of eclipse. In all these cases the power of the hour comes from the stars and planets, and as the hour is a time of transition from one *śakti* to another, one *śakti* as it were incoming and one outgoing, it is characterized by both good and evil potentiality. Besides these there are fourteen *Manvādi*[1] days which are also *parvakāl*, the

[1] *Manvadi* (*manu* and *adi*) is the accession day of Manu. There are fourteen Manus in all, the rule of each being four *yugas*, and this period is called *Manvantar*.

power of which is not based on planetary influence though a few of them are *Pūrṇimā* and *Amāvāsyā*. These days are Chaitra,[1] sud. 3; Chaitra Pūrṇimā; Jyeṣṭh Pūrṇimā; Āṣāḍha, sud. 10; Āṣāḍha Pūrṇimā; Śrāvaṇ Vad. 8; Bhādrapad, sud. 3; Āśvin, sud. 9: Kārttik, sud. 12; Kārttik Pūrṇimā; Pauṣa, sud. II; Māgha, sud. 7. Phālgun Pūrṇimā and Amāvāsyā. Certain days and months of another category are also *parvakāl*. Rāmnavamī the ninth of Chaitra; Akṣayatṛtīyā the third of the first half of Vaiśākha; Narsinh Jayantī the fourteenth of the bright half of Vaiśākh; Hanuman Jayantī the full-moon day of Chaitra; Gangotpatti in the month of Jyeṣṭha; Vatsavitri the full-moon day of Jyeṣṭha; Gokulaṣṭamī the birthday of Kṛṣṇain the second half of Śrāvaṇ; Anantacaturdaśī the first ten days of Āśvin and known as Navrātri; Dhanatrayodaśī the thirteenth day of Āśvin; Narakacaturdaśī the fourteenth of Kārttik; the Amāvāsyā, the Balipratipadā the Yamadvitīyā which fall during the festival of Divāḻī; Kārttik Ekādaśī the eleventh day of Kārttik; Vaikunṭa Caturdaśī the fourteenth of Kārttik; Makar Sankramaṇa in the month of Pauṣa; Rathasaptamī the seventh of Māgh; Hoḻika and Śivrātra. Of the months Śrāvaṇ, Kārttik, Māgha, Chaitra, and Vaiśākh are *parvakāl*.

There are certain characteristics in common of *parvakāl*. The powerful influence of the planets at these times adds to the power of all things. Because water gains enhanced power at a *parvakāl* bathing in rivers is common at this time; mantras are learnt and used for magic purposes; libations of water are made to the *pitṛs* who are associated with all *parvakāl*; *ugra* gifts to avert evil can be made. On the other hand there is evil in the power of a *parvakāl* due to the excess of *śakti* therein and to the fading of one form of *śakti* as it gives way to another. All *parvakāl* are followed by a *kari* period or period of danger; marriages and other *sanskār* cannot be performed on days of *parvakāl*; agricultural operations are tabooed; fairs and festivals cannot be held; images of gods and other media through which *śakti* is invoked cannot be installed; ceremonies of *śakti* such as a *śānti* and of *puṇya* such as a *vrata* cannot be carried out. For all these rites dependent on *śakti* a good *muhūrtta* must be found, and this, though it may coincide with a *parvakāl*, is not based on a *parvakāl*.

The first Manu was Svayambhuva Manu, from whom came the Manu Smṛti. At present is the rule of Vaisvasvat Manu, who has passed three *yugas* (Kṛta, Tretā and Dvāpāra) and is now in his Kāḻiyuga.

[1] Each month has two halves: the bright half called *śuddha*, 'pure' or 'clear', or *śukla*, 'white'; the dark half called *vadya*, 'blameless', or *kṛṣṇa*, 'black', or *bahūḻ*, 'dark'.

A *muhūrtta* is a period of two *ghaṭikā* during which the *tithi*, *vār*, *nakṣatra*, *yog* and *karaṇ* are all auspicious with reference to the horoscope. A *vār* is a day called after one of the seven planets. Its coincidence with a *nakṣatra* may make the day favourable or unfavourable. Sunday, for instance, coinciding with the star *Hasta* produces an auspicious moment, coinciding with *Anurādhā* it makes a bad moment. There are fifteen *tithi* in a fortnight, some of them good, some bad. If a good *tithi*, for example *Daśamī* or *Pancamī*, falls on a Tuesday it produces a very bad combination called *mṛtyyog*. Of *nakṣatra* there are twenty-seven, some good and some bad; if a favourable one fall on a Sunday it is a bad union.

There is a cycle of twenty-seven *yog* each of which is like a *tithi*, a period of about twenty-four hours, or sixty *ghaṭikā*. The duration of each is determined by the position of the stars; some of them are favourable, some entirely bad. The *yoga* are Viṣkambha, Prīti, Āyuṣmān, Saubhāgya, Śobhana, Atigaṇḍa, Sukarma, Dhṛti, Śūla, Gaṇḍa, Vṛddhi, Dhṛva, Vyāghāta, Harṣaṇa, Vajra, Śiddh, Vyatīpāta, Varyāna, Paridha, Śiva, Śiddhi, Sādhya, Śubha, Śukla, Brahmā, Aindra, Vaidhṛti. Those of Vyatīpāt and Vaidhṛti are wholly bad and no good work is attempted during their duration; the first half of Paridha is bad as are also the first three hours and thirty-six minutes of Vajra, the first seventy-two minutes of Viṣkambha, the first two hours of Vyāghāt, and the first two hours and twelve minutes of Atigaṇḍa and Gaṇḍa. The remaining *yoga* are auspicious.

There are eleven *karaṇ*: Bava, Bālava, Kaulava, Taitala, Garaja, Vaṇija, Viṣṭi or Bhadra, Śakuni, Catuṣpād, Nāga, Kimstughna, each with a presiding deity (*adhidevatā*), respectively Indra, Brahma, Mitra, Aryamā, Pṛthvī, Lakṣmī, Yama, Kāli, Śankar, Sarpa and Vāyu. These all depend upon *tithis*; the first seven are called *cara*, 'moving' and the other four *sthira*, 'fixed'. The seven follow in a series beginning from sud. Pratipadā of each month until vad. 14; the four have certain fixed *tithi* from vad.14 to sud. pratipadā of the next month. The duration of each is thirty *ghaṭikā*, that is twelve hours. During the continuance of each *Karaṇ* some specific work can best be performed. Bava is a good *karaṇ* for every auspicious work such as the taking of medicine or beginning the construction of a building; Bālava is a good *karaṇ* for discharging duties towards others or making presents to win *puṇya*; during Kaulava one should attempt to win love and friendship; during Garaja agricultural operations should succeed and during Vaṇija all sorts of contracts are best executed. None of these works assigned to these *karaṇ* will succeed in Viṣṭi which is an appropriate *karaṇ* for exorcising spirits or working evil or learning charms. Śakuni is the time for taking omens, for gambling or astrology. Immovable property and cattle are best dealt with during Catuṣpād and at this *karaṇ* war is best conducted and treaties are best made. Nāga is the *karaṇ* during which sacrifices should be made and acts which involve cruelty. Kimstughna is a propitious time for all good work. The Viṣṭi *karan* is peculiar. It occurs four times during the bright fortnight when it is called *sarpiṇi*, 'snake', and four times during the dark fortnight when it is called *Vṛścika*, 'scorpion'. A snake has poison in its head and a scorpion its sting in its tail and these names indicate that the first half of this *karaṇ* in the one fortnight is a time of danger, and the second half in the other fortnight, whilst the second half in the bright fortnight and the first half in the dark fortnight are harmless.

SANDHYĀ

Derived from the word *sandhi*, 'union', the term *sandhyā* is applied to the morning and evening twilight, to a period of forty-eight minutes between night and day, and also to midday, the time of union between forenoon and afternoon. These hours of dawn, noon and sunset are *parvakāl* or hours of *śakti*. To the Muhammadan these hours are *ghoro* or *vazandār*, 'heavy'. The same idea of a transition as appears in the word *Sandhyā* underlies the Muhammadan's description of noon as 'the day is between two needles', *dinhan bini suyunje vich men ahe*.

Precisely because these hours are hours of power, there is a close similarity in the restrictions imposed on man's actions at noon or in either of the twilights. Sleep [1] is forbidden to both Hindu and Muhammadan. A Muhammadan who sleeps in the morning twilight loses all the *barkat* of the whole day; to be awake at this time confers the same blessing as prayer. At sunset it is equally imperative to be awake; one cannot even lie on a cot at this time and the sick are made to keep awake and sit up. A Hindu who sleeps at these hours falls ill or endures poverty; worse than this, spirits enter the sleeper, make his ears ring with their jabber and finally cause his death, so all who sleep are awakened by others.

When the sun sets, rises or stands in the middle of the sky he

[1] Vide *Grihya-sutra of Hiranyakesin*, i, 5, 16; 15–16; *Apastamba*, ii, 5, 12, 13–14; *Laws of Manu*, ii, 219–21; iv, 55; iv, 37; iv, 69; *Institutes of Viṣṇu*, lxx, 17.

must not be gazed at. The Hindu will not look at the sun when it is at the height of its power, nor at twilight when it is struggling with the demon of darkness. In Sind a popular belief is that a Muhammadan who faces the sun at dawn gets a headache, which grows worse and worse till it reaches its climax at noon, and can be cured only by a Mulla taking the sufferer to a well another day before sunrise, reciting over him the Koran and sprinkling him with water. This process of cure and the headache itself are called *sajavati*.

The Prophet forbade his followers to commence their prayers exactly at sunrise, sunset or noon, because infidels worshipped the sun at such times. *Nimaz* and *Sijdah* are not performed at the three hours the Hindu calls *Sandhyā*. The noon prayer should begin after *zavāl*, a period of prohibition determined by the shadow of a stick held straight in the sun. At dawn, sunset and at noon the Koran should not be read and recital of the book should cease. Hindu practice has much that is similar. The *Veda* must not be recited [1] in the twilight and their recitation cannot be begun at noon. At noon the important details of the *Śrāddha* ceremony cannot be carried out. Before dawn and before sunset the *Agnihotrī* takes out his fire, but he performs his *hom* after sunrise and after sunset.

Drinking and eating are forbidden [2] in the twilight and at noon. If one drinks or eats, the Hindu thinks, the spirits join in the meal. The Muhammadan believes that if a man gets into the habit of taking water at sunset, he will when the darkness of death approaches imagine it is sunset and ask for water, whereupon Satan will give him unclean water and rob him of all his *imām* or faith. It is bad for even a sick man to take water or medicine; children in the evening must wait till the lamps are lighted before they can drink, and neither at noon nor at sunset is water drawn or carried. One reason given by the Hindu for avoiding food and drink in the twilight is that Yama, the god of death, chooses this time for practising penance.

Chastity is imperative.[3] A Hindu fears that a child begotten at noon will be deformed, and one begotten at sunset will be a demon. Children born with teeth are usually considered demons. Women who are *enceinte* at these hours are in great danger. In Sind such women are never left alone. A Hindu woman who is

[1] Vide *Manu*, iv, 113.

[2] Vide *Manu*, iv, 62 and iv, 55; *Institutes of Viṣṇu*, lxviii, 11, 12.

[3] 'He must avoid connubial intercourse, and in a temple and at the root of a tree or shrub, and in the daytime and in the twilight.'—*Institutes of Viṣṇu*, lxix, 7–10.

with child must not stand in the doorway at sunset or she will harm the unborn child; she must avoid also seeing the cattle returning from pasture in the twilight as spirits attach themselves to their feet, attempting in this way to gain entry to the residences of man. Children also are to avoid the returning cattle, but as cattle are more often than not shepherded by children, practice does not follow theory.

Other acts which the Hindu would call acts of *himsā* are also forbidden. A Muhammadan will avoid washing clothes or bathing at noon, sunset or dawn; he will not even give clothes to a washerman in the twilight. He avoids also shaving or cutting his nails; sweeping and grinding; he will not cut a tree and will not allow children to climb trees or pluck flowers. Hindu practices are on the same lines. The Hindu ceremony of *Caul* or tonsure cannot be performed at noon. If a Hindu woman or child cuts the hair at *Goraj* the youngest son of the mother dies.

It is very dangerous to take an oath or utter a curse at any of these hours. The Muhammadan considers an oath taken either in the twilight or at noon very dangerous; the Hindu thinks an oath taken at sunset is more dangerous than at any other time, and the worst curse is one uttered at noon. Bad intentions entertained at dawn, noon or sunset draw power from the hour, and lead to ill. At these critical hours, all forms of abuse or quarrelling and untruth must be avoided; even to play at quarrelling brings its sequel of evil.

The complex character of power; its potentiality for good and at the same time its inherent element of danger, is manifested by the confusing medley of practices at the hour of sunset. *Godhūḻi* or *goraj* is a period of twelve minutes before and twelve minutes after actual sunset. It takes these names from the dust kicked up by cattle as they return to their stalls from the fields. It is, on the one hand, an auspicious hour, an hour of *Lakṣmī*, the goddess of good fortune, an hour of creative activity, a time which some consider most propitious for the celebration of a marriage,[1] independently of whether or not it coincides with a good *muhūrtta* related to the horoscopes of the bridal pair. A man who dies at

[1] Even if a marriage be performed at sunset, and this is far from being a rule, the *akṣat* thrown on the bridal pair must be thrown at the correct *muhūrtta*, and the rites of *Lājāhom* and *Saptapadī* must be performed after sunset, as the bridal pair must see certain stars, Dhruva and Arundhati.

Cp. *The Mystic Rose*, E. Crawley, 1927, vol. ii, p. 41: 'Weddings very commonly take place in the evening or at night, a custom natural enough for its convenience and its obviation of dangers, such as that of the evil-eye and those connected with human, and especially female, shyness and timidity.'

this hour is said in Gujarāt to go to heaven. At this time the homeward wending cattle bring fortune, says the *Mahār*, in their trail if they pass the open door of a house and the inmates wisely remain silent and at peace. A woman desiring issue chooses this time to throw rice on the roof of a neighbour and draw an omen from the chance conversation she overhears. Women obtain an easy delivery at sunset; if a pregnant woman enters at this hour a temple of Mahādev she delivers prematurely, so women whose delivery is overdue go to such a temple at sunset. To avert evil-eye from a woman after her delivery water is poured over the rear fold of the *dhotar* of a pure person at sunset and given her to drink, whilst if she awaits delivery the front part, *niryas*, of a woman's skirt is waved up and down in front of her, a skirt being taken from a woman who usually has easy deliveries. Another practice is for the husband when his wife is in travail to place his turban on her body at the time the cattle return home, and unwind its folds in the reverse way. *Svāmīs* and *sannyāsīs* enter villages at sunset in search of hospitality. When an epidemic is imminent, several kinds of grain are boiled together and sprinkled on the village confines before the sun sets.

At sunset the Hindu performs a double rite which itself demonstrates the dual nature of the power of the time. To scare away *Alakṣmī* or bad fortune, a lighted wick is carried round all the nooks and corners of the house, beginning at the back door, and ending at the front door, and whilst this is done a winnowing-fan is beaten with a stick. After this an attempt is made to encourage *Lakṣmī*, the goddess of good fortune, to enter the house by lighting another wick and carrying this through the house beginning from the front door.

The inherent danger in the hour of evening twilight leads to a very large number of taboos. One must be careful not to give many things away. The Sindi Muhammadan will not give away anything white such as lime, eggs, white cotton, milk, salt or curds; he will not give away fire or fruit. In the Karnāṭak the Hindu will not give away a winnowing-fan, a sieve, a pestle or mortar, a broom, curds or milk, lime or salt, garlic, grain, fire, or a lamp, butter or money. A man who gives away lime finds himself saddled with a daughter. Money transactions at this time mean loss of wealth and are avoided; money cannot be changed. A guest will not want to depart nor will he be allowed to do so; a journey cannot be begun. As no bad act is to be done because it draws power from the hour, and as in general no good act can be done, sunset becomes an hour of rest. Weeping of any kind would bring a sequel of ill. It is dangerous to be called at sunset or to make anxious inquiries about the health of another. It is rash to attempt a good action lest it should fail; it is equally rash to entertain an evil purpose, for evil thoughts materialize at this time.

The Sindi Muhammadan calls sunset *nahas*, 'inauspicious'. He also says *sanjho danjho*, 'Evening is calamity'. Many acts are avoided at this time from a fancied association with death, which may, however, not be primitive in thought. Sleep is an impure state destroying *barkat*, and all impure acts are forbidden at noon and in the twilights, but sleep also resembles death; bathing washes away *barkat*, but it also suggests the purification that is imperative after a funeral; cowdung cannot be brought home, because cakes of this are used at a cremation; fire cannot be extinguished nor water be thrown away, because these things are done on a death and also at an eclipse. The Muhammadan is enjoined at sunset to remember the darkness of the tomb; to eschew all evil acts and to pray for forgiveness of sins.

A man who dies at sunrise, *gopāl*, is said in Gujarāt to go to heaven and a birth at dawn is auspicious. Unless the day be an *Amāvāsyā* one may set out on a journey any day at dawn without considering the *muhūrtta*; dawn itself is called *Gargacārya muhūrtta*. As dawn approaches the Muhammadan believes that Khwāja Khizr visits the market-places and assists to success those he meets; this is, too, the time when holy men pray and called on this account *piro fakirji mahal*, 'the hour of Pirs and fakirs', a holy hour when it is good to grind grain. Noon is associated with spirits as well as with the *śakti* of a *parvakāl*. All *himsā*, such as sweeping, grinding, the cutting of the hair and nails, cutting trees or plucking flowers, is tabooed to a Muhammadan as to a Hindu. It is forbidden a Muhammadan to sell or buy; to fetch water or go on a journey; continence is imperative. The Hindu will not give alms at noon and should a beggar come to him will give him food but not alms. Milk cannot be carried or the person carrying it loses *barkat*; water must not be drawn, and there must be no manner of abuse or crying. Like the Muhammadan the Hindu must avoid washing clothes or bathing at noon, and I have found Hindus who say that no offering can be made in a temple at noon.

AMĀVĀSYĀ

Umās (Sin.); *Amāsi* (Kan.)

The new-moon day is *ghoro* to the Muhammadan and a *parvakāl* to the Hindu. The moon on this day surrenders its power to the sun, and there results a combination of great power. The word *Amāvāsyā* is derived from *ama*, 'together' and *vas*, 'to dwell'.

As a time of great power *Amāvāsyā* is associated with the same prohibitions as the *sandhyā* and other hours of power. Strict chastity is imperative for both Hindu and Muhammadan. There can be no grinding and no washing of clothes. The Sindi Muhammadan will not bring grain to the threshing-floor, will not reap his crops, will not cut the hooves of his horses or cattle, will not shave or cut his own hair or nails. There is some difference of opinion as to whether sweeping also is forbidden, but with this exception Hindu and Muhammadan practice is the same. The *Jain* will not cut cloth on *Amāvāsyā*. Another act which always has its dangers is that of spinning or that of weaving, and *Kuruvinaru* weavers will neither weave nor spin on *Amāvāsyā*.

All *Umās* days to a Muhammadan in Sind are 'bankrupt days', *khutal tarikhun*. Nothing done for love or livelihood on these days will succeed; no new work can be commenced, and if a journey is attempted the wanderer loses his way. To a Hindu an *Amāvāsyā* is an *anadhyā* day. This term literally meaning 'not studying' implies a time when anything learnt is not remembered; it refers, in particular, to days when the Veda are not to be studied, days that include the first, eighth and fourteenth of each month, *Pūrṇimā* and *Amāvāsyā* and stormy days accompanied by thunder and rain. It is also used with a more comprehensive meaning referring to any work that is fruitless. According to *Manu*, the new-moon day destroys the teacher, the fourteenth the pupil, the eighth and the full-moon days destroy all remembrance of the Veda.[1] The destruction of memory on an *Amāvāsyā* is called *pāṭhanaśa*. Private schools close on the day of no-moon, Sanscrit Pāṭhśālā keep holiday and Puraniks do not recite the *Purāṇa*.

New clothes and ornaments cannot be purchased on an *Amāvāsyā*; a lamp cannot be bought; the first entry of a new house cannot be made, and the agriculturist not only cannot perform those operations of agriculture such as reaping and threshing which are destructive, but he cannot sow. No *sanskār* or *śānti* can be performed and no *kamya karma* or rite with a specific and declared object as distinguished from *nitya karma* such as the *Sandhyā*, the *Balīharana* and the *Vaiśvadeva* which have no *sankalpa* or declaration of purpose. *Amāvāsyā* is the one day that makes inauspicious the time just before dawn, the *Gargacārya muhūrtta*. It is bad to be born on *Amāvāsyā* and one so born develops into an irascible adult. A calf born brings evil to its owner and is

[1] *Manu*, iv, 113–14.

therefore given away. The day is a fateful one for the sick and certain diseases such as typhoid and plague are at their worst during the four days ending with *Amāvāsyā.*

Amāvāsyā is a *bhūtveḻ*, a time when spirits are active. Strange fires by the sea or in lonely places denote the presence of spirits on this day, and one way to prevent being accosted by spirits is to pass or walk between cattle. The prince of spirits, *Vetāḻ*, permits his followers to wander when there is no moon. On an *Amāvāsyā* which coincides with a Sunday a charm is made to protect cattle from ticks. A shallow dish is taken; on the inside of this is drawn with lime a pentacle and on the other side of the dish the hideous face of a spirit *Rav.* The plate is held in the smoke of burnt alum and then hung inside the cattle-shed near the entrance so that the cattle will have to pass under it. As a propitiation of spirits a coconut is sometimes kept in a niche and renewed every *Amāvāsyā*; in the Karnāṭak this is called *kervan māḍā*, 'niche of the black-faced spirit'. On *Amāvāsyā* a man wishing to control spirits invokes the *śakti* of *Yakṣiṇī* the wife of *Vetāḻ* into a plant called *raktabutali*, and then severs a branch which he ties to a beam in a temple or in a saint's *maṭh* that it may be free from all *suher* and *sutak* impurity, that is from the contagion of a woman's impurity or that of death. Whenever he wants to achieve anything he then obtains a paste, *gandh*, by rubbing the branch, and with this paste writes charms on burj-leaves. If *Amāvāsyā* falls on a Sunday mantriks practise *jap* or silent prayer to add efficacy to their charms; on any *Amāvāsyā* mantriks prepare *yantras*. On an *Amāvāsyā* a mantrik will take earth on which a man has urinated and making from it an image and worshipping this with a thousand Kaṇgal flowers, subdue a spirit through whom he can work evil.

Besides the magic of mantriks, many other magic rites are performed on an *Amāvāsyā*. Rags are tied to trees and nails are driven into trees to avert evil-eye; charms are written on paper and, inserted in bored copper coins, are worn as talismans against evil-eye. Salt is placed before a god's image on *Amāvāsyā* to free afflicted cattle from pests; charmed salt is given to the sick. Medicinal herbs or herbs credited with curative power are uprooted in silence on *Amāvāsyā*. As at an eclipse trees that remain barren are coerced to become fruitful; deep cuts are made in jack-fruit trees by a naked person, and tamarind-trees are thrashed with sticks. On *Amāvāsyā Kumbhārs, Lingāyats, Kurubas* and others bathe a married woman who has many children in a river or pond, and issueless women sit near so that they may be wetted with water splashed from her body. When *Amāvāsyā* falls on a Monday, *Somvati Umās*, to acquire *puṇya* Hindus rise before dawn and without speaking take a bath in a canal, river or tank and return home; this is called in Sind *gongi tubi*, 'dumb bath', and in the Karnāṭak *mukaniru*.

Some *Amāvāsyā* are of particular importance. The *Amāvāsyā* of Bhādrapad is associated with the worship of all the *pitṛs*; *Sarvapitrī Amāvāsyā*. This is celebrated throughout the dark fortnight which in Kanara is called *Mahālaya* and in the Karnāṭak *Pakṣa* or 'fortnight'. It should be performed on the day the *yajamān's* father died; in calculating this fifteen numbers are counted and then again the numbers one to fifteen, so that if a man died on the sixteenth his *Darśa Śrāddha* is celebrated on the first. At an ordinary *Śrāddha* three *piṇḍa* only are offered to the dead, but at *Mahālaya* one is offered for every departed soul, and as the names of the dead are not remembered *piṇḍa* are offered in the names of gods for each deceased ancestor up to three generations back. Another slight difference of ritual distinguishes the *Śrāddha* on this day from the ordinary *Śrāddha*, for at the latter the *piṇḍa* only are offered to the crows whilst on *Amāvāsyā* all food prepared for the dead is so offered. *Mahālaya* is performed by the eldest son of the last deceased ancestor; if the younger brothers are living in the same house they join the elder son in the worship, but if separate they offer *tarpaṇ* only, an oblation of water to the *pitṛs* on *Amāvāsyā*. On *Amāvāsyā* also *Śrāddha* must be performed by all who have omitted to perform it on the correct day.

Parvakāl are associated with the light and heat of the heavenly bodies. The *pitṛs* are supposed to be fond of light and heat and are called 'drinkers of heat'. Offerings to them, therefore, are made when there is heat and light more than usual, and this happens at conjunctions (*parva*). Even on *Amāvāsyā*, though no moon is apparent, the sun and moon rise together and set together producing enhanced heat.

The *Kātkarī* has no calendar of his own and takes the Hindu feast days for his own ceremonies of which he claims his *Sarvapitrī-Amāvāsyā* is one. Many *Kātkarīs* celebrate this but once a year; others celebrate it on *Phālgun Amāvāsyā* as well, whilst some of the *Dhor Kātkarīs* celebrate it three times a year. Food such as the dead are supposed to relish, particularly the flesh of the iguana, is brought, as also samples of the new crops. On the ground is placed a basket containing the images of the ancestors, *yir* and *supli*, to which coconut red-powder, liquor and a fowl are offered. Amongst *Dhor Kātkarīs* the clan consumes these articles and nothing is offered to crows; grain from the different crops is placed in the basket before the first-fruits are given to children to eat. *Son Kātkarīs* in the Kolaba district have a ritual slightly different. The cooked food is offered to crows by the eldest male member of the family who is not allowed to shave for a whole month previously. The spirits come through the doors which are left open all the night and leave next day when the crows have gone to sleep. Dancing at night is indulged in vigorously in order to keep the dead awake; a smell of burnt rice announces the presence of the spirits, one of whom enters a medium and reveals his identity. Amongst *Dhors* the clan meets for this celebration in the house where the symbols of the deceased ancestors of the tribe are kept, and only failing such place in their own houses. As a rule, *yir* and *supli*, representing respectively male and female ancestors, are kept only as long as the son is alive, and considerable secrecy, I find, is maintained as to the precise house wherein they are kept.

On *Amāvāsyā* things that represent the goddess of fortune, *Lakṣmī*, such as rice and money, are not given away. The day before the dark night of *Āśvin Amāvāsyā* is considered a day of the goddess who is worshipped through her symbols to dispel her enemies who come with the night. All professional castes worship then the implements of their profession, whilst some castes do this every *Amāvāsyā*; *Śikārīs* their guns, snares and axes; *Kumbhārs* their kiln, wooden patter and stirring-rods; merchants their stores and account books. *Koravas* worship their implements of crime. When implements are worshipped the usual rule is that the wife of the worshipper should join in the worship, but on *Amāvāsyā Koravas* exclude altogether women from such worship, and *Vaddars* who allow their womenfolk to assist in the worship of their tools on *Dasarā* forbid them to do so on *Amāvāsyā*. The worship of implements is by some castes also celebrated on *Kārttik Amāvāsyā*, whilst in the Karnāṭak on the *Amāvāsyā* of *Jyeṣṭha* earthen models of bullocks are worshipped and a plough bullock is brought home in the evening and also worshipped. This use of earthen models gives to this *Amāvāsyā* the name *Mannettin Amāvāsyā* (*mannu* is clay; *ettu* is bull).

The threshing-floor central pole is often cut as by *Talwārs* on an *Amāvāsyā* that it may acquire the *śakti* of the day. On the *Amāvāsyā* of *Āśvin Jains* cut a pole of kaki (Cassia fistula), worship it with *akṣat*, food and sandal-paste and keep it in the house until used a month later on the threshing-floor.

Amāvāsyā, like other *parvakāl*, is a good day for bathing in river or in sea. On the *Amāvāsyā* of *Māgh* called *Mahāśivrātri*, *Samud-*

rasnān or bathing in the sea is very meritorious; children and even the sick bathe and in Kanara there are pilgrimages to the sea.

On Pauṣa vad. 30, when the *rabī* crops have matured, the white millet, *śaḻu*, is ready to be reaped and the cotton buds begin to open, a feast is held in the fields called in the Karnāṭak *hatti holada charagā*. The *charagā* is a preparation of the white *jvārī* in the form of cakes, *soragaḍabu*, and is prepared in honour of the cotton crop. The farmer gets up before sunrise and goes to his fields taking the *charagā*; he ties together chosen plants in the fields, and robes them in the clothes of a woman, worships them with *akṣat*, flowers, *haḻad* and *kunku* and offers them a portion of the *charagā*. This done he throws *charagā* from a large basket in all directions along the boundaries of the fields. This must be completed before sunrise. He then remains in the field until his guests arrive when a feast is held; the cattle and bullocks are fed also with the same preparation and in the evening the merry party returns home bearing with them selected plants which they tie in an arch, *toraṇ*, to their doors and over the place where they keep their gods. This ceremony and feast is intended to avert evil and to bring *barkat* to the crops. For the *kharif* crops a similar ceremony is performed on the full-moon day of *Āśvin*. *Bhils* and *Koḻīs* also choose an *Amāvāsyā*, Śrāvaṇ 30, for a ceremony called *Pithora* in honour of all ripe crops. A bamboo canopy is erected under which, before various goddesses, garlands of all kinds of grain, grass and vegetables are hung.

Guḍhī Pāḍvā or New-Year's Day is the worst *Amāvāsyā* in the Hindu year. On this day parents press their children to eat lest they should be short of food throughout the ensuing year. New clothes are given to children; schoolboys worship their slates; women put turmeric on the handle of the churn and churn butter. Dishes are prepared from the tender leaves of the nim and eaten to bring health and happiness throughout the year, and villagers even meet in bodies at their temple and eat such leaves together. On the last day of the departing year no *himsā* can be done; no ploughing; no grinding; no shaving or hair-cutting; no new work can be begun.

Criminal tribes, on the whole, look upon the night of *Amāvāsyā* as an auspicious time for crime. The facile explanation that appears in some books of this choice as determined by the darkness of the night concealing movement, is hardly correct. There is an element of evil in moonlight recognized in many ways, whilst there is a *śakti* conducive to success in an *Amāvāsyā*.

AN ECLIPSE

Current accounts of the customs associated with an eclipse of the sun or moon accept in their literalness the mythological and other stories that explain an eclipse, and so doing offer a very narrow interpretation which isolates an eclipse from other hours of power. According to story, the *daitya* or demon *Rāhu* drank of the nectar produced at the churning of the ocean and became immortal. He was detected by the sun and moon who informed *Viṣṇu,* and the latter cut off the demon's head and arms. The head and tail of the demon were thereupon transferred to the heavens where he wreaks vengeance on the sun and moon by swallowing them. Urdu almanacs picture a snake swallowing the celestial orbs. Other stories make the orbs overshadowed by the shadow of Mount Meru, or by that of a Bhangi creditor as *Rāhu* and *Ketu* collect their debts. Demons are *tamorūpī*, ' dark in form ', and the original character of *Rāhu* as a demon is retained in the name of the two planets *Rāhu* and *Ketu* which are called ' shadow planets ', *chāyāgrahā*.

In *Religion and Folklore of Northern India,* W. Crooke, 1926, p. 40, an eclipse is described as a ' crisis, a time of danger ', because demons are abroad. In *India in the Dark Wood,* Dr. Nicol Macnicol, 1930, p. 53, is another description assuming that an eclipse is an hour of demons : ' For example, when there is an eclipse of the moon, that is when, according to the popular notion, a great demon is threatening to devour the moon, the members of one of those outcaste groups go from house to house crying " Give us a gift and we shall have the moon set free ". The high-caste Hindus accordingly propitiate them with gifts, evidently because they are supposed to have relations with the demon world.'

Now such an assumption that an eclipse is a time when spirits are abroad must explain first of all why this time is not recognized by the Hindu as a *bhūtveḻ,* ' a time of spirits ', unless it happens to synchronize with one. The second assumption that the gifts made at an eclipse show a connexion between the depressed castes and the world of demons, if logical, would charge other classes also with being in league with this world of demons, for the type of gift made at an eclipse is also made to other classes, and on occasions also other than at an eclipse.

Gifts made at an eclipse are called *ugra* or ' fierce '. The fierceness, ' *ugraṭa* ', of a gift is determined by the occasion, for the same things may be given on two different occasions ; on one of these the gifts will remain ordinary gifts and at the other they will transfer to the recipient a burden of ill or sin. When the planets are propitiated, for instance, and worshipped during a *sanskār* or a *śānti*, or in performance of a *vrata*, with the object of attaining success or winning *barkat*, gifts are made to priests and are not *ugra*. When the same gifts are made to avert evil resulting from the evil influence of the planets, their *pīḍā*, the gifts are *ugra*; the priest by accepting them loses some of his *śakti* and has to perform a *prayascitta* to regain his lost power. At a marriage, again, gold can be given to a bridegroom, but when this is given to a priest during obsequies it becomes an *ugra* gift. Gifts of a cow, land, vessels, and clothes at a marriage bring happiness and fertility; when given during obsequies they bring evil. On the day of the consummation ceremony bedding is given to the bridegroom, but when this is given to a priest at obsequies it is the worst of gifts to accept.

All gifts to priests during obsequies are *ugra*; gifts made at the *Karka Sankramaṇa* are also *ugra*, as are those made when the bad *yogas*, *kuyoga*, of *Vaidhṛti* and *Vyatīpāt* fall on a *Pūrṇimā*, *Amāvāsyā* or *Sankramaṇa*. At a funeral therefore the chief priest chooses a particular priest to accept such presents with their burden of evil. In the second half of *Bhādrapad* on the anniversary of all the *pitṛs*, black sesamum is offered to priests, and fodder is thrown on the road for passing cattle to eat, so that the sins of the dead may be transferred. This is another example of an *ugra* gift.

The gifts made at an eclipse are of this character. When an eclipse of the moon occurs in a man's star zodiac he gives to a priest a small image, *bimba*, of the moon and one of a snake, or if the eclipse be solar occurring in one's *janmarāśi* or *janmanakṣatra* a gold image of the sun and of a snake. These images are placed in a copper plate filled with ghee and given to the priest. At an eclipse all forms of alms draw power from the power of the time. The Hindu says they are ten times more efficacious than at ordinary moments; they avert calamity and they convey or transfer sins. In Sind charity is advised at this time to lessen the punishment of the planets who are being punished for their sins. A *corpus vile* is not unnaturally the best medium for transferring sin or evil.

The various cries uttered at an eclipse by those who receive gifts are instructive. In the Deccan the *Māng* goes about calling '*Īḍā pīḍā dyā*', 'Give away your evils', a phrase commonly used when a lamp is waved round a person's head to avert evil. In the Karnāṭak *Māngs* call '*Kari dana kodri*' or merely '*Kari kari*', 'Evil time; give charity'. In Gujarāt *Ravalias* cry out '*Sonadān, rupadān, tāmradān vastradān*', 'Give gifts of gold, silver, copper and clothes'. In Sind sweepers call out '*Kar kalyān sada kalyān*', 'Do good and you will always have good' or '*Jati satika dān*'. One cry of *Māngs* is '*Chute grahaṇ de dān*', 'Free the eclipse, give alms', but I am unaware of this ever being interpreted as implying that the freeing of the eclipse is achieved by the *Māngs*, and the gifts are actually made when the eclipse is clearing. *Vedh* is the nine hours before a partial lunar eclipse and the twelve hours before a full lunar eclipse or a solar eclipse whether full or partial. It does not include the period of eclipse, but ends when the eclipse begins. To ascertain when an eclipse has actually begun, a wooden pestle is placed erect in a shallow dish containing water and cow-dung, an iron article being placed near. If the eclipse has begun the pestle will stand erect. The beginning of the eclipse is called *sparśakāl*, the middle time *madhyākāl* and the time of clearance *mokṣakāl*. In the first period the Hindu has to bathe and recites *jap* or mutters silent prayers; the second period is for worship and during the third *śānti* is performed and gifts are made to avert evil. The final clearance of the luminary is followed by a period of twelve hours, a *kari* or evil time, such as follows all *parvakāl*, called *grahaṇdakari* and during this many auspicious ceremonies cannot be performed. A thread ceremony or a marriage cannot be celebrated for four days before and for three days after an eclipse.

Gifts made when the eclipse is clearing away are many. A figure of the eclipse is drawn in a basket or winnowing-fan with grain, and the whole is then given to a *Māng*. A pot of oil in which the donor has looked at his own reflection, and to which he adds a copper coin, is given away. Hindus in the Deccan give away shoes; rings of five metals or of copper inscribed with the letter K; the Muhammadan in the Deccan gives away salt and uḍid (Phaseolus Mungo), a marking nut pierced with needles, oil, fibres of a broom and the hair of a woman; in Sind the Hindu also gives away iron nails. In the Karnāṭak nine grains of different kinds representing nine planets, *navgrah*, are given to *Māngs*, as are also pieces of coal. Because gifts at an eclipse bear with them a transferred evil, Brahmins will accept nothing but cash. At Sangam Mahuli near Satara, a Raja of Satara wished to make a gift of land as an endowment to Brahmins, but they would not accept it when made as it was the time of an eclipse, so the Chief Minister of the Peśwa, the *Pratinidhi*, accepted the land himself and bestowed it on the Brahmins after the eclipse had passed.

It is only by visualizing the hour of an eclipse as an hour of great power, as a *parvakāl* and as *ghoro* or *vazandār*, that the ritual associated with it can be given an accurate perspective. It is not a mere hour of demon activity, it is not a *bhūtveḷ*. On the other hand, a portion of the period of an eclipse is a *puṇyakāl*, a time when *puṇya* or 'merit' can be won, and the *Institutes of Viṣṇu* (xc, 29) speak of the manifold advantages attending an eclipse which can be obtained. At an eclipse all water has the *śakti* of the Ganges; every gift has the value of a gift of land, and every Brahmin has the *śakti* of *Vyas*, the composer of the *Purāṇa*. At an eclipse the *śakti* of man is the greater and therefore his worship of images adds the more to their *śakti*.

Of these advantages one is the absolution of sin which can be secured by bathing in river or sea. The bathing [1] which is so common a feature at an eclipse, is done with the intention of sharing in the enhanced *śakti* of water at this time, and through it of winning absolution. Another illustration of the power of water during an eclipse is the repetition of mantras whilst standing in water so as to add to their *śakti*.

The eclipse which has no existence apart from the luminaries eclipsed is itself *dev*, and must be protected from every manner of uncleanness. Sleep as a state of impurity is forbidden and even children are kept awake. Relieving nature is forbidden and any sexual indulgence. An unclean person may not look at the eclipse, for not only will he himself suffer from the resentment of its *śakti* but the period of the eclipse will be prolonged. A pregnant woman must not see the eclipse, and in Sind a proclamation is made warning all such women. Even pregnant cattle must not be allowed to wander and are tied up in their stalls. Sindi Muhammadans think God punishes the luminaries as an example to men to pray and repent, and as repentance and prayer require complete purity, remain aloof from all unclean acts, fearing a prolongation of the eclipse if they do not do this. The penalties of a breach of these injunctions are many. A child conceived at an eclipse is born blind or with hands and feet reversed. If a pregnant woman sees the eclipse her child is born blind; if pregnant cattle are not kept at home they have a miscarriage.

All forms of *himsā* are forbidden at an eclipse. The reaping of crops, for a crop reaped at this time will eventually be consumed by fire. Sweeping is tabooed, and as everything must be clean

[1] Cp. *Religion and Folklore of Northern India*, W. Crooke, 1926, p. 41: 'Bathing in a sacred place is the most effectual way of relieving sun and moon from the attack of the demon, because bathing removes a man's pollution and renders him pure enough to recite the mantras or holy texts which scare the demon.' I am afraid that an obsession that everything done at an eclipse is to be explained by fear of demons, robs most of the ritual followed of its real meaning.

when the eclipse begins the house is swept and cleaned before it begins. Clothes and vessels are washed and a bath is also taken before the eclipse appears. The cutting of hair and nails; shaving; grinding and threshing are equally prohibited. When such destructive acts are done by a pregnant woman her *śakti* makes the act the more dangerous and her child suffers in consequence; if she sews or cuts anything the child will bear the marks of the cutting and the sewing on its body. These restrictions, however, on the conduct of a pregnant woman at an eclipse are not peculiar to this time. In the dark half of the month she is never allowed to look at the moon for fear of harm to the fœtus; acts of *himsā* are always prohibited to her from the beginning of her pregnancy or shortly afterwards, and the restrictions applied to her on *Nāgpancmī* are much the same as those she must observe at an eclipse. During an eclipse a *Haranṣikārī* woman, if pregnant, cannot make bread or break a stick; a *Māngarudi* woman cannot cook or grind; and a *Ghattivaddar* woman is required to sit perfectly still.

In other respects, too, a time of eclipse is similar to other *parvakāl.* Food taken at an eclipse is poisonous and brings illness if eaten, and from the beginning of *vedh* food [1] and water cannot be taken. Work must cease or one suffers bodily pain and the labour is fruitless. Trees, for example, planted at an eclipse would never bear fruit. The recitation of the *Veda* must cease and even the daily *sandhyās* are interrupted.

At an eclipse the *śakti* of the sun or moon is in trouble; it is polluted. To say that the eclipse is unclean and to say that the *śakti* of the eclipsed body is reduced is one and the same thing. The myth of *Medinī* makes unclean the ground, contact with which destroys *śakti.* The term *suher* which refers to the impurity associated with birth, is also applied to the period of an eclipse. In precise proportion, however, to the reduction in the *śakti* of the luminary the *śakti* of a mantra or *yantra* may be increased. Mantras already learnt are repeated at an eclipse to add to their power; a *yantra* prepared at an eclipse is very powerful and when an eclipse begins goldsmiths melt metals for use as caskets for charms. Metal sheets for the preparation of *yantras* are obtainable in every bazaar,

[1] 'He must not eat during an eclipse of the moon or of the sun.'—*Institutes of Viṣṇu*, lxviii, I.

'The Vedas are not to be recited when *Rahu* by an eclipse makes the moon impure.'—*Manu*, iv, 110.

'In the case of an eclipse of sun or of the moon . . . the recitation of all the sacred sciences must be interrupted from that hour until the same hour the next day.'—*Apastamba, Aphorisms*, i, 3, 11, 30.

'On an eclipse of the sun or of the moon the study is interrupted until the same time next day.'—*Grihya-sutras of Gobhila*, IIIP, 3K, 18.

and mantriks keep a stock of them. When one is required, mantriks inscribe a charm on a piece and worship it in a *śaktisthān*, such as a temple, throwing over it *akṣat*, making *ārtī* and performing *jap* or silent prayer. Deccani Muhammadans put on their arms at an eclipse a new *tawiz* which they renew at the next eclipse. The time of an eclipse is the only time when a magician will give away to others the secrets of his charms. The power of an eclipse adds power to many an act dependent on power for its efficacy. At an eclipse nails are driven into barren trees, or they are stabbed with a sickle to coerce them to become fruitful. As this is done the tree is threatened with complete destruction if it does not heed the prickings and give fruit.

The impurity which is supposed to affect the eclipsed bodies pollutes other *śakti*. Fire must be extinguished; all water in the house must be thrown away; food remaining uneaten is thrown or given away; costly things, such as milk, butter, clothes and books, are protected by leaves of the tulsī (Ocimum sanctum). Pickles are protected by a circle of wool or silk. Darbha grass is also used to protect valuable articles and nothing really in the house can be touched. After the eclipse is over the old sacred thread is thrown into running water or at the root of the tulsī and a new thread is substituted. One explanation, too, of the immersion of the *kul devatā* at an eclipse is that it protects them from the *suher* of the eclipse.

The religion of the Prophet has not prevented popular Muhammadan practice approximating to that of the Hindu. On the day of the death of his son Abraham, which synchronized with a complete solar eclipse, the Prophet ascended the pulpit and addressed the people saying: 'Surely the sun and moon are the signs of Allah; they do not become eclipsed in consequence of the death of any one nor on account of any one's life, so when you see this call on Allah and magnify Him and pray to Him and give alms.' The belief of the masses, however, is that charity at an eclipse lessens the punishment of the sun and moon, and assumes that the period of the eclipse will be prolonged if good Muhammadans do not repent and pray. Hindu practice, too, is inspired by a belief that man's action may control the duration of the eclipse. *Akṣat* is thrown towards the eclipse to free the luminary and after the eclipse is over is thrown again in gratitude for its release. More than this, the family gods are immersed in a pot of water and kept so immersed till the eclipse is over, whilst the *yajamān* performs *jap*. This is a coercion of the *śakti* of these gods to free the eclipsed planet from the eclipse. When the eclipse is a lunar one Muhammadans recite the *namaz khusuf* and when it is solar the *namaz kusuf*; in Sind either prayer is said by individuals or in congregation, but Deccani Muhammadans pray in congregation only at a solar eclipse.

The Hindu recognizes an eclipse as a *parvakāl*, the Muhammadan as *ghoro* or *vazandār*, and both consider that the power of the hour adds to the danger inherent in taking an oath. Both again forbid all destructive acts which destroy power; eating and drinking which militate against the winning of *barkat* in an hour of power, and both enjoin strict continence.

HOURS OF DANGER

In every Hindu day there is a period of three and threequarters, *ghatikā* called *kāḻveḻ* ,' black time'. This is a time when death comes and any one who dies on a particular day dies within its *kāḻveḻ*, which occurs once in every twenty-four hours. Following every *parvakāl* also is a *kari* or time of evil.

There are, moreover, days full of danger, *ghātvār*. On these no good work can be done; no journey undertaken; no auspicious ceremony celebrated, and on which a Hindu may not shave. Determined, too, by the zodiac of his birth there are also dangerous *tithi*, *nakṣatra*, months and *prahar*, the last a period of three hours, the day being divided into eight *prahar*.

Zodiac of birth	Day of danger	*Tithi* of danger	*Nakṣatra* of danger	Month of danger	*Prahar* of danger
Aries . . .	Sunday	3.6.11	*Maghā*	*Kārttik*	Fourth
Taurus . .	Saturday	5.10.15	*Hasta*	*Mārgaśirṣa*	Fourth
Gemini . .	Monday	2.7.12	*Svātī*	*Āṣāḍha*	Third
Cancer . .	Wednesday	2.7.12	*Anurādhā*	*Pauṣa*	First
Leo . . .	Saturday	3.8.13	*Mūlā*	*Jyeṣṭha*	First
Virgo . . .	Saturday	5.10.15	*Śravaṇa*	*Bhadrapad*	First
Libra . . .	Thursday	4.9.14	*Pūrvāṣādhā*	*Māgha*	Fourth
Scorpio . .	Friday	1.6.11	*Revati*	*Āśvin*	First
Sagittarius .	Friday	3.8.13	*Bharaṇī*	*Śrāvaṇ*	First
Capricorn . .	Tuesday	4.9.14	*Rohiṇī*	*Vaiśākha*	Fourth
Aquarius . .	Thursday	3.8.13	*Āradrā*	*Chaitra*	Third
Pisces . . .	Friday	5.10.15	*Āsleṣā*	*Phālgun*	Fourth

The birthday of a man, *Vadhadivas*, is also a time of danger and this not only for the man himself but for his father. On that day neither he nor his father can commit any form of *himsā*; they may not cut their hair or nails; they must remain strictly continent;

must avoid eating flesh and bathing with hot water. All kinds of quarrelling must be avoided; they cannot go on a journey; celebrate any auspicious ceremony; begin any new work such as digging a well, laying the foundations of a house or entering a new house for the first time. Religious instructions, *mantropadeś*, cannot be taken from a teacher; no debt can be incurred, and if he be a king his coronation cannot take place. The *nakṣatra*, *vār* and the *tithi* of birth are equally dangerous.

The Hindu calendar has other days which, though not exactly dangerous, are in some degree devoid of *śakti*, so that acts done thereon are not as efficacious as at other times, and this especially when the winning of *puṇya* is the object. Such days are the *kṣayatithi* when one *tithi* merges into another; the *kṣayamās*, which occurs once in a hundred and forty-one years, when the year has only eleven months and the two fortnights of the last month called *kṣayamās* are counted as two months. Besides these, there is the *adhikamās*; once in thirty months the year has thirteen months; the ordinary last month is then called *nija* and the name of this month with the suffix *adhik*, 'more', is given to the additional month.

The days of the week have each their own power. On different days it is dangerous for a Hindu to go a journey in a particular direction. On Saturdays and Mondays he should not travel towards the east; on Sundays and Fridays towards the west; and on Wednesdays and Tuesdays towards the north. If unavoidably he has to travel in a direction which has its dangers he attempts to avert evil by eating certain foods which vary according to the direction in which he is to travel. Should he be going east he is to eat curds; he is to take oil if he goes south, jaggery if going west, and certain preparations of milk if he travel north. Apart again from the direction in which a man starts out on a journey the mere setting out on a journey demands certain precautions which vary according to the day. A man setting out on a journey on a Sunday should first look into a mirror; on Monday he should use sandalwood oil; on Tuesday should eat coriander seed; and on Wednesday raw sugar. If he sets out on Thursday he should take two or four grains of mustard; on Friday should take curds; and on a Saturday *vāvḍing* (Embelia Rives).

SUNDAY

Sunday is not a good day for a Hindu. Nothing new should be commenced; buttermilk should not be prepared and gourds should not be cut. The day is a negative day, save that it is a good day for deeds of magic. It is a good day to take the first draught of a new medicine; to collect medicinal herbs; to begin to wear a new charm. Above all, it is a good day for the preparation of *yantras* for the cure of evil-eye, spirit possession or diseases of children caused by impure contacts. On Sundays salt is usually charmed, the ruī-tree is worshipped by women who crave issue, and astrologers predict the future.

An ordinary Sunday is of little importance to a Muhammadan, but the first Sunday of each month is one of the best days for writing charms before sunrise, for taking measures to avert evil-eye, and for rendering services such as sweeping or filling water-pots at shrines from which comes *barkat.*

MONDAY

A Hindu woman will not sew on Monday because this is a day sacred to the god Śiva and the vernacular word for 'to sew' is similar to the name of the god. To clean cotton on Monday brings a man to ruin, *hatti kaladre halaguttade.* Women who have sons will not eat in the evening or they will have no more male issue. If a woman combs her hair she brings danger to her brother; if she takes an overhead bath her husband will die if he chooses the same day to shave. If the husband shaves on this day he brings danger to his son. Agriculturists will not plough on Monday; butter and ghee cannot be made; a bullock cannot be yoked to a cart; wheat cannot be ground. The eating of sesamum and of butter must be avoided and a man with a son must not take a meal in the evening. It is a good day for the first wearing of new clothes and for measuring grain.

The first Monday of a month is a good day for a Muhammadan; it is for him good to be born on that day; to travel; to begin new work; to write a charm or to be circumcised.

TUESDAY

It is calamitous for a Hindu to start a journey on this day; to settle any agreement; to wash the floor; to plough or reap. No consultation should be held on Tuesday, and a dumb man is said to consider every day a Tuesday. It is bad to change money or prepare a bodice. Anything said or done on this day leads to nothing, though it is considered an auspicious day for planting sugar-cane.

A Muhammadan considers it an inauspicious day, as *nahas.* The construction of a house cannot be begun. A child born on Tuesday brings *barkat* to none nor to himself. Spirits are very active and unmanageable and cannot be exorcized. Charms are written on Tuesdays for evil objects, and blood-letting is done to get rid of evil blood. Guests are not welcomed, but their departure is welcomed as they take away with them on departure the evil of the day. There can be no shaving on a Tuesday.

WEDNESDAY

Hindu women will not leave their homes on Wednesday for fear they should not return, *Jaśil budhi yeśil kadhi.* It is a bad day for reaping or measuring grain; a journey made on this day is fruitless; it is bad to lend or borrow money; it is bad for a woman to bathe; it is bad to eat gram; and a father will not on Wednesday send his daughter to her husband's house. It is a good day for shaving and for cutting wood for a building.

A Muhammadan considers Wednesday a lucky day; it is 'the father of profit', *Alarb'a Abularabih.* It is good to be born on this day; good to wash clothes; to begin ploughing; and it is a good day for a circumcision. The last Wednesday of *Safar* is a very auspicious day when sweets are prepared and given in the name of the dead. Grain, however, cannot be measured; and if blood-letting is performed, leprosy ensues.

THURSDAY

This is an auspicious day. It is good for a journey or for any agricultural operation. For both Hindu and Muhammadan it is an excellent day for witchcraft and magic. A Muhammadan child born on Thursday night has special *kudrat,* and such children are called *Juman rati sayad.*

FRIDAY

Friday to a Muhammadan is a day of great *barkat.* It is good to be born on Friday, as it is to die on this day. According to Muhammadan calculation, the night of any day is the night that precedes the day and therefore Thursday night, according to the English idea, would be for the Muhammadan the night of Friday. This is the holiest day in the week; alms given on Friday acquire for the giver great merit. Charms written before sunrise are very potent. It is the best of times to bring home a bride. It has, however, a dangerous element which leads to restrictions on action. It is bad to go out for *shikar* on Friday; bad to start a journey before the noon prayers; it is bad to receive condolences and one must avoid quarrels.

Hindu mantriks choose Friday for their magic because they are under the influence of a *Śakti*; precisely for this same reason on this day, as on Tuesday, grinding of grain and pounding are forbidden as these cannot be done when any form of worship of power is performed. A bride cannot be taken from her husband's house to that of her parents. It is dangerous to make a decision or form any project on a Friday, as such programmes are never realized. It is, however, a day of *Lakṣmī*, and so milk must not be drunk or gram eaten; cash and ornaments must not be loaned to others as they will not be returned. In the evening a pot of milk and gram must be placed before the *kul devatā*.

SATURDAY

This day is associated with Saturn and is accordingly one of evil power. It is a bad day for ploughing, or the commencement of a journey; for shaving or wearing a new garment. As oil, salt and sesamum are among the offerings usually made to *Śani*, to buy them on a Saturday is bad; to buy fuel or oil in the evening portends death to the chief member of the family. A Hindu must not break an earthen pot on a Saturday; must not cut certain varieties of gourd, eat gram, or drink milk. He chooses Saturdays for measures to dispossess spirits or avert evil; trees with power to avert spirits are cut on Saturdays, on which days spirits are active. Merely to say 'Born on Saturday' is a remedy against the effects of evil-eye; shoes are waved over the victims of evil-eye and other precautions taken to avert this evil *śakti*.

For a Muhammadan it is a bad day for a wedding or a circumcision; it is also dangerous to quarrel on a Saturday. On the other hand, he will write charms intended to work evil on this day.

The Hindu regards this day as a good day for *shikar* in the belief that *Śani* demands a victim on Saturday.

MONTHS

The same meticulous taboos apply to many of the months. The months of *Vaiśākh* and *Chaitra* are called *vasantṛtu*, 'the season of spring', and bathing in rivers at early dawn is enjoined. During *Vaiśākh* there is no restriction on celebrating any auspicious or inauspicious ceremony but *Chaitra* is not a month in which to lay a hearth, grind or store turmeric, retouch the grindstone, commence a vow of *Brahmacārya* or perform a marriage or thread ceremony. During *Jyeṣtha* a thread ceremony, or the marriage of an eldest child is not performed. *Kārttik* and *Mārgaśirṣa* are auspicious months for all purposes; on the twelfth of *Kārttik Kṛṣna* awakes from his long sleep of four months. *Pauṣa* is a month of bad portent; it is known as *Śūnya māsa* and *śūnya* is used to describe something void of *śakti*; no auspicious ceremony can be performed, no consultation about a marriage or comparison of horoscopes can be made. In this month in the first year after her marriage the bride cannot live with her husband. If a cow gives calves in this month they are given away to a saint or *guru*. When plague or other epidemic breaks out in India and people abandon their homes and take up their residence in hastily-constructed shelters in the fields, the inauspiciousness of this month is often their salvation. As every district officer at times laments as soon as deaths cease in a village, the people who have evacuated it haste to return to their homes, with the result only too often that there is a recrudescence of the epidemic. When, however, the month of *Pauṣa* intervenes no movement of any kind can be made until the month is over, and a longer evacuation of the village results. *Māgha* is a good month for all purposes and bathing in the early morning is a duty. If, however, buffaloes have calves in this month they are given away to a holy person. *Phālgun* is an inauspicious month. *Caturmās* is a period of four months during which the gods are supposed to be asleep and so no auspicious ceremony can be performed; in some respects this is a sort of Lent for the orthodox, abstinence from many luxuries being practised.

The taboos and the duties associated with individual days and months are manifold in detail. There are probably, however, few Hindus or Muhammadans acquainted with them all, and the list I have given has been prepared from information given by many informants.

CHAPTER XII

THE POWER OF COLOURS

OMENS of pending evil are drawn from objects of black colour. Dreams of black things, excepting a black cow, foretell illness or even death. It is bad to meet a black animal in the morning, such as a black cat or dog, if one has set out with a purpose, and if such an animal enters the *mandap* where a marriage is being celebrated the marriage will bring disaster. If one meets a person carrying something black, as oil or tar, one should return home and set out afresh. A *Telī* woman still warns those she meets of the ominous burden of oil she carries, so that they may return home and wash their feet before setting out again. It is equally bad to meet a person carrying a sooty pot or pan.

A horse with a black roof to its mouth brings disaster to its owner. The ominousness of a crow is obviously due to its black colour. Should a crow touch a man's head he will soon become poor, involved in a serious quarrel or may be he will die; if the crow touch his shoulder or waist he will be stricken with morbid fear; should the crow touch a woman her husband or son dies shortly afterwards. The touch of a crow, however, is powerless to harm a man if he be sitting under a tree, carrying curds, or eating cooked food. The assembling of many crows betokens an impending epidemic. If a crow enters a house it is usually vacated for three months, and on one occasion I found a whole college perturbed, and its daily routine all upset, because in the morning a crow had entered the kitchen. If a Hindu sees two crows mating or quarrelling he should at once write to a relative informing him of his decease, and the relative's tears at his bereavement will avert the impending evil. Crows to the Hindu are messengers of *Yama*, god of death. On the thirteenth day of their *Śrāddha* ceremony Hindus give a quarter of the feast to crows saying: 'Be you *Yama*, messenger or crow, I worship you, oh crow; let the sacrifice be eaten that I offer for my sins of seven lives.'

It is bad to meet a person dressed in black in the morning. In Sind if a man meets a *Sidi*, an Abyssinian, he calls upon him to show his white teeth at once. No black vessel can be used by a

Hindu in an auspicious ceremony, and baked earthen vessels are on such occasions splashed with white lime. A black *sāḍī* cannot be given at a joyous gathering; the bridegroom should not wear a black coat and a black winding-sheet must not be used for the dead. If a Hindu woman wearing a black *sāḍī* approaches a man who has been bitten by a snake there is no hope of the man's recovery. It is ominous also if a girl attains puberty just when she is wearing a black garment, and the mischance necessitates a special *śānti*.

On the tenth day of *Muḥarram*, Muhammadans eat cakes of wheat in memory of the martyrdom of Imām Ḥusain. In the preparation of these cakes the greatest care is necessary. No impure woman may enter the house, the strictest continence is enjoined until all the cakes have been consumed, and no woman wearing a black *sāḍī* may enter the room in which the cakes are prepared or baked.

There is a general reluctance to use black tiles in roofing a house, and though a black blanket serves the Baluch as a tent, tent-cloth of black colour is usually avoided. In the Karnāṭak is a saying, 'If a jet-black bullock is brought; if the daughter-in-law with black eyes comes home, the evil effects cannot be averted'. In Sind if a man has been cursed he is said to have stepped on black, '*hunjo kari te per payo ahe*', and the tongue of a man whose curse is effective is said to be black, *kar zibanyo* or *tunhji ziban kari ahe*. The Sindi believes that the gift of a black animal to secure a bride will lead to an unhappy marriage. A married woman or a maiden in Gujarāt will not wear a black *sāḍī*. Presents of black animals must be given away, and the offer of anything black is the more dangerous if made in the morning. If the heart of a slaughtered animal is black evil befalls the man who killed it. There are some families that will avoid black clothes of any kind. A black hen in Sind is used to promote quarrels between friends, and if a Sindi can but get another to tie a knot in a black thread, he can himself wear the thread and by so doing keep the person who tied the knot in subjection.

Though, however, black is so ominous a colour in some cases it works good, and it is often used to avert evil. The milk of a black goat or cow is supposed to have more *śakti* than that of other milch cattle, and is given to a woman in her confinement. The milk of a black cow is also used for the *abhiṣek* of an image. The commonest of animal sacrifices is that of a black goat and this animal appears among the *devak* of the *Marāṭhā Śeḻārs*. A Muhammadan uses the milk of a black goat to cure whooping cough. A

Vaddar gives the milk of a black goat or black cow to sick children. A black horse is a possession to be treasured. To a Sindi Muhammadan a black ant, a black cat or a black horse brings *barkat.* A black cock reared in a house will protect any woman of the household when *enceinte.* A black blanket because of its approximation in colour to a rain-cloud is used by *Dhangars* in rites practised to bring rain. Sindi Moslems believe that congress with a negress cures venereal disease, and that harmony can be restored between a husband and wife by means of the bile of a black cat.

Objects of black colour are used in many ways to avert evil. As a protection against evil-eye armlets of black thread are worn; the combings of black hair and marking nuts are tied to the necks of cattle; the faces of young children are marked with black pigment and the use of soot and antimony to keep away evil-eye is very general. A black cloth with uncooked bread is waved across the face of one victimized by evil-eye and then thrown away. Until recently ornaments worn in the ear to avert evil-eye, and now made of pearls and gold, were made of black beads.

Fig. 120.

The thigh-bone of a black sheep killed on a Saturday also averts evil-eye. The *dṛṣṭimaṇī* worn by children and the *mangaḻsūtra* worn by a married Hindu woman contain black beads (*tāḻi*).

Black things are a protection against spirits. In Sind sacrifices to spirits are usually black and are called *kali bala*, ‘ black calamity ’. Figures in black are drawn on the doors of the room of a woman in confinement, and on the front door of a house to avert spirits, and with the same object paddy grain is coloured black and scattered on the *rās* or heap of grain gathered to the threshing-floor. Black thread is freely used in the preparation of *yantras* or charms against spirits, and black clothes are given away to stay the persecution of a ghost. To prevent the ghost of the dead returning to haunt the living, black grain *rāḻā* (Panicum Italicum) is thrown behind the departing bier. A black cord, *bhāldorī,* is tied round the neck or foot of a milch animal to prevent spirits drinking from its udders. Inhaling the smoke of a black cloth burnt on cinders with chillies, is a cure for spirit-possession. As a preventive of the attentions of spirits some castes blacken their teeth.

In transferring evil to others black things are used to ensure success. A black goat in Sind is waved round a sick man, then killed and given to fakirs to eat, and thereby accept to themselves the illness of the patient. In the Deccan a black goat or hen is waved round a person supposed to be possessed and then allowed to wander away. If a man has indigestion some of his food is given to a black dog, and his illness goes if the dog eats the food.

The evil influence of Saturn or *Śani*, the *pīḍā*, is defeated by the use of certain black objects. A horseshoe from the foot of a black horse, picked from the road on a Saturday and nailed to the threshold averts this *pīḍā*. When silent prayer or *jap* is resorted to, to avert the influence of Saturn, a black animal or black grain is used in offerings. The efficacy of iron in dispelling the influence of Saturn is in part due to its black colour. Besides iron, other black things are used; a black rag is worn in the pocket, a black coat, a black turban, black shoes and even a *dhotar* with a black border afford protection against Saturn's *pīḍā*. Black gram is an offering to Saturn. On Saturday an iron image of Saturn is made; this is put in a pot of oil, it is covered with black blankets and after worship is given to a black priest, *Kriṣṇa Brāhmaṇ*. Black cloth is also an offering to the inauspicious *Rāhu* and *Ketu*.

When a house is built a doll or image made of rags and wood is hung up in the house covered with a black cloth, to avert the evil associated with the *pāyguṇ* of the new. When a visitor arrives and is suspect, to prevent his renewing his visit a black earthen pan covered with soot is thrown to the ground behind him as he departs, and to remove the apprehended results of his visit black *rāḻā* grain is thrown behind him. When an owl hoots a black thread is taken and at each hoot of the owl, a knot is tied in the thread to forestall evil.

WHITE

White is often a synonym for 'auspicious'. When a new cow or bullock is bought a Hindu pours milk on its hooves, that its innate *pāyguṇ* may be white. Trees with milky sap and trees that drop white powder, *Śīr khiṣt*, are credited with miraculous powers. White is the colour of Śiva's laughter and white things are welcomed by him, and therefore bring good fortune. White thread, camphor, white flowers, milk and silver all bring *barkat*. White fowls are given by *Marāṭhās* to the chief relative of the bridegroom and at his betrothal a silver coin is given to the bridegroom.

The tying of a knot in a thread in the process of invoking power is a marked feature of Hindu ceremonial. White threads alone are used when the beneficent power of gods is invoked and black when the power of spirits is invoked. In all auspicious ceremonies, *mangalkārya*, white threads must be used.

White clothes are pure to a Hindu and even if they be touched by an ' untouchable ' can be used without being washed. Because, however, of the association of white with a funeral, for in severe mourning white is used and the winding-sheet of the dead is white, pure white is usually avoided by a Hindu. White sandalwood-paste is used in *Śrāddha* ceremonies, but white *dhotars* without a coloured border are seldom worn ; if the walls of a house are white-washed they are usually splashed with colour or designs and lines in colour are drawn on them. A bridegroom must never wear pure white clothes and his clothes if white are splashed with colours. Different families of *Marāṭhās* dress their bridegrooms in different colours ; the *Bhoites* and *Chavans* in yellow, the *Pisals* in green, and the association of a *Marāṭhā* family with a particular colour was a very close one a few decades ago.

Certain white markings make a goat very auspicious to a Muhammadan ; on an inquiry of Moses which colour was the best of colours God is supposed to have chosen white. A white umbrella is a sign of royalty. Lime-water wards off evil-eye from gardens, and power is invoked into stones merely by smearing them with lime. A mixture of white with another colour, particularly with black, is very auspicious. The horse sacrificed in the old horse-sacrifice, *Aśvamedha*, was a black one with white ears, and oxen with white spots on their heads and knees were chosen for ploughing the site of the old Aryan village. Animals that are purely white are not used in sacrifices. The *panc kalyāṇ* horse with white marks on the feet and forehead is *sadoro* or ' lucky ' in Sind and to both Hindu and Muhammadan is a valuable possession. According to Abū Qatādah the Prophet said, ' The best horses are black with white foreheads and having a white upper lip ' ; according to Abū Wahhāb the Prophet considered a bay horse with white forehead and white fore- and hind-legs, the best of horses.

GREEN

Green is an auspicious colour. Muhammadans think that green clothes are worn in Paradise and that the soul saw green before entering the human body. When a Sindi purchases an animal he takes with him a bunch of green grass, so that the results of his purchase may be green or lucky. Thirty days after *Muḥarram* Moguls, men and women, discard their mourning garb and picking up a bunch of green grass, attempt a transfer of its *kudrat* to themselves saying, ' Let greenness come to us '.

When a Hindu woman becomes *enceinte* for the first time she must use green plantain-leaves as a plate; in the fifth month of her pregnancy the *Lingāyat* and the *Namraddi* parents give her a green *sāḍī*, green bodice-cloth, and green bangles (*hūmuḍisuvadu*). The first *sāḍī* a Hindu woman wears after the settlement of her marriage should also be green. At the first and second tonsure of a boy a green bodice is given to his mother. Green bangles are offered to goddesses and the bangles of a bride should be green. The *devak* is often placed in a winnowing-fan along with a green bodice-cloth (*khaṇ*).

Green, however, is to be avoided by a Hindu woman who has a first-born son still unmarried; she cannot take her meals from green leaves; she cannot go under a green bower, or wear a green *sāḍī* or green bangles.

Of all colours red and yellow have the most power and of these the power of red is the greater.

RED

Red is associated very directly with *śakti* by the Hindu. A worshipper of *śakti* must wear red clothes. Goddesses are worshipped with red cloth and the image of Gaṇpati is painted red *Kunku* and *haḻad*, the former red and the latter yellow, are both necessary in the worship of *śakti* and an invariable feature of ceremony.

In magic rites red clothes are often prescribed. The Muhammadan practising *Ḥāḍrat Jinn*, or the control of spirits, clothes his medium in red clothes, whilst the Hindu wears red clothes himself when preparing many a *yantra*.

Akṣat is coloured red; the *akṣat* thrown on the bride and bridegroom; the *akṣat* placed on the *āsan* on which images are placed when installed or on which *ārtī* lamps are placed. The *mantrākṣat* given by *svāmīs* to their devotees as a blessing is always coloured red. When giving a verbal invitation to an auspicious ceremony red *akṣat* is given by the host or a priest to the guests invited. Invitation cards for a marriage or other important ceremony are coloured the same colour.

Red is an ever-recurring colour in a marriage ceremony. The posts of the marriage *manḍap* are coloured red and white. A red design is drawn on the wall near which the bridal pair has to sit (*bhorajgali*). Red figures of a svastika are drawn on gifts made to the bridal pair. The bridegroom, his father and the father of the bride should wear red turbans. A *nivāḻi* of red water is waved round the bridal pair, as it is round the *vaṭu* at his thread ceremony, or round a bull or horse which has been taken in procession. In the *surgi* bath taken by the bridal pair red water is sprinkled on the pair; the bride and bridegroom also throw red water, *vokḻi*, on each other. When a man marries a widow as his first wife, in castes permitting the re-marriage of widows, the dagger to which he is married is tied with red cloth (*alvan*).

In car festivals after the car has been drawn the deity is taken into the jungle. On return from the jungle a ceremony called *Okaḻi* is performed, and red water is sprinkled on the deity and all the assembled persons to ward off the effects of evil encountered in the jungle.

Married women put red marks on their foreheads, and red sandalwood-paste on their nails and palms and even on their feet in the month of Chaitra. A married woman, however, will not wear a red *sāḍī*, the garb of a tonsured widow, unless it be wholly of silk, nor wear red bangles without other bangles of another colour. The clothes of *gurus*, *svāmīs* and *sannyāsīs* are red; those of the boy at his thread ceremony in some Brahmin sects must be coloured red. The whitewashed niches in which the image of *Gajanana* is placed, and the *Tulsī Vṛndāvana* are coloured red. The Hindu every day and in particular on holy days marks his forehead with red sandalwood-paste; his threshold he washes with red earth, and his whitewashed walls he splashes with red colouring. *Vokḻi* or red water is thrown on each other by those who join in the celebration of *Hoḻī*; red water is applied to the foreheads of friends when lights are waved at *Divāḻī*, and when a wife attains puberty red colour is thrown on the husband. *Baḻī* offered to spirits in the evening should be red.

The Muhammadan boy wears a red *lingota* at his circumcision; the bridal pair wear red clothes as does a girl on attaining puberty. Red sheets are placed on the tombs of saints, and red flags at the top of trees to obtain *barkat*.

YELLOW

Saffron is used in writing mantras and the clothes of the Hindu bridal pair are sprinkled with saffron. Turmeric is a substitute for saffron. Any cloth put with the *devak* is usually coloured yellow as is the *antarpāṭ* or curtain which shields at one stage of the marriage ceremony the bride and bridegroom from each other's evil-eye.

Hindu brides are given yellow *sāḍīs* at a wedding; the *kankaṇ* worn by the bridal pair are yellow and have a piece of turmeric tied to them. Married women use turmeric every day as a sign of *saubhāgya* or married felicity.

Turmeric powder (Curcuma longa) must not be trodden nor touched by an unclean person. The *Haḻdi* ceremony consists in covering the bodies of the bridal pair with turmeric (*ariśiṇ*), and this is practised by Muhammadans also in the south of the Presidency, though not in Sind. *Haḻad* and *kunku* are applied to all new things, even to a *dhotar* or *sāḍī*. Continuous application of *kunku* prolongs a husband's life. Svastikas of turmeric and saffron are drawn on the feet of the bridal pair and of their parents. A yellow *dhotar* (*pitambara*) is worn when making *pūjā* of images. The skin of a tiger is a common *āsan* for a worshipper, though a Brahmin is forbidden to use it. Any cloth placed on the image of Viṣṇu must be yellow.

Yellow things are chosen to avert evil. Yellow slippers protect a Sindi from evil-eye. In the Sholapur district a man suffering from boils places on a public road a knotted yellow cloth in the hope of transferring his ills to others. When sheep are attacked by a disease called *arisin* shepherds take turmeric dates, dry coconut and tie these in a yellow cloth in the semblance of a doll and bury the bundle beyond their village boundary. To cure abscess three kinds of grain are tied in a yellow rag, waved round the affected person and thrown at cross-roads. When a man enters a new house or begins a journey he makes a knot of cloth which he carries with him, and this knot must be yellow and contain turmeric and gold.

CHAPTER XIII

THE POWER OF NUMBERS

ONE is an ominous number. It is bad, when on a journey, to meet a single Brahmin, or a person carrying a single pot of water. A person blind in one eye is a destroyer of the world; a person lame in one leg is the bane of all men. According to a Kanarese saying, an only son is not a son at all.

In auspicious ceremonies presents made must not be of single things, for such presents mark only inauspicious ceremonies such as obsequial rites and *Śrāddhas.* One must not use a single leaf of tulsī (Ocimum sanctum) in the worship of a god; one must not take a single fruit, flower or other thing as offering when going to perform *darśan* of a god or of a saint; that is when seeking *barkat* by the sight of power. With the exception of the moon all planets bring evil in the first zodiac; the first month in the Hindu calendar, *Chaitra,* is not one in which auspicious ceremonies can be performed. There are twenty-seven rains related to the *nakṣatra*; if the first of these, *Aśvinī,* be abundant it brings famine and a dearth of milk. One is avoided in counting on the threshing-floor, and it is inauspicious for one person to wave *ārtī,* or for *ārtī* to be waved round one person only.

TWO

A union of two forces is always necessary to produce fertility, and to make active a dormant potentiality. The number two is therefore associated with *barkat.*

The second of the twenty-seven rainy *nakṣatra* brings abundance of grain; it rains 'golden bricks'. In all auspicious ceremonies, *mangalkārya,* the *ārtī* used must have two wicks to each of its two lights. To meet two Brahmins or a person carrying two pots of water is a presage of success.

There is, however, evil in the *śakti* of the number two. A Hindu should not marry in the second year after the death of his former wife. Charity in gifts of even number is avoided. Though, too, invitations may be issued to two persons, it is dangerous for a sick man if two friends simultaneously go out to bring him a doctor.

THREE

The Hindu and the Muhammadan both associate finality with the number three. When finality is desirable three is deliberately chosen as a limit, but when finality means disaster three becomes a number to be avoided. *Murinda muktāya* (Kan.), 'With three it is ended'. *Ijā bijā āṇi tijā* (Mar.), 'A thing which has happened twice must occur a third time also'. *Murakhe mukti* (Kan.), 'To the third is completion'.

Anything said or done by a Muhammadan three times acquires a legal sanction, *tre dafah shari*. He pronounces his *tilak* or declaration of divorce three times; the bride acknowledges three times her acceptance of the bridegroom, *ijāb kabul*. To invoke the blessing of God the hands are raised three times after prayer; three recitations of the Koranic verse, *Kul Huvallah*, are equal to one recitation of the whole Koran. The purificatory ablution of the Muhammadan involves washing the hands thrice; gargling thrice, taking water in the nostrils three times, and thrice washing the face and feet. When three Muhammadans sit down to dine together the angels of God come and pour *barkat* upon them. To avert or transfer evil, articles are waved thrice round a stricken person; three marks of black on the face keep away evil-eye; and a lamp placed where three roads meet cures fever.

In making a *yantra* a Hindu repeats three times the mantra that invokes power. A Hindu's word repeated thrice must be accepted as truth, for by this repetition he speaks for the present, the past, and for the future. An extract from the *Veda* must be recited with three specific accents, *udātta, anudātta* and *svarita*, for void of accent a mantra would kill a person using it as if it were a thunderbolt. On the completion of a sale the sale price is mentioned three times. The water of the *mangalsnān* taken by the bridal pair and on occasions other than marriage by others, is sprinkled thrice to bring *barkat*. The *arghya* is offered three times; when *ācaman* is made in an auspicious ceremony it is done thrice.

To cure a snake-bite a banyan-tree is encircled three times. In the removal of evil, *utāra*; in measures taken to avert evil-eye or evil *pāygun* three is a determining number. The articles waved over the stricken or suspected person are frequently chosen in threes, or in some way distinguished by the number three. Three pieces of salt or bread; three pieces of wood taken from the roof of a house or pieces of straw and wood taken from three roofs;

a lemon cut in three pieces or a lemon marked with three lines; grain of three kinds; thread of three colours; three burning wicks; earth collected from three roads. These are typical of the things waved to avert evil. Besides this, the articles are waved three times and finally thrown where three roads meet. Among the tattoo-marks used by the *Kātkarī* in the Konkaṇ are three dots representing the triangular hearth and three lines, *titha*, representing cross-roads.

To appease the ghost of a deceased wife a custom of the Deccan is for castemen and a *bhagat* or magician to eat three kinds of grain in company. To cure an abscess three kinds of grain are tied in a yellow rag and waved round the patient by an elderly person and thrown at the meeting of three roads. The *mangaḻsūtra* of a married woman and the Brahmin's sacred thread consist of three strands. At a Brahmin marriage two copper pots are placed on an *āsan* of rice; they are filled with water, sandal-powder, flowers and saffron, and are covered with mango-leaves. To avert evil from the bridal pair they are brought in contact with the foreheads of the pair three times. *Tilagars* wave bread thrice round animals newly purchased; in a dangerous illness they take rice three times on the back of their hand, three times on the palm, wave round the sick and throw away.

Coming to an end, however, may mean loss or disaster. *Muru andre muravatti* (Kan.), 'Three; that is spoiling'. Three is always 'destructive', *mukkabaddi* (Kan.). Should a Hindu when engaged on some work chance to hear another utter the word 'three', the success of his work is forthwith ruined.

Charity cannot be given to three persons at one time nor can it take the form of offering three things; if three pieces of bread are offered to a child in Sind one piece is broken so as to make four pieces, Three and only three things must not be made at one time; three persons cannot set out together on any good work; three animals cannot be bought together; an agriculturist cannot store his grain in three places; three men must not hold an animal when it is slaughtered; three bearers must not carry the dead; the agents to a marriage must not be three; three bullocks must not be yoked to a plough. It is of evil omen to meet accidentally three persons; to travel on any day which by any computation can be regarded as a third day is dangerous. As the number five is associated with finality just as the number three, a number that is the sum of three and any multiple of five is a number to be avoided. The third, eighth, thirteenth, twenty-third, and twenty-eighth days of a lunar month to a Muhammadan are *nahas*, are inauspicious, are *ghoro* or *bhāro*, 'heavy'; if a Muhammadan dies on one of these days unless a piece of iron is placed in his mouth his relatives in turn will all die in a short time. In gambling three means the loss of everything. If a son be born after three daughters, an elder male of the family will die; if a girl follows three boys the girl brings calamity to the family of her husband and that of her parents. The Hindu in such an eventuality performs a *śānti*, *Trikaprasav Śānti*.

Na gacchet brahmana trayam, 'Three Brahmins will not go out together'. A Hindu considers it disastrous for three persons simultaneously to summon a doctor; to answer to a call that is repeated thrice is dangerous, for evil spirits call thrice. To carry three offerings to a temple or make three offerings to a god; to join two others in worship; to issue an invitation to three persons; to plough with three bullocks; or use a *nandādīp* with three wicks entails a sequel of evil. Three Hindus will not leave a house at the same time, or save at a *Śrāddha* sit down to a meal together. In one marriage *manḍap* there must not be just three *suvāsinīs*; when *ārtī* is waved round children, as on the birthday of a son, if there be only three children in the house a neighbour's child must be brought in for the occasion to avoid the number three. If a man loses his first wife and does not remarry in the year of her death, he must wait till after the expiry of the third year. *Pānsupārī*,[1] the commonest of courtesies offered to guests, cannot be offered to three persons. Three is avoided in measuring grain on the threshing-floor, and the Hindu considers three, with thirteen, nine and eighteen so fateful that they are used together as an expression connoting disaster or failure.

Perhaps the most interesting aspect of the finality attributed to the number three is the explanation it affords of certain forms of mock marriages. *Arka vivāha* is the marriage of a bridegroom to a ruī-tree (*ruī*, *ruiṭi*, *ark*, *ankdo*, *ekki*), Calatropis gigantea. There is no reference to this form of marriage in Vedic literature nor is it included among the eight forms of marriage mentioned in the *Smṛtis*. Later authorities, however, prescribe its ritual and emphasize the dangers associated with a third marriage. According to *Garga* ṛṣi, 'no one should marry a third wife for the attainment of love; if through infatuation or ignorance one takes a third wife one will no doubt perish'; 'The third human girl should not be married for she will die or become a widow. Therefore in the third place one should marry an arka-tree'.

[1] The gift of pan-leaves and supari nuts; the leaves are folded round the nut, held together by a clove and often covered with gold leaf.

A man marrying a third wife selects an arka-tree bearing fruit and blossom, and this on a Saturday, a Sunday, a day having the *nakṣatra* of *Hasta* or any other auspicious day. A priest is selected to give away *Kanyādātā*, the tree-bride, the *Arkakanyā*, 'daughter of the sun'. The bridegroom anoints himself with sandal-paste and puts on flowers, and makes his *sankalpa* or declaration of object saying, 'I perform this *Arkavivāha* to avert the guilt arising from my marriage with a third human being'. The priest worships the tree with red *akṣat*, sandal-paste and offerings; ties yellow cotton thread round the tree, places a woman's *sāḍī* near it and sprinkling water three times round the tree says, 'I give this daughter of the sun to the bridegroom'. Then the bridegroom sits on a *pāṭ* or wooden stool, and the priest offers him the usual *madhupark* of honey, sugar, water, milk and ghee and washes his feet. A screen, *antarpāṭ*, is held between the tree-bride and the bridegroom, and *akṣat* is thrown on both. Cotton thread is wound five times round the tree and round the bridegroom, and out of this thread *kankaṇ* or wristlets are made for the tree and the bridegroom. The bridegroom prays, 'Oh lustrous sun; the seven-horsed resident of the three worlds, ward off from me the evil arising from my third marriage and make me happy'. Meditating on the sun dwelling in the tree he mutters a hymn, *Ablinga*, encircles the tree with white cloth and thread and walks round it; then he offers the tree rice and molasses and again circumambulates it saying, 'This venerable woman whom I have now touched and who bestows love upon me, and who is created by Brahma from the sun, may she now protect me'. This action he again repeats with the words, 'I bow to thee, auspicious deity, to thee, the daughter of the sun. Oh goddess, protect me. You have come here as my wife. Oh sun, you have been created by Brahma for the good of all living beings; you are the presiding deity of the trees and the promoter of love among gods, please destroy forthwith the sin of my third marriage and also death'.

The priest gives away the bride with these words: 'I give this daughter of *Arka*, the granddaughter of *Savitu* and the great-granddaughter of *Aditya* to you who belong to the family of —— and bear the name of ——. May you resort to her.' As the priest encircles the tree and the bridegroom with thread, he utters the *Gāyatrī* mantra and as he ties the wristlets repeats a hymn called *Bṛhatsama*. The bridegroom ties a *mangaḻsūtra* to the tree and then standing to the north of the tree, proceeds to name the five gods for whom the bridal *hom* is prepared. The priest makes a fire, *yojik*, and offers oblations to *Agni*, *Indra*, *Vayu*, *Surya* and *Prajapati* and prays to the tree to bless the bridegroom with issue.

This is the detailed ritual of the Brahmin ; non-Brahmins merely seat the bridegroom near the tree on a *pāṭ*, and throw saffron and *akṣat* on the tree and the bridegroom, after which the bridegroom ties to the tree a *mangalsūtra* containing a piece of gold and black beads. A copper coin placed on *nāgvel* is offered to the tree to free the bridegroom from sin and avert spirits.

In the Kanara district the term *Arkavivāha* is usually applied to the marriage of a *Brahmacārī* when he dies unmarried, to a ruī, with a view to preventing his becoming a *rākṣasa* or ghost. When a man takes a third wife, a marriage is performed with a plantain, and this is called *Kardalī* or *Rambhāvivāha*. In this marriage a plantain-tree is chosen some four to five feet high and one that has never flowered but is virgin. After the marriage the tree is cut some three feet from the ground and the severed piece representing the head of the bride, is thrown at the stump. Both pieces should then be burned with darbha grass (Poa cynosuroides), and the obsequies of the tree should be performed, but as the tree is green the cremation in practice is a nominal one. In this marriage also the ritual of an ordinary marriage is followed. There is the same *vāgdān*, the same *kanyadān* or gift of the bride ; the encircling of the pair with thread ; the tying of a *mangalsūtra* to the tree bride, the offer to the tree of a coconut, plantain and bodice-cloth in a *sāḍī* wrapped round the tree, *uditumbodu* ; the same cancellation of the wife's *gotra* and the substitution of her husband's *gotra*. *Kan Divars* and *Madivals* choose a plantain far from the house of the bridegroom who, after the marriage, strips the tree of its ornaments and chops it down. In some of the States bordering on Gujarāt a man who makes a third marriage is married to a Śamī-tree (Prosopis spicigera).

In the case of the marriage to a ruī there is some variation in the manner in which the final disposal of the tree is made. In the Deccan it is abandoned, but the bridegroom and bride and their relatives may never look at it and it is supposed to wither and die. In the Karnāṭak the same practice is followed by some castes ; *Raddis Sonārs* and *Lingāyats* cut it down, whilst another practice is to uproot it, but, as it is a sin to kill a tree, to transplant it elsewhere. In the Konkaṇ a *Kātkarī* who has been married to a ruī-tree will never in his life cut down a ruī-tree. Because the ruī-tree is so often used in mock marriages it is usually, though not invariably, avoided in the *pancpālvi* used in a marriage ceremony, whether this be used or not as a substitute for a *devak*. In such cases of its use at an ordinary marriage, as have come to my notice, the ruī-tree used is a male one.

Among *Komarpaiks* in Kanara if a woman marries for the third time, she is married to a cock and the throat of the cock is cut after the performance of the mock marriage. This non-Brahmin custom which assumes the same ominous sequel to a third marriage performed by a woman, as a Brahmin attributes to a third marriage made by a man, is valuable evidence as to the potentiality of the number three. In all these mock marriages substituted for a third marriage death is the evil feared, and the mock bride or bridegroom dies instead of the real partner.

Another series of mock marriages is also based on the fear of death. When the horoscope of a girl shows the influence of the stars to be adverse, it is presumed that after her marriage she will lose her husband and become a widow. To avert her widowhood she may be married to a ruī-tree, but more commonly other mock marriages are found for her. *Vaidhavyahār kumbha vivāha* is the marriage of a girl at an early age to an empty pot. This is a practice consequent upon the custom of marrying girls before they attain puberty. In this marriage, which is performed at the girl's house, the usual ornaments and *mangaḻsūtra* are tied to the empty pot, but the *saptapadī*, which in the real marriage is a rite to obtain issue, is omitted. The pot after the marriage is sometimes kept and even used for domestic purposes, for it is assumed that the evil feared has passed not into the pot, but into the air; in the Karnāṭak more generally the pot is broken and thrown into a river, implying the death of the girl's first husband. At Indi in the Bījāpūr district I learnt of the marriage of a girl whose horoscope showed the evil influence of Mars, to a he-buffalo calf which died shortly after the marriage. In Madrial a girl was married to a ram. Among the less-advanced communities these marriages are performed with a cock, a sheep, a dagger, a doll or even with a woman's *sāḍī*. When the mock partner is an animal it is killed after the marriage but cannot be eaten by members of the bride's family, and is usually given away to outsiders; when inanimate objects are used these are buried after the marriage. In the Kanara district, to remove the fear of widowhood a mock marriage is celebrated below an aśvath-tree (Ficus religiosa) with the *hāḻkumbha*. The bark of five trees possessing milky sap is put in a pot, and this is placed near the sacred fig-tree by a *suvāsinī* who has a husband living. The pot is then brought home covered with a cloth as a protection against the evil eye of the sky; a garland of branches from the same five trees is placed on the pot and children go round it five times. The pot is then placed in front of the bridegroom, and water from it is sprinkled over the bridal pair by five married women (*Halvakki Vakkals*; *Nadors*; *Gam Vakkals*; *Madaris*). Among *Rajputs* when the star of a girl is bad in its influence she is given in marriage to a pipal-tree, with a prayer to the tree to remove any sin she may have committed in a past life, which would cause her in this birth to become a widow before attaining puberty.

When a bachelor marries a widow many communities celebrate a mock marriage. This form of marriage is naturally not found among Brahmins who do not allow the re-marriage of widows. When, however, a girl has been married, but in consequence of some defect in the bridegroom, such as lunacy or consanguinity, the marriage ceremony was interrupted before the *saptapadī* was performed, on her re-marriage, the second bridegroom, whether a bachelor or a widower, has to marry first a ruī-tree. *Calwadis* and *Korgars* marry the bachelor to a doll which is buried after the marriage. *Kurubas, Talwārs, Songars, Raddis, Lamānis* and *Gollars* marry him to a tree to which they tie a *hungnul* of white cotton, which remains so attached for five days and on which they throw *akṣat*. *Vaddars* marry the bachelor to a ruī-tree, or failing this to a dagger on which is stuck a lemon; the tree is adorned with red coral beads and a bridal garment, whilst the dagger is covered with red cloth (*alvan*). After the mock marriage the bridegroom cannot touch the particular tree used, nor any other ruī-tree on a *Pūrṇimā* or an *Amāvāsyā*; when a dagger is used he may never touch the dagger. One particular feature distinguishes this form of marriage from other mock marriages. There is no idea that the tree-bride withers or dies. *Vaddars* even say that the tree becomes more fertile after the marriage. The marriage is not a device to protect the one or the other of the bridal pair from death. A bachelor's first wife must be a virgin or otherwise the issue is not legalized.

One more form of mock marriage is the marriage of a dead person to a ruī-tree or branch. Brahmins do this when a *Brahmacārī* dies before marriage; *Lingāyats* perform this marriage both when a girl dies a virgin and when a man dies unmarried. When the deceased is a girl a male ruī is used, and a female tree when the deceased is a man. Sometimes the body is taken to a standing ruī-tree in the cremation ground; sometimes a twig of the tree is brought to the house where the dead body lies. The twig and the corpse are smeared with turmeric powder and covered with yellow clothes; the two are tied together with thread, *akṣat* is thrown on them and sacrificial *hom* are performed. The tree after being uprooted or the twig is burnt and the obsequies for thirteen days are performed in the usual way. The basis of this form of mock marriage is the belief that any one dying with unsatisfied desires returns to this world as a ghost in a vain attempt to realize his desires. This fear has created in India quite a number of dreaded ghosts. *Khavīs* is the spirit of a strong man who dies with his wishes unfulfilled; *Jhoting* that of one who dies of violence. There is the ghost of the man who dies childless; the *Munjā* or ghost of the boy who has taken his thread ceremony but has not taken a wife; the ghosts of those who have left estates without an heir or competent manager, and the fearsome *Heḍalī*, the ghost of a woman who dies in childbirth. This marriage is performed to satisfy the supposed desire of the deceased for a partner; to prevent the deceased returning restlessly to earth to haunt the living.

This mock marriage of a dead person is the only form of mock marriage in which the fear of ghostly persecution is at all admitted, and even in this there is no question of persecution by the ghost of a deceased partner. Western authorities have advanced many theories to explain these mock marriages; there is the theory of an initiation into the totemic clan which has now been abandoned; there is the theory that the mock marriage is a fertility rite, which I need not dwell upon in the absence of evidence to suggest its truth; there is also the explanation that the mock bride is a scapegoat to which some evil is transferred.

It is with this last theory only that I would deal, confining myself, of course, to the evidence I have been able to collect in Western India. In *Religion and Folklore of Northern India*, W. Crooke, 1926, p. 415, it is suggested that when a widow or a widower is married to a tree, the wrath of a deceased partner is diverted to the tree. In *Ritual and Belief*, 1914, pp. 230–1, in a chapter on 'The Haunted Widow', Mr. Hartland suggests that the mock marriage on the death of a second wife is consequent on the failure of other devices to keep quiet the ghost of the first wife, and that 'after the death of the third wife the evil influence of the first is deemed to be exhausted'.

Now measures are certainly taken in India to secure a living wife or husband from the jealousy of a deceased partner. In Khandesh among *Marāṭhās*, *Māḻīs* and *Koḻīs*, when a man who has lost two wives remarries he keeps near him during the ceremony a hen, and a woman who has lost two previous husbands keeps near her a cock. In the Konkan the bridegroom who marries a widow carries a cock under his arm. There is a definite admission in these cases that the ghost of the deceased partner enters the hen or cock and kills it, thus freeing the living partner from further persecution; to make sure, too, that the wrath of the ghost is diverted to the hen or cock the animal is usually killed or crushed to death. A *Bhil* bridegroom marrying a widow who has lost one or more husbands holds a bamboo stick during the marriage ceremony and eventually throws this away. A widower among *Bhils*, *Mavchis* and *Konkanis* on marrying again, carves a picture of a woman on a large stone, and burying this so that the figure remains visible above the ground, offers it periodic worship (*Vaḍ Dakhaṇī*). To avert the jealousy of a deceased wife, a woman marrying a widower wears a round piece of gold or silver carved with the impression of a pair of feet, called 'sister-in-law'; ascribes her own issue to the deceased wife, and in her honour wears a second mark of saffron on her forehead. A *Lingāyat* bride or bridegroom who has lost a partner has to make *pradakṣiṇā* of a patri-tree to calm the spirit of the deceased. Offerings of clothes are again made with the same object, to married women in the name of a dead wife. *Jakhaṇī*, the name of such a gift, comes from the word *Yakṣiṇī*, a female spirit. The present appeases the spirit of the deceased wife. *Jakhaṇī* is also the name given to the worship with red flowers of a twig of red Kaṇgal-tree into which the ghost has been invoked.

Though, however, many measures in these ways of protection are taken against the ghost of a deceased partner, I can find no evidence at all to support an assumption that a mock marriage has a similar object. When the ghost of the dead is feared there is no reluctance to admit this fear, but in all the many cases of mock marriages that I have examined, all idea of ghostly persecution is unequivocally denied, save in the case of the marriage of a deceased person to a ruī-tree, and in this case also there is no question of a deceased partner. In the Konkaṇ the ghost of a deceased husband is called *Puruṣvāra*, but this ghost is never associated with a mock marriage. The measures, indeed, which are taken against a ghostly persecution are independent of the mock marriage; they are a feature of ordinary marriages which are not preceded by mock marriages, and they may mark the marriage which follows a mock marriage. When a bachelor marries a widow there is not even any idea of evil diverted to the mock bride, and the tree-bride does not suffer but actually becomes more fertile. To ensure the object of this mock marriage, namely, that the first wife of a bachelor be a virgin, it is not imperative that the mock bride should die.

Each form of mock marriage has its specific object. The one is to prevent the deceased becoming a ghost because his earthly desires were unsatisfied; another is to prevent widowhood or widowerhood, and a third is to escape the restrictions on marrying a widow. In no one of these is there any belief in persecution by a deceased partner. Still less is there any such idea in the mock marriage of the bride or bridegroom who contemplates a third partner. The evil to be avoided here is that of death, the finality associated with the number three. There is again absolutely nothing in the ritual of the *Arka vivāha* and cognate marriages to restrict it to cases where a bridegroom has lost two previous wives; the determining factor is the number three; if with one wife or two wives living he takes a third wife the mock marriage is imperative. In the *Journal of the Asiatic Society of Bengal*, lxx, part iii (1901), p. 28, as quoted by Sir James Frazer in *The Magic Art*, vol. ii, p. 57, Captain Wolseley Haig, speaking of third marriages among the *Velamas* of Berar, stresses the same point, that the evil of the third marriage is independent of whether the bridegroom's former wives be alive or dead. As further corroboration, too, of my conclusion that it is merely the finality of the number three that determines the mock marriage that precedes a third marriage, I would add that localities can be found in which the same mock marriage is insisted upon before a fifth marriage. As fifth marriages are not numerous it is not surprising that the belief in the evil sequel to a fifth marriage is held somewhat diffidently, but both in the Karnāṭak and in the Konkaṇ and the Deccan I have found families who hold this belief. Here again the mock marriage bears the same meaning. Five is as final as is three. *Aidu saidu* (Kan.), ' Five it ends '; the finality of five makes the fifth marriage as dangerous as is the third marriage.

Among non-Brahmins in some parts no danger is attributed to the third marriage of a widow, but in the coastal tracts her third marriage is as dangerous as that of a man who marries for the third time. The ritual of the Brahmin, restricted only to the marriage of a bridegroom, refers to the sin of a third marriage, yet even this ritual defines the sequel of death. It does not therefore seem rash to surmise that Brahminism has given the sanction of religion to a prohibition originally based on a belief in the evil *śakti* of the number three.

FOUR

Four is an auspicious number. To the Muhammadan it is a substitute for a whole. ' One should not go against the will of four persons.' To say that four good men came is the same as saying that many came.

To the Hindu the fourth day of the week is an auspicious day, as is the fourth day of the lunar or solar fortnight associated with *Gaṇpati*. Whenever three is avoided one more is added frequently to make a fourth. When three persons dine together a fourth plate is added; when three pieces of bread are baked or given, one piece is broken in two, so that there are actually four pieces or an extra piece of bread is baked; when there are three children only in a house at the time of waving *ārtī* a fourth child is brought in from outside. A *nandādīp* may have four wicks.

FIVE

Five is a most auspicious number. To the Muhammadan it is wealth or *ganj*, and on the threshing-floor when measuring grain he says '*ganj*' when counting five. The Hindu uses the number to win success. *Pancmukhi Parmeśvar*, 'There is God in the mouth of five persons'. *Panc tethe Parmeśvar*, 'Where there are five there is God'. *Pancamam karya siddhisca*, 'The fifth is the fruition of the act'. *Aidu saidu*, 'Five it ends'.

Five is an ever-recurring number in the practices of non-Brahmins and of primitive tribes. *Kal̲l̲ Koravas* as a *bal̲ī* kill a cock where a man has expired and then bury it near the body, bringing it back later and eating it. Five plates of cooked rice, wheat bread, jvārī bread, milk, curds, and liquor are also taken to the funeral site; there one plate is placed near the stone which is put near the head of the dead, two plates are put near the feet of the dead, and one plate on the right and another on the left of the grave, and these are all abandoned. In the practices of the *Kātkarī* five is a number constantly recurring. On the fifth day celebration after a birth the whole village is represented by five elders; when the body of a deceased *Kātkarī* cannot be obtained for disposal, at the obsequies five children call out the name of the dead; the marriage of a *Sōn Kātkarī* may be made binding merely by waving in turn five heaps of rice in a pan with a lamp round the bridal pair.

There are five practical duties of Islam 'pillars of religion': the recital of the creed or *kalimah*; compulsory prayer five times a day; fasting between dawn and sunset during the month of *Ramaḍān*; charity or *zakāt* at the rate of two and a half per cent. of one's income, and the pilgrimage to Mecca. With three and seven, five is a number generally used in measures to avert evil. A Muhammadan uses thread of five colours to form a *hisār* or barrier against spirits; when a Muhammadan has fever five pieces of bread are given to a Mulla at a mosque or are placed beneath the sick man's pillow and given to beggars the next morning. Another cure for fever is to place five utensils of clay under an isolated tree. A child at birth is protected from spirits by four arrows and a sword. At a wedding five or seven lemons or flowers are put in water, and waved round the heads of the bridal pair, and finally thrown at the feet of the horse ridden by the bride in procession. If a child or an adult is attacked by evil-eye or by spirits, five leaves, *panjpati*, or five flowers of different kinds are dipped in water taken from seven wells; turmeric, lime and pepper are added and the water is then waved at sunset round the patient and thrown at cross-roads. To cure snake-bite five pebbles are waved over the bitten part in the name of *Ādigudi Imāmsāb* of Bījāpūr by Muhammadans of the Karnāṭak.

Any comprehensive dictionary of one of the chief vernaculars of the Presidency would give a tedious list of words beginning with 'five'. Many of these, such as the fivefold division of the science of medicine or the art of Government, are of little practical interest, and it would be meticulous to repeat them in detail. There are, however, many groupings of five which are strictly maintained in actual ritual.

There are groupings of gods in fives, *Pancāyatan*, which when worshipped are placed in cross formation, the principal symbol in the centre and the other four symbols at the corners of a square around. In all *Śānti* ceremonies the *Pancratna* or five gems are necessary, sapphire, diamond, ruby, pearl, and coral; in the worship and the bathing of sacred images *Pancāmṛt* are used, milk, sugar, ghee, curds, and honey; the materials of worship are kept in a vessel of five compartments, *Pancpātra*. An amalgam of five metals is credited with special *śakti*. Five varieties of fruit are offered in worship and also in *Oṭī bharaṇī* when the lap of a woman is filled in the hope that she may have issue. There are five daily sacrifices, *Pancmahāyajna*, a calendar treats of five things, the *vār*, *karan*, *tithī*, *yog*, and *nakṣatra*, and the *muhūrtta* is a combination of these; five products of the cow, milk, curds, ghee, urine, and dung, are used for purification and form the *Pancgavya*.

One of the commonest groupings of five is that of five leaves, *Pancpallav* or *Pancpālvi*. In Brahmin ritual *pancpālvi* are used in all the Sanskār save the sixteenth, that of the obsequies, and on all other occasions when *kalaśas* are installed. Text-books of ritual prescribe particular trees to be used by the Brahmin for his *pancpallav*; the aśvath (Ficus religiosa), the bilva (Aegle marmelos); the banyan (Ficus bengalensis); the dhatri (Phyllanthus emblica) and the asok (Saraca Indica), but in actual practice there seems much local variation in the choice of five trees.

Five leaves are used in many ways by non-Brahmin castes. The *Kātkarī* uses five leaves to sprinkle water on the feet of those who visit a woman in confinement; on the remarriage of a *Kātkarī* widow by the *pat* ceremony which is a less respectable form of marriage than the ordinary one, five fig-leaves are placed near the door of the house for guests to use in washing their feet; on the fifth day after a birth the *Kātkarī* performs his *pāṭā* ceremony and at this time places five mango-leaves on five paths leading to his house. In the event of illness a *Bhil* offers five leaves from five different trees to his gods. *Marāṭhās* and others place five different leaves beneath the central pole on the threshing-floor, whilst it is a very common practice to place *pancpālvi* in the drain leading from the room in which a woman is confined, or on the roof of a new house when first entered upon.

Lingāyats in their *Puṇyāhavācan* ceremony install two *kalaśas* on an *āsan* of rice and place in them the leaves of the mango, umbar, pipal, dhatri, and jambul. Some sub-castes of *Lingāyats*, before the marriage ceremony begins, install a flag-post with an image of *Nandī* the bull at its base, *Nandīdhvaj*; on the site where the post is erected five leaves are placed. *Lingāyats* also put five leaves into the water in which they wash the feet of their *guru*. Brahmin women worship Mangaḷagaurī, Hartalika and Durgā with five leaves; *Konchikoravas* use for their *hālgamba* a branch with five leaves. *Pancpālvi* are tied to the same post as the *devak* of *Marāṭhās* and other castes in the Deccan and Konkaṇ. In parts of the Karnāṭak five bundles of twigs are used in the *hālgamba* ceremony and after the marriage thrown on the roof of the house. On the sixth day after the birth of a Muhammadan child five leaves of the pipal (Ficus religiosa), the sirih (Albizzia Lebbek), the jamun (Eugenia jambolana), the babul (Acacia arabica) and the ber are dipped in broth; the little finger of the child is dipped in this broth, which is then given to other children to drink.

Several explanations are offered of the *śakti* of the number five. The body is made up of five elements and to avert the evils attaching to the body five things are necessarily offered in worship, and an image is circumambulated five times with five prostrations. The number five is also closely associated with the cross; the pour points of an equal-limbed cross and the centre make five and these determine the number of articles used in ritual. A Kanarese figure for five, an auspicious sign written by boys on their slates when they worship them, follows exactly the formation of a cross. At a *Lingāyat* marriage near the *bahul* or platform on which the bridal pair sit, a figure of two squares is drawn in rice on a white cloth. Within these squares five copper pots are placed in a cross formation and on each five leaves of mango.

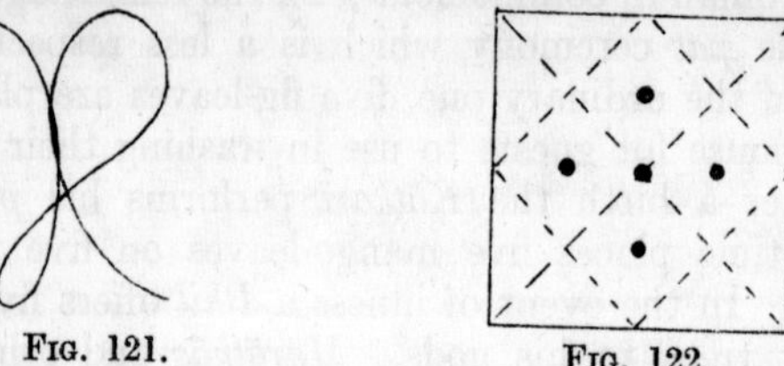

FIG. 121. FIG. 122.

After a *Marāṭhā* marriage two or four singers, *Gondhalis*, sing a prayer in obscure *Marāṭhī* which has to be interpreted to the listeners ; at this time a cross is marked on the ground and in the centre is placed a small copper cup of water. In front of the cup or at each corner of the cross and in the centre are placed five pairs of betel-leaves and on the cup itself five such leaves.

At every *Ankurāropaṇ* celebrated by the Brahmin five gods are invoked into five betel-nuts placed on the earth in which the seeds are sown ; these nuts are arranged in a cross formatiin and the invocation of *śakti* into them produces a *dikbāndha* or fortification of the quarters. In the Karnāṭak during a marriage a piece of ground is purified with cowdung and on it with rice of different colours (white, red, green, blue, and yellow) a svastika is drawn. First a square is drawn with white *akṣat* and around it squares with the other colours. Five *kalaśas* are placed on this design ; one at each corner and one in the centre ; each *kalaśa* has a plate as a cover and on this a burning light. Five persons comprising the bridal pair and relatives go round the square five times. This is the *Airaṇī* ceremony.

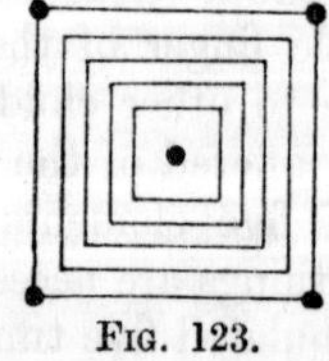

FIG. 123.

During the obsequial rites of a Brahmin five *pinḍa* or balls of cooked rice and sesamum are offered to the dead on the tenth day after the death. Blades of darbha grass are put on the ground to form a cross and on this five leaf cups, *droṇ*, are placed, each of which holds one *piṇḍa*. The five cups are joined together by cotton thread passed round them five times before the *piṇḍa* are offered. This is called *Pancodan piṇḍa*.

FIG. 124.

An *āsan* frequently is a design of a cross or two intersecting squares.

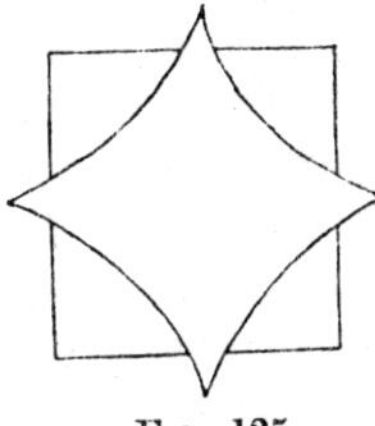
FIG. 125.

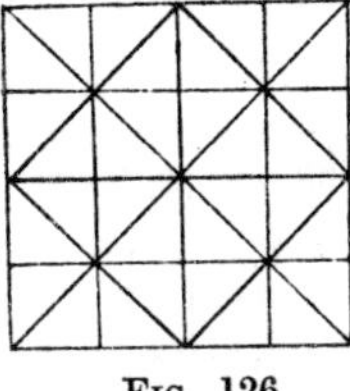
FIG. 126.

When the marriage of the tulsī plant is celebrated in the month of *Kārttik,* lamps of ghee are placed at the four corners of a square and an image of Kṛṣṇa is placed in the centre. The offerings made are all in fives; five stalks of sugar-cane and five garlands of flowers are placed in the centre and at the corner, whilst in front of the image are placed five almonds and five dates and supari-nuts.

Examples of the use of the number five can easily be multiplied. The *Marāṭhā bahul* or seat for the bridal pair is an earthen construction of five steps surmounted by a mango-twig, and painted with lime and red earth. In front of this are placed in a square four sets of five earthen pots of diminishing size; against or around each pile of pots are placed five stalks of sugar-cane or jvārī. Within the centre of the square the bridal pair sit when *akṣat* is thrown. In the Karnāṭak at the back of the bridal pair where they sit when *akṣat* is thrown, a design called *bhorajgali* is drawn, or a special erection in the same design is made on a dais; this is very similar to the *Marāṭhā bahul.*

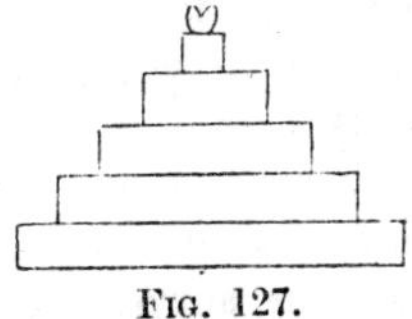
FIG. 127.

When the seeds of pumpkin or cucumber are sown, five seeds only are sown in each bed and these in a cross formation. Before applying oil to their body women first drop five drops on to the earth in the same cross formation. Five is used in a representative sense by the Hindu. When *akṣat* is thrown on the bridal pair the priest says, 'Let five grains be sprinkled'; when a host speaks of his guests having come he says, '*Panc pannas*'. A feast to Brahmins or to *suvāsinīs* should be to not less than five or to multiples of five. At a tonsure ceremony five measures of rice are pounded by five *suvāsinīs*; the first fruits offered to the *kula devatā* consist of five stalks or ears; the things put in the lap of the bride are in fives. Five stones are used to represent a deity, particularly if it be inconvenient to visit his shrine. Five *suvāsinīs* bathe the bride; wave *ārtī* round the bridal pair; fetch water for the *mangalsnān*; throw *akṣat*; and in other ways play a prominent part in a marriage ceremony. When *kumārikās* or children are used in ritual their number is usually five. The same representative use of five is common even among non-Brahmins and in primitive communities. The *Marāṭhā* feeds five children on the fifth day after a birth; the *Naikda* feeds five children nine days after a funeral; the *Kātkarī* bathes five children over the stone of life.

The finality of five, its power to avert evil, and equally to collect or gather *śakti* from the directions makes it an almost indispensable number. The bride and bridegroom pledge their loyalty by tying five betel-nuts in each other's garments; the fathers of the bridal pair on effecting a betrothal offer each other the same token of agreement. When the bridal pair go round the central pole of the marriage *manḍap* or round the marriage *hom* they do so five times. Trees are encircled with thread five times to effect cures or exorcize spirits; the thread that is wound round the four sides of a *dikbāndha* is wound five times. A *yantra* is tied to the neck or the wrist with five threads; charity is given in multiples of five.

In spite, however, of its auspiciousness in general there remains an element of danger in the number five. *Pancamim na tu pancamim.* The fifth girl in relationship is not to be taken in marriage. There are families which make a mock marriage when a man takes a wife for the fifth time. Five posts are avoided in erecting a marriage *manḍap*. *Śani* is feared in the fifth house of a man. The area covered by the dwelling-house of a Hindu should always be square or at least a triangular or five-sided area must be avoided. In town-planning schemes the survey often leaves such irregular areas the disposal of which the district officer finds very difficult. Because three and five alike are associated with finality their combination is inauspicious; a combination of three and a multiple of five makes the eighth, thirteenth, eighteenth, twenty-third and twenty-eighth days of the lunar month *nahas* to the Muhammadan, whilst the Hindu regards three, thirteen, nine and eighteen as an expression of disaster.

SEVEN

Number seven figures prominently in the theology and in the ritual of the Hindu. There are seven sages, seven sacred rivers, seven sacred islands, seven principal centres of pilgrimage, and the creative energy of the principal gods is personified as seven divinities, *Saptamātṛkā*.

Saptak or a period of seven days is a common period fixed for following a course of medicinal treatment; multiples of seven days, such as twenty-one and forty-nine, are also auspicious periods. Illnesses are supposed to show a change every seven days. *Yantras* are worshipped for seven days; *jap* or silent prayer is maintained for the same period and sacred texts are read for seven days.

In the orthodox marriage ceremony the marriage becomes irrevocable when the bride and bridegroom have taken seven steps together, *Saptapadī*. Water drawn from seven wells is a cure for barrenness; the husband collects the water in the morning in silence and the wife bathes with it also in silence. Seven kinds of earth are used in the installation of *kalaśas*, and a *parḍī* when not of five compartments has seven compartments.

Seven is a number of constant occurrence in measures taken to avert evil. In the transfer of evil to others, in practices adopted to cure or avert evil-eye, it is as common a number as three or five. To avert evil the *Jain* carries round the marriage *manḍap* a thread containing five or seven knots. The *Bhāt* to avert spirits waves a pot of water seven times round the head of the bridegroom before throwing the water to the ground. In Kanara, to scare away field pests the rayat sticks branches of the bagni-tree (Caryota urens) in seven places in the field. The tiers of water-pots which are placed in a square as a *dikbāndha* to protect the bridal pair contain each seven pots of different sizes. *Olānḍā* is a rag with seven knots and containing seven marking-nuts thrown on a public road by a person afflicted with boils; it is also the name for the disease contracted by stepping over such a rag. The Muhammadan uses thread with three, seven or nine knots as amulets against evil.

Seven is a number dear to *Maruti*, to whom offerings are made of seven cakes or seven kinds of grain. The seventh lunar day in *Māgh* is an auspicious day for on this day the sun ascends his chariot. On the other hand, a child begotten on a seventh day proves to be a daughter destined to have no issue.

In a *Lamāni* marriage ceremony seven is a determinant of ritual. Two poles, four to five feet long, are erected six feet apart, and adorned with mango-leaves and garlands of marking-nuts. Near these posts a square is formed of piled-up pots painted red, in each of which twigs of seven trees are tied. The bridal pair, during the ceremony, go to a small heap of dried cowdung and each strikes it seven times with an axe. After their bath the bride and bridegroom walk round the two wooden posts seven times carrying a rupee, a betel-nut and a cowrie in their hands.

The Muhammadan has his seven heavens, seven earths and seven seas. *Surahs* are recited seven times to obtain control of their innate power. If a goat does not give milk it is taken seven times round the shrine of a saint. The Muhammadan bride goes into *Vanvāha* three, five or seven days before the first day of the marriage. When a child is just beginning to walk, to give it strength, its foot is placed on seven loaves of bread, *per mani.* After the *nikah* the Muhammadan bridegroom is taken into the bride's house; his mother and six married women lightly place on his head the corner of a sheet, and his best man covers him with the corner of his scarf (*palao vijhan*), and they escort him to a basket. Under the basket are placed an earthen lamp cover and an earthen lighted lamp. The bridegroom is made to sit on the basket seven times; each time he rises he is given water and molasses. The basket is removed and the bridegroom then kicks the articles underneath the basket into fragments. This same ceremony is performed for the bride, but the best man of the bridegroom kicks the lamp and cover. This Sindi custom is dying out, but in Gujarāt there is a practice somewhat similar. When the bridegroom in Gujarāt arrives at the bride's house the priest shows him a churning-rod, a pestle, a cart-yoke and the needle, *trāk,* of a spinning-wheel as symbols of the new life he will live. The priest then throws jvārī grain in four directions to remind the bridegroom that it is still not too late for him to go where he will and decline to accept the responsibilities of marriage. An earthen bowl of curds is covered by another inverted bowl and placed on the ground; the two bowls are tied together with thread. Over these bowls the bridegroom who accepts his new responsibilities walks breaking them to pieces (*samputֽ*).

Groups of seven saints associated with one site are not uncommon. The seventh month of a Hindu woman's pregnancy introduces for herself and her husband increased disabilities; in this same month the Muhammadan offers miniature boats to Khwāja Khizr. In a Muhammadan marriage ritual the number seven frequently occurs. Seven married women perform a ceremony called *Buki*; seven dates are tied to a grindstone in a piece of red thread. Each woman takes one date and gives the grindstone a turn. The red thread is then tied to the wrists of the bridal pair, for each of whom this ceremony is performed separately. An old man ties the thread to the wrist of the bridegroom with some wheat and a small iron ring; the bridegroom's sister ties the thread to the bride's wrist. When the heads of the bridal pair have been brought together and this is done three times, an elderly woman holds a bit of cotton over the head of the bride and asks the bridegroom to pluck cotton from it, which he does seven times. Then the bride and bridegroom dip their fingers in milk, throw this to the four directions and apply to each other's forehead; then they each take seven morsels of powdered sweet cakes, *kutti*, and seven sips of milk.

EIGHT

To a Hindu eight is a lucky number. There are eight things of good omen, the *Aṣṭamangal*; a lion, a bull, an elephant, a water-jar, a winnowing-fan, a flag, a trumpet, and a lamp. A girl should be married in her eighth year and a boy should perform his thread ceremony in his eighth year. The eighth lunar day in *Āśvin* and the eighth in *Śrāvaṇ* are auspicious days. Obeisance to a god is done with eight parts of the body. When blessing women a form of good wish is to say, '*Aṣṭaputra saubhāgyavatī bhav*', 'May you have eight sons and live a *suvāsinī* until death'. The verses repeated to bring blessing when the *akṣat* is thrown on the bridal pair should not be less than eight in number.

Siddhi or abnormal *śakti* acquired by penance is eightfold, comprising *aṇimā* or the power to become as small as an atom; *laghimā*, the power to become ethereally light; *prāpti*, the power to obtain anything at will; *prākamyam*, irresistible will-power; *mahimā*, the power of increase; *iśitvam*, superiority; *vaśitvam*, the power to conquer; and *kāmāvasāyitā*, the power to suppress desire.

The number eight is very common in the details followed in preparing *yantras*. The *yantra* is written with eight kinds of powder mixed with water; the eighth day of the second fortnight of the month is chosen for writing the *yantra*, and a lotus figure of eight or sixteen leaves is a common design. As examples of the use of this number the *Jayavaha yantra* consists of a lotus of eight leaves drawn on a round surface with the object desired written in the centre; this is folded twice and immersed in water for twenty-one days to subject the wicked to one's desires and for forty days to dispel all delusions. The *Lalita yantra* is a lotus of eight leaves with a *trikoṇa* in the centre drawn on a stone with turmeric; worshipped with flowers it brings rain; worshipped for seven days it brings all desires. The *śakti* invoked into the *yantra* is that of the earth and another name for the charm is *Saubhāgyadan*. A *Jvarahara yantra* consists of two squares drawn with *datura* on cloth which has been worn at a funeral, and on the eighth day of the second fortnight of the month. The intersecting squares produce eight *koṇ* or compartments; in the middle sixteen lines are drawn and all the names of the cardinal directions are written in the middle figure. This *yantra* must be worshipped in a cemetery and is a powerful charm to cure fever. Sixteen leaves of a lotus are drawn on metal with *haḻad* and saffron to form the *bandhamokṣakrit yantra*; sixteen vowels are written on the leaves and two consonants on each leaf. A square is drawn round the whole figure and it is worshipped for seven days with lotus flowers to free the worshipper from anything that restricts him. A square is drawn on a leaf with haḻad and saffron to form the *Śantikara yantra*; eight lines are drawn horizontally and eight lines vertically crossing the former. It is worshipped for three days and three nights and then worn on the neck to remove evil. If the same figure be drawn on a lotus of eight leaves this charm removes ghosts from a house.

A lotus of eight leaves is used as an *āsan* for fire taken from a cemetery which is shown to the cardinal directions day after day until after twenty days of worship it prevents an enemy from going to heaven, whilst if the *Agnibhayahara yantra* is worshipped when wearing red clothes and accompanied by the feasting of a *kumārikā* the enemy is removed altogether.

The accompanying designs show how frequently the number eight or its multiple is a feature of *yantras*; eight, in fact, represents the cardinal points and its use is to draw *śakti* from the directions. In the tattoo-marks of the *Kātkarī* the cross is called lotus, another illustration of the symbolic use of the lotus design.

Fig. 128.

Fig. 129.

Fig. 130.

Fig. 131.

Fig. 132.

Fig. 133.

Fig. 134.

Fig. 135.

Certain numbers possess a magic power and are used as a key number in making a charm. A square containing sixteen small squares is drawn and in each small square a number is placed, so that the four numbers in each horizontal, vertical, or diagonal row total to the same number. Thus the number one hundred scares away ghosts if embodied in a charm in this way.

8	1	48	43
44	47	4	5
2	7	42	49
46	45	6	3

The number twenty-four produces a charm which when buried in a field scares away pests.

4	11	2	7
6	3	8	7
10	5	8	1
4	5	6	9

Numbers thirty-four, sixty-four, and fifteen will assist a woman in travail; fifteen cures fever; forty is another number that will free a field from pests.

The key number of a charm may be arrived at by taking certain names and giving to each letter thereof its numerical value. Thus to seduce a woman the names of the woman and her would-be seducer are taken; if a married pair desire issue their names are necessary; if a man desire to make the friendship of another his own name and the name of the friend he seeks are required. When a key number has been taken thirty is subtracted from it and the remainder is divided by four; or twelve is subtracted and the division is by three. The resulting number is the number which is first placed in one of the squares of a larger square which in the first case consists of sixteen and in the second case of nine squares. The figure of sixteen squares is used in general to secure a good object and that of nine squares to accomplish an evil desire. The name of the mother of the person using the charm is added when the figure has sixteen squares but not when the figure of nine squares is employed.

When the design of the charm contains sixteen squares the first small square filled with a number is the top right-hand square. When the design is a square of nine small squares the centre squares on each side are the important ones. The centre square on the top line is called *Fire*, that to the left *Wind*, the bottom centre square *Water*, and the centre square on the right *Earth*. To cure a cold the *yantra* would be written beginning with the fire square; to cure fever it would begin with the water square; to cure wind with the earth square; to bring a person from a distance the *yantra* would commence in the wind square and would be tied to a tree so as to be shaken by the wind. To bring rain the letter values of *mekā'īl*, 'rain', are added together, the *yantra* is begun from the water square, whilst the letter V has to be repeated forty times and the words '*Va Ya Mekā'īl*'. To stop rain K is repeated forty times and the words '*Ka Ya 'Azrā'īl*'; '*Azrā'īl*, enigmatically meaning fire; the *yantra* is begun from the fire square. The *yantra* to bring rain is actually based on the number fifteen.

8	3	4
1	5	9
6	7	2

Whilst the writer writes these charms he is required to keep sugar-candy in his mouth; when he writes the Fire *yantra* must have cotton in his ears and nostrils and when he writes on paper must use paper without holes. Sometimes he is required to eat bread and salt only for forty days before writing the *yantra*. When possible, a pen of bamboo should be used; both the writer and he who uses the charm must be ritually clean, and the place where the writer sits must be purified with cow's urine. Special days and times, too, are fixed for the preparation of the *yantra*; the hour of sunset or that of an eclipse; Saturdays and Sundays and the fifteenth and thirtieth of the month.

Besides these *yantras* which have a key number there are *yantras* whose number is legion which combine several numbers, in the choice of which caprice apparently has been the only guide. There are combinations which cure pain; remove the effects of snake-bite; which scare thieves; remove fear of lightning; bring customers to a shop; keep snakes from a house; keep one of a married pair in subjection to the other; promote unity among relations; secure a magician's tricks from discovery by his audience; concealed in his turban, keep the audience of a public speaker enthralled; which increase the supply of milk; bring rich fruit to crops; which buried at a shop door bring quick profits; enable a sleeper on waking to interpret his dreams; which bring wealth and prevent abortion. There is no ill of human kind, in fact, which a *yantra* in the belief of the masses will not cure, and no desire, good or evil, it cannot satisfy. Such, too, is popular credulity that if a *yantra* fails to produce the desired and expected effect, disappointment blames the person using the *yantra* for lack of care and not the *yantra* itself.

Muhammadan charms do not differ materially from those prepared by Hindus, and the classes who resort to such charms are quite ready to test the charms of another, no matter of what religion he may be. Besides the ordinary charms based on numbers the Muhammadan gives a numerical value to verses of his Koran and from this acquires a key number which often runs into many thousands.

The numerical value, for instance, of the *āyatu'l kursī* gives him the following charm which secures immunity from illness.

10545	10548	10543
10540	10542	10544
10551	10546	10539

A pregnant woman is protected by a chart containing the numerical value of the *sūrah Luqman.*

39739	39753	39756	39732
39757	39743	39748	39754
39744	39758	39751	39747
39752	39746	39725	39758

To cure illness or overcome calamity the numerical value of the *Sūratu'l-fatḥ* and the *surah Muzammil* produce these charts:

2340	2343	2346	2334
2345	2333	2329	2344
2334	2348	2341	2338
2342	2337	2335	2347

32566	32559	32564
32561	32563	32565
32562	32567	32500

and the combined value of the *sūrah ikhlās* with other *sūrahs* forms the following chart:

3540	3542	3546	3532
3545	3534	3539	3544
3535	3548	3541	3538
3522	3547	3546	3547

ODD AND EVEN NUMBERS

Although there is no auspicious number which is not at times inauspicious and no general rule to which there are not many exceptions, odd numbers in general are credited with beneficent power.

Pradakṣiṇā or the circumambulation of sacred objects is done an odd number of times up to a hundred after which the number is immaterial; after the birth of a child Hindu women visit a temple in a month that is odd when counted from the birth; *Annāprāśan* or the first giving of food to a child should be done in an odd month of an odd year calculated from the day of birth. In practices to avert evil and, in particular, evil-eye, the numbers three, five and seven almost rule out other numbers. Vedic magic is full of reference to three, seven and twenty-one, and these numbers still determine the days *yantras* are worshipped or repeated. Vigils of prayer to bring rain are for seven or twenty-one days. Knots tied in threads as amulets against evil are usually odd in number. The new-born infant is bathed on the first, fifth, seventh and eleventh day after birth, and thereafter every day for eight months to keep away spirits. The cutting of a child's hair should be performed in the first, third, fifth and seventh years. *Lingāyats* make presents to their priests (*uttarakriya*) on any odd day after a death.

A Muhammadan says, 'God is odd; He loves the odd'. After the last compulsory prayer at night and after the prayer before dawn the Muhammadan offers ordinary prayers, *rek'āt*, in an odd number of three, five or seven.

CHAPTER XIV

THE POWER OF SWEET THINGS

SWEET things confer *barkat.*

When a Muhammadan leaves home on a pilgrimage all those who remain at home attempt to secure for him the fruition of his object by eating sweets. At a marriage the distribution of sweets is common. Sweets and coconuts are given to the families of the bridal pair; at a betrothal the parents of the Muhammadan bride give the bridegroom a scarf, *bochhan,* in which sugar-candy, almonds, pieces of coconut and small balls of sugar, all called *mura,* are tied, and the bridegroom's people in turn give the bride a red sheet called *khumunbo* in the four corners of which the same *mura* is tied with lip-salve, henna, a gold ring and a rupee. On the sixth day after the birth of a son friends take coconuts and sweets to the house and in return the father distributes molasses to all his visitors. At a circumcision sweets are distributed among all the guests present. On the third day after a death Muhammadans perform *Jārata* in which sweets are freely distributed to bring the dead *barkat.* After *Muḥarram* on the third day subsequent sweetmeats are distributed to friends in honour of the *panjā* installed in the Karnāṭak. When a Persian wheel is erected in Sind rice and molasses are placed beneath the pole of the wheel; sweets are distributed among all the workers and at home the women dole out sweetened rice. Before the measurers of the threshed grain enter the charmed circle drawn round the pile of grain sweets are distributed in measure or in value multiples of five, and sweets are placed on the stack of grain to increase its *barkat.* During *Ramaḍān* on the twenty-third, twenty-seventh and thirtieth a *Hafiz* blows upon sweets which are preserved by those who receive them; after completion of the recital of the Koran in every mosque sweet dates are given away, these are subscribed for by the worshippers and given to the crowds that gather. On the eleventh of each month sweets are distributed in the name of *Pir Dastagir* of *Baghdad* and whenever a boon has been obtained from a *Pir* or a shrine, sweets are given away in the name of the person from whom the blessing came. When writing charms the Muhammadan must often hold sweet things in his mouth.

The fruit of the umbar (Ficus glomerata) is supposed to be always sweet, and to promote sweet relations between the bride and the bridegroom the Muhammadan in the Deccan, at a marriage, fixes a piece of umbar in the marriage booth. He pours milk on to this post when it is fixed and also when it is removed. A piece of cloth dyed yellow with turmeric, rice coloured in the same way and a betel-nut are tied to the post with a red thread which the bridegroom unties on the fifth day after the marriage. Perhaps the same idea underlies the use of umbar by other communities. The *Jain* bridegroom sits on a seat of umbar; the *Kabbaligar* throws a log of umbar into a well, and unwidowed women bring it home after sunset, and from this two posts are made for the marriage booth. *Dhangars* place blocks of umbar at the corners of bamboo baskets on which grindstones are laid for the bridal pair to stand upon.

At a Hindu marriage the fathers of the bride and bridegroom touch the mouth of the bridegroom with sugar and then the mouth of the bride, and all the relations follow suit, with the object of making the married life of the pair a sweet one. The Hindu pilgrim, like the Muhammadan pilgrim, is helped on his way by those who stay at home eating sweets at the moment of his leaving home. At a birth honey is given on the fifth day to young girls when the child is named and dried coconut is given to all visitors. Sugar and sugar-candy are given to a boy when he is adopted; at a thread ceremony all those present are given sweets. At *Mahi Sankrānt* sesamum coated with sugar is exchanged between friends and the exchange should be accompanied by the words, '*Til gul̲ ghyā āṇi goḍ bolā*', 'Take sweet sesamum and speak sweet throughout the year'. On the day following *Makar Sankramaṇa* in the Karnāṭak a ceremony called *Kariyariyona* is performed to avert from young babies evil-eye and evil arising from the conjunction of the sun and Capricorn. Infants are bathed in the morning; in the evening they are dressed in new clothes and placed in the laps of their mothers or on carpets. Then sweets, bits of sugar-cane and seeds of green gram are put in a pot and this is emptied over the infants. *Ovāl̲aṇī* is also performed, that is, an auspicious lamp is waved round the infants. On *Makar Sankramaṇa* and on *Rath Saptamī* sugar-cane and sweets are poured over the heads of children to secure them a long life. On the latter date, *Māgh* sud. 7, young married girls go from house to house with earthen vessels containing sugar-cane, ghee and carrots which they distribute to *suvāsinīs*.

In agricultural rites the distribution of sweets is common. They are distributed during ploughing and when grain is collected on the threshing-floor, a distribution which averts evil-eye from the grain. If the central pole of the threshing-floor in Sind becomes loose both the Hindu and the Muhammadan avert evil by free distribution of sweets. Every Friday sugar and fried gram is distributed in honour of the goddess Lakṣmī. At a betrothal (*vilāya*), *Lingāyats* and *Namraddis* distribute sweets and the latter give sugar to the betrothed girl. After a birth, unless the child be still-born; at a cradle ceremony; at *Vāstuśānti* on entering a new house; after *akṣat* has been thrown on the bridal pair sweets are distributed. *Marwaris* and *Gujarātis* distribute milk and sweets in large quantities on the death of young children. In the Karnāṭak Hindus make a distribution of sweets whenever any good news is received, or any success has been achieved; when any danger has been surmounted and whenever a man returns home after a long journey. On a Hindu attaining the age of sixty he is weighed against silver coins and sweets are distributed. When a thirsty person calls for water he is first given something sweet. *Lamānis* give sweets to children on the third day after a birth. Whenever Hindus leave home to attend an auspicious ceremony sweets are first prepared at home and eaten. On the thirteenth day after a death sweets are eaten, as also when a bride first comes to her husband's house. Muhammadans place sweets in the palanquin of the bride when she goes to the house of her husband, and when they purchase a cow make a purchase at the same time of grain and of sweets that the purchased cow may bring *barkat*, and also distribute sweets to onlookers.

Sweet things accompany the bride to make her *pāyguṇ* sweet; the Muhammadan, besides the purchase of sweets when he buys cattle in the bazaar, gives away sweets when his mare foals to render the *pāyguṇ* sweet of the newly-born animal. Sweets are used on the threshing-floor to avert evil-eye.

Where there is honey, the Muhammadan believes, there gather angels of *barkat*. Honey is *riqunabi*, 'the spittle of the Prophet'. 'In honey there is healing for men' (Koran, cap. xvi, 69). Angels always come to a house where there is honey unless disturbed by a black dog, by musicians or other untoward presence. To eat honey is a virtue. The Prophet passed much of his time with Ayesha, the youngest of his wives, and when his other wives complained of neglect he said he did this because *Ayesha* gave him much honey. If any one sees another carrying honey he should dip his fingers in it and the person carrying it should offer him honey; an offer of honey must never be refused. The Muhammadan gives honey to the dying to confer *barkat*; he offers it to a guest; after a betrothal it is sent to the betrothed girl; on the third day after a marriage it is served to the bride and bridegroom.

To the Hindu honey is one of the *pancāmṛt*. It is taken to a shrine and then to the field or the threshing-floor to confer *barkat* on the grain; it is a common ingredient in the *naivedya* offered to standing crops. On New Year's Day it is offered to all. It is used in the preparation of the meal taken at a *Śrāddha*; it is used in *abhiṣek* or the bathing of images; it is used in *madhupark*, offered to guests, the bridegroom, pilgrim, a king and to saints. Because of the power honey possesses it may be a source of danger. A Hindu cannot decline an offer of honey without incurring disaster; if bees make a hive in the uppermost part of a house some inmate of the house will die; the collection of honey necessitating as it does *himsā* is considered dangerous to the prosperity of a family. To spill honey or touch it with the foot brings a sequel of ill, whilst mixing milk and honey in equal parts brings illness. Honey must be preserved from all impure contacts, and absolute cleanliness is imperative when collecting it.

If sweet things confer *barkat* and avert evil it is natural to assume that there is evil in sour things. *Mahārs* say that in a thunderstorm one may rest in safety under a sweet tree such as a banyan or a sweet mango, but it is dangerous to rest under a tamarind, a bitter mango or a wood-apple-tree. If the first eating of a dish which is good tastes bitter it is ominous to the *Mahār* of the early death of some near relative. In Sind the offer of a lemon embitters friendship, though in the Karnāṭak the district officer is constantly receiving small lemons offered to promote friendship. In Sind if a schoolboy eats sour things his intelligence is supposed to be impaired.

Things or mixtures that are purely sour cannot be offered by a Hindu as *naivedya*; a mantrik may use lemons and other sour things in charms but may not eat sour things, for eating is a kind of sacrifice. If a Hindu has a sour taste in his mouth he must stop the recitation of the *Veda* and sip water, *ācaman*, for if he persist otherwise in the recitation it has no effect. Flowers that smell sour cannot be offered to an image and a person practising penance or *jap* avoids sour things.

There are, however, bitter things which are used to obtain *barkat*. The leaves of the nim (Melia azadirachta) are bitter, but they are used by many castes to avert the contagion of death. *Baris* sprinkle nim-leaves round the lamp which they place at the spot where the deceased expired ; *Bhils* light a fire outside the house of the deceased and, throwing nim-leaves into it, purify themselves after a funeral by rubbing their faces and hands in the smoke ; *Dhors* use a nim-leaf to sprinkle *gomūtra* on themselves after a funeral. On the Hindu New Year's Day a tall bamboo is tied to a pillar in every Hindu's house. This *guḍhī* is erected in the name of Kṛṣṇa ; to the top of it are tied the *sāḍī* and bodice of a woman and a twig of nim-leaves. At the temple, too, nim-leaves brought by a priest are crushed and eaten with raw sugar to bring *barkat* for the coming year.

A decoction from nim-leaves is given to a woman in her confinement ; branches of nim-leaves hung over her door keep away spirits and the feet of visitors are washed with water by means of nim-leaves. Branches of nim are used in the exorcism of spirits and leaves of this tree are used medicinally and in bathing. On one occasion during an epidemic the dying were brought nightly to a nim-tree at my garden gate in the hope that through the power of the tree they would recover. The Muhammadan also thinks the nim brings *barkat* ; he plants it in graveyards so that its shadow may bring *barkat* to the dead. At *Hoḻī* the *Lamāni* wears nim-leaves in his turban. In the worship of the tulsī twigs of the tamarind and dhatri are used, although these are bitter.

CHAPTER XV

THE POWER OF TREES

THERE is no manifestation of power which illustrates better than does the power of trees all the complex and often contradictory ideas associated with power. Trees contain the *śakti* of the planets and of all the five primary elements of creation; to their possessing fire is due their fertility.

It is this innate power of trees that is recognized in Indian practices rather than the divinity which popular belief has attributed to certain particular trees. Certain trees are the abode of gods and some are the abodes of spirits, and it may be that the same tree shelters a god in the morning and a spirit in the evening. From constant contact with the divinity of a god there are trees that acquire special *śakti*, just as there are trees which after the death of a saint may be worshipped as saints because they acquired power from the saints who observed penance beneath them. In general, however, the term *dev* is not applied to trees, and like the ritual of the threshing-floor, the cult of trees illustrates concepts earlier than those of animism.

Trees are often the abode of spirits. When a Muhammadan passes beneath a tree he utters *bismillāh* and the Muhammadan woman covers her head. Sleeping near a tree is always dangerous because of the possible visitation from spirits. The Muhammadan calls trees which are haunted by spirits *ghoro* and gives them names which end in *lain* or 'accursed'. *Iblis lain, Shaitan lain,* which trees include the sirih, ber, lao, bar and babur. To harm another person a Muhammadan will sit on the top of a tree and recite after midnight the *sūratu'l-jinn*, the seventy-second chapter of the Koran. When a man is haunted by a spirit a mantrik lashes a tree; the effects of the laṣhing are repeated on the possessed man himself and the spirit then leaves its victim. Another cure for spirit possession is to make an image of a spirit and nail it to a tree, or inducing a spirit to leave its victim drive a nail into a tree saying as one does this, 'Be you for ever fixed in this tree'. When, too, a haunted tree is cut down special precautions are taken to provide the spirit with another home. A cock is sacrificed to the tree and as a notice to the spirit to quit, a copper plate on which a svastika has been drawn is attached to the tree. Then another tree is chosen for the spirit to move into; around this is built a small platform and a stone is placed at its base and, with the tree, sprinkled with saffron and oil. Copper coins are placed near this second tree; incense is burnt and a piece of cloth to provide the spirit with clothes (*āvaran*) is thrown upon the tree. When the spirit changes from the one tree to the other a branch of the tree it abandons usually breaks and falls; should there be no sign of the spirit willingly leaving its tree, it is bottled up in the shell of a coconut, or in a bottle, and tied to the second tree.

Particular diseases have, according to the Hindu, their governing deities. When a man is sick a relative takes an earthen pot half-filled with water, covers it with an earthen lid and places it on an *āsan* of rice sprinkled on the ground. Blades of darbha grass are then placed on the lid and on these an image of the deity associated with the man's illness, this in gold, silver or clay. With the grass the water from the pot is sprinkled on the sick man, and then the image is fixed to a tree with nails.

Spirits again cause barrenness in trees as they do to animals and human beings. Spirits that haunt trees are called *Māsti* or *Cauḍi*. When a tree is haunted stones are placed at its roots, whilst in Kanara wooden posts are fixed around in which are many wooden pegs.

Particular spirits and ghosts haunt particular trees. The pipal, banyan and umbar trees, all varieties of the fig-tree, are haunted by the spirit of a pandit who died without imparting his knowledge to others (*Brahmarākṣasa*); the bamboo is haunted by the spirit of a *Brahmacārī*; the ghost of a woman who dies in childbirth (*kāminī bhūt*) haunts a tamarind, the nux vomica. the tumri (Trewia nudiflora) the casuarina and the jali (Acacia arabica). The worst type of sinners occupies the marking-nut tree and the nuggi, whilst other haunted trees are the kari (Maba nigrescens), and the basari (Ficus infectoria). If a bel tree (Aegle marmelos), a pipal (Ficus religiosa), and an audumbar (Ficus glomerata) or a samī (Prosopis spicigera) grow spontaneously on a grave it is a sign that the dead has returned.

Although, however, trees may be the temporary abode of spirits; though spirits may by man's art be driven into and confined in trees, yet the power of trees is a protection against spirits. In the Deccan if a man possessed by a spirit hugs and climbs a tree he will fall off the tree senseless, but relieved. To free a man from the persecution of a spirit the banyan and the pipal tree are embraced; stones tied in a cloth are hung to a nim or to a tamarind, or the dry leaves of a pipal and a nim which have been married, torn off the trees on Sunday and Thursday, and preferably when there is a new moon, are used in fumigation. Roots of the bhūtakeś (Mussaenda frondosa) buried at the four corners of her cot, protect a woman in confinement from spirits, and nim-leaves tied to her bed serve the same purpose.

Many trees are called by names incorporating the word bhūt, 'spirit', such as bhūtya, bhūtkeś, yet even the branches or leaves of these are used to keep away spirits. The stealing of milk and butter is a pastime of spirits, and with their assistance witches play the same game. A witch imitates the action she wishes to profit by; if she wishes to steal flour she imitates grinding, if she wishes to steal butter she pretends to churn with water in a pot. To defeat her wiles a peg is prepared from bhūtya and used to tether the cow. Then a seer of milk from another cow is poured over the peg. The firmer the peg is fixed in the ground, the firmer it nails down the power of the witch. The cow whose milk the witch is stealing is then milked, and the first few drops of milk yielded by her are thrown on her back and she is patted.

The combined *śakti* of a pipal and a nim cures from spirit possession women who make a *pradakṣiṇā*. A branch of pandhari (Croton reticulatus) cut on Saturday or Sunday averts spirits if held in the hand or tied to some part of a house. Branches of ankola (Alangium Lamarckii) collected on a Wednesday in the month of *Pauṣa* are hung in a house. The threshing-floor in Khandesh is protected from spirits by a pole of bhūtkeś placed near the entrance of the floor; cattle-pens are protected by Muhammadans with black wood and branches of kanda. Merely carrying a nāg betha (Calamus tigrinus) or a branch of ulpi (Grewia salvifolia) is a protection against spirits. The encircling of a patri-tree (Aegle marmelos) by a Lingāyat averts the attentions of the ghost of a deceased partner. In Kanara when the first sowing is made early in the morning a twig of kyadgi (Pandanus odoratissimus) or of mundki (Pandanus fascicularis) is buried in the fields, and again when the crops are mature, soon after nightfall twigs of the same trees are buried in different parts of the fields to scare away spirits. The pestle of a churn is usually made of ari (Bauhinia racemosa) because this tree keeps away spirits; the pole of the threshing-floor is for the same reason in the Deccan often of saundad (Prosopis spicigera) and leaves of this tree are used in *pancpālvī* which the *Marāṭhā* ties as a protection to his *devak*. The tulsī (ocimum sanctum) keeps a house free of spirits, and the Muhammadan attributes the same power to a stick of olive.

The power of a tree is sensitive to impure contacts. A woman in menses may use plantain-leaves as plates, but she is not to use the leaves of the paḻas (butea frondosa); a tree withers if the shadow of such a woman fall on it. If a barren woman bathes in the shade of a tree the tree dies or becomes barren; it also withers if a girl attaining puberty does but touch it. An unclean person fails to climb a tree, for attempting this he falls down. Nothing unclean can be done near a tree and as sleep is an unclean state, one should not sleep near a tree. Cattle are not allowed to rest under a tree in blossom lest they should pollute the vicinity of the tree. In Sind if a man with a black mole on his tongue praises the fruit of a tree it forthwith withers; if one speaks of the dead under a tree it dies. A tree is destroyed by evil-eye, as a protection against which garlands of marking-nuts, turmeric and sandals are tied to its branches. Plantain-trees are protected by the skull of a cow stuck on a post of bamboo. As an ordinary precaution, too, visitors to a garden may be required by the gardener before entering the garden to wash their faces.

Though sensitive, however, to evil-eye trees and their leaves or fruit are the commonest protection against evil-eye. In fumigation the Hindu uses the leaves of the betel, the seeds of madarangi (Lawsonia alba); pieces of black-wood (Dalbergia latifolia); coconuts; nuts of the marking-nut tree; leaves of the nim; pieces of bagni (Caryota urens); leaves of viṣapanjar (Erythraea Roxburghii), of isbandari (Plantago ovata), tamarind-wood and sandalwood. Beads of ruī are worn on the wrist as amulets and in Kanara cow-pens are protected by branches of kenjigangidā. A rope made from the bark of asuna (Briedelia retusa) protects cattle from evil-eye. The Muhammadan burns in Sind ak (Calotropis procera) to avert evil-eye. To prevent the return in convalescence of a disease through inadvertent exposure to evil-eye branches or leaves of pancundra (Diandria monogynia) and pacva (Grewia microcos) are used, whilst beads of the fan-palm, bajar battu (Corypha umbraculifera), protect children and handsome men.

A garland of pundi (Hibiscus cannabinus) tied to the neck of a milch animal with black thread secures it against the evil-eye of a witch, and if a witch can be found, a beating with a branch of ruī (Calotropis gigantea) destroys her power.

The effects of evil-eye can be transferred from a victim to a tree, causing the withering of the tree. To cure a child affected by evil-eye its clothes are thrown on a green tree. On Sundays,

Thursdays and *Amāvāsyā* rags are tied to trees and nails are driven into trees to avert the effects of *dṛṣṭi.* A Muhammadan waves the liver of a sheep round a victim of evil-eye and throws this at the root of a tree, or places a glass of milk in front of the victim and, taking him to a tree, throws the milk at the base of the tree and drives a nail into the trunk. Needles are also brought in contact with the afflicted and then stuck in a tree to effect a transfer of the evil, or oil in which an afflicted child has seen its own reflection is thrown on thorny bushes or on the golgolki.

Transfer of evil predicates the aid of power and the power of trees enables many evils besides that of the evil eye to be transferred to them in the distress of man. To cure fever Sindi Muhammadans throw their clothes on a pipal or a sirih tree. When a child suffers from anaemia (*muḍadoṣ*) caused by the touch of an impure woman the worn-out clothes of the child are thrown on a thorny tree on a Sunday or Thursday. The person who throws the clothes is required to say 'Let the evil of the child remain in this thorny bush'. In the Karnāṭak clothes of the child are thrown in this way on successive Sundays and Thursdays for several weeks until the child has no clothes left that it has worn, and then the cure by transfer becomes complete. When the Sindi bridegroom is taken in procession on horseback a tuft of his hair is buried at the foot of a tree to transfer all his evils to the tree. In Kanara the nail and hair clippings of the sick are wrapped in an old rag and tied to a tree; the bark of the tapasī tree is tied first to the neck of a sick child for a fortnight and then to a tree; when a boy suffers from rickets thread is tied round his neck for one, three, or seven days and then thrown on a tree, which withers at once. To remove jaundice threads are tied to a tree on Sundays and Thursdays after being brought in contact with the sick; to cure glands and recurring fever mantras are recited over trees three or five times in the Karnāṭak and then the trees are uprooted in the name of the sick. If a man suffers from fever another man gazes at him intently, and then seeks a pikjali-tree (Acacia Farnesiana) in the forest without talking to the sick man; muttering the name of the sick man he then uproots the tree and ties to the man's neck a piece of the tree's bark. Nine kinds of grain are tied in a cloth and with a copper coin waved round the sick and tied to a tree that has a milky sap; the same remedy is used to cure cattle in an epidemic, but the tree chosen must then be one outside the village and on a public road. To cure fever or the bite of a scorpion the Muhammadan recites the name of the sufferer and that of his mother over a thread and ties this with a knot to a tree. To cure whooping-cough a thread is tied round the neck of the patient and then to a green tree; to cure anæmia the thread is thrown on a kākī-tree (Cassia fistula) on a Sunday.

The shadows of the sick are allowed to fall on a tree and then a nail is driven into the shadow; this is done when a man suffers from megrim or a child from anæmia. *Vaddars* choose Thursday or Sunday for this practice and drive nails into a nim-tree before sunrise and in silence. Another cure for megrim is for the sick man to rest against a tree, and for some friend to draw lines on the tree in a line with the man's temples, cheeks and neck, choosing three successive days for doing this.

Contact with the tree in many cases is even more direct than through the shadow. The sick man may actually embrace, bite, climb or in other ways touch the tree. Sick people climb a mango on Tuesdays or a banyan on Wednesday for seven weeks in succession. A person suffering from epilepsy is tied to a nim-tree the moment he has an attack and the leaves and branches of the tree are wrapped round him. When suffering from fever *Bhils* and *Koḻis* go on alternate days and either at dawn or at sunset and without speaking embrace a toddy palm (Borassus flabelliformis) or a bari-tree (Periploca aphylla); as they embrace the tree they say, 'To-day to me, to-morrow to you'. To cure a cold a pipal is embraced; to cure ague a plantain. Touching a vedi babul (Acacia arabica) with the right arm followed by the left on a Saturday or a Sunday is also a cure for ague. In Sind the Muhammadan to cure fever embraces at the top any *ghoro* tree or any tree of particularly fine appearance. If several children in a family die a surviving child is made to embrace a tree that stands by itself, to avert the contagion of death. A man bitten by a snake recovers if he bites a gaṭṭmalligi-tree, a tamarind or a nim; one suffering from malaria bites the bark of a tapasī-tree (Holoptelea integrifolia). Sindi Moslems bite a pipal (Ficus religiosa) to cure fever. In Sind, too, a sirih-tree (Albizzia Lebbek) is embraced before sunrise to cure fever and as he embraces the tree the sick man says, 'I transfer my fever to you'.

When the products of trees are applied to the bodies of the sick or are used to form potions, it is often difficult to say whether any other power is attributed to the trees than a Western science might concede. There are, however, myriad illustrations of the use of these products based on the belief in the magic power of trees. In the Konkaṇ to cure spleen the bark of the moho-tree (Bassia latifolia) is taken and from it a figure, half human, half toad-like in shape, is made and applied externally to the spleen. The figure is then hung over a stove for a year or so to dry and as it dries the spleen also is supposed to dry. In Kanara the bark of the samī and of the kesarigonde trees are removed with a stone in silence and before dawn and tied to the neck or arm of a man suffering from fever. Then prayers are offered to the tree to bestow *śakti* on the bark; these prayers are repeated seven times and at each recital a knot is tied in the bark to tie up the power of the tree.

The power of trees ensures women an easy delivery. Charms to assist a woman are written in the shadow of a kaṇgal-tree (Pongamia glabra) that they may acquire *śakti* from the tree. The bangle of a woman in travail is with copper coins, rice and jvārī placed at the foot of a ruī (Calotropis gigantea); a piece of the root of the tree is put in her hair, and after the birth of her child, to prevent prolapsus, this root is taken back to the tree and camphor is offered to the tree. The woman's marriage necklace is also buried under a ruī with a prayer to the tree to grant her an easy delivery. In lieu of the ruī sometimes a rasabali or a plantain tree is used in the same way. To stop premature delivery pains nine threads are tied round a banni-tree (Acacia ferriginea). The root of a nim-tree is tied round the waist of the expectant mother, or a piece of utrani (Achyranthes aspera). In parts of Gujarāt a stem of punmadi is placed on her abdomen and its roots are tied in her hair. In Sind charms are written by Moslems on mango or jamun leaves and placed on her stomach. A piece of erand (Rhus cotinus) is another substitute tied to her hair, or a piece of vekhand (Iris pseudacorus) to her waist, whilst the worship of a śamī-tree also facilitates delivery.

By the transfer of the *śakti* of a tree a woman may be made fruitful. In Khandesh *Bhils* make their marriage booths from branches of savar (Eriodendron anfractuosum) and sayphal (Nyctanthes arbor tristis), or from kakad (Flacourtia Ramontchi). Nine branches of the kakad-tree are fixed in the ground; to these rafters of teak are fastened and on these again are placed branches of jambhul. When savar and sayphal are used two poles only are fixed in the ground. These branches or poles are left after the marriage to take root and blossom, and by so doing confer issue on the bridal pair in proportion to their own fruit. Sometimes the *Bhil* spreads branches of umbar (Ficus glomerata) bearing blossom on the marriage *maṇḍap* roof and shakes the fruit of the umbar branches on to the bridal pair as they sit below. In the Karnāṭak the *hālgamba* is associated with the fertility of the married pair. It is allowed by many castes to remain after the marriage and take root, bringing issue to the bride and bridegroom. *Mahārs* make two miniature *āsan* from their gular (Sterculia urens) representing a boy and a girl infant, and married women preserve these in a bag of rice during the marriage ceremony. Another practice is to make two small dolls from the same wood as the milk-post and for the bride to hold these when she takes her *mangalsnān* with the bridegroom. *Kaḻḻ Koravas* have a custom according to which at a marriage five married women take five earthen pots to a well and fill them with water. One pot is distinguished by spots of white lime and sandal-paste ; a branch of basari (Ficus infectoria) is placed on this pot, brought to the *maṇḍap* and placed in front of the married pair on an *āsan* of jvārī grain, and kept for ten days after which it is thrown into a well, the water of which is later used for cooking purposes. This basari-twig is supposed to bring the bridal pair issue and is only used in this way at a marriage. Brahmin priests give the bridal pair coconuts to ensure that they have issue and in some cases the bridal pair embrace a coconut-tree after they have been sprinkled with *akṣat*. In Sind the Muhammadan bride embraces a kandi-tree (Prosopis spici gera) and vows if she gets issue to tie to it a green thread. The marriage *maṇḍap* of the Muhammadan in Sind is constructed of date palms which bring issue and peace to the bridal pair. Another Muhammadan custom is after the marriage to write charms, mix them with manure, and in this plant a flowering tree which must, however, not be a sirih-tree ; when the tree flowers the bride eats of the blossom, but after congress with her husband must not touch the tree or it withers. It is the parents of the bride who plant the tree.

The audumbar and the banyan are generally planted before the temples of goddesses and are called *Devarmara*, 'the tree of the deity'. Issueless women worship them to get issue. A barren woman to obtain issue goes barefooted round an aśvath-tree a hundred times a day, and after obtaining issue hangs a cradle on the tree ; she may also go round the tree five times carrying two pots of water and pouring this round the tree on her final circuit. On the first *Jyeṣṭha-Pūrṇimā* that follows a marriage the newly-married pair go round the same tree. To obtain issue women bathe in a tank and then go to a temple holding a branch of lakki (Vitex negundo) ; at Hegade in the Kanara district they make a round of a temple wearing round their loins twigs of nim or of lakki. In the same district there is a grove of trees where annually at a fair married couples sleep in the hope of getting issue.

In Sind a woman desiring issue takes water and goes a little beyond a pipal or a nim tree ; then eases herself, uses half the water she has brought to purify herself and then throws the remainder at the root of the tree, returning home without looking back. This is done every day for forty days, after which period the tree in a dream asks the woman what she desires and, learning this, grants her her longing. Hindu women in Sind rub themselves against a pipal-tree to get issue.

The planting of a tree is supposed to bring issue to the planter, and the worship of a mango-tree during the rains has the same result. Sindi Muhammadans pour water at the root of a tree so that a barren woman may get issue. As gifts made by a Hindu are decided by the nature of the boon desired by the donor, the giving of fruit is a means whereby fertility may be obtained in return. Fruit is offered to a god and the worshipper, the *pujārī* of the temple, gives some portion of the offering back to the suppliant as *prasād* of the deity. A woman without issue in the same way offers a coconut to a god and the priest gives it back to her without breaking it (*pūrna phala*). A bridal pair is also given coconuts by one of the priests at their marriage. Eating fruit ; riding a fruit-tree at night and then eating its fruit ; rolling under a fruit-tree and then eating its fruit ; stepping on fruit, followed by congress, are some of the ways in which issue can be obtained by the transfer of fertility from trees and their products.

At a marriage *Marāṭhās* sow bhopaḻi (Curcubita maxima) seed in the house-yard to encourage the fertility of the married pair ; it is tended until ten or more pumpkins have appeared and is then destroyed. A woman without issue in the Deccan goes to a mango or a tamarind tree, choosing a tree which is in blossom, places five stones in a line radiating from the trunk and on each places a piece of bread and turmeric. Then she prays, saying, 'May all the fruit of this tree be destroyed and may a child enter my womb'. The tree is supposed forthwith to wither and the woman has a child. If a married woman fail to have issue a palm-leaf is tied with a string of jute round her neck and she becomes *enceinte* within three months. In Sind issueless women make a vow if they have a child to place on particular trees a preparation of ghee and powdered wheat called *kutti*.

The *śakti* of the cosmos being one and every manifestation of fertility a single form of active potentiality, the power of trees fosters the increase of grain and other crops. In Kanara on *Karka Sankramaṇa* a branch of ketgi (Pandanus odoratissimus) is stuck in a field early in the morning with as much noise as possible of tom-toms and other music and this branch is treated as the husband of the crops. At sowing, pieces of sugar-cane are stuck in the ground to bring increase to the grain sown. When the picking of cotton is begun a garland of marking-nuts, vekhand (Iris pseudacorus), turmeric, coconuts and garlic is tied to five plants of cotton in the field to increase the yield of cotton (*Bajantri Koravas*). The threshing-floor pole is chosen with care in all districts in the belief that its wood adds to the increase of the grain. In Kanara it is usually cut from a tree with milky sap, the umbar (Ficus glomerata), the banyan, the dhatri (Phyllanthus emblica), the shalmali (Bombax malabarica), the kalli (Euphorbia tirucalli), the saptapurna (Alstonia scholaris), or the gambhari (Gmelina arborea). In Sind a tree that is considered *ghoro* is chosen for the pole. When the grain has been gathered on the floor the *Marāṭhā* scatters on it flowers of the ruī (Calotropis gigantea); in the Karnāṭak before the measuring of the gathered grain begins a little of it is placed at the foot of a tree, usually the ruī or the tarvad (Cassia auriculata) or flowers of these trees are placed on the *rās*. To increase the grain on the threshing-floor a custom of the Karnāṭak is to place leaves of the banni (Acacia ferruginea) and ari (Bauhinia racemosa) beneath the floor, and a very common practice in the Konkaṇ, the Deccan and the Karnāṭak is to place five leaves of different trees in the pit in which the central pole of the threshing-floor is erected.

A branch of mundaki (Pandanus fascicularis) is also stuck in the standing crops; branches of the thorny lavangi kante are in the Karnāṭak fixed amid the crops. Crops are supposed to show a great yield if the creeper Lepidagathis cristata be planted in the fields, whilst rice crops grow best in the vicinity of a karanja tree (Pongamia glabra).

At every new agricultural operation some prominent tree, if any, in the field is worshipped, non-Brahmins in particular worshipping the nim-tree at both the rabī and kharif harvests. In the Karnāṭak a garland of marking-nuts and turmeric is tied to a billa-tree (Chloroxylon Swietenia) if there be one near the field. When the kharif crops are harvested a banni-tree (Acacia ferruginea) is worshipped in a small *pandal* made of sugar-cane stalks. A brass or copper pot of water with five leaves of *pān* in it and a coconut over it, is placed in front of the tree. Five marks in saffron and turmeric are made in a horizontal line on the coconut and it is decorated with a bodice, a *sāḍī* and the gold ornaments of a woman. Five married women wave *ārtī* and *naivedya* is offered to the tree.

Muhammadans in Sind throw leaves of sirih into a garden to make it fruitful; if these are thrown into a granary the store of grain never grows less, however much grain be removed. When a cow bears a calf the placenta is placed on the top of a tree to increase the supply of milk given by the cow. In the Deccan boys throw stones into a milkbush (Euphorbia tirucalli), the *śer*; these stones are then collected and waved three times round the udders of a cow or goat to augment its milk. The stones are also heated and placed beneath the animal as it is milked. Waved round the breasts of a woman they produce the same effect.

Increase, however, is only one form of *barkat* and trees may be used to obtain *barkat* of other kinds.

Through the medium of a tree a Sindi Muhammadan can subdue the spirits of water. By throwing a leaf into a river the water spirits are brought into the service of man. To force a woman, for instance, to come to him he writes her name every day for forty days on leaves of sirih and throws these into a river. After the object desired has been obtained a goat is sacrificed to the tree or flags and rags are tied to it. It is to be noted that in these practices the name of Khwāja Khizr is never taken. To obtain wealth a Hindu rises two *ghaṭikā* before dawn on *Ugadi* or *Yug-pratipadā* (Chaitra sud. I) and embraces a nim-tree, and continues to do this hopefully every day throughout the year. Trees are planted in the names of others and carefully tended so that they may grow, and with their growth the persons on whose behalf this is done may also live. Trees are planted by the Hindu over the buried navel-cord of a child to bring the child *śakti*, and the cord is enclosed in a gourd to prevent the death of the child or of later-born children of the same mother.

In Kanara if a traveller meets a wild dog he takes a twig of a tree and, without looking back, points it in any direction he wishes and says to the dog, 'Go in that direction and seek your prey'. Pieces of kāre (Nux vomica) are thrown on the bier of a man who was notorious for evil living in order to prevent his returning as a ghost. Though the rule is barely observed nowadays, strict orthodoxy requires that all torn garments should annually be thrown on or near a tree on *Ekādaśī* of *Āṣāḍha*. In the Dharwar district to prevent a dead man troubling the living as a ghost a piece of his garment is tied to a tree, and the ghost remains with the piece. On Chaitra sud. I, in every Hindu house a very tall bamboo is tied to a pillar. At the top of this *guḍhī* is put a brass utensil inverted and below this are tied the new garments of a woman, and a twig of nim. The pole is worshipped to secure peace and happiness during the coming year. At the entrance to the marriage *manḍap* Sarasvat Brahmins tie to a post a twig of pāngārā (Erythrina Indica); the post with the red rice, turmeric and a yellow-coloured rag tied to it, is called *Senāpati* and averts evil.

TREES AND RAIN

When rain fails in the months of *Jyeṣṭha, Āṣāḍha Śrāvaṇ* and *Bhādrapad* trees like the pipal are worshipped with *mahā mahā abhiṣek.* The water used in bathing the trees must be allowed to reach the sea, for on the day it reaches the sea heavy rain will fall; the water is therefore thrown into a river or nullah. A śamī and a nim trec growing side by side are called *Maḻi*, 'rain', and *Appyya*, 'father', and are worshipped to obtain rain.

In Sind there is a practice which will soon have died out, of filling a jar with water from a well and tying it to the top of a tree with a prayer that water should come from above in the form of rain, or from below in the flood of the canals. The Muhammadan ties many of his written charms to trees, and among these is one based on the key number fifteen which he ties to bring rain.

THE TYING OF RAGS AND THREADS

The tying of rags and threads to trees is a practice which admits of several interpretations. When a thread is first tied round the neck of a sick person and after it has thus been in contact with him for a fixed number of days, is tied to a tree and the tree withers and dies, it may be assumed that a transfer of evil has been made, which in essence does not differ from the transfer effected by throwing on trees clothes worn by the sick or the hair and nail clippings of the sick. When the *Kātkarī* ties grass to a tree to cure fever and chooses a tree near a public path he contemplates the transfer of his illness to others.

There are, however, many other cases in which a thread or rag is tied to a tree, in which no harm ensues to the tree and the rag or thread has not been in contact with any form of evil contagion. There are, too, trees which are always covered with pendent rags and threads, which in Gujarāt are called *Chintharia*, in the Deccan and the Karnāṭak *Cindyā Dev*, 'rag god', and in Sind *Chindhi Pīr*, 'rag pir'. These trees receive fresh adornments from passers-by, for they are usually on the edge of public highways.

Threads, nine in all, are tied round a banni-tree (Acacia ferruginea) to stop the pains of premature delivery. To obtain issue *Raddis* tie thread to a nim-tree, *Kabbars* to a banni, Brahmins to a śamī, a bel (Aegle marmelos) or to a pipal which has grown united to a nim or to a single pipal of which the thread ceremony has been performed. Rags are tied with the same objects. In West Khandesh many castes tie thread round an umbar; the *Gujar* ties it to the joint trunk of a pipal, nim and banyan (*tirpindi*); the *Kātkarī* ties black thread to a ruī (Calotropis gigantea).

Several reasons are given by those who resort to these practices. It may be that in the presence of the sick a thread is taken and by the recital of charms the evil *śakti* which causes the illness is brought into the thread, which is then tied to the tree merely to prevent its touching the ground. A more common interpretation is that the thread annoys the *śakti* of the tree and coerces it to grant the relief or boon asked for. When white thread is tied round a śamī or bel tree to obtain issue the person who tied the thread says, 'I have tied you round until you grant me my desire'. After the desire has been granted the thread is removed from the tree; a pit is dug near the tree in which the thread is placed. Milk and ghee are then sprinkled on the thread, perhaps with the object of cooling its hot *śakti*, leaves are scattered and on these a stone is placed and finally with earth the pit is filled in burying the thread. Precisely the same ritual is followed in tying white thread round a bor (Zizyphus jujuba) before the sun rises far enough to cast shadows with the object of curing a fever, or in tying thread round a pipal before noon-time at which time *Agni*, who resides in the tree, leaves it.

Between the invitation of *śakti* to come to a particular place and its coercion the difference is negligible. To both Brahmin and to primitive tribes like the *Bhil*, *Naikda*, and *Koḻī* the tying of a thread round a tree is an invitation to the tree. The *Bhil* ties a thread round his kadamb-tree before he cuts a branch to bring to his marriage *manḍap*. Brahmins tie a thread round a tumbi (Diospyros ebenum), invoke the *śakti* of the tree, and as they tie the thread, ask the tree to accept the thread as an invitation to come to the celebrant's house. The next day the plant is uprooted, taken home with the thread, and tied to a beam root upwards. The plant must not be touched by any tool of iron, and after the patient has been cured the root is always thrown on something green. In a similar way a thread is tied to a castor-oil plant as an invitation to come to the house of the sick, and the root of the plant is tied to the arm or neck of the patient in a cloth, the thread still attached to the root.

Muhammadan practice is similar. Rags are tied to trees to transfer evil, but also to force a tree to grant a request. The Muhammadan significantly calls the tying of rags and threads to trees *mair*, which connotes coercion. He ties thread to a kanda-tree to secure the fruition of any object. Sometimes he ties rags and flags to a tree not antecedent to obtaining a boon, but after his wishes have been granted. To cure fever or the bite of a scorpion or snake the Sindi recites the name of the sufferer and that of his mother over a thread and ties to a tree. If he wishes to transfer the illness to the tree he must tie a knot in the thread; if he wishes unkindly to transfer the illness to another person he must not tie a knot, but must attach to the thread the written name of that other person and of his mother, and remove the thread from the tree.

There is yet another type of practice in which a thread is tied to a tree. When issue is desired a thread is tied to certain trees, but always in some castes by a *suvāsinī*. The *Raddi* who follows this custom says the thread tied is merely a *hungnul* or sign of married life, the tree being treated as a married woman. The *Kabbar* gives the same explanation of the tying of a thread five times round a banni to cure a person possessed by a spirit.

The practice of driving nails into trees also admits of more than one interpretation. The *Marāthā* drives nails into a ruī to cure a cold or ague; *Vaddars* drive nails into any kind of tree to cure megrim. In the Konkaṇ, where the practice is very common, the *Kātkarī* drives nails into the hivar (Acácia leucophloea) or the saitan (Alstonia scholaris) to cure fever; into mango-trees and mad (Cocos nucifera) to cure ague and fever; into the bori or the banyan to cure toothache; and to cure fever into a babul at the spot where three branches meet. On Sundays nails are driven into pipal-trees to cure any disease, and on Sundays, Thursdays and Amāvāsyā into trees to cure evil-eye.

In Kanara the practice of driving nails into trees as a cure for disease is the profession of a special class of men called *Ghadig*. The usual procedure is to place the nail in the hand of the sick man and then place it with its supposed burden of ill on a plank where it is charmed with mantras. The nail is then driven into a tree outside the village bounds and woe betide any person who sees or touches the nail after it has been driven into the tree. At the same time an unhusked coconut which has been waved round the patient is tied to the tree, and fowls which have been similarly waved are let loose near the tree or sacrificed at its base. In Sind the alphabet is written in numbers on a paper and this is tied to a tree; a nail is driven into letter after letter until a desired cure is effected. When the *Kātkarī* drives a nail into a tree he bows to the tree and requests it to take away the illness of the sick patient. If one may roughly define geographical areas in which the idea of a transfer of evil or that of coercing the *śakti* of the tree predominates, I would say that in Gujarāt and in the Karnāṭak the driving of nails into a tree seems to be a mere transfer of evil by contact, whereas in the Deccan and in Sind the idea of coercion of power is more manifest.

The tying of a thread or the driving of a nail is not the only way of coercing the power of a tree. In Kanara if a tree remain barren it is threatened by a man who goes round the tree saying, 'I will cut you'. If a tree be barren when an eclipse occurs the owner, without washing his face, takes a log of wood with an iron ring at the end of it and early in the morning strikes the tree thrice. This treatment, if it does not make the beaten tree fruitful, at least terrifies the other trees into bearing fruit to avoid a beating. In Sind if a tree does not give fruit one man threatens the tree with an axe, and another man intervenes and offers himself as surety for the tree's behaviour.

The *Kātkarī*, when ill, bends down the branch of a tree with his left foot and places on the bent branch a heavy stone, saying to the tree, 'So long will you remain thus until my illness is cured'. When the patient recovers, some one, not the patient himself, removes the stone. In Sind if a Muhammadan wants a woman to come to him he writes her name and that of her mother on a piece of paper and ties this to a tree and then presses down a branch and covers it with a heavy stone. The tree so roughly treated is supposed to pass on to the girl the pressure of the stone. In the Konkaṇ there is a practice of coercing creepers such as that of the pumpkin to bear fruit. As this must be done in complete silence the practice is called *Muṭṭas* (*muṭṭ* means 'silently'). The creeper is slit open and powdered asafoetida is put in the slit, which is then bandaged.

Stones are piled round the stems of jack-fruit trees at the joints of branches to make the trees give fruit in proportion to the weight of the stones. Stones are also tied to trees to cure illness. They are tied to babul and nim trees to cure malaria and to nim-trees to cure snake-bite. On a śakuni-tree stones are placed to remove any kind of calamity.

Although the planting of trees is represented in the sacred books of Hinduism as an act of merit; although wealth, power, longevity, issue and other forms of *barkat* follow from the planting of trees, yet there are trees the planting of which is so dangerous that the young cannot plant them. There are trees that are therefore left to old men to plant. Sindi Muhammadans leave the planting of the lai (Tamarix Indica), of the sirih (Albizzia Lebbek) and of a small species of nim to the old. A ruī tree is not planted by a Hindu near a house, nor is a bel (Aegle marmelos) save in the compound of a temple; a pipal is not planted near a house. The atti (Ficus glomerata), the alli (Memecylon edule) the a'l (Ficus Bengalensis) and the betel-tree are not planted by the young. Beyond these the habit of punning on words which itself moulds much Hindu ritual, is probably responsible for other restrictions on planting. The jamun-tree (Eugenia jambolana) is also called *niralu*, which is a compound of *ninu*, 'you' and *iralu*, 'living'; the tree therefore is supposed to say '*Na iralyo ni iratiyo*', 'I should live or you should live', threatening the planter of the tree with death if the tree survive. In much the same way the plantain-tree called *bāli*, which means 'having survived', is supposed to say '*Na bāḻalyo ni bāḻatiyo*', 'I should survive or you should survive', linking the life of the tree with the death of the man who plants it. The śevga-tree is alternatively called *nuggi*, and *nuggu* means 'having crushed'. The person who plants a nuggi-tree is crushed and calamity comes to his family; even one who passes in its shadow has to perform his thread ceremony, if already performed, a second time. When these trees, *bali*, *nuggi*, *niralu*, are planted, the planter does not return home the day he plants the tree, but goes to another village. This is done to save himself and the tree, for by going away to another village he replies, as it were, to the tree by saying, 'I go away', i.e. I do not survive and you had therefore better survive. The tree thereupon is consoled and attempts to grow and, having once resolved to grow, does not change even if the planter returns the next day.

Banana-trees when putting forth fruit are supposed to make a slight sound which when heard is a presage of death; a banana-tree should therefore never be planted near a house. When any of these trees of ill omen are planted, old men are chosen to plant them, as they have presumably less years than the young to live, and by reason of their innate power have greater immunity from evil.

If the planting of certain trees is a hazardous task, the cutting of trees is accompanied by still greater danger. Cutting a tree is a form of *himsā* and all *himsā* destroys *barkat*. Cutting a tree before beginning a journey dooms to failure the object of the journey; the cutting of trees when crops stand mature in the fields destroys the *barkat* of the crops. Forest contractors may prosper for some time, but in popular belief end their days in poverty. Muhammadans share with the Hindu the belief that cutting a tree means non-fruition of purpose. Mythology makes

Yakṣiṇī, a demi-goddess in the service of Kuber, king of wealth, guardian of forests, attacking all who cut or fell a tree without authorization.

In all parts of the Presidency, varying from district to district, there are trees preserved from destruction by a reverence in many cases based on the fear of consequences. There are tracts where reckless destruction has made the landscape a treeless waste save for one or two varieties of trees. The *Marāṭhā* will not cut down the ruī and in some places he protects the nim. Fear of death, if it be cut, often preserves the blackwood-tree. The pipal and the śamī are cut only if they wither; the Brahmin will not cut the sandal-wood tree nor the dhatri (Phyllanthus emblica) and fears leprosy if he cut the aśvath, the audumbar or the banyan. Non-Brahmins will protect the toddy-palm and the surangi (Calophyllum inophyllum). In 1930 political agitation was accompanied by widespread destruction of trees, but even politics had to recognize the forces that protect the coconut-tree.[1]

When trees of necessity have to be felled or cut, it is not uncommon to find the task of destruction committed to some one other than the owner. It is a Muhammadan belief in Sind that a young man must not cut a nim, sirih or lao, but must leave the work to the old. A Hindu who plants a plantain-tree will not himself cut it down; the owner of a nim (Melia azadirachta), of a banni (Acacia ferruginea), of a patri (Aegle marmelos) or arli (Ficus religiosa) always employs some one else to cut down his tree. Throughout the greater part of the Presidency at a marriage a branch of a tree is installed in the marriage *manḍap*. When

[1] The coconut, so long as it contains milk, is to a Hindu full of *śakti*. The milk of an unbroken coconut which has not touched the ground represents the holy Ganges. Coconuts are offered to gods; in constructing a marriage *manḍap* the milk of a coconut is sprinkled on all sides to avert evil; a coconut is placed over the foundations of a house under construction; it protects the walls when they rise and is placed on the threshold or on a beam when the roof is about to be put in its place. At a marriage the bridegroom keeps a coconut with him until he reaches his own home and must not lose it; the lap of the bride is filled with unbroken coconuts and she must not lose the coconut which she takes to her husband's house, where it is broken and distributed. At a Hindu marriage several hundred coconuts are given to all women guests; women when *enceinte* are given a coconut from which they must not part till their child is born; when a married woman leaves a house to go to her husband's house, she is given a coconut with its fibre intact. Coconuts are thrown into a river or the sea when tides or floods are high to prevent their rising further. A coconut must not come in contact with impurity; it must not be thrown into fire nor stepped over.

Before the Muhammadan bridal pair put on their wedding garments a coconut is tied above their waist; on the fifth day after a wedding a broken coconut is distributed. In the Deccan the Muhammadan sprinkles the milk of a coconut in the four corners of his marriage *manḍap*. A coconut has the form of a human head and to see it in a dream is a sign of fertility.

in Gujarāt the ruby pillar *Manekstambha* is erected the tree used for it is cut by *Koḻis* and *Sutārs* and not by the father of the bride or bridegroom; in the Deccan when a tree is cut to provide a twig for the *devak Koḻis, Bhils* and *Guravs* in some districts are employed to cut the branch. In Kanara before going to a marriage, *Jains* cut a plantain-tree bearing green fruit which the party of the bridegroom bears to the house of the bride, after worship of the tree with turmeric and coconut. The actual cutters of the tree are considered murderers and so a generous reward is offered to others to cut the tree. The tree has, further, to be cut with the left hand and the axe must be worshipped before use; after the tree has been felled a new tree is planted in its place and an offering of curds in propitiation of the tree felled is made. A tree cut should always be cut or felled in silence.

At *Soḍamunj*, when the Brahmin bridegroom ceases to be a bachelor he still takes an oath in Sanscrit not to cut or climb a tree. The offer of an apology to a tree when cut is a common practice. In the Dharwar district when the jungle is cleared for cultivation or withered trees are felled, the owner worships one representative tree with burning camphor, a broken coconut and turmeric before he hands over the work of destruction to his workmen. When an *Agnihotrī* cuts a tree he apologizes to it; when a Brahmin cuts one of his five sacred trees he implores the axe not to hurt the tree, and as soon as the tree has been felled, pours ghee over the stump and prays it to grow in a thousand shoots. The *Jain,* the day before he cuts his khijda-tree to use as his ruby pillar, goes to the tree and invites it formally to the marriage, and the next day cuts the tree, saying, 'Do not be angry as we want you for a good purpose'.

When timber has been used in the construction of a house, a sacred car, or a temple, a sacrificial *hom* is performed by the Brahmin before he enters the building or uses the car, to appease the trees that supplied the timber, and the spirits that may have taken up their abode therein. Before the leaves of betel-trees in a garden are plucked one tree is worshipped with *akṣat* and saffron; when the tapping of toddy-palms begins for the first time in a season one tree is worshipped and a coconut is broken on the tree. The milk of the coconut is sprinkled on the tree and pieces of the kernel with parched rice are distributed among those present as *prasād.* Even when the bark of trees is removed, generally on Sundays and Wednesdays, to be tied as a cure to the arm or neck of a fever-stricken patient, an apology is offered to the tree, and its name must not be uttered.

Power is attributed to trees according to their more obvious characteristics. The banyan-tree's habit of throwing down tendrils which take root, and become massive trunks before the parent tree has even withered, not unnaturally suggests longevity; planting a banyan-tree is one way of attaining long life. The pipal-tree, another variety of fig, is also associated with fertility, but the pipal has a habit of growing in walls and crevices and eventually destroying the wall in which it grows. There is no tree that in this way causes more ruin in India than the pipal. It is therefore worshipped when the suppliant wishes to accomplish the destruction of his enemies; it is never planted near a house, for if its roots get under the house the householder will have no progeny. In the case, then, of a pipal-tree a Hindu woman will do *pradakṣiṇā* of the tree a hundred and eight times or a number of times which is a multiple of this number, in order to obtain issue, yet the planting of the same tree near a house destroys the hope of issue to the occupant.

In the Konkaṇ when the ploughman has finished his task he erects a branch of the silk-cotton tree in one field, as its straight shoots will ensure a regular spacing in the seedlings of the rice crops. Trees with many thorns are avoided in selecting timber for building; to build a house with wood from a thorny tree means that the future of the household will be thorny. On the other hand, thorns are a protection, and thorny trees, therefore, very useful in averting evil. Thorns are used to avert evil-eye, to protect the grain on the threshing-floor from theft by spirits; a thorny tree is usually selected when the clothes of the sick are thrown on a tree. If a *Kātkarī* thinks a ghost is following him he cuts some thorny twigs and puts them under a stone by the side of a road, and believes he has pinned down the ghost. Thorns are planted or strewn secretly at the door of a tenant who will not leave a house when asked to do so, and then he has to choose between complying with the notice to quit or meeting an early death. In collecting the names of trees used for the *Marāṭhā devak* and for the *Hāḻgamba* of the Karnāṭak I was struck by the number of thorny trees used, and was given the explanation that these are chosen to symbolize the thorns of a married life, and by this representation to make the course of married life smoother for the bridal pair.

In Mallad tracts of the Karnāṭak when the central beam of a tiled roof is laid in its place it is worshipped with saffron and *akṣat* and to it is tied a clump of lavaḻasar (Aloe vera). This is supposed to grow for years without needing water and suggests, therefore, the growth of the family occupying the house. Durva grass is very hardy and continues to grow when cut freely; it is therefore placed on the head of a child on its birthday to procure it a long life. In some Brahmin families the child's birthday is celebrated every month for a year. The mother with her baby sits near the *Kadagol Khāmba*, a post some four and a half feet high to which the string of the churn is tied, and holding the child near the pillar says, 'Be tall like this pillar'. Then she places cotton on the child's head and says, 'Live long till your hair grows white like this cotton', and then, placing durva grass with its roots on the child's head, says, 'May your lineage grow like this durva grass'.

The presence of sap also determines the choice of many trees. In parts of Gujarāt the principal post of the marriage *maṇḍap* must be one with much sap, and so the gugal (Boswellia serata) is usually chosen. The central pole of the threshing-floor must be cut from a tree with a milky sap. The majority, again, of trees used to supply the *Hālgamba* have milky sap. Trees with milky juice are chosen for the transfer of illness by tying to them threads or other objects. Things with inherent or invoked *śakti* after use are thrown away under trees with milky juice instead of into water; examples of these are the *kankaṇ* of the bridal pair and the *hālgamba*-twigs.

The banyan, pipal, umbar and allied trees apparently produce fruit without blossom. They are the *Vanaspati* or lords of the forest, though this word has lost its precise meaning and is now generally applied to trees in general. Trees, again, that drop white powder, *śīr khiṣt*, are credited with miraculous power.

TREES AND THE DEAD

Trees in Muhammadan belief have tongues and always praise God. During *Muḥarram* shrubs are placed on tombs and leaves of mango and jamun trees to confer *barkat* on the dead. Trees are planted on graves with the same object; the pomegranate, the mendi and the bor being commonly used for this purpose. When visitors to a Muhammadan grave find trees on the grave they assume that funeral prayers have not been said, and so offer prayers for the dead. If the grave of a Muhammadan be shaded by a tree he will not be punished after death. The leaves of date-palms are sprinkled on graves whenever visited to bring the dead *barkat*.

Non-Brahmin Hindus also place trees on graves, usually the basari, the bel or the śamī. When a revered old person dies *Lingāyats* bury him in his own yard or field or in the compound of a *maṭh* and plant a bel-tree on his grave. This bel is worshipped regularly and even daily in the belief that the dead will watch the interests of the living.

Muhammadans think that the souls of the virtuous become parrots and other birds and sit on trees; it is an act of merit to pour water at the root of a tree. The Hindu thinks that on *Sarvapitṛī Amāvāsyā* the spirits of the dead swing on the tendrils of a banyan; at *Prayag* pilgrims perform a *Śrāddha* for the dead under a banyan and the annual *Śrāddha* that all Hindus perform was, it is supposed, originally always performed under a banyan. An aśvath (Ficus religiosa) is planted near a tank so that leaves may fall from it into the water; these fallen leaves are regarded as *piṇḍa* offered to his ancestors by the man who planted the tree. During the rainy season the *pitṛ* reside in trees, obtaining nourishment from nectar in the rain itself; in the rains, therefore, trees are not to be cut. During the dry months of *Chaitra* and *Vaiśākh* a vessel of water is hung to a pipal-tree for the *pitṛ* to drink, and water sprinkled at the root of a tree reaches the *pitṛ*.

If a bel, pipal, umbar or śamī grow spontaneously on a grave, it is supposed to be the dead returned. At Siddapur in the compound of a temple of Śankardev is a coconut tree which is supposed to have been fertilized by the spirit of a *Brahmacārī* buried there some ten years ago.

Lingāyats make *pradakṣiṇā* of a patri-tree (Aegle marmelos) to avert the attentions of a deceased partner's ghost; the marriage ceremony of a nim and of an aśvath after the thread ceremony of the latter is performed by Brahmins to avert the attentions of the ghost of a deceased wife.

MARRIAGES OF TREES

When a date-tree flowers *Koḻīs* and *Bhils* in the eastern parts of Gujarāt put up the tree a branch of a toddy-palm without which the blossom of the date-tree withers without giving fruit. When a mango-grove gives fruit for the first time, one of the mango-trees is married to an avali (Phyllanthus emblica) or other tree before the fruit is plucked or eaten. The marriage of a nim to a banyan or to an umbar is performed, but more common still is the marriage by Brahmin and non-Brahmin of the nim to an aśvath; the trees are planted and reared together and if one dies it is replaced. The thread ceremony of the aśvath is first performed and after this the marriage to the nim. The marriage of the nim, which is regarded as feminine, is performed with the main object of averting persecution by the ghost of a deceased wife. When the married trees are worshipped they prevent the death of future issues born to the worshipper.

In Sind Muhammadan children play at marrying tree to tree.

Another tree that every year is married by the Hindu is the tulsī (Ocymum sanctum). In every Hindu house there is a pot containing a tulsī-bush, the *Tulsīvṛndāvan*; this pot is always square with the tulsī in the centre and is aligned to the cardinal points. This *tulsīdev* guards the Hindu house from spirits. Every day women sprinkle water over it to obtain issue, and even a widow is allowed to worship it. All the sacred *tirths* are supposed to lie at its root, all the gods to live in its middle and all the *Veda* are at its summit. Even Yama, the god of the world of the dead, dare not look at a person on whose head there is a *tilak*-mark made with mud from the foot of the tulsī. Oaths are taken by the tulsī and if the oath be broken the tulsī dries up. At an eclipse tulsī-leaves are placed as a protection on milk, butter, food, books and clothes; mantras are written on tulsī-leaves; wreaths of its leaves are tied round the neck of the dying; its leaves are dropped on the dead or placed in the mouth of the dying. Tulsī worn in the ears or on the head not only averts evil, but prevents the telling of a lie. The *darśan* of the tulsī brings *śakti* and *puṇya*.

The *Tulsīvivāha* is performed on the twelfth bright day of the first half of *Kārttik*. In the centre of the *Tulsīvṛndāvan* near the plant is placed an image of Kṛṣṇa about three inches high. At the four corners are placed lamps fed with ghee; at each corner and in the centre are placed stalks of sugar-cane, and five garlands of flowers are placed at the corners and centre respectively, whilst five almonds, five dates and five supārī-nuts are placed in front of the image. Twigs of avali, dhatri, tamarind and bor are placed with the image. The tulsī may also be married to the *śāligrām*; this stone embodies the *śakti* of Viṣṇu and its marriage is really the same thing as a marriage with Kṛṣṇa.

Mythology does not give much assistance in interpreting this marriage of the tulsī-plant. The day of its celebration, the twelfth of *Kārttik*, follows immediately the close of the *Caturmās*, during which the gods are supposed to sleep, awaking on the twelfth of *Kārttik*. The *Tulsīvivāha* is thus a celebration of the awakening of the gods. On this same day the sun enters the constellation of *Tula*; the sun is known as Kṛṣṇa or black, and one interpretation of the tulsī marriage is that it is a symbolic representation of the union of the sun and of *Tulārāśi* which opens the day for the gods. During *Caturmās* Hindus do not perform marriages (Āṣaḍha sud. II to Kārttik sud. II) but await the annual marriage of the tulsī. Another explanation of the tulsī marriage is that the tulsī represents the green and living and Kṛṣṇa the dry. The marriage of the dry with the green would then be paralleled by the use of a dry and a wet twig to produce fire, and by the use of a *halh*, 'barren', or dead twig and a *hasar* or living twig at a marriage. On the other hand, there are Brahmins who deny that any marriage of the tulsī is made; they say that the god merely is worshipped below the tulsī and that this worship is only *Tulsīpūjā* and not *Tulsīvivāha*.

TREES AND OATHS

The Hindu takes an oath touching or holding certain trees such as audumbar, tulsī, banni or patri. The *Mahār* swears by grass; the *Kuruba* by the shadow of a tree. In Sind the Muhammadan takes an oath by the leaves of trees or standing on the top of a tree, in which case if a false oath is taken, the taker of the oath falls from the tree. The cutting of a tree adds to the danger in an oath taken by a Muhammadan.

In Chota Udaipur after a betrothal has been accomplished, the party of the boy, after leaving the house of the prospective bride, plant a twig of beri (Zizyphus jujuba) on the outskirts of the village to keep the girl's father to his word. When any contract has been settled *Bhils* stick in the ground branches which are thrown away if the contract be broken by either party.

THE WORSHIP OF TREES

Particular trees are the residence of gods who take up their abode therein for different periods. The tulsī, dhatri and atasi are the abode of Viṣṇu; the bel of Mahādev. The śamī and the nim are the abode of Lakṣmī and the latter also of Sarasvati and of Pārvatī. Dakṣaprajapati resides in the mango during the rainy season; the jambu-tree is frequented by Manmatha, the son of Śrī Kṛṣṇa. Independently the aśvath, the vat and the audumbar are not the abode of a god, but when their thread and marriage ceremonies have been performed they are visited by gods; the aśvath and nim by Viṣṇu, the audumbar by Brahma, Viṣṇu and Maheśvar. The ruī-tree is associated with the sun.

Though popular credence goes further and identifies the tree with the god, strictly speaking, all worship of trees is worship of the gods that frequent them or propitiation of the spirits that haunt them. Trees worshipped during the daytime are worshipped with a sixteen-fold worship, *Sodaśopacāra Pūjā*, which includes invocation of *śakti*, *āvāhan*, and the use of an *āsan*; when worshipped at night a shorter worship of five elements, *Pancopacāra pūjā*, is performed.

The vicinity of a tree is often chosen for the worship of deities. In Malnad tracts in the Karnāṭak to protect cattle from the ravages of wild beasts the tiger-god, Hulidev, is worshipped through the symbol of a stone placed near certain trees. On *Amāvāsyā Sarvapitṛī* stones called *pitṛ* are also placed below trees and worshipped.

CHAPTER XVI

THE WEATHER

ALTHOUGH Indian practice recognizes the unity of Nature, it does not predicate a cosmos following a fixed law; the source of all causation is man's own *śakti*, and his control of the *śakti* of other entities. This is very apparent in the ritual followed to control the weather.

In the Kolaba district in the precincts of the temple of Rameśvar at Cheul are supposed to be three *kuṇḍ* or pits; these pits enclose fire, wind and rain. The position of the three pits is in front of the gong of Rāmeśvar, Gaṇpati and Viṣṇu respectively, but the actual sites of the fire and wind pits have been lost to knowledge. In A.D. 1857 the rain-pit was discovered, but before this the pit had been opened in 1653 of the Hindu Śālivāhan era or A.D. 1731 by Srimant Sarkār Sahkojine Angre. In A.D. 1857 it was opened by Pingalnama Sanvascara on the seventh day of the bright half of *Śrāvan*. It was also opened in A.D. 1877 and in 1899.

The pit is four cubits in measurement all round. The person who digs the first sod or spadeful of earth in opening the pit is supposed to die within a year. The actual ceremony of bringing rain consists in the installation of the nine planets, with a sacrifice to propitiate them which requires a thousand oblations. Ghee is poured continuously into the sacrificial fire with sesamum; the *hom* entails a lac of offerings of sesamum and ghee and in A.D. 1731 cost five thousand rupees. Water is poured through a pierced pot on to the image of Rāmeśvar and then a silken garment dipped in ghee is thrown into the fire with coconuts and fruits. Finally an oblation of boiled rice is put in an open cart and with tom-toms taken in procession through the village, and thrown outside the village bounds. The opening of the pit is resorted to only when dire famine occurs, which along the coast of the Konkaṇ is a rare event.

A very large number of rites performed to bring rain are marked by the sprinkling of water in one way or another. In Gujarāt women and girls of low caste parade from door to door carrying on their heads a wooden plank on which are mounds of earth decorated with vegetation. As they proceed they call to the god of rain, Meghrājā, and other women drench them with water. In the Jambhughoda State a procession is formed in which a wooden camel or a wooden frog is carried to the accompaniment of tom-toms. All the women of the village gather to drench with water the wooden images, and the members of the procession. Among *Mārwāris* in Gujarāt girls carry a pot of water on their heads and are drenched as they pass through the town.

In the Satāra district five heaps of cowdung are placed on a board covered with turmeric and vermilion and this board is carried by a naked child through the village and beyond its bounds. As the child passes from door to door a woman of each house comes forth and pours water on the boy as he spins round. The *Citkoba*, as the board with its burden is called, is finally brought back to the village by a number of boys who go the round of the village collecting gifts of grain. Another Satara custom is for naked boys to carry round a board bearing an image of Mahādev or a live frog; these also are drenched by the villagers. Girls in the Sholapur district collect together in the evening and prepare a ball of earth and put this in a small pot, erecting in it a stalk of grass. This *Cendkoba* they carry from house to house singing '*Bhunde bhunde paus de*', 'Bhunde, give us rain'.

The carrying of some symbol suggestive of rain or the fertility that comes with rain and the drenching of the bearers, again suggesting a fall of rain, are features of similar rites in Khandesh, the Deccan and the Karnāṭak. *Bhils* of the Navapur Peta make an image of earth adorned with green plantain-leaves and flowers and place on a board, which an unmarried girl carries through the village, accompanied by other women singing rain songs and praying for rain. At each house she passes she receives grain and is drenched. *Pavra*, *Naira* and *Nahal Bhils* perform *Varhatya*. Boys and girls below nine years of age go from house to house on four successive nights, accompanied by men bearing torches which simulate lightning. The girls who are drenched at each house sing:

'*Dondya Dondya pāṇī de*
Sāḻ dāḻ pīkne de
Juvār bājrī pīkne de.'

'Dondhya, Dondhya, give rain.
Make rice and pulse grow.
Make jvārī and *bājrī* grow.'

Tadvi Bhils send a boy round the village bearing a pot of water with leaves of the nim-tree tied round his head ; a band of dancers accompanies him. *Dublas* in West Khandesh dance from house to house with green branches when rain withholds and are drenched by the householders.

The Karnāṭak has many customs of similar nature. Pigeons are drenched with water and set free. *Ambigers* and *Kurubas* send out children of both sexes carrying pots to which a live frog is tied (*guraci*). *Talwār* and *Korava* girls carry from house to house a brass plate on which a ball of cowdung is placed with durva grass stuck in it ; sometimes this cowdung, called *Gorji*, is made conical and ornamented with the hair of a bullock as is the *Būdā* on the threshing-floor. Water is poured over the girls as they go about singing:

'*Gorji Gorji yalyādi bande*
hallā kollā ulyaḍi bande.'

Gorji is also the name given to the girl and the song runs:

'Gipsy, whence after playing have you come ?
After rolling through brooks and dales you come ? '

Another variant of this rite is for the girl to carry a large frog on the heap of cowdung, covered with the shell of a nut. The girl's hair is left dishevelled. An alternative practice is for a man to go in silence from house to house with a water-pot to collect water ; whenever any one gives him water he waits till the donor has turned his back and then dashes the water against the threshold of his house. In the months of *Jyeṣṭha*, *Āṣāḍha*, *Śrāvan* and *Bhādrapad*, trees like the pipal are given a bath, *mahā mahā abhi ṣek* ; it is essential that the water should reach the sea, so it is made to flow into a river or ditch and heavy rain is supposed to fall when it reaches the sea.

In the Deccan *Māng* boys carry a plank on their heads and call out:

'*Pāus pāṇī paḍu dyā. Ābādāni hou dyā.*
Ambar umbar pīku dyā. Solā khanḍyā viku dyā.'

'May we have ample rain and prosperity ;
May the sky and umbar-tree yield good harvest ;
May corn be sold at sixteen khandis.'

Other rain songs are as follows. The first song is sung by *Bhils* in Khandesh and also by *Kātkarīs* in the Konkaṇ, who to bring rain ascend a hill and dance with branches of trees.

'*Dhondya Dhondya, pāṇī de sāy māy pīku de*
yere yere pāvasa tulā deu paisā
paisā paḍalā khoṭā pāus ālā moṭ' ī
pāṇī āyā jangalme ardhi roṭi bagalme.'

'Dhondya, give rain. Make blossom fruit and flower.
Come, rain, come. I will give you a pice.
The pice has become a false coin and great rain has come.
Water has come in the jungle. In my arm is half a loaf.'

'*pāus pāṇī ābādānī abhāḻ bharale pānyane*
khaḻe bharale dāṇyāne yere pavasa tulā deto
paisā paisā jhala khoṭā pāus jhala moṭhī.'

Abundance of rain gives us prosperity. A sky full of clouds,
A threshing-floor full of grain. Come, ye rains. I will give you
A pice. The pice has become a false coin and rains have come in plenty.'

In the Panch Mahāls *Bhil* boys and girls parade the streets with branches of khukra or paḻas and dash the branches against the doors of houses. *Koravas* imitate thunder by beating drums. *Dhangars* wave black blankets in the breeze to imitate the dark rain-clouds. In parts of the Dharwar district when there is a long break in the rain, *Hanabars* carry their deities to a hill in a palanquin. Shepherds accompany them. The villagers stand in a row holding their black blankets in their hands and the shepherds passing along the line jerk up the blankets and call up the rain with cries of '*Mali ba mali ba*', 'Come, rain'. Hills so associated with the bringing of rain are called 'water-hills', *Niragudda*, one example of which is at Kasba Artal in the Bankapur taluka. *Dhor Koḻīs* to bring rain make a long-drawn sound like a bird, *doho*, associated with rain and pray to the sun and moon. In the Sakri taluka a common practice is to tie a live frog by its legs to a tree; the cries of the frog are supposed to bring rain. In Gujarāt and in the Konkaṇ Muhammadans parade the streets with flags and banners praying loudly; the fluttering of the flags, like that of the dishevelled hair of the girls who carry the *Guraci*, the *Gorji* or the *Cendkoba*, raises the wind which is the necessary prelude to rain.

In many of these rites some one is liberally drenched with water. The person drenched not infrequently spins round as the water is thrown upon him, and this in the direction that it is hoped the rain will follow. This drenching, besides imitating the fall of rain, has in some cases the object of eliciting abuse or curses. In the Panch Mahāls a person of some importance is followed quietly and, when possible, is drenched with water ; in another district filthy water or even ordure is thrown, to make sure of obtaining a curse in return. Curses and abuse bring *barkat.*

Persons who are credited with an evil eye deliberately enter a stall of others where cattle are being milked or a house where the occupants are dining, knowing that because evil-eye is most dangerous to milk and particularly baneful during the taking of a meal, they are sure to be cursed. From the curses they receive they hope to derive a cure for their own evil-eye, and with the same hope the hapless possessor of an evil eye picks quarrels with persons of choleric temper. Similarly, a curse may mollify the effects of an evil-eye. By teasing or enraging a man who inflicts evil-eye the power of his eye is rendered less potent.

In Kanara the man who is the last to finish reaping is pricked with thorns and other sharp things to make him angry, for the more he curses, the greater will be the yield of the crops. There are saints in Sind called *majzub* who are teased to elicit their curses. In Ahmednagar there is a saint whose good words actually bring evil but who confers *barkat* when he curses or beats a suppliant. The priest who officiates at a Hindu marriage is often maltreated to make him angry. *Gondaligirs* throw *akṣat* into his eyes or prick him ; *Lamānis* prick their priest with needles ; *Arers* insert twigs of mango stealthily in his turban, or tie stones to his hair while he is occupied in uttering mantras. Among *Deśastha Brahmins* the bridegroom's mother is taken in procession at the close of her son's marriage. She is seated in a chair or on a wooden stool called *cauk* ; she is adorned with a garland of onions and treated as a mock queen. She is given abusive epithets ; she is called *Caukrāṇī* or the queen who halts and sits on a cauk at important cross-roads only to vomit and evacuate. To imitate her evacuations leavings of food mixed in coloured water are thrown before and behind her whenever she halts in procession. A similar treatment is given by the bridegroom's party to the bride's mother and by this both families are supposed to derive *barkat* and immunity from illness.

When the sun enters the *Kanyarāśi* the influence of the moon is baneful and particularly so during the first four days after the sun's entry into this *rāśi.* On Bhādrapad sud. 4, *Gaṇesa Caturthī,* it is dangerous to see the moon ; even the wild boars hide their heads so as not to see the moon. On this day many things are done by the Hindu to provoke his neighbours to curse ; manure and other filthy things are thrown at the doors of others and fruit-trees are pillaged. A very close parallel to this practice is that followed in Kanara on *Narak Caturdaśī* which falls on the fourteenth of the second half of *Āśvin.* On the night previous to this day petty thefts are committed from neighbours and ordure is thrown into their verandahs so that when the day breaks they may curse and confer *barkat* by their curses.

To cure a sick child its excrement is thrown on the roofs of others to force a curse which will cure the child. At *Hoḻī* indecent marks are made on the clothes of passers-by and *vokli* or red-coloured water is freely thrown about with the object of annoying and winning *barkat* through a curse.

In the Sakri taluka of West Khandesh among *Bhils, Mavchis* and *Konkanis,* five unmarried girls go by night naked to the house of a *Mahār* and steal a water-pot, *ghagar.* This pot is then buried in a dungheap and rain is sure to come if the *Mahār* remain ignorant of the place where it is buried, or of the identity of the person who stole it. If rain does not fall the pot remains buried, but if rain falls the *Mahār* is told where he can find the pot and it is returned to him filled with grain. *Tadvi Bhils* in the Satpura range steal combustible material from others and burn it to bring rain. A common Hindu practice is to steal an image of Gaṇpati from another and break open its stomach in a field.

This thieving naturally elicits a curse which brings *barkat,* but another idea underlies a practice which is adopted on many an occasion other than those on which attempts are made to control the weather. When a gift is made it is the donor and not the recipient who acquires *barkat.* A stolen article, on the other hand, does not deprive the taker of the *barkat* that it may bring. In the celebration of *Hoḻī* the fuel for the fire is stolen ; at the festival of *Kollappa* held at Hampi the fuel for the pyre is also stolen. On *Gaṇesa Caturthī* and in Kanara on *Narak Caturdaśī* petty thefts are committed from the gardens of others. To obtain issue childless women on *Gaṇesa Caturthī* steal images of Gaṇpati ; images of Basavanna are stolen from temples or clothing from the images. During a marriage thefts are often committed by one party to the marriage and his family, from the family of the other party. Flowers voluntarily given cannot be used in worship and these are stolen to ensure that the full benefit of the worship performed goes to the worshipper. This association of *barkat* with a stolen article is confined to the Hindu ; the Muhammadan has no parallel concept.

The friendship which is supposed to exist between milk and water suggests the sprinkling of milk as a bait to bring rain. In Khandesh milk is sprinkled at the entrance to a well. Another custom is to carry a pot of milk along the village boundary, allowing the milk to fall through a hole in the pot.

Ceremonial weeping or lamentation acts as a rain-charm. In Khandesh a sleeping man is carried by night through the village to the accompaniment of loud lamentations and shouts of '*Rām bolo bhai Rām*'. In the Karnāṭak plays full of pathos are acted to bring rain through the tears of the audience. One such play is the story of a king who went to look for a bride for his son *Kumār Rām* but himself fell in love with the girl he had selected. Whilst the king was hunting the son happened to go near the palace to search for a ball encrusted with pearls that he had lost, and the queen, seeing him and smitten with love, attempted to seduce him but in vain. When the king returned the disappointed queen told him that his son had attempted to molest her, and unless executed would encompass the death of the king. The king thereupon ordered the boy to be beheaded and his head to be hung in front of the queen's chamber. A minister, however, approached the executioner and substituted another boy with similar features and sent the prince to a distant kingdom. After some time the queen was stricken with remorse and the king who had loved his son went mad. The minister then brings back the prince, the king recovers and the queen becomes an ascetic. The pathos of the story which is supposed to bring rain reaches its climax when the prince is saying good-bye to his young wife whom he is leaving on the point of having a child.

In the up-Ghāṭ districts of the Karnāṭak there is a funeral of *Jokumār* which is supposed to bring *barkat* to the standing crops and also to bring rain. *Jokumār*, 'Hail young boy', is the image of a boy with a face painted black, the crown of his head white and his forehead red. It is seated in a basket and covered with nim-leaves breast high, leaving its face and hands exposed. This boy is supposed to have been born on the eighth night of *Bhādrapad* in the house of a *Barker* between 8 and 10 p.m.. On the next day a feast is held in honour of the birth and for the next six days *Kabbaligar* women take the image round the village from house to house. In these rounds boys and girls dance round the carried image and a woman from each house pours water over the image. *Jokumār ālā pāus ālā*, 'Jokumār has come ; rain has come', is the burden of the cries. Rain is expected when a hundred pots of water have been poured on the image. As the image is borne along the villagers give to the bearers millet for the image and the women bearers in return give black paint, nim-leaves and boiled flour of millet. This black paint, made from burnt plantain-leaves and sweet-oil, is smeared on the face of the image, and any paint that remains over is, with the millet preparation and the nim leaves, buried in the fields among the standing crops to bring *barkat*.

On the full-moon day the parading of the image ceases ; *Barkers* worship the image outside their houses and then *Holers* come and warn the people that *Jokumār* will die that night and that it is dangerous to pass or meet those who will carry the corpse. The *Holers* then take the image to the quarters of the *Mahārs* where a knife is put to its throat in punishment for misbehaviour with women, and it is buried outside the village under the stones used by washermen for beating their clothes. This is done at midnight, as any one seeing the *Holers* returning after doing this will die in three days.

The following morning the washermen discover the image and bury it properly and with their womenfolk observe mourning for three days, during which they abstain from their ordinary work. On the fourth day they take a bath of purification and hold a feast. In the actual funeral no woman can take part. On the same day after the completion of the mourning food is offered to the buried image, and this is thrown later on the boundaries of the fields to bring *barkat* to the crops.

Personal sacrifice is not unnaturally expected to bring its return. The opening of the rain-pit at *Cheul* entails the death of the man who is the first to assist in its opening. In the Panch Mahāls the village *badva* or necromancer observes a fast and sings songs as he sits in the middle of a stream from which he does not rise till the water rises and covers his head. He may also go to the top of a hill and remain there till there is a deluge of rain. A person again of reputed sanctity is asked to sit in an old abandoned temple outside the village bounds and remain without food till rain falls. In the Belgaum district at Gurlhosur there is one *Kaggappa Kurab* whose austerities are supposed to bring rain within two or three days. In Gujarāt to stop rain a man with no social ties and with no children weighs water five times against a ten-pound weight and then throws the water back again into a river. As it is a sin to weigh water the man doing this sacrifices all hope of ever having issue.

The god of rain is worshipped under many names by different communities. The image of Mahādev is, in his shrine, immersed until completely covered. The image of Ganpati is also immersed. The outlet to his shrine is closed and *abhiṣek* is performed until the image is quite covered with water. The water is then allowed to pass to the fields through pipes made from the sheath or covering of plantains, and rain is expected as soon as the water reaches the fields. This immersion of images is unaccompanied by worship or offerings, and would seem to be a combination of the coercion of 'power' and of homœopathic magic. *Mavchi* and *Katone Bhils* bury an image of Maruti in mud and cowdung and pass night and day dancing and singing. In Satara a vigil is kept without a break for seven or twenty-one days, each celebrant being relieved after two or three hours, and a continuous prayer is maintained which is not broken even at night. This practice is called *Satpa* and implies a coercion of the god addressed. In the Kumta taluka to bring rain the image of Narsinh is smeared with a paste made from green chillies.

The cursing of a god to obtain the grant of a request is resorted to on many occasions. If a child falls ill an image is made from the worn-out clothes of the child and placed in an earthen plate on which ashes from a potter's kiln are sprinkled. This image is called *Nanjina Jvaradammā* (Kan.) and represents the dame who causes illness. She is then abused by old widows and old women who call: 'You are a woman yet you have no shame. How is it that you do not blush to come to a house where no respect is shown you. You are a woman with issue, yet you plague and tyrannize over infants.' This said, the image is beaten with a whip and finally thrown away at the village boundary. Another custom of the Karnāṭak on the repeated death of children at an early age is to abuse the goddess *Sheṭigemmā* on the fourth day after the birth of a child. Old widows again hurl their abuse saying, 'You have taken the life of so many babies; you call yourself a goddess yet you do not blush to kill infants. By killing our babies you kill your own. Children are children whether they be ours or yours. Are you not ashamed of child murder?' To cure pneumonia *Gurammā* is cursed; to cure smallpox *Gul̲l̲ammā*; to cure stiff joints, *Guddammā*; to cure fits, *Sheṭigemmā*, and to cure cholera, *Durgammā*. *Mahārs* on New Year's Day curse their goddess *Gal̲idurgamma* so that she may not send them disease during the year. *Śikārīs* curse stones and trees which they regard as *van devatā*, 'deities of the jungle', if they fail to get good sport. During the fair of *Dyamava* a special class called *Asadaru* of *Madigars* is set apart to abuse the goddess. In the same way to bring rain the god *Indra* is cursed and a curse is embodied in the mantras used in his worship.

Noise is a feature of a large number of practices adopted to bring rain. Loud cries; the noise of tom-toms mark processions. Besides this, the prayers uttered are usually said very loudly.

Bhajan or uninterrupted prayer for a long period by a succession of worshippers is performed in a roaring voice. The Muhammadan utters his prayers for rain, *barani nimaz,* loudly in congregation, and when he makes a procession with flags calls out his prayers in a loud voice.

Dancing is an equally marked feature of these rain-producing rites; dancing with or without some carried object which suggests some aspect of a rainstorm. Of the dancing of girls and boys carrying planks bearing some such object I have already given several examples. In the Karnāṭak when the sky is overcast children, mainly girls, waltz with dishevelled hair, imitating a rain-storm, and singing:

'*kāḻe māḻe kappat māḻe*
suṇṇā koḍateni suriyale maḻiye
baṇṇā koḍateni bārale maḻiye
basari giḍadag Basappa kuntān suriyale maḻiye'

Of this stanza the first line is an address to rain; the second, roughly translated, is 'Pour down in torrents, I will give you lime'. The next line is 'Come down, I will give you colour' and the fourth, 'Pour down in torrents for Basappa is now sitting in the grove of basari trees'.

In a very large number of these rites the performers are naked. Now nakedness is to be avoided in rites strictly religious. The worshipper must not be naked. Among Brahmins he must tuck the end of his *dhotar* into his waist behind (*Kaccheda kodu*) or is considered naked and unfit to worship a deity. Young children often wear but a string round the waist (*uḍadāra*) and until they take their thread ceremony they are considered clothed by this string, but without it cannot touch a sacred image. As soon as a child is born it is customary for Hindus to tie a girdle string round its waist; this string is worn even by adults who wear *dhotars* and those who do not wear one are called *muḍadār*, 'ungodly', a word which is used by some Muhammadans to indicate something unfit for use or not dedicated to God. Besides the requirement that the person worshipping must be clothed, the thing worshipped must also not be naked. When trees such as the pipal, banyan, and audumbar are worshipped a thread is tied round the tree to remove its nakedness; then a garland of cotton is offered as clothing (*āher*) which in Marāṭhī is called *sutputaḻyā*. In the same way when the *śakti* of Gaṇpatī is invoked into a betel-nut, when that of Varuṇa is invoked into a *kalaśa* at *Udakśānti*, or that of Nārāyaṇ into the *kalaśa* of Satyanārāyaṇ, the symbols are first invested with a cotton thread. The twigs and leaves used for invocation of the *manṭapadevatā* at a marriage or at other ceremonies are similarly invested with a thread. During a *Śrāddha* ceremony a piece of thread is placed as an offering of cloth on the *piṇḍa* offered to the *pitṛ*. *Akṣat*, again, is often thrown on an object worshipped as a substitute for clothes; it is, for example, thrown on sheaves of crops standing in the fields with the words, '*Vastra samarpayāmī*', 'I offer clothes'.

If, however, in religious rites nakedness is avoided as destructive of *barkat* it is a very marked feature of rites that are magical or are connected with the control of spirits. A mantrik reciting mantras to get control of spirits must be naked during his recitation and cannot wear even his girdle string. If he be a Brahmin he must divest himself also of his sacred thread, and if a *Lingāyat* of his linga. Medicinal herbs or herbs through whose inherent power it is hoped to effect a cure are collected in a naked state. A man learning charms stands naked in water during an eclipse. When a child is suffering from *muḍadoṣ* it is given the urine of a cow, but both the child and the person administering the urine must be naked. The nudity, therefore, that characterizes many rites practised to bring rain is not peculiar to these rites alone but distinguishes them from ritual that is essentially religious.

Communal feasting is characteristic of most of these rites. When objects are carried round the village by children a band of other children goes from house to house collecting grain which is later consumed at a caste feast. There is also a more direct recognition of corporate interest in the general picnicking that takes place when rain withholds. *Bhil* women in the Panch Mahāls are not allowed when rain fails to prepare any meal in their house; *Bhils* and *Konkanis* in Khandesh take their meals in the fields (*ujalani*); in Gujarāt Muhammadans and Hindus picnic outside the boundaries of their villages. In Khandesh when clouds appear the villagers flock *en masse* beyond the village bounds where curds and rice are distributed. Village feasts are held near temples, near rivers and on high hills. A custom of the Karnāṭak is to collect all the villagers by beat of drum and to form a procession with a palanquin bearing the image of Nandī. The image is borne to a water-course where a rock is worshipped and a general feast is held (*parva*). On their way home the party is supposed to meet with torrential rain.

In Sind and in parts of the Deccan the plough is washed to bring rain. A plough, however, is more commonly used to stop rain. With this object *Thakurs* burn an old and useless plough. In the Panch Mahāls a man born in an auspicious month is bathed and then, naked, strikes the share of a plough on an anthill.

Standing still in the rain and getting drenched is supposed in the Karnāṭak to lead to a greater fall of rain. *Bhils* take a pot of curds to a place where they see the rain actually falling in the distance and there allow themselves to be drenched and try to lead the rain on to their village. *Marāṭhās* go to the boundary of their village when they see clouds gather, with an empty palanquin and receive the rain formally by blowing a horn.

Leprosy in India is concealed as far as possible and a leper's body is often buried without its contagion being known. This burial is supposed to drive away the rain clouds, so when rain fails relatives of any buried leper go to his grave with a lamp in an earthen dish which they invert in the grave and in its flame burn a picture or drawing of the leper. This is supposed to be equivalent to a cremation of the body, though religious injunction forbids cremation and prescribes for the body of a leper throwing into water or burial.

In Khandesh on the failure of rain dead trees, if any, standing in the village site are cut down. In the Karnāṭak obscene plays are performed by *Killikyats* with dummy figures. In Kanara an image of the supposed descendant, *Rasyasringa*, of a family which according to the *Purāṇa* possessed a diamond which always ensured its possessor timely rains, is installed and worshipped for seven days. Other districts have families credited with the power of bringing rain by their prayers, as, for example, the families of *Dhaguji* and *Meghuji* in the Satāra district.

In Sind when rain is wanted the whole village in congregation performs *barani nimaz* in a loud voice. For three days the Prophet is invoked and charity is given to children and to the poor. The Koran and other sacred books are carried in procession with flying flags. After the *nimaz* the preacher changes his mantle from the right shoulder to the left and back again,[1] with the object of bringing rain as quickly as the change of the mantle's position is made. This action is called *istisqā*. The whole ceremony consists of two *rek'āt* or ordinary forms of prayer, two sermons and one *du'ā* or supplication. In the prayer the ordinary formula is changed and in lieu of the words '*Allahu akbar*', 'God is most great', '*istagfir Allah*' is said, 'I implore the forgiveness of God'.

The Muhammadan also walks in procession to the shrines of his saints and there recites portions of the Koran and sacrifices

[1] In the Karnāṭak when a man sets out on a journey his women-folk at home reverse their bodices, so that he will return quickly.

sheep and goats. In procession he must have his feet bare and his head uncovered.

In the stopping of rain the natural antagonism between water and fire suggests certain measures. In the Deccan a naked woman carries fire into the rain; in Sholapur a naked man carries a lighted torch into the rain. *Bhils* and *Marāṭhās* throw live coal or embers out of the house into the rain. In Kanara burning cinders are thrown on the roof of another by a naked person; water-carriers who would lose business if rain were continuous are supposed to do this frequently. In the Karnāṭak torches are thrown high into the sky and also stones made hot in a fire.

Salt attracts moisture and can therefore be used to stop rain. In the Panch Mahāls one custom is for a naked man to bury a coconut in salt. *Kātkarīs* in the Konkaṇ place salt in an earthen jar or a copper pot and cover with a piece of paper or an aloe-leaf, and then invert this pot in a plate of water and place over a stove. The covering of the pot must be tied by an unmarried virgin.

An unmarried girl in the Karnāṭak throws soil into the rain. A practice of the Ron taluka is to put an old shoe in an earthen plate and, spinning it, to throw it into the falling rain.

A doll is frequently used to stop a fall of rain. *Bhils* tie up a doll upside-down in the rain. *Bhils* and *Mavchis* of the Sakri taluka West Khandesh make a black bull stand on an anthill and then remove the earth trodden by the bull and from this fashion two dolls. These dolls are buried close together in the anthill from which the earth was taken. Then loin-cloths are torn in shreds and thrown away and, naked, the celebrants dance and return home. Within a fortnight from the beginning of sowing operations the dolls must be unearthed. In the Satara district a doll of rags is hung on the door-frame head downwards and beaten with shoes every time an inmate of the house goes out or comes in.

Many a rite to stop rain is performed at a river. Men and women in Gujarāt proceed in procession to the noise of tom-toms to a river or tank. Here they float on the water an earthen pot containing curds. The pot is covered with a red cloth and garlands of flowers are tied to it and as it floats away rice is thrown at it. Sometimes along with the pot is floated a lamp made of large leaves burning ghee as oil. If the pot or the lamp continues its course down the river the rain will cease, but if it comes ashore anywhere the rain will continue. One singular feature of this rite is that the headman of the village who accompanies the procession must wear a woman's bracelet of ivory or celluloid and on his head the red garment of a woman. In the Panch Mahāls curds, coconut and vermilion are put into the earthen pot, taken to the river, and the headman cuts his little finger and lets blood drip therefrom into the river. Among *Bhils* of the Navapur Peta an unmarried man brings an earthen pot filled with curds and after a bath carries it to a river; he then throws the pot into the river with eyes turned away and returns home without looking back. Five married women in the Karnāṭak offer a river in flood the bodice-cloth of a woman; chaste married women or prostitutes are also taken in procession to a river and there asked to take water three times from the river in a winnowing-fan and throw away. Before she does this the chaste married woman says, 'Oh goddess, abate if you think me chaste'; the prostitute on her part says, 'I am full of sin; heed not the sin and abate'. Married women having husbands alive also wave a winnowing-fan in the air to drive away the rain clouds.

Prognostication of the monsoon is regularly made. Elsewhere in this work details have been given of the prognostication made by performing the rite of *Ankurāropaṇ*, and also made during the celebration of *Holī*. In the Deccan a rope some two inches thick is made from the unravelled thread of two turbans and tied at one end to a temple of Mahādev and at the other to a pole sixty feet away. If this rope breaks the monsoon will fail. Another practice is to fill two pots with water in the cold weather and place them aside and to fear the worst if the water dries up. When rain seems to be failing rice is spread on the ground in the Karnāṭak and on this is placed a pot of water. Then *suvāsinīs* place both their palms on the pot and if rain is coming the pot spins, but if no rain is coming remains unmoved.

Ten only of the twenty-seven constellations are supposed to bring rain, and a popular saying is, 'Subtract ten from twenty-seven, what remains? Nothing', '*Satavis me das gayeto kya rahe? Matti*'.

Scattered clouds of smoky colour forming in a clear sky are the fœtus of the monsoon rain, *garbha*. If these are observed in the second fortnight of *Bhādrapad* the outcome can be judged in the second fortnight of *Jyeṣṭha*, a wind blowing east to west will bring good rain, a wind in the reverse direction means no rain. If these clouds are observed in *Āśvin* the effect follows in *Āṣādha*, but if in this month a cloud assumes the form of a cat, the cat will devour the foetus and there will be no rain. If the *garbha* are seen in the month of *Kārttik* the rain fœtus will deliver rain in *Śrāvaṇ* if the wind blow towards the south and the cat-like cloud can do no harm. Should the rain fœtus be observed in *Mārgaśīrṣa* the delivery occurs in *Bhādrapad*; should it be seen in *Pauṣa* the fœtus is supposed to have miscarried owing to excessive heat and no delivery is expected in the monsoon month of *Āśvin*. In the month of *Māgh* the fœtus is not observed, but gathering clouds bring rain in the autumn.

On the fifth of the bright half of *Chaitra* a cart-like formation of stars is watched. If the moon is in front of these stars rain will be heavy but poor if the moon be behind, for the moon is considered to be a trader; if he precedes the cart he is hurrying on the cartman in anticipation of his gains; if he be behind he is merely anxious to protect the cart. On the third of the bright half of *Vaiśākh* there appears a cluster of stars in the form of a scythe. If the moon passes through the handle there will be no occasion to use the scythe, that is there will be no harvest; if the moon passes through the centre of the cluster the year will be an ordinary one, but one of great plenty if the moon passes by the point of the scythe.

Prognostications from the blossoming of trees or from the actions of animals are not unnaturally very common. If the thorny tree kanthar bears a multitude of black berries there will be heavy rain; the paddy crop will be a rich one if the *khakhar* bears heavy pods. Crows building their nests in the middle of trees indicate their fear of heavy rain; if they build on the exposed tops of trees rain will fail. If the buds of the nim-tree wither or if dogs sleep flat on the ground in summer rain will be scanty. The loud and sustained barking or the long-drawn howl of a dog on a dunghill or on the roof of a house in the rainy season is presage of heavy rain. If doves sing or if sparrows sprinkle themselves with dust, rain can be expected.

Throughout the year certain acts must be avoided or the monsoon months will not bring rain. In Sind if the bridal pair speak at moments when silence is enjoined there will be drought. Stepping over grain reserved for seed or sitting on a grain measure provokes the resentment of *śakti* and leads to drought. When the rain clouds gather again certain acts must be avoided. Fire must not be taken out of doors or the rain will vanish; on Fridays and on Saturdays there must be no grinding which as a destructive act will destroy the prospects of rain, and in the Deccan the *Marāṭhā* will not kill a sheep.

Ceremonies to bring or stop rain emphasize the lingering corporateness of the Indian village. In the Deccan any one who does not reside in the village is called *sivdhada*, 'beyond the boundary'.

23

The village is the enclave of the village god ; so long as the *devak* is installed at a marriage the bridal pair cannot go beyond the village boundary. *Sīmāntapūjā* is the reception of the bridegroom at the boundary of the village. In agricultural rites the deity of the village boundary is worshipped ; in the Karnāṭak when the blood of *Durgā's* buffalo is sprinkled on rice, famine follows if the rice be taken by any one beyond the village boundary. When epidemics rage the village is again the unit and scapegoats are abandoned at the boundary ; spirits are driven across the boundary and the practice of *Utāra* is sometimes spoken of as the 'driving across the boundary' ; along the village boundary, too, in time of epidemic grain is scattered or milk and ghee are sprinkled. If a hyæna be killed the body must be buried at the entrance to the village or all the *barkat* of the village will pass to another village.

The life of India is divided into compartments. There is the compartment of the family very prominent in the ritual of the threshing-floor ; there is the seclusion of the individual most marked in the religious ritual of Hinduism and in magic practices ; there is again the unity of the village that characterizes measures taken in the face of calamities such as epidemics, drought and flood and to some extent the practices of agricultural ritual.

CHAPTER XVII

THE RITUAL OF AGRICULTURE

PLOUGHING

IN Khandesh, ploughing is not done on Monday as this day is sacred to *Śiva* and bullocks are his vehicle. The last day of the month, Saturdays, Sundays and Tuesdays, are also in some places avoided. Some ploughing is done on *Agoṭ* or *Guḍhīpādvā*, the first day of *Chaitra* and the Hindu New Year's Day. In the Karnāṭak ploughing is avoided on the eighth day of the lunar fortnight for fear that if used the bullocks will go lame, and the avoidance of ploughing on an *Amāvāsyā* is general. The Muhammadan in Sind begins his ploughing on an auspicious day chosen by a Mullah, Maulvi or Pandit, though this ploughing may only be nominal. In Chota Udaipur, Thursday, Friday and Monday are considered auspicious days; whilst in Kanara Saturday and Wednesday are good days to begin ploughing.

Ploughing is often begun before sunrise so that no one will talk to the ploughman as he initiates this important work. It must be done in a certain direction. On the first day of ploughing it can never be done facing south ; in Sind the usual rule is to plough in the direction of the north or the west ; in the Deccan it is habitual to plough towards the east ; in the Karnāṭak the north is the direction in which the first ploughing should be done. In West Khandesh it is forbidden to plough in an easterly direction on a Monday or a Thursday, towards the west on Sundays or Fridays, towards the north on Tuesdays and Wednesdays, and on Thursday or on the first day of ploughing towards the south.

The ploughman in the Deccan and in parts of the Karnāṭak must be a man of good character, and it is not uncommon to find several landholders employing the same man, because of his repute for good living, to begin the ploughing of their fields. He must remain celibate so long as he has to return to the field to plough ; he must take a bath before going to the field or his plough will break and his cattle will be injured. A belief in the Karnāṭak is that his bathing also prevents the possibility of a drought. When the ploughman has left his house to go to the field he must not turn back even if called by his wife, according to Muhammadan belief, but in the Deccan a Hindu cultivator will turn back if called by his wife, for she is to him *Lakṣmī* or *Gṛhlakṣmī*. In Sind if he be called back he must be approached from the front; he may then return home, sit there awhile and start out to his work afresh. He is not allowed to shave till the work of ploughing is complete. A man who has ridden an elephant or a *Telī* whose profession is that of crushing oil-seed would not be employed as a ploughman.

If when ploughing a yoked bullock suddenly sits down and rises again at once it is a forecast of early rain. If the yoke of the oxen breaks the farmer will die, and so in ploughing a new yoke is necessary.

In Sind, Kanara, the Deccan and in other parts it is considered bad to take earth of one field by the foot or by the plough to another field, for every atom has its own inherent power and such transfer of earth may effect evil. In Khandesh the plough is frequently washed before use; in the Deccan the washing of the plough is forbidden, but it is distinctly the older generation that respects this prohibition. In the Konkaṇ there are talukas like that of Karjat where the plough is washed after use, but other talukas like the Pen taluka where this is forbidden as destructive of *barkat*. If the plough be washed in Kanara it must not be used again the same day, for it is assumed that the washing has lulled to rest the power inherent in the plough so that it cannot be used for some time. This is another way of saying that the washing washes away *barkat*. A guest coming to the threshing-floor brings *barkat*, but he must not wash his feet or the *barkat* will be lost; those who are threshing refrain from washing till the threshing work is complete. In the Karnāṭak bathing is forbidden before the threshing or the measuring of grain is finished and so also is the washing of clothes. In the Ahmednagar district and again in the Shikarpur sub-division of the Sukkur district of Sind I found instances of the plough being deliberately washed to bring rain.

The plough must never be left in the field pointing towards the south, and the bullocks when unyoked must be left with their heads towards the north or east.

It is a custom of the Karnāṭak to rub the ploughshare with a piece of gold that the crop may grow golden. That the crop may be vigorous and strong the bullocks must not be castrated; that the grain itself may be white the bullocks should be white and the ploughman should wear a white head-dress. If black bullocks are used the millet crop will suffer from smut. To ensure that the crop drives its roots deep into the earth the bullocks used should have long hairy tails. The first five furrows ploughed are of great importance. They must be straight and unbroken and no stopping of work should be made until they are complete. Of these five furrows the first, third and the fifth, which naturally run northward as ploughing is begun in that direction, are believed in the Karnāṭak to bring respectively success, increase of wealth and abundance of grain.

In Sind with some exceptions the prevailing custom is to use bullocks of uneven number; in the Deccan, on the other hand, their number must be even. In threshing, however, the grain on the threshing-floor, even in the Deccan, three bullocks are often used.

Amongst *Ko̱līs* and *Bhils* there are rites that evidence a fear of spirits of the ground disturbed by the plough. When a new plough comes from the carpenter *Rathwa Ko̱līs* go to a *bhava* or exorcist and obtain from him a charmed thread which is tied to the plough to avert the spirits of the ground and prevent the breaking of the plough. When ploughing, *Dharala, Baria,* and *Palia Ko̱līs* sprinkle kunku on the ground and cover it with rice and pice, and then light a fire, in which they throw ghee and before which they break a coconut. The foreheads of the bullocks are then anointed with turmeric and a red thread is tied to the right hand of the ploughman, the right horns of the bullocks, and to the end of the plough. *Rathwa, Dhanka Ko̱līs* and *Bhils* sprinkle the blood of a goat or fowl on the ground and on the plough and the horns of the yoked oxen. In the Godhra taluka a fowl is offered to the family god, *Baba Khatri,* represented by a wooden nail, and the blood of the fowl is sprinkled on the main ridge of the house to which a white thread is tied.

When the agricultural season opens, *Lingāyats, Marāṭhās, Lamānis* and *Badigas* in the Karnāṭak dress the plough, to which all the implements of sowing have been tied, in the garments of a woman. A week before a marriage the agricultural *Raddis* dress the plough in the clothes of a woman and sprinkle on it camphor. The yoke pin of the bullocks' yoke is at the same time dressed in the garments of a man and marked with the *ṭilak* which a man wears on his forehead. Another example of the association of a woman's fertility with an agricultural implement is the dressing of the seed-drill in the garments of a woman at *Divāḻi,* the day before *Divāḻi,* and on days when sowing is actually done. The *Hālgamba* twigs in the Karnāṭak are sometimes tied to a plough instead of to a post in the marriage *manḍap.* When a milch cow or buffalo fails to have calves it is yoked to a plough or to an oil-press that it may acquire the *śakti* of grain with which these implements in different ways are associated.

On *Ṛṣi pancmī* in the month of *Bhādrapad* seven betel-nuts are placed on rice sprinkled on an *āsan*, and before each are placed a pice, another nut, two betel-leaves and a dried date ; flowers, haḷad and kunku are sprinkled on the nuts. This is done to bring *barkat* to the *pitṛ*, and in the case of women to secure physical purification. On this day nothing can be eaten which has necessitated the use of a plough, and not even grain which has needed the employment of bullocks.

SOWING

Lāvaṇī

Grain put aside for sowing must not be stepped over ; if stepped over it will not germinate and a famine ensues. It must not be eaten or illness and poverty follow. In the Karnāṭak, however, there seems to be no fear of evil consequences on eating the reserved grain or on stepping over it. Separate portions of grain have to be put aside to satisfy the claims of the *balutedārs* or village menials, who in return for services rendered to the village community have an ancestral right to a portion of each year's grain. The seed must not be mixed with other grain. In the Belgaum district the person who brings the grain out of the house must keep apart from others and see that no one other than himself touches the seed. In some districts where *Marāṭhās* predominate the seed must not be touched by a child or by an unmarried person, for this would destroy all prospects of his future marriage.

When the seed is taken from the granary a small portion of it is put back again in the store, so that the stock shall never be exhausted. This portion so taken out and then replaced in the granary is in the Deccan called *ubhār*. The same principle governs a number of practices throughout the Presidency, though I have not found any word parallel in meaning to *ubhār* outside the Deccan.

When bags are filled on the threshing-floor in the Karnāṭak preparatory to removing the grain to the store, some grain from the filled bags is always put back again in the *rāśi*, so that the pile of grain on the floor may increase. When a horse is fed a small portion of the grain in its nosebag is taken out and reserved, to be added to the feed of the next day. When grain is measured the measure must never be quite emptied nor must the grindstone be cleaned after grinding grain. In accepting gifts also it is habitual for the recipient to return to the giver some portion of the thing given. To add to the *barkat* of the crops grain is given in alms to beggars who in the Deccan are called *Kaḍak Lakṣmī* ; in Kanara the gift of such alms is called *hurūsalu*. These alms are presented in a winnowing-fan and it is essential that the recipient should return the fan to the owner with some grain. Even gifts on ordinary occasions to friends or relatives are treated in the same way. If food is given on a platter the vessel must never be washed but returned with a little of the food. In Gujarāt when a milch animal gives birth to young, its milk for two or three days is given away and the receiver must return the pot in which it was sent, filled with staple grain.

At the end of the first day's sowing, if any of the seed taken to the field be left over it must be given away ; in Sind it can be eaten, but only after first giving away some share in charity ; in parts of the Karnāṭak also it is eaten, but it can never be sold.

In Sind when the seed is taken out of the granary seven handfuls of it are given to an unmarried daughter or sister of the cultivator to protect the grain from evil-eye. The Muhammadan considers it a good omen for the seed to be touched and brought out of the granary by a maiden or, failing a maiden, by a married woman if pure, whereas in the Deccan an unmarried girl will not touch the seed.

There is considerable variation in districts as to the restriction on certain persons sowing the seed. In the Ahmednagar district a woman may sow ; in the Kanara district the first seed sown should be sown by a *muttaidi* or married woman with her husband living ; in some parts of the Deccan any one may sow provided the seed is given to the sower by a woman with a husband of good character. Sometimes a woman is allowed to hold the grain and even to drop it into the sieve, but she may not in the Deccan touch the sieve itself ; in Sind after the seed has left the house no woman can have anything to do with it. In no district would a barren woman be allowed to sow, and when a woman is allowed to sow, one with many children is usually preferred.

The sower must be free from all defects as defects will be reproduced in the crops, and as defects mean a proportionate loss of *śakti*. In Sind the sower is followed to the field by his friends who call attention to any defects he has and if these be serious, insist upon another sower being substituted. *Lingāyats* will similarly not allow any man with defects to sow the first sowing. If he be a leper, lame, deaf or dumb, if he has a finger missing, a diseased nose, or only one eye, they consider the crop in some way or other will fail to reach perfection.

Raddis will not permit a man with blood on him to sow. In Khandesh and in the Karnāṭak the sower for the first sowing is chosen according to his birth star. He is subject to a strict code of rules limiting his actions. When he leaves his home for the field like the ploughman he must not turn back if any one should call him. He must be ritually clean or he will break his foot or wrist; he must remain continent. These restrictions are observed, even by primitive races such as the *Bhil* and *Kan Divar*. He must not shave or cut his hair nor bathe until the sowing is finished. He must not break the sowing of the first line in the field and must now allow his bullocks to stop until he has completed the first line or the produce of the field will be reduced. If he be sowing millet he must not touch the ear of a yoked bullock or the mature crop will suffer from smut.

Practice differs so far as sowing on an empty stomach or after a meal is concerned. In Khandesh the sower may not sow on an empty stomach. In Kanara sowing is done at first in the early morning facing the rising sun in order that the seed may thrive as the rays of the sun give increasing light, and therefore it follows that the sower has not broken his fast. Before reaping jvārī reapers usually fast. A Sindi Muhammadan will not eat during the measuring of grain. The difference in practice is not difficult to explain. On the one hand, if the sower sows on an empty stomach it is thought that the ears of the crops will be without grain; on the other hand, a full stomach is regarded as destroying *barkat.*

Whilst the grain is being sown a mystic relation exists between the future crops and the action of those left at home. During ploughing, sowing, reaping and the measuring of grain the women at home cannot braid their hair, spin or sew. Whilst sowing is proceeding the women at home must not grind, bake or roast grain; they must avoid, too, speaking ill of the sowers or of the seed. At home no one must shave, clothes must not be washed, nor can even the house be cleaned with cowdung. Those at home, in fine, must not commit *himsā*, must not do anything destructive of *śakti* lest they thereby destroy the *śakti* on which depends the *barkat* of the crop. In the Mallad tracts of the Karnāṭak an elderly woman of the household fasts on the night previous to the first sowing.

The first sowing is done at a good *muhūrtta.* In Kanara *Akṣayya-tṛtīyā* or the third day of *Vaiśākh* is generally chosen as a good *muhūrtta.* Early in the morning a twig of kyadgi or mundki (Pandanus odoratissimus) called bechu, 'scarecrow', is buried in a prepared plot. It is worshipped with sandal-paste, *akṣat*, flowers, coconuts and plantains, and *ārtī* is waved round it. The object of this rite is to scare away spirits. Then the sower scatters seed towards the rising sun, first sowing on the edge of the field with the cry '*Bahu bagya*'. Subsequent sowings may be done at any time save on Saturdays, *Amāvāsyās*, and on days of eclipses. Non-Brahmin *Gunagā* or *Gauḍā* add another ceremony before actually beginning the sowing. This is *Gaḍi pūjā* or worship of the change of the season. The local deities, usually *Jatka*, the spirit of a warrior, *Mhasti*, *Vandevatā* and *Bete Devaru*, the god of hunting, are worshipped with boiled rice, coconuts and plantains, and in some places with a sacrifice of fowls or goats. In Khandesh on the day fixed for the first sowing, the sowing implements and the sower himself are worshipped by a married woman; then the sowing implement is covered with a woollen blanket and taken to the field. On his way to the field the sower places a little seed before the village god, then sows a little in the field and returns to a feast at which all the family members are regaled and the bullocks are fed. In Kanara, too, before sowing, the plough oxen and the seed basket are worshipped, and after the sowing is over the plough is taken home and worshipped and a caste feast is held, *Kūrine Habbā.* In the Karnāṭak the forehead of the sower is smeared with sandal-paste on which grain is thrown, the plough is held over a svastika made in the field and the seed-drill is dressed in the clothes of a woman and worshipped.

Whilst sowing jvārī all the sowers wear rings of gold in order that the grain of the crop may be golden. The seed of cotton is mixed with fried jvārī which is white, to make the cotton crop white, and this is one of the objects of sprinkling milk over the cotton crops on *Pūrṇimā Pauṣa.*

In the Karnāṭak it is thought that should seed be sown on a Tuesday the crop will be eaten by rats; if sown on Saturday it will be destroyed by insect pests. Early jvārī is sown in the *Rohiṇi nakṣatra*, a popular saying being to the effect that if sown in *Rohiṇi* the streets will be full of grain.

An interesting custom which illustrates how agricultural ritual is dominated by the idea of 'power' is that found in the Karnāṭak of making the sowers on their return from the field sit on the ground and wash their faces, hands and feet with cold water. The sowers have been in close contact with the power of the seed; they return home hot with *śakti* and to that extent are dangerous to their fellow-men. By washing with cold water they are made 'cool'; by sitting on the ground a contact is established which draws away their *śakti*.

There are many family prejudices about different crops which are not always easy to explain. A frequent factor which induces a particular family to avoid sowing certain seed is that at some time or other that same seed was sown and produced an exceptionally good crop with which disaster was associated. Sometimes an accident to a member of a family whilst eating a certain food, or as in one case that I found, an accident whilst cooking a certain food, leads to a tradition in a family that certain grain should not be cultivated. *Lingāyats* and *Raddis* have a reluctance to cultivate sanabu [1] (Crotolaria juncea), though Muhammadans and castes that eat meat will cultivate it; it is associated with the demon world and its flowers resemble the nails of a tiger. To the cultivation of tobacco [2] there is a widespread aversion in some districts. In Kanarese there is a saying, '*Tambaka hachidavarige timbaka kulu illa*', which means that those who plant tobacco have no food to eat. When the tobacco plant attains maturity it is trimmed at the top and this leads to further sprouts which have in turn to be lopped away; this trimming of the plant is supposed to resemble the sin of killing a child, and planting tobacco is the sin of killing a woman. When tobacco plants are pruned women who have no issue are employed, for if women with issue were employed their children would die. There is also a white pumpkin the cultivation of which is supposed to bring death as the pumpkin is *rākṣas*, 'demonaical'.

Many omens are drawn from accidental happenings that occur during the sowing of seed. If the person carrying seed to the field steps on any cowdung the crop of jvārī will suffer from smut. The same disease attacks the crop should the sower meet a woman wearing a black *sāḍī*, one with pigment between her eyes or a

[1] When Rama invaded Lanka to recover Sita from the demon king, Ravan, a battle was fought in which Ravan was killed. A woman came forward and prostrated herself before Rama, who blessed her saying, 'Be not a widow.' Rama did not know that she was Mandodavi, the loyal wife of Ravan, but when she begged for the restoration of her husband, he kept his promise by saying, 'Let Anabi (mushroom) and the flowers of Sanabu grow on earth as your husband's brain and finger-nails.'

[2] *Tammakka* was the unfaithful wife of a great man. At a meeting called by the god *Kṛṣṇa* this man and his wife were invited and the wife at the *pānsupārī* was given four *pāns* instead of two. This led the man to question *Kṛṣṇa*, who told him that two of these *pān* were for the child in the womb of *Tammakka*. Her husband thereupon in a rage killed her and her child on the spot. *Tammakka* resolved to associate freely with all even after death and grew into a plant on the spot where she was murdered; as tobacco she is still the associate of all.

woman who has just become a mother. If the bullocks yoked to the seed-drill attempt to shake off their yoke there will follow some kind of evil; if the main beam of the drill gives way the whole crop will be destroyed by fire. If the sower be a woman and the fold of her *sāḍī* in which she holds the seed gives way she will become a widow. If a widower or a childless widow passes in front of the sower; if a single bird, *pingla*, passes by or a lizard makes a noise for a moment and then suddenly ceases, the future of the crop is imperilled. Should all the bullocks that are used in the sowing, during an interval of rest go to sleep with their right side touching the ground, the cultivator considers himself blessed, returns home at once and keeps holiday, feeding his bullocks with choice food.

A belief that explains many an agricultural rite is the belief that a maturing crop is as a woman in her pregnancy. If the seed of the sower is blown by chance on to a public footpath and mature ears of corn appear on the path, the path is abandoned from fear of harming a pregnant woman. *Bhils* and *Konkanis* in Khandesh for the same reason will not allow children to pluck ears of grain in the field. When a crop is mature, passing through it, whatever its utilitarian necessity, is forbidden lest harm should befall the pregnant crop. The Hindu sacred books are full of regulations prescribing the care which should be shown to a pregnant woman, and the practice of to-day of offering tasty and delicate foods to standing crops, is interpreted as a literal carrying out of the injunctions of *Manu*.

The crop is supposed to have a husband. The songs of the reapers allude to the husband of the crop. In Kanara, when the crops are almost ripe for reaping, sheaves are cut and stuck in the ground to represent a husband whose guardian care is best for a woman when pregnant. In or after the month of *Śrāvaṇ* pieces of Pandanus odoratissimus are planted in the fields in the belief that thereby the crop is united to her husband.

In some ceremonies two sheaves are worshipped and called *Lakṣmī* and *Nārāyaṇ*. On Dasarā or on *Gangaṣṭamī*, the eighth day of the second fortnight of *Āśvin*, is celebrated the *Hosahabba*, 'the new harvest' or *Muṣṭi muhūrtta* in Kanara. A priest accompanied by Brahmins and to the sound of music goes to the paddy-fields, and ties together two sheaves, each containing a handful of full ears. In the field they are given a bath of milk (*abhiṣek*) and offered sandal-paste, saffron, flowers, coconuts, plantains and betel-leaves, whilst *ārtī* is waved round them and *akṣat* is thrown on them. The throwing of *akṣat* is a substitute for clothing the sheaves. Then the sheaves are cut with a sickle which has been worshipped previously, and placed in a copper plate, *harivāṇ*, and taken home. In the house the sheaves are placed in a square made from flour in front of the *Tulsīkatta* ; the same offerings are made and then the sheaves are taken to the family god. After this once again the same rites are performed and special cakes called *kadabu* (Kan.), *kānule* (Mar.), are included in the offerings. The ears of the sheaves are then tied one by one to the shrine of the family god ; to the granary and the cattle-shed ; to the yard gate and to the main pillar of the house, to the cash-box and the pot in which rice is stored, to the child's cradle and to the pestle, churn, grinding-stone and plough. No reaping in the field can be begun until after the celebration of *Hosahabba*, and every cultivator going to a field worships two sheaves for himself.

On the full-moon day of *Āśvin* known as *Śīgī Huṇṇivi* (Kan.) a feast is held in the fields. This feast is the *Śīgī Huṇṇivi Charagā*, also called *Bhumi Hunnima Habba* or *Bayake Habba*, in the belief that the crops are then pregnant. The preparations for the feast are various kinds of puddings and cakes with vegetables, the principal preparation being one of boiled jvārī (Sorghum vulgare). Before sunrise the farmer goes to his field with these comestibles ; he gathers and ties together some jvārī plants and dresses them in the clothes of a woman and worships them with *akṣat*, flowers and turmeric. Then he makes his offering of food to the plants and having done this, worships five pastoral deities under a tree. The five pastoral deities are represented by five stones behind which is placed one black stone called 'thief', *kāllā*. The *naivedya* offered to the black stone is offered separately and is buried in the ground near or under the stone. The five stones are called *Pāṇḍavā*, whilst the name of the sixth stone is possibly a corruption of Karna, a brother of the *Pāṇḍavā*. These *Pāṇḍavā* are also worshipped on other occasions ; along with a scythe they are worshipped before an elderly man initiates the reaping of the crops, and they are again worshipped on the threshing-floor.

After worship of the representative stones the cultivator throws along the boundaries of the field and in all directions his preparation of jvārī, *honnuggi*, to satisfy the pastoral guardians of the field ; as he does this he calls '*Hulgyā, hulgyā*', 'Increase, increase'. All this he must accomplish before the sun rises and then he awaits the arrival of the guests invited for the feast ; these guests are all men, but women join the party on its return home. On the arrival of the guests the cattle also are fed with the *honnuggi* and the merry party does not return home till evening, when they take ears of jvārī and tie them as a *toraṇ* or arch over the shrine of their family gods.

A feast of the same kind is held when the rabī or later crops are mature and the buds of cotton are ready to burst. This feast is known as *Hatti Holada Charagā*. The *charagā* in this case is made from *śalu*, jvārī, and the cakes prepared from it are called *sora-gadabu*. This feast is usually held on *Yal̲l̲a Amāsi*, that is on Pauṣa vad. 30 which falls in February. In both these feasts no meat or fish can be used, for these are taboo to a pregnant woman.

In the Konkaṇ after the transplanting of the rice seedlings *Kātkarīs* and others hold a feast called 'The Fair of the Field'. In this fair after the sun has set, a basket, containing camphor, incense, a lemon and the bangles of a woman, is placed on the boundary of a field. In the Karnāṭak, after the transplanting work is finished and before the seedlings begin to sprout, coconuts and plantains are offered to the field and village deities; this is called 'green worship', *Hasrupūjā*.

In the Karnāṭak when sowing is begun, again when the crops are advanced and just before reaping, a feast is given to a pregnant woman with the object of benefiting the crops. On Bhādrapad sud. 9 a pregnant woman is asked to grind grain and with the flour resulting from her labour and with water a man sprinkles the standing crops. It is imperative that the grain chosen by her for grinding should be the same as that maturing in the field. Another custom of the Karnāṭak is before reaping the millet crop to tie together five stalks of the crop with a sickle at their base and to pour over them milk and ghee.

On the full-moon day of *Jyeṣṭha* to discover what crop will be a good one, a rope of mango and nim leaves is tied over the entrance to a village, with a dry coconut hanging in the centre. This arch of leaves, *toraṇ* or *mālā*, is called *kari*. The plough bullocks the day previous to the full moon are given boiled millet, crushed wheat or gram, whilst on the full moon day eggs are broken and with oil forced down their throats. The horns of the animals are gaily painted; gay quilts are put on their backs marked prominently with an impression of a hand in red colour; the ornaments and anklets of women are put on them and round their necks are strung rings of fried gram. Then selected bullocks are taken a mile or so without the village and driven in a race to the *kari*, and from the colour of the winning bullock an omen is drawn as to the crop which will be the best in the coming season. As the bullocks reach the rope *Mahārs* try to grasp the rings of gram and tear them from the bullocks, and when the leading bullock reaches the *mālā* a gatekeeper throws a rope on to it which brings the suspended coconut down on to the back of the bullock and breaks it. In the Dharwar district in each village there are two families, *Kattimani* and *Metimani*, who take a red and white bullock in turn and give them complete rest for six months before the race. The success of the red bullock means a good crop of red millet or paddy; the victory of the white bullock means a good crop of white millet and of cotton. When a race is run with black bullocks the winning of the black bullocks brings a rich crop of uḍīd. Should the victorious bullock wander away into another village the village in which the race was run loses the right of holding the race within its bounds. This bullock race is called *Kari Hariyona*, 'doing away with inauspiciousness', and the day itself is known as *Kar Huṇṇivi.*

REAPING

Tuesdays and Wednesdays are to a Hindu inauspicious days for reaping, whilst Thursdays, Fridays and Saturdays are auspicious. As reaping is an act of destruction it should not be done on a day sacred to the village deity, and if reaping be done on a full-moon day, a new-moon day, at an eclipse or under an inauspicious *nakṣatra* the grain will eventually be consumed by fire.

Before reaping begins one sheaf of the standing crop is worshipped with haḻad and kunku and the offering of a woman's folded bodice-cloth (*khaṇ*). In the Konkaṇ five ropes are made from the crops with grass tied into a knot and hung over the images of the family gods, where they remain for six months.

In reaping, small patches of rabī jvārī, late millet, ground-nut, sugar-cane and other crops are left unreaped for the poor to glean or for animals to eat. These patches are called *bījvad* in the Deccan, and it is assumed that the gratitude of the gleaners brings *śakti* and therefore *barkat* to the owner of the field. The Muhammadan in Sind leaves, similarly, a portion of his field unreaped for fakirs to glean; this is called *Pirjo bharo*, 'The Pirs' portion', or *numberjo khair*, 'the charity of the field'. A deserving man is sometimes given the first sheaf reaped in charity. In the Deccan the last sheaf is given in charity and the unreaped patch of field left to gleaners is in places called *Sītā Devi*.

The last sheaf reaped receives many names. In Kanara it is *ari, holigattu* or *Benappa*, the last perhaps a synonym for *Gaṇpati.* In the Deccan it is *Sītā mai; Sital devi; Sītā devi*: *Bhils* call it *hotri* or *dharmādāya*, 'charity'; *Gujars* call it *Devāca bhāg*, 'God's portion' and reserve it for the god of boundaries. This last sheaf or the last few stalks of grain reaped, receives special treatment, for into it is supposed to retreat the whole power of the grain of the entire crop. When *Bhils* bring this last sheaf to the threshing-floor they actually ask the whole virtue of the crop to enter into it. In Kanara the last five stalks of grain reaped are called *belimumbu*, which means 'future growth', for they are believed to contain the very essence of the crop.

In the Dang parts of the Kalwan taluka when reaping begins five handfuls of the grain and a branch of the apta-tree are worshipped, and the rest of the reaping is resumed three days later. The last few stalks reaped are called *rānā* and made up into a bundle, *ranyaca bhara* are tied to the central pole of the threshing-floor after the rest of the gathered grain has been threshed.

The last sheaf is removed in Kanara with its roots and attached earth and placed on the top of the pile of grain on the threshing-floor with a tuft of karad grass beneath it. When the threshing begins it is removed from the pile of grain and placed aside; after the threshing is over it is again placed near the grain and worshipped before the grain is removed from the floor. Before, too, the threshed grain can be taken away to the granary this sheaf must be thrown into a river, a tank or a well. It contains special *śakti*; it must not be stepped over or trodden upon and throwing it into water prevents such a happening. *Kan Divars* and *Madivals* have a practice very much the same as this. The last few stalks must be uprooted in a particular way; the sickle must be inserted under their roots in criss-cross lines and the whole root left attached to the stalks. These stalks are then placed on the pile of grain on the threshing-floor and with them are placed a flowering plant and a branch of mango. When the threshing is complete these stalks are taken to water; grain is sprinkled on the roots and then the stalks are thrown into the water to bring *barkat* to the crops and their owner. In the Sakri taluka of West Khandesh it is customary for the reapers before leaving the field to unfasten the ends of their turbans and bow to the last stalks left for gleaners.

Among reapers there is usually a good-humoured competition to avoid being the last to finish reaping, for the reaper who finishes the last is called by nicknames such as *heḍi*, 'laggard', *kadinumba*, 'last left' or 'the man with bangles'. In Kanara he is set upon by the others, who prick and tease him to elicit his abuse, which is supposed to add *barkat* to the crops. In Chota Udaipur State the reapers make a rush at the wife or daughter of the owner of the field, or at a new bride and, dragging her from the field, hold her as forfeit.

Whilst reaping inauspicious words must be avoided. It is bad to use the word 'reap' and instead of this the reaper speaks of stretching his hand to the field, *gaddage kai hāku*, and when the reaping is over the reaper says the crop has grown, *beḻe beḻesitu* (Kan.). *Bhil* women as they reap repeat the following song:

oḍo bhoḍī huyo bāli nā ki i
tu helako hai ke hijaḍo hai.

'Though you have grown so big, you have no bride;
You must be of low caste or neuter.'

In the Deccan the reapers call 'Lakṣmī give increase'. In the Chota Udaipur State they sing:

'Lakdi comb her hair; send *Dhondi* to her husband.'

In some districts the first five stalks of grain must be reaped by a woman with a living husband, and are then placed on a coconut near the pole of the threshing-floor. A quaint custom of the Dharwar district is to pay a pregnant woman who reaps double the ordinary wage, in recognition of the *barkat* she brings to the crop.

In the Deccan after the reaping of the first minor crops a tug-of-war is held called *Mahānguḻī*, 'great finger'. This takes place on the first day of *Mārgaśīrṣa*, called *Thorli Divāḻī*. A rope of green grass is made in three strands and sheaves of corn with ears (*ghāns*) are inserted in the rope in nine places which represent nine rainy constellations. The rope is then hung over the entrance of the village for the cattle to go under and thereby obtain health and long life. Then a tug-of-war with the rope is held at sunset, some seventy persons a side, who in some cases represent village factions. The object of the contest is to get the sheaves woven into the rope; any portions won are called *sānjī*, 'emblem of plenty', and taken home by the *rayat* to add to his store of grain or fodder, to ensure it against loss.

Reaping, like ploughing and threshing, is forbidden on certain days. It is an act of *himsā*. All agricultural operations have to cease on the day sacred to the village god; on *Nāgpancmi*, the fifth day of the first fortnight of *Śrāvaṇ*. There is, too, a lull in agricultural work on days of *parvakāl*, on *Amāvāsyā* and *Pūrṇimā*, at an eclipse, at a *Sankramaṇa* or at the hour of sunset. If there be a dead body lying still unburnt or unburied the *Marāṭhā* in the Deccan and the *Kātkarī* in the Konkaṇ and others will not work in the field.

THE THRESHING-FLOOR

Khaḻe (Mar.)

The threshing-floor is to a Hindu a hallowed spot. In some *Marāṭhā* families the marriage *devak* is taken to the threshing-floor before it is installed in the marriage *manḍap.* At *Divāḻī, Raddis, Mahārs, Talwārs* and some other castes take kavci (Muciena pruriens) grass, a herb called brahmadandi (Argemone Mexicana), spear-grass, uttran (Achyranthes aspera) and the flowers of tarvad (Cassia auriculata), and a twig of banni (Acacia ferruginea) and with these decorate a piece of cowdung on the threshing-floor and worship it as the goddess *Lakṣmī.*

There are no agricultural rites of greater importance than those observed on the threshing-floor, because it is on the floor that the grain is supposed to increase in measure, and the ritual followed by the cultivator has the one and only object of producing a calm atmosphere in which the power inherent in the grain may work its will undisturbed.

No one can enter a threshing-floor unless clean. *Bhils* and *Konkanis* require the chance stranger to purify himself with *gomūtra* before admitting him to the floor.

A site for the floor is chosen with care. In the Karnāṭak a spot near a growing śamī tree (Prosopis spicigera) or an arka tree (Calotropis gigantea) is preferred ; in any case the vicinity of a creeper called pātāḻgarḍī or bhūtkesī must be strictly avoided. In Sind several private threshing-floors are united in one *dera* and surrounded by a hedge. In the northern Konkaṇ, besides the individual floors there is one floor called *mahākhaḻ,* 'great floor', owned by a family with prescriptive right in which, after the threshing is over in all the private floors, a sacrifice is made on behalf of the community and the threshing of the village is brought to an end.

In most threshing-floors there is a central pole, *tivaḍā* (Mar.), *nih* (Sin.), *meṭigūṭā* (Kan.), round which the sheaves of grain are stacked and round which the bullocks go as they tread the grain. Sometimes in the Konkaṇ and in Sind there is no pole.

The choice of a tree for this pole is a matter of great importance, for the pole may hinder or induce the increase of the gathered grain. Whenever increase is looked for the power of any tree used is an important factor ; the ari, for instance, is specially chosen for the pestle of a churn and the jack-tree is used for making a grain measure. There are no trees that bring more *barkat*, according to a Hindu, than trees with a milky sap, and in general he chooses such a tree for the central pole of his threshing floor. The *Marāṭhā* uses the śivri (Bombax heptaphyllum); the umbar (Ficus glomerata) or the auspicious mango. In the Karnāṭak the cultivator chooses the kaḻḻi (Euphorbia tirucalli), the basari (Ficus infectoria), the dhātri (Phyllanthus emblica), the sālmalī (Bombax malabaricum), the gambhārī (Gmelina arborea), the saptapurṇa (Alstonia scholaris), the āl (Morinda citrifolia), the ari (Bauhinia racemosa), or the banni (Acacia ferruginea). In Eastern Gujarāt one finds the banyan and mhowra among the trees used for the pole, and strippings of bark from the same trees are tied to shrubs on the four sides of the threshing-floor. The *Bhil* makes his pole from khākar (Butea frondosa) which protects the grain from the malicious art of evildoers. *Konkanis* in West Khandesh use a pole of teak or paḻas. In the Sholapur district the commonest choice is that of the saundad-tree (Prosopis spicigera), for it has the property of scaring away witches and others who attempt to steal the *barkat* of a threshing-floor. The *Jain* in the Karnāṭak cuts his pole from the kākī (Cassia fistula) or from the tumri (Disospyros melanoxylon). A choice of the kākī-tree, however, by a cultivator rouses the resentment of other cultivators, for though it brings abnormal increase to the grain on the floor where it is erected, it reduces proportionately the *barkat* of adjoining floors; the use of this tree, therefore, is dying out. The Sindi Muhammadan has no particular preference for a tree with milky sap and will even use the babul-tree (Acacia arabica) which is taboo to the Hindu, but it is significant that the trees he uses on his threshing-floor, the babul, the lai (Tamarix Indica) and the ber are to him *ghoro* or ' heavy with *kudrat*.

By cutting the pole on special days or erecting it on the floor on auspicious days the power of the pole may be enhanced as it will draw power from the day. *Talwars* and *Jains* cut their pole on the *Amāvāsyā* of *Āśvin*, throw on it *akṣat*, offer it sandal-paste and food and preserve it until it is actually required on the floor. In Kanara also the pole is usually cut on the first day of *Divāḻi* and erected on a Thursday or a Friday. In the Dharwar district the pole is cut before sunrise on the first day of *Kārttik* and is erected before sunrise. *Bhils* and *Konkanis* choose Thursday for erecting their pole, and those who erect it must not face west or south. On the *Amāvāsyā* before *Divāḻi* a practice of *Lingāyats*, *Marāṭhā Upars* and others is to take home a branch of banni

(Acacia ferruginea), alad (Ficus Bengalensis), or ari (Bauhinia racemosa). A square four feet wide is walled round with cowdung and in the middle four heaps of cowdung are placed, shaped like an egg with a small ball on the top of it. These represent the *Pāṇḍavā.* The pole is then placed in the centre cross-wise, leaning against a wall; a broom, a rope and a pumpkin are placed near it. The *śakti* of the goddess *Lakṣmī* is then invoked into the pole to secure the *barkat* of the crops; lime is applied to it and an offering of food is made. This branch is used later as the central pole of the threshing-floor.

Before the pole is erected the Sindi Muhammadan places in the hole or small pit prepared for it, a piece of paper on which he has written the mystic word *bismillāh*, for this is the key to the door of the treasures of God, *hast kalid dar ganj hakim.* The *Marāṭhā* places in the pit an egg and the leaves of five different trees which must not include the tree of which the pole is made. If the pole be not made from saundad, the leaves of this tree are included in the five representative leaves, *pancpālvi*, because of its magic power in defeating the art of the malicious. *Bhils* and *Konkanis* place in the pit a lemon, two copper pice, five marking-nuts, an egg and some grain. A custom of the Deccan is to place beneath the pole a marking-nut pierced with needles, and to drive into the ground until invisible two to seven nails. Milk and curds are also poured into the hole. In the Deccan and Karnāṭak incense is burnt on erecting the central pole and a lemon dipped in turmeric is tied to the post.

To protect the grain on the floor from evil-eye and from theft by spirits a number of precautions are taken. *Bhils* place near the entrance of the floor a branch of bhūtkes (Mussaenda frondosa); near the pile of grain-sheaves an inverted shoe is placed and in the pile a piece of iron, whilst seeds of jvārī (Sorghum vulgare) coloured with turmeric and marking-nuts Ibhilāvā (Semecarpus anacardium) are thrown on the pile. In the Panch Mahāls before threshing begins a broom is placed on the floor and after the threshing is complete a lamp is placed on the pile of grain, *rās*, and around it towards each of the cardinal points four other lamps. *Raddis*, as the pile of grain rises around the central pole, tie to the top of the pole a black blanket, *kambali*, in semblance of the human head, and pile up the grain below until nothing of the pole is visible. With the same object of concealing the pole from the view of spirits the cultivator of the Deccan ties to the summit of the pole one or two sheaves; this is protection, in particular, on full-moon and no-moon nights when spirits are very active. Muhammadans in

Sind tie to the pole an iron ring which serves the double purpose of an attachment for the ropes of the bullocks and of averting spirits; on the completion of the first day's threshing they also tie to the pole hair from the tails of the bullocks, in doing which they are said to take *rākh* of the bullocks. The same term is used for another Muhammadan practice of drawing with the end of the winnowing-instrument a line around the stack of grain and another around the floor, and uttering the word, '*bismillāh*'. In Kanara a charmed coconut is placed on the floor and a goat, sheep or cock until the threshing is finished. In Gujarāt two or three conical heaps of cowdung are placed round the floor. Other common practices are to tie a lemon in a cloth to the central pole; to hang a doll made from black rags with a cowrie attached to its neck at the entrance to the floor; to place a shoe upside-down at each end of the path which leads to the floor, or to tie a shoe to a tree close by. In the Sholapur district a circular line is drawn around the whole floor and on it the seed of black rāḷā (Panicum Italicum) or of uḍīd (Phaseolus mungo) is thrown. *Kātkarīs* place a sickle and a coconut on the floor and pile up on these the sheaves and grain. A line as a protection against spirits is drawn round the pile of grain and chaff with the ashes of burnt chaff in many districts. Auspicious designs are drawn with ashes or with turmeric and camphor on the floor and on the pile of grain. To prevent any decrease in the grain which is attributed to spirits the cultivator in the Panch Mahāls draws with ashes a figure of a tree on the pile of grain; in Khandesh the marks of a svastika and of a double triangle are drawn, and in the Karnāṭak figures of the sun and moon and symbols of *Gaṇpati*.

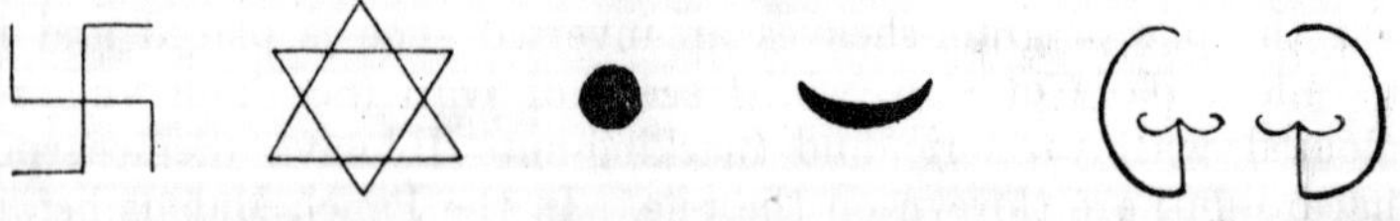

Fig. 136.

A familiar feature of the threshing-floor in the southern districts of the Presidency is the *būdā*, an image of a spirit which presides over the floor. This is made of cowdung into which hair from the tails of the bullocks used on the floor is stuck to form a crest; sometimes it is made from a sheaf of grain with a broken jar for a head on which with lime white moustaches are painted. Curds and cakes of rice are offered to it in propitiation of a spirit called *Jeṭṭi*. This image is carried round the *rās* to the cry of '*Huli libho*', and when the grain has all been heaped around the pole all the agricultural tools are placed near the image. When the grain is finally removed from the threshing-floor the image is allowed to decay or is brought home with the grain.

In the Dharwar district a sheep is sacrificed to avert evil-eye and then food mixed with flesh from the stomach of the sheep is thrown on the outskirts of the field in which lies the threshing-floor, to quench the thirst of spirits. In Kanara, when threshing begins, an unhusked coconut, symbol of the three-eyed *Śankar*, monarch of spirits, is placed on a stool or seat on the floor. Mango-leaves and flowers are tied to the stool or placed near, and *akṣat* is thrown on the stool. An offering of boiled rice is made, and placed on four plantain-leaves, is deposited on the four sides of the floor to defend it from spirits as a *dikbāndha*. If threshing take several days this is done every morning to avert spirits.

To secure the co-operation of spirits a sacrifice is made called *ḍavrā*. A *ḍavrā* is made before ploughing, reaping, measuring, or before drawing water from a new well. In some districts only certain shepherd castes resort to this practice. In the Konkaṇ a goat is sacrificed and dragged round the *rās* on which the blood of the goat is sprinkled. In the Deccan the blood of the goat is sprinkled at the four corners of the threshing-floor. *Naivedya* is offered to the spirits and this must be prepared by a clean person from cooked rice, bread and mutton. No woman can be present during the feast which follows a *ḍavrā*, though later the food that remains over is taken home and shared by the women-folk.

It is impossible, however, to make a sharp distinction between the ritual that essays to appease spirits and that which attempts to secure the favour of deities, for the worship of the deities that guard the boundaries of the fields operates to frustrate the activities of spirits. The *Bhil* encircles his threshed rice with the blood of a fowl and liquor and then worships *Śivarya*, the god of boundaries, with an egg and *śendūr*. In Kanara after the grain has been collected on the threshing-floor the *rayat* takes a bath and with wet clothes goes round the heap of grain three times. He sacrifices a cock and offers boiled rice to the field deities and later mixes the rice with the grain on the floor that it may increase. The *Marāṭhā* places five small stones on his *rās* to represent the five *Pavlīs* or goddesses that guard the boundaries of the fields. Before the measuring of the grain begins each of these stones, *Pancpavli*,[1] is sprinkled with turmeric, a *parḍī* is offered to them and a coconut is broken before them. The *parḍī* is a sort of frame made from stalks with five or seven points or compartments, *khān*, in each of

[1] *Pancpavli* must not be confused with *pancpālvi*.

which representative offering is placed. At each point is placed a cake of bread, oilseed cake, a ball of baked wheaten flour, a pudding of the same flour, sugar, coconut and a lamp of wheaten flour with a cotton wick fed with ghee. After offering this *parḍī* to the deities the owner of the threshing-floor in the Deccan gives away the contents of the outside compartments, four or six, to the owners of the fields which adjoin his own, giving to each the offering in the compartment which points towards his fields. In other words, he gives away towards each of the cardinal points. The offering in the centre of the *parḍī* he divides into two portions, retaining one himself and giving the other to a cow to eat. After use the frame is thrown into water. The offerings of a *parḍī* cannot be eaten by a woman. If there be no boundary guardians in the *rayat's* fields he does not offer a *parḍī* until after the measuring of the grain is over, and then the *parḍī* must consist of some, but never of all, of the following ingredients, viz. bread made from three or seven kinds of grain, to which an egg is added when the grains used are seven, and sweet-oil and chillies when the varieties of grain used are three ; bread made from wheat flour, the measure of flour being a handful or one and a quarter times any regular measure, and lastly the earthen bowl of a smoker's pipe, *chilam.* Another deity of the boundaries is *Mhasoba,* who is represented by a single stone placed under a tree ; a goat is offered to this deity after the threshing and at some distance from the threshing-floor. The worship of *Mhasoba,* if there be one of his symbols near the village, is always performed should any worker on the threshing-floor or any of the bullocks used on the floor feel any kind of pain or illness during the threshing of the grain. He is also worshipped with the sacrifice of a goat (*pānjī*) when the pressing of sugar-cane begins.

In the Deccan five stones are placed near the best sheaves which have been placed to the north of the central pole ; they are covered with red lead and when the measuring of the grain begins, rice and curds are offered to them. These stones represent the *Vanaspatis* or sacred trees among which the tree from which the central pole is cut is included, making a representation of six trees in all. On *Āśvin* vad. 30 five stones called *Pānḍavā* smeared with lime are placed in each field and in one field an earthen pot called *Sānj Moravā* in which turmeric, pice and a lamp are kept. These stones, with the pot, are worshipped ; the pot is then buried in the field and in the field a feast is held by the members of the cultivator's family. When the threshing-floor is ready for the threshing the buried pot is taken up and placed near the floor with a stone and a ball of earth called *Lakṣmī*. Over these a shelter is formed with five sheaves of millet to which boiled rice is offered. Five other sheaves called *Behaḻecyā* are placed on the low raised edge made around the threshing-floor; five other sheaves, *Pāḻicyā*, on the border of the floor itself, and a single sheaf called *Tivaḍā peṇḍī* is tied to the central pole. When the threshing is ended the grain from these sixteen sheaves must be taken home and eaten by the members of the cultivator's family, but by no one outside the family. Another form of this rite is to place five stones, *Pāṇḍavā*, just before the winnowing begins, outside the floor and anoint them with rice and curds to bring *barkat* to the grain. Castes that make an offering to the *Pāṇḍavā* do not make an offering to the *Pavlis*. In the Kalwan taluka on the completion of the threshing the threshed grain is heaped over a plough and a stone representing *Gaṇpati*; a hen or goat is sacrificed and eaten. In the Sakri taluka this stone, which has been brought from a river-bed, is placed in the western part of the *rās*, and after the close of the threshing is preserved in the cattle-shed till the next year.

The threshing-floor cannot at any time be swept with the ordinary broom, as this is destructive of *barkat*. To allude to sweeping is also forbidden on the floor, and in Kanarese districts the word *saḻḻuhoḍi* is used instead of the ordinary word *kasāhoḍi* for sweeping. In the Deccan the floor is brushed with coconut fibre, stalks of tur (Cajanus Indicus), the stalks of aghāḍā (Achyranthes aspera), with nirgūḍ (Vitex negundo), or with any green leaves. In the Kanara district sweeping with a broom made from the leaves of the toddy-palm (Borassus flabelliformis) is tabooed.

The manner of threshing and the number of threshings made vary in different localities. Stone rollers are occasionally found, but in general are considered to destroy *barkat*. In the Konkaṇ the nāglī grain only is trodden by bullocks and the other grains are beaten by hand on a central stone. In the Deccan the best stalks of grain are selected and placed to the north of the floor where they are beaten with sticks or with the legs of the stool on which the winnower stands. At the time these stalks are threshed no woman can be present. This threshing by hand of a few stalks is done either before the threshing of the other grain is begun or after all the other threshing has been finished. The practice in Kanara is to take the best stalks from a portion of the field which has been tended with special care, and place them on the top of the pile of sheaves. As they rest on the pile they are beaten with an iron rod before the general threshing is commenced.

Apart from this threshing of selected stalks the crop receives two threshings in the Deccan. The first threshing and the grain which results therefrom is called *madan.* By this the heavier grain is separated and this is then measured. A small portion of the *madan* is given to a priest in return for his services in covering with red lead all the stones in the fields which represent bouṇdary deities and in breaking a coconut at the first measuring. The second threshing separates the inner and smaller grain and is called *ākaṇ*; the grain from this second threshing is in turn measured and should there still remain any grain in the ears they are beaten by *Mahārs* with sticks and the *Mahārs* are allowed to take away what grain they find, which is called *nisarvā.* When a third treading of the grain is made it is called *nikaṇ.*

The number of threshings in the Karnāṭak varies according to the crop. In the case of the jvārī crop the sheaves are first stacked in the field, *gūḍuhāku*; their ears are there separated and taken to the threshing-floor and placed round the pole where the bullocks tread them. This threshing is called *teni tuḻisuvadu.* After winnowing, the result of the first threshing comes the second threshing or *kaṇki,* which completes the separation of the grain. In dealing with the produce of the wheat crop there are four operations. The first threshing, *hullu tuḻisuvadu,* removes some of the grains; the second, *kaḍḍi buḍḍi,* separates the husks from the stalks; the third, *maḻalu,* separates the grain from the husks; and the fourth, *kaḍigāṇā,* is a final threshing.

When the tired oxen are unyoked the Deccani *rayat* holds two handfuls of the threshed grain near the foreheads and the tails of the bullocks, this after the threshing of jvārī, and allows the grain to fall to the ground. This fallen grain or *sānjī* is supposed to add *barkat* to the yield and five grains with five hairs from the tails of the bullocks are tied in a long cloth to the top of the central pole of the floor. This tying is called *sānj ghene*; *sānjī* means a cornucopia or horn of plenty and is applied also to the sheaves won in the *Mahānguḻī* tug-of-war which also bring *barkat* to the stock of grain.

The key, and the only key, to the ritual of the threshing-floor is the belief that the grain possesses an inherent power, *śakti,* by virtue of which it can of its own accord increase in measure. This belief is common in almost every part of the Presidency, though it would seem absent in some tracts of Sind and Gujarāt. An increase of measure, if within certain limits, is a gift of *barkat,* but it is a veritable danger if in excess and brings ruin of some kind or other to the cultivator. In the Deccani maund there are sixteen *paillis* and in the same measure in the Konkaṇ twelve *paillis*;

the *rayat* in both parts expects an increase in measure of four *pailiis* in the maund. In many parts of the Karnāṭak no standard of increase is fixed as auspicious, but in others a 50 per cent increase is hoped for. Should the grain increase in measure within this limit and not beyond it, it is said to have brought *barkat, holā hulasu ātu,* but should the increase pass beyond this limit it has boiled over, *rāśi ukkeritu.* There is a similar belief respecting butter when churned and oil when pressed.

The agriculturist fears an abnormal crop as he fears any excess of power. If his yield of grain boils over he fears even death. If his chilli crop is very good he fears an outbreak of plague or other virulent epidemic. He fears death if a field that usually yields a poor crop provides suddenly a very good one ; he expects famine if his vegetable crop is above normal. The only crop whose abundance he does not seem to dread is the brinjal crop and an excellent crop of brinjal portends a good cotton harvest. Besides grain, butter and oil, jaggery also may 'boil over' and cause death. Fear of an excess of power was explained to me pithily by one who said that sufficient rain was good but an excess of rain destructive, and a few children were a blessing but a large family a curse.

There is really no moment when the spontaneous increase of grain becomes impossible. Grain increases during the threshing ; it increases again as soon as it is touched by the measure, when it is taken to the granary and even later than this. *Bhils* and *Konkanis* in Khandesh store their grain in a granary called *kanaga.* As they empty their baskets of grain and fill the granary they cry '*Bharbar kanga Mahādev*', and if when they have stored all their grain the granary should not be full they take the grain out again and then replace it, believing that at the second filling of the granary the stock of grain will be the bigger. Whenever, too, grain receives by contact a fresh accretion of power, it increases in measure. If a precious stone be placed in grain it increases in measure. At a Muhammadan marriage the measuring of grain by the bridal pair, *rās mojne,* results in its increase. At a *Śrāddha* ceremony the priests who represent gods or *pitṛ* throw rice over the celebrant who lets it fall into his hands and then adds to his store of grain to increase its *barkat.* Even grain picked up from the ground and placed in the granary enhances the measure of the store. Before installing a sacred image a test is sometimes made by Brahmins whether the image is such as will bring its worshippers *barkat* or not. It is buried in a specific measure of grain and if this increases it is presumed that the image will bring *barkat,* whilst if the grain does not change or if it decreases in measure the image is not installed. More instances of this kind will be found in other parts of this book. It is primarily, however, on the threshing-floor that grain increases in measure.

The increase in the grain on the threshing-floor is to a considerable extent within the control of the cultivator. It is for him to secure the peaceful atmosphere free from evil power in which alone the power of the grain will act. On the other hand, the increase may pass beyond his control. If the grain increases to excess he may place on the *rās* a sickle with its edge upwards or throw at the heap of grain a sandal or shoe in the hope that these things will arrest the growth of the grain, but his hope is a slender one, and he is generally content with distributing the grain among the poor, as charity averts evil, and with avoiding in future the cultivation of that particular kind of grain. No belief could be a greater obstacle to progress or to the efforts of organization to increase the productivity of the soil.

The Karnāṭak provides the best illustration of this concept of power ruling agricultural ritual. Threshing must be done at night, as the sun must not shine on the threshing-floor whilst threshing proceeds. As dawn approaches and the farmer begins to make with his bullocks the last three rounds round the central post he joins with his companions in the following dialogue in song. The first three couplets, each containing a question and its answer, all refer to the increase in the grain.

Q. Oh bull, why are you walking so very slowly ?
A. The grain which was so long under my ankle has increased till I am now walking in it knee-deep.

Q. What is *Būdā* doing seated near the heap ?
A. He is giving us grain, basket upon basket.

Q. What is goddess *Lakṣmī* doing who resides in the fields ?
A. She is so mightily pleased that she now sports about wearing her rich pearl ornaments.

These three couplets of song are then followed by a shout from all the workers in unison :

'We have been using a pearl broom and that is why our heap of grain has increased till it touches the sky. Hence, oh *Huligyā*, scatter and toss the grain to the sky in wanton joy.'

In these songs the *būdā* is the image of the spirit presiding over the threshing-floor securing the calm atmosphere requisite for the increase of the grain. *Huligyā* is a personification of *barkat* or increase. In various forms this word appears again and again in the cries of the threshing-floor. *Ho halyan halyo* is a refrain that ends most of the songs sung on the floor. When the winnowing is done the winnowers are allowed to utter one word only, '*huligyā*', and this is in invocation of the wind necessary for winnowing. If there be again any occasion to use the word fire on the floor it is alluded to as *huligyā*. The same word is also used when measuring in lieu of numbers considered inauspicious.

Whilst these songs are being sung which terminate the night's work of threshing, a closing which is called *Huligyānnā Hariyodu*, the man who drives the bullocks round the post carries in his left hand a pot of water and in his right hand a broom, *śal̲l̲u*, made from aghāḍā (Achyranthes aspera), with which he sprinkles the water on the central post, the heap of grain and on the bullocks. When, too, the bullocks are finally unyoked he dabs a little water between their eyes. Here again we have the association of power with heat, for the use of this water is to cool the hot *śakti* which suffuses the grain and through contact with it the threshing-floor, its parts and also the bullocks.

The dust from the threshed grain which clings to the bodies of the bullocks is carefully brushed so as to let it fall on to the floor, for if it be blown away it will carry the *barkat* of the floor to other threshing-floors.

Threshing songs are numerous, but for the most part merely illustrate the light-heartedness of the workers, though they usually end with a shout for *barkat*. The following are typical songs:

'How could young Nilava (the cow) the wife of Basavanna work when suckling her young calf?'

'The young cow bows to the bull, as his horns appear above the flooded river he is crossing.'

'Eight bullocks are in yoke facing the east. The last two are chafing. Our Basavanna loves a necklace of jingling silver beads.'

'When the six bullocks of an elder brother, the three of my younger brother and the sixteen of my father come, the earth of my village trembles.'

'Tiresome is a cart to the banta (a Y-shaped frame that supports the beam); loathsome is a young woman to an old man, and an eyesore is a widowed daughter to the family of her father.'

'If our Basavanna dies the Holers take away the body and with great relish consume its flesh.'

'The tottering cart of my friend moved down the slope with uncertain gait.'

'Who is he who rides on the stone pavement with a grey horse? He is Rajappa and his horse swims in the battlefield.'

'Holding a drill and a silver whip in his right hand with the help of a pair of bullocks he sowed gold on the riverside.'

'How are the crops and how is the rain on the river's further side? The rain is good and the crops are full; the grain of the white millet is big and shining as golden beads worn round the neck.'

'Do not cry, Rama, your mother will soon be here.'

'Take away your guldali, if you wish. I do not want to be vexed by your remarks on my ugliness and black colour. The world is wide enough for me.'

'Stay awhile, good lady. I will accompany you. If you do not stay I tell you, by yourself, your pitcher and your bracelets, evil will befall you.'

'To the first bullock is tied a beautiful feather, and to the last a jingling ornament.'

'The bullocks of Hundekar eat safflower cake and drink water from the pond.'

'The dust clings more and more to the white bullock and mantles over the red.'

In varying degree from district to district a woman is not allowed on the threshing-floor until after both the threshing and the measuring of the grain is finished. In the Kolāba district strict exclusion of women is observed only in the case of the most important grains, but a woman is always denied entry to the *mahākhal̲* when the threshing of the whole village is brought to an end with sacrifice. Even the noise of a woman's bangles would destroy the *barkat* of this rite. The *Bhil* and the *Konkaṇī* in Khandesh are strict in excluding women; in Sind the Muhammadan makes a general warning to all the women of the village not to approach the *dera* in which several threshing-floors are incorporated. The *Marāṭhā* allows no woman on his threshing-floor whilst the threshing of selected stalks is being made; he allows no woman to eat of a *parḍī*, and no woman can be present when the *ḍavrā* sacrifice is made. On the other hand, the possibility of a woman's co-operation in winnowing is shown by a *Marāṭhī* saying that if ā woman, no matter whether married or not married, catches the wind made by another woman winnowing, she will have twelve daughters. *Sūpācā vārā āṇi mūḷi hoti bārā.* In Kanara no woman is allowed to see an image which is made on the floor from burnt husks of grain after the winnowing is finished. The great agricultural community of *Raddis* will not allow women on to the threshing-floor until the first basketful of grain has been separated from the ear. In the Dharwar district grain is usually not measured on the floor, but put into baskets; women assist in emptying the baskets into carts, but cannot be present where the men fill the baskets. There seems little or no exclusion of women in Gujarāt; in the Karnāṭak communities like the *Vaddar*, *Madival* and *Kan Divar* allow their women to work on the floor, and a not uncommon practice in the Karnāṭak is for married women to enter the floor, after the threshing and worship the *rāśī* waving *ārtī* round the heap of grain.

Until the threshing is over there is a general prohibition of bringing meat on to the threshing-floor. In the Karnāṭak the workers can bring on to the floor bread, cooked rice and curds, and are supposed to keep a stock of these sufficient to regale any two chance guests or strangers that should visit the floor whilst threshing is proceeding. They may not, however, bring curry which contains meat on to the floor, and when they drink they must not make a sipping sound which destroys *barkat*. In Khandesh and in many villages of the Deccan no food or drink can be taken on the floor. When a goat is sacrified to *Mhasoba* it is sacrificed at a distance from the floor; when the *ḍavrā* is offered to spirits it is consumed in the fields. The *parḍi* also is not eaten on the floor but on its outskirts. In the Deccan no one is allowed to approach the floor carrying water, as this would reduce the yield of grain, and all water-pots brought by the family on to the floor must remain empty, save one which is filled to remove the evil consequences attributed to empty pots. In Kanara meat cannot be taken to the floor until after the threshing, when a feast called *Kāṇhabbā*, 'the granary feast', which is similar to the *Gaḍi pūjā* described before, is held, though even then the preparation of the sacrifice and feast is made away from the floor. Similarly, in the Karnāṭak a feast, *Rāśi butti* or *Khanad habbā*, is held on the floor after the threshing. Muhammadans have no scruples about taking food or drink, except meat, to the floor.

A barber, a eunuch or a tattooed man may not enter the field in which there is a threshing-floor, the barber because his profession is one of *himsā*, the eunuch because he is mutilated and so destructive of *śakti*. All who enter the floor must remove their shoes [1] but cover their heads.

Charity is a marked feature of every stage of agriculture and, in particular, marks the ritual of the threshing-floor. When the jvārī crop is almost but not quite ripe it is a widespread custom to invite all and sundry to a feast at which the unripe grain is roasted, and eaten with coconut and garlic after five ears have been offered to the village god. This *Hurḍā* feast is one of the most familiar sights in season of the countryside. Similarly, when

[1] Shoes are removed when shearing sheep, when eating, on entering a temple or a crop of sweet potatoes, chillies, plantains and betel-nuts. It is forbidden to walk in a cultivated field, as distinct from on its embankments, wearing shoes. On crossing water or a bridge, on entering a boat, on lighting a lamp, on milking a cow, on ploughing or sowing and when passing a temple, the shoes should be removed. A distinction is made between wooden and leather shoes. Wooden shoes may be taken across the threshold of a house and on to the threshing-floor, but not even these into the inner shrine of a temple; an *Agnihotrī* can wear wooden shoes but not leather ones.

sugar-cane is being pressed, the farmer welcomes any who choose to come and eat of the *gūl* or pressed-out sugar juice. When ploughing is begun molasses are distributed to visitors. During the reaping of crops there is the *nisarvā* given to Mahārs, the *Sītādevī* and the *Bījvad* left for gleaners or for the birds. Before measuring the grain in the Karnāṭak, to prevent any decrease in the measure of the grain, five small heaps of grain are put aside called *nidhi* or wealth, and given to a *Mahār*. When the grain is collected on the threshing-floor Muhammadans distribute some of the grain among the poor and among *Sayads*. If the central pole of the floor becomes loose in Sind, a very dire portent of coming evil, sweets are distributed; before the measurers enter the protecting circle, which after threshing has been drawn round the pile of grain, sweets are freely given away and thrown on the grain in multiples of some standard measure or in value multiples of some standard coin. In Khandesh when the grain has been brought to the floor a little is put apart and sold and with the sale proceeds sweets are purchased and given away. The separation of this grain for sale is called *bālājī Kāḍhne*, 'to take out *barkat*' or 'increase', and it protects the grain on the floor from evil-eye. In all districts and among all castes and tribes the chance-come visitor to the threshing-floor is regaled and feasted with the object of adding increase to the grain. Any beggar who passes by when measuring is going on must be given alms. After measuring, *Mahārs* take five ears of grain and hang them in the verandah of their house for birds to eat.

The object of all this charity is the averting of evil and the concomitant winning of *barkat*. The gratitude of the recipient of alms, the blessing of man or bird, is a force which conveys *śakti*; good wishes have their innate power and these transferring *śakti* to the donor bring *barkat*, which on the threshing-floor always means an increase in the yield of the grain. Closely allied to this distribution of charity is the practice of taking earth from beneath the pole of the threshing-floor and scattering it where many will tread it underfoot. The cultivator is not content to rely upon his own 'power', but attempts to draw upon the power of others.

In many ways the *rayat* hopes to obtain *barkat* from the power of trees. He chooses for his central pole on the floor a tree to which he credits abnormal power; he places beneath that pole the leaves of five trees; he represents trees by five stones placed on the floor and he makes on his pile of grain the figure of a tree. Finally, before he begins to measure the grain he takes a little of the grain and throws it at the foot of a tree, and brings back the flowers of the tree and throws them on the pile of grain. In the Deccan he chooses for this purpose the ruī (Calotropis gigantea) and the tarvad (Cassis auriculata), in the Kalwan taluka the paḻas (Butea frondosa) is often used; in the Belgaum district no distinction is drawn between trees. To increase the yield of the grain, in West Khandesh branches of bor are spread in the field and on these further branches of apta and ruī and on these again five stones over which five sheaves are placed in a pyramid with other sheaves around.

WINNOWING

Vāḍhaviṇe

Winnowing is done before each measuring. The farmer stands on a stool holding high his basket of grain, which he allows to fall steadily to the ground. He must never winnow if the wind be blowing from north to south; if the wind comes from the east he must face north, and must face south if the wind be from the west. To test which way the wind is blowing an earthen pot of water is put outside the threshing-floor and in it jvārī grain is boiled, producing a smoke which indicates the way of the wind.

Both when winnowing and when measuring the *śakti*, *Rāhubal* of the planet *Rāhu* which is always considered inauspicious must also be considered. The *rayat* winnowing or measuring must not have *Kāla Rāhu* behind him or to his left and as *Rāhu* is in different quarters on different days the *rayat* must change his own position accordingly. *Rāhu* is in the east on Sunday and Thursday; in the south on Monday and Friday; in the west on Tuesday; and in the north on Saturday and Wednesday.

The light grain that falls during the winnowing that follows the final threshing is called in the Deccan *maṇi*, *phanjaṭ* or *varaḻe*.

The man who winnows should keep absolutely silent save for uttering '*Huligyā, huligyā*'. When he lays aside his basket he must always leave some grain in it or his stock of grain will come to an end, and for the same reason he must never place the basket upside-down.

MEASURING

The measuring of the grain is the most important operation on the threshing-floor, and there is more uniformity in the ritual connected with this than in any other ritual of agriculture.

If an inauspicious day be chosen for measuring there will not only be no increase in the grain, but a positive decrease. Saturdays and Tuesdays are bad days. Mondays and Thursdays, on the other hand, are good days for measuring grain. Unimportant grains can be measured at any time, but the really important grains only after sunset, or in the Konkaṇ after sunset or before dawn. The measurer must also face an auspicious direction as he works; in the Konkaṇ he usually looks towards the east; in the Deccan and in Sind towards the north, and in either case no one must pass in front of him.

Certain persons are better measurers than others, bringing more increase to the grain. In Sind an old man is preferred because of his greater *kudrat*; in the Karnāṭak a man whose wife has attained puberty but whose marriage has not been consummated brings special *barkat* to the grain. A man of good character brings to the grain all the power associated with his piety and in Sind and in the Karnāṭak is chosen when available as measurer. In no case can a man who has any physical imperfection measure; deformity and mutilation imply loss of *śakti*, and if the measurer be lacking in power it cannot be expected that the grain will show increase. A man who has ridden an elephant cannot in the Deccan measure, and the *Telī* whose profession it is to crush oil-seed cannot anywhere measure grain on the threshing-floor. No *barkat* can be expected from measuring done by one whose trade it is to destroy *śakti*.

The measurer cannot cut his hair and nails or shave until his work is finished on the floor; he and all who assist him must be clean and remain continent. In these restrictions, again, the concept of *himsā* enters. The measurer and all who are present on the threshing-floor must keep their heads covered; they may wear sandals, though these be of leather (*kālmari*), but they cannot enter the floor wearing boots or shoes (*joḍā*).

In Sind the measurer muffles his face, saving his eyes, and measures with bent head, never looking at the top of the pile of grain, for his satisfaction with the height of the pile might foster the evil power of his eye. Measuring is done almost in silence; those who help the measurer must remain absolutely silent whilst the measurer utters his numbers in a whisper. Two persons sometimes do the counting and silence is observed only during the first measuring. Silence is observed not only because of the *barkat* that silence brings, but in order that others may not hear what yield the grain has provided. Good fortune must not be proclaimed abroad. The *rayat* hesitates, as every district officer knows well, to admit a good crop; he will not reveal how much butter he has obtained in churning; he will not weigh water or even food, and on the same principle when the moon is full he will not speak of its large size.

The first grain measured is put aside as a gift for a priest. In the subsequent measuring all inauspicious numbers are avoided. One is universally avoided, *lābh* or 'gain' is used as a substitute in many parts, *hechu* with the same meaning in Kanara, *bāḻāji* in Khandesh, and *barkat* in Sind. Instead of two, *barkat* is usually said; in the Sholapur district *savai*, 'more', and in Sind *bahu barkat* or 'great *barkat*'. For three in the Deccan *nyāhār* is said, but no one has been able to give me the meaning of this word, which seems to be a borrowed word; in the Sholapur district the same enigmatic word is used for four, and *barkat* is used for three. Five is nowhere avoided, as it is an auspicious number, but the Sindi sometimes calls it *ganj* or wealth. The Kanarese word for eleven, *yelu*, when used as an exclamation means also 'rubbish', 'go to the dogs', and so is avoided on the threshing-floor. In lieu of this *aru huli*, 'six and more', is said. In the Sholapur district *sānj* is substituted for seven, whilst in the Karnāṭak as a whole *huligyā* is used. *Adhik*, 'more', is a synonym for eight in Sholapur; *mattondu*, 'one more', for eleven in Kanara, and *hadināru huli*, 'sixteen and more', for seventeen, whilst in Sind 'big nine' is said for ninety-nine. Before any counting begins the measurer generally says something meaning 'good luck' such as '*bahu bagya*'.

When once measuring has begun it must not be stayed until the whole grain has been measured. In parts of the Karnāṭak there seems to be no fear of theft by others of the *barkat* of a man's threshing floor, but it is very prominent in the Deccan and in the Konkaṇ. A *Ceṭakiṇ* or *Ceṭakyā* is a woman or man who works through the help of spirits; one who borrows for a time a *Pitar*, a spirit who assists its devotees to steal from others the *barkat* of grain when measured, of butter when churned, and of oil when pressed. The image of this spirit in human form has no particular features, but his worship can be performed only in a state of uncleanness. In the Deccan it is said that all the *pitar* come from the Konkaṇ. When the devotee of this spirit wishes to steal the *barkat* of a neighbour's threshing-floor, he watches for the time when his neighbour begins to thresh and sprinkles on his own floor ears of grain already emptied of their grain (*piśā*) and then spirits bear the *barkat* of the one floor to the other. Many of the precautions already detailed to keep spirits away from the floor, such as the nails, marking-nuts and eggs placed beneath the central pole, or the line of black seed drawn around the *rās*, and the

25

marking-nuts pierced with needles or the small wooden measure placed beneath the *rās*, are directed against the spirits in the employ of a *ceṭak*. The prohibition of staying the work of measuring before it is all finished is, in those parts where *ceṭak* are believed in, a final measure of precaution against their malice.

During the measuring of grain, water-pots on the floor must remain empty save one. If a woman passes by bearing an empty pot of water the measuring must be stopped. Work, too, must stop if a widow passes by or a person known to have an evil eye or if a cat crosses the floor from right to left. Should an owl or a crow settle on the top of the central pole the *barkat* of the measuring is lost. If a scorpion, a snake or a fox be found on the floor the omen is a good one. The best of omens, however, is for a flock of sheep to wander on to the floor and eat the grain; the sheep are not disturbed at all and the shepherd is taken home and feasted. It is also portent of good luck if an ass, which is usually considered an inauspicious animal, comes by chance to the floor. If the moon rises or a jackal calls as measuring begins, the cultivator may expect great *barkat*. A good omen, too, is drawn from the unexpected coming to the floor of a *Māng*, especially if he carries a rope. It is ominous of evil to sneeze or cough on the floor.

A few additional precautions against evil-eye and spirits are taken on the floor just before the measuring begins. A coconut which must be unbroken is in the Deccan placed in the *rās* and the milk of a broken coconut is sprinkled round the *rās*. On the pile of grain are placed a black blanket and a white cloth, *pāsoḍī*. In Sind pieces of bread and sweets are placed on the grain, whilst in Kanara a piece of bread made from the new paddy crop is placed on the *rāśī*. In the Deccan rice and curds are sprinkled round the floor before measuring, and *Mahārs* sprinkle the blood of a goat at the four corners.

After the grain has been removed from the threshing-floor the floor is swept and the threshing-post is removed. In the Deccan a coconut is usually placed in the hole from which the post is removed, and this remains in the hole till the next year, unless it is taken by a *Mahār*. In the Karnāṭak before the pole is taken from the floor milk and ghee are poured on to it to cool its hot *śakti*.

Agricultural ritual affords many illustrations of this association of power with heat. The sowers, as we have seen, on their return from the field are required to cool their hot *śakti*; during threshing the bullocks and the threshing-post are kept cool with water.

Raddis pour milk and ghee into the pit in which the threshing-post is erected; when the threshed stalks of millet are stacked for fodder, milk and ghee are first poured on the site to cool it. When milk and curds are sprinkled round the *rās* or the threshing-floor the object would seem to be the same, the cooling of hot *śakti* for milk does not scare away spirits. The offering again of milky foods to the crops, and the pouring of milk and ghee over standing sheaves is in part based on the assumption that the crop should be treated as if a pregnant woman, but there is also the idea that milk should be offered in *naivedya* to cool the hot *śakti* of the grain.

When the grain is ready for removal from the floor women come to assist their men-folk. In the Karnāṭak the women cannot approach the spot where the men fill the baskets on the floor, but they help to empty the baskets into carts. In the Konkaṇ as the women remove the grain from the floor they touch the grain and then their foreheads with their right hands in an effort to add increase to the grain.

There are many ways of storing grain. There is the granary, *koṭhā* (Sin.), *kaṇagā*, *kaṇang* (Mar.). In black cotton soil tracts grain is stored in pits lined with kadbi grass and covered with a stone lid, *hage*; inferior grains are merely put into bamboo baskets which are placed on stones, *panat*, *khanaj*. Those who place grain in the store must be ritually clean, but there is diversity of practice subsequent to the filling of the granary. In Kanara widows and unclean persons are not allowed to remove grain from the store. In Sind boys who have not yet completed their study of the Koran are not allowed to approach a granary lest they, as semi-infidels, destroy its *barkat*. In many parts, however, there is no insistence on cleanliness when grain is removed from the store. In the Deccan no grain can be removed without leaving the level of the store quite smooth, and if grain be given out of the house it must not be given without being measured. The store of grain in the Deccan is protected by ashes from the *Hoḻī* pyre; in Kanara the roots of cuscus grass, bāḻdevaru, are put with the store of rice; jvārī and wheat grain reserved for seed is protected by nim-leaves and asafœtida.

I have already made reference to the possibility of the store of grain increasing in size after it has been placed in the granary. When a saintly visitor visits a house he is given grain; some of this he returns and it is added to the store of grain in the granary to add to its increase. On the day she enters her husband's house for the first time (*gharbharaṇī*) the bride is required to kick over a measure of grain to avert the evil potentiality of her *pāyguṇ* ; this grain is subsequently added to the granary. Those who observe a Somavati vow give grain to a priest who returns three handfuls to the giver ; this too is added to the granary. During *Navrātri* many families beg grain from house to house, not from any need but to obtain grain to add to their store. Every Friday in the month of *Śrāvaṇ* women visit the temple of a goddess, preferably *Lakṣmī* and while on their way back try to find grain lying on the road to add increase to the *barkat* of their household store.

THE WINNOWING-FAN

The winnowing-fan separates the grain from the chaff; it is therefore credited with a power of scattering evil and banishing spirits, and this power is associated with *Mariammā.*

When a child is attacked by smallpox a winnowing-fan is used to create a wind and the child is supposed to be relieved as it is fanned ; boiled gram, too, is often put in the fan and waved over the child. A winnowing-fan is used by all communities to avert evil and epidemics. The *Kātkarī*, when there is an epidemic of fever, takes a winnowing-fan and places in it a coconut, liquor, and a fowl with two or three images of flour in human semblance and carries it to the village boundary, where the comestibles are eaten and the fan is left for the next village to pass on in turn to its neighbour. When small-pox comes to his village he deposits at the boundary of his village a winnowing-fan containing a coconut and leaves of the nim-tree (Melia azadirachta). Cholera he attempts to avert in much the same way by placing a coconut and a fowl in the abandoned fan. In forest villages of the Karnāṭak on an outbreak of plague old winnowing-fans are deposited in a line on public roads or on the joint boundaries of villages. When cholera breaks out non-Brahmins in the Karnāṭak take a sheep, a miniature cart and a winnowing-fan to the boundary of the village ; the fan contains coconuts, lemons, untwisted thread and the bangles of a woman. On the tenth day after a man has been smitten with small-pox *Kātkarīs* call seven girls and one boy and feast them ; the boy is given a stick of bamboo and each girl has a winnowing-fan. At sunset the Hindu housewife, to drive away *Alakṣmī*, the personification of ill luck, goes round every corner of her house with a lamp the while some one else beats a winnowing-fan with a stick.

In the practice of *Utāra*, in which things are waved round a sick person and deposited at cross-roads in the hope that the sickness will be transmitted to others, a winnowing-fan is the usual receptacle in which the waved objects are placed. If a child be born at an inauspicious moment it is placed in a winnowing-fan with grain and placed before a cow which eats the grain and smells and breathes upon the child, thus removing the anticipated evil. When a Hindu is dying, millet is placed in a winnowing-fan and this is distributed in the name of the dying man after he has inserted his hand in the grain. If a mother has lost several children at birth, on another birth sweepings are placed in a winnowing-fan with the child; the fan is taken out of doors, the sweepings are thrown away and the child is brought back in the fan covered with a cloth. This prevents the premature death of the child or that of future issue. When a child suffers from chicken-pox, dry manure is winnowed so as to sprinkle the child. On the sixth day after a birth when the goddess *Ṣaṣṭhī* is worshipped along with the instrument with which the child's navel-cord was severed, a winnowing-fan containing rice, coconut and a *khaṇ* or bodice-cloth is given to the officiating priest or his wife.

To increase the longevity of their husbands all *suvāsinīs* make presents on certain days of two new winnowing-fans to other married women. This is done on days when *Gaurī* is worshipped; whenever rivers are bathed in on *parvakāl*; on every twelfth day of the fortnight and when the donor's husband is dying, as this will necessarily be the last occasion on which she can do this. Two new fans are taken; with lime and red colour a line is drawn at the bottom of the fans from corner to corner; in one fan are placed rice, coconut, five bangles, turmeric, saffron, dried coconuts, cash and a new *khaṇ*. The second fan is inverted on the first. The *suvāsinī* who receives this gift must sit on a wooden plank with her face to the East; her lap is filled (*oṭī bharaṇī*) and then the fans are gently placed in her hands.

Giving away a winnowing-fan has its dangers. A winnowing-fan cannot be given away or lent at sunset, and a woman when *enceinte* can never give one away. A fan must never be touched with the feet and never sat upon.

One explanation given of the frequent use of a winnowing-fan is that it is a *vanśapātra*, a utensil made from *vanśa* or bamboo. The bamboo is called the progenitor of the race, and as *vanśa* also means 'race', a winnowing-fan is used at a birth, the beginning of the human race, at a marriage which is the increase of the race, at death, the end of the race, whilst it is used as a receptacle for grain, the support of the race. This has all the appearance of being another example of the insidious habit of playing on words so characteristic of Hindu ritual.

PESTS OF THE CROPS

On the *Sankrānt* night preceding the *Māghanakṣatra* soon after nightfall twigs of kyadgi and munḍaki are buried in different corners of the fields. The person who buries these twigs makes a shrill noise in imitation of scaring away mice and hares, and he must let no one see him burying the twigs. Branches of baiṇī are also stuck in the ground with the same object of keeping away these pests, and providing sentinels who will protect the crop in its state of pregnancy.

To keep away jackals from a field of sugar-cane an image of a jackal is made out of sugar-cane and put in the middle of the plantation with a prayer to the jackal to keep away his tribe. Pieces of the tops of the cane, *vāḍe,* are made into images of a man and of a tiger and placed at different ends of the fields, and the human image is supposed to keep away tigers. When there is an epidemic of mice an image of a mouse made from wheat flour is put at the mouth of a mouse-hole. A field, however, may contain small images which are not intended to scare away pests. When sugar-cane is planted an image of an elephant is made from the severed tops of the cane, about ten inches long and six inches high and placed in the field so that the crop may grow as strong and high as an elephant. This image is worshipped with haḻad and kunku, and a strange feature of the worship is that as the worshipper returns home another person beats him with sugar-cane until he howls, for if he does not howl then, he will howl later when he finds his crop a poor one.

The bājrī crop is damaged by an insect called *baḻī.* To scare away this pest a *baḻī* is caught and placed on the palm of the hand with its head towards the finger-tips. Then the *rayat* strokes it from head to tail facing the direction opposite to that from which the insect came. The insect, however, responds to this treatment only on Saturdays and Sundays.

To free a field from locusts in Sind earth blessed by a *Pīr* or Shaikh (*mākri pīr*) called *khāk* is sprinkled over the soil. *Mavchis, Bhils* and *Konkanis* catch a locust and worship it with a bangle, red ochre, red and yellow turmeric, camphor and a coconut. The locust with all these things is placed in a new basket of bamboo along with a lemon, an egg and a chicken ; four flags of red cloth are stuck at the four sides of the basket which is called 'the cart of the goddess'. The basket is then taken to the village boundary where another village takes it on further until it reaches finally the temple of the goddess at Khed Kochra in the Shahada taluka where it remains. In Khandesh locusts are also driven away by making images of a locust from earth and placing these on the village bounds. Locusts are also caught in an earthen pot and the pot is dashed in pieces at cross-roads after dark. In Sind certain *Pīrs* and fakirs have the power of driving away pests. Locusts have a king who guides them on their flight; through charms the *Pīr* approaches the king who closes the mouths of the locusts as they fly over particular fields, rendering them innocuous. The *Pīr* also writes charms which are buried in the field or are hung to branches in the fields or makes rings round the fields with charmed sand and earth.

The Hindu also buries *yantras* at the four corners of his fields as a protection against pests. On some crops like brinjal he sprinkles ashes from a potter's kiln; on his grain he scatters ashes from the *Hoḻī* pyre. When a pest actually attacks a crop, one plant infected is taken and its leaves are tied to a plough, and then at early dawn unobserved by any one a naked man inverts the plough. As a protection against deer or grasshoppers a charmed black thread with many knots is tied round the corners of a field. In the Deccan to free a field from locusts a woman in her menses is asked to walk through the field rubbing in her hands four locusts and four ears of bājrī.

CHAPTER XVIII

THE POWER OF GRAIN

THE ritual of the threshing-floor preserves the *śakti* of grain from injurious contacts. With the same inconsistency, however, that marks other forms or manifestations of power, the power of grain is itself able to avert evil.

On the threshing-floor every effort is made to prevent the stealing of grain by spirits, yet at the same time grain itself scares away spirits. Scattered towards the cardinal points it is one of the commonest forms of *dikbāndha* or barrier against the entry of spirits. When a *Kātkarī* woman after the birth of her child is haunted by spirits grain is put down her clothes. When illness in Gujarāt is attributed to spirit activity a pile of wheat is boiled and deposited at the junctions of roads; in the Deccan when epidemic approaches several kinds of grain are boiled and sprinkled after sunset on the village boundary. Sprinkled over a person possessed by a spirit; eaten by him or tied to his person, grain exorcizes a spirit. At a *Lamānī* marriage five kinds of grain are placed in two earthen pots, waved in front of the bridal pair and thrown away to the south. These pots, which after being waved must not be seen by the bridal pair, keep away spirits. During *Airaṇīpūjā* in the Karnāṭak the bride's mother holds a winnowing-fan containing a heap of rice; this is covered with another fan as a lid and on this is placed a lamp. The mother finally takes grain from the heap and scatters in all directions to keep away spirits. Even the threshing-floor and the pile of grain *rās* is protected from spirits by sprinkling round in a circle the grain of rāḻā or uḍīd (Panicum Italicum, Phaseolus mungo).

When a Muhammadan woman dies in childbirth mustard seed is thrown behind the corpse to prevent the ghost *Ruh* of the dead returning. When a Hindu loses his wife in some castes grain is thrown behind the corpse as it is carried to the pyre, to prevent the return of the ghost of the deceased, should the husband remarry; if the woman has died in travail her ghost *Hedalī* or *Churel* is one of the terrors of India, and the attentions of this ghost are averted by throwing *rāḻā* seed after the corpse.

If anything with *śakti* which should not touch the ground, does so touch the ground, the Hindu sprinkles rice to avert evil, and if milk boils over into a fire, throws rice into the fire. The Muhammadan under similar circumstances would weigh against grain the object which has touched the ground and give the weighed grain away in charity. When a pilgrim returns from his wanderings grain is sprinkled on him and also is thrown about. At an eclipse gifts of grain are made to avert evil. *Lingāyats*, *Tilagars* and others in a dangerous illness put rice three times on the back of their hands and thrice on their palms and throw away; *Kan Divar* and *Madivals* in illness tie nine kinds of grain in a cloth with copper coins to a tree, choosing a tree outside the village and near a highway if the illness has affected their cattle.

Grain is used in many ways to render innocuous the potentiality of *pāyguṇ*; a gift of grain to a priest, *navgrahadān*, averts the evil influence or *pīḍā* of the planets. Grain is an ingredient of things waved round a person and thrown at cross-roads to avert ill, and though seldom used to avert evil-eye, it is with this object waved round the Hindu bridal pair when they return from their procession. In all auspicious rites *Puṇyāhavācan* is necessary; both in this rite and when a *baḹi* is offered to gods in a *śānti* ceremony to avert evil, the celebrant takes grain and water and sprinkling them on the ground says, 'May every kind of evil be driven away'.

The most interesting aspect, however, of the power of grain appears in practices in which it is used to control *śakti* in the interest of man. There is no feature of Hindu ritual more common thatn the throwing of *akṣat* or unbroken rice, and hardly less common is the use of grain, not necessarily unbroken, as an *āsan* to insulate *śakti* from the ground.

An *āsan* of grain is always used for *kalaśas* installed in all *śānti* ceremonies; in all ceremonies the betel-nuts and coconuts representing *Gaṇpati* are placed on grain as are also the nuts representing the *Saptarṣis* or the *Navgrah*. Certain images are always placed on an *āsan* of grain; that of *Gaurī* worshipped on Bhādrapad sud. 3, that of *Gaṇpati* installed on *Gaṇesacaturthī*, of *Anant* installed on *Ananta caturdaś*; the image of *Durgā* installed during *Navrātri* and that of *Ṣaṣṭhī* worshipped on the sixth day after a birth. Symbols into which *śakti* has been invoked, such as images and the *devak*; things which by association with something possessing power have themselves acquired power such as the *ārtī* waved around an image; persons again who for the moment have abnormal power, such as the bridal pair; all these are placed on an *āsan* of grain. As an *āsan* grain not only protects a thing possessing power from the drawing away of its power through contact with the ground, but it adds to its *śakti.* The grain on which the bridal pair sit is not merely an *āsan,* for beneath the grain there is already an *āsan,* a blanket or *pāṭ*; it adds to the *śakti* of the bridal pair.

In other ways, too, grain and in particular *akṣat* adds to the *śakti* of the object on which it is thrown. When *ārtī* is performed of an image all who are present throw rice on to the image and thereby add to its *śakti.* In the worship of every image each portion of the image is worshipped in turn and rice is thrown on to each limb and part. This is *Angapūjā* and adds to the *śakti* of the image. During the worship of every deity save *Viṣṇu* coloured *akṣat* is applied to the forehead of the image.

The invocation, *āvāhana,* of *śakti* is usually accompanied by the throwing of *akṣat* on to the symbol into which the *śakti* is invoked. It is thrown on an image at its installation; it is thrown on to the *devak* and the *hālgamba,* on to the betel-nuts, coconuts and other symbols into which *śakti* is invoked. The invocation of *Agni* into all *homs* or sacrificial fires; that of *Varuṇa* into *kalaśas*; the invocation of the *navgraha* or planets, that of *Gaṇpati,* of the family god and of other deities is always done with the throwing of *akśat.* It is with *akśat,* too, that invoked *śakti* is finally dismissed, *visarjan.*

Akṣat is used to invite *śakti.* When medicinal herbs are required *akṣat* is placed near the herb or tree before it is cut as an invitation to it. *Akṣat* is given to all gods in temples as an invitation to them to be present at the rites contemplated. As a form of invitation it is also offered to human beings. At a thread ceremony, a marriage or the feast which follows a birth the host brings a bowl of *akṣat* containing a betel-nut and gives to the assembled guests, who add another betel-nut and return the offering. At the beginning of the *Navarātri* festival *akṣat* is given to elderly persons, touched by them and given back. At a Brahmin marriage the parents of the bridal pair go in procession to the temple of *Gaṇpati* and request him to come to the marriage. Betel-nuts and *akṣat* are placed in front of his shrine, and a printed invitation card bearing the names of the bridal pair is placed before his image and before the *kula devatā.*

When in worship some requisite article is not obtainable, *akṣat* may be substituted. In the worship of standing sheaves in the field *akṣat* is thrown on the sheaves in lieu of ornaments and clothes, and the celebrant, as he throws the *akṣat,* says, '*Vastra samarpayami*', 'I offer clothes'; similarly, when flowers cannot be obtained it is sufficient to say 'I offer flowers' and throw *akṣat.*

Akṣat effects a transfer of *śakti.* At the beginning of every *hom akṣat* is placed on a leaf near the fire and this is applied by the *yajamān* to his forehead in order to transfer to himself the *śakti* of the fire. A blessing is a transfer or transmission of *śakti*, for there is *śakti* in will and in wishes. The bridal pair throw *akṣat* on each other; when *ārtī* is waved round a person *akṣat* is thrown on him; it is thrown by all assembled upon the bridal pair and on the *vaṭu* at his thread ceremony. *Akṣat* is thrown on the Hindu child after his tonsure; at *Sīmāntonayan* performed in the seventh or eighth month of a woman's pregnancy it is thrown on the woman and her husband and also on both of them at *Garbhādhān* and at *Pumsavan.* When a *svāmī* blesses he gives *akṣat* and throws *akṣat, mantrakṣat.* In all these cases there is an acquisition of *śakti* by the person blessed.

At a *Śrāddha* on completion of the ceremony the Brahmin representing God and those representing the *pitṛ* throw rice over the *yajamān* and wish him long life and prosperity. At the first and second tonsure of a child rice is applied not only to the boy's forehead but to that of his mother. When the sun is worshipped *akṣat* is thrown towards it. In the first year after her marriage and in the month of *Śrāvaṇ* each Monday the Hindu bride worships *Śiva* with a hundred and eight handfuls of *akṣat* to win long life and issue for herself and her husband. *Suvāsinīs* or married women are always to receive in their lap rice and other grain before they leave a house, in order to make more sure their enjoyment of *saubhāgya*, or the blessings of married life. In a marriage ceremony grain is used in several ways. During *Saptapadī* the bride walks on seven heaps of rice to acquire *śakti*; just before the gathered guests throw *akṣat* on the bridal pair and immediately after the screen or *antarpaṭ* between the bride and bridegroom is drawn aside, the bridal pair standing each on a heap of rice and facing, the bride east and the bridegroom west, throw *akṣat* and cumin seed on each other's head. At every marriage, too, the bridal pair worship *Gaṇpati* in a betel-nut placed on an *āsan* of grain, and the grain and the nut are then tied in the corners of their clothes. In every auspicious rite, in the introductory and in the closing ritual alike, the *yajamān* throws *akṣat* and water on the ground saying, 'May there be more auspicious rites in this house, abundance of grain, accomplishment of objects, long life to all, health and happiness'.

The object, then, of using grain and *akṣat* varies in detail considerably. At one time the hoped-for good is fertility itself, a manifestation of *śakti*; at another it is longevity; at another the averting of evil; at other times it cannot be defined more precisely than as the acquisition of *śakti* from which all *barkat* flows. When *akṣat* is thrown by a large number of people, as at a marriage, not only is the *śakti* of the grain transmitted but also the *śakti* of the common goodwill of those that throw the grain. This same variety of object distinguishes another class of rites; the rites of sowing seed ceremoniously called *Ankurāropaṇ* or in Kanarese *Sasimuḍisuvadu*, which are known to Western scholars as the cultivation of Gardens of Adonis.

ANKURĀROPAṆ

On the first day of a marriage, among *Lingāyats* and *Raddis*, when the bridal pair are anointed with turmeric powder and coconut oil, earth is taken from an anthill and put in an earthen dish. Then the priest takes five kinds of grain, unhusked rice, wheat, millet, gram and black gram and mixes them together. In the dish of earth he prepares five small basins in a cross design. The *śakti* of *Pṛthvī* or *Bhūmātā*, mother earth, is then invoked into the earth, and as he sows the seeds in the five hollows the priest invokes into them in turn the *śakti* of *Sadhyojāt*, *Vāmdev*, *Āghor*, *Tatpuruṣ*, and *Iśān*, which are all different names of *Śiva*. He then takes more grain and throws over the grain already sown, and after this waters the basins, but invokes no *śakti* into the water. The seeds are watered daily for fifteen days by the families of the bride and bridegroom. On the sixteenth day the party of the bridegroom go in procession to the bride's house, taking a dish of seedlings from which at the bride's house some are taken and with seedlings from the dish of the bride are put in the hair of the bride by a *suvāsinī*, usually the mother of the bridegroom. The seedlings that remain are distributed among all the married women who have gathered. This ceremony is called *Sasimuḍisuvadu*.

In much the same way seedlings are cultivated by *Lingāyats* a week before *Nāgpancmī* and used afterwards in the worship of the snake-god on the *Cauthī* and *Pancmī* days. Another *Lingāyat* ceremony is to sow seed in large earthen basins on the second Monday in *Śrāvaṇ* and to keep the seedlings till the last Monday of the month, when a *manḍap* of bamboo is made and decorated with betel-leaves. *Suvāsinīs* take this *manḍap* with the seedlings in procession to a well with an image of a bull of clay (*Basappa*). The image and the well are worshipped with *akṣat*, saffron and coconuts and the seedlings are thrown into the well; the betel-leaves are distributed with fried rice among those assembled. On the full-moon day of *Gaurīhuṇṇivi*, the season in which wheat is sown, *Lingāyats* perform a ceremony known as *Hangoḍā*. A fortnight before the full moon seedlings are sown in large shallow earthen basins. On the full-moon day a *suvāsinī* carries a pot of water worshipped with flowers and *akṣat*, and other married women carry the basins to a well which is also worshipped. Then the seedlings are set afloat on the water and the pot of water is brought back, adding to it water from the well. Fried rice and copra are distributed as *Gangāprasād*.

In the month of *Chaitra* Brahmins and their women-folk worship *Gaurī*, preferably on a Tuesday or Friday. This is the *Haḻad kunku* ceremony. The earth used for sowing seeds is taken from an anthill; the seeds are watered every day and then on an auspicious day at the end of the month are taken with the image of *Gaurī* and thrown into water. In this month the seeds of the kharif or first season crops are sown; in the month of *Vaiśākh* the seeds of the rabī or second cultivating season would be sown. The object of this ceremonial sowing is to foretell the harvest.

When a Brahmin dies his son sows seeds in an earthen dish and keeps for ten days at the spot where his father died. A lamp is also kept burning at the same place for fourteen days. On the tenth day the lamp, which is covered, and the plate of seedlings are taken to the spot where the customary obsequies are performed. There the lamp is used to kindle a fire; a calf is allowed to wander in the name of the dead so that by grasping its tail the dead may be assisted to cross the river *Virja nadī*; *piṇḍa* are offered to the deceased and in these *piṇḍa* some of the seedlings are stuck or the seedlings are placed on the *piṇḍa*. Finally, the *piṇḍa* and the remaining seedlings are thrown into water. Into the seeds when they are sown the *śakti* of the deceased is invoked. The object of this ceremony is to prevent the deceased going to hell or becoming a ghost, and it is thought he has attained salvation if the seeds germinate.

Even among more backward communities examples of ceremonial sowing can be found. In the Chota Udaipur State *Koḻīs* and others have an example of *Ankurāropaṇ* which they call *Jhanāria ind.* This sowing of seed accompanies the invocation of the *śakti* of *Ind* into five or ten twigs of kalamb (Anthocephalus cadamba), in fulfilment of a vow made in the hope of getting married, getting issue or recovering from a dangerous illness. Early in the morning men and women, with music, go to a kalamb-tree, taking with them a hen and a goat which are offered to the tree in worship. Then a bachelor, who must have fasted the last twenty-four hours, cuts the twigs, which have to be caught by others before they touch the ground. Then the party returns home and must be received on arrival by an old woman. The yard of the house is cleaned with cowdung and a hole is made for each twig; in each hole is placed rice and copper coins, save in one hole in which a rupee is put. Near the twigs is placed a raised seat of rice on which are placed one, two or three stools with a coconut on each. Nine kinds of seeds are sown in baskets and placed on the stools; before each stool is placed a small earthen pot of liquor, a larger pot of water and in a dish of khakhar-leaves five leaves of the bili-tree. There are also a silver twig, a silver pot and a silver stool. Early in the morning the *badva* walks from twig to twig, each of which is as thick as a man's ankle and at the root some five or six inches thick, and over the earthen pots without touching the ground. His ability to accomplish this depends upon his own continence and that of the inmates of the house for the previous three nights. The priest grasps the first twig with the right toe of his right foot and must not relinquish this hold until he has grasped the next twig and so on until he has walked over all the twigs. After this has been done a fire is lighted; the head of the goat, coconuts and bread, prepared the day before by four unmarried girls, are offered to the fire; a general feast follows and the twigs are then thrown into a river. The sowing of the seeds is done by the *yajamān* himself and the seeds are watered daily, but the rite can be performed without the sowing of seeds and is then known as *karodiya*.

At the fair of *Lakṣmī* or *Dyamava* performed in parts of the Karnāṭak once in twelve years, in some places once in thirty years, and at Sirsi once in three years, a buffalo is sacrificed, after which seedlings are cultivated, and the failure of these to germinate is regarded as a sign that there will be trouble in the village before the next fair. Story relates that a *Mahār* once obtained a Brahmin wife by deceit; his wife once asked for a betel-nut cracker and he inadvertently gave away his origin by saying he could crack nuts without a cracker as he was accustomed to breaking bones. When the *Mahār* was found out and was pursued, he entered the body of a buffalo by the process called *parkayapraveś* and this buffalo was killed. The ritual of the fair is in this wise. A buffalo is killed; a lamp is lighted and placed for one day on the severed tongue of the animal and for eleven days on its head. On the eleventh day a fire is kindled from that lamp; the severed head of the buffalo is placed on a raised platform and is covered with a basket. One man watches the lamp by day and by night and the obsequies of the buffalo are supposed to be performed by the Brahmin wife of the story called Lakṣmī. On the same day the image of Lakṣmī is taken outside the village; her garments are removed and her bangles are broken. Her *mangaḻsūtra* symbol of married life, the broken bangles and the seedlings are buried outside the village, and a new simple white garment with red border is given to Lakṣmī as a sign of her mourning. A small hut is erected over the head of the buffalo and when the image of the goddess is taken outside the village, the hut and the buffalo's head are burned and the flesh of the buffalo is eaten by Mahārs. One small detail observed is to place the right foreleg of the buffalo in its mouth. After all this, the image of the goddess is brought back with its face covered and kept in a temple with closed doors for three days, after which the image is placed in a *pandal* before the temple. The villagers are divided into two parties which represent the family of the Mahār husband and that of Lakṣmī's parents. One person from each party, accompanied by his wife, brings for the goddess a *mangaḻsūtra,* a bodice-cloth (*khaṇ*) and other clothes, and after this other devotees bring clothes. The *śakti* of *Dyamava* is invoked into the seeds sown and the object of the *Ankurāropaṇ* is the general welfare of all.

On *Ghaṭasthāpana* day, the first day of *Āśvin,* grain of all kinds is placed before the household gods and water is poured on the grain. The seeds are sown in small plates of brass or earth. The earth in which they are sown must be brought from a north-easterly direction after worshipping the instrument of digging and the spot whence the earth is dug. On the tenth day which is *Dasarā* the seedlings are thrown into the fields to fertilize the kharif crops. On this day it is considered lucky to cross the boundary of a village and some of the seedlings are worn in their turbans by people who make a point of crossing the bounds of their village. The pot in which the seeds are sown along with a *kalaśa* covered by a coconut is called *ghaṭa,* 'joining together', and this gives its name to the day.

At every *Ankurāropaṇ* performed by Brahmins five gods are invoked into five betel-nuts, and these are placed on the earth in which the seeds are sown. These five nuts are placed in the formation so customary in Hindu ritual, that of a cross. The nut, which is the symbol into which Brahma is invoked, is placed at the centre and the other four nuts at the four cardinal points around, Indra in the east, Varuṇa in the west, Soma in the north, and Yama in the south. These five gods guard the directions, their invocation forms a *dikbāndha* and they themselves are *dikpālakā,* 'guardians of the directions'. The basket in which the seeds are sown and the symbols of the gods are placed on an *āsan* of leaves from the bel, aśvath and śiriś tree with darva grass, and white rice is thrown on the earth before the gods are installed. When the invocation of the gods is made the celebrant says, 'I bow to the lords of the cardinal points who bring success in every work; may they make my present rite a success and always accomplish what is auspicious for me'. After the invocation of the guardian deities the rite of *Ankurāropaṇ* is begun with the *Sankalpa* or declaration of intention as follows: 'That I may succeed in this rite I undertake and that this may create my future success and above all with the object of pleasing the Supreme Being I am going to perform this subsidiary rite.'

Ankurāropaṇ is performed by Brahmins in all auspicious ceremonies at *Caul*, at a marriage and at a thread ceremony; at a car festival and at *Grahyajna*; when an image is first placed in a temple, *devatā pratiṣṭā*; before entering a house for the first time. It is also performed in obsequial rites. It is also performed in almost all the *sanskāra*. Some exceptions to the ceremonies in which it is performed afford a clue to its real meaning and object. *Ankurāropaṇ* is not performed in *Garbhādhān* or the ceremony of consummating a marriage. In this ceremony several *hom* are lighted; one of these is the *Garbhādhān hom*, the *hoṁ* of impregnation at the close of which the *yajāmān* is required to put juice of durva grass in the right nostril of his wife and offer prayers to the sun to make both of them fertile by removing any obstructions to fertility (*sūryopasthan*). *Ankurāropāṇ* is also not performed in the ceremony of *Sīmāntonayan* celebrated in the seventh or the eighth month of a woman's pregnancy; in that of *Jātakarma* on the twelfth day after a birth, nor in the naming of a child *Nāmakarana*. It is presumably not performed in the consummation ceremony because the seed of fertility is otherwise sown, nor in the other rites mentioned because the realization of fertility has already been achieved.

Conceding, however, that one of the objects of *Ankurāropaṇ* on many an occasion is fertility, it is, I think, easy to emphasize unduly its connexion with fertility. Fertility, after all, is but a manifestation of the activity of power; *barkat*, the fruit of *śakti*, includes other objects of desire, and it seems to me that no co-ordination of a multitude of examples of *Ankurāropaṇ* is possible save on the assumption in general terms that the cultivation of seedlings is to produce power. *Ankurāropaṇ* is a marriage of two *śakti*; that which is invoked in the earth and that which is invoked in the seed; when performed in a *jatrā* it is part of the marriage ceremony of the deity. It adds to the *śakti* of a deity and can be performed for all gods and goddesses. Fertility can hardly be associated with the *Ankurāropaṇ* performed when a *Śāstrī* for seven days in Bhādrapad reads to an audience of listeners. At a tonsure ceremony it brings the welfare of the child and this includes *vidyākāmuka* or wisdom; at a thread ceremony it helps the boy to remain a celibate; it brings happiness and as a necessary preliminary to this *pāpaparihār* or the wiping away of sin. On their New Year's Day Persian Moslems, at a particular hour fixed by their priest, place on a table grain which for five days previously has been soaked in water and allowed to germinate. This grain with eggs, fish, fruit and a hen is consumed and distributed among friends to win *barkat* during the year which has just opened. *Tamil Christians* sow seed around their 'foundation pole' in the marriage booth to secure happiness for the bridal pair and after three days throw the seedlings into water. In the case of a death there has been a distinct break with fertility, and though there is a belief that in the sowing of seed during the obsequies fertility is preserved, an avowed object of the sowing is to add to the *śakti* of the deceased, preventing his becoming a ghost or going to hell.

Many authorities [1] treat the ceremony of *Ankurāropaṇ* as intended merely to ensure the fertility of the earth and of mankind, and accept the final throwing of the seedlings into water as a charm to secure a due supply of fertilizing rain. The *Gardens of Adonis* are taken as the best proof that Adonis was a deity of vegetation, and Sir James Frazer emphasizes that the sowing of the seed was done chiefly or exclusively by women, whilst in *Religion and Folklore of Northern India* it is stated that at marriages, thread girdings and pregnancies the Mother is invoked to enter the seedlings.

In suggesting a new co-ordination I would invite attention to the following details of the ceremonies I have already described. At a car festival, at *Grahayajna* and at *devatā pratiṣṭā* it is the priest who sows the seed; at a marriage or at a thread ceremony a father sows the seed, but must, as in many Hindu rites, be accompanied by his wife, and should the father of the *vaṭu* or of the bride or bridegroom have no wife, the seeds are sown by a relative who has a wife. At obsequies it is the son of the deceased who sows the seed; in the Kanarese ceremony of *Sasimuḍisuvadu* it is the *ayya* who sows the seed. There is nothing, in fine, in Hindu ritual

[1] Vide *Religion and Folklore of Northern India*, W. Crooke, 1926, pp. 257–8; *The Golden Bough*, Part iv, vol. i, pp. 239 sqq. 'The Position of Women in Rabbinical Literature', E. M. Ezekiel, *Journal Bombay Branch Royal Asiatic Society*, vol. iii (new series), 1927, p. 182: 'Barley was sown in flower vases a few days before the wedding as a symbol of fecundity.'

to suggest that the sowing of the seed is the work of women because of the fertility of their sex.

There is again no restriction of this ceremony to deities associated with vegetation; it may be used in the worship of all gods and goddesses and the *śakti* of the particular deity worshipped is invoked.

The final throwing of the seedlings into water also bears for me quite another meaning from that which is usually attributed to it. It is quite impossible to associate all the occasions on which *Ankurāropaṇ* is performed with operations or seasons of agriculture, and the throwing of the seedlings into water is paralleled exactly by the habitual throwing into water of all symbols into which *śakti* has been invoked. In Hindu ritual it is impossible to get away from the practice of throwing into water things which have once been the tabernacle or repository of *śakti*. Images of gods and goddesses after invocation of power on special occasions and these are usually of clay; the betel-nuts into which the *ṛṣis* are invoked on *ṛṣipancmī*; the *piṇḍa* into which the *śakti* of the dead is invoked; the *hāḷgamba* and the *manekstambha* which have possessed the invoked *śakti* of the family god; the *Aśmā* or *Jīvkhaḍā* stone which has enshrined the *śakti* of the dead; the images of bulls worshipped on the *Amāvāsyā* of *Jyeṣṭha*, and the image of the snake-god worshipped on *Nāgpancmī*; the image of *Gulkavva* installed by *Lingāyats* during *Śrāvaṇ*; images of *Śiva* worshipped daily as *Pārthivaling* on the palm and renewed every day; images of *Gaurī* worshipped on *Gaurītṛtīyā*, of *Gaṇpati* worshipped on *Gaṇeśa caturthī*, of *Kṛṣṇa* on *Gokulaṣṭamī* and that of *Kṛṣṇa* worshipped on *Śrāvaṇ* vad. 8 when made of clay; all these are thrown after use into water. When a new sacred thread is substituted for an old one the discarded thread is thrown into water, for in its strands and in its knot it has enshrined the *śakti* of many deities.

Things which have acquired *śakti* by contact are also eventually thrown into water. The *kankaṇ* and the *bāśing* of the bridal pair; the *kankaṇ* or wristlets worn by the *yajamān* at a car festival; the severed navel-cord of a child; flowers and leaves used in worship when removed at a subsequent worship; offerings of *naivedya* made to *Gangā* on *Karka Sankramaṇa* and regarded as the leavings of the goddess which none must eat; the leaves on which Brahmins dine at a *Śrāddha*.

Even to a Muhammadan the idea that a thing which has once possessed power, kudrat, must be thrown into water is not unknown. Arabic writing found on the ground is thrown into water;

a hearth when broken or a talisman which has served its purpose or in which faith has been lost. The seeds of dates over which verses of the Koran have been recited; the remnants of food prepared during the ten days of *Muḥarram* in the name of the martyrs and food prepared in the name of *Piran Pir*; the wristlets of the bridal pair, *ghāna*; worn leaves or bindings of the Koran and even old books are all thrown into water. Remnants of food prepared from a sheep into the mouth of which the *kudrat* of the Koran has been blown, and the bones of the same sheep. In the month of *Rajab* Persian Moslems put foods of various kinds into seven, twenty or forty pots, in memory of *Ḥaḍrat 'Ali*; when the name of the saint is pronounced his *kudrat* enters the pots, and so after the food has been consumed the pots are thrown into a river.

Various explanations are offered of this practice of throwing things into water. After the dismissal of *śakti*, according to the Hindu, the object which once enshrined *śakti* becomes the 'leavings' of *śakti* and these are thrown into water that they may dissolve into an element from which they were evolved, that they may be preserved from impure contacts and that they may not be stepped over. Muhammadans explain their similar practice as a measure to cool hot *kudrat.* The pots into which Persian Muhammadans have invoked the *kudrat* of *Ḥaḍrat 'Ali* are eventually thrown into water 'to make them cool'. Muhammadans in Sind use the same phrase with reference to the throwing of the garlands and wristlets of the bridal pair into water, and precisely the same explanation is given of the throwing of the *tāzias* in Sind and of the *panjā* in the Karnāṭak into water during *Muḥarram.*

The assumption of Western writers that in many rites the throwing of water or the throwing of a thing into water is to ensure a supply of fertilizing rain can hardly be made on the basis of Indian practices. The splashing of water on those, for example, who return from sowing is interpreted as a rite to bring rain, but as I have described before, in the Karnāṭak sowers have on return from the field to wash with cold water to cool their hot *śakti*, and the threshing-post and bullocks used on the threshing-floor are sprinkled with water with the same object. The regularity of the Indian seasons again forbids any assumption that rites carried out throughout the year can have as their object the bringing of rain which out of season would entail disaster.

The *Ankurāropaṇ* ceremony, if I am right in following the guidance of those who practise it, is nothing more than a rite intended to produce an increase of power and all that this connotes. When at the close of the rite the seedlings are thrown into water they are so thrown because they have been the residence of power, and quite probably because it is necessary to cool their hot *śakti.*

Accepting, too, the premise that power whether evil or beneficent is associated with heat, it does not seem rash to assume also that whenever anything is ritually thrown into water it is to avoid some danger and to cool some manifestation of hot power. The *baḻī* offered to avert evil in a *śānti* ceremony performed to escape the anticipated sequel to an ominous happening is thrown into a river, but primitive communities in India have many practices that suggest the same object of cooling hot power. If a man be attacked by small-pox a *Kātkarī* hangs over his bed a garland of flowers ; after some time this is taken to a river in complete silence and thrown away by a crowd. During an epidemic of cholera the *Kātkarī* takes plantain-leaves, marks on them with soot and red powder the impression of a hand and, adding a ball of rice, waves round a stricken person and throws into a river. On the fifth day after a death *Kātkarīs* hang up a garland of flowers ; at dawn the elders from the land of the dead are supposed to come and take away the soul of the dead and then the garland is thrown into running water or a well. In the event of a great disaster attributed to the agency of spirits the *Kātkarī* takes a lemon, red powder, a comb, red and yellow thread and, tying all these in a basket with black thread, gives to a *bhagat* who lashes himself and howls as if possessed by a spirit, and goes to a river, followed by a noisy crowd. The basket is then thrown into the river after which the crowd remains silent for some minutes.

As disease, death and spirits are all associated with hot power it is possible that in these practices of the *Kātkarī* a manifestation of hot and evil *śakti* is cooled by the throwing into water of something which is supposed by contact to have become itself suffused with that power. I have not, however, as in the earlier practices described, been fortunate enough to find admissions that support this suggestion.

CHAPTER XIX

THE POWER OF BREAD

BREAD has *śakti* or *kudrat* derived from the grain of which it is made. Its power averts evil of many kinds.

Bread is a medium commonly used for destroying the evil *pāygun̦* of the unknown. *Marāṭhās* wave bread round newly-purchased animals. When their cattle give birth to calves away in the jungle bread is waved round them when they return to their stalls. *Tilagars* wave bread twice round their purchased cattle and then throw it to dogs. Another common practice is to place a preparation of bread called *puran̦pol̤ī* on the back of a horse or bullock after purchase; the bread is slapped whilst it is on the back of the animal and is then given the animal to eat. The giving of bread to an animal before putting it for the first time in its stall is also a widespread custom.

When a person returns from a journey or comes from another village, bringing perhaps strange spirits with him, or having, it may be, encountered the evil-eye of others, bread is used to protect him. In the Karnāṭak bread is waved round the returned traveller or the pilgrim who has been afar. When a woman with her child returns from a journey bread is waved round the child and thrown away; in Gujarāt this is done to protect the child, but in the Deccan the bread is waved round the woman to protect both her and her child. When a woman leaves her own village and goes to another village for her delivery bread is waved round her when she returns with her child. *Telīs* wave bread at sunset round any one who returns to his village, and throw it away. *Marāṭhās* do the same, but late in the evening place the bread outside the village gate.

A bridegroom coming to his bride's village crosses a boundary, and boundaries are the haunts of spirits,[1] whether these be the boundaries of villages or, as are thresholds, of individual houses. *Sīmāntapūjā* is the reception the bridegroom receives at the bound-

[1] Makār old men say that their fathers believed that the spirits of their ancestors sat on the village boundary.

ary of the bride's village before he enters its confines. In this reception bread is waved round him; this is repeated when he reaches the bride's house, bread being waved round both him and the bride and this again when the bride leaves her own house to go to that of her husband. When the bridegroom or the *vaṭu* at his thread ceremony goes in procession he exposes himself to the risk of evil-eye, so after the procession bread is waved over or thrown across him. Bread is waved near the face of any one the victim of evil-eye, spat upon by the victim and then thrown away.

Bread is also used in the transference of evil, in *Utāra*, *ghorā* (Sin.). It is waved round a sick person and thrown at cross-roads; the Muhammadan places cooked bread on the head of the sick and then throws it to dogs, or like the Hindu, waves it round the sick and throws away. The Muhammadan can direct the transference of his evils to an enemy by throwing the bread so waved at the door of that enemy. If a child does not sleep *Mal̲īs* wave bread round the child and throw away; when eating near a well the Hindu throws bread into the well or puts bread on the parapet of the well to avert spirits, and when eating in the open always satisfies the spirits by throwing bread in all the four directions.

A solution in Sind for a bad dream is to bake bread, place an onion on the bread and give it to a beggar.

The *Marāṭhā devak* and its *śakti* is protected from evil by a preparation of bread, *puraṇpol̲ī*,[1] and the *hāl̲gamba* of the Karnāṭak by a similar preparation called *hurand holgī* tied to it. In Gujarāt when a dead body is taken to the burning ghāṭ bread is thrown to dogs to rest the soul of the deceased, and if a man is persecuted by a ghost he throws bread outside his door.

The power of bread not only operates to avert evil, but more directly it confers *barkat*. To a Hindu bread is one of the things which should never be sold; to a Muhammadan an offer of bread confers *barkat* on the person who gives it, whilst it is dangerous to refuse such an offer. If a Hindu finds bread lying on a road, or if he sees a dog carrying bread from one house to another he should pick up the bread or snatch it from the dog and in silence bury it beneath his threshold, thus bringing himself great wealth in the near future. In the Deccan bread is placed on the heap of grain, *rās*, on the threshing-floor, to add to its increase, and still

[1] Cp. *Indian Antiquary*, May, 1895, p. 126, vol. xxiv: 'One of the *devaks* or wedding guardians of the Dekhan Mhars is a piece of bread tied to a post in the marriage porch.' This is inaccurate; the puraṇpol̲ī is not a *devak*, but protects the *devak*.

more common is the habit of mixing with the *rās* pieces of the bread used in the feast held during the threshing. In the Karnāṭak also before their meal on the threshing-floor the threshers throw bread not only on the pile of gathered grain, but also on the central post of the floor and on such agricultural implements as are on the floor. *Per mānī* is a Muhammadan practice followed to make a child walk well; when an infant first attempts to walk, seven loaves of bread are piled one on the other with a cord on the top of them. The child's foot is placed on the pile and at one blow the maternal uncle of the child has to cut with a knife the cord and at least one cake.

Precisely because of its intrinsic power bread is subject to many taboos. It must not be stepped upon; he who steps upon it will suffer from *tangi* or scarcity of food. It should not come in contact with the ground. Bread found on a road is put away from contact with the ground; in the Deccan it is powdered and thrown to fish to eat; should a Hindu throw bread to a dog it must be thrown in small pieces so that the dog will not drop any, or it should be placed on a prepared mound. The *tavā* or flat iron plate on which bread is baked derives power from its contact with the bread and a number of restrictions governs the use of the *tavā*. If the *tavā* be washed or cleaned after lamp-lighting time the cattle of the household will fall ill. The woman who places the *tavā* on the fire must also be the person who removes it, for if some other woman removes it the daughters of both the women will have disastrous quarrels with their husbands or their relations. A *tavā* cannot be placed on the hearth on *Nāgpāncmī* day nor when a corpse lies in the house. Three pieces of bread can never be roasted at the same time or the person so doing will fall in debt; either two pieces must be roasted or a fourth piece of nominal size should be added. Some of these illustrations are a recapitulation of the substance of other chapters in this book.

The drawing of omens implies the existence of a causative power and many omens are drawn from a *tavā*. If after it has been removed from the hearth and placed upright against a wall it sparkles with sparks, it is supposed to be laughing at the prospect of the good harvest that is coming. If when placed on the fire it makes a noise called *bhar bhar*, it indicates the immediate coming of a guest.

CHAPTER XX

THE POWER OF ANIMALS

THE HORSE

TO the Muhammadan in the Deccan a horse is *ghazi mard*; in Sind it is *malaik* or angel and *firishta*, 'God-sent', names that are also applied to a child with its special *kudrat*. The Prophet swore by the horse and the sparks from its hooves, and to possess a horse is as meritorious as entertaining forty Hafiz. A horse prays for itself and for its owner; from morning to afternoon for its owner and from afternoon till sunset for itself. When it bends a hind leg until it touches the ground it is making *fat'ha* on behalf of itself and its owner. Khwaja Ḥassan Basari had sold his horse, but bought it back at an enhanced price when in a dream the Prophet asked him why he had sold an animal that for long had prayed for blessings in Paradise for its master.

The nodding of a horse brings prosperity to its owner. Its stamping on the ground also forebodes success, but should it dig with its hooves disaster will follow. If its owner go on a journey attended with danger, a horse can see the danger and by unusual sounds and sudden stops will warn its rider. A horse can see the dead in their graves and the punishment therein of the sinful dead, so when a horse is lethargic, has stomach complaints or any bad disease, it is taken round a graveyard for twenty minutes that it may receive a shock on seeing the dead.

A horse that is *sadoro* scares away spirits when it neighs and protects its rider. To ensure that it bring *barkat*, when a horse is purchased the Muhammadan breaks an egg against its forehead. When a Hindu buys a horse he washes its feet, gives it bread to eat and applies turmeric and gold to its forehead to make its *pāygun̥* good. If its *pāygun̥* be auspicious a horse averts evil-eye and scares away spirits. Its hair is an amulet and Hindu children wear jewels threaded on the hair of a horse to keep away evil-eye, or the evil effects of contact with an impure woman. Horse-shoes, particularly on Sundays and Thursdays, avert spirits; they are also used to avert evil-eye.

A horse brings wealth. Muhammadan dealers in horses are proverbially lucky. To a Hindu a horse with auspicious markings brings all kinds of wealth, and if a Hindu cannot afford to keep a horse he tries at least to get a hair of a horse. At a Hindu marriage a horse and not a mare is used to bring *barkat*, though on the other hand *Mahārs* will not allow a bridegroom to ride a horse because they think this would be an affront to *Lakṣmī* and Saturn might carry off the bridegroom. Out of respect for the horse the Muhammadan abstains from eating horse-flesh, and the aversion to using horses in a plough is universal.

In some Hindu ceremonies orthodoxy requires that the earth used should have been trampled by the hooves of horses, *Aśvakrānte*, and in the ritual of the daily bath taken by the Hindu the earth is addressed as *aśvakrānte*.

When a mare foals the Muhammadan owner distributes sweets to every family in the village and the recipients are supposed to bless the mare and foal. The Hindu under similar circumstances treats the day as a holiday and worships the mare to get riches.

A pregnant woman or a bride newly married is not allowed to ride a mare. Before riding a horse one must be ritually clean, for an unclean rider harms himself and the horse. A Hindu, if unclean, cannot even salaam a horse and he cannot give food to a horse.

The lather of a horse in Sind is a cure for the bite of a scorpion, and the hair and the shoes of a horse are used in magic to create love. A Hindu gives the dung of horses to milch cattle to increase their supply of milk, and he makes people of wanton habits sit in a stable for some days as the odour of the mare's urine and excrement effects a cure. Both Hindus and Muhammadans think that frequent riding reduces sexual power, and that an ordinary saddle, not to mention the saddle of a saint, has its dangers. A Muhammadan utters *bismillāh* when he puts a saddle on a horse.

In Bombay at Nauroz, the New Year, when according to Persian Muhammadans the bull that supports the earth changes its burden from one horn to the other, a horse, fully harnessed, is kept outside their houses to indicate by the shaking of its harness the precise moment when the earth trembles in consequence of the shifting of the bull's burden. During the celebration of *Muḥarram* in Sind all horses are supposed to mourn the death of the Shahids of Kerbela and a feature of this celebration is a framework covered with a cloth which is ridden astride as if a horse; these horses are called *duldul* after the horse of *Ḥaḍrat 'Ali*, and to them women make vows in order to get issue.

If a mare is barren or its foals die it is in Sind taken round a saint's shrine and earth from the shrine is tied to its neck. If a horse has a habit of running away its halter is left at a shrine or the peg to which the horse is usually tethered is taken to a saint for him to blow over it.

THE ASS

A Muhammadan considers a donkey an accursed animal. Satan rides on its tail and Anti-Christ will ride a donkey. It is bad to keep a donkey because it is always praying for misfortune to come to its owner. The Koran is said to condemn its bray as the worst of all sounds. The sexual organ of a donkey is used as an aphrodisiac and for medicinal purposes; its milk cures whooping-cough and makes children sleep, but it destroys the intelligence of the child who drinks it. Intercourse with a female donkey is a stimulant, it is believed, of sexual power.

To touch, see or ride a donkey brings misfortune to a Hindu save at *Hoḻī*, when it is auspicious, and donkeys are ridden almost to death. The milk of a donkey, and in particular of a black donkey, is the best cure for bronchitis; fumigation with the smoke of its burnt excrement is a medicinal cure; a piece of the ear of a donkey is hung round the neck of children in a covering to make them strong, and the semen of donkeys is taken in other medicine to cure sexual impotence. The burnt hair of a donkey is used in fumigation, and in Sind a piece of donkey's dung is hung over the door of the room where a woman awaits her delivery as a protection against spirits. The sight of a donkey seen when going on any business means failure of object; the braying of an ass with its nose in the air is ominous of good fortune, but to see asses fighting brings disaster. If a pregnant woman sees asses mating her children will be born strong.

THE CAMEL

Eating the flesh of a camel is to a Muhammadan an act of piety. In the Karnāṭak and in Sind on *Bakri 'Īd* a camel is obtained by public subscription and its flesh is distributed. The camel is an animal of Paradise. The Prophet rode a camel and took an oath by a camel. The hair of a camel keeps away spirits and its flesh is a cure for rheumatism.

The Hindu thinks that the nails of the left foot of a camel kept in a house scare away mice. Its flesh is used medicinally and its dung when burnt cures many diseases.

THE SNAKE

A snake to a Muhammadan is either a saint or a spirit. If a snake appear at the shrine of a dead saint it is supposed to be the saint himself. At shrines snakes are fed with milk. If a snake appear when a house is being built it is called the master of the ground. A snake in the granary is called the *barkat* of the house. Where there is a snake there is usually wealth and it is bad luck to kill a snake.

To the Hindu also a snake is either a saint or an evil spirit. A good snake always departs when asked to do so; he is *jātivant*, 'born of a good family'; he is a saint who has not yet completed his penance. Some families have snakes that not only do them no harm, but actually protect the family and its buried wealth.

A snake is killed only when it shows it is a bad snake by not going away when requested. In contrast, however, with this idea is the belief of many primitive communities that to let a snake go free when it is met on a journey destroys the fruition of that journey's object. When a man is bitten by a snake mantriks throw water on him, and he is then able to relate the history of the snake and the reason for its reincarnation as a snake; a greedy man on reincarnation becomes a snake. If a person dies from snake-bite he is reborn in a royal family. It is lucky to see a snake in a dream, for it is a sign that a son will be born to the dreamer. If in a dream a snake passes over one's foot without biting it, it is a sure sign of success in any undertaking.

Barrenness is attributed to the killing of a snake in the present life or some past life. *Nāgbaḷī* is a kind of funeral obsequies performed with a snake made from darbha grass, to remove the curse of some snake killed which obstructs fertility. In Kanara among Brahmins on the fifth day of a marriage the snake-god is propitiated with the object that the bridal pair may have issue. *Nāgpancmī* is the day of the annual worship of the snake-god; on this day no life of any kind can be destroyed; there can be no ploughing, reaping, no plucking of fruit or plant; no grinding or other form of *himsā*. On the sixth of *Mārgaśirṣa*, known as *subrahmanya ṣaṣthi*, barren women observe a fast known as *ṣaṣṭhī* or *champa ṣaṣṭhī* and worship an image of the snake-god with soaked gram, sesamum, milk, flowers and saffron. They consume fruit, but must not touch salt nor eat any kind of grain, cooked or uncooked. This fast is sometimes observed on the sixth of every month until the women performing the worship obtains issue.

If a cobra be accidentally killed it is burnt after putting milk and a copper piece in its mouth.

THE COW

The cow to the Hindu is full of *śakti.* To see a cow averts the evils of the day. One who rears a cow never wants and one who has more than five cows has every form of wealth, *godhana.* The sight of a cow is equal to the sight of all the holy tīrths, whilst bowing to a cow secures the grant of one's prayers.

A cow confers *barkat. Mahārs* think that if a cow passes an open door at sunset and the occupants of the house remain at peace they will have *barkat,* but illness if at that moment they quarrel. In Sind a Hindu will not disturb a cow that enters a granary, for it brings *barkat* to the store.

A child born under a bad star is made to pass several times under the belly of a cow, or it is placed in a winnowing-fan full of grain and as the cow eats the grain it breathes on the child. The supposition is that the child enters the womb of the cow and is delivered by the cow free of sin, *goprasav.* When a new house is entered upon for the first time a cow is driven across the threshold before the owner enters. When a man leaves his home for some long time, on his return he sends a cow into the house, for the cow's body contains thirty crores of gods, as many a highly coloured picture in the bazaar shows, and these will drive away any evil spirit that has settled in the house during the owner's absence. At the time of performing worship a cow should strictly be tied near and within the sight of a worshipper, and the shrine of the *kula devatā* should be an area which a sitting cow would cover. The footprints of a cow bring blessing and Hindu royal processions used to be headed by a cow. When a goddess is to be installed, marks representing the footprints of a cow are made with powder and the goddess proceeds on a way marked with such footprints.

The dust kicked up by the feet of cows, *goraj,* is applied by some castes to the body of a new-born child to avert evil-eye ; the same dust should be sprinkled on the bridal pair, though this seems rarely done, and when water is not available as an offering to the sun in the daily *arghya, goraj* dust can be used.

On the twelfth of the dark fortnight of *Āśvin* Hindu women with children fast till evening and then worship a cow to secure the *kalyāṇ* of their children. On the twelfth day after a death Brahmin priests should be given a cow in the name of the dead to secure the absolution of the deceased and to give him assistance after death, for the tail of the cow will help the deceased in crossing the dread river of *Vaitrani* which separates this world from the next.

When a cow is about to calve, if a man encircles it three times, *pradakṣina*, this is equivalent to going to Benares; it is equal, indeed, to going round the earth, earth in this context being the old conception of India. This is *Bhūpradakṣiṇā*. On the twelfth of *Māgh* women without issue worship five cows with calves to obtain children.

The five parts of a cow have *śakti*. *Pancgavya*, that is curds, milk, ghee, urine, and dung. *Pancgavya* is given in small quantities to the *vaṭu* at his thread ceremony; at the annual renewal of the sacred thread, *Śrāvaṇī*, it is given to all who may be present; after a death it is sprinkled all over the house of the deceased after the removal of the corpse; after a birth it is sprinkled over the mother's room and over her clothes. These products of the cow taken together free from sin. When a vow is taken *pancgavya* is taken. Women are given it when they complete the third month of their pregnancy; elderly women perform a fast on *Ṛṣi Pancamī* and purify themselves with the same products. When clothes are brought back from the washerman they are sprinkled with *pancgavya* and when a man from one caste is admitted to another he is sprinkled with the same as a purification.

Gomūtra or the urine of a cow is used in many ways. In chronic cases of anæmia of a child caused by the touch of an impure woman, the mother in a naked state bathes the child in the urine of a cow. *Gomūtra* is as sacred as the water of the Ganges. On the eleventh day after her delivery a Hindu mother is sprinkled with this; on the eleventh day after a birth or after a death the house in which either of these happens is also so sprinkled. Children are bathed in it periodically to remove an evil anticipated after some ominous happening or to avert the evil of the eye or of spirits. *Bhils* and *Konkaṇīs* in Khandesh will not allow any stranger to enter their threshing-floor until he has been purified with *gomūtra*. Diseases of children are removed by a bath in *gomūtra* or by a draught of it.

When a cow calves it is said to have two heads, *dvimukhigo*; it is worshipped and the worshipper goes round the cow and the calf. The sight of a cow on waking brings *barkat*. Some orthodox persons worship a cow every morning and give it food which they themselves take at midday. When a cow drops dung, grain found in the dung is washed, cooked and eaten. A sick child can be cured by waving over its face three times the tail of a cow, or by taking it the same number of times round a cow. When new cloth or new clothes are purchased they are first placed on the back of a cow so that they will last long and bring *barkat*. Muhammadan children in Sind, to avert evil-eye or cure its effects, are given clothes which have been previously placed on a road for cows and other cattle to soil.

Milk confers *barkat.* A tradition of the Prophet is that he said, 'He who has no milk has no friend'. In Sind milk is *Khīr Pīr.* A Kanarese saying is that 'Peaceful is the house in which milk boils'.

It is forbidden to a Hindu to sell milk. To a Brahmin selling milk is as great a sin as one of the five great sins. Its sale is denounced, along with that of other things, in the phrase, *ras vikraya*; selling milk brings disaster, loss of wealth and harm to the children of the seller. The Muhammadan has an equal aversion in Sind to selling milk. A district officer in camp has much difficulty in forcing acceptance of payment for milk supplied to his camp. Many families in Sind will never sell milk, and on the eleventh of every month owners of herds of cows also refuse to sell milk and distribute it free to add *barkat* to their future supply of milk. This distribution of milk is made in honour of a saint, *Yarhienavara,* whose death occurred on the eleventh of a month. It is dangerous to spill milk; spilt on the ground it harms the cow and reduces the supply of milk. The Muhammadan covers spilt milk with earth or attempts to put it back in its vessel and then carrying it to a quiet spot, pours it away. *Mahārs* think that milk spilt should be dried at once with a cloth or with the hand before any one sees it, as otherwise the person spilling the milk will fall ill.

Milk should not be allowed to boil over into a fire; to prevent this, water is added to it before it is boiled and this prevents the udders of the cow being burned and the supply of milk failing. Though, however, it is unlucky to spill milk or allow it to boil over, on the seventh of the first fortnight of *Māgh* earthen pots of milk are boiled until the milk boils over and the side on which it overflows denotes the direction from which prosperity will come during the year. This milk is boiled by Brahmin women who have previously bathed with ruī leaves on their heads. Images of the sun and of his car are drawn with red sandalwood-paste on a wooden board and worshipped with flowers by men and women. The milk is boiled near the tulsī plant and the overflow is supposed to reach the sun.

Milk cannot be cooled by blowing on it or it brings blisters in the mouth. It must never be trodden upon. Curds and sweet oil must never be mixed, and ghee and sweet oil cannot be mixed nor even carried at the same time. An offer of milk cannot be refused. To a Muhammadan the gift of milk is a gift of God and to refuse it is sin; it is a worthy gift, *naimat uzmai.* When a

Muhammadan accepts an offer of milk he should give in return a coconut or grain, but sometimes this is done only when the first milk of a cow after calving is given away. A Hindu cannot refuse an offer of milk, but must at least dip his fingers therein; refusal of milk brings probable death to the mother of the person bold enough to refuse it and is particularly dangerous on a Friday. After accepting an offer of milk if the recipient leaves any milk this must be given away also or thrown away.

The *barkat* of milk can be stolen, leaving attempts to make butter from it futile. Several measures are taken to prevent the theft of this *barkat.* A churn pestle made of hivar wood cut on a Saturday is itself supposed to keep away a witch; a squirrel skin stuffed with earth from where the witch has urinated and hung to the rod of the churn and beaten, rendering the witch helpless, is another measure of protection. Beating the door of the room in which butter is being churned with a shoe or marking it with a marking-nut on a Saturday or a Sunday also prevents theft. The Muhammadan in Sind suspends a dead hoopoe or the teeth of a hyena over the churn.

At the time of milking animals are given cotton-seed soaked in water to eat; the seeds that the animals allow to fall on the ground are stolen by others and given to their own milch cattle to increase their milking capacity. To increase the yield of butter from one's own milk the last remnants of butter wiped from the churn are thrown into the churn of another man; this reduces the yield of butter obtained by the other man and to a corresponding extent increases one's own yield of butter.

Milk is peculiarly sensitive and attracts evil-eye. Muhammadans say this is because of its white colour. It is therefore always covered when carried out of doors. Muhammadans put sugar in milk when it is carried out of doors and cover it with leaves, paper or cloth. The Hindu puts in the milk as a further protection a blade of green grass. When milk is boiled to avert evil-eye marking-nuts are put in the milk.

Milk also attracts evil spirits. When children have just drunk milk they are not allowed to go out of doors for fear of being persecuted by spirits. Any decrease in the supply of milk given by a milch animal is attributed to a spirit called *Kusḻiṇ.* If a bowl of milk falls it is supposed that a spirit has attempted to drink it. Milk cannot be given away at sunset because those who do this are attacked by spirits; it cannot be given away even after the lighting of lamps, but buttermilk can be given away at that time.

Milk is associated by the Hindu with *Lakṣmī*, the goddess of good fortune. When a man sets out from home on a journey, to secure his safe return *patavadya* is given him before setting out; this is a preparation of gram pulse mixed with water and condiments, but milk is often used in the same way. In Gujarāt milk is poured round the village boundaries on Bhādrapad sud. 14, to prevent the appearance of any epidemic within the village. During an epidemic in Sind Muhammadans distribute milk among their fellow-villagers. Milk is also used to lessen the dangers of cutting the hair; at a thread ceremony the razor with which the *vaṭu's* hair is shaved is dipped in curds; at a tonsure the priest marks with milk the hair that is to be cut. In the Karnāṭak milk is sprinkled along the village bounds to prevent drought.

During a marriage ceremony milk is extensively used in one way or another by all communities. At a *Jain* marriage the guests dip ornaments in milk and present them to the bride, and the bridal pair give each other sugar and milk. In Sind the Muhammadan bride and bridegroom dip their fingers in milk and sprinkle it on each other; they sip milk from one dish and then the guests, to get *barkat*, sip from the same dish. *Vaddars* take grass and a woman's nose ornament and put them in a pot of milk and then pour this on the shoulders, back and front of the bridal pair. *Māḻis*, just before the wristlets of the bridal pair are worn, place curds in a saucer made from leaves on posts above the heads of the pair and at the corners of a square in which they are seated. When the groom leaves his own house, milk brought by one of the bride's parents is given him at his house; when he reaches the boundary of his bride's village he takes milk in his hand and at the door of the bride's house he is again given milk. When the married pair later return to the bridegroom's house they are both given milk, and when she enters the bridegroom's house the feet of the bride are washed with milk. Later again, when she returns to her parents as she leaves her husband's house she is given milk. The wristlets which the bridal pair have worn are, after removal, washed in milk to remove, according to one explanation, any evil they may have acquired in their defence of the bridal pair.

In the Deccan milk is used in many ways at a Muhammadan marriage. For three days before the marriage milk is sent every morning by the bride's family to the bridegroom and by his family to the bride. Before the bridegroom dons his festal clothes and leaves his own house to go to that of the bride his feet are washed in milk. The feet of his horse are also washed in milk, and an egg is placed beneath a hoof of the horse for it to crush. At the door of the bride's house the same thing is done and again an egg is crushed and the feet of the bridegroom's horse are washed in milk. During the marriage milk with rice is put in an earthen pot and all the women guests partake of it; this is done to invoke the assistance of the good spirits and, in particular, the spirit *Bibi Pari* and thereby add to the *barkat* of the marriage. The thumb of the bride is washed in milk which the bridegroom then drinks in order to foster their mutual love. After the marriage ceremony is over milk is given to all the guests and when the married pair leave the bride's house milk is given them. Finally, when the bride reaches the bridegroom's house her feet are washed in milk, and this is then sprinkled over the whole house, and especially in the four corners.

The Muhammadan explains this frequent use of milk at a wedding as intended to make the marriage white and prosperous. The bringing of *barkat* and the averting of evil are beyond a doubt also one of the objects with which the Hindu uses milk, but there are two examples of the use of milk at a Hindu wedding which bring in another idea with which I have dealt more fully in another chapter. The *kankaṇ* of the bridal pair are dipped in milk after their removal to cool their hot *śakti* and on the sixteenth day after the marriage milk is thrown on the marriage *maṇḍap* again to cool hot *śakti*.

Oaths are taken by milk and conditional curses are imposed by an offer of milk. A *Rāmośī* and a *Bhil* will not commit theft in a house wherein they have accepted an offer of milk; *Rājputs* offer milk to an unknown guest as do Sindis and, like the Deccani Muhammadan, they turn away a guest who will not take milk.

THE JACKAL

It is a good omen for a jackal to call whilst corn is being measured or whilst ploughing is in progress. 'Have you seen to-day the face of a jackal?' is a popular way of asking if all is well, for it is a good omen to see the face of a jackal. A jackal is one of the few animals the form of which a spirit will not assume. Its thigh-bone is used to avert evil-eye and is tied round the neck or round the feet of prized cattle.

If a jackal is met going from left to right of the traveller the omen is good; the howl of a jackal in broad daylight betokens danger; its howl in answer to another jackal, and this when it is looking south, means the death of the person who sees it, and if it be looking west, means the death of another person by drowning.

THE SHEEP

A sheep to a Muhammadan is holy. The Prophet said a man who wishes to prosper should buy a few sheep. The ram has much kudrat, for it descended from heaven as a substitute for the son of Abraham.

To a Hindu, on the other hand, it is an animal associated with evil. Devout priests will not touch it and a Brahmin would not rear one. It is one of the things which are used in making a gift the object of which is to transfer evil, and it is frequently a scapegoat.

The thigh-bone of a black sheep killed on Saturday averts evil-eye provided it has not had a hole made in it by a butcher.

THE CAT

One of the Prophet's disciples was called *Abū Hurera*, 'the father of a cat'. The cat received a blessing from the Prophet, and kept in a house brings *barkat.* Cats are kept at Muhammadan shrines and food touched by a cat remains clean to a Muhammadan. According to a tradition, cats are not impure; they keep watch around us. The Prophet used water from which a cat had drunk for his purification, and his wife ate from a vessel from which a cat had previously eaten.

Many omens are drawn from the movements of a cat. A cat coming towards a person when he rises in the morning means for him a bad day and a fruitless journey if the cat be met when he sets out. A cat's mewing from the west is a good omen and success comes to a man if a cat comes out of his house along with him. If a cat walks where a Hindu woman in menses has sat or taken a meal it does not by contact carry contagion. A cat's placenta buried under the threshold of a house brings good fortune to the inmates, and the bone of a cat ground into paste is a remedy for a wound caused by a rat.

THE BUFFALO

Although it would be hard to find an Indian village without its buffaloes, the buffalo is to the orthodox Hindu an unholy animal; its milk is not used in religious ritual and those who drink its milk or ride it are supposed to become dull-witted. To see a buffalo early in the morning is a presage of evil and to dream of one brings death. It is a demon *Mahiṣāsur*, the vehicle of the god of death. It is one of the objects given away in *ugra* gifts and, like the sheep, is often a scapegoat during an outbreak of epidemics.

THE DOG

It is a happy omen when setting out on a journey to see a dog with meat in its mouth, but a bad omen if the dog be carrying a fresh bone, and it is ominous of death if it be carrying a glowing piece of wood. A dog entering a house with a dry bone warns the householder of some great danger. It tells of coming rain if it barks loudly or utters long-drawn howls on a dunghill or roof of a house during the rainy season, but if it does this in another season it gives warning of a great fire or other calamity. If a dog plays with cattle there is happiness in store for the owner of the cattle; if it licks a man's shoes it is a sign that he will travel.

A dog crossing the threshing-floor when the grain has been gathered for threshing brings *barkat.* If a dog steals a piece of bread or other cooked food from a man and takes it to the field or threshing-floor of another man, the latter will have great *barkat.* If a dog jumps up on a man and embraces his neck the omen is also a good one.

Should a man going to a temple to worship see a dog chewing a shoe he cannot go to the temple till he has taken a bath. If when marriage negotiations are being conducted a dog touches the back of the negotiator the bridal pair will suffer harm, but the bridal pair will be very happy if the dog puts its nose in the face of the person opening the negotiations. Should a dog enter a house and carry away any kind of food the family will suffer poverty. The yell of a dog near a house is a warning of a coming death in the house or the illness of one of its inmates.

To the taking of omens from animals there is no end. A goat that drinks its own milk brings death to some member of the owner's family. The crow-pheasant used to live near the hermitages of saints and on behalf of the dead *vāyasbaḻī* was formerly offered to it, as it is by the Hindu of to-day to crows. To meet a crow-pheasant (*bhāradvāj, sambāra kāgi*) on a journey means success if it passes on the left, and encircling it sunwise brings *barkat.* The *tās* (Coracias Indica) is equally a bird of omen. If it flies from the right to the left in the first watch of the day it brings a man friendship, *mitralābh,* in the second watch it brings *annalābh* or food; in the third *dhanalābh* or wealth; and in the fourth *strīlābh* or the good fortune of a good woman. The great *Marāṭhā* leader, Śivājī, saw a blue jay flying in an auspicious direction when he set out to capture the fort of Torna whence he got much treasure. The hoopoe, *hudhud,* should not be killed and is an auspicious bird to meet. The pigeon to a Muhammadan is a *Sayad*; it is a sin to kill a pigeon and its cooing brings *barkat.* A peacock is a bird that receives respect from both Muhammadan and Hindu. It is not eaten by Muhammadans; tame peacocks are kept at Muhammadan shrines and called 'angels'. Feathers of a peacock are kept at shrines and placed inside the Koran; brooms are made from them and at circumcision a peacock's feather is tied to a boy's wrist to keep away spirits and retained until the boy's wound has healed. To a Hindu the peacock is the *vāhan* or vehicle of Saraśvatī. Its feathers are used both to invoke and to scare away spirits; the eyes of the feathers are with mercury put in an empty coconut and used to exorcize a spirit; the feathers are tied to the arms of children as a protection against evil-eye and when burnt are used medicinally.

CHAPTER XXI

SPIRITS

ACCORDING to both Muhammadan and Hindu belief, spirits are a creation apart. The Muhammadan believes they were created from fire; that they consist of two communities, one which has accepted the message of the Prophet, and the other bad souls, *arwah khabisah,* intent merely on doing mischief to man.

Usually invisible spirits may assume many forms, though they cannot pose as inanimate objects, such as stones. Their forms may be those of animals, such as buffaloes, goats, kids, dogs, sheep, cats, cocks, tigers and asses. Except when guarding buried treasure they are not supposed to take the form of a snake and they never take the form of a jackal and very rarely that of a horse. Besides animal forms, they assume forms semi-human or human. They can assume the form of a man who has died; their semi-human forms are many. They may have their feet reversed; their eyes in their foreheads looking upwards; long hair sweeping the ground; they may be headless or without thumbs. Whatever their form, they have no shadow and avoid contact with the ground. Hindu spirits are often of tremendous height, but the Muhammadan seems to picture his spirits as of shorter proportions, resembling more a water-skin. The form the spirit takes is largely determined by the person who sees the spirit, for it is a creation of man's imagination.

Spirits propagate and are very fertile. There are men who have had visions of their colonies and seen them swarming with children. They breed in more ways than one, for they breed by mental *śakti,* yet there is a *yoni* of spirits and intercourse between human beings and spirits is not uncommon. Of instances of such supposed congress I have come across two. In the one case one of my staff whose work I had found very indifferently performed justified himself by saying he was perpetually persecuted by an amorous female spirit; in another case a municipal servant went to a well with his wife but found the water in the well very low and his ropes not long enough to reach it. To his horror, from which he died, his wife stretched out her hand many feet until she reached the water with her pot, and the unfortunate husband discovered he had married a spirit. Women without hope of issue are also said to go naked by night to cemeteries and *ghāṭs* in the hope that spirits will there make them *enceinte*.

Spirits eat and drink somewhat after the fashion of men; they actually eat the food of man and are fond of blood, but they avoid salt and water and they feed in strange ways, drawing sustenance for a time merely from smells, emptying a coconut of its milk without breaking the shell, or drinking from the udders of milch cattle.

Some people have an uncanny capacity for seeing spirits which is denied to others. People who are haunted by spirits are naturally able to see them; people with spots on the pupils of their eyes can see them; children born with the foot presentation are able to see them, and pregnant women have the same power. Those who have this power of seeing spirits are said to have *ravagannu* eyes. Animals have the same power, and this is one reason why so many portents are drawn from the sounds and movements of animals; animals are able to see the evil that spirits are plotting and attempt to give man a friendly warning.

Besides being visible in animal or semi-human forms, spirits betray their presence in other ways. They make tree branches shake violently; on full-moon days and at other times they show their presence in sudden fitful flashes of light in unaccustomed places such as a lonely forest or on the banks of rivers or the shore of the sea. Their weeping, yelling, talking and laughing in isolated spots away from the haunts of men can be heard; they rush past with the sound of wind and from this characteristic are called *ghāḻi*, 'wind'. A whirlwind is called *Devvaghāḻi* or 'the demon's wind'. When a person is possessed by a spirit, though an ignorant man, he may suddenly deliver learned lectures and speak Sanscrit; constant yawning is another sign of spirit possession, as is eating heartily but without satisfaction or a nervous shaking of the head, *lahar*, when music is heard.

There are many names given to spirits in general and individually. The Muhammadan calls them *Sayad, Fakīr* and even *Pīr* or saint; he calls them *Iblis* or *Saitan* but his general term for them is *jinn, jinnat*. The Hindu word *dev* for 'god' is derived from the Sanscrit 'div', 'to shine'; the gods of the Hindu are shining, his spirits, on the other hand, are supposed to be dark. From the same word *dev*, however, is taken the Kanarese *devva*, which is applied to a spirit and to anything huge or grotesque. The two words, *dev* and *devva,* are applied to objects that excite wonder and suggest power; the latter word connotes something which seems contrary to the normal, but it is obvious that there must be many objects which the dweller in the wilder parts finds a difficulty in classifying as *dev* or *devva.* Both words express a recognition of something out of the common, something supernatural and inexplicable by ordinary experience.

Bhūt or 'spiritual being' is a Sanscrit word still used, and *pret* is another such word. It is dangerous, however, to speak of spirits by name individually or collectively, for this is equivalent to summoning them and so many words are used to avoid this danger. They are referred to as *piśitāśina piśāca,* 'eaters of flesh and blood'; *niśācara,* 'wanderers in the night'; *ghāḻi,* 'wind'; *riṣādah,* 'eaters of dead bodies'. They are also called even *graha* or planets; the spirits which dwell near ponds, in forests and in trees are collectively called *yakṣagaṇ* and a female spirit of this class *yakṣiṇī* or *jakhīṇ.*

Spirits bring evil to man. They cause epilepsy, convulsions, rheumatism and madness; they cause fear and, according to some thinkers, this is the only way in which they can cause death, as birth and death are beyond their control. They steal things possessing *śakti,* such as milk, buttermilk, butter, bread and grain; they actually steal milk from the cow. Spirits cause barrenness in women, in trees and in animals; they dry up the supply of milk that milch cattle give. They steal cattle and make them wander and they remove babies from their cradles. They obstruct the delivery of a woman and delay the attaining of puberty by a maiden. The tricks they play to annoy man are legion. They will turn his cooked rice into worms, his butter into clay and his milk into blood; they will set fire to his house or his stack of hay; they will drop excrement into his plate as he dines. When stones rattle on the roof and pieces of the ceiling or its beams persist in falling, it is certain that the jealousy of a spirit has been aroused. A problem I once attempted to solve, and unsuccessfully, was to induce masters and children to return to a school which, newly opened, had been abandoned immediately because every child who attended the school returned home covered with weals on its back caused by spirits.

Spirits reside near hidden treasure, in abandoned houses, old wells and graveyards; they haunt trees, waterfalls, caves and huge boulders and any feature of Nature which the peasant does not consider sacred. At the gate of a village and the threshold of a house spirits congregate, awaiting an opportunity to obtain entry into the village or house by clinging to the feet of men or cattle. Mountains, marshes and water are haunted by them, as are fire-places and all unclean places.

Wherever there is beneficent power there will be found spirit activity. To remain some time in a temple is a cure for spirit possession; when women are possessed they are sent to a temple and the other women-folk of their household don the garments of a man. Spirits, however, lurk in the precincts of a temple and every temple has a bell which a devotee visiting the temple must ring, saying as he does so, 'Ring the bell that God may come and spirits haste away'. Water in which the feet of a saint have been bathed scares away spirits; spirits are driven away or exorcized by the mere name of a saint; some saintly shrines are famous for their power to cure possessed persons and some saints are supposed to have spirits in their command, and yet saints take iron filings to keep away spirits. In the same way the bridal pair requires special protection from spirits, though the water in which the feet of the bridegroom have been bathed itself keeps away spirits. Trees are often haunted and many of them have names which include the word *bhūt*, yet even these and their parts are used by man to defeat spirits. Grain is stolen by spirits and half the ritual of the threshing-floor is directed to protect the grain against spirits, yet grain is used in many ways to keep away spirits or form a barrier, *dikbāndha*, against them. Fire and allied things are destroyers of spirits; ashes, lamps and soot keep away spirits, but the fire hearth is a haunted spot and spirits oft appear as flashes of fire. There is nothing more generally used then water to keep away spirits and yet water is haunted. Of all animals the horse is supposed to have exceptional power to resist spirits; it protects its rider and its hair and shoes are amulets against spirits, and yet a spirit may take the form of a horse. Spirits again are most active on certain days of *śakti*; on *Pūrṇimā*, *Amāvāsyā* and on holy days. Man himself labours incessantly to protect himself and his rites from spirits, but his spit averts spirits; the combings and cuttings of his hair when burnt protect a woman in her confinement and free a victim of spirit possession, whilst his shadow falling upon a spirit causes the spirit to faint.

The religious ritual of the Hindu, lastly, always has two aspects of which one is the taking of measures against spirits. Evil spirits come from all quarters to obstruct the performance of religious rites, and so before beginning any religious rite such as *jap*, a *sanskāra* or the installation of a god, protection against spirits is imperative. The *dikbāndha* or barrier against spirits is a common feature of ritual; the snapping of the fingers and clapping of the hands is another measure of defence.

The fear of the threshold, which is as common in India as in other parts of the world, is explained by the Hindu as a survival of the fear of spirits who used to obstruct the sacrifices which of old were performed on the threshold, the *Vedi* or *Yajnabhūmi.* To-day the threshold in common belief is the abode both of beneficent and of evil *śakti.* It is the place where formerly prayers were made for wealth and happiness and therefore still associated with *Lakṣmī,* the goddess of good fortune; it is also the dreaded haunt of evil spirits. The many taboos connected with the threshold are determined by one or other of these characteristics of the threshold. As associated with *Lakṣmī* it is forbidden to step on the threshold and the bridal pair are lifted over it. Muhammadan practice, particularly in the Deccan, is very similar to that of the Hindu. In Sind the Muhammadan bride is lifted across the threshold of her husband's house; in the Deccan the boy whose circumcision is to be performed goes to a mosque and at that time is lifted over the threshold by his nearest male relative; when a Muhammadan pilgrim returns from pilgrimage he is lifted across the threshold of his home; at a Muhammadan marriage the bride is lifted by her brother or maternal uncle across the threshold of her own house. Early every morning Hindu women worship the threshold, sprinkling water mixed with cowdung and making designs on it of good luck with powder. After the worship of the tulsī plant (Ocimum sanctum) in *Śrāvaṇ* the threshold is always worshipped before those who have worshipped the tulsī re-enter their house. The threshold must not be touched by the feet, and acts of *himsā,* such as cutting wood, grass or betel-nuts, must not be done on the threshold. Nothing should be passed across the threshold by one person on one side to another person on the other side; a lamp burning oil of ground-nut must not be placed on the threshold, and only a child with its great *śakti* can sit on it with impunity. To sneeze on the threshold is dangerous, and water must at once be sprinkled on it and on the framework of the door. As the entrance to the dwelling of man it is naturally on the threshold that horse-shoes are nailed and lemons are hung to keep away spirits.

Certain classes of persons are frequently or generally haunted by spirits. Women, in general, are associated with spirits. *Nārī pratyakṣa rākṣasī.* They are beautiful and spirits assail beauty; they have periods of impurity which attracts spirits; they have milk and this also attracts spirits. They are also weak, and weak people are haunted. People who are sick are also liable to be haunted, for the weakness of their mental power makes them prone to visualize their fears and these bring spirit apparitions. Anger or fright, again, exposes a man to spirits. Religious people are particularly exposed to spirit molestation, and one proof of this is that whenever they commit a breach of the rules of *dharma* they suffer ill which is attributed to spirits. Persons who have eaten meat, as a protection against spirits, should not leave the enclave of the village-god for some time ; persons who have smeared themselves with turmeric attract spirits, and this attraction is given as one reason for the measures taken to protect the bridal pair, for in most communities the bride and bridegroom are anointed with turmeric. Prostitutes are another class of persons liable to be haunted.

The ordinary man, however, is attacked by spirits only when he happens to hurt them, and this he may do by thoughtlessly throwing out of door after dark the sweepings of his house, by spitting or treading on them. Talking whilst doing an unclean act also brings spirits.

Spirits have great power. According to Muhammadans, they have the *Ism Azam*, a word which confers great power only less than that of God. They can speak any language and a gibberish attributed to them by Hindus is largely made up of Sanscrit words. They can tell the past of a human being and see his future. They can say where lost or stolen property lies, whether the sick will recover or die and can prescribe the treatment which on occasion may even be advice to worship a god.

On the coast of Kanara castes like *Halepaiks, Bhandaris, Matkars* and others depend almost entirely on a professional class who can summon spirits in any difficulty. These *Ghaḍiga* place rice on a board or *pāṭ*, pass their right palm over the rice and summon spirits, from whom they inquire as to the action the applicant should take. Through the agency of spirits both good and evil can be wrought. A spirit, too, if treated with respect may become the guardian of a household, and on the threshing-floor the co-operation of spirits is always sought to secure the maximum increase of grain.

Muhammadans also have their methods of summoning spirits. Suleiman had a ring which gave him power over the spirits as well as over the winds and the animal creation, a ring which had been given him by Allah. This ring he lost but discovered later in a fish he was about to eat. Before his death Suleiman was told by God to throw this ring into the well of Zemzem within the precincts of the mosque at Mecca. Though the ring, however, of Suleiman is no longer in the possession of any mortal, there are people who have rings of Suleiman, *Khātim-i-Suleiman*; these are ordinary rings to which they apply a black dye and give to a small boy to hold and gaze at till mesmerized, when Suleiman is invoked and comes in pomp, bringing the spirits with him.

By summoning spirits one may find out the person responsible for a theft. A boy or girl above ten years of age but below puberty, whose body is without blemish, is bathed and dressed in red clothes. On a piece of paper a Koranic verse is written and the paper is stuck on the child's forehead. The child is made to sit on a clean spot over which incense has been burned, and two or three pious persons sit with the child. The following chart is then written on a plate with a dot of black ink in the centre at which the child gazes whilst a reader reads forty times the *Surah Azimat.*

Michael		Gabriel
Israel		Israfil

The boy is then asked what he can see; at first he replies that he can see spirits like men; then he is told to summon sweepers to sweep the ground and to sprinkle the ground with water; the sweepers come and then a man comes and spreads a carpet, and finally the child sees in the dot the arrival in pomp of the King of the Spirits. The reader then tells the child to salaam the king and to demand the name of the thief and the site of the stolen article. The king of spirits writes out this information which the boy, though illiterate, is able to read. Another practice is to write the same chart on a plate or inside a cup which the boy holds as the *sūratu yā sīn* is recited. The plate or cup held in the boy's right hand will lead the boy to the site of the stolen property.

In Kanara one may find wooden images of spirits which receive regular worship as gods do; in the Konkaṇ there are stone images called *pitar*, the worship of which gives command over spirits. Then, too, there is the worship of *Vetāḻ*, prince of spirits. It is characteristic of the worship of spirits that the same cleanliness is normally required as in the worship of gods; the dealing of men with spirits, however, involves the strict exclusion of women whose participation would result in the control of man by the spirits and not that of the spirits by man. A mantrik avoids food prepared by a woman just as rigorously as a saint avoids it; acts of *himsā* are as destructive of a mantrik's art as they are of the *barkat* of one who resorts to religious ritual to win power. A mantrik must not hear the sound of grinding during his meals nor when preparing a charm; *Bhils* will not sweep in the presence of one practising the magic art, and quite a general practice is not to sweep whilst such a practitioner is dining.

The evil power of spirits is invoked into objects in the same way as beneficent *śakti* is invoked. One use that is made of this invoked *śakti* is to invoke it into images or into the skull of a woman who died in childbirth and use the image or the skull to protect gardens against trespassers. The *śakti* of *Yakṣiṇī*, the wife of Vetāḻ, is invoked into a branch of raktabutale, and this is kept tied to a beam in a temple or at the tomb of a saint to keep it immune from impure contacts. The mantrik uses this branch whenever he wants paste to write charms, and it is worshipped every *Amāvāsyā* which is a *bhūtveḻ* or day of spirits.

Various forms of power keep away spirits. Childless women wear a tiny copper box to keep away the spirit which causes barrenness; a copper bracelet worn at an eclipse assists a woman in travail, protecting her from the spirit that obstructs delivery; copper coins offered to trees in mock marriages free the bridegroom from the attentions of spirits. Iron and things of iron are used on all occasions when spirits are active; they protect the new-born infant and its mother; they protect the dead on this earth and even on their way to the next world; they protect the bridal pair and the boy at his circumcision; they protect the invoked *śakti* of the *devak* and of the *hāḻgamba*, the grain on the threshing-floor, the girl who attains puberty and the pregnant woman. Saints find in iron a protection against spirits; iron articles guard the threshold and protect cattle; they drive spirits from trees or fix them helpless in the trees.

Salt, again, protects a corpse; a woman on her delivery; children and the bridal pair; it drives away spirits from a newly constructed house or well. Stones may be used as a *dikbāndha* against spirits and are carried as a protection by travellers. Invested with *śakti* they protect cattle-sheds and are buried in fields, houses and gardens. Earth, fire and water avert spirits. Bread is a protection against spirits, as is grain; grain is sprinkled on a person possessed and is used as a *dikbāndha*; it protects the *rās* on the threshing-floor and a winnowing-fan associated with grain has the same protecting power. Black things defeat the activity of spirits; certain combinations of numbers are potent charms against them, whilst the number of trees and plants used to keep away spirits is very large.

There is power in certain names to avert spirits; the names of gods such as *Dattātreya* or of great mantriks such as Basappa of Betigeri. Sacred passages drive away spirits; the prayer *Rāmrakṣa* and the hymn *Ratrisukta.* The *sūratu yā sīn* is the heart of the Koran and its great power drives away spirits; the *āyatu'l-kursī,* the 256th verse of the second chapter of the Koran, the *sūratu'l jinn,* the seventy-second chapter and the hundred and twelfth chapter, the *sūratu'l ikhlās,* also defeat spirits. The *bismillāh* itself is uttered by every Muhammadan on every occasion when he anticipates evil, including the evil that spirits bring; it is said when he goes near a tree, when he saddles a horse, before he begins to eat; written on paper it is placed below the pole of the threshing-floor. Besides the *bismillāh,* 'in the name of God', another phrase commonly used to keep away spirits is *Bismillāh r-rahman r-rahim,* 'In the name of God the merciful, the compassionate'. The whole *barkat* of the first chapter of the Koran which itself contains the whole *barkat* of the Koran, is to be found in this latter phrase; the *barkat* of the phrase is to be found in the letter B with which it begins and of this letter the *barkat* lies in the dot below it. The recital of the kalimah or creed is a defence against spirits, and this is contained in the twenty-first verse of the forty-seventh chapter and in the twenty-ninth verse of the forty-eighth chapter of the Koran; it is a declaration that there is no god but God and that Muhammad is his apostle. The numerical value of verses of the Koran is also taken to form charms against spirits which are tied to the arm or neck of a haunted person, buried in the western wall of a house to prevent spirits throwing stones on the roof, or washed in water which is then drunk by a person possessed.

3912	3911	3904	3909
3913	3960	3908	3910
3902	3907	3912	3905

6	7	2
1	5	9
8	3	4

11	8	6	2
6	2	6	6
6	2	6	6
6	6	66	9

7823	7817	7824
7823	7821	7819
7818	7825	7820

429	453	450	446
452	440	445	451
441	455	448	444
449	443	442	454

Sometimes beneficent power, though requiring protection itself against spirits, transmits to objects which have been in contact with it a power to avert spirits. The two best examples of this are the power of *prasād* and that of *tīrth*. The *prasād* of a god or of a saint and the *tīrth* of a god or of a person with special *śakti* have power to keep away spirits. The sweepings of a temple, again, though not considered *prasād*, are put in water and sprinkled over a house to scare away spirits, or over children suffering from convulsions caused by spirits. Water in which a god has been bathed, water in which the feet of a bridegroom or a saint have been bathed, keeps away spirits ; ashes from certain *homs* have a great power in scaring away spirits, in particular the ashes from a temple of Maruti which are preserved as a permanent prophylactic.

If all forms of beneficent *śakti* are really manifestations of one cosmic *śakti* there is also a marked bond of relationship between different forms of evil *śakti*. There is evil in the *śakti* of *pāyguṇ* at times; there is always evil in the *śakti* of *dṛṣṭi*; there is evil in the *pīḍā* of the planets; evil in the power of spirits and even in beneficent *śakti* itself an element of evil. Between all these there is a similarity in the effects they produce and in the measures taken to avert those effects the similarity is very close.

Pāygun̩ and *dṛṣṭi* are closely related; terminology makes them identical; they both cause minor illnesses such as nausea and indigestion and abdominal pain. Bread is used as a defence against both evil *pāygun̩* and against *dṛṣṭi*; water deprives the former of its evil potentiality and averts evil-eye; iron and gold again are as effective in warding off the one evil as the other. Both of these forms of evil *śakti* again are related to the evil *śakti* of spirits. Washing the feet is a measure of protection against evil-eye, against *pāygun̩* and also against spirits who attach themselves to the feet of men. Grain is used to render *pāygun̩* innocuous and is widely used to exorcize spirits or avert them. Fire, which is so commonly used to burn the evil of the eye, is a potent defence against spirits and is used to make *pāygun̩* harmless. When a man sneezes water is sprinkled to avert spirits, but at the same time water is applied to his eyes. All these forms of evil *śakti* are lastly closely related to the evil power of the planets. Planets inflict evil-eye; the *śakti* of a man is drawn from the planets and evil *pāygun̩* is decided by the horoscope; spirits are actually called planets and measures taken to protect *śakti* from the sun are explained as protection against evil spirits and the evil-eye of the planets. The effects attributed to the adverse influence of the planets and to the activity of spirits are often identical; to the *pīḍā* of planets are due disasters such as madness, epilepsy, hysteria, fits and even death, but these are also caused by spirits. Eggs are used to avert the evil of the eye, but also as a bait for spirits when a woman is in travail. Black things protect man against spirits, against the *pīḍā* of the planets and against evil-eye; trees avert both spirits and the evil of the eye and many other articles such as brooms, shoes and winnowing-fans are employed to avert all these forms of evil *śakti*. The activity of spirits, moreover, is very marked on days such as Tuesday and Saturday when the influence of the planets is also baneful.

There remains the evil that beneficent *śakti* occasions when in revolt, and here again this evil is hardly distinguishable from the evil caused by spirits. When the *śakti* of a holy place is in revolt against the contact of an unclean person madness is often caused, but this is one of the ills brought by spirits. In many cases the revolt of *śakti* is admitted to bring in the activity of spirits. When an unclean person attempts to collect honey the revolt of the *śakti* of the honey results in his being stung by the bees, but the bees are instigated to do this by spirits; when an unclean person insults the *śakti* of a tree by climbing it, it is a spirit which makes him fall from the tree. One can collect honey without being stung if one has previously propitiated *Vetāḻ*, who rules the spirits. At certain hours of *śakti*, *parvakāl*, some forms of *hiṃsā* are strictly forbidden and the penalty of disregarding these injunctions brings in the agency of spirits to enforce the inevitable penalty. If one sleeps at hours of *śakti*, spirits enter the ears of the sleeper and make them ring; if one violates the injunction not to eat and drink, spirits join in one's meal; if one is unchaste, spirits again work their will; if one sweeps at these times, one hurts a spirit and incurs its wrath. If one sleeps on the day following the fast of Ekādaśī, one must besmear the soles of one's feet with ghee to deceive the spirits. Another example of the close relation between the evil that beneficent *śakti* may cause and the evil worked by spirits lies in the fear the *rayat* has of an undue increase of grain on his threshing-floor. In the Deccan this abnormal increase is attributed to the *śakti* of the grain, but the evils that follow to the activity of spirits; in the Karnāṭak the increase itself may be due to the agency of spirits, but whether due to beneficent or to evil *śakti* the remedy against such excessive increase is to throw a shoe at the pile of grain, and a shoe is a sovereign defence against spirits.

Muhammadans and Hindus alike associate spirit activity with the evils that follow the outrage of beneficent power. Pollution of a mosque brings in the agency of spirits and those who sleep in a mosque are disturbed by *jinn*. If a Hindu eats food before he has made an offering to a god spirits seize the food.

We can thus make our way in circles through the seeming maze of Indian thought. The law of *dharma*, the keys to the attainment of power and of *puṇya*, are from one point of view the conservation of beneficent power; when the rules that these dictate are broken there follows *pāp* or sin, a form of evil power which reduces for the Hindu his fund of *puṇya*. *Pāp* is the revolt of *śakti* and the revolt of *śakti* brings in the agency of evil spirits. A religious man more than any other is haunted by spirits who act as ministers of the law, enforcing a penalty whenever there is a breach of the rules of *dharma*.

Beneficent and evil power are never quite separated. No beneficent *śakti* is quite immune from molestation by the *śakti* of evil, though the aged and the devout *Brahmacārī* are supposed to approach this immunity. Images of deities need protection from evil-eye and temples from spirits; the *devak* and other symbols into which beneficent *śakti* is invoked require protection; persons who possess great *śakti* similarly need defence, and neither the saint, the child nor the god-like bridegroom is safe from evil. Always closely connected, the unity in the effects produced by evil suggests that there are moments when beneficent *śakti* stands aside and allows evil *śakti* to work its will, but the frequency or rarity of such moments is for man to attempt to determine.

CHAPTER XXII

CURSES AND OATHS

THE Indian Oaths Act, 1873, Section 8, allows witnesses or parties in any judicial proceeding to give evidence on oath in any form common amongst or held binding by persons of the race or persuasion to which they belong, and not repugnant to justice or decency and not purporting to affect any third person. It is rare, indeed, however, that a magistrate comes across any of the multitudinous forms of oath which are used in everyday life.

An oath is a simple assertion that the taker of the oath is speaking the truth, or a form of curse in which he calls down upon himself some punishment if he speaks false. Whichever form, however, the oath takes the person who takes it swears by something that possesses power.

Oaths are taken by persons possessed of power. Oaths are taken by a child and by its neck or blood. The Hindu when taking this oath says, 'If I do this I will be drinking the blood of my child', 'If I do this I will eat my child', 'I take my child or this child in my hand', 'A child is near me'. He also adds to the power of his oath by placing the child before an image of a god. Both Hindus and Muhammadans place their right hand on a child when swearing, though sometimes the child is not touched. Another practice is to establish a contact with the child by stepping over it, an act itself full of dangers. Oaths are taken by parents or grandparents. One Hindu oath is 'If I were to drink the blood of my parents, then only would I do this'. Oaths are taken by relatives, but oaths by distant relatives are not considered dangerous. Relatives swear, touching the neck of another, and more often than not the oath is taken by a female relative. A Hindu swears by a saint, 'I am sitting before the saint', 'My face is towards the saint', 'The saint is behind me'. He swears by the feet of a *svāmī*; by the house or the *maṭh* of a saint, by his raised seat or, as he swears, he touches the tomb of a saint. The Muhammadan takes an oath at the shrine of a saint, keeping his hand on the door of the tomb or on its covering and repeating the name of the saint; he swears by the house of a living saint; he also swears by the cot of an elderly person, a leader or Sirdar, by the matting of a Sirdar *tadejo kasm*, and by the beard of an old man. Both the Hindu and the Muhammadan swear by a bridegroom and the Muhammadan swears by the pilgrim returned from Mecca, *haji sagorejo kasm ahe.*

Objects possessed of power are sworn by. Oaths are taken by grain, 'I am sitting on grain', 'I hold grain in my hand'. In taking such an oath the swearer prays that he may die of starvation if false. Oaths are taken by the threshing-floor, 'I am standing in the threshing-floor'; by a vegetable garden, by the standing crops and by a crop after it has been reaped. *Mahārs, Vaddars* and *Calvadis* swear by grass. The Hindu, in general, swears by trees such as the tulsī and the banni, the bel and the audumbar. Oaths are taken by the leaves of the pipal (Ficus religiosa) which the swearer crushes in his hands and prays that God will similarly crush him if he speaks false. *Kurubas* swear by the shade of a tree. Fodder is touched as an oath is taken, or coconuts and betel-leaves are held in the hand. The Muhammadan takes an oath by green verdure but, as a rule, does not touch it any more than he would touch the branch of a tree when swearing, from fear lest he should wither as all green things eventually wither. He swears by the leaves of trees and sometimes climbs a tree to take an oath, for if his oath be false he will fall from the tree.

As a Hindu or a Muhammadan takes an oath he will sit on the ground or lay his hand on the ground. The Muhammadan believes that if such an oath be falsely taken the earth will crush him in the grave after death. Oaths are taken by water, 'I hold the Ganges in my hand', 'I stand in the water of the Ganges', 'I am standing in a river', 'I have bathed'. An oath by water or by the river Indus is equally common among Muhammadans, who also swear by Khwaja Khizr with whom water and vegetation are associated. Fire is the subject of an oath. When an oath is taken by fire an earthen pot containing fire is touched. The Hindu also swears by a lamp, 'I hold a lamp', 'I am under the light of a lamp', 'A lamp is before me'. In the case of an oath by a lamp the man demanding an oath may light a lamp which the person taking the oath extinguishes saying, 'If I speak false may there be no lamp in my house'. In this phrase the lamp in the house means progeny. In Bombay *Moguls* swear by a lamp, *jotki kasm.* The Muhammadan swears by fire, holding his hand over it, or offers ashes to another by which to swear.

Artisans and craftsmen, whether Muhammadan or Hindu, swear by their implements of trade; agriculturists by their ploughs and bullocks, clerks by their pens, potters by their kilns, warriors by their swords, and a barber by his razor.

An oath by salt is common among Hindus but not among Muhammadans; it is quite common among the more primitive races and tribes. The *Bhil* swears, 'I am touching salt' and the *Ghattivaddar* swears in the same way. Oaths are taken by bread, 'I hold bread', 'I am seated at table', 'I am under your roof'.

Hours and days of power are sworn by. The Hindu swears by sunset and by dawn; Among Muhammadans in Sind I have found oaths by sunset and dawn, by an eclipse, by the full moon and the new moon and by the first Monday of a month. Other Muhammadan oaths are by the month of *Ramaḍān*, by the nights of festivals such as *'Īd Mulūd, Shah-ba-rat*, the night of Friday, and by sacred days such as the first or the twenty-seventh of *Ramaḍān, sagori ratjo kasm ahe.*

The Muhammadan takes an oath in a mosque in front of the *miḥrāb, Khudajo ghar*; an oath taken in a *Jama Masjid* is considered very dangerous, whilst an oath may be taken by repeating the name of a mosque or by using the word mosque only without reference to any particular mosque. A Hindu also takes an oath in a temple, and some temples, as those of Durgava, Mahārudra and Mahākāli, make an oath very serious. In the temple an oath is taken by the *bel bhanḍāra* or the turmeric powder used in the worship of Khandoba, and this form of oath is very common in the Deccan, 'I have lifted the *bel bhanḍāra*'. The feet of the image in the temple may be touched; the sacred ashes, *angār*, may be held in the hand. The swearer sometimes says, 'I am standing in a temple'; sometimes he takes the name of the temple, and a particularly dangerous oath is to take the name of a temple which in ordinary conversation has to be avoided. Stones representing gods are sworn by and an oath is most dreaded if the god sworn by be Narsinh or the family god. Oaths are also taken by flowers removed from a divine image.

Calvadis swear by the graves of their ancestors. *Ghattivaddars* by a graveyard and by bones and skulls. *Ghantichors, Bestars, Dong Dasaris* and *Korvars* swear by a skull. A Hindu oath may be taken by the tomb of a man murdered innocently; by a corpse, 'I do not lie as I carry a corpse'. A criminal may swear by the gallows. Shepherds carrying a basket filled with the dung of sheep walk round a flock of sheep as an oath and are supposed to lose all their sheep if they speak false. Butchers swear by raw meat. *Vaddars* who are stone-cutters swear by a heap of stones.

Muhammadans swear by any book of religious learning, and if they be sitting with an *'Alim* swear ' by the learning which is in your chest '. The Koran is kissed, placed on the head whilst the swearer turns towards Mecca. Other Muhammadan oaths are taken by cattle; by henna; by one's livelihood, *rozi*. Women swear by their own eyes, *nurjo kasm*; oaths are also taken by the foot of another person, *tumare payko hath lyakar kahta hun*; by a rosary and by milk, *khir bhatarojo kasm ahe*; by pet animals, by the moon and by the sun. Among Hindu oaths are oaths taken touching a religious book; by the sun, moon and stars; by the feet of bullocks, by a cow or calf, the swearer holding its tail, touching its back or pointing towards it; by turmeric, by the trefoil bel leaf; by the rosary used in *jap*; by a man's sacred thread or a married woman's *mangaḻsūtra* (*guḻdāṇi*, Kan.); by the *dhupārtī* or pot of incense placed before the image of a god. *Bhils* swear by a tiger, ' Tiger will eat me if I am false '; *Ghatti-vaddars, Ghantichors, Bestars, Dong Dasaris* and *Korvars* swear by manure and *Bhils* by cowdung. *Chapparbands* swear by articles they have stolen.

Hindus swear saying, ' I am speaking *Rāmvacan* ', a reference to the truthfulness of Rama, or, ' I am taking the *bhīśma pratidynā* ', ' I take the vow of Bhisma, ancestor of the *Pāṇḍavās*, who never broke a vow '.

Some oaths are far more dangerous than others. An oath taken by a Hindu on Saturday, *Ekādaśī, Amāvāsyā, Pūrṇimā*, at sunset, at an eclipse, or on a day of fast are dangerous oaths deriving their enhanced power from the power of the time. The Muhammadan also attributes greater power to an oath taken at an eclipse, at dawn or sunset, at full moon, or on the first Monday and Friday of a month.

An oath is the more serious if taken in a place full of power, such as in a graveyard, the *dargāh* of a saint, a mosque or a temple. If the taker of an oath be unclean at the time he takes an oath the danger of swearing is the greater; if a pregnant woman takes an oath she does harm to her future child, nor should a woman within forty days of her delivery take an oath. An oath taken after sexual intercourse or after easing oneself is very dangerous. On the other hand, wearing wet clothes is a proof of ritual cleanliness after a bath and an oath is the more serious if taken when wearing wet clothes. An oath is more binding if taken on an empty stomach or in a state of nakedness. Among Hindus there are practices of covering the body, though the swearer is still considered to be naked. Those who have as their family goddess, *Yellava*, discard their clothes and twist round their waist the small twigs and leaves of the nim-tree, and then take an oath by the temple of the goddess. Others cover their body thickly with sandalwood-paste. The first of these practices is called *uṭigi* and the second *gandhad uṭigi*.

Himsā of any kind adds danger to an oath. An oath is worse if taken after cutting grass or cutting a tree, after shaving or cutting the hair, after grinding or even in front of a grindstone. One is well advised not to take an oath when standing on grass, sitting on a stone or standing near water or fire. To add efficacy to an oath the swearer stands on a stone, holds a stone or maybe even breaks a stone. Burning hair-combings or nail-clippings or grinding stones when an oath is taken makes the oath very dangerous.

Eating or drinking the thing sworn by effects a contact, as does touching or holding the object, which transmits the intention of the person taking the oath and makes the object sworn by carry out his wish and cause injury if he be treacherous. Because of this transmission of intention by assimilation a Sindi Muhammadan, as a rule, will not even drink water when swearing.

There are several sayings which emphasize the danger of taking an oath. The Muhammadan says, '*Na kasm dian chango; na kasm khanan chango*', 'Not to give an oath is good; not to take an oath is good'; '*Kasmi khan bhaj pare*', 'Run away from one who takes an oath'. The Hindu shows reluctance to giving hospitality to one who has taken an oath and avoids being present at a temple when an oath is taken; people seeing a man going to a temple to swear will try to dissuade him from going.

To avert the effects of an oath charity is given. If a man, for instance, take an oath by his child the mother will protect the child by giving charity. Another measure of defence is for the child to spit or for the mother to spit or even any one in whose presence the oath has been taken. Hindus also to avert the effects of an oath press their tongue between their teeth.

CURSES

Śāp

A curse may take the form of an appeal to God to injure some one, sometimes stating some definite harm which the person cursing hopes another will receive. Curses may, however, be uttered without an appeal to a divine person; they may also be pure invective, but in general this form of curse is not combined with one that includes an appeal to God.

The curses of some persons are far more dangerous than those of others. 'The houses on which female relations not being duly honoured pronounce a curse, perish completely as if destroyed by magic' (*Manu*, iii, 58). The *śakti* which a woman possesses in her pregnancy adds force to her curse; the special power of the old makes their curse more dangerous, and in the same way the power of the bridal pair or of a guest adds power to their curses. Parents, as far as their children are concerned, are possessed of special *śakti*, their curse is very dangerous; the curse again of a saint is very dangerous and nothing can mitigate its deleterious effects save the hand of God.

When a man curses he considers his tongue defiled and therefore washes his mouth. A *Lingāyat* woman, after uttering a curse, will not touch her baby until she has washed her mouth and her feet. The same idea of defilement leads to a person who utters a curse going outside his house before he curses.

An undeserved curse can effect no harm to the person cursed, but it recoils on the head of the person who uttered the curse.

MAIR

Mair is an expression used in Sind only. Literally it means 'a meeting of persons', but in practice it is used to describe an act by which a conditional curse is imposed or transferred to another person should he not accede to a request. The original meaning of the word is more or less retained when a large number of people are taken to a man suspected of theft to force from him a confession, and the *mair* derives its force from the number of the people and not from the special power of any individual among them.

This transference of a conditional curse is sometimes expressly stated by the person who brings *mair* to another or threatens to bring it, 'If you do not do this as I wish I will bring you *mair* of the Koran'.

Mair is said to be 'upon' a person and *mair* is 'brought'. '*Hane mair andi-sun*', 'We have now brought *mair*'. A person to whom *mair* is brought may decline to accept it, saying '*Man tho mair vijhain*'.

Mair is effective only with those who fear, but on the other hand there are phrases which make it a slur on a man to refuse to accept *mair*. '*Hik chae biyo na mane tanhiji saji rab bhane*"

'One man says, another does not hearken, God breaks his unbroken things'. There is, however, something dangerous in *mair*, 'May the effect of *mair* befall no one', and a person who often takes *mair* to other people is avoided and considered a bad person.

Mair has many forms. It may consist in nothing more than touching the turban or the chin of the person to whom *mair* is brought; touching his feet, placing one's turban at his feet or touching his horse or his reins. A dangerous form of *mair* is to place a son in his father's arms and say, 'Here is his *mair*', for there is associated with this *mair* the possibility of the child's death if the request demanded is not granted.

There is the *mair* of old men and there is *mair* in the repetition of the personal names of saints. The *mair* of a virgin is equal to that of seven Korans, and to force the grant of a request a young girl is taken to the person from whom a request is demanded and left with him till the boon is granted. There is *mair* of a guest, *mihmanji mair*, and fear of this is one of the factors fostering hospitality. Whilst the Muhammadan bridegroom sits in *Vanvāha* he should not speak, and so the fear of evil consequences should he speak makes his *mair* the more dangerous and he is taken to others to force a request. A bride is not used in *mair*, but a small child, a *Maulvi* and a pilgrim are all used as *mair*.

Other forms of *mair* are *saje danyaji mair thi*, 'the *mair* of the whole world', *Rizkji mair thi*, 'Let there be the *mair* of food', *chain nyaninji mair*, 'the *mair* of four virgins', *chain fakiranji mair*, 'the *mair* of four fakirs', *Koran mair thi, murshid mair thi, Pir mair thi* and *Rasulji mair*, the *mair* of the Prophet. There is the *mair* of green verdure, *sai savalji mair*. Snake-charmers bring the *mair* of Suleiman to their snakes.

When an oath takes the form of eating or drinking the object sworn by, it is usual to speak of *mair*. An oath by milk is *khirji mair*, an oath by salt is *lunaji mair*, and an oath by grain is *anaji mair*.

Mair may be brought not only to human beings but to trees. When a nail is driven into a tree the person driving the nail says, '*Khudaji mair thi* or *Rasulji mair thi*', 'May there be the *mair* of God or the *mair* of the Prophet'. *Mair* is also used to coerce a dead saint. A stone is thrown on his shrine; rags and hair-combings are tied to his tomb or to the trees around; the leaves or twigs of trees near the tomb are twisted in knots, and knots are tied in the covering of the tomb. All these practices are spoken of as *mair*.

CHAPTER XXIII

THE INVOCATION OF POWER

ĀVĀHANA

THE invocation of 'power' is a practice common to all communites and castes, though the Brahmin has given it a special importance in the developed ritual of Hinduism. The *Koḻī* invokes the power of Ind into twigs of kalamb-tree; the *Bhil* invites the *śakti* of a tree to grace his ceremonies by tying a thread round the tree; non-Brahmins invite power into their grinding-stone, pestle and mortar, their seed-drills, their yokes, carts, water-pots, oil-presses and into stones. The *Marāṭhā devak* of the Deccan and the Konkaṇ and the *hāḻgamba* of the Karnāṭak illustrate the widespread prevalence of the idea of invoking power among castes which are not Brahmin. The rite of *Ankurāropaṇ*, again, though one of meticulous detail among Brahmins, involves even among non-Brahmins the invocation of power. *Lingāyats*, *Marāṭhās* and others invoke *Lakṣmī* on the *Amāvāsyā* before *Divāḻī* into a pole which is eventually used for the central post of the threshing-floor; *Marāṭhās* and others invoke power into the *guḍhī* or pole of bamboo which is erected in the verandah of every household on New Year's Day.

The invocation of power is by the Brahmin effected by the use of appropriate mantras and the throwing of unbroken rice or *akṣat*. *Āvāhan* is the invocation of power into a medium or symbol; *visarjan* is the eventual formal dismissal of such invoked power.

Prāṇpratiṣṭā is the invocation of power into an image. Strictly speaking, the invocation is that of life and *śakti*; the mantras uttered at the time of invocation when *akṣat* is thrown on the image invoke all the organs of sense, the mind, speech, the organs of the eye, ear, nose, tongue; the hands, feet and even the anus. In the Belgaum district the shrine of the saint, *Chidambar Doxit*, receives annual reverence from devotees, because the saint even at the age of twelve was able to infuse life into clay elephants during the celebration of a *Prāṇpratiṣṭā*. In the degeneracy, however, of to-day man is unable to master completely the mantras used at a *prāṇpratiṣṭā*. The mastery of the *Gāyatrī* mantra requires twelve years' assiduity and other mantras can be learned only at particular moments such as the hour of an eclipse, and in all cases to produce its full effect the *śakti* of a mantra must be supplemented by the *śakti* of the person using the mantra. The mantra used at a *Prāṇpratiṣṭā* contains mystic syllables which invoke life, and others which invoke *śakti*, but owing to man's incomplete mastery of the mantra a *Prāṇpratiṣṭā* of an image does not to-day result in the image becoming alive.

The actual ceremony of *Prāṇpratiṣṭā* consists in placing the image, first of all, in a copper plate and bathing it with water and the five products of the cow, *pancgavya*. Then a rite called *Angyuttaraṇa sanskār* is performed, the object of which, as declared by the *sankalpa*, is to remove the ill effects produced by the use of fire and iron instruments in the manufacture of the image; in this rite the image is bathed simultaneously with milk and water. The image is then placed on a prepared *āsan* to insulate it from the ground, and after meditation the *yajamān* throws choice flowers on it, which is followed by the throwing of *akṣat* and the invocation of power.

By such a *Prāṇpratiṣṭā śakti* has been invoked into the image. How much has been invoked depends upon the *śakti* of the celebrant and as charity increases the *śakti* of the donor charity is enjoined at a *Prāṇpratiṣṭā*, in the form of cash presents (*dakṣiṇā*), gifts of clothes (*aher*) and grants of land or gifts of cows and gold. A pious man has more *śakti* than one less pious, and if a *sannyāsī* throws the *akṣat* (*Akṣatāropaṇ*), lays his hand on the image and utters the mantra of invocation, the image is suffused with the greater *śakti*. In the *Purāṇa* are many images described as installed by great saints, and these, called *Purāṇaprasiddh*, have special *śakti*. Examples of such images are those of *Vir Nārāyaṇ* and of *Trikuteśvar* at Gadag, of *Banaśankar Mahakuteśvar* of Badami and of *Virupax* at Hampi.

Even after *śakti* has been invoked into a symbol the power remains to a great extent within the control of man. The *śakti* of a *pratimā* or image is enhanced by the worship of a pious man; it is enhanced by worship in hours of power when man's own *śakti* is great, and different gods are associated with different hours. Monday is the day for the worship of *Śiva*; Wednesday for *Vithoba*; Tuesdays and Fridays for *Durgā* and *Lakṣmī*; Thursday for *Dattātreya*, Sunday for the sun, Saturday for *Maruti* and *Rūdradev*. *Ekādaśī* is the best time, and then early in the morning, for the worship of *Viṣṇu*. By celebration also of the rite of *Ankurāropaṇ*, or by celebrating the marriage of a deity the *śakti* of an image is increased.

On the other hand, there are many ways in which the invoked *śakti* of an image may become less or even lost altogether. Its *śakti* must be constantly replenished, unless it be a *svayambhū*, 'self-existing', image which suffers no loss of *śakti* on neglect. If an image is not worshipped for one day it must be worshipped twice the next day; if it be neglected for two successive days a special worship, *mahāpūjā*, is imperative on the third day. After a neglect of three or more days a *samprokṣan* or ceremony of purification must be performed, whilst if the neglect is prolonged for a month a fresh ceremony of invocation is necessary. Besides neglect, there are many contacts which destroy the invoked *śakti* of an image. An image loses its *śakti* if it touches the ground; if rain-water falls on it or the full power of the sun shine upon it; the touch of a woman not ritually pure, the touch of a thief, of a *Mahār*, and of certain animals such as a horse, dog, or donkey, destroys its *śakti*. Worship of an image by the impious, by mourners, by a glutton or miser destroys its *śakti*, and this also fades away if during worship the worshipper cuts his finger and allows blood to fall on the image. If a person dies in the inner shrine of a temple, or if the temple be burned by fire, the power of the image is lost, whilst as *śakti* will not abide in a broken tabernacle if the image be broken its invoked power vanishes.

The Hindu *Śrāddha* provides another illustration of the invocation of *śakti*. In this rite blades of darbha grass are spread on the ground with their tips pointing south; the *yajamān* then pours water and *til* over the grass and places on the grass one ball of cooked rice, *piṇḍa*, in the name of the deceased whose *Śrāddha* is being performed, and two other balls in the name of the male or female grandparents, according as the deceased was a man or a woman. Then *akṣat* is thrown on the *piṇḍa* with words of invocation and the *pitṛs* are supposed to leave the world of shades and come to the feast. After the celebration is over the *yajamān* asks the priest for permission to dismiss the *śakti* of the dead, and this he then does by moving the *piṇḍa* with his hand, neither using mantras nor *akṣat*. If before such dismissal one of the *piṇḍa* cracks of its own accord the early death of the *yajamān* is considered certain.

Śakti is invoked into many mediums. It is invoked into knots; *akṣat* is thrown on the knot to the accompaniment of mantras which bid the *śakti* be present, *sannihito bhava*. At a birth a knot is tied with white thread, *akṣat* is thrown on it and the *śakti* of *Agni* is invoked to protect the child, who is made to wear it, from evil-eye. At a tonsure the same invocation is made; at a thread ceremony three threads are knotted into one and the *śakti* of *Agni*, *Candra* and *Varuṇa* is invoked into the threads by *akṣat*. At a Hindu marriage four threads are knotted as a *kankaṇ* and tied to the right wrist of the bridegroom and to the left wrist of the bride, and into these is invoked the *śakti* of *Pṛthvī*, *Varuṇa*, *Agni* and *Vāyu*. At the celebration of the *lājāhom* during a marriage two pieces of cloth are held by the bridal pair called *pancā*; these are knotted together and the pair hold the ends thereof on their way to, and their return from, a temple, until they bow together before their *kula devatā*; into the knot of these *pancā* is invoked the *śakti* of *Lakṣmī Nārāyaṇ*. At a *Śrāddha* ceremony a piece of sesamum and darbha is tied in the *dhotar* of the *yajamān* on his right side, *nivi bāndhan*: this knot remains until the end of the celebration and keeps spirits away from the *piṇḍa*, for it contains the *śakti* of *Janārdan* which is invoked and dismissed by mantras. Another knot containing the same *śakti* is tied in nine or ten pieces of darbha grass and then dipped in water which is sprinkled round the dishes used in the *Śrāddha*. At a *Vāstuśānti* on entering a new house for the first time, a white thread is knotted and tied round the house and into it is invoked the *śakti* of *Indra* and of *Viṣṇu*. Once a year, on the fourteenth of *Bhādrapad*, *Ananta* is worshipped through the medium of a snake made of darbha grass; thread is brought from the bazaar already knotted with two knots of silk and placed near the medium; by throwing *akṣat* and the recitation of mantras the *śakti* of the god is invoked into the thread which is worn that day, and then put in a box and preserved till the next year, when it is again worn for a short time until a new thread has been sanctified (*anantadhar*). On the eighth of *Bhādrapad* threads are prepared, one for each member of a Hindu family; in each thread knots are tied, two knots if the wearer be a man, and one knot if she be a woman. Into these knots the *śakti* of *Gaurī* is invoked and the threads are worn until meals have been taken and are then buried near the *kula devatā*. Each day after his bath and before reciting his *sandhyās* the Brahmin ties a knot in his lock of hair, *śenḍī*, and invokes into it the *śakti* of *Aparājita* which averts spirits; after his prayers are over the knot is untied and the invoked *śakti* departs. The sacred thread of a Brahmin consists of three strings and a knot, and each string is made up of nine strings. *Akṣat* is not thrown on the thread, but the thread is hung on the thumb of the left hand and nine turns are made with the thumb of the right hand as each mantra is repeated, invoking the *śakti* of gods. In one string the *śakti* of *Onkār* is invoked, that is the power of *Brahma, Viṣṇu* and *Śiva*; in the second string the power of *Agni*; in the third that of the serpents *Nāgan*; in the fourth that of the moon; in the fifth that of the *Pitṛs*; in the sixth *Prajapati*; in the seventh *Vāyu* or wind; in the eighth the sun and in the ninth all the gods; in the knot itself, *Brahmagāṇṭh*, the triad of gods, take up their abode. Because of this invoked *śakti* the sacred thread averts all manner of evil; shown to the sick it effects a cure; dipped in water it gives curative power to the water. Another example of *śakti* invoked into knots is the thread which *Jains* carry all round the marriage *manḍap*, at a height from the ground higher than that of a man; this thread has five or seven knots into which *śakti* is invoked.

Invocation of power accompanies the coercion of power by tying threads. When threads are tied to trees or plants to coerce their *śakti, akṣat* is thrown on the thread and some particular *śakti* is invoked. To obtain issue, white thread is tied round a śamī-tree and into this thread the *śakti* of *Mahākālika* is invoked; after the *munji* of a pipal-tree has been performed by men, women tie thread round the tree to get issue and invoke therein the *śakti* of *Kṛṣṇa*. Thread is tied round a combined pipal and nim tree seven times and when *akṣat* is thrown on this, the *śakti* of *Nārāyaṇ* and of *Lakṣmī* is invoked.

Śakti is invoked into *kalaśas* in all the sixteen *sanskār* save that of the obsequies, *antyeṣṭi*. In all *śānti* ceremonies, too, *kalaśas* are required and the *śakti* of *Varuṇa* is invoked; in addition the *kalaśas* are used as an *āsan* for the principal deities to be propitiated; on each of the *kalaśas* a plate is placed and on this the metal image of the deity whose *śakti* is invoked. The *kalaśa* in all cases is a means whereby the *śakti* of the invoked deity, for which it serves as an *āsan*, is transferred to the *yajamān* through the sprinkling of the water from the *kalaśa*.

Power is invoked into trees. Before beginning a *munji* or thread ceremony the parents of the boy, *vaṭu*, go to a śamī-tree and after its worship bring back a twig and throw it on the roof of the *manḍap* and then casting *akṣät* on it invoke into it the *śakti* of *Lakṣmī*. After the *Munji* ceremony is over the boy accompanies a priest to a pa̱las-tree where, repeating a mantra after the priest and throwing *akṣat* on the tree, he invokes into it the *śakti* of *Brahma*, to whom he then prays to make him a learned man. On New Year's Day a branch of flowering nim-tree is brought and by means of *akṣat* the power of the moon as *amṛt* or nectar is invoked into it; the leaves and flowers are then eaten with salt, sesamum, lemon-juice and jaggery. In the Karnāṭak the *śakti* of *Mahādev* is often invoked into the pole which is placed near the pyre of *Hoḻi*.

The *śakti* of *Agni* is invoked into the kankaṇ of the bridal pair, and I have found the same *śakti* invoked into the *hāḻgamba*. The *akṣat* thrown on the bridal pair both invokes and transfers to the pair *śakti*; the *śakti*, according to the Brahmin of the gods, the stars, the sun and moon, of days and seasons, of the rivers and mountains, of the *Veda* and *Upanisads*, of the *ṛṣis* and of the blessed dead. In the installation of the Brahmin *devak* (*Nāndisthāpan*) the *śakti* of various deities is invoked into leaves. *Karnāṭakaru* Brahmins take a wooden hammer, *koḍatī*, dress it in a *khaṇ*, throw *akṣat* on it and invoke therein the *śakti* of *Soma*, a washerwoman who restored a bridegroom to life.

As a medium for the invocation of the power of Indra, figures of his vehicle the elephant are made in rice and salt, and on these, after the throwing of *akṣat*, the bridal pair is required to step. Brahmins invoke the *śakti* of the seven goddesses of wealth who bring longevity into a comb-like figure drawn on the wall with lime and turmeric juice, on which they cast *akṣat*. Drawings and

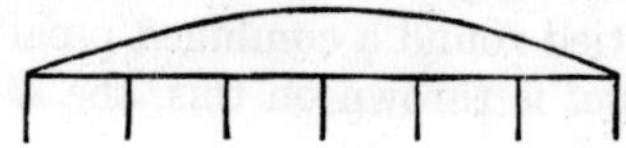

pictures are frequently used for the invocation of *śakti*. Even written words may be used as a medium and at thread and marriage ceremonies *akṣat* is thrown on the words *Śrī Ganeṣa yanama* painted on a wall. The *śakti* of the *diggaja* or eight mountains that were created to keep the earth steady by their weight is invoked into the doors and into the window-frames of a house when constructed. The *śakti* of *Mailarlinga* is invoked by his devotees into the feather of a peacock after a marriage or a thread ceremony; the power of *Rāhu* is invoked on *Āśvin Pūrṇimā* and *Amāvāsyā*, *Bhādrapad Amāvāsya* and *Śrāvaṇ Amāvāsyā* into darbha grass.

A betel-nut is perhaps the commonest medium into which sacred *śakti* is invoked. This medium is used for invoking power in *Ankurāropaṇ*; on the first day of *Navrātra* the *śakti* of the planet Rāhu is invoked into a betel-nut placed on darbha grass; at the beginning of every auspicious ceremony the *śakti* of *Gaṇpati* is invoked into a betel-nut; into betel-nuts the *śakti* of the eight elephants of the cardinal points is invoked when a new well is used for the first time; the *Lokpālā* when invoked are invoked into eight betel-nuts; in the rite called *Grahamakh* or invocation of the planets before a marriage or a thread ceremony, as many as forty-two betel-nuts are placed in a winnowing-fan, for besides the planets, nine *Adhidevatā*, nine lower gods, *Pratidevatā*, seven *Vinayaks*, 'leaders to the good path', and eight *Lokpālā* are represented.

CHAPTER XXIV

TOTEMISM AND THE *MARĀṬHĀ DEVAK*[1]

THERE is probably no 'ism' that has played more havoc with the interpretation of Indian customs than 'totemism', and both English and Indian writers have constructed comprehensive theories of totemism on little more than apparent resemblances.

Of the survival of a genuine institution of totemism a few examples in the Bombay Presidency are still to be found. The *Kātkarī* illustrates a totemistic organization which for practical purposes is now a thing of the past. He calls his totem brother, and has vague ideas that he may be reborn as his totem; he also pays a certain respect to the totem, but this figures in none of his ritual. It plays no part in his celebration of *Sarvapitrī Amāvāsyā*, when through the medium of symbols, usually *ṭāk* or engraved pieces of copper, he invokes the spirits of his dead, and its absence from his marriage ceremonies is still more marked.

It is not always easy to say how much the sophisticated *Sōn Kātkarī* has borrowed from his Hindu neighbours. In the Thana district he has a *devak* synonymous with his family gods which one may not rashly assume he has borrowed, but granting that this institution is borrowed, it is clear that he does not imagine he has borrowed the totems of others. In the Kolaba district the *devaks* of the *Kātkarī* appear more or less identical with those of the *Marāṭhās*, but here again tradition makes one and the same original families such as the *Powar* and the *More*, the *Mukane* and the *Hilam*, which have different *devaks*, and in marked contrast to his totem his *devak* is a very important feature of a marriage ceremony.

The *Kātkarī* accordingly suggests the impossibility of attributing to the *devak* a totemistic origin. *In primis* he has both a totem and a *devak*; the former is not brought into any ceremony of to-day, the latter is a well-marked feature in the important ceremony

[1] This chapter appeared in a modified form in the *Review of Philosophy and Religion*, vol. ii, no. i.

of marriage, and again, whilst every family or *kul* is supposed to have its own totem, a single family on partition takes different *devaks*.

Existing definitions of the *devak* are many. In *Totemism and Exogamy*, vol. ii, 1910, pp. 376–7, Sir James Frazer, quoting from the *Census of India of* 1901, writes of the *devaks* as sacred symbols which appear to have been originally totems. Mr. R. E. Enthoven in several publications has given a fuller account which again, however, accepts the connexion between the *devak* and totemism. In the *Encyclopaedia of Religion and Ethics*, vol. ii, p. 338, 1909, he calls the *devak* a marriage guardian; in *Tribes and Castes of Bombay*, 1922, he speaks of it as a 'god of the exogamous section', whilst in his edition of *Religion and Folklore of Northern India* (W. Crooke, 1926) he describes it with fuller detail as 'the totemistic spirit contained in some tree, animal or material object which in addition to being the subject of special worship, regulates the marriage laws of many primitive sections of the population. In origin it appears to have been an ancestral spirit'. Finally, in *Tribes and Castes of Bombay*, 1922, vol. ii, pp. 282–3, he identifies the *devaks* of the Pardeśī *Kumbhārs* with their family deities or *dhiradis*, and elsewhere (*idem*, vol. i, p. 61) the *devak* of the *Baris* with their 'house goddess'. Then again there is the definition made by Sir James Campbell of the *devak* as a 'marriage guardian' or 'wedding guardian'. It is at the outset obvious that these various definitions cannot have the same connotation; the family gods of the Hindu, his *kula devatā*, are not ancestral spirits. No *Marāṭhā* would accept the identity of his *devak* with an ancestral spirit; none of the offerings that are usually made to the *pitṛs* are made to the *devak*; and lastly, a ceremony of invoking an ancestral spirit at a marriage, the *Mūḻapuruṣa* as it is called, has not yet quite fallen out of practice among castes that have *devaks*, and this ceremony has no connexion with the installation of the *devak* and may even be performed along with the latter at a marriage. The only explanation that the *Marāṭhā* offers of the diversity of his *devaks* is that the *devak* was originally something by which his family took an oath.

One deduction that has given colour to the theory of totemism is that drawn from the identity of names that undoubtedly exists between some families of *Marāṭhās* and their *devaks*. It is easy, for instance, to find families of *Mores* who have as their *devak* the *mor* or peacock; to find *Sāḻunkes* with the *sāḻunkī* bird as their *devak*, *Śelārs* with the *śeḻī* or black she-goat and *Kalambes* with the kalamb-tree. It is, however, equally easy to find *Mores* with the *maryādvel* or *pānkaṇis* as their *devak*, and *Sāḻunkes* with the śahāmṛg, the nāg, the śamī, sūryakiran, bhāradvāj, bhārang, umbar and conch, or *Śelars* with the kalamb, whilst I was fortunate in finding in Wai, a village of the Satara district, a family of *Śeḻārs* who within living memory had the banyan-tree as their *devak* but changed this subsequently to the *śeḻī*, on their becoming meat-eaters. When one remembers that punning and false etymologies lead to restrictions on the cutting or planting of trees, decide the form of charms, and expand the meaning of a *devak* as when those who have as *devak a dhār* or edge of a blade, avoid garments with a coloured or pronounced edge, one can easily concede that a pun may have led to the choice of a *devak*. Among the *Kātkarīs* a play on the words *śindī*, 'wild palm-tree' and *śindaḻī*, 'a kept woman', leads to the injunction [1] that those who have lost their totems should take the wild palm-tree as their totem. So far from concluding, then, that the family name was taken from that of the *devak* there is reliable evidence to suggest that the *devak* is often chosen from a play on the name of the family, on the principle perhaps that there is *śakti* or 'power' innate in a name. The number of families with names similar to those of their *devaks* is in any case small in comparison with that of families between whom and their *devaks* there is no such connexion. Sometimes, too, a particular *devak* is not possessed by a family with the same name as that *devak*, but by another family of another name; a *Kaḻambe* among *Kunbis*, to give a single instance, may have as *devak* the conch, whilst a *Kadam* or a *Śhetge* family may possess the kaḻamb-tree as *devak*.

A second deduction that has frequently been made is one drawn from the respect paid to the source from which the *devak* is taken. In *Tribes and Castes of Bombay*, vol. iii, p. 131, Mr. Enthoven writes: 'These *devaks* are totemistic as the objects representing them are not touched, cut or otherwise used.' There are several inaccurate surmises in this assumption. In the first place the *devaks* include objects which on grounds other than their being *devaks* are reverenced by Hindus in general, and in the second place it is easy to multiply instances of trees from which *devaks* are cut that receive themselves no reverence at all save on the occasion when the *devak* is cut. Further than this, even should one concede that the parent source of the *devak* always received reverence, one would not be justified in assuming that the *devak* is a totem. It is not unusual to find reverence paid to a thing which at times is used in a special ceremony; the *Marāṭhā* has

[1] *Jyālā nāhin kulī tyānen dharāvī śindicī muḻī.*

a disinclination to cut the ruī-tree, as he uses this in the worship of *Gaṇpati*, and the Brahmin, of course, is equally reluctant to use for ordinary purposes the five trees he burns in a *homa*.

There are other considerations that discredit the theory of totemism as applied to the *devak*. A family that divides sometimes extends the meaning of its *devak*. *Powars* have as their *devak* a sword or knife ; on the point of this the *Dhār Powar* sticks a lemon ; the *Hār* branch puts a garland of onions or of umbar ; the *Lend* subdivision puts on the end of the blade a piece of white cāmphā wood and the *Ghār* subdivision attaches a feather of a *Ghār* bird. Many families have more than one *devak*, sometimes two, sometimes even three, which they use alternatively ; one of these usually being some object easily obtained ; families that claim no interrelationship at all have the same *devak* ; contrariwise, families that cannot intermarry because of consanguinity have different *devaks* and families making division take different *devaks*. The substitution of one *devak* for another is very common, particularly if some similarity of name suggests this ; the *garudvel* is substituted for the *garud* ; *bharangvel* for the *bhāradvāj*, a yellow piece of cloth in lieu of the yellow cāmphā ; the sunstone is substituted for the sunflower and a trinket of gold is used in place of the *sonvel*. Then again there are villages in which a number of races entirely different, even different sects, share a common *devak*, and it is quite common for a family migrating from one village to another to assume the *devak* it finds common in its new abode. No principle, in fine, of totemism rules the adoption or the abandonment of a *devak*.

To return to the many current definitions of a *devak*. If one rules out the possibility of a *devak* being an ancestral spirit, is it possible to accept it as a 'marriage guardian' or as a family god ? Now there are several vernacular names for a *devak*.[1] In the Konkaṇ among the *Agris* and again in Khandesh among the *Konkanis* the *devak* is called *vārak*, which I presume means 'defender' or 'that which wards off' ; in other districts it is frequently called *māi devatā*, and a more esoteric definition is the 'abode of God', *isvarāce adhiṣṭhān*. The key, in fact, to the problem of the *devak* is nothing more than the Hindu practice of invoking *śakti* into symbols, the practice of *āvāhana*. The *devak* of the *Marāṭhā* and other castes is a symbol into which the *śakti* of the village or the

[1] Several explanations are offered of the origin of the word *devak*: (*a*) The 'k' is a diminutive. This explanation seems improbable in view of the importance of the *devak*, the worship of which must be performed by a married pair ; (*b*) Devak is an abbreviation of *devakuṇḍ*, as one manner of installation is to put the *devak* on two earthen pots of water placed in a small pit ; (*c*) Devak is an abbreviation of *devata karnam*.

family god is invoked, these being often identical. By this invocation the presence of the deity is ensured during the marriage ceremony within the marriage *maṇḍap* or booth and when, as occasionally happens, a marriage is performed in a temple in pursuance of a vow, the *devak* is not installed because the deity is already present in the temple.

The details of the ritual of installing the *devak* follow exactly the ordinary canons which guide the practice of *āvāhana*. Should the *devak* be a branch of a tree it is severed from the tree with certain formalities which, in general, constitute the only reverence which is paid to the parent tree. Whatever be the *devak* it is first taken to a spot considered sacred; this is usually the temple of the village god. In the Konkaṇ one practice is to sever a twig from the parent tree and place it near the *tulsīdev*; at the time of *Puṇyāhavācan* it is brought into the house in a *parḍi* of rice and kept on a *pāṭ*. Some *Marāṭhās* take the *devak* to the threshing-floor; some *Koḻīs* to the cattle stand, whilst by depressed castes it may be taken to the site of the *Hoḻī* fire. Another alternative practice is to take it direct to the shrine of the family gods, where it may be placed in a winnowing-fan with a bodice-cloth before the gods. Whether, however, it is taken to the one or to another of these places the subsequent ritual is the same. The *devak* is insulated from the ground by an *āsan* or seat of rice and *akṣat*, unbroken rice, the usual medium for invoking *śakti*, is thrown on it, conjuring therein the power of the family god. It is from this moment that the object really becomes a *devak*, the repository of holy *śakti*, and henceforth ritual consists in providing the symbol with protection from influences that would destroy its inherent *śakti* and finally in its final dismissal, *devak-utthāpan*.

First and foremost the *devak* must be protected from the sun; when it is carried to the marriage *maṇḍap* four persons hold over it a *cāndvā* or canopy, which in the centre is held up with an axe by a male member of the family, who walks under the canopy with his wife, their clothes tied together. In the marriage *maṇḍap* it is then once more isolated from contact with the ground by being tied to one of the posts of the marriage booth. Along with it are tied a cake of flour, *puranpoḻī*, an axe and five leaves, *pancpālvi*, the object of which is to protect the *devak*. *Marāṭhās* also tie a lamp which is a betel-nut wrapped in cloth and lighted in groundnut oil, and it is a bad omen should this lamp fall. Occasionally a comb, a wooden bowl and other objects are also tied to the post. In the Konkaṇ where one practice is to place the *devak* in a *parḍi* or bamboo frame, a lemon, coconut, almonds, plantains and copper pice are placed along with the *devak*. It is very essential to emphasize that none of these objects constitute the *devak* or even part of it. In the *Indian Antiquary*, May, 1895, vol. xxiv, p. 126, however, Sir James Campbell writes that one of the *devaks* of the Deccani *Mahārs* is a piece of bread tied to a post, whilst in *Tribes and Castes of Bombay*, Mr. Enthoven seems at times to confuse all the articles so tied.

The last item in the ritual of the *devak* is its formal dismissal and the request made to the deity to return again when asked. This is the ordinary practice of *visarjana*, the dismissal of invoked *śakti*. In the Konkaṇ one common method of dismissing the inherent *śakti* of the *devak* is to shake it, just as the *śakti* of the manes is dismissed in the *Śrāddha* ceremony from the *piṇḍas* when the *yajaman* moves them. After this *visarjan*, the customary practice is then to throw the *devak* into a well or running water, which again is after the general procedure following the dismissal of *śakti*. *Dhangars* and *Cāmbhārs* in some cases take the *devak* of a branch of a tree back to the parent tree under a protecting canopy and leave it there, whilst in the Konkaṇ it is often abandoned near the *tulsīdev*.

From the beginning, therefore, to the end of the *devak* ritual, it is treated as something embodying the *śakti* of a deity. It is protected from contact with the ground, from uncleanness of all kinds, from being stepped over; it is shielded from the sun, and when tied to the post is protected from evil *śakti*. Yet another provision or rather prohibition which illustrates the power of the *devak* is the prohibition of all forms of *himsā* during the time the *devak* is in its position on the *maṇḍap* post. Grinding, washing, sweeping, shaving or the cutting of nails, the eating of meat are all prohibited, whilst continence is insisted upon. As, too, in the case of the worship of a god, if the worshipper wears silk or wool he need not wash his clothes, but if his clothes are of cotton it is imperative to wash them. The importance of the *devak* is further evidenced by the fact that it must be worshipped by a married pair with *śakti*.

In appendices I have given the *devaks* I have myself collected among some six thousand examined. The majority of these consists of trees and creepers; there are also symbols which represent beings and animals of Hindu mythology that could hardly be 'aboriginal', and among the metals used there is the significant absence of iron into which *śakti* cannot be invoked. The individuality of the *devaks* accordingly seems to support other evidence that the *devak* is nothing more than a symbol into which the *śakti* of a deity is temporarily invoked.

Criticism of my explanation of the *devak*, however, may still urge the possibility of a totem having been perpetuated in use as a symbol, and point to the influence of the *devak* in restricting intermarriages.

Now the possession of a common *devak* is by no means a universal bar to intermarriage, and there seems little more ground for arguing that present practice discloses the one-time prevalence of prohibitions based on the *devak*, than for thinking that the practice of to-day may have followed the wholesale alteration of *Marāṭhā* names that occurred under Muhammadan rule. The association of family unity with a particular symbol is not unknown even among *Deśastha Ṛgvedī Brahmins* ; I found six instances of such Brahmin families using in their worship of their family gods, special grasses and herbs ; davana (Artemisia vulgaris), kevada, durva (Cynodon dactylon), bamboo leaves and bailghata grass. In one case a family used as a canopy within the marriage *maṇḍap pariṭācīghaḍī*, which is a *devak* of the *Marāṭhās*. There are too—and this has been forgotten—a few instances among *Marāṭhās* of families which use their *devak* every day in the worship of their family gods but do not use them in any special way at a marriage.

To return to Mr. Enthoven's account of the *devak*. He frequently asserts that the commonest form of *devak* is the *pancpālvi* or five leaves. As the number of trees used in the *pancpālvi* is distinctly limited and no permutation or combination thereof can reach a very large figure in proportion to the number of *devaks* known, and as the *pancpālvi* does not operate as a bar on consanguineous marriages, it would follow that the *devak* seldom restricts marriage, a deduction inconsistent with Mr. Enthoven's assumption that it does so generally. The recurrence in ritual of the *pancpālvi* has apparently led to some confusion. Mr. Enthoven writes, for instance, that one of the five leaves 'as the original *devak* of the section is held specially sacred '. Now it is true that the saundad-tree is credited with the power of scaring witches, and on this account is included in the *pancpālvi* tied to the *devak*, and still more frequently in the *pancpālvi* placed beneath the threshing-floor post. As a *devak*, however, the use of this tree is comparatively rare, and I have been unable to find any evidence that one leaf in the composite *devak* receives special reverence.

One might easily multiply illustrations of the *pancpālvi* in Hindu ritual. The Brahmin uses it in the installation of *kalaśas*, and in the *puṇyāhavācana* ; the *Marāṭhā* ties it to his *devak* ; *Konchi-koravās*, in times of marriage, tie a branch of five leaves to their *hālgamba* ; *Bhils* offer the leaves of five trees to their gods during an epidemic; *Kātkarīs* place five leaves on five roads after a birth on the fifth day and at a marriage sprinkle water on the feet of their guests with the same number of leaves. *Marāṭhās* place the *pancpālvi* beneath the pole of their threshing-floor, and on entering a new house tie five leaves to the roof; along with many other castes when they take away their image of *devi* from the goldsmith they carry five leaves with it. One might even go beyond Hindu rites and adduce the customs of the Sindi Muhammadan which entail the use of *panjpati*.

As to the use of the *pancpālvi* as a *devak* there would seem to be very precise restrictions. Though, for instance, when so used the name of the family goddess is taken when the leaves are tied to the post I have found no single instance of the *pancpālvi* being taken to the *kula devatā* as other *devaks* are taken. In many cases, too, though the *pancpālvi* is used as a substitute for a lost *devak* it is not called *devak*, and sometimes the number of leaves is three and not five, or the *pancpālvi* is a misnomer as the five articles used are not all leaves. Above all it is a short step from tying the *pancpālvi* to every *devak* to using the *pancpālvi* independently when the original *devak* has been lost or forgotten.

In a similar way there seems to have been a confusion as to the use of craft tools as *devaks*. Here again a multitude of craftsmen tie their tools to the *maṇḍap* post but do not call them *devak*, and according to their own explanation, do so in order to secure that they are not used on the marriage day, and again as a substitute for the ordinary axe that is generally tied with the *devak*. It is obvious, too, that in any case if the whole of a class of goldsmiths were to use their pincers or blow-pipe as a *devak* that *devak* could not possibly operate as a bar to consanguineous marriages between families, but would prevent marriage altogether save with other castes. Whatever the explanation, accordingly, of the use of tools as the *devak*, several of the ordinary conclusions applied to the usual *devak* cannot be applied to a tool used as a *devak*. There is yet another possible explanation of this use of craft tools as *devak*. The Brahmin custom of installing at a marriage *Bhagvatī Śastragarbha* signifying the inherent *śakti* in a weapon suggests a parallel which may have influenced the practice of non-Brahmin craftsmen. It may also be to the influence of Brahmin custom that the use of the *pancpālvi* is due, for I examined a large number of such *devaks* and in every case I found that at some time or other those who used the *pancpālvi* as a *devak* had employed Brahmin priests.

In speaking, therefore, of the *pancpālvi* or of craft tools used as a *devak* it must be recognized that the term when applied to them is used with a much looser connotation than is implied in the ordinary use of the term, and, above all, in their case the grounds which have been adduced as evidence that the *devak* is a totem are quite irrelevant.

The internal evidence of the *devak* and its ritual warrant, in my opinion, the assumption that it is but a medium for the invocation of divine power. There are fortunately many customs very similar to that of installing a *devak* which force the same conclusion. The *devak* is an institution prevalent in the Deccan and Konkaṇ and, I suspect, having its origin in the Konkaṇ. In the Karnāṭak one finds the *hāḻgamba* or 'milk-post'; in Gujarāt the *manekstambha* or 'ruby pillar'; among Tamil Christians the *Arasani Kallu,* among Rājputs the *Vedīkhāmb,* and among Ahir Gaulis immigrants from the Mysore State the *mandā.* Between all these customs there is a remarkably close affinity which must be accepted in discussing the meaning of the *devak.* The *hāḻgamba* is a post in the marriage booth to which symbols are tied. The affinity between this custom and that of the *devak* is so close that the *Marāṭhā* of the Deccan with his *devak* can accept the *hāḻgamba* when resident in the Karnāṭak, and the *Lingāyat* of the Karnāṭak when resident in the Deccan can take the *devak* instead of his *hāḻgamba.* Some families in the Karnāṭak even call their *devak hāḻgamba.* The symbols tied to the *hāḻgamba* are usually two or three branches of different trees, though the practice of using a single tree and a single branch is not unknown. A few hours before the marriage ceremony begins a man, who is neither a widower nor unmarried, is sent to the parent tree which he worships before he cuts the *hāḻgamba.* He then takes the severed branch to a temple or throws it into a tank or well; in the temple the twig is worshipped on an *āsana* of two pots of water brought by two married women and *akṣat* is thrown on it. From the temple or well it is then taken in procession to the marriage booth under a canopy (*taḻī, chatra*); if brought from a well it is first placed on an *āsana* of the same wood and *akṣat* is thrown on it before it is tied to the post where it becomes the *kalpavṛkṣa.* The person bearing the twig is treated with respect; a lamp or *ārtī* is waved round him and a woman pours water on his feet. Along with the twig are tied to the post coloured rice, five pieces of turmeric and five pies wrapped in new cloth and a coconut.

In some cases in lieu of being tied to a post the *hāḻgamba* is tied to the yoke of a cart erected in a pit in which the *pancāmṛt* have been placed and over this five pies, pice or rupees; lime and red earth are applied to the yoke. When the *hāḻgamba* consists of several twigs, these are made up into five separate bundles. Of these bundles one which is the *hāḻgamba* proper is made from two trees and the remaining bundles are composed of twigs of a third tree. The first bundle is then installed to the right of the *manḍap* whilst the four bundles are thrown on the roof of the booth and after the completion of the marriage ceremony all five sheaves are thrown on the roof of the house. Supplementary practices are to make two dolls out of the *hāḻgamba* wood and give these to the bride to hold when she takes the *mangalsnān* or auspicious bath, or to make from the *hāḻgamba* two miniature *āsan* and place these in a bag of rice which five married women must carry throughout the marriage ceremony. One doll and one *āsan* represent male issue and the other female issue.

Now to revert to the affinity between the *devak* and the *hāḻgamba*.

1. The *hāḻgamba*, like the *devak*, is the tabernacle of invoked *śakti*. In the temple or in the marriage booth five married women throw *akṣat* on the symbol and invoke the presence of the marriage deity. At one *Lingāyat* marriage that I attended the *śakti* of *Agni* was invoked into the *hāḻgamba*; in other cases the family god was invoked, and when the five bundles of twigs are thrown on the roof of the house these are held to embody the *śakti* of the family god. Sometimes, again, a distinction is made between two posts of the *manḍap* and the *śakti* of *Varuṇa* is invoked into the *Hasargamba* with the object of averting a spirit, *Yakṣa*, who molests the bridal pair.

(2) Like the *devak* the *hāḻgamba* is protected. It is primarily protected from contact with the ground; it is again shielded from the sun and carried under a canopy held up by four persons. Castes that eat flesh seem invariably to use a canopy; vegetarians sometimes do not use a canopy. One quaint form of protection that I found in one village was the provision of the bride's uncle who carried the *hāḻgamba* with an umbrella to which were attached old shoes and torn rags, with a garland of brinjals, onions and old brooms, with old clothes and torn blankets and an earthen pot marked with soot. As in the case again of the *devak*, widows or unclean persons cannot touch the *hāḻgamba*. Corresponding to the *puranpoḻī* which protects the *devak* is the *hurand holgī* which protects the *hāḻgamba*.

(3) The dismissal of the *hāḻgamba* requires the same precautions as the *visarjana* of the *devak*. The *hāḻgamba* must not be thrown on the ground where it might be stepped over; it is thrown after use on the roof of the house, at the root of a tree or into water.

(4) The same restrictions as to committing *himsā* prevail during installation of the *hālgamba* as during that of the *devak*. All grinding is prohibited; sweeping, if done from necessity, cannot be done with a broom but only with a cloth; the baking of bread is tabooed. Amongst flesh-eaters no flesh may be eaten or any animal killed; haircutting and shaving are forbidden as is the threshing of grain. In the case, therefore, of the *hālgamba* we have the same practice of *āvāhan* and of *visarjan* as in that of the *devak*. We have different families possessing separate symbols, though family exclusiveness is not as marked as among *Marāṭhā* families with their *devaks*; these symbols, however, are not connected with any restrictions on intermarriage and the most ardent enthusiasm would not attribute to them a totemistic origin.

To pass to the customs of other castes. *Tamil Christians* in their turn pay deference to a pillar of the marriage booth. To this they fasten mango-leaves and at the top a crucifix. Around this post of bamboo the bridal pair turn, followed by married women throwing grain at the foot of the pillar and sprinkling milk on the grain. The catechist reads the marriage prayers near the pillar, the family of the bridal pair standing close by. On the third day of the marriage all seize the pillar together and shake it, after which the pillar is thrown away. It requires little imagination to trace in this practice, particularly in the shaking of the pillar, the memory of a custom of invoking *śakti* into the pillar and of eventually dismissing it.

Among *Rājputs* a platform or *vedī* is built in the west of the *manḍap* and behind it a branch is fixed in the ground of gular or mango, and to this *halad* and *akṣat* are tied. The branch is called *vedīkhāmb*. This branch, after severance from the parent tree, is first taken to a temple and thence brought in procession to the *manḍap* under a canopy (*chat*); in the *manḍap* the priest invokes into it the *śakti* of the family god.

Jains of the Karnāṭak have their *manekstambha*,[1] a familiar institution in Gujarāt. I have also found Jains with a *hālgamba* (Ficus infectoria) which illustrates again the affinity between all these cognate customs. A khijda-tree (Prosopis spicigera) is usually cut for this post through the agency of *Kolīs* and *Sutārs*, as there is danger supposed in doing this cutting; when the tree is cut it is addressed with these words, 'Do not be angry with us as we want your wood for a good purpose'. The branch is then

[1] Cp. *Religion and Folklore of Northern India*, W. Crooke, 1926. I can find no evidence that the 'Ruby-pillar' is so called because it gleams with blood. All Jains whom I have consulted explain the name as meaning only 'valuable pillar'.

taken to the marriage booth and before its erection cotton thread coloured red, mendphul, kangani and an axe are tied to it. The post is then placed in a pit on the right side of the bridegroom's *manḍap* and to the left of that of the bride. *Akṣat* is first thrown into the pit. No respect is shown to the khijda-tree save on the occasion of its use at a marriage. The post remains erect for some days during which no widow or unclean person can touch it as it is supposed to be the residence of the family god. On the seventh day a ceremony of dismissal is performed and until this is over no grinding of grain is permitted. After this dismissal of the inherent *śakti* the pole is thrown into a river or well by a member of the family of one of the bridal pair.

Among *Ahir Gauḻīs* at a marriage the maternal uncle of the bride worships a mango-tree and severs a branch some five feet long which is taken direct to the house where the marriage is celebrated and erected in front of it. Then a small earthen pot besmeared with cowdung and rice is taken; a half-anna piece and leaves from the mango-branch (*mandā* or *mānda*) are placed in it and the pot is put in front of the branch. During the marriage ceremony the bridal pair go round the pole every day five times, and on the third day when *kankaṇ* or wristlets are tied to the wrists of the bridal pair similar *kankaṇ* are also tied to the post, and these with the post are thrown into running water. Though it is not an invariable practice, some *Ahir Gauḻīs* bring the mango-branch to the *manḍap* in procession under a canopy coloured with turmeric.

In all these kindred practices, therefore, there are many features in common. In the care taken to protect the branch from the contact of the unclean or from that of the ground and to shield it from the sun; in its formal dismissal and the final throwing of the branch into water there is proof that the branch is believed to embody the *śakti* of a god, and in some cases there is direct evidence of the invocation of such *śakti*. In the Kanara district in some communities the word *hāḻgamba* does not appear commonly used, but the symbolic post used at a marriage is called *Muhūrtta Meda, Muhūrtta Khāmba* or *Hālekhāmb*. *Sherugars* take two twigs of Ficus glomerata and two of Alstonia scholaris and place at the entrance of the *manḍap* after keeping them near their family god. Among *Kharvis* some men have the prescriptive right of fixing twigs of hale, atti, jīṇā, and sātīnā (Pisum sativum) at the entrance of every marriage booth. *Hālakki Gauḍās* make two arches from three branches of atti under which the bridal pair sit. *Kumris* take five twigs of heddi, yarjal (Mimusops elingi), atti, kavargi and the silk cotton tree and form a circle enclosed with thread within which the bridal pair is seated; one twig of each tree is placed near the *Tulsīdev* and one near the family god; *akṣat* is used in invoking and in dismissing the twigs. When finally dismissed the twigs, which are called *Sāyakanḍ*, are taken to a tank and left with their ends in the water.

In the case of the *mandā*, the *manekstambha* and the *vedīkhāmb* a whole caste uses one and the same symbol; in the case of the *hālgamba* there is some variation in the symbols according to families, but the number of symbols is very limited. Between these symbols and restrictions on intermarriage there is no connexion. If then we pass from these customs to the institution of the *devak* it seems unnecessary to assume at once that because the symbols used are more numerous they must necessarily represent family unity in the sense of entailing restrictions on consanguineous marriage. To go from the *mandā*, the *manekstambha*, and *vedikhāmb* through the *hālgamba* to the *Marāṭhā devak* is merely to proceed in orderly stages from the use of a single symbol by a whole caste to a differentiation of symbols among families which reaches its most perfect form in the *devak*. To assume *a priori* that the *devak* is a totem is to neglect altogether these other customs which are so alike in ritual detail and meaning and to which no totemistic origin can be attributed. The whole theory of totemism in fine as applied to the *devak* institution is a loose construction based on deduction from a few premises, moulded by assumed analogy and framed without consideration for one of the principal and fundamental axioms of Indian thought.

APPENDIX I

Devaks

(1) Miscellaneous

Vāgh—The skin, claws, or flesh of a tiger.

Bhāradvāj—Bhārgavarāma, Kuḍkumbhā, Bharat, Sonkāvalā. The crow-pheasant.

Rājhaṁs—The goose.

Vangāy—The hair of the wild ox.

Mor, Lāṇḍor—Peacock and peahen.

Śeḷī—The hair or head of a black she-goat with issue.

Garuḍ—A mythical animal half man half bird represented by a species of eagle, or more generally by Garudvel.

Śahāmṛg—The eggs of an ostrich; also the feathers.

Parī—A fabulous bird represented by a water-bird.

Dahyali—A bird.

Kaṅk—A curlew or heron.

Parthin—The wing of a pied wagtail.

Baḻi—The cattle egret. Bubulcus coromandus.

Hastidant—The tusk or image of an elephant.

Gāy—A cow; also Gāyīcegomūtra.

Baji Potira—A bird.

Ghār—A kite.

Kombḍā—A hen.

Dukar—A pig.

Sāḻūnkki—Gracula religiosa.

Kāsavācī Pāṭh—Tortoise-shell.

Kolisara—A lynx.

Sāyalāce Kāṇḍe—A porcupine quill.

Bail—An ox.

Cātak—A bird, Cuculus melanolucus.

Śankpāl—A lizard.

Nāg—A snake; Nāgācī Phaḍī. The hood of a cobra.

Sone—Gold.

Tāmbe—Copper.

Śaṅkh—Conch.

Viṭkar—Burnt powdered brick.

Ghāgarī—A small bell.

Dive—Lamps to the number of fifty or 360.

Dhār—A blade with a lemon at the end of it; a blade with a garland of onions or umbar at the end; a blade with a piece of white Cāphā wood; a blade with the feather of a kite. The lemon at the end of the blade is also called Dhāreca Phul or the sparks that fly when steel is edged.

Paraṭācīghaḍī—A fold of cloth washed by a washerman and brought from his house.

Jakeri—A lamp of flour placed in an earthen pot and taken to a stream covered with cloth.

Poṁvale—Coral.

Kāndyāncī Māḻ—A garland of onions with gold.

Rudrākṣāncī Māḻ—Berries of Eleocarpus ganitrus with gold.

Sūryakānt—Suryamaṇi; Sunstone; Crystal.
Leṇḍ—Dung.
Sugar.
Hār—Garland of onions or the fruit of the umbar tree.
Nāraḻ—Coconut.
Bhomad—A large ant-hill.
Vāruḻāce Sing—The upper part of a white ant-hill.
Vibhūti—Ashes.
Kāḻī Māṭī—Black earth.
Cotton wool.
Ukirḍā—Rubbish.

(2) Trees and Creepers, etc.

Mārvel—Andropogon scandens.
Nirguḍi—Vitex negundo.
Rui—Ruchkin; Calotropis gigantea with white flower.
Mandār—Calotropis gigantea with grey purple flowers.
Agasti—Sesbania grandiflora.
Kaḻamb—Kadamb. Stephegyne parvifolia.
Anjan—Hardwickia binata.
Karanj—Pongamia glabra.
Nāgcāphā—Mesua ferrea.
Pivaḻā Cāphā, Kāncan—Michelia champaca.
Pimpal, Aśvath, Ravi, Bari—Ficus religiosa.
Umbar—Ficus glomerata.
Vaḍ—Ficus Bengalensis.
Jāmbhuḻ—Calyptranthes jambolana.
Saundad, Śami—Prosopis spicigera.
Bel—Aegle marmelos.
Kaḻak—Bambusa arundinacea.
Veḻu—Dendrocalamus strictus.
Paḻas—Butea frondosa.
Bhāraṅg—Clerodendron serratum.
Rothi—Malva rotundifolia.
Khair—Acacia catechu.
Aghāḍā—Achyranthes aspera.
Vet—Calamus rotang or verus.
Moh—Bassia latifolia.
Gugul—Balsamodendron mukul.
Ketak, Kevaḍā—Pandanus odoratissimus.
Kamaḻ—Lotus.
Lokhaṇḍi—Ventilago maderaspatana.
Kiṅkar, Devbābhal—Acacia latronum.
Śiras—Mimosa sirisha.
Rāi—Sinapis racemosa.
Dhapāḻī—Juniperus Lycia.
Kambaḻ—Hymenodyction excelsum.
Śisav—Dalbergia Sisu.
Āptā—Bauhinia racemosa.
Śevrī—Bombax heptaphyllum.
Nimbuṇī—Citrus limonum.
Ain—Terminalia tomentosa.
Śevrā—Toxotrophis Roxburghii.
Tivar—Avicennis officinalis.
Dhotarā—Datura.
Śindī—Phoenix sylvestris.
Kāvaḻī—Sterculia urens.
Mandra—Marlea begonifolia.
Somvel—Sarcostemma brevistigma.
Jāicāvel—Jasminum grandiflorum.
Salpi, Salphali, Salai—Boswellia serrata.
Drākṣācāvel—Vitis vinifera.
Maratvel, Bel—Aegle marmelos.
Darbha—Eragrostis cynosursides.
Moriel, Morbel, Morvel—Clematis gouriana.
Vasanvel—Cocculus villosus.
Guḻvel—Tinospora cordifolia.
Garuḍphul—Anamirata cocculus.
Pānkaṇis, Pānedicekaṇis—Typha augustata.
Maryadvel, Marjadvel, Margati, Ranjai, Marjavel—Ipomoea biloba.
Pānvel—Piper betle.
Cāndvel—Macaranga Roxburghii.
Payaṇi—Vateria Indica.
Maricivel—Piper nigrum.

Asanvel—Pterocarpus marsupium.
Ḍavṇā—Artemisia Sieversiana.
Basundrivel—Rubus biflorus.
Jāsvandice Phūl—Hibiscus rosa-sinensis.
Sonvel Amarvel—Cuscuta reflexa.
Mogarī—Jasminum Sambac.
Phaṇsice Jhāḍ—Carallia integerrima.
Mircī—Capsicum frutescens.
Vaghanti—Capparis Zeylanica.
Śerṇi—Adelia neriifolia.
Kākaḍ—Garuga pinnata.
Maharukh—Ailantus excelsa.
Vasundarivel—Cocculus villosus.
Kaṇherī—Oleander odorum.
Kaṇikānche Jhāḍ—Paramignya monophylla.
Bhadarāce Phūl—Artocarpus Lakoocha.
Margali—Garcinia indica.
Bāṇḍguḻ—Epidendron tesselloides.
Garuḍvet—Anamirta cocculus.
Rāmbāṇ, Ramhan—Typha elephantina.
Pāṅgārā—Erythrina indica.
Madhvel—Combretum ovalifolium.
Khuḻkhuḻā—Crotolaria retusa.
Kātvel—Cucumis trigonus.
Sūryakānti—Ionidium suffruticosum.
Sūryakamaḻ—Helianthus tuberosus.
Gangavel—Cucurbita maxima.
Karal—Bauhinia malabarica.
Mendī—Lawsonia alba.
Kumbhā, Vakumbhā—Careya arborea.
Nirvel—Limacia cuspidata.
Vāghācā Chāmpā—Michelia exelsa.
Vāsukīcāvel—Chenopodium ambrosioides.
Maredi—Erigeron asteroides.
Agasvel, Akāśvel—Cassytha filiformia.
Sūryakiran—Sun lotus.
Vaghoti—Capparis horrida.
Devpāyarīcakaṇis — Ficus Rumphii.
Sumudravel—Argyreia speciosa.
Marelīcāvel—Allophylus Cobbe.
Revatavel—Jasminum angustifolium.
Haraḻ, Durvā—Cynodon dactylen.
Gaurī—Calamus acanthospathus.
Araṇi—Clerodendron phlomoides.
Kāṭe Kaḻak—Bambusa arundinacea.
Moḻ—Pyrus Pashia.
Arkhaḍ—Rhus Punjabensis.
Ghevaḍā—Dolichos lablab.
Asvalī—Vitex glabrata.
Bilāyat Jhāḍ—Feronia elephantum.
Pal—Mimusops hexandra.
Surad—Laportea cranulata.
Koch—Curcuma aromatica.
Garuḍāsan—Anamirta cocculus.
Lenḍphūl—Salacia macrosperma.
Kaval—Helicteria Isora.
Gahū—Wheat.

(3) Other *Devaks* but not identifiable

Āgvel, Mirgaḻvel, Bhārgavvel, Vasanilīcāvel, Mālvel, Mragvel, Vasudicāvel, Vasanīcāvel, Markatvel, Mariticāvel, Davshel, Asapursh, Javayelu, Katvat, Cephul, Mukapicāvel, Rohita, Pāhiṇī, Daigaḍyācāvel, Marlivel, Vasamcāvel, Udabrā, Pacamīcāvel, Singanvel, Kamalnal, Virchatra, Vadvagni, Śūdhravivel, Margalvel, Sukharvicāvel, Mundravel, Dangdīcāvel, Madhura, Kanholi, Kandādicavel, Jibkāpi, Ghodyacijibh, Gharvel, Devaruticephul, Karalicavel, Marmedicavel, Mudrolvel, Magajyacavel, Ban.

APPENDIX II

The *Pancpālvi*

Khair—Acacia catechu.
Hivar—Acacia leucophloca.
Phaṇas—Artocarpus integrifolia.
Tarvaḍ—Cassia auriculata.
Cinc—The tamarind.
Bor—Zizyphus jujuba.
Rāmphaḻ—Anona reticulata.
Karvand—Carissa carandas.
Śitāphaḻ—Anona squamosa.
Pimparṇi—Thespesia populnea.
Yirval—Salicineae tetrasperma.
Toraṇ—Zizyphus rugosa.
Ḍāḻimb—Punica granatum.
Āvḻi—Phyllanthus emblica.
Payara—Ficus Rumphii.
Perū—The guava tree.
Cāmphā—Michelia champaca.
Nimb—Melia azadirachta.
Temburṇi—Diospyros melonoxylon
Nāgvel—Piper betle.
Supārī—Areca catechu.
Paḻas—Butea frondosa.
Saundad—Prosopis spicigera.
Vaḍ—Ficus Bengalensis.
Rui—Calatropis gigantea.
Salai—Boswellia serrata.
Ambā—Mango tree.
Moh—Bassia latifolia.
Arkhaḍ—Rhus punjabensis.
Jāmbhuḻ—Calyptranthes jambolana.

The mango, umbar and the jāmbhuḻ trees are almost without exception an invariable ingredient of the *pancpālvi*. To these two other leaves are added and castes choose different trees.

Mahār—Rāmphaḻ; Karvand; Bor; Sitāphaḻ; Saundad; Pimparṇi; Pimpaḻ; Yirwal; Cinc; Jack; Rava; Banyan; Cāpā; Rui; Toran; Kalamb; Perū; Betel leaves and nuts and jvarī are also added to make up the number of five things.
Telī—Banyan; Saundad; Ber; Pimpaḻ; Karvand.
Nhāvī—Śamī; Cāphā; Karvand; Bor.
Dhangar—Hiwar; Bor; Tarvad; Paḻas; Khair; Pimpaḻ.
Cāmbhār—Śamī; Cāphā; Bor; Pimparṇi; Āvḻī; Pimpaḻ; Rui; Limb.
Lohār—Karvand; Jack; Rava; Bor.
Vāṇī—Bamboo, Ḍāḻimb.
Māng—Pimparṇi; Bor; Hivar; Tarvad; Saundad; Karvand; Jack; Rava.
Parīṭ—Saundad; Pimpaḻ.
Koḻī—Saundad; Karvand.
Kumbhār—Bor; Āvḻi.
Rāmośī—Bor; Rui; Pimpaḻ; Payaran.
Māḻī—Bor; Saundad; Pimpaḻ.

APPENDIX III

The *Hāḻgamba*

Ekki—Calotropis gigantea.
Alad—Ficus bengalensis.
Kari, *Pimprī*—Ficus infectoria.
Basarī—Ficus infectoria.
Aśvath—Ficus religiosa.
Cakki—Artocarpus integrifolia.
Gular, *Atti*—Ficus glomerata.
Śend, *Kallī*—Euphorbia Tirucalli.
Niral—Eugenia jambolana.
Mullu-Mutala, *Halival*, *Halvan*—Erythrina Indica.
Ippi—Capparis sepiaria.
Mar-Audla—Jatropha Curcas.
Dagaḍī—Cocculus villosus.
Apa—Typha angustifolia.
Banni—Acacia ferruginea.
Ingal—Balanites Roxburghii.

CHAPTER XXV

THE COERCION OF POWER

NIRBANDH

THE coercion of the *kudrat* or *śakti* of a saint is practised in much the same way by the Muhammadan as by the Hindu, and their ways of coercing the power of a tree do not differ. A piece of paper is folded and tied round the neck of the sick and then thrown before a saint with the words, 'The cure has begun, you must finish it'. When stones are placed on tombs or at the roots of trees; when branches of trees are weighed down by stones; when knots are tied in the coverings of tombs or pieces of cloth are tied in the branches of trees there is ample evidence of words being uttered which imply that the intention is to coerce the power of the saint or tree. The driving of nails into trees or the tying of thread round trees are also methods of coercing power.

When one passes to the coercion of the power of gods one finds this coercion admitted in many phrases such as the *Marāṭhī* phrase, *devāvar bhār ghālṇe*, 'to impose a weight on a god', and the Kanarese phrase, *devarannu sankaṭadalli hākoṇa*, 'to place a god in a dilemma'.

A god may be coerced through his name, for the name is stronger than the god. *Nāmasmaraṇ* is the continuous repetition of the name of a god by relays of people, *bhajan* is prayer night and day by relays of suppliants. *Dharṇe* is sitting at the door of a temple and fasting till the god grants a request. *Pranacar* is lying prostrate before a god or at a saint's tomb and refusing to get up or take food till a desired request has been complied with. The immersion of a god in water till it is quite submerged is done on many occasions. An image of *Gajāna* is immersed to assist a woman in her delivery, and the image is not freed till delivery has taken place; an image of *Gaṇpati* is immersed if a man does not return home when expected; at an eclipse all images are immersed to hasten the delivery of the luminary from the eclipse; when the monsoon delays an image is immersed without worship or offering to bring the delayed rains. Immersion of images is performed whenever loss of livelihood is anticipated.

In time of danger an image of *Gaṇpati* is put in a glass case and kept immured till the danger is over. On *Gaṇeśa Caturthī* when people enthrone images of *Gaṇpati* a barren woman will steal the image of another and enclose it in a niche in a wall and keep it there until she gets issue. There are, moreover, various ways of irritating a god so that it will grant a request. His image is worshipped at improper times or it is circumambulated in the reverse way; a temporary benefit may even be obtained by worshipping it with unclean things. The sticky juice of the ruī-tree is smeared over an image; in the temple of Narsinh near Nāgatirth in the Kumta taluka when rain withholds, a paste of green chillies called *lavangīmircī* is applied to an image from head to foot. Images of gods are made to lie on their stomachs in the field and are there smeared with cowdung and even with ordure. To bring rain one practice is to steal an image of *Gaṇpati* and break open its stomach in a field.

The use of mantras again is a form of coercion of *śakti*, for the mantra is stronger than the god. *Mantradhinum tu daivatum*, the mantras are gods.

CHAPTER XXVI

THE DESTRUCTION OF POWER

THE ANTIPATHY OF TWO POWERS

UNLESS they belong to a *pancāyatan*, a group of five inter-related gods, the images of two deities cannot be placed on the same *āsan*. The images of *kula devatā* of different families cannot be brought together; on the fifth day after the birth of a *Marāṭhā* child the mother receives many women visitors, but no woman may visit her who has a family god different from that of the mother. The *jatrā* or fairs of two deities of one place cannot be held at one time or evil befalls the village. About twenty years ago the fairs of Dyamava and Durgava were held together at Dharwar on the same day; the deities were driven in the same car and placed on the same *āsan* in the *manḍap*. During the night the deities fought and in the morning their broken bangles and hacked swords were found on the ground, whilst later there was a virulent outbreak of plague.

In Sind a mosque cannot be built near another mosque; if any second mosque is so built it is called *Masjid zarar* or the mosque that harms and it is unlawful to enter it.

In Sind two pregnant women must not have their delivery in the same house or the life of the children or of one mother is endangered. Sisters-in-law among Hindus must not meet when they are pregnant. In the Deccan any near relationship prevents the meeting of two women when *enceinte*. In the Panch Mahals a pregnant woman must not meet or see a woman who has just delivered. A restriction prohibiting two bridegrooms from seeing each other's *bāśing* is a common one and prevents the holding simultaneously of a marriage in each of two opposite houses. Two sons of one father cannot have their thread ceremonies at the same time, and two *munjā* or *vaṭu*, if they meet, must hide their faces. Two *Pīrs* should not meet nor two *sādhus*, for quarrels ensue from their meeting; persons who blow pipes to charm snakes will not allow another charmer to blow his pipe at the same time as they blow their own.

Two Muhammadan *tābūt* should not meet ; men who have been working in one *dera* or threshing-floor are not allowed to enter another threshing-floor, for fear of conflict between the *kudrat* of the two floors. Two wells cannot be dug near to one another ; two grinding-stones, two saddles or two brooms cannot be placed together. In Sind two white things should not be put together, and so milk and curds cannot be mixed. A Hindu will not place a broom and a winnowing-fan together, the pestle and mortar after use, or place together the hammer used to fix the peg of the grindstone, *gunḍakallu,* and the pestle of the mortar, *kabbagunḍu.*

MUTILATION

After the invocation of power into an image the *śakti* of the image is lost if the image be broken. During the annual festival of *Gaṇeśa Caturthī* care must be taken that the image of *Gaṇpati* used is not broken before it is finally immersed. The bangles of a married woman lose their *śakti* if they break ; the *mangaḻsūtra* of a married woman, if torn, must be replaced, and if the Brahmin tears his sacred thread he cannot take a meal until he has sanctified a new thread. A temple bell, a conch, a hearth lose their *śakti* if broken.

In Hindu ritual no article is more commonly used than *akṣat* which is unbroken rice grain ; cotton thread, too, is used in its simple untwisted state. Untwisted thread is tied round *kalaśas* ; is used in the *mangalsnān,* in making *kankaṇ* ; it is used to avert evil-eye and to tie an amulet. When leaves of the bel are offered in worship they must not have been damaged by insects ; the leaves used by Brahmins and by *suvāsiṇīs* as plates should be intact. In some cases perfection is associated with a certain number ; when leaves of tulsī are used in worship they must be in pairs ; plantains should be in unbroken bunches of five, though some castes permit the use of any odd number of plantains when an offering is made to a betrothed girl. In all auspicious ceremonies, in *vratas, śāntis* and in *Śrāddhas* the Hindu should not wear singed, torn or knotted clothes, and in strict theory ought annually on *Ekādaśī Āṣādha* to throw his worn clothes beyond the village boundary on or near a tree.

Imperfection destroys *śakti,* which will not abide in an imperfect tabernacle. As a corollary to this, imperfection destroys the *śakti* which results from performing a rite. Paper used for writing charms must have no holes. A sacrificial victim must be without blemish. There is a story well known in Sind of the Mogul emperor, Akbar, being wounded by a knife which left a scar on his hand. A Mulla Dopiaza who saw the scar gave thanks to God, whereon one Biral pointed out to the emperor the delight of the mullah and secured his imprisonment. Some days later the emperor when out hunting was separated from his retinue and captured by wild tribesmen who were seeking a human sacrifice to bury beneath the foundations of their fort. They were on the point of burying the emperor when they discovered his scar and set him free. On his return to the palace the emperor, of course, set free the unfortunate mullah and rewarded his prescience.

Not only, too, must a victim be unblemished but the *yajamān* or celebrant must be without stain. The *Lingāyat* will not allow an imperfect person to begin the ploughing, the sowing or to measure grain; the Muhammadan has the same restrictions, and when the sower goes forth to sow, his friends follow him to the field in Sind to see if he has any physical blemish and in that case substitute another sower. A defective or mutilated person cannot cut the branch used for the *hālgamba* or bring it to the marriage *maṇḍap*; he cannot prepare a charm; he cannot take part in any *Mahāyajna*; if he be an *Agnihotrī* he cannot celebrate a *hom*; though he may carry the corpse of one who is a near relative he cannot bear the corpse of one who is not a relative, for nothing that he does can bring *śakti* to another. *Lingāyats* call defective persons *mūḻā* and exclude them from all ceremonies in which boys, virgins or *suvāsiṇīs* are to be feasted. In one sect of *Lingāyats* celibates who have vowed to remain unmarried are called *Paṭṭdayyā* or *Caraṇṭayyā* and receive much reverence; the water in which their feet have been bathed is sprinkled over others and the leavings of their food are treated as *karuṇa prasād*, but should these celibates in any way become imperfect their special *śakti* vanishes and with it the reverence paid to them.

When practising *Ḥāḍrāt jinn* to get control of spirits the Muhammadan makes use of a boy or girl as a medium, but the medium must be without blemish. In a mosque a defective person cannot conduct the prayers; he could not conduct funeral prayers; he cannot slaughter an animal and he should not even be present when others are discussing something of capital importance. To meet a defective person when going on an errand is as fatal to the success of the journey in the eyes of the Muhammadan as it is in those of the Hindu. A Muhammadan excludes a defective person from the room of a woman in confinement and from the *davan* ceremony when thread, to be used eventually for the trousers of the bridal pair, is wound round the big toe and the thumb of the bridegroom. The destruction of beneficent *kudrat* which mutilation is supposed to cause brings in the activity of evil-eye.

As corollary to the axiom that mutilation or imperfection destroys power, husbands whose wives have mutilated limbs are not allowed to participate in a marriage ceremony. There are many ideas that contribute to the disabilities of the widow in India, but into her exclusion from ritual enters in some degree the idea that she is imperfect and therefore destructive of *śakti.* Castes that permit widow remarriage usually debar from auspicious ceremonies those that have married widows. The barren woman again is considered imperfect, and her exclusion from ceremonies the object of which is the winning of *barkat* is common to all communities. Insistence on perfection leads also to the requirement that a *yajamān* should have with him his wife, that his child should be associated with him, and on occasion that he should have parents living on both sides.

The befouling contact of deformed persons is a standing subject in the ancient books of Hinduism. Deformity is destructive of *śakti,* destructive of *barkat.* To break a thing is to make it void of *śakti.* Muhammadans avoid meeting in the morning a man with one eye, for Anti-Christ will have only one eye, and a person with six fingers, *changho,* is equally inauspicious and, if met, brings bad fortune during the day.

Although, however, imperfection drives away power or possibly because it drives away *śakti,* a broken thing is often used to avert evil, such as the evil *śakti* of evil-eye, of spirits and of disease. Broken images of sandal-wood, broken coconuts, broken *śāligrām* stones, broken conches, cowries and bells ; worn-out brooms, baskets and winnowing-fans afford protection against evil *śakti.* Tattered rags are called *piḍā* or *kāli,* 'calamity', and the gift of these to others transfers evil, but they are also used to avert evil.

SILENCE

By speaking, *barkat* or *kalyāṇ* may be lost and the efficacy of a rite destroyed.

If after a meal a man washes his dirty hands and throws away the dirty water accidentally hitting some one, the latter will obtain *barkat,* but only if he remains silent. Another belief of *Mahārs* is that if a cow passes by an open door at sunset it will confer *barkat* on the occupants of the house if they remain silent. On seeing a dog carry away a piece of bread from a house one may obtain *barkat* by snatching the bread from the dog and burying it beneath one's threshold, but one must do this in silence ; bread found on the road also brings *barkat* if buried in silence. A good dream should not be related to another or its *barkat* is lost. If one finds a piece of asafoetida in one's curry one should tell no one of one's discovery. Advice given by a *guru* must never be told to another, and if a *Pīr* in Sind give a *vazifa* or prayer to a disciple it must not be disclosed to any other person. Magicians when they discover a new charm must tell no one about it and exorcists must make no display of their knowledge.

In Sind if a Muhammadan hears of the death of a near relative he remains silent in the hope of winning *barkat.* Many of the Caliphs are said to have buried their own children with their own hands in silence. According to tradition, the Prophet said that a good dream should not be told to any one other than a beloved friend, and a bad dream should not be mentioned to any one so that evil may not come. In the month of *Rajab* Persian Moslems serve several dishes in large earthen pots, in one of which a two-anna piece has been concealed ; the lucky guest who finds the silver coin must tell no one of his fortune.

The efficacy of a magic rite depends upon the observance of silence. When a child is a victim of evil-eye it is shown its reflection in a dish of oil and this is taken in silence to a temple where it is burnt. Silence characterizes some rites performed to bring rain. Nails are driven in silence into trees to cure or transfer illness. In the practice of *Utāra* things waved round the heads of the sick are deposited or buried at cross-roads in silence. Herbs are uprooted in silence at an eclipse or on an *Amāvāsyā* ; medicinal herbs are collected in silence and medicines are administered in silence. When the aid of mantriks is sought and objects are taken to them to be charmed or brought back from them silence must be maintained. Incantations made over the sick must be made inaudibly, for if the patient hear them they are inoperative as cures. A person over whom the Koran is recited must remain silent, and when writing a charm a Muhammadan remains silent. Silence is imperative when a bath is taken in charmed water, a dumb bath, *mukaniru,* to drive away disease or to obtain issue. This bath is also taken as a preliminary to rubbing oneself against a 'breathing stone', a *usala kal* ; this stone is found in front of temples of Hanuman, and by rubbing against it five times on each of three days a strain which affects the breathing can be cured, but only if silence be maintained. When the *Kātkarī* coerces the power of a ruī-tree by placing a stone on a bent branch he does so in silence ; when asafoetida is rubbed into a cut made in a barren pumpkin creeper this must be done without speaking.

Barkat is lost if one speaks when taking grain from a granary ; when removing grain from the threshing-floor or when measuring grain, silence is necessary. Coconuts and plantains should be gathered in silence and betel-leaves plucked in silence; butter should be churned in silence or the butter will congeal; honey should be collected in silence and cattle should be milked in silence.

To help a woman in her travail water is passed from a well along a long line of persons and given her to drink; it is essential that all these persons should remain silent or the *śakti* which the water acquires from the common will of all and the piety of any pious person among them is lost. A talisman loses its power if when tying it to one's person one speaks.

The Muhammadan observes silence after the preliminary *bismillāh* on slaughtering an animal until he has rinsed his mouth and washed his hands. The success of *Istikhāra* depends upon silence being maintained. When *naivedya* is offered by a Hindu to a god; when *akṣat* is thrown on the *vaṭu* at a thread ceremony, on the bridal pair during a marriage, or on an image save when its *śakti* is dismissed, silence is incumbent. The sun is worshipped in silence on Sundays; the bride worshipping *Gaurī* and *Śankar* does so in silence; the propitiation of *Vetāḻ* is accomplished by silent worship and Hindu women worship *Lakṣmī* in silence at *Divāḻī*. Among non-Brahmins when a sick person recovers from a severe illness and goes to a temple to express his gratitude he must worship in silence. *Pancāḻs* worship the patri and the banni trees in silence before dawn. In Khandesh the hour before dawn is chosen for the first ploughing, and *Jains* choose the same hour for the first sowing because it is a time when the probability of being accosted is least. At *Śimgā Bhils* of the Taloda taluka dance from village to village in silence and keep silence when objects pledged to a god are taken from one village to another, for the breaking of silence would mean death. In the Karnāṭak a Hindu travelling to a temple of Southern India will not speak until he reaches the temple even if accosted, and *Kuravas*[1] cover their mouths so as to make speaking impossible. In Sind some Muhammadans observe silence on their way to a saint's *dargāh*, and according to tradition, he who goes to a mosque without talking to any one on the way is rewarded by God, who records for him a virtuous deed equivalent to a duly performed pilgrimage. When a Hindu paces round a temple in fulfilment of a vow he must do so in silence. Fire for a sacrificial *hom* must be brought in silence and the *hom* must be kindled in silence.

Silent prayer is recognized by Hindu and by Muhammadan alike. According to *Manu*, 'an offering consisting of muttered

[1] Vide *The Land Pirates of India*, W. J. Hatch, 1928, p. 143.

prayers is ten times more efficacious than a sacrifice performed according to the rules of the *Veda*; a prayer which is inaudible to others surpasses it a hundred times, and the mental recitation of sacred texts a thousand times'. The *Sandhyā* and the *Gāyatrī* mantra are repeated inaudibly, and *jap* or silent prayer is a recurring feature of Hindu ritual. The *Grihya-Sutras* have many examples of the injunction to maintain silence. The bride had to be silent till the rising of the stars; after concluding his period of studentship the *Brahmacārī* had to enter a cowpen before sunrise and keep silent till the stars appeared, and at *Sīmāntanayan* the woman remained silent till the same moment when the stars appeared. A Muhammadan has his prayers at midnight and in the afternoon which, if not uttered in congregation, are muttered in silence; all his prayers are followed by a silent muttering or *sukut*, and after the midnight prayer silence is sometimes maintained until the morning prayer (*tahajju*).

A restriction forbidding the bride or the bride and bridegroom at various stages of the marriage ceremony to speak is common to all castes and creeds. Strictly speaking, the Muhammadan bridal pair should be silent for the day of marriage, the day that precedes it and the day that follows it, but in practice silence is often maintained only until the *jalvan* ceremony when the pair for the first time see each other's faces. Among Hindus the bride must not speak when *akṣat* is thrown on her and the bridegroom; when her *mangaḷsūtra* is tied round her neck; when the marriage is made irrevocable by the *Saptapadī* or seven steps taken by the bridal pair together, and when the thread from which the wristlets of the pair are made is passed round the pair five times by the officiating priests. In communities which have the *Dhāre* ceremony, in which after the tying of the wristlets to the wrists of the bridal pair milk and water are poured in turn over their hands, the bride must remain silent during the ceremony. The meal again taken by the bridal pair as an integral part of the marriage ceremony must be taken by them together in silence.

From the moment the hands of the Muhammadan boy at his circumcision are dyed with henna until the henna dries, the boy must remain silent.

Though silence, however, brings *barkat* there are occasions on which prayers are deliberately said loudly. In rites intended to bring rain loud prayers are more habitual than silent ones; when the sacred thread is renewed annually a loud prayer is uttered to *Yama* ten times. The repetition of mantras may be in whispers or in a loud voice. In *Candipūjā* a *sātkoṇ* is drawn on a lotus-leaf and at each cardinal point a goddess is invoked; *Brahma Viṣṇu* and *Maheśvar* are invoked in whispers. On the other hand, with the object of attaining wealth the *Kukkutamantra* is repeated a thousand times by the *yajamān* who sits on a mountain or the bank of a river and invokes *Śankar* and other deities in a loud voice.

SUNSHINE

Śakti must be shielded from the sun. The Bombay Presidency is rich in cave temples, the construction of which was perhaps dictated by no architectural need, but by the desire to escape from the sun. The darkened shrine of the modern Hindu temple repeats the protection from the sun which the cave temple afforded; the sun is not allowed to enter the *Garbhāgudi* or innermost sanctuary of a temple, the shrines of *Śiva* and of *Durgā* only, whose *śakti* is stronger than that of the sun, permitting the entry of the sun for a brief time on the first of the Hindu year. No image can be worshipped in the sun, and the sun must not fall on the head of a divine image, though it may fall on the feet, and in some temples, as in that of *Vir Nārāyaṇ* at Gadag and of *Mahālakṣmī* at Kolhapur, a small aperture in the wall admits the rays of the sun for a few moments on certain days. When a sacred image is borne from one place to another it travels in a palanquin which protects it from the sun. The *Gondhalis* carry their *triśul* under a canopy, and symbols such as the *Marāṭhā devak* and the *hālgamba* into which *śakti* has been invoked are protected from the sun by a canopy until they reach the marriage *manḍap*.

At his *lingapūjā* the *Lingāyat* chooses a shadowed spot to uncover his *linga* twice a day. The *pādukā* of saints are carried in a palanquin and fan-shaped *abdāgīr*, now little more than ornaments of pageantry, recall a one-time protection against the sun. An ordinary conch can be placed in the sun but not a conch used in worship. An *ārtī* must be protected from the sun; fire to be used for a *hom* must be covered when carried out of doors, as must also offerings to be made to deities.

Sunshine destroys the efficacy of prayer. Hindu saints retire from the sun when they perform penance and when they pray clouds are supposed to gather. To a Muhammadan no blessing can come from God in the full sunshine. When the Prophet moved from place to place he was traditionally protected by clouds, and when a Muhammadan saint moves about he shields himself by making cloudy weather. Though the skies of Sind for many months in the year are cloudless there are people who sing songs composed by Shah Bitai, and when they sing the clouds gather, bringing *barkat*. A Muhammadan performing penance for forty days, *chillā*, chooses a deep cave in which the sun does not enter, and the Prophet himself before he attained his prophetship prayed in a cavern on Mount Hira. The congregational prayers of the Muhammadan are of necessity often finished in the sunshine, but a prayer should be begun in the shade; the *miḥrāb* is always in the shade and so is also the raised *nimbah* on which the *khatib* prays.

The Muhammadan will not place the Koran nor *hadis* in the sun; the Hindu keeps the *Veda* protected from the sun. A *yantra* may not be dried in the sun nor can a mantra or even water in which a mantra has been dipped be placed in the sun. Flowers and leaves collected by a Hindu for use in worship must be collected before the sun rises; worship which has a special object is performed before dawn; sages perform penance before sunrise. The hour before dawn is to the Muhammadan in Sind the hour when holy men remember God, *Piro fakirji mahal*.

The absence of the sun is one of the factors giving a special value to this hour before dawn. In the Konkaṇ in many *Kātkarī* villages the measuring of grain must be done before dawn or after sunset. In Khandesh and in the Karnāṭak the first ploughing is done before sunrise; in the Dharwar district the threshing of the major grains is begun after midnight and completed before dawn. A journey is well begun if begun before sunrise. Many a magic rite has to be completed before sunrise; nails are driven into trees, trees are embraced, charmed medicines are brought from mantriks before sunrise. The threshing-floor is swept before dawn; the pole of the floor is cut before dawn and erected on the floor before the sun rises. Before the sun appears at the time of sowing or reaping, agriculturists in the Karnāṭak cut up a coconut and sprinkle the pieces over the fields; in other parts of the Karnāṭak *charagā* or boiled rice is sprinkled round the field and threshing-floor at the same early hour. Many charms are written before sunrise.

Milk and all food are protected from the sun by the Hindu and by the Muhammadan. *Śilavant Lingāyats* cover all water when they draw it from a well. There are castes that invariably roof in their wells, and the ordinary step-well now being superseded in the interests of sanitation, shielded its waters from the sun. One section of the *Lingāyats*, the *Dhūḻpavads*, ‘dust-purified’, because the sun shines on streams and pools, draw their water from holes dug for the moment in the river-bed, and close the hole as soon as they have filled their water-pots.

Persons with special power must not go in the sun. The Muhammadan bride and bridegroom and also the bridegroom's best man, *anar*, cannot go in the sun for a definite number of days; the non-Brahmin bridal pair are also subject to the same restriction, which may be extended even beyond the day of marriage. The mother after her delivery and her child cannot go in the sun for some time; the *Haranśikārī* forbids her doing so for five days, the *Marāṭhā* for five weeks, the Muhammadan for forty days. The Brahmin mother is now under no such restriction, but the *hom* called *sūryāvlokan* which strict orthodoxy requires at the end of her confinement seems to suggest that she should not go in the sun for three months. This *hom*, 'the sight of the sun', is not celebrated nowadays. If a *Vaddar* woman miscarries in her fourth or eighth month of pregnancy, she is shut up in a dark room for a month and not allowed to see a light or expose herself to the sun. A Hindu or a Muhammadan girl on attaining puberty is not allowed to go in the sun for some time. The Muhammadan boy at his circumcision should not go in the sun for three days, but in practice does so as soon as his wound is healed. In the *Grihya-sutras*, the Brahmin boy at the end of his studentship had to enter a cowpen before sunrise, and remain there till the stars appeared; perhaps it is a memory of a restriction on his going in the sun that to-day during the *Samāvartan* ceremony which ends his studentship he is given an umbrella denied him during his studentship.

Several explanations of this fear of the sun have been offered or accepted by Western writers. The familiar story of *Danae* has given support to the assumption that the sun is avoided because it causes impregnation. Sir James Frazer (*Balder the Beautiful*, vol. i, p. 75) writes of the Hindu ceremony of *Garbhādhān*, 'the impregnation rite', during which the bride is made to look towards the sun or be in some way exposed to its rays. This to the best of my knowledge is not quite accurate. After the celebration of a *hom*, *Agnupasthān*, the husband puts the juice of durva grass in the right nostril of his wife and both then offer prayers to the sun to remove any impurity or obstacle that impedes fertility. This actual invocation of the sun is called *Sūryopasthān*, but the pair do not go into the sun. The power of the sun purifies. If a man whilst worshipping hears a menstruous woman talk he becomes pure again by gazing at the sun, and the sight of the sun purifies him should he have touched a human bone without flesh. On the eleventh day after her delivery and after her bath, the Brahmin woman is required to have a sight of the sun, and to hold up a churning instrument or *ravī*, a word which with different accent also means sun (*ravi*). This looking at the sun is intended as a prayer to the sun to make her pure.

It seems to me impossible to isolate particular illustrations of the fear or avoidance of the sun, and give to them an explanation which will not apply to others. The *Lingāyat* avoids the sun in all religious exercises, considering the sun a *śūdra* or one without a *linga*. The common rule that the bridal pair should not go in the sun is explained by those who follow it in many ways, but never by attributing to the sun the power of impregnation. Exposure of the bridal pair to the sun it is thought brings disaster to their parents; *Raddis, Kabbars, Gollars* more emphatically believe that an evil spirit attacks the bridal pair if they venture into the sun; *Talwārs* keep the girl on her attaining puberty and the mother after her delivery out of the sun from a fear of the evil eye of the sun. Sindi Muhammadans also associate the sun with evil-eye and with evil spirits. *Dinhan tato jinn mato*, 'When the day is hot the spirits are active'.

The restriction on going in the sun is frequently accompanied by a restriction on touching a light or fire. The *Haranśikārī* mother after her delivery must not touch fire or a light for five days as well as not go in the sun; the *Valdar* woman who miscarries is not to see a light for a month. A girl on attaining puberty must not light a lamp or touch fire. There may be in this, from one point of view, the objective aspect of taboo; fire must be protected from pollution, but I think another explanation also is possible.

The Muhammadan will not allow a man who is seriously ill to go in the sun. This prohibition must also be explained along with other similar restrictions, and in this instance there can be no question of impregnation. Now illness is caused by hot power. If a Muhammadan lies seriously ill, children are made to eat food and sprinkle over the sick man the water in which they have washed their dirty hands, and this to cool the hot power which has caused his illness. If a household is visited by small-pox all the members of the house every evening soak their clothes in water and throw the water at the root of a tree, and in any serious case of illness the hands of the sick are dipped in water which is thrown on his face and at the root of a tree before sunrise. The Hindu pours water on the *pādukā* of the deity to whom he attributes small-pox to cool her hot *śakti*. Heat, again, is associated with a woman in her confinement and with a child for some days after birth. The movable grate used in the confinement-room has to be cooled by being sprinkled with milk and ghee; the bathing of the child, too, has among other objects that of cooling its hot *śakti*. Once again the whole atmosphere of a marriage is charged with hot power; on the sixteenth day after a Hindu marriage milk is sprinkled on the *maṇḍap* in which the marriage was held to cool its *śakti*, whilst the Muhammadan puts the discarded wristlets and the garlands of the bridal pair into water to make them cool.

To keep cool, *thaṇḍa*, or calm, *śānt*, is the aim of much ritual both of the Hindu and of the Muhammadan, and it seems only logical that measures adopted to prevent an access of heat should accompany measures adopted to attain coolness. Evil spirits are as one form of power associated with heat, and the non-Brahmin explains his restrictions on going in the sun as an avoidance of evil spirits.

In face of the general denial of any fear of impregnation in some of the rites I have just described, and the impossibility of associating any such fear with other rites, another explanation of the avoidance of the sun must be sought, and this, I think, is to be found in a fear of heat which destroys *barkat* and brings a train of evil.

HIMSĀ

There are features of the respect shown in India for animal life that are more than familiar; the extreme respect of Jainism, the motive for such respect introduced by the belief in metempsychosis, the intimacy which prevails in India between animals and men. These and other features of this respect for animal life are not within the limits I have set to this book. I wish to treat of *himsā* or the destruction of life in general terms and in so far as such *himsā* affects man's control of power from which comes *barkat*. The sacred books of Hinduism enjoin respect for animals; the Koran speaks of beasts and birds as being nations like unto those of men, but again I do not propose to deal with the religious sanction of any of the great creeds of India, or with the Puritanism of any sect that avoids the eating of flesh.

In the *Bombay Gazetteer*, vol. ix, part i, p. 178, it is said that *Bhavsars* or calico-printers in Gujarāt will not dye during the four rainy months because the slaughter of insects in the dye adds to the evil of the southing time. Here is an example of *himsā* being avoided because it enhances the evil *śakti* of time. It is on similar lines that I wish to illustrate how *himsā* as a destructive act destroys *barkat*, destroys *śakti* and *kudrat*, and how many practices of the Hindu and of the Muhammadan are based on the same idea that *himsā* destroys the fruition of purpose. In this idea there enters no question of religious sanction, though sacred books may refer to it; it is a basic idea earlier than the growth of the present creeds of India, it may be found in the same detail among tribes barely within the pale of Hinduism and even among those that for practical purposes are without it, as among the more advanced castes of Hinduism. However intimate its connexion with modern Hinduism or the religion of the Prophet, the belief that *himsā* operates to destroy a mysterious 'power' is infinitely older than either of these. The various forms of *himsā* I now propose to deal with are grinding, washing, the roasting of grain, the cutting of hair and nails, sweeping, the eating of flesh and incontinence, between which an undoubted bond of union can be traced.

GRINDING

There is a story of the saint *Ramdas* weeping when he found a woman grinding grain and telling her she was destroying life. The grindstone is one of the five destructive domestic implements called *pancsunā*, one of the five 'slaughter-houses' mentioned by *Manu*,[1] one of the five places where, according to the *Institutes of Viṣṇu*,[2] life is ignorantly destroyed. A hearth, a grinding-stone, a broom, a pestle and mortar and a water-pot cause the destruction of life binding the Hindu, in the words of his sacred books, with the fetters of sin to expiate which five great sacrifices are prescribed.

Grinding grain destroys the *śakti* of the grain, eliciting the curse of the grain. Grinding, like other acts of destruction, destroys *barkat*. In Sind the professional grinder of grain, *chāki*, is supposed to be always in adversity, just as grass is always green, but the cutter of grass always unfortunate, *gāh sadāi sāo magar gāhi sadāi sunjo*. The *Macchī* or fisherman in Sind never prospers, for he lives by destroying life, as does the butcher. The *Telī* is accursed by reason of his profession of crushing oil-seed. According to *Manu* (iv, 85) one oil-press is as bad as ten slaughter-houses. A man with a house adjoining that of a *Telī* never prospers; the sight of a *Telī* or the sound of his press in the morning is to be avoided; in agricultural operations he is tabooed.

Grinding is forbidden during the celebration of any form of worship,[3] as it would render nugatory, through its destruction of *śakti*, the efforts of the worshipper to win *śakti*. It is forbidden

[1] *Manu*, iii, 68–9.

[2] *Institutes of Viṣṇu*, lix, 19, 20.

[3] Cp. *Indian Antiquary*, vol. xxiv, p. 229, 1895, 'Notes on the spirit basis of Belief and Custom', J. M. Campbell: 'During the festival of *Dyamava* in Dharwar no corn-mills may grind corn, apparently from the fear that as *Dyamava* is more of a fiend than a guardian the blessed influence of corn-grinding may annoy her, may even put her to flight.' This is quite a wrong interpretation of the prohibition of grinding. Grinding is forbidden at all fairs or *jatrā*, as are other forms of *himsā*.

when instruments of craft are worshipped, and how far this is because it destroys *śakti* is clear from the simultaneous restriction of threshing, sweeping, washing and shaving by *Pancāḻs* and *Tiglars*. There can be no grinding whilst the *Marāṭhā devak*, the *manekstambha* of Gujarāt or the *hāḻgamba* of the Karnāṭak remains installed without the prior dismissal of its *śakti*. It is forbidden on any day specially set apart for worship to avert a calamity; when rain fails there can be no grinding on days sacred to *Indra*; during an epidemic it must not be indulged in on days sacred to the goddess responsible for the visitation of the epidemic, and in the Karnāṭak in time of epidemic drums are beaten to warn people to stop grinding for five Fridays and five Tuesdays, the breach of which warning would add to the number of victims claimed by the epidemic.

During hours of *śakti* it is essential to do nothing that destroys *śakti*. Grinding, therefore, is forbidden at an eclipse, on *Amāvāsyā* and on some *Pūrṇimā*; at sunset, dawn, midday, and at midnight. Grinding on *Ugadi* or during *Divāḻī* entails hardship throughout the following twelve months; on Fridays and Saturdays in the month of *Śrāvaṇ* and also on *Nāgpancmī* grinding is forbidden. The Muhammadan, similarly, will not grind at an eclipse, at noon or at sunset, nor throughout the first ten days of *Muharram*.

When a male member of a household leaves his house to go on pilgrimage or a journey, acts of destruction would destroy the fruition of his purpose, and must accordingly be avoided by those who stay at home. *Ghantichors*, *Bestars*, *Dong-Dasaris* and *Koravas* do not allow their women-folk to wash the day their menfolk leave home, and consider that grinding after the final good-bye means disaster to those that have left home. The Muhammadan also refrains for the day from grinding when some one in the house sets out on a journey. When an animal has just been purchased its *pāygun* is still a matter of doubt; nothing must be done to make evil the potentiality of the animal, and so until the animal is properly tethered neither a Hindu nor a Muhammadan will grind. After any new purchase, indeed, or after receiving a gift a Muhammadan will not grind, nor will he do this after the birth of a calf. *Māḻīs* believe that if there be grinding within an hour of the birth of a calf the hair of the calf will always remain erect.

After the birth of a child the Muhammadan forbids grinding for forty days; at the time of delivery and also just before delivery grinding is equally forbidden. Hindus believe that harm will befall the mother if grinding be indulged in within a day from the birth of her child. After a death, again, grinding is prohibited to a

Muhammadan for three days; grinding whilst a body remains without disposal means to a Hindu long illness for the women relations of the deceased's family in consequence of persecution by the ghost of the dead. When a Muhammadan is dying grinding is forbidden as a protection to his relations, and in some communities, such as that of the *Kātkarī*, even distant relatives of the deceased in other villages must cease to grind on hearing of his death. There are similar prohibitions after a marriage in order that the *barkat* of the marriage may not be lost. The *Marāṭhā* and the *Telī* bride cannot grind for sixteen days after her marriage; the Muhammadan bride is restricted for six or twelve months, and a Brahmin bride cannot grind or touch a grindstone for a year after her marriage. Grinding during a marriage, save when ceremonial grinding is necessary as part of the ritual of the occasion, is generally prohibited, whilst *Ghattivaddars* for five days forbid grinding as well as sweeping and washing.

When seed is being sown those at home must not imperil the success of the sowing by grinding; when a guest arrives and when he departs the *barkat* expected from his visit must not be jeopardized by thoughtless grinding. A man practising charms should not hear the sound of grinding, and should a man dream of seeing a woman grinding, death, calamity or illness will come to his next-door neighbour. Mantras recited whilst grinding is being done lose their power and are without efficacy. In the Karnāṭak, but not in Sind, the Muhammadan installs dead *Pīrs*, and at *Muḥarram panjā* or hands are held aloft which are called *pīrān*; grinding is forbidden for five days after any such installation.

The destructive act of grinding, like other forms of destruction, destroys *barkat*. There may, however, be occasions on which its very destructive potentiality is a desired asset. The efficacy of a curse is enhanced if the curse be accompanied by an act of destruction. A Hindu adds to the power of his curse by cutting blades of grass, breaking branches or twigs of trees, by pulling out his hair or by breaking one stone on another. A Muhammadan considers an oath a very serious one if it be taken after cutting grass, after hair-cutting, in front of a grindstone or to the accompaniment of grinding. An enemy of one who is taking an oath will try to make the consequences of that oath the more serious by grinding stones.

SWEEPING

A broom is another of the five domestic implements of destruction. It sweeps away both good and evil. A broom is a remedy against the evil eye; in Gujarāt a broom is waved over the afflicted person and fibres of a broom are tied to his wrist; the handle of a broom with chillies and salt is placed on a tile and this after being waved round the victim is placed at cross-roads. A broom drives away evil spirits. If a child at lamp-lighting time cry, a broom is beaten on the threshold, taken out of the house and again brought back to scare away spirits. In the Karnāṭak a broom with a round stone is placed near a woman awaiting her delivery as a protection against evil. If a man has bad dreams caused by spirits he keeps a broom near his pillow. A broom is waved over a person possessed by spirits or the person's shadow is beaten with a broom. Beating the ground with a broom drives away the evil *śakti* of disease. After an epidemic of cholera *Kātkarīs* sweep clean the whole village, not from any modern idea of sanitation but in the belief that the disease is thereby driven away. Sweeping drives away the evil *śakti* of *pāygun̩*; when an unwelcome guest departs from his host's house the steps are well brushed with water. In Bombay prostitutes if they fail to find a client take a broom and beat the ground. In Gujarāt when a house is vacated it must first be swept clean, and this again not from any advanced motive of cleanliness but from the simpler desire to avert evil.

Though, however, the broom is used to sweep away evil it remains an implement of dangerous potentiality. It must never be touched by the foot and it must never touch the person of any one. A boy beaten with a broom of grass becomes lean; sitting on a broom leads to bleeding sores; if a woman be beaten with a broom she becomes a bad character and a person so beaten never has any issue. If in Gujarāt one man beat another all the *puṇya* of the first man is swept away and all the sins of the latter are transferred to the former. It is bad to see a broom as the first thing in the morning; it must never be left vertically against a wall but always flat on the ground, or family quarrels will ensue. At night a broom must be kept in a safe place lest it fall into the hands of a thief who, by making passes with it over a sleeping household, can keep all the members asleep whilst he plunders them. A new broom should not be bought on a Saturday or on a new-moon day, and when bought it must be sprinkled with turmeric to render its *pāygun̩* harmless to the owner. A broom should never be brought home on an auspicious day and never carried on a journey; it should never be picked up off a road, never given away, or, at any rate, at night or sunset, and it must never be burnt.

Restrictions on sweeping follow very closely those on grinding.

When a respected guest arrives there can be no sweeping or the *barkat* of his visit will be lost; sweeping would be a hint to him to depart and sweeping after his departure is a method of getting rid of the evil his *pāygun̩* has brought. When a man leaves home on a journey of importance or on a pilgrimage there must be no sweeping in his house on the day of his departure; in the Dharwar district when a man goes on a pilgrimage his wife cannot sweep with a broom until he returns, and if sweeping be necessary, gets some one else to do it for her, an evasion of issue not uncommon in Hindu practice. Sweeping is forbidden during an auspicious ceremony; during worship; on fair days and car festivals; on the anniversary of the dead; during meals which are a form of sacrifice and during a conversation of importance. In Khandesh and in the Karnāṭak it is forbidden whilst sowers are sowing in the field. When the Koran, the *Veda* or the *Purāṇa* are being read sweeping must cease.

At certain hours of power sweeping is rigorously forbidden. In the twilight; at an eclipse or at midday. If it be necessary to sweep at sunset the sweepings must be stored in a corner and thrown away in the morning. The Muhammadan will not sweep on an *'Id* nor on certain Fridays.

After the birth of a child the Muhammadan refrains from sweeping for some hours as he does after receiving a valuable present, after buying a valuable animal or after his cow has given birth to a calf. To the Hindu sweeping is tabooed after a birth till the sixth day. During and after a marriage there are restrictions on sweeping. The Muhammadan will not sweep during a marriage and the Muhammadan bride cannot sweep for seven days or seven weeks after her marriage. The Hindu cannot sweep even the storeroom during a marriage, and if sweeping cannot be avoided whilst the *hālgamba* is installed, it must be done with a cloth and not with a broom. *Vaddars* will not purchase a new broom for a year after a marriage. Sweeping immediately after *Ovālaṇi* or the waving of *ārtī* would destroy the *barkat* of those rites. A Muhammadan will not allow sweeping whilst he is performing *Ḥāḍrāt Jinn*, or attempting to receive a prophetic dream. A Hindu cannot sweep the threshing-floor until all the threshed grain has been removed from the floor; he cannot sweep a granary with a broom and must clean his cattle-shed with his hand. After a death so long as the body lies in the house there can be no sweeping, and even after the body has been removed from the house only the track followed by the body can be swept.

THE HEARTH

Roasting grain or baking bread is one of the five deadly sins of a Hindu. It is forbidden during the celebration of any auspicious ceremony such as a marriage, a tonsure or a thread ceremony. When an epidemic visits the Karnāṭak villagers are warned by beat of drum not to roast grain. During the sowing of seed the roasting of grain is forbidden, though during the sowing of cotton-seed jvārī is roasted to see whether the crop of cotton will be a good one or not according to the swelling of the roasted seed. The Muhammadan will not roast grain when a man lies very sick for fear of making his illness beyond cure; whilst sowing is proceeding; on the eighth day of *Bakri 'Id* until prayers have been offered, on the tenth of *Muḥarram* and for three days after a death.

WASHING

Just as the *Telī* or oil-man by reason of his profession brings misfortune to others, so the *Dhobī* or washerman is a person associated with ill. The *Dhobī* woman is generally regarded as a witch; the Deccani Muhammadan will not take food at her house and calls her *bala* or calamity. A washerman washes away the *barkat* of a house, *dhoban ghar dhokar lejati hai.*

Washing is forbidden on certain days and at certain hours. It is bad to bathe in the twilight; the washing of clothes is forbidden at an eclipse or at sunset; even the Muhammadan will not give clothes to a washerman in the twilight. A Muhammadan will not wash clothes or himself on *'Id*, at midday, midnight, sunset, sunrise and in many cases at an eclipse. Washing clothes at an *'Id* or for ten days at *Muḥarram* washes away the *barkat* of the time.

Bathing and the washing of clothes are forbidden in the Karnāṭak before ploughing, sowing, measuring or threshing grain or reaping crops. In Khandesh sowers will not bathe till they have completed their task, nor till the sowing is finished can the house be washed or clothes be washed at home. A bath during the threshing of grain or after the floor has been prepared and until the grain is brought to the store, destroys all hope of any increase in the grain. A guest or stranger visiting the threshing-floor is not allowed, any more than is one of the threshers, to wash his feet. In general, too, the plough cannot be washed till the ploughing is over. When a man leaves home the rest of his household cannot bathe the same day; *Ghantichors, Bestars, Dong Dasaris* and *Koravas* think that the bathing of the women at home would cause the death of the absent man. As, too, the man leaves the house he is given curds in his palm which he must eat, but after eating which he must be careful not to wash his hands and thereby destroy the *barkat* this gift imparts.

In the performance of great sacrifices the celebrant and his wife do not take a bath until the last day of the sacrifice. When visiting a god a suppliant must see the image without having previously washed his feet (*dhūḻdarśan*, ‘ dust sight ’). Unless one has stepped on something impure one cannot wash one's feet after returning from a temple or one loses the *barkat* of one's visit to the temple. After offering *naivedya* to a god a Brahmin cannot immediately bathe or even wash his clothes, nor can he do so after witnessing a procession of a sacred car. A Hindu over whom *ārtī* is waved must not bathe or he loses the *barkat* of that rite. In Kanara at an eclipse the man who beats barren trees to coerce them to give fruit must not wash his face or his efforts are in vain.

Whilst the *hāḻgamba* is installed any washing of clothes that is necessary must be done at the house of another and not in the house wherein the installation has been made. Among *Haviks* the bridal pair must not bathe for four days from the installation of *Nāndi*.

When a man dies Muhammadans believe that angels and the souls of relatives visit the dead bringing *barkat*, and that any kind of washing whilst a corpse remains unburied will deprive the dead of *barkat*. From the day the Muhammadan pilgrim puts on the garb of a pilgrim until he reaches the sacred *Ka'bah* he should not bathe unless he has suffered pollution. The Hindu, save at an eclipse and in the event of hearing of the death of a near relative, avoids bathing after a meal.

SHAVING AND HAIR-CUTTING

The hair and the nails grow spontaneously; they contain life and *śakti*. Their cutting is to a Hindu a form of *himsā*, a destruction of life. The sin of cutting the hair or the nails involves purification, *prayascitta*, by bathing. After shaving a Hindu is as impure as a woman in her menses until he bathes; he cannot touch any one, he cannot enter the shrine of a sacred image, he cannot enter the kitchen, and the very orthodox after cutting their hair or after shaving will slip round to their bathing-place without entering their house. The place where a Hindu has had his hair cut ought strictly to be cleaned with cowdung; the purificatory bath he takes should not be taken in the customary bathing-place, and that he may not touch with his impure hands the bathing utensils the water of his bath should be poured over him by another. After cutting his hair a Hindu without first bathing cannot pray or perform his *sandhyā*; he cannot do any agricultural work; he should not eat nor drink; he cannot grace any auspicious ceremony by his presence; he cannot cohabit with his wife; even his clothes are impure and should be washed. The barber whose profession it is to cut hair is another example of a profession tabooed because it is associated with *himsā*. Clothes touched by a barber must be washed; his shadow falling on a sacred image makes purification imperative, *samprokṣaṇ*. The name of a barber cannot be mentioned after sunset; it is a bad omen to see a barber when one rises in the morning and particularly if he carries no tools. In the Karnāṭak when a man suffers heavy loss in his business he is said to have had his head shaven, *bolu ketti hoitu*.

The opening of barbers' shops in India has destroyed many of the old customs relating to hair-cutting, and especially the restriction which confined this form of *himsā* to certain hours. The very orthodox, however, who will not visit a barber's saloon call the barber to their houses and will still not have their hair cut at noon.

This idea of impurity associated with the cutting of the hair or the nails, is not confined to the Hindu. After shaving or being shaved a Muhammadan must bathe ere he can enter a mosque, touch the Koran, go to a graveyard, measure grain, or even sit under certain trees such as the bar and pipal. Some Muhammadans take a bath before they think of cooking food after being shaved or having their hair cut.

Shaving and hair-cutting at forbidden times shorten life; they destroy *barkat*. When of old a new king had been consecrated he might not shave his hair for one year, and none of his subjects might cut his hair during this period save Brahmins, and even horses were left unclipped.[1] The husband of a pregnant woman cannot cut his hair from the sixth month of her pregnancy till the tenth day after her delivery; in practice he does not do so for the ten days after her delivery and for two to four weeks before the child is born. The penalty of breaking this injunction is harm to the child and the shortening of the father's life.

In order that the dead shall not lose *barkat* mourners must observe strict purity; they must remain chaste and should not shave or cut their hair and nails. On the day of his father's or mother's death the son only shaves before he performs the funeral rites; this shaving is not considered *himsā*, but any subsequent shaving during the period of mourning is forbidden as entailing

[1] Satapatha Brahmana, *Sacred Books of the East*, vol. xii, pp. 126–8.

the offer of something unholy to the spirit of the dead. Sindi Muhammadans forbid shaving and hair-cutting for four days following a death. After completion of the mourning Hindus shave on the eleventh day after a funeral; *Gaud Sarasvats* require all male cousins of the deceased who have no parents to shave even their moustaches. If a Hindu woman loses her husband whilst she is *enceinte*, as a protection to the expected child, she is not tonsured during the obsequies, but her hair is left uncut for several months.

Hair-cutting is forbidden a Hindu on his birthday, on days of *Śrāddha*, and on the anniversary of a saint. If a child is smitten with small-pox no one of the household can shave or cut his hair before the goddess associated with the disease has been worshipped. When a Hindu makes *darśan* of a temple, that is seeks *barkat* from merely seeing the temple, he cannot cut his hair till the third day subsequent or he destroys the *barkat* of his *darśan*. A Hindu cannot cut his hair on a day sacred to *Gaṇpati*; on a day of fasting or on days dedicated to special deities. He must not cut his hair during the performance of a vow or of a sacrifice; after meals he cannot shave, because no bath can be taken after a meal save when after a meal a man goes to a funeral, on return from which he must bathe.

Devakārya is a worship of the *kula devatā*. Guests are invited, and after *mangalārtī* or the auspicious waving of *ārtī*, throw flowers and *akṣat* on the images. Each of the bridal pair performs this ceremony separately; it is also performed in a thread ceremony and when a pilgrim returns from pilgrimage. On the day this worship is performed before a marriage the father of the bride, the father of the bridegroom, and the bridegroom cannot shave or cut their hair. At a thread ceremony, again, the *vaṭu* himself cannot cut his hair or shave, nor can the returned pilgrim when *Devakārya* is performed on his return.

During a marriage ceremony hair-cutting and shaving are forbidden. For sixteen days, too, after a marriage the bridegroom and all male members in the families of the bridal pair cannot shave.

When a man goes a journey or on a pilgrimage he should not cut his hair, if not for the whole period of his absence, at least for the day of his setting out. There are some sacred places of pilgrimage where the Hindu must shave before performing ceremonies for the *pitṛs*, but save for these places shaving and hair-cutting are forbidden during a journey made with a religious object. The injunction on the Muhammadan pilgrim to the sacred places of Arabia is equally strict. During his performance of penance, *chillā*, again the Muhammadan is forbidden to cut his hair or nails. The other restrictions which apply when a Hindu or Muhammadan goes on a journey or on a pilgrimage, emphasize that hair-cutting is forbidden, not because of any possibility of his shorn [1] hair falling into the possession of another person who may through its possession do him harm, but because any act of *himsā* imperils fruition of purpose. When a Hindu goes a journey or on a pilgrimage, food that is sweet must be eaten by all his household to bring him *barkat*, and that the *barkat* may not be lost by a destructive act, clothes cannot be washed in his house, the house cannot be swept, other male members of the household cannot shave, relations cannot bathe or throw away water and, after the pilgrim has said good-bye, grinding would bring him disaster on his way. The Muhammadan pilgrim after assuming the *ihram* cannot cut his hair or nails, cannot kill any animal save dangerous creatures, cannot cut grass, a tree or a plant. During *chillā* also a Muhammadan cannot kill animals or cut grass or a tree. The doctrine of *himsā* is as familiar to the Muhammadan [2] as to the Hindu and moulds his practice.

Among Muhammadans when a member of a household lies sick all in the house must refrain from cutting their hair or nails until the sick man has passed his crisis or they imperil his life; when the hair of a child is cut or when a boy is circumcised, again all male members of the household refrain from such destructive acts for one or two days.

As an act of *himsā* the cutting of hair and nails cannot be done by a Hindu in hours of *śakti*, at an eclipse, at noon, on an *Amāvāsyā* or *Pūrṇimā*, though *svāmīs* and *sannyāsīs* shave every *Pūrṇimā* and an *Agnihotrī* every *Amāvāsyā*. At a *Sankramaṇa* such acts are forbidden and at midnight and sunset. If the hair of a child be cut at sunset his younger brother will die. A Muhammadan likewise will not cut his hair or nails at an eclipse, at sunset or dawn, on a full-moon day or at midday.

CHASTITY

In Sind when the foundations of a house are laid and again when the principal beam of the roof is placed in its correct position, all members of the household of the owner must remain continent.

[1] Cp. *The Golden Bough*, 'Taboo and the Perils of the Soul', p. 361: 'The reason for this custom is probably the danger to which, as we have seen, a traveller is believed to be exposed from the magic arts of the strangers amongst whom he sojourns; if they got possession of his shorn hair they might work his destruction through it. The Egyptians on a journey kept their hair uncut till they returned home.'

[2] Vide. *The Holy Cities of Arabia*, vol. i, p. 99, Eldon Rutter, 1928.

When a *Muhāna* or fisherman builds a boat all those who are engaged in its construction are required to be continent until the boat is ready for use. Sexual indulgence whilst sugar is being pressed reduces the yield of sugar and prevents its setting firm; if those engaged in sawing stones are not continent till their work is finished the stones break in irregular lines. On digging a well continence is imperative until the water actually gushes forth, and is equally necessary when a Persian wheel is being erected until the work of erection is complete. During the sowing of seed, ploughing, reaping and, above all, during the measuring of grain, all members of the household of the *rayat* must remain continent or the seed will not germinate, and the gathered grain will give a reduced yield. For a week before marriage the parents of the bridal pair remain continent; when a Muhammadan boy is circumcised his parents remain chaste until his wound is healed and in all for about a month. Before the first catch of the season the fisher class in Sind remain continent for two or three days. Professional thieves abstain from congress for a day before they set out to commit a crime. The day a man sets out on a pilgrimage, or goes on a visit to a Pir or a saint, he must remain chaste; every one who attends a marriage should be continent during the course of the marriage ceremony. Before taking up a new employment a wise man remains continent for some days. To a Muhammadan sexual congress is also avoided at an eclipse, at sunrise, sunset or midday; before visiting a graveyard, riding a horse or entering a boat.

Passing to the occasions on which continence is enjoined for the Hindu the similarity of Muhammadan and Hindu practice is very marked. Fishermen remain chaste the first day of the fishing season; *Telīs* when the pressing of oil begins. *Chapparbands* when they go out on what they call *pheri*, that is on an expedition to coin false coins, remain continent, just as *Delhiwal Bauriahs* when they go on an expedition of crime, *muśāfrī*, keep away from their wives for six months. *Kuravas* remain apart from their womenfolk for a whole month before they determine to commit a dacoity, and on their return with their booty must not see any woman, even their wives, for a week. *Kātkarīs* and many another tribe addicted to catching animals in the forest and jungle remain chaste so long as they are occupied with the chase, fearing otherwise they will have no captures. *Berads*, *Tudugoddars*, *Kaikadis*, *Ghantichauders*, *Haraṇśikārīs*, *Lamānis*, and *Bestars* remain continent for three days before they set out to commit crime, or during the whole period of their absence from home.

The *Bhil* before he visits his goddess *Devmogri* at her shrine in the Sagbāra State keeps away from his wife for fifteen days. On the night previous to a special *abhiṣek* or bathing of the image of *Śiva* with the object of bringing rain, the priests employed must remain continent. On the day previous to the celebration of a *Śrāddha* the *yajamān* and the invited priests must be chaste. A man who intends to take an oracle must first fast and remain continent. One who walks through fire or takes cakes out of boiling oil in fulfilment of a vow must be strictly continent or will not be immune from burning. If a man with his wife go on a pilgrimage together they must observe the same restriction for the whole period of their joint pilgrimage. The *Agnihotrī* must follow the same rule the day previous to performing *āgrāyaṇī*, when on *Āśvin sud. Pūrṇimā* he offers with rice the powdered grain of the new crops to his fire, and he and his wife must remain chaste for three days before they make fire by friction.

On days of power the Hindu must remain chaste ; at an eclipse, at sunset or dawn or at noon ; on an *Amāvāsyā* or a *Pūrṇimā*, on *Karka* or *Makar Sankramaṇa*, and on his monthly or annual birthday.

During agricultural operations the Hindu is as strictly continent as the Muhammadan. Chastity adds to the return of the crops, whilst illicit intercourse on the part of the ploughman, the sower or the reaper destroys the yield of the crops. The parents of the *Korava* bridal pair remain continent for five weeks until the bridal pair have finished their weekly bathing which lasts five weeks ; the parents of a Brahmin bridal pair remain chaste for three nights [1] in order to bring *barkat* to the bride and bridegroom. Continence is required from the man who presses sugar-cane and even from all who come from far and wide as uninvited guests to taste the *gūḻ* or raw sugar. When any one is afflicted by a contagious disease all the male members of the household must remain continent for nine or eleven days. Chastity is incumbent at the time the *manḍap* is erected for the celebration of a marriage, and an injunction that commands considerable respect in the Karnāṭak is that of continence whilst one's cattle are grazing, to prevent loss by theft and the barrenness of the cattle.

Eminent authorities have offered various explanations of this enforced continence. Dr. Westermarck (*The Origin and Development of the Moral Ideas*, 1926, vol. ii, p. 417) writes as follows :

[1] Cp. *Grihya Sutras of Apastamba*, 3, 9, 4 : 'One (for instance, the wife's father) who wishes that the hearts of both (husband and wife) may be in accord should observe chastity through at least three nights. . . .'

'Holiness is a delicate quality which is easily destroyed if anything polluting is brought into contact with the holy object or person. The Moors believe that if anybody who is sexually unclean enters a granary the grain will lose its baraka or holiness. A similar idea probably underlies the belief prevalent among various peoples that incontinence, and especially illicit love, injures the harvest.'

In a foot-note (7) he rejects the explanation offered by Sir James Frazer (*Golden Bough*, ii, 209 sqq.), namely, that uncivilized man imagines 'that the vigour which he refuses to expend in reproducing his own kind, will form, as it were, a store of energy whereby other creatures, whether vegetable or animal, will somehow benefit in propagating their species', and adds :

'This theory entirely fails to account for the fact that illicit love, by preference, is supposed to mar the fertility of the earth and to blight the crops, a belief which is in full accordance with my own explanation, in so far as such love is considered particularly polluting.'

Continuing, Dr. Westermarck remarks that

'an act generally regarded as sacred would, if performed by an unclean individual, lack that magic efficacy which otherwise would be ascribed to it.'

Now in suggesting my own interpretation of the many examples of enforced continence, in the light of Indian belief, I would invite attention to the frequency with which a prohibition of sexual indulgence is accompanied by a prohibition of several other acts which can all be included under the Hindu term *himsā*. Chastity, for instance, during agricultural operations is enforced simultaneously with the prohibition of grinding, of cutting the hair and nails, of bathing or washing, of baking or roasting grain. The ploughman must not shave till his task is finished; during the sowing of seed the sower cannot shave or cut his hair, the roasting of grain is forbidden and the women at home must not grind grain nor wash clothes; the house cannot be covered afresh with cow-dung and the sowers themselves cannot bathe till they have finished their work. When grain is measured the man measuring must not shave or cut his hair; a *Telī* who always crushes grain cannot approach the threshing-floor and even the chance visitor to the floor is not allowed to wash.

In the same way when a man sets out on a pilgrimage or an important journey continence is enjoined, but the day he leaves home the house cannot be swept, clothes cannot be washed, family relations cannot bathe or even throw away water, inmates of the house cannot grind grain, nor cut their hair or shave.

If any one is lying seriously ill the male members of his household remain continent for a number of days; at the same time grinding is forbidden, grain cannot be roasted, and until the patient has passed his crisis no one in the house can cut his nails and hair or shave. The celebration of a marriage, again, is accompanied by rules enjoining continence, and also prohibiting grinding, sweeping, the roasting of grain, washing and the cutting of the hair. The same unity of idea appears in Muhammadan practice; in *chillā* a Muhammadan is forbidden to cut his hair or nails; the pilgrim to Mecca or Medina from the moment he assumes the *ihram* must be continent, but he must also refrain from cutting his hair or nails, and from destroying the life of animal, tree or grass. And lastly, in hours of *śakti,* in hours that to a Muhammadan are *ghoro,* continence is enjoined, but acts of *himsā* are also forbidden.

The universal belief that sexual congress is weakening has been often commented upon. If a *Brahmacārī* during sleep has a nocturnal emission he should pray to the sun to restore his strength, and this strength is something more than mere physical force. The *jivātma* or principle of life is supposed to enter the body of a man through the food he eats and to pass into the semen where it remains three months, after which it is ready to enter the woman's womb and assimilate blood. A child is described as the product of semen and blood and accordingly is considered to derive soul and *śakti* from the father. From a union of these ideas comes the belief that in the sexual act soul or life is transmitted or even destroyed. From this point of view the sexual act is an act of *himsā,* it destroys *śakti,* and is therefore on a par with other acts of *himsā* and prohibited when such other acts are forbidden. It destroys *śakti,* and in order to get *śakti* the organs of procreation of horses, asses and sparrows are often eaten.

Though, then, a sense of pollution attaches to the sexual act, if there were only a question of ceremonial purity Hindu ritual provides many a means of purification. If a *Brahmacārī,* an ascetic or a saint passes semen intentionally his vow is quite broken. The stringent injunction of continence is more than an insistence on ritual purity, and it is impossible to separate it from the rules which forbid such destructive acts as the cutting of the hair, grinding grain, washing and sweeping, or the more direct destruction of life.

EATING OF MEAT

The eating of meat destroys *barkat.* There are communities in India that avoid eating meat altogether, and this axiom can only be illustrated from the practice of flesh-eaters who avoid eating meat on special occasions, and this not, as has sometimes been suggested, from the influence of castes that never eat flesh.

A very common practice is to avoid animal food during a marriage ceremony, and this at the house of the bride as well as that of the bridegroom. *Kabbaligars* in the Karnāṭak; *Lamānis, Gollars*; *Kabbars*; *Vaddars*; *Mahārs* and *Talwārs* observe this prohibition, as do the *Bhils* of West Khandesh. Muhammadans in Sind forbid the bridal pair to eat meat for two days before and one day after their marriage, the bride even avoiding meat for seven days. *Vaddars* will not kill an animal or eat meat even during the *udki* marriage of a widow.

Talwārs abstain from killing animals during all auspicious ceremonies, and a person who has killed an animal save as a sacrifice cannot worship a deity. After eating meat a *Vaddar* or a *Telī* cannot worship an image for a day. A *Vaddar* woman cannot cook or eat flesh whilst her husband is absent on a pilgrimage. Eating meat is forbidden to a *Vaddar* before he lays the foundations of a house or enters for the first time one he has newly constructed; during the construction of a well till the water gushes forth; before going to a religious fair; for three days whilst the impurity [1] of death abides; for five days during the continuance of the impurity associated with a birth. A *Telī* will not eat meat in the sight of his oil-press nor whilst the pressing of oil proceeds. *Konchi Koravas* will not eat meat for three days after a birth until the child has been named. *Mahārs* and *Talwārs* will not eat meat on the day a sacred car is drawn; on days sacred to their respective deities; on the day subsequent to the third or fifth month after a birth when the grandparents bring the mother a cradle; during the continuance of a vow; when seed is being sown in the field or grain is measured on the threshing-floor, whilst their mantriks avoid meat when preparing a charm. A *Bhil* will not eat meat when any death or birth has occurred in his family.

The eating of meat is avoided by those who worship their professional implements on *Amāvāsyā*; the *Gondhali* avoids meat when he worships his symbols on Sundays and *Gondhal* day. *Dhōrs* will not touch meat or even a raw hide on Monday, the day of their *guru*, and abstain from flesh on *Amāvāsyā*. If a Hindu falls victim to small-pox the inmates of his house must avoid meat for seven days, and during an epidemic of cholera meat is tabooed. At all *parvakāls* and on holy days meat is avoided.

When *Mahārs* kill a goat as a sacrifice for a goddess the animal is killed outside the house of the worshipper and the image of the

[1] Cp. *Gautama*, xiv, 39; *Institutes of Viṣṇu*, xix, 15.

deity is taken outside the house, for meat must not be brought near a sacred altar. The *Mahār*, like many another, will not take meat on the threshing-floor nor near a buffalo or other milch animal for fear of stopping its supply of milk. Taking meat near cattle is supposed to bring foot-and-mouth disease; meat cannot be taken near a plough, near butter, curds or plantain-leaves. Meat must not be brought near any agricultural implement or near a fruit-tree; the worship of crops is performed without the use of flesh. The *Marāṭhā* says that a man after eating flesh is haunted by spirits and must not leave the protection of his village god. One of my own servants once came to me with a severe abdominal pain which he said had been caused by his going beyond the village bounds after indulging in a feast of meat. The agricultural community of *Raddis* will not allow a man to sow who bears the mark of blood, whilst if a woman pricks her finger causing blood to flow she cannot take grain from the granary nor milk a cow.

A Muhammadan in Sind may not eat meat at an eclipse nor at sunset; he may also not do so for fifteen and it may be for forty days during *Muḥarram* and for seven days after the death of a relative. After the circumcision of a Muhammadan boy the boy and all his household refrain from meat for two days, and when a Muhammadan goes on a pilgrimage all the rest of his family abstain from eating meat for one or two days. When a Muhammadan measures grain the eating of meat is forbidden in his house; it is forbidden if any inmate of the house lies seriously ill. Meat cannot be taken near the Koran or under certain trees that are *ghoro* and, in general, it cannot be taken on the threshing-floor. A Muhammadan preparing a charm avoids all meat and even fish, and both these things are avoided before any undertaking of great importance is entered upon. If he be a mourner a Muhammadan may not eat meat for three days subsequent to the death.

An *Agnihotrī* should not even speak of meat or blood, and the Muhammadan during *chillā kashi* cannot eat meat.

The injunction not to eat flesh on certain occasions is closely related to other prohibitions which forbid all forms of *himsā*. This is particularly noticeable among the more backward communities such as *Vaddars* who, during the period of mourning, may not even kill a rat, or *Konchi Koravas*, who will not kill any animal during the period of *suher* following a birth. The illustrations I have already given of occasions on which grinding, sweeping, and other forms of *himsā* are forbidden will show how closely these occasions approximate to those on which the eating of flesh is forbidden. Muhammadans in the Karnāṭak provide another illustration of the prohibition of *himsā*. To the *Mulla* falls the task of offering sacrifices with its concomitant slaughter of animals. As one therefore who often destroys life he cannot be chosen to officiate at a *nikah*, at a circumcision, or to assist in the ritual of *namaz*. At a Muhammadan funeral all the mourners offer prayers in common for the welfare of the soul of the dead. They stand in three rows and one man is chosen to begin the prayers. This chosen person, called *peshimām*, must be a man of strict religious habits and one who has not committed *himsā*. As soon as the body is laid in the grave and before the grave is filled in, the *peshimām* and the other mourners take five clods of earth in their right hands and utter over them a sacred text. The *peshimām* then arranges his five clods about the head of the deceased and his example is followed by the others. This placing of sanctified clods of earth in the grave is supposed to add to the power of the dead to fight evil spirits; their number, five, is reminiscent of the use of that number in making a *hisār*, or to use the Hindu term, a *dikbāndha* against spirits, whilst the belief that common will effects a transfer of power finds expression in the idea that the greater the number of the mourners who perform this rite, the greater the power that the dead receives. As the leader in these rites at the graveside must not have destroyed life a *mulla* can never be a *peshimām*.

UNCLEANNESS

Uncleanness is a form of evil power inimical to *barkat*, and certain forms of impurity are identified with 'hot' power. Uncleanness, however, is something more and something less than the word implies in the languages of the West. To a Hindu products of the cow which a Briton might consider unclean are not unclean. To a Muhammadan uncleanness includes lack of faith, the eating of onions and the chewing of tobacco. According to the Koran, 'idolaters are nothing but unclean' (Koran, c. ix, 28), intoxicants and games of chance, sacrificing to stones are only an uncleanness (c. v, 90). An animal not slaughtered with the name of God is also unclean. Uncleanness to a Muhammadan is *janabah*, a state of separation, a condition that separates him from *barkat*.

Uncleanness is destructive of *barkat*. Reciting the Koran or the *Veda* is without effect if the reciter be unclean. An unclean person prays without effect. One must be clean when visiting a shrine or when entering a temple or a mosque to obtain *barkat* from one's visit. Cleanliness is essential for the success of any enterprise, and failure of purpose is, in general, attributed to some uncleanness. Butter churned when unclean remains liquid; a cow fed or milked by an unclean person ceases to give a good supply of milk; if an unclean person attempt to collect honey he is merely stung for his pains; if a ploughman is unclean his plough only breaks, and an unclean sower breaks his wrist or foot. Those that sow, reap, weed, thresh, or measure grain must be clean; those that watch the threshing-floor by night must do nothing unclean; those that remove grain from the threshing-floor, set up the central post on the floor or take grain from a store must be clean. The *amil* who practises *da'wah* or invocation of God's help must bathe constantly, sleep as little as possible, for sleep is an impure state, and must purify his house. Uncleanness on the part of one who uses words and names destroys their power.

A Muhammadan dies a sinner if he be not absolutely clean at the time of his burial. It is therefore imperative that all who wash the body should be ritually clean; the deceased, too, will not attain salvation if all the persons taking part in the *janaza namaz* and forming part of the funeral procession are not clean. The Hindu dead also loses merit or *puṇya* if the mourners do not observe strict cleanliness. The moment when the disciples of a Hindu *svāmī* receive an order from him is a moment of *barkat*. When such an order comes the disciples take a bath and assemble in a state of ritual cleanness, *sonvale*; the order is placed on an *āsan* of wood in a clean spot; rice coloured with turmeric and flowers are thrown on the order, camphor is waved over it and coconuts are broken and offered to it. The disciples then prostrate themselves before the order; the priest reads out the order and the chief person present then places the order to his forehead and touches the signature of the *svāmī* with both his eyes.

Persons who visit temples when unclean are affected in their sight and are unable to see the sacred image the *darśan* of which would bring them *barkat*; they are worried, too, later by horrible dreams, high fever and pain. In Sind unclean persons who have visited the shrine of Lal Shahbaz have died instantaneously or become blind or permanent invalids. At Kallur in the Ramdurg State is a *Lingāyat* temple of Siddeśvari, and at Gajendragad another, Kallakmallesi; both of these temples have a *tīrth* or sacred pond. If an unclean person touches this water he is attacked by bees which do not leave him until they have killed him, and to escape them he is forced to enter the temple and do penance. If an unclean person enters the temple of Śiddha on the bank of the Kalinadi in the Supa Peta Kanara he is stung by bees; if he enters the temple of Kārtik Svāmī in the Sandur State he goes mad.

In the Satara district there is a mosque which was burnt to the ground because of an unclean act done in it, and the offender still lives in a state of great poverty. In the village of Yanin in Kumta taluka Kanara is a temple of Jotadhari Iśvar on a hill; it is also protected by bees which chase any unclean person beyond the bottom of the hill. At Chandragutti in Sorab taluka of Mysore, seven miles or so from Siddapur of the Kanara district, is a temple of Amma on a hill; here again unclean persons are prevented by bees from ascending the hill. In some cases snakes defend temples in a similar way, as at the Subramanya temple in Goondapur, at the Mangeśi and Śantadurgā temples in Goa and at the Śivanath temple at Magali in the Karwar taluka. Sometimes unclean persons approaching a temple become mad, and this is supposed to happen at the temple of Narasobavadi at Kurundawad, at the Ganagapur temple in Moglai, at that of Avadumbarvadi in the Tasgaon taluka and at the temple of Parśuram in the Chiplun taluka.

An unclean person may not touch fire or light a lamp; cannot enter a boat; cannot ride or feed a horse or camel; cannot bathe in the sea. If an unclean person witness the circumcision of a boy the boy's wound will not heal, and if an unclean person sees one who is smitten with small-pox the patient will become worse.

THE IMPURITY OF BIRTH

Suher, *Suver*

From the sixth month of his wife's pregnancy a Hindu becomes tainted with impurity and is under several disabilities. The woman herself is also impure to the extent that she cannot cook the food required in a *Śrāddha* or touch the articles used in performing this rite. Besides the husband, however, no other relatives of the woman are affected.

If in the first three months of her pregnancy a Hindu woman has an abortion she is impure for three days, and if this occurs in her fourth month her impurity lasts for four days. Her husband and his *sapiṇḍā* can remove their impurity by a simple bath. If abortion occurs in her fifth or sixth month she becomes impure for five and six days respectively, and her husband and his *sapiṇḍā* are impure for three days.

When a child is born during the seventh or any succeeding month of a woman's pregnancy the woman and the *sapiṇḍā* observe impurity for ten days among Brahmins, twelve among *Kṣatriyas*, fifteen days among *Vaiśyas* and a month among others. A cowife also becomes impure, but can remove her impurity by a bath.

Sapiṇḍā mean all the male relatives of the father and their wives and children excluding married daughters, up to twelve degrees, beyond which there is no impurity. Between the eighth and the twelfth degrees a Brahmin is impure for three days only. If a woman delivers at her father's house her brothers have to observe impurity for one day, her parents for three days and the other *sapiṇḍā* of her father for one day. If delivery takes place at her husband's house her father, mother and the *sapiṇḍā* of her father do not become impure. If a child be still-born the full period of impurity is observed by the mother and the *sapiṇḍā*, and there rises no question of the impurity occasioned by a death; if the child born alive dies before the navel-cord is severed the Brahmin mother is impure for ten days and the *sapiṇḍā* for three days. If the child dies after the severing of the navel-cord and within ten days from birth the full period of impurity is observed by the *sapiṇḍā*, but there is no observance of any impurity in consequence of the child's death. If a father hears the news of the birth to him of a child after ten days he need only take a bath; if he hears the news earlier he observes only the unexpired period of impurity.

Whilst they are impure the relatives of the woman cannot cook food to be offered to a god, bring water or flowers to be used in worship; they cannot enter the inner shrine of a temple or worship the family gods. They cannot offer twilight prayer or make offerings to the sun, *sandhyā vandan*. Before renewing their usual religious tasks they must change their sacred thread and take *pancgavya*.

For ten days after her delivery the Brahmin woman is very impure. If a stranger touches her he has to take a bath and change his clothes, for she is as impure as a woman in menses. Her *mangalsūtra* is removed before her delivery and replaced on the twelfth day after the birth of her child; her glass bangles are also removed and new ones substituted. In castes or tribes that retain the idea of communal corporateness, such as the *Kāṭkarīs*, the impurity of birth affects the whole village. Among *Kātkarīs* on the fifth day after a birth, coconut pieces are sent from the house in which the birth has occurred to all the women in the village for them to cleanse therewith their hair and bodies. After ten days have passed, a period of impurity less marked follows until the *niṣkramaṇa* or 'going out of the house for the first time', which generally is fixed for a good *muhūrtta* after three months from the birth. In this period of modified impurity the mother can cook and others can eat food prepared by her, but this food cannot be offered as *naivedya* to a god, nor to the *pitṛs* or to priests.

At the close of his *vrata*, at the close of his *Brahmacārya*, a *Brahmacārī* has to observe three days as if impure, on account of deaths or births occurring in his family during the period of his vow. During these days he cannot worship and is under all the disabilities imposed by *suher*.

Among Muhammadans the impurity of birth is recognized so far as the woman is herself concerned, but it does not extend to the husband and relations. A Muhammadan woman after the birth of her child is impure for twelve to forty days during which she cannot touch or recite the Koran or *Hadis*, cannot pray or touch any green living thing, cannot cross a river, take grain from a store, sit under a tree or wear a charm. No one, however, becomes impure by touching her. Should she die within the period of impurity, *nifās*, she becomes, according to some Muhammadans, a martyr and goes to heaven, but in the belief of others, as she dies impure, becomes a ghost, *Chudel*.

Vaddars and *Kurubars* recognize a *suher* of five days only, some castes limit it to three days and the *Lingāyat* does not recognize *suher* at all.

The idea of *suher* is applied also to the calving of a cow. The milk of a cow which has calved is not drunk but solidified by boiling with sugar and made into *kharvas* and distributed freely to others, but many refuse the offer of *kharvas* by reason of the *suher* of the cow. After the birth of a calf the milk of the cow cannot for ten days be used in *abhiṣek* or offered as *naivedya* to a god. *Suher* cannot attach to a *Brahmacārī* during the continuance of his *vrata*; to a *jogī* or *sannyāsī*; after the installation of the *devak Nāndi* the bridal pair, their parents and all the family members of the house in which a marriage is celebrated are not affected by any birth until after the dismissal of the *devak*. In car festivals the *yajamān* and priests, and at great sacrifices the officiating priests, are invested with wristlets of thread, *kankaṇ*, and until these are removed the wearers are immune from any *suher* arising from a birth among their relatives.

VIṬĀḶ

A menstruous woman is described as a *Caṇḍāḷī* or outcaste on the first day of her menses; as a *Brahmaghātaki* or 'slayer of Brahmins' on the second, as a *Dhobī* or washerwoman on the third, as a *Patyanukūlā*, 'useful to her husband', on the fourth, and as pure for all purposes on the fifth.

The shadow of a menstruous woman falling on a child gives it intestinal ailments; falling on a pregnant woman harms the unborn child, which is born rickety. Her shadow must not fall even on the cradle of a child or on the bed of a woman who is *enceinte*. It must not fall on a god-room, *devārā,* and tender plants, creepers and flowers wither under it; it is deadly for a cobra, and if it falls on a dying man the woman herself suffers harm.

Her touch is destructive. Seed sown by her develops disease; a cow fed by her dies; a victim of small-pox touched by her loses his sight or maybe life; if she sits among locusts they die; fruit-trees and trees with scented blossom wither at her touch. If she touches a man he loses his sight; a person who eats flour ground by her is attacked by leprosy. Vegetables and fruit, though not major grains, are ruined by her touch; if she touches the water in the step-well at Hangal (Kusbarbhavi) within three days the well is full of red worms; if she dips her foot in the temple well at Jambunath near Hospeth the well dries up until a purificatory ceremony has been performed. Grain and earthen pots touched by her must be thrown away; the leaves she uses as plates must not be given to a cow. She is not allowed to touch implements; to wash clothes in a river; to enter a granary or a vegetable garden; to bring water; to touch fire or milk; to go near a sugar-cane press; to bathe in water used for the irrigation of crops. She causes an abortion if she touches a pregnant woman or a pregnant cow or mare.

If a man touches her he has to change his clothes, bathe and wear a fresh sacred thread, and this he has to do also if he treads where she has trod or sat. A person who has bathed cannot speak to her and if she speak to him must bathe again. One who does no more than step over the spot where she has sat or slept acquires the contagion of her virus. Orthodox Brahmins, should they see her and should they hear her speak, purify themselves by looking at the sun.

The glance of a woman in menses spoils pickles and, if she meets a man, foils the purpose of his going. If she travels on a boat she should, with her clothes, be drenched with water; when her condition is known boatmen refuse her passage on a boat lest the boat should sink. She cannot help to unload fish; she is not allowed to speak whilst elder women are eating; she should not speak haughtily or angrily or weep, must not apply oil to her person or saffron and black pigment; she should not laugh loudly; she cannot touch anything in the house, is served separately and removes her plate herself. She cannot comb her hair; she sleeps alone, and the place where she has slept must be covered with cowdung before another can touch it. At an eclipse she must bathe and allow her wet clothes to dry on her body, but save at this time she is forbidden to bathe for three days.

On the night of the fourth day after sunset she is purified by water poured over her through a sieve and is free from *viṭāḻ*, but the food she can cook on this night can be eaten only by her husband and children and not by others. On the fifth day she is pure for all purposes.

Among the Muhammadans of Sind a woman in menses cannot touch the Koran and a Koran cannot be placed above the spot where she sleeps. She cannot touch a green tree, fruit or flowers, implements or a newly born infant. She cannot enter a mosque or *dargāh*; sit under a big tree which is considered *ghoro*; enter a cultivated garden; milk a cow or sow seed; draw water or approach a river; she cannot give in charity or attend a wedding; she may not approach another woman for forty days after her delivery and cannot go near the sick or the dying. She is not allowed to come near a circumcised boy and cannot cook food in honour of a saint or a Pīr.

In some very important details, however, the Muhammadan concept of her impurity varies from that of the Hindu. The Muhammadan does not regard her as ordinarily making others impure by contact; the place where she sleeps need not be isolated nor eventually purified; she can normally touch others and her touch does not entail the purification of the person she touches; she is allowed to touch fire, and though she is haunted by spirits, her peculiar condition is not supposed to make her evil-eye more baneful. There is again nothing in the ideas of the Muhammadan corresponding to the Hindu idea that the husband participates in the disabilities of his wife. During his wife's menses the Hindu cannot worship deities, perform *jap*, perform a *Śrāddha*, and is an unfit person to whom gifts may be made.

Both the Hindu and the Muhammadan share the belief that a menstruous woman may harm herself through the resentment that contact with her arouses. The Muhammadan believes that she suffers if her shadow falls on the dying; the Hindu that she loses her sight if she makes *darśan* of the image of *Venkateś* at Giri, and that bees attack her if she climbs the hill of Kalakaleśvar near Ganjendragad.

On the fourth day of her menses a woman's evil-eye, according to the Hindu, has the greatest virulence. It is then that a barren woman in order to obtain issue bathes and, wringing the water out of her hair, puts it into the mouth of another's child which forthwith wastes away, transferring its vitality to the woman; on this day a woman may transfer the vitality of a child to herself by merely touching it, the vitality of a tree bearing fruit in the same way and that of a mother of many children by flinging in her face the end of the *sāḍī* she has been wearing.

The Hindu will not use the milk of a cow in heat, and considers a river in flood to be in menses and will not use its waters for drinking, bathing or washing.

THE IMPURITY OF DEATH

Sutak

Just as there are castes that do not recognize any impurity following a birth, so there are communities that do not observe a period of pollution consequent upon a death. When a *Lingāyat* is dying, some two hours before his expected death a *svāmī*, or still better a *Pattada Svāmī* or *Caramūrtti*, is called. The dying man is given a bath with a sponge or wet cloth and the *svāmī* also takes a bath. Then the *svāmī* performs *Śivapūjā* and comes near the dying man; the *svāmī's* feet are washed and the water used is sprinkled over the dying man and a few drops of it are put in his mouth. Food is then given to the priests present, but not if the man dies earlier, as then the household is unclean. If whilst the priests are being feasted the dying man expires the feast is not stayed, and as the relatives of the deceased are considered pure there is no mourning. When the man dies the *svāmī* places his right foot on the head of the body. This whole ceremony is called *vibhūti vile*. After this ceremony there is no mourning, and as the corpse has been touched by the *svāmī* its contact is not unclean. If this ceremony be not performed during the life of the deceased the mourners are unclean, but this only until the body has been disposed of, after which they bathe and clean their houses. If the deceased be himself a *svāmī* the feast to the priests is not stayed even if he die before the feast begins, but in the case of an ordinary man food is not given to priests subsequent to the man's death. Drinking water in which the feet of their *guru* have been bathed, *dhūḻpādodak*, also frees *Lingāyat* mourners from pollution, whilst sprinkling such water over their heads is called readmission, *vaḻage togombona*. A wearer of a *linga* cannot in theory be impure. *Lingāyats* of the lower classes, however, do not abide by this strict axiom, and among some *Lingāyats* death causes impurity for five days.

Orthodoxy prescribes a period of ten days' impurity for the

Brahmin, fifteen for the *Vaiśya,* twelve for the *Kṣatriya* and a month for the *Śūdra.* This applies only to the *gotraja* and the *bhaīband* of the deceased. Those not close relations of the deceased who assist in carrying the corpse or accompany it must not take food or drink till the stars are visible if the body be cremated by day, or till sunrise if the cremation be by night. After seeing the stars and bathing they are pure. Inmates of the house of the deceased who are not his close relations and have not touched the corpse become pure by bathing after the removal of the body.

During the period of *sutak,* mourners are under many disabilities. Their shadows should not be allowed to fall on pure objects or persons or on sacred images. Other people will not touch them, and should they visit the houses of others they are required to sit apart. If there be a distant relative not also under taboo he or she prepares food for them ; otherwise they prepare their own food and no one else would partake of food cooked by them. The dishes they use are thrown away if not valuable or are purified by being passed through fire, or cleaned with cowdung. Mourners may not recite Vedic hymns ; cut their hair or nails ; make or touch a *yantra* ; worship a god or take part in any ceremony ; they cannot sow seed or reap crops ; except for the *barkat* of the dead they can give nothing in charity. If a mourner touch another person he not only harms that person but also harms the dead. A mourner in *sutak* on account of the death of a relative cannot touch the corpse of one who is not a relative ; if he have a father alive he cannot assist in carrying the corpse even of a relative, for if he did this he would lose his own father.

At the close of his *vrata* the *Brahmacārī* observes three days of *sutak* on account of deaths that have occurred among his relatives during the period of his vow. A man and wife observe the same period of *sutak* who perform *Nāgbaḻī,* that is, in the belief that their failure to have issue is due to the killing of a cobra in a past life, perform the obsequies of a cobra with an image made of flour. A period of three days' *sutak* is also observed when *Nārāyaṇbaḻī* is performed. The *sankalpa* of this ceremony is the removal of the *pretatva* of a person whose death has not been followed by the proper rites. The non-performance of the necessary *Śrāddha* has led to the deceased becoming an evil spirit and as such obstructing the generation of his family. *Nārāyaṇbaḻī* is therefore performed to free the spirit of the deceased and enable the living to have issue. The ceremony consists in installing *kalaśas* ; sometimes two, on which are placed images of *Viṣṇu* and of the *Pret,* sometimes five, on which are placed images of *Brahma, Śiva, Yama,* and the *Pret* ;

ten *piṇḍa* of cooked rice with honey, ghee and sesamum are offered to the *Pret*; priests are feasted, but the *yajamān* fasts the whole night and remains awake, and the next day performs the *Śrāddha* of the *Pret* and again offers *piṇḍa*.

Death is visualized as contagion. In Sind among Muhammadans when several children of one mother have died the next-born child is passed through a ring of unburnt clay and then one of burnt clay, as a sort of barrier between it and the contagion of death. Another practice of Muhammadans is to write the *surah yā sīn* on a piece of paper and to make a large hole in the paper through which the child is passed. Almost identical is the practice of *Śimpīs*, who make a hole in the wall of the house and pass the child through the hole. Many other Hindu castes pass the child through a hole in the door, and this is done when a child is born under a bad constellation ominous of death. The placing of a barrier against death in this way is paralleled by other practices adopted to escape evil. The great *Marāṭhā* leader Śivājī is said to have crawled though a perforated stone to escape the ghost of the Mogul general he had killed, and at Gokarn is a cave through which pilgrims pass to free themselves from sin. Iron is very commonly used to check the contagion of death. Opprobrious names are given to children to preserve them from death when previous issues have died, and akin to this practice is that of Muhammadans who, if one child survives but another dies at birth, seat the living child on a bag of grain and give it to eat powdered sweet baked bread called *kutti*; as the child eats this *kutti* it is made to say that it loves the *kutti* more than it loved the deceased child.

The throwing away of cooked food left in the house of mourning at a death illustrates the same idea of contagion. The restrictions on association with mourners; the disability imposed on the priests who officiate at the obsequies which forbids them during the period of mourning taking part in any other ceremony enforce the same idea. Among Muhammadans after a death for one year no marriage can be held in the family of the deceased unless a child has been born in the house and evidenced the cessation of the contagion.

If a man dies within the inner shrine of a temple the god's image therein loses all its *śakti* and a fresh *prāṇpratiṣṭā* is called for. On the other hand, there are many cases in which power seems to be above the impurity of death. The impurity of *sutak* affects the Brahmin, the *Kṣatriya*, the *Vaiśya* and the *Śūdra* in different degrees; the varying *śakti* of these persons leads to a difference in the length of the period of impurity. A child's innate *śakti* again enables it to touch a corpse with immunity and to eat food where a mourner could not do so. The sacred fire maintained by an *Agnihotrī* destroys any impurity attaching to his dead body or to that of any inmate of his household. The *vrata* of the *Brahmacārī* renders him immune from *sutak*; *jogīs* and *sannyāsīs* are exempt by reason of their power; so long as the *Nāndi* remains installed the parents of the bridal pair and all the family members of the house where a marriage is celebrated cannot be contaminated by the contagion of death; in great sacrifices and in car festivals the *yajamān* and priests are protected from impurity by the *kankaṇ* which they wear and which tie up *śakti*. *Manu* (v, 96 ff.) explains the immunity of a king whilst performing his duties as because he incarnates the eight guardian deities who remove impurity, but the real reason must be the king's own *śakti*.

Death in Indian thought is the result of power, though often vaguely conceived. It is attributed to the malicious craft and intention of enemies; to the influence of the planets; to the resentment of outraged power, to evil spirits and even to uncleanness. The *Kātkarī* touches the corpse of a dead tribesman with a faggot and says 'Go to that which caused your death', for he is unable to explain what he regards as an interference with the ordinary laws of Nature. In Chapter I, I have given illustrations of the common concept of death as a form of hot power in which the *Katkarī*, unless his practices be borrowed, would also seem to share in spite of his doubts.

EXCREMENTAL IMPURITY

Excremental impurity destroys *barkat*. No prayer is effective if offered near excrement. Excrement cannot be thrown in fire; it cannot be brought near water, though unfortunately this rule is sadly broken in practice; it cannot be brought near any tabernacle of *śakti* such as a *devak*; it should not, though again theory is disregarded in practice, be brought near a tree, and cattle should not be allowed to graze under trees for fear they cast pollution. The enclave of the village god coincides with the boundaries of the village, and there are still orthodox Hindus who will not relieve nature within the village bounds as this offends the village god, but for their needs go just outside the boundaries. When evacuating a Hindu should first protect the ground with leaves.

After urinating or evacuating the hands and feet should be washed and clothes should be changed. A mantrik who does not observe these rules of cleanliness is overpowered by the spirit he would otherwise control. In the Dharwar district I found one story of a mantrik who on his way from Ron to Gadag had no water with which to cleanse himself, and was therefore seized by spirits and thrown into a clump of prickly pear. A cartman passing by heard the cries of the mantrik Betgeri Basappa and brought him water with which he cleansed himself and recovered control of the spirits. A Hindu may not urinate or evacuate facing the auspicious north.

A Muhammadan may turn his back on Mecca but cannot face Mecca when he urinates; when evacuating he cannot even turn his back on Mecca but must face the south or the north. He may not relieve himself near a mosque, under a tree, in a graveyard or even at a Hindu burning *ghāṭ*, or near water. If he does this near a store of grain he destroys the *barkat* of the grain. As cowdung to a Muhammadan is unclean, though he uses cowdung in many of the not insanitary ways the Hindu employs it, he will not clean with cowdung his hearth or the spot where he prays.

SLEEP

Sleep is a state of impurity, for during sleep one may have a nocturnal pollution, make water or break wind. It is also a state in which the activity of all faculties or perception and action is suspended, and the whole object of life is to acquire knowledge and perform good actions. After sleep, therefore, ablution is necessary for both the Hindu and the Muhammadan; the Hindu after sleeping must perform *Ācaman*,[1] which consists in sipping water from his palm three times.

In the innermost shrine of a temple and in the adjoining room sleep is forbidden; even the recognized *pujārī* or worshipper of a temple must not sleep therein. A Muhammadan may not sleep in that part of a mosque which is reserved for *farz namaz*, the compulsory *namaz* as distinguished from the optional prayer, *nafal namaz*, which is performed at home. The souls of holy persons and angels attend the mosques for *namaz* at night after twelve o'clock and throw out those they find there sleeping, or so disturb them that they are compelled to leave. The holy spirits, however, listen to those engaged in religious exercises and bring them *barkat*; *Khwaja Khizr*, too, questions them about their desires and reveals to them secrets of Nature.

The Hindu is forbidden to sleep[2] at hours of *śakti*, or on holy days such as all Tuesdays in *Śrāvan*, the night of *Ekādaśī*, the

[1] *Manu*, v, 145: 'Though he may be already pure, let him sip water after sleeping.'

[2] Vide *Manu*, ii, 219–21 and *Institutes of Viṣṇu*, lxx, 1–17.

night before *Dasarā*, the full-moon night of *Śrāvaṇ*, on *Gokulaṣṭamī*, *Durgāṣṭamī* and on all days on which *vrata* are observed. The Muhammadan who sleeps at dawn loses the *barkat* of the whole day, and the call of the morning *muezzin* reminds him that prayer is better than sleep. He will not sleep again on the 'night of destiny', *Lailat-ul-qadr*. Persian Muhammadans in Bombay will not sleep on the night of *Nauroz* when the bull that holds up the earth shifts his burden from one horn to the other, until a priest intimates that the change of the earth's position, *sat tahvil*, has been effected.

The same fear of losing *barkat* forbids a Hindu sleeping during a religious ceremony, or during a sermon; before he visits a shrine or *tīrth*, before he writes a charm, during the visit of a *svāmī* or revered guest or whilst a *Purāṇa* is being read. A Muhammadan saint performing the penance of *chillā* sleeps as little as possible, as do saints under discipline, *ahl riyazat*. A Muhammadan refrains from sleep just before writing a charm, whilst the Koran is being read, and before visiting a shrine. Before he sleeps, too, a Muhammadan will remove any charm he is wearing.

The Hindu will not sleep near certain objects possessing power, fearing the resentment of their *śakti* if he does so. He will not sleep near a grindstone or a broom; on the bed or even in the presence of a *guru*; under a biba or a pipal tree; near a river or well; near the hearth or near the tomb of a saint. A strange prohibition is that which forbids his sleeping with his head towards the fringe of a rug or blanket unless the fringe has been turned over. A blanket has evil *śakti*. It is forbidden a Hindu to use more than one blanket to sleep upon; to use a blanket as a pillow; many blankets in a house bring poverty and the gift of a blanket transfers the evils of the donor. A Muhammadan will not sleep near a grindstone, fire, water or trees; he will not sleep on grain nor in the shadow of a human being; he will not sleep with his feet towards Mecca.

Sleep destroys the hope of *barkat*; it provokes the wrath of outraged power and it destroys also, according to Hindu belief, merit or *puṇya*. The goddess *Mohīnī* steals the merit earned by fasting on *Ekādaśī* from one who sleeps after his midday meal the next day.

EATING

Barkat is destroyed by eating. A sacrificial animal should fast. At *Sirsi* after each fair or *jatrā* at which a buffalo is offered to the goddess *Dyamava* the priests purchase another buffalo which is allowed to wander where it wills, is never beaten, and is offered food wherever it goes. Nine days before the next *jatrā* it is tethered and given nothing to eat or drink save lime-water. At big *yajna* the victim of sacrifice is always to fast two or three days, and in the Karnāṭak Muhammadans also observe the same rule regarding sacrifices.

At a Hindu wedding five persons from the side of the bride and that of the bridegroom are supposed to fast; the *yajamān* and his wife fast until the *devak Nāndi* has been dismissed; the bridal pair and the *yajamān's purohit* or family priest fast until the *Lājāhom* has been celebrated, and the marriage has been made irrevocable by the *saptapadī*. At a thread ceremony the father of the boy *vaṭu* and the family priest fast till the end of the ceremony. In a *Śrāddha* the *yajamān* fasts on the previous night and on the night subsequent, and the invited Brahmins must not eat on the evening of the actual day of celebration. The *yajamān* fasts also in a similar degree when he offers oblations, *pakṣa*, to the dead in the sixth month after the anniversary of death.

In hours of *śakti* the Hindu must not eat or drink; at an eclipse, at sunset, noon, midnight; at equinoxes, solstices, conjunctions of planets and on the days of the new and the full moon. To avert the evil influence of the stars fasts are observed on the days associated with the respective stars; on Sunday to avert the influence of the sun; on Monday to avert the influence of the moon; on Friday that of Venus, Saturday that of Saturn, Thursday that of Guru and on Wednesday the influence of Budha. On *parvakāl* the *yajamān* fasts until the moment when *puṇyakāl* commences; on *Gokulaṣṭamī* until 12 p.m. the birth time of *Kṛṣṇa*; on *Rāmanavamī* till the birth time of *Rāma* at noon. When the *Bhagavata Purana* is recited the *Purāṇik* fasts for seven days. The *yajamān* fasts during *Yajna,* and all penances, *jap,* and all *karma* are performed on an empty stomach. When an *Agnihotrī* intends to make fire he and his wife must fast for three days. In car festivals fasting is necessary until the car has been drawn past one's own lane; disputes often arise in consequence of this restriction and to satisfy various claimants the same car has to be drawn on more than one day. When setting out on a pilgrimage the pilgrim should fast and also on his return for half a day. On holy days fasting is performed to win the *barkat* of the days. An empty stomach is required when cutting one's hair or shaving; when collecting herbs of magic power before sunrise; when preparing charms to effect evil; when collecting flowers to be used in worship, and mantriks often fast when attempting a cure until the cure is achieved. When a man worships *Vata Savitrī* on the full-moon day of *Jyeṣṭha* his wife and not he himself must fast, and it is she who fasts also during *Naurātra*.

The Muhammadan fasts at an eclipse; at sunset and noon; from the first to the thirteenth of *Muḥarram*. He fasts on holy days to obtain the *barkat* of those days; on the twenty-third of *Rajab*, on the twenty-seventh of *Rajab* when the Prophet went to meet God; on the fifteenth *Sa'bān* when at night angels carry to God for sanction the requirements of man's livelihood for twelve months. An empty stomach is imperative when a Muhammadan makes *istikhāra* or *Ḥāḍrāt jinn*; when he prepares charms or collects herbs. Whilst grinding grain, eating and drinking is avoided, as also when curds are churned or a cow is milked. Those who sow and plough fast early in the morning; those that measure grain also fast. The whole household fasts when a woman approaches her delivery, and the parents and all the inmates of the house fast for a few hours before a Muhammadan boy is circumcised. Brides and bridegrooms sometimes fast a day before their marriage, but this is far from being a general custom. Fasting is essential when a corpse lies unburied; before the Koran is read early in the morning; before morning prayers and before the prayers on *Bakri 'Id*, though these are offered at ten or eleven o'clock in the morning.

Both the Muhammadan and the Hindu think that an oath or a curse is the more serious if accompanied by fasting. 'One must not insult a Brahmin who has an empty stomach' is a popular saying.

In contrast to this injunction of fasting in order to win *barkat* is the prohibition of fasting in some districts during the sowing of seed. In the Dharwar district jvārī must not be sown on an empty stomach and in Khandesh no seed can be sown unless the sower first take a hearty meal; an empty stomach would, it is thought, be reflected in the empty ears of the grain.

Fasting is a means of obtaining *barkat*. Gluttons are supposed to have an evil eye, and in Sind there is a proverb, 'Keep your inside empty of food in order that you may find the light of divine perception'. One interpretation of *upvās*, 'fast', is that it means 'sitting near' and therefore drawing *śakti*. Among Hindus there is the idea that it is dangerous to partake of food before a god has had his share; food taken by man before it is offered to a god is called *rākṣasī āhār* or 'demoniacal food'. This explains why a Brahmin does not partake of food before he has offered *Vaiśvadeva* and why *naivedya* is always offered to a deity on an empty stomach.

So long as a dead body remains unburied or unburned a *Kātkarī* cannot take food. The whole village, in fact, is under the same restriction, and, should the funeral procession pass by a house in another village where *Kātkarīs* are eating, their meal must be stopped. This prohibition of food on a death, however, is exceptional; in general there is no fasting among Hindus and Muhammadans after a death, but flesh-eaters abstain from flesh and persons other than mourners avoid eating with mourners who in many cases may not prepare food for themselves. The *Kātkarī* practice, however, draws attention to the marked resemblance between the restrictions observed during hours of power and period of impurity. During all *parvakāl* flesh-eating Hindus abstain from eating flesh and the Muhammadan observes the same restraint at an eclipse and at sunset. After a birth the eating of flesh is forbidden for a varying period to both Hindu and Muhammadan, and on a death, again, both of these abstain from flesh. Grinding, again, is forbidden at *parvakāl* and during a varying period after a birth or a death. The rules about sweeping, washing, hair-cutting and the cutting of the nails also illustrate the similarity of restrictions applied to hours of power and of impurity. In the beliefs associated with an eclipse there is even a fusion of the idea of power and of impurity; a multitude of practices bear witness to the power of the hour whilst, on the other hand, the word *suher*, which is the general term applied to the impurity following a birth, is applied also to the dangerous elements in the same hour of an eclipse.

STEPPING OVER
Orāngin (Sin.)

To step over a thing effects a contact of a particular kind. It brings the power of the person who steps over into conflict with that of the object stepped over. There is some difference of opinion as to the effect that follows an accidental stepping over. The Sindi says that accidentally stepping over an object brings no harmful sequel as there is no question of an exercise of will; that it does no more harm than would the accidental breaking of a fast. In the rest of the Presidency, however, accidental stepping over an object is considered even more dangerous than a deliberate act of the same nature. When a man deliberately steps over an object there is at least a conflict of two powers, his own and that of the object stepped over, and the victory of either *śakti* must in effect be a kind of compromise; when, however, a man accidentally steps over an object possessing power his own will is dormant, there is no opposition to the unrestricted working of the *śakti* of that object and the result is the greater injury to the man. This manner of argument, perhaps, is not followed with absolute coherence, for a Hindu loses *puṇya* if he touches elders with his feet but not if the contact be effected accidentally.

It is forbidden to step over any form of implement or weapon; stepping over an agricultural implement destroys the hope of agricultural gain. The punishment is always fitted to the crime. If one steps over a pestle (*musaḻ*) one will have swelling of the knee-cap; boils are the penalty of stepping over a grindstone; cattle die if one steps over their yoke. Disease is the sequel to stepping over a *vaniki* or rod for cleaning rice. Stepping over the ropes of a boat or the tethering ropes of a horse or cow brings harm to the owner of the boat or animal. Stepping over a winnowing-fan brings itch. Seed stepped over will not fertilize and famine ensues; stepping over the black seed of papyra brings blindness; stepping over cotton-seed or custard apples brings blindness at night. Stepping on a grain measure means that the measure will not be required or, in other words, the rains withholding, there will be famine. If a child or unmarried person steps over grain reserved for seed the offender will never marry. Stepping over bread entails loss of all future income (*tangi*, Sin.); no form of food, in fact, can be stepped over.

Fire, if stepped over, attracts the life of the person who steps over it; a Sindi Muhammadan throws into water a broken hearth to prevent its being stepped over. Even an empty fireplace must not be stepped over. Stepping over water in which a *tavā* or plate used for roasting bread has been washed, is said in the Deccan to produce a black kind of eczema.

The growth of a new tooth is prevented if one steps over a discarded tooth. A Sindi loses all hope of future *śikār* if he steps over the produce of his sport. To step over a buffalo is to incur the risk of having an intelligence as stupid as that attributed to a buffalo. It is dangerous to step over the coronet of a bridegroom or the wristlets of the bridal pair; only the owners can do this, but others imperil their own *śakti*. The 'stone-of-life', if stepped over, attracts to itself the *śakti* of the offender. It is dangerous to step over the buried navel-cord of a child.

Nothing into which power has been invoked can be stepped over. This is one of the reasons why the *devak* and the *hāḻgamba* are tied to a post in the marriage *manḍap*; it is also one of the reasons why such symbols after the dismissal of their *śakti* are thrown into water.

Persons with *śakti* or *kudrat* must not be stepped over. One must not step over a saint; over a child or even its clothes or the growth of the child is stunted. If her husband steps over the stretched-out legs of his wife her issue will be male, and that issue will always resemble the person who steps over the mother. There is also a danger that the mother will become lame if any one step over her when pregnant, but this danger can be averted by again stepping over her in the reverse direction. If a pregnant woman steps over the tethering-peg of a horse she will have an extended period of pregnancy like a horse and probably will succumb; similarly, she will have a prolonged pregnancy of eleven months if she step over bath-water which has issued from the drain of a room wherein another woman has delivered within ten days. Death comes to a man who is stepped over while he is asleep,[1] and malicious story says that police guards are able to get rid of prisoners by stepping over them in their sleep. Stepping over elderly people is dangerous; it is equally dangerous to step over the property of others; dangerous for the owner at times and at other times hazardous for the person committing the offence. In Sind a wife cannot step over her husband's shoes or turban or even his urine; the clothes of a respected person, the shoes of a Pīr or of a sādhu cannot be stepped over. There is a story that before the Battle of Panipat Sadaśirao was implored by his aunt not to go forth; he would not listen, so to force her advice upon him she threw down her shawl. In a fit of obstinacy Sadaśirao at once stepped over the shawl and thereby lost the battle. A tiger-skin is the *āsan* used by ascetics; for an ordinary Brahmin to sit or step over such a skin would mean a death in his family. If one steps over the dishes from which another person is eating the penalty is severe colic.

Articles of *nivāḻī* deposited at cross-roads transfer their peculiar burden of ill only if their insulation from the ground is preserved when they are touched, but merely stepping over them without actual contact brings its penalty in *databakki* or eruptions on the legs.

A charm will not be stepped over by a Muhammadan and a Hindu charm loses its power if stepped over by man or animal.

[1] Stepping over a sleeper is dangerous, because during sleep a man's *jīva* leaves his body and wanders. The popular Hindu belief is that there are two *jīva*, the major *jīva* which leaves the body and the *pāngūḻ jīva* which remains. *Pāngūḻ* means 'without the use of the legs' and the heart is called *pāngūḻ jīva*. It is equally dangerous to bind the feet or hands of a sleeper or mark his face lest the *jīva*, on its return from wandering, should not recognize the body. It is dangerous to sleep with the mouth open lest a spirit should enter the body and so prevent the entry of the returned *jīva*.

A Muhammadan will not step over the tomb of a saint ; over the Koran ; over thread, a drawn line, a heap of green verdure, new clothes or cloth, a grave or a dead body, an animal, over his own spittle or excrement ; over a comb, a mirror, a pen or antimony ; over the garlands of the bridal pair ; over all kinds of food ; a pot of water ; fire or a fire-place ; over a child or its clothes ; over tools or the ropes of a boat.

Fear of the dangers following stepping over an object with power enters into practices which admit also of other explanations ; it is one of the reasons, I have said, why certain things are not placed on the ground, why things with dangerous potentiality are thrown into running water, and it is also a reason why things with dangerous power are tied to trees.

In the preceding chapters I have attempted to explain the 'Keys of Power', those axioms and rules of conduct that man frames in his effort to control power for his own purposes ; to preserve it, to transfer it, to coerce or invoke it. I have sketched, too, the factors which destroy power and lead to a set of restrictions of conduct. There is, however, one way in which the rules of conduct are disregarded and the prohibition ceases to restrain. *Kari na kari* or 'do that which should not be done' is accepted as a guide to conduct in some families ; it leads to a reversal of every ordinary detail of ceremony and to a ritual which the ordinary canons forbid.

APPENDIX A

HINDU AND MUHAMMADAN CHARMS

Hindu Charms

To accomplish any good objects.

		1		
	6		2	
7		10		3
	8		4	
		9		

Tied round the neck to cure a pain in the neck.

87	104	88
102	100	88
101	86	13

Tied to the arm or hand to cure stomach-ache.

1	18	2	7
6	3	13	2
15	10	8	1
4	5	11	14

or

24	31	26
28	27	25
22	23	30

To cure snake-bite.

7	9	8
2	6	4
3	1	5

Tied to the neck to obtain a son.

8	1	13	10
11	12	4	5
7	2	9	14
11	12	6	3

Tied to the hand of a woman in travail.

46	53	48
51	48	47
50	45	52

To scare thieves.

12	24	36	48
7	1	3	6
5	3	20	29
10	18	8	18

To remove fear of lightning.

16	23	2	7
6	3	20	11
22	27	8	1
24	5	18	24

Retained to get wealth.

	66	66	
BHOJ			putra
	33	33	

Tied round the neck to cure ague.

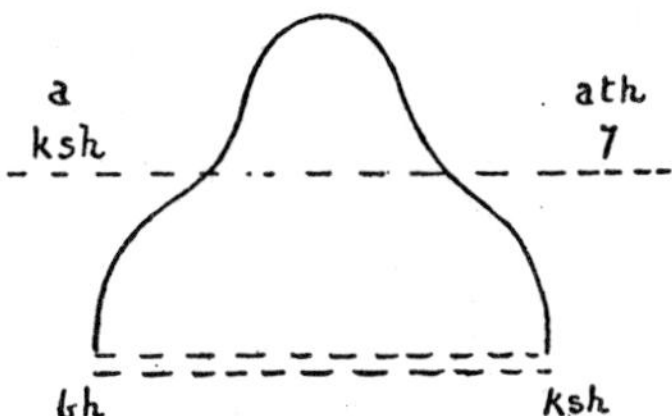

To stop a child's crying; tied to its neck.

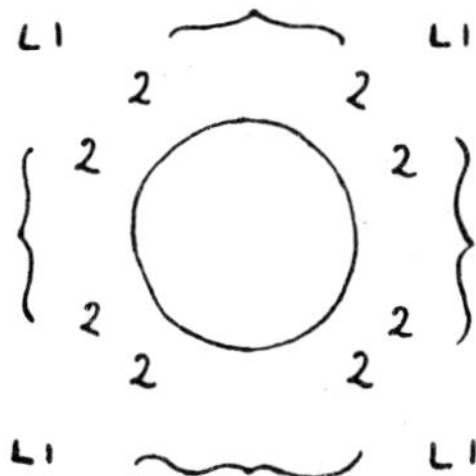

To effect an easy delivery.

9	16	2	7
6	3	13	12
15	10	8	1
4	5	11	14

To remove pests of crops.

4	11	2	7
6	3	8	7
10	5	8	1
4	5	6	9

To scare away ghosts.

8	1	48	43
44	47	4	5
2	7	42	49
46	45	6	3

Buried in fields to remove pests.

	Rhi	Rhi	Rhi	Rhi	
Rhi	12	19	2	7	Rhi
Rhi	6	3	16	15	Rhi
Rhi	18	13	8	1	Rhi
Rhi	4	5	14	17	Rhi
	Rhi	Rhi	Rhi	Rhi	

To cure fever. Written on betel-leaf; incense thrown on fire and sugar offered to the *yantra*. Finally eaten with nut and lime.

1	2	3
5	6	4
9	7	8

An expectant mother looks at this charm which is written with sweet oil and red lead.

8	3	4
1	5	9
6	7	2

Written in ink on paper and tied to a cow's horn to increase her supply of milk.

$\frac{3}{4}$	$2\frac{1}{4}$
$\frac{3}{4}$	$2\frac{1}{4}$
$\frac{3}{4}$	$2\frac{1}{4}$

Buried at a shop-door to increase profits.

50	57	2	7
6	3	54	53
64	57	8	1
4	5	51	55

Written on betel-leaf and eaten to cure malaria.

1	2	3	4
6	7	8	5
11	12	9	10
16	13	14	15

Buried in a field to increase the produce of crops.

2	20	2	8
7	3	84	23
26	81	9	1
4	6	22	24

Tied to the necks of cattle to cure disease.

8	11	35	10
1	44	4	12
2	7	9	66
63	15	5	3

Kept by a magician so that the audience will not spot his tricks.

11	18	2	7
6	3	15	4
17	12	8	1
4	5	13	16

Kept on his head under his turban by a public speaker so that he will control his audience.

88	92	36	12
33	99	39	12
94	39	37	31
31	44	54	62

To win over whom one wishes.

3	2	5	6	2
1	94	1	8	12
11	13	11	4	13
16	18	6	3	2
9	18	21	7	8

Tied to the arm to cure fever.

24	43	2	7
6	3	38	37
40	15	8	1
4	5	6	35

Worn on their hands by wives to subject their husbands.

4	92	34	36
8	32	34	As
11	40	V	SH
34	KM	RM	VM

To promote unity among relations.

RHI	RHI	RHI	RHI
RHI	RHI	RHI	RHI
RHI	RHI	RHI	RHI
RHI	RHI	RHI	RHI

To keep rats out of a house.

8	3	4	0
1	5	16	0
60	2	17	0

To cure cold or fever; tied to the neck.

6	1	8	JVA
7	5	3	LA
2	9	4	MUKHI

(*Jvālāmukhī* means 'volcano')

To prevent abortion.

3	9	5	6	N
2	9	6	4	7

Muhammadan Charms

To cure fever.

6	1	8
7	5	2
2	9	4

To cure small-pox.

22	25	28	15
27	16	21	26
17	30	23	20
24	19	18	29

To cure headache.

27	30	29	36
32	31	32	37
32	35	34	31
29	24	29	40

To cure a pain in the neck.

389	384	2815
3810	3088	386
385	3812	387

To cure melancholy.

153	157	160	146
159	127	152	158
168	162	155	151
156	150	149	161

or

8920	893	5927
8226	8924	8922
8921	8922	8934

To cure kidney pain.

8	6	2	2
2	3	0	0
6	8	2	2
4	2	0	6

To cure stomach pain.

1000	1500	5187
1009	1004	1004
1001	1008	1002

To cure stone.

3	8	6
9	5	1
4	2	8

To ease the travail pains of a woman.

1	12	12	6
3	7	4	12
6	6	6	13
10	[illegible]	6	10

APPENDIX B

HINDU FESTIVALS ON WHICH CERTAIN FORMS OF *HIMSA* ARE FORBIDDEN OR ALLOWED

Month.	Festival.	Hair-cutting.	Grinding.
Chaitra . . .	*Ugadi*	Forbidden	Forbidden.
,, . . .	*Rāmanavamī*	,,	,,
Vaiśākha . . .	*Akṣayyatṛtīyā*	,,	,,
,, . . .	*Narasinhajayantī*	,,	Not forbidden.
,, . . .	*Agi-huṇṇivi*	,,	,, ,,
Jyeṣṭha . . .	*Mannettina-Amāvāsya*	,,	Forbidden.
Āṣāḍha . . .	*Prathama-ekādaśi*	,,	,,
,, . . .	*Karka-Sankramaṇa*	,,	,,
Śrāvaṇa . . .	*Nāgpancmī*	,,	,,
,, . . .	*Gokul aṣṭamī*	,,	,,
,, . . .	*Śrāvaṇi*	,,	Not forbidden.
Bhādrapad . .	*Gaṇeśacauthī*	,,	Forbidden.
,, . .	*Yeliaṣṭamī*	,,	,,
,, . .	*Ananta-caturdaśī*	,,	,,
,, . .	*Pakṣamāsa*	,,	,,
Āśvin . . .	*Navarātra*	,,	Not forbidden.
Kārttik . . .	*Divāḷī* (3 days)	,,	,, ,,
,, . . .	*Sud. ekādaśī. Tulsī vivāha*	,,	,, ,,
Mārgaśīrṣa . .	*Campa-ṣaṣṭhī*	,,	,, ,,
Pauṣa . . .	*Makara-sankramaṇa*	,,	Forbidden.
Māgha . . .	*Ratha-saptamī*	,,	Not forbidden.
,, . . .	*Śivarātri*	,,	,, ,,
Phālgun . . .	*Holī-huṇṇivi*	,,	,, ,,

N.B.—Sweeping is not forbidden on any of these days for the whole day but only at certain hours. On *Ugadi* it is allowed through the agency of servants.

APPENDIX C

UTĀRA IN THE DECCAN

TO avert and transfer evil the following objects are waved round the afflicted person and then placed on a public highway, at the meeting of cross-roads or occasionally thrown in running water in the direction from which it is assumed the evil is approaching. Animals waved round the afflicted person are either slaughtered or allowed to wander loose. The articles deposited on the road are insulated from the ground by leaves, grain, tiles or by a winnowing-fan.

A. To cure the effects of evil-eye.
   Sea salt; mustard; salt and mustard; chillies; salt and chillies; red powder; lemons, these sometimes pierced with needles.

B. To prevent molestation by a spirit or ghost.
   Uḍīd; the eggs of a hen. A round thick cake (*poḻī*) made of seven cereals and pulses, including *uḍīd*. A cake of seven cereals and eggs. Stale bread. Powdered bread with chillies and oil. A chicken. A hen or cock preferably grey in colour and with reversed feathers. Curds and cooked rice. Coconuts. A clay pipe used for smoking hemp. Liquor. A black sheep. A black female goat that has never had young. Water.

C. To transfer illness.
   Curds; cooked rice. Coconut; gold; money. A child is obtained secretly from another family, waved round the sick and quietly restored to its parents. *Uḍīd*; root of turmeric. A narrow strip of cloth made yellow with turmeric and knotted with an uneven number of knots which contain *uḍīd* and turmeric.

APPENDIX D

RESTRICTIONS ON INTERMARRIAGE BETWEEN DIFFERENT *KUL* OF THE *KĀTKARĪS*

In the *Roha* taluka

A Yadhav cannot marry a Jadhav.
Hilam ,, ,, Jadhav, Rao, Powar, Vaghmare.
Jadhav ,, ,, Yadhav, Sinde, Hilam, Dongarkoli.
Powar ,, ,, Hilam, Śeḻār, Dongarkoli.
Vaghmare ,, ,, Hilam, Valekar, Dongarkoli.
Rao ,, ,, ,, ,, ,,
Jagtap can marry only a Vaghmare and Valekar.

In the Karjat taluka

A Jadhav cannot marry a Mukane or a Powar.
Hilam ,, ,, Vagh or a Mukane.

In the Umbergaon taluka

A Kambdi cannot marry a Bhoya, Kavra or Ravalya.
Kavra ,, ,, Ravalya, Bhoya, Kambdi.
Mukna ,, ,, Gangoda, Bhoya, Mukne.
Ravalya ,, ,, Kambdi, Kavra.
Gangoda ,, ,, Mukna, Tumbda.
Bhoya ,, ,, Tumbda, Ravalya, Kambdi.

In the Dahanu taluka

A Bhambera can marry only a Diwa, Vagh, Powar, Savra, Ghatal.
Diwa ,, ,, ,, Bhoya, Bhambera, Valvi, Lakhan, Gangoda.
Vagh ,, ,, ,, Bhambera, Vardi, Bhoya, Savra, Mukne.
Vardi ,, ,, ,, Vagh, Bhoya, Śeḻār.
Bhoya ,, ,, ,, Diwa, Vagh, Vardi, Powar, Valvi, Lakhan, Bhandar, Gangoda, Tumbda.
Powar ,, ,, ,, Bhambera, Vagh, Bhoya, Misal, Bhandar Gangoda.
Savar ,, ,, ,, Bhambera, Vagh, Bhoya, Powar, Mukanya, Bokya, Śeḻār, Misal, Tumbda.
Mukanya ,, ,, ,, Vagh, Savra, Valvi, Lakhan, Gangoda.

Ghatal	can marry only a	**Bhambera, Śeḻār, Bhandar, Gangoda.**
Bokya	,, ,, ,,	Savra, **Śeḻār, Lakhan, Bhandar, Gangoda.**
Dhulya	,, ,, ,,	Tumbda.
Śeḻār	,, ,, ,,	Vardi, **Savra,** Ghatal, Bokya.
Misal	,, ,, ,,	Powra, **Savra.**
Valvi	,, ,, ,,	Diva, **Bhoya, Mukanya.**
Lakhan	,, ,, ,,	Diva, **Bhoya, Mukanya, Bokya, Gangoda.**
Bhandar	,, ,, ,,	Bhoya, Powar, Ghatal, Bokya.
Gangoda	,, ,, ,,	Diva, Bhoya, Powar, Mukanya, Ghata, Lakhan.
Tumbda	,, ,, ,,	Bhoya, Savra, Dhulya.

I have given in some detail the restrictions on intermarriage between the clans of the *Kātkarī* to illustrate how impossible it is to attribute these to the possession of a common totem or *devak*. A clan that can marry into another clan in one locality cannot do this in another locality; a clan that can give a daughter in marriage to another clan cannot take a bride from that clan. The Hilam and Mukane were formerly one; the Powar and More were traditionally once one clan; the Yadhav and the Jadhav; the Śeḻar and the Powar, the Jadhav and the Sinde were originally one. If one follows the restrictions on intermarriage between these families, one finds within the same circle of restrictions many *devaks*.

Another feature is that in different localities one may find a family that can marry with one other family only, and on the other hand a family that can marry with all the other *Kātkarī* families at pleasure.

If one goes beyond the limits of the *Kātkarī* tribe there is a striking similarity of restrictions. Among the *Thakurs* the Yadhav and Jadhav cannot intermarry; among the *Dhor Koḻīs* the Gangoda, Dagla, Bendkol, Mondha, Bhoya, Gaikwad, Powar, Potinde, Vagh, Ardhe, Dodka, Bhadage, Ghumal, Singada, Valvi, Pardhi, Lokhandi families have more or less the same restrictions on intermarriage as the families of the same names among the *Kātkarīs*.

APPENDIX E

THE POWER OF THE CARDINAL POINTS

THERE are many unadvanced tribes in the Presidency that are still unacquainted with the cardinal points. The *Kātkarī* and others call the East and the West the 'rising' and the 'setting', *ugvat*, and *maulat*, but have no idea of the South and North. The *Kātkarī* when indicating a direction describes its position to his right or left; others speak of the south as 'towards the sea' and of the north as 'towards the mountains'. This ignorance of the cardinal points has an important effect when such tribes accept the religion of their Hindu neighbours, for in the everyday ritual of orthodox Hinduism the cardinal points are always recognized, and orientation is habitual.

The two wicks of the *nīrānjan* lamp used in *ārtī* are placed across each other pointing in the cardinal directions. *Tulsīvṛndāvan* is the earthen receptacle which contains the household tulsī plant (Ocymum sanctum); this is always square and aligned to the cardinal points. The *mangalsnān* of the bridal pair is taken within a square; the common *pāṭ* used as an *āsan* is always square; the area occupied by a Hindu house should strictly be square; ceremonial *manḍaps* are square; and *homakunḍ* or the pits used for sacrificial fires are also square.

The cardinal points may also be regarded as eight, each of which has its own *śakti* which is invoked by man. If in spite of his efforts evil comes from the directions it is beyond his control and a post-Vedic word, *diśāsūḻ*, is used to describe this evil. At the respective cardinal points are eight elephants created to hold the earth steady by their weight; these are worshipped in the thread and the marriage ceremonies of the aśvath-tree, and in *pūrt* ceremonies, including those connected with the construction of a reservoir, a well, or garden. In these ceremonies a *manḍap* is built with four doors towards the four chief cardinal points, over a pit *kunḍ* in which fire is consecrated. At each door two elephants are worshipped through the medium of betel-nuts placed on a plate previously sprinkled with rice which covers a water-pot or *kalaśa*; of water-pots there are eight in all.

The eight points again with the centre are identified with the nine planets. Each point has also a guardian, *Dikpālā*; these guardians are invoked into betel-nuts. At a marriage or thread ceremony before the shrine of the *kula devatā* and also in the marriage *manḍap* a bamboo frame, *parḍī*, is placed on the ground; in this is put a cloth washed with turmeric and on this again rice is sprinkled with a svastika drawn on it in red powder, which serves as an *āsan* for eight betel-nuts placed at the points, a ninth betel-nut being placed in the centre to represent *Gaṇpati*. At every *Ankurāropaṇ* five gods are invoked into betel-nuts placed at the centre and at the four points of a cross.

Besides actually invoking the cardinal deities by name, *śakti* can be gathered from the cardinal points by use of the cross or the svastika, and these same figures also scatter evil to the cardinal points. On celebrating a *hom*, a cross is made of darbha grass or with twigs of umbar on the *āsan* of sand or black earth prepared for the *hom*. When a platform is made for the bridal pair to sit upon, bricks and betel-nuts are placed on an *āsan* of rice or wheat following the cardinal points. To assist a woman's delivery a svastika is marked with turmeric over the door of her room; a svastika is drawn on the feet of the *vaṭu* and on various parts of the *manḍap* used at a thread ceremony; it is drawn on the screen held between the bride and bridegroom; on the grain gathered on the threshing-floor; and on the *āsan* on which the bridal pair sit.

Each point has its own *śakti*. The south is associated with death. On a death a lamp is lighted where the deceased expired and its wick is turned towards the south, but no other lamp can face the south unless another lamp be placed opposite it. In agricultural ritual the south is studiously avoided, particularly in the furrows of the plough; one must not take medicine facing the south or the medicine will fail to save the patient, and one must not sleep with one's feet towards the south. A house must not face the south, and a horse must not be tethered to face the south. In modern days of travel it is still possible to find persons travelling in public conveyances, turning their faces aside when the conveyance happens to take a direction due south. In witchcraft and magic the practitioner faces south.

The East and the North are auspicious directions, and whatever can be practised facing east can usually be done also facing north; one exception is the ceremony of *Puṇyāhavācan* in which the man and his wife must face east. In all auspicious ceremonies the *yajamān* must face east or north; the bridal pair, the *vaṭu*, the *yajamān* celebrating a *hom*, the celebrant worshipping a deity or performing *jap*. When, too, a Hindu is shaved he faces the east, and faces the same direction when before bathing he applies oil to his head.

Houses, as far as possible, should face north or east. The front of a *manḍap* erected for some ceremony should face the east; the temples of all gods, except some temples of Maruti, should face the east. There may be many temples of Maruti in a single village that do not face south, but the temple of Maruti as the presiding deity of a village faces the south so that Maruti may scare away the spirits that haunt the south. Threshing-floors are placed in the north-west corners of fields; cattle-sheds to the south-west of a dwelling-house, wells and bathrooms to the west and the hearth to the south-east.

INDEX

Printed in Great Britain by Butler & Tanner Ltd., Frome and London